Naked Visionary
Seize Your Sparks of Inspiration...

Faith Lynella

Naked Visionary: Seize Your Sparks of Inspiration...
Faith Lynella (1944)
Also published as Dr. Lynella Grant and Lynella Faith Grant

Copyright © Off the Page Press, 2012

Radiant Library is an imprint of Off the Page Press

Softcover Version: ISBN-13: 978-1888739-56-5 ISBN-10 1-888739-56-8

All rights reserved. Produced and/or printed in the United States of America. No part of this publication may be reproduced, stored in a retrieval system or transmitted in any form or by any means, electronic, mechanical, photocopied, recorded or otherwise without the written permission of the publisher. Reviewers may quote brief passages to be printed in a magazine, newspaper, or on the World Wide Web.

NOTE: Some BonBons are from *BonBons to Sweeten Your Daily Life* by Faith Lynella, © Off the Page Press, 1996. Others are from an upcoming book of BonBons.

Portions of this book are taken directly from *How to Survive a Spiritual Hangover* by Faith Lynella without attribution. © Off the Page Press, 2007

"Binkle" is a registered trademark and copyright belong to The Binkle Foundation,

Faith Lynella, and Off the Page Press. All rights are reserved.

Websites for Readers
http://NakedVisionary.com
http://FaithLynella.com
http://VisionaryFountain.com

Contents

Contents	3
List of BonBons	4
Acknowledgments	5
Introduction Bringing a Vision Down to Earth	7

Part I The Visionary Process Goes Inward and Outward — 11
- Chapter 1   Treading New Ground — 13
- Chapter 2   Tracking the Visionary Process — 35
- Chapter 3   Stripping Down to Essentials — 59
- Chapter 4   Bridging Between Vision and the World — 87
- Chapter 5   Going to Extremes — 117
- Chapter 6   Finding a Paramount Vision — 143
- Chapter 7   Bringing a Vision to Life — 171

Part II Grounding Insight in Practical Ways — 201
- Chapter 8   Tackling the Challenges — 203
- Chapter 9   Identifying the Spectrum of Change — 233
- Chapter 10 Packaging a Vision that Resonates — 261
- Chapter 11 Engaging the Visionary Drive — 277
- Chapter 12 Seeing "Outside the Box" — 305
- Chapter 13 Developing Our Energetic Intelligence — 331
- Chapter 14 Practicing Visionary Leadership — 357
- Chapter 15 Building Supportive Environments — 383

Part III Spheres Where Vision and Practice Meet — 409
- Chapter 16 Opening to the Transformative Power of Art — 411
- Chapter 17 Following Science and the Route of the Mind — 431
- Chapter 18 Following the Spiritual Route of the Heart — 449
- Chapter 19 Shifting the Paradigm — 475
- Chapter 20 Creating an Incubator for Visionary Thinkers — 503
- Chapter 21 Taking the Next Step — 519

Back
- Appendix A 50 Ways to Get Naked — 529
- Glossary — 537
- References — 641
- Index — 551

BonBons in Chapters

Chapter 3	Inner Work	83
Chapter 4	Ship Ahoy	115
Chapter 6	Beyond Knowledge	170
Chapter 7	Ode to Being "Had"	176
	Energy Policies	189
Chapter 8	Ligatures of Devotion	212
Chapter 9	Fresh Truth	239
	Beware of Potential	244
	Getting All You Pay For	256
Chapter 11	Opportunity Knocks	282
	Opportunity Knocks Again	283
	Jailbreak	301
Chapter 12	Life is But a Stream	324
Chapter 13	Smash the Mid-Range	347
Chapter 16	Art, Music and Beauty	423
Chapter 17	Make a Space for Grace	461
Chapter 18	"Do Not Judge" Is a Place, Not a Verb	491
	Democracy Through Action	495

Acknowledgments

This book could not have been written without the loving encouragement of some very devoted supporters. They were my cheerleaders and a kind hand to hold when I hit a wall. Each of them played a vital role in keeping me sane and on task for the four years of writing it (besides the years that prepared me for the task).

How blessed I feel to have such a strong circle of practical and emotional intimates. They did much more than help and encourage me, since each of them brought greater clarity about what this project could be as they urged me on. It takes a special person to help to hold a vision during the long, uphill phase when it is not evident if the goal is possible. These stalwarts have not had an easy task on what can only be described as a "high maintenance relationship" with me.

Naked Visionary was a visionary journey that itself tracked the whole dynamic process. Much of it was internal — getting an explicit handle on the journey's interior reality. I was compelled to verify the accuracy of what I wrote about by putting it to the test in my own circumstances. The heart, mind, body and spirit all insisted on being involved in the narrative.

My closest ally every step of the way has been Paulette Pohlmann. She is a skilled writer and editor, but beyond that she has a rigorous crap detector that refuses to tolerate any lack of precision. She and I split hairs and fine-tuned each element that was encountered on the search for Truth. Close behind, I drew on the emotional and intellectual strengths of: Pat Troyer, Charlotte Hardwick, Mary Hungerford, P. J. Bauer, Madelon Mottet, and Jim Norman.

My children, Jessica Bundschuh and Ross Grant (both writers of a philosophical turn of mind) deserve special recognition. We engaged in the kind of highly-focused give-and-take seldom seen outside of academia. But their added love and wit made it apparent our aims were always in service to uncompromising clarity. It would be unfair not to mention their spouses, Emily Arsenault and Steffen Bundschuh, who were as supportive of my vision as they've been.

Sir Isaac Newton said, "If I have been able to see farther than others, it was because I stood on the shoulders of giants." Some shoulders I stood on were the far-seeing visionaries who inspired me. Foremost among them are Evelyn Underhill and Ralph Waldo Emerson, as well as other great thinkers who represent the Liberal Arts ideal.

Other shoulders belonged to exceptional mentors I encountered along the way. My mother was first, and significant in raising my sites high — while brooking no excuses. My Spiritual Teacher for 18 years assured that I developed the rigor necessary to engage the Absolutes.

I also note two specific mentors, David King, Tribal Leader of the Fort McDowell Yavapai Nation (Arizona) and Cavett Robert, who launched the motivational speaking industry and founded National Speaker's Association.

To each of these, and so many more who remain unnamed, I humbly express my gratitude for your influence on me and this undertaking.

Dedication

To the Visionary Spark and those noble souls
with the courage and determination to serve it—
Without counting the personal costs or
the indifference of the world

Introduction - Bringing a Vision Down to Earth

*"Once you have flown, you will walk the earth with
your eyes turned skywards, for there you have been,
and there you long to return."* Leonardo da Vinci

A Journey of Self-Discovery

The visionaries are the high flyers of the creative contingent. They refine the abilities both to fly (via vision and imagination) and to land — to bring what they see down into the everyday world. The process they're committed to is as much an inner journey as it is about solving thorny practical challenges.

Given the amount of chaos and dysfunction rampant in public and private life these days, the world badly needs some farsighted and revolutionary answers. We need visionaries, with their clarity and determination to defy the odds and obstacles. We need their uncompromising commitment and resolve. And we need some of that unstoppable foolhardiness.

Visionaries function in the field of potential — what *could be*. They are change agents who must master their inner demons and doubts, while struggling to communicate a compelling message to an unreceptive world.

The visionary journey is a long and convoluted process, only partly defined by the igniting vision or how the world responds to what the person does with it. Distinct stages and trials test anyone who walks that path. Those challenges arise without regard for the individual's personal qualities or preparation.

This book looks at the qualities that many visionaries share, or that set them apart from the larger community. But being a visionary is not an all-or-none designation. Each person who goes that route will be altered by the experience, for it is a journey toward greater self-awareness. Most of those travelers master the necessary skills gradually, so their point of view changes along the route and over time.

"Naked Visionary" Symbolizes the Unfolding Process

"Naked" speaks to the flesh — the warm, soft, unprotected flesh and bones of the human animal. But within, the mind and emotions complete the physical package. "Visionary" speaks to the spark of inspiration and vision. It includes the act of seeing something remarkable, as well as the unbroken view it shows.

Naked Visionary Incorporates Contrasting Elements:
- Both near and far — across time and space
- Both inner and outer in direction
- Both vision (insight) and what becomes grounded in tangible ways
- Both masculine can-do and feminine imagination; a combination of abstraction and execution
- Both particular and personal and on the grandest scale
- Both here and now and off in the clouds (somewhere down the road)

- Both clear and fuzzy for some of it is outside of everyday reality
- Both personal and for the larger community, or even humanity

And these are all happening simultaneously. There is something going on in the lives of travelers that is much more than logical either-or thinking can comprehend.

This is a journey from the familiarity of customary awareness to a degree of integration, wherein each dissimilar element is recognized as relevant and connected.

But all these elements work together as a unit—each adding to wholeness. The journey is about the vision, the person, the vantage point (where they look from) and the broad horizon. Visionaries are engaged and poised for action, changing what is to what it *could be*.

Naked Visionary is about the inner work, not just about the outer work. It cannot pander to the ego, which is eager to take credit for originating the vision—as well as what flows from it. The visionary path has a quality of a humble, solitary pilgrim embarking upon the mythic Hero's Journey.

That path is initially undertaken with humility, devotion, and innocence, and might only later act as a messenger for the divine. At any time upon that journey, if the ego claims ownership, disappointment, tragedy and/or suffering follow.

Where We're Headed

Let's fan the flames of vision wherever they arise. It is time to embrace each other's brilliant notions for their own sake, and for the sake of a splendid future we can envision.

It's time to tackle the challenges of reinventing our way of life so it is more respectful of vision and deeply-held human values.

We should, however, make changes intelligently, drawing upon the strengths that each of us represents. Imagine what can be gained when we build upon each other's contributions for the good of us all.

My Mandate to Write This Book

I've been preparing to write this book for more than 50 years, so it reflects a lifetime on a rather quirky scavenger hunt. The information presented is a mix of my personal insights, a range of research, and the grand scale, of heart, mind and emotions—all mixed in together. It shows my journey, but also the larger journey of the visionary path.

My mother was a *bona fide* eccentric who never found a place she could fit until moving to Alaska before the 1940s. That untamed way of life brings forth inner resources not demanded or tolerated in more cultivated settings. Living on "the last frontier" permitted her to stand tall for the first time in her life.

She was a pioneer in many ways. But as a child I saw her take too many hits because of it. In the writing of this book, I was able to see more clearly than ever before that she was a visionary, one who was broken by the process. So I know the upsides and the downsides of this journey intimately. Nevertheless, she equipped me to understand the value of vision and the freedom necessary to follow it.

My mother taught more by example than by precepts how to be a survivor, without sacrificing the grand view. I was encouraged to push against my limitations and to function from an inner integrity, rather than trying to satisfy external expectations—even hers.

I've walked the visionary path most of my life—all the while as a student of the process. That has been combined with the rigor of a scientist, a philosopher, and a reporter. My eclectic training and careers refined the skills needed to stalk an elusive quarry, as the visionary process has proved to be. But I've learned its scent and can usually spot its signs. The chapters to come detail what I've found.

Center for Visionary Brilliance

This is not simply a book for and about visionaries. It points to the mindset and dynamics of visionary thinking that are *available to anyone*. It is my sincere hope that what I've written will lead to more discussion about the role visionaries play in driving cultural change. And that, in turn, will lead to greater acceptance.

In my mind, I see the possibility of a community forming (a virtual one). For now, it is in its earliest stages. But I expect it to develop further as attention grows. I consider this book a starting point, an invitation to public discourse. During the entire writing process, I felt that this subject has a life of its own.

I am very excited to find out what people can do with what I've written—and where they can fill in the gaps. As only one person, I cannot satisfy all the roles such a significant subject warrants. That is the purpose behind the Center for Visionary Brilliance.

This non-profit organization (described more fully in Chapter 20) will serve as an advocate and resource for the visionary process. It is itself a visionary undertaking, and will only thrive if it fills a need and serves those deeply engaged in these concerns.

I hope to speed up the understanding of a crucial topic that has too long been ignored. I encourage anyone seriously concerned about the visionary process to help me to chart it. Our combined knowledge and insights could aid those anywhere along the visionary path. I sense a community forming around this topic, where an exchange of discoveries can shed more light in this barely-explored terrain.

Part I - The Visionary Process Goes Inward and Outward

When there is no vision, the people perish.
Proverbs 29:18 King James Bible

Say it the other way around: Where there is vision people thrive and bloom. Vision sustains and enriches life beyond bare survival. It permits us to see more than the mundane, to experience the grand and glorious. It vivifies, inspires, and animates us.

Vision is powerful out of proportion to its duration. Its uplifting effect on those who led humanity forward has enriched us all. Vision ignites in us the spark of truth, of insight, of awe, of inspired clarity — which releases a burst of creative energy. Our visions can animate our ideas, encourage worthy deeds, galvanize new directions of thought.

The force of vision shines brighter in some individuals and in some circumstances, but its capacity to inspire resides in everyone. Vision motivates someone to bridge the gap between a dazzling insight and building something tangible from it.

Vision exists in the world of possibilities — a glimmer of what could be, just out of reach. Tantalizing. Some people reach out for it, then follow wholeheartedly where it leads. Those are the visionaries. Where that commitment takes them is on a journey of self-discovery, even while they attempt to ground what they en<u>vision</u> in practical ways.

This book is organized in three parts. Part I deals with the elements of the visionary process: who, how, stages, and turning points. Part II is about bringing the vision to life. Part III describes several specific arenas where visionaries ply their trade: the scientist, the artist, the spiritual searcher.

Section I Contents

Chapter 1   Treading New Ground
Chapter 2   Tracking the Visionary Process
Chapter 3   Stripping Down to Essentials
Chapter 4   Bridging Between Vision and the World
Chapter 5   Going to Extremes
Chapter 6   Finding a Paramount Vision
Chapter 7   Bringing a Vision to Life

Chapter 1 - Treading New Ground

There is a rich vein of information about the visionary journey, and the non-conforming individuals embarked on it, that has never been mined very deeply.

Balanchine and Me

I can clearly remember the evening about twenty-five years ago when I was hit by the insight that eventually led to writing this book. I was watching a PBS (Public Broadcasting System) program about George Balanchine, the choreographer credited with creating modern ballet.

I knew little about ballet, beyond enjoying the graceful beauty of it. Yet as the program described how Balanchine experimented with novel ways to develop a gesture or stretch the body's capabilities, I was amazed. *But that's what I do. That is how I push the limits too.*

Although the form of expression for his field and mine were vastly different, *how* he and I approached what we do was very similar. Both of us were working to discover previously unexplored methods of communicating the inexpressible.

I realized that his *manner of relating to his craft* overlapped my own in numerous ways I could not have imagined. I intuitively appreciated *how he worked* and understood the man himself — from the inside.

Balanchine communicated through the medium of living flesh. He developed novel ways for his dancers to correspond to the flow of music. He exaggerated certain elements of the dance in order to present a different kind of visual form. His dancers used their limbs and gestures in inventive ways that stretched their craft, as well as their bodies.

Balanchine's work grew out of his philosophy about beauty. Without relying much on words, he developed a language of movement that expressed what he could envision. His work with his dance troupe pushed the human body past what was considered doable, so they could display something both pleasing and unexpected.

An aspect of his artistic mastery was his ability to transmit moods and emotions to his dancers through choreography. They were, in turn, able to communicate those sentiments to the audience as a beautiful, deeply moving performance.

In his own words — from *George Balanchine: The ballet maker* by Robert Gottlieb:

> When I stage a ballet (I don't use the word 'create' — God creates and I assemble what already has been created), I try to find interesting proportions of movement in time and space because music is time. It's not the melody that counts. It is the time it gives you. It's up to the choreographer to know what sound represents harmonically, and melodically, and rhythmically and then manipulate the gesture into the time and see if it gives any visual pleasure when you look at it.

Steps don't exist in themselves. There is no such thing as a ready-made combination. You have to use your legs and hands that are ready to move in any direction or any speed at any time, the maximum the body can do.... Eventually, when the whole thing comes to life, they [dancers] will understand what it is. But before it does, you cannot improvise, you have to devise, separately analyse, sift through and slowly feed them and while you're doing that you have to show them every possible position.[1]

Balanchine's unique conception of movement and emotional expression left an indelible mark on classical ballet. His extensive creative output demonstrated something fresh that changed what ballet dancers, composers, and audiences could expect or would try to replicate. As such, he contributed a new model of what was possible in his field. That is one of the defining characteristics of a visionary.

Spotting the Visionary Markers

Since the insight about Balanchine, it has gotten much easier for me to notice the signs of visionary thinking by others—even from seemingly incoherent crumbs. There is an energy and cohesiveness about such originality as clear and distinctive as a bird song. My attention is always scanning popular culture and publications for those unique twerps and trills that stand out from the background chorus.

Unlike then, I am no longer surprised that unique and clear voices go so often unrecognized and unappreciated—especially by the singers of those trills. Sad to say, a visionary is often late to learn his or her unusual approach has much value.

To be a visionary, one must discover at some point what one is passionate about is not as weird as one was led to believe by those devoted to being "normal."

In some ways, the visionary's recognition of the worth of their own distinctive voice is even more important for them than the eventual public acceptance of their inventive ideas. In taking that step, the person claims a right to be heard and leave their one-of-a-kind mark.

Claiming one's uniqueness is crucial to anyone undertaking the visionary path (although it is not always seen at the start). That discovery helps them frame their message and a long-term legacy.

In my opinion, there is a rich vein of information about the visionary journey, and the non-conforming individuals embarked upon it, that has never been mined very deeply. My aim is to describe the influences, rewards, and obstacles that characterize the visionary path.

---

[1] Gottlieb, Robert, *George Balanchine: The ballet maker* (New York: HarperCollins, 2004), 204.

Like an Indian scout who tracks wildlife by reading the bent twigs and disturbed blades of grass they leave, I have honed my stalking skill — alert for subtle and elusive signs that reveal the visionary process at work. What sets those who travel that demanding path apart from their contemporaries? What motivates them, or stops them cold? What is the normal progression most share on the journey? What are the earliest signs of visionary tendencies?

Focusing on the visionary process itself ignores what happens to any specific vision or to its proponent. The approach taken here deals with the *patterns of the journey* — those influences that rise above particular individuals. It provides a rough roadmap of what lies ahead for those on the visionary path, in one guise or another.

Merging the Vision, Messenger, and Mission

A vision or creative discovery often starts as an abstract and electrifying idea. What gives it life, substance, and relevance comes from devoted efforts by the specific person (or core group) who brings it forth into reality. They will do it *their way*. And taking on that responsibility has personal consequences for them separate from the fate of their vision.

The visionary path is transformational, certainly for the person who develops a new creative platform, as well as for his or her community. Stories of *who did what* and *how they did it* are easy to find. In contrast, the path visionaries travel is not well known. It rises above the personalities and specifics, linking them to greater universality.

Those who are lauded as visionaries make up but the tip of the iceberg of those who demonstrate visionary qualities and motivations. Most of them function out of the public eye. They share certain similarities and priorities in the way they work, as well as certain qualities that set them apart from their peers. By disregarding the specifics of a particular person's culture or field, it is easier to notice some of those common influences.

Known or unknown, successful or not, tormented or acclaimed — those are secondary considerations dictated as much by happenstance as by the person's efforts or the value of what they contribute. The visionary process is partly personal, but in many ways it is impersonal and generic, serving up comparable challenges and rewards to all comers.

Studying the process casts light on the commonalities among visionaries. Each visionary is unique in the way he or she chooses to nourish their vision and message; in the ways they respond to common obstacles; in the impact they make, both in their time and later. How each traveler decides to navigate the journey is every bit as idiosyncratic and revealing as their igniting vision.

Off the Beaten Path

Abraham Lincoln said, "Towering genius disdains a beaten path. It seeks regions hitherto unexplored." Whatever their differences might be from each other, the visionaries among us are the ones who leave the beaten path of conformity and security in search of something else.

Anyone who goes that route does not have to be a "towering genius," since it is impossible to know until much later. There is a price for doing so, but most who choose that path will claim, if asked, they could not have done otherwise.

I consider the visionary spirit a treasure that deserves to be sought and nurtured. It is a vital resource to be tapped—and not just for the financial rewards it could bring. Yet this resource of inestimable value has never been appreciated sufficiently in its own right. Nor is it encouraged to grow much except around the edges.

"We can do better" is the credo of those who see beyond what already exists. Then intrepid souls set out to prove it in a myriad of ways. I think all of us could do better about encouraging sparks of genius to shine brighter—whether our own or those found in others.

The urge to explore the unknown is wired into each of us, but most people do not take it to heart. Something changes for those who do, as detailed in the following chapters.

Very real differences exist between a performance artist, a biologist, and a politician, even when each personifies the visionary process. The individual's sphere of interest, or the style of contribution permitted in it, must also be considered in order to make meaningful statements about the type of challenges most likely to be encountered.

On one hand, it is over-simplistic to treat all visionaries like they are the same, or on the other hand, to act like these individuals are too unique to be categorized at all. It is impossible to put their collective personality traits in a blender and come up with a typical visionary. Besides, the ubiquitous stereotypes about creative types are largely off the mark.

A visionary's sphere could be in areas as dissimilar as spiritual matters, scientific or artistic fields, philosophy, or re-directing social conventions. Each sphere has its own sub-set of standards, challenges, and nomenclature particular to its participants. But whatever one's unique qualities might be, anyone rigorously engaged in the visionary process participates in experiences that are not solely *for them*—or *about them*.

The visionary path represents an identifiable process, irrespective of the uniqueness of the individuals who walk it. It is lawful and progressive, with specific stages and rites of passage.

Elements of the Visionary Process:
- The vision and subsequent message and mission (Chapter 6)
- The person who champions a vision (Chapter 4)
- The context in which the process occurs—the time, place and zeitgeist; also, the specific field of endeavor involved
- The challenges—both internal and external (Chapter 8)
- The package for the vision, and sometimes a protective organization
- The impact of the visionary and the vision
  - Effect on the visionary personally (and the supporting organization)
  - Effect on the world, the future, and those who follow it

My challenge in writing about this topic involved being specific enough to bring fresh thinking about the visionary process, without resorting to generalities that mask relevant distinctions about it, or about members of this group. (However, using "group" to describe such unique loners does not imply customary group dynamics, or that individuals know and influence each other directly.)

From Traveler to Chronicler

Some years ago, in the heat of an insight about visionaries, I called a close friend to chew over the implications. I hadn't said much before she stopped me with the shocking announcement,

"But you know you're not a visionary, don't you?"

"How can that be? I have been on this journey almost my whole life. It is who I am," I sputtered.

She replied, "That's right, and it was true for you until now. I am not saying you *haven't been* a visionary. You were, but you are no longer wedded to a particular vision in the way most visionaries are. I noticed that something has changed for you. I think you have become a *visionary about the visionary process itself.*"

New idea! As we talked further, I came to realize she was right. I had changed my frame of reference about my relationship to the visionary path. I was still on it for my own growth arc, but I had assumed another responsibility toward the experience as well. I was also a witness.

It was not just about me following my personal journey and my own visions any more. I had also become a chronicler who could report about the nature of the path itself.

Because of that conversation, I adjusted my attention to identify the features of the journey with greater care. The visionary process itself had become a primary focus of mine I had not noticed until then.

Here is an example of how an intense interest with lots of insights can take on the nature of a vision over time, supplanting a person's other interests and priorities.

So I ponder: What are its underlying dynamics? What "goes with the territory"? What challenges signify common markers and turning points? What constitute the land mines and quicksand? Are they avoidable? What must occur for a spark of vision to be sustained over time? Where do most visionaries encounter their greatest frustration? Satisfaction? Lots of questions…

My Motivation

Finding such answers has been a lifelong pursuit of mine since I feel a deep kinship with those intrepid explorers off the beaten path. I have known its triumphs and defeats first hand, and second hand, and third hand—and often enough to see past the drama, the guts and gore. Yet I am also objective enough to acknowledge its setbacks and challenges are beneficial in making those who face them grow stronger still.

My innumerable learning curves and eclectic range of careers refined my skills for stalking the elusive visionary process—often nearby but largely unseen. I learned to recognize its scent and sometimes spot its presence, even when it has not yet fully developed in someone. By comparison, spotting it through the ripened fruit it bears is somewhat easier.

The chapters ahead detail much of what I have found about the visionary process. But my involvement with it goes way beyond writing this book because encouraging visionary sparks on a larger scale has become a life mission of mine as well.

I was born and raised in Alaska, which is called The Last Frontier. Growing up at the edge of civilization brings forth inner resources, neither demanded nor tolerated in more cultivated settings. The dominant culture of Alaska back then was of misfits.

It is summed up by the old saying: "Everybody in Alaska is wanted—or not wanted." It is not exactly true, but points to their rugged individualism and a preference for being a step removed from normal society.

That environment, and my hugely eccentric mother, made me a frontier thinker—as are many visionaries. (I can now, in retrospect, recognize so many of my mother's unconventional ways as signs of visionary thinking, even though it made me "roll my eyes" back then).

Perhaps the quirkiness in how I grew up gave me an appreciation of how those out of the mainstream or ahead of the curve operate (including myself). I have long wondered why vision-driven nonconformists are so uniformly mischaracterized and misunderstood. Despite that, more people keep heading off on this journey, without regard for the high personal costs.

Giving Credence to the Quest

What drives us? Us—yes, I must declare I speak as a member of that company (nowhere near a public figure, however). For my part, I strongly feel a personal responsibility to act as a spokesperson for those who have not been inclined to speak out in their own defense.

There is a need to set some matters straight, to cut through the fanciful assumptions about what visionaries are up to. In my opinion, it is time for the world to look at those who wear the visionary mantle in a different way, without the distrust and rejection that has so hobbled those who "bring fire from the gods."

That refers to Prometheus, who stole fire from the gods and gave it to humans. According to Greek myth, Zeus punished Prometheus (who was immortal) by chaining him to a rock and having an eagle peck out his liver, which grew back each day, only to be pecked out again. Human beings accepted the gift, but without much appreciation for his sacrifice.

The myth also relates to vision, the spark of inspiration that has a godlike quality about it. Vision transcends the tangible human world and unites us with a larger, inspired view that is beyond our usual limits. The visionaries among us attempt to bring visions into the world, and like Prometheus, often suffer for it.

I am humbled by the scope of the task and ask, what gives me the right? So I apply the twin tests I must be clear about whenever deciding whether to proceed with something new: Why me? Why now?

- **Why me?**
  I care enough to be as objective and honest as the task demands. I have spent sufficient time in the trenches to get past the glamor of it. I respect the visionary process and trust its overall purpose, though it is a tough taskmaster. I have lived almost every phase of it—and that required many years of intense sustained effort.

  This path has been a compelling influence on how I operate and who I have become. Thus I can spot its "fingerprints" in the lives of others. Besides, I seem to be uniquely wired up for the undertaking.

- **Why now?**
  The world, with all its urgent problems and ill will, sorely needs what visionaries can bring—and soon, too. Just as important, it is time for more visionary thinkers to come out of the margins, so they can launch what shines bright in them. They are needed, and I sense a new receptivity to fresh thinking is emerging.

My being humbled and awed by this task, yet taking it on anyway, characterizes an early phase of visionary undertakings (that most on the path have decided "yes" to). I have accepted the charge and am committing to taking it as far as I am able. It feels like my destiny to do this.

To quote Emerson, "Do not go where the path may lead, go instead where there is no path and leave a trail." Here is my effort to bushwhack a trail through the underbrush. I encourage others to help build the road.

Taking the Fork in the Road

Plenty of Detours, But No Shortcuts

There are both inner and outer battles to be waged early on, and more encountered along the visionary path. Each visionary is on his or her own personal journey as they promote their particular vision.

However, the obstacles encountered are not merely personal, as they mark distinct stages of the process. Almost every traveler encounters them, and some challenges are essential to refine both the vision and the visionary.

We do not need to agree about who is or is not a visionary. It is enough for our purposes to recognize a person exhibited certain signs of visionary thinking and that they acted on some non-mundane and original notion with unyielding determination to make it happen. It does not depend on their ultimate achievement.

Looking at the visionary process as one of personal growth and evolution recognizes a particular person's degree of refinement changes along the way. The path is not static or homogeneous from end to end. While the form of the process is tailored for each traveler, it has defining and shared characteristics. And there are major differences between those embarked on this journey and their contemporaries who are not.

Its route leads somewhere — somewhere travelers only recognize in retrospect, through their direct experience and the lessons learned along the way. The purpose of the path is not just to guide travelers to the finish, but to assure they grow through the experience.

Additionally, certain difficulties only present themselves after others have been successfully overcome.

The visionary path is long and complicated, given its extended duration and the variety of terrain encountered. It reflects a timeline and orderly progression. Also, different phases of it call forth different skills. The protracted time the journey takes helps to assure the visionary and their message mature in sync.

The journey cannot be rushed. Besides, as Beverly Sills, the opera singer, said, "There are no shortcuts to any place worth going."

While it is a pathway walked by others over the years, the form it takes is also unique for each traveler. Many who followed it perished without ever passing on their bright light. Think of all those who never got far enough to leave a lasting mark: the cure for diabetes, an abundant green energy source, a resolution of bigotry — who knows...

I came to know (among other things) a vision has certain qualities that are distinctly different from a good idea. Having the vision does not make a visionary. Many people have worthy visions, lots of them. Few commit to them or see them through. Fewer yet devote their lives to bringing their inspired insight to fruition. Intense dedication and single-mindedness are needed for the making of a visionary.

Charting the Route

Most of what has been written about visionaries has been a specific person's story, or something that tells about what someone accomplished — the fruits. There is scant information about the process itself. Yet those farthest ahead of the curve walk common ground with those who acted on earlier visions.

And they keep smashing into many of the same obstacles that appear in diverse guises across different times and cultures.

Since many such difficulties are identifiable, it should be easier for travelers to steer around them — if the signs can be clearly identified from the outset. That's my theory, anyway.

Looking at the lives of visionaries as though they are engaged in a process gives an overview — a context beyond individual lives and circumstances. Surely, if budding visionaries understood they were embarking on a journey with identifiable choice points and hazards, more of them might be able to navigate through the obstacle course successfully.

They could also spot the difference between fellow travelers and imposters, who fail to engage beyond platitudes. Those on the visionary path can usually recognize others who are dealing with comparable issues intrinsic to the process. There is something like a dog-whistle that is quite audible to others who are similarly engaged. So they often recognize each other as fellow travelers or forerunners.

A mythology has grown up around well-known visionaries that makes such individuals seem different from the rest of us. Much such iconic admiration is derived from an inaccurate picture of what actually occurred for the visionary in real life. Fanciful assumptions about them does not give a sense of the authentic person.

Looking at the process cuts through the myths, and lets us see visionaries (be they grand or budding) without their story getting in the way of appreciating their ordinariness reaching for extraordinary.

What Makes a Visionary, Anyway?

The word "visionary" has been thrown around rather casually. It is as likely to be bestowed on a mediocre leader or the latest fad as to a significant change agent like Gandhi, Edison, or Disney, who forever altered the culture or their field.

This book sets out to ascertain qualities most visionaries have in common. What are the identifiable traits and motivations of a budding change agent? Why do some thrive while many more languish?

An important factor in the visionary process is the social environment in which it occurs. Change does not occur in isolation. How well the visionary is able to chart the waters of his or her milieu may well determine whether there will be an enduring impact from their contribution. (See Chapter 9 about change.)

Visionaries function in the field of potential. They create the bridges whereby what is seen as possible in the far-off scheme of things becomes tangible in the here and now. Visionaries appeal to the truth in the "knowing place" within each of us.

Their concept of what is possible appears to be unconnected because the dots from A to Z are not obvious yet. The visionary flair is in connecting those dots — often in startling ways.

During their lifetimes, such individuals are likely to look like crackpots because what they are up to is not understood by the larger community. They challenge common wisdom to varying degrees. What drives them to be so contrary? It is not the contrariness we should notice, but *what they are contrary about*.

They are trying to build a case for another way of understanding what the rest of us assume we already know. We ignore or dismiss those individuals to our peril.

Those on the visionary path are learning the abundant differences between the conventional worldview and what is required to hold a larger-than-life view. They confound normal expectations and throw sand in the gears of business as usual. In the process, such individuals demonstrate the forces of novelty at work.

The visionary process expands the perspective of those who go through its tutorials (real-life experiences). They are compelled to see beyond simple, self-centered, self-interest rooted in the short term. At their best, the visionary is not thinking about what's in it for *me*, but what is in it for *us*. They adhere to a longer time horizon, which includes the brighter future they are trying to create.

Defining a Place for Themselves to Stand

Here are several rough categories to sort those immersed in the process. Bear in mind, each field of interest influences the ways participants differ in their style, influence, and impact. One sphere is not better than another, and a particular person or subject matter can inhabit more than one sphere simultaneously or sequentially.

Flavors of visionary-ness:
- Innovators, futurists, and abstract problem solvers
- Spiritual or religious — prophets, mystics, shamans
- Scientific or technological discoverers, inventors, researchers
- Creative artists — music, writing, painting, film, dance, architecture, etc.
- Political and organizational leaders who significantly alter the social framework

- Crusaders who lead the charge for beneficial social, political, or scientific changes
- Philosophers, systems builders, theorists

By the same token, such is the nature of innovation it is possible for there to be a field of interest with only a single person in it initially. Someone could plant a flag in previously unsuspected or unexplored territory. Those committed to the visionary process exhibit a disregard for defined categories and boundaries. Such individuals can discover new frontiers in the midst of what is already considered to be well-tilled fields.

As they stretch the scope of what human beings know, creative types sometimes find it necessary to create whole new places for their vision to thrive. This could occur on an individual scale or by establishing entirely new domains of knowledge.

Mihaly Csikszentmihalyi describes the immensity of creating whole new professions to accommodate visionary discoveries in *Creativity: Flow and the psychology of discovery and invention*.

> Creative individuals usually are forced to invent the jobs they will be doing all through their lives. One could not have been a psychoanalyst before Freud, an aeronautical engineer before the Wright brothers, an electrician before Galvani, Volta, and Edison, or a radiologist before Roentgen. These individuals not only discovered new ways of thinking and of doing things but also became the first practitioners in the domains they discovered and made it possible for others to have jobs and careers in them. So creative individuals don't have careers; they create them. In addition, these pioneers must create a field that will follow their ideas, or their discovery will soon vanish from the culture. Freud had to attract physicians and neurologists to his camp; the Wright brothers had to convince other mechanics that aeronautics was going to be a feasible career. Because careers can take place only within fields, if a person wants to have a career in a field that does not exist, he or she must invent it. And that is what people who create new domains do.[2]

Visionaries "See" Something More

Humanity stands on the shoulders of a long procession of unidentifiable visionaries. They made the evolutionary leaps that launched waves of progress. Without those willing to make such efforts we would still be living in the trees. Humanity, left to its own safe and predictable preferences, would not have advanced so far without what curious forerunners found. This book grew (in part) from my desire to honor the efforts of our visionary predecessors.

Nicholas Nassim Taleb, a writer about change, said ,"History and societies do not crawl. They make jumps. They go from fracture to fracture, with few

---

[2] Csikszentmihalyi, Mihaly, *Creativity: Flow and the psychology of discovery and invention* (New York, HarperCollins, 1996), 193.

vibrations in between. Yet we (and historians) like to believe in the predictable, small incremental progression."[3] It is mostly the visionaries who make those jumps, creating new paths where the rest of us could follow.

- "Vision is the art of seeing what is invisible to others." (Jonathan Swift)
- "Visionary people are visionary partly because of the very great many things they don't see." (Eric Hoffer)
- "Every creative act involves … a new innocence of perception, liberated from the cataract of accepted belief." (Arthur Koestler)
- "The idealists and visionaries, foolish enough to throw caution to the winds and express their ardor and faith in some supreme deed, have advanced mankind and have enriched the world." (Emma Goldman)
- "The visionary is the one who brings his or her voice into the world and who refuses to edit, rehearse, perform, or hide. It is the visionary who knows that the power of creativity is aligned with authenticity." (Angeles Arrien)
- "A visionary is one who can find his way by moonlight, and see the dawn before the rest of the world." (Oscar Wilde)
- "Part of understanding the creative urge is understanding that it's primal. Wanting to change the world is not a noble calling, it's a primal calling." (Hugh MacLeod)
- "Vision without action is merely a dream, action without vision just passes the time, vision with action can change the world." (Joel Barker)
- "It is not the earthquake that controls the advent of a different life but storms of generosity and visions of incandescent souls." (Boris Pasternak)
- "True originality consists not in a new manner but in a new vision." (Edith Wharton)
- "You are not here merely to make a living. You are here to enable the world to live more amply, with greater vision, and with a finer spirit of hope and achievement. You are here to enrich the world, and you impoverish yourself if you forget this errand." (Woodrow Wilson)

Visions and Visionaries Are Unique

The force of the igniting vision inspires innumerable descriptions—all inadequate. In the case of any particular visionary, there is a specific defining vision, or there is not. It can be a singular event, or a frequent occurrence; experienced after long preparation, or in a flash—without any prior efforts.

---

[3] Taleb, Nassim Nicholas, *The Black Swan: The impact of the highly improbable* (New York: Random House, 2007), 11.

Visionaries are exceptional, and how they came by their visions are likely to be as atypical as what they decide to do about them.

Visions arise as the offspring of inspired clarity. The whole out-of-this-world experience feels full and complete (fulfilled). Some people find themselves forever altered by what became apparent for them through a vision.

Someone might feel inspired to start a new scientific specialty, for instance, or put gears in motion — gears that change the world (or some pocket of it).

It could take a religious or spiritual form, in a context divorced from practical considerations. Maslow believed at the core of every known high religion could be found "the private, lonely personal illumination, revelation or ecstasy of some acutely sensitive prophet or seer."

What such individuals encounter as they attempt to ground what they discovered corresponds to the visionary process. Robert and Michele Root-Bernstein are experts in creativity. In *Sparks of Genius* they said:

> At first the impulse, the vision, the feeling, is unspoken. But in the end it must come to words. Once the poet or writer has received inspiring or troubling images and feelings, the problem is the same one shared by scientists and artists: how to translate these internal feelings into an external language other people can experience.[4]

Taking the steps to communicate and ground the vision that shines bright for them moves someone from the tried-and-true, into unfamiliar territory. The person feels they absolutely must do something concrete with what they discovered. The determined efforts made to express what they see allow others to experience it too.

Making Something Out of Nothing

What visionaries seem to have in common is an insistence their "dream" be brought into our waking reality. They heed the advice of Thoreau: "If you have built castles in the air, your work need not be lost; that is where they should be. Now put foundations under them."

Edison defined the visionary process in his famous saying: "Genius is one percent inspiration and ninety-nine percent perspiration." The initial work of visionaries is in getting prepared and holding a state of readiness for a spark of insight — the "1% inspiration." Then comes the never-fully-completed task of grounding it in the world of matter, where "99% perspiration" applies.

The visionary process alters all who undertake it. The degree of change is proportionate to the amount of diligence required by the visionary to ground their inspiration. What a visionary contributes is more than the concrete fruits of

---

[4] Root-Bernstein, Robert and Michele, *Sparks of Genius: The thirteen thinking tools of the world's most creative people* (New York: Houghton Mifflin, 1999), 9.

their vision, but it also shows itself through the quality of who they become via the trip.

One of the consequences of the visionary process is a forging of a vision-visionary dyad. The relationship between the vision and the visionary is symbiotic. As the vision and visionary become more enmeshed and representative of each other, it is an identity changer.

The visionary path is not for the faint of heart. It does not go quickly, but proceeds at its own pace, which cannot be rushed. It takes its travelers on a life-long experience. Once they commit to the process, it alters who they are and what they do in a decisive way. For some notions, what was set in motion continues to play out long after the visionary dies.

After the Vision

The visionary's challenge, once they return to their everyday frame of mind, is not so much to find a way to return to the otherworldly state of amplified clarity, but to establish a way to function in everyday life again. Finding a course of behavior that respects what was seen so clearly in their vision, yet allows them to function *in the world,* is the visionary's first, ongoing, and most daunting task.

The monumental difficulty in making them work together accounts for why so many visionaries were treated as weirdoes—even while their innovative efforts may have been adopted. Those who attempt to ground their visions have a foot in two competing realities, and they must find a way to reconcile them.

Initially, the visionary path leads to the person's divergence from their familiar and conventional worldview. He or she is on a journey that takes them both inward and outward, in order to ground what their insight revealed.

Much later, the visionary path leads toward a reconciliation of the two competing views because the individual became adept at functioning with both.

The vision's out-of-this-world qualities are nearly impossible to describe after they fade away. Besides, there are inherent problems in discussing something the human brain, language, and memory are not equipped to handle. Transcendent experiences are dynamic and are not fixed in time.

According to Charles Sigismund, author of *Champions of Silicon Valley*, "Real visions are alive and organic, changing over time, as are people's skills in creating, communicating, and executing them."[5]

The endless challenge for a visionary is to find ways to bring the spark of vision into his or her everyday life, so their existing circumstances or behavior will shift in its direction. Visionaries put together the intervening steps between their

---

[5] Sigismund, Charles G., *Champions of Silicon Valley: Visionary thinking from today's technology pioneers* (New York: John Wiley & Sons, 2000), 4.

bright idea and something tangible. Once they do so, other people can experience something of what they foresaw.

The Big Tent of "Vision" Meanings

"Vision" will be used throughout the book in many different ways. Since these connotations overlap and are not exclusive of each other, readers must take their cues from the context.

Meanings of "vision" (in no particular order):
- The moment of greatest inspirational clarity—the igniting experience
- What is perceived in a profound state—the whole of it or aspects of it
- The culmination of multiple significant insights or breakthroughs
- What the visionary sees and serves—the person's turning point and touchstone
- The memory of what was experienced—*after* the full intensity has faded, all someone can hold onto; the residue of inspired clarity
- The direct awareness of Unity (the sense that everything is connected), along with all the profound truths related to it
- The sense of knowing one's purpose and place in the larger scheme of things; held in one's "knowing place"
- The Spark of Truth received in a moment of clarity; what the visionary attempts to embody, express, and make tangible
- The ability to see beyond the everyday realm of existence; to see with the inner eye; usually short-lived leaving a pale memory
- The core insight transmitted from the visionary to others
- The subsequent message developed by the visionary; the package (vessel)
- The supernatural or psychic experiences that might accompany the event(s) when it arose
- The guiding beacon that leads the visionary while acting; the espoused mission
- The part of the abstract notion that can be grounded and made concrete
- The sound bite or slogan the public receives about the message—a mere crumb

Also bear in mind "vision" is both about the *process of seeing* (whether with the inner eye of imagination or the physical eyes) as well as *what is being seen*. Chapter 12 describes how Visual Seeing and Naked Vision differ from normal vision—both of which are sharpened on the visionary path.

Because visions are dynamic, expansive, and fluid, any vision resists being nailed down too precisely. It would be inaccurate to treat any person's vision as a single, integrated, or cast-in-stone incident, or to compare visions as though it were. Each vision is very personal, as is the individual's reaction to it as it occurs.

Visions often reveal beauty or a larger view of life far beyond simple survival. It is married to the heart and our "higher angels," which insist, "This is the only thing that matters now. You must act!"

It urges us to pay attention to the fuller experience of what is going on, to sense it completely and in as many ways as possible. Then it urges us to behave accordingly. The visionaries among us take that charge to heart.

Surviving the Visionary Process

Survival Tools for the Trek

The visionary path can be lonely, distant from familiar roadways and companions. Solitary travelers often find they must "invent the wheel" about how to proceed—on top of the difficulties inherent in pursuing their vision.

Given that other audacious travelers have gone ahead of them on the path, why aren't there time-honored markers and tools for dealing with the likely difficulties?

Imagine how much less struggle they would face if visionaries knew themselves to be engaged in a long-term process with specific obstacles and rites of passage. They would realize that some difficulties they endure are not entirely personal, or a consequence of their failings. They would be better able to read the signals and pick their battles from the outset. They would gain—we all would gain.

I like to think it is possible to hand out maps and wheel-making advice for those who set out. As the likely obstacles inherent in the path are better mapped and understood, more travelers could find their way through the inhospitable territory, as they follow their inventive pursuits.

Although reference is made to a visionary path throughout the book, it is not to restrict or dictate any traveler's options. It is not a set path, but the opposite of that, since it expands the possibilities for each individual.

Nor am I implying I know "the way" or what somebody should do. Those who take the path are making their own route, each step and decision along the way.

The precise course each person takes is of their choosing. Nothing in the chapters ahead should be construed as telling someone what they *should do* or *should not do*—particularly if it conflicts with their sense of purpose. Each reader should pick and choose from this smorgasbord of information and decide what is helpful or fits their circumstances.

Equipped for the Long Slog

While writing this book, I visualized myself packing a backpack readers could take on their tramp off the beaten path. It includes: rough maps of trails, warnings about critical dangers to watch for, advice, and assorted gear to help traverse the perilous terrain.

Nobody needs everything that is tucked in, and the value of some of it only appears when deep in the swamp. But every bit of it could be heartening to someone who is struggling on the frontier.

No cookbook approach is possible for something as idiosyncratic as the visionary path. This book is not a how-to manual explaining how to become a visionary. But it might help anyone recognize and respect their own sparks of genius (because they come to all of us). Some might even feel emboldened to take timid steps—setting them on a new course.

The visionaries among us who have made the leap are already committed to leaving the safe and familiar behind. They will read this book very differently than others because of being immersed in the process. Those well along the path will recognize it describes issues and concerns they've been living through.

This is not a travel guide for people who are not inclined to take the trip. Nothing in it will make a person imbued with conventional thinking bother with the visionary path. More likely, a clearer perception of the inherent difficulties involved would convince them they are right not to bother.

Everyone has moments of inspiration and creative urges. Most people do not feel the need to respond by making the major life changes that characterize the visionary path. There are innumerable ways to ground their insights within normal life activities. The actual percentage of devoted visionaries in the population is small. But the number who find ways to nurture a mini-vision is immense.

Some readers may be emerging visionaries, who sense their own urges to act on a vision growing stronger in them. What I have written could help him or her to understand what is involved—both the risks and benefits.

What they consider to be just about them is, in truth, part of a larger view and greater opportunity. If they leap, they will have a better sense of why.

In this time of social unrest and widespread instability, more and more individuals are looking around for where they belong. They sense they do not fit in the broader culture or want what it offers. As a result, many feel driven to find their own place or path. Such individuals are feeling the pull of innovative thinking, and looking for ways to leave their mark.

To those readers who recognize a resonance with the visionary process as discussed here, I say: You could be a visionary thinker. Your dreams and frustrations are not flukes but calls to greatness.

Who Needs to Understand the Visionary Process?
- Visionaries and creative types of all stripes, who exert an innovative influence in the world
- Educators and therapists who work with children, non-conformists, and individuals attracted to unconventional strategies
- Those on the vanguard of the massive shifts afoot (at whatever scale)

- Leaders and social influencers in a position to direct or support large-scale constructive change
- Those sensing the pull of their own "distant drummer" or "wee small voice" and do not know what to make of it
- Close family, friends, and supporters of someone showing visionary tendencies, who want to understand what is going on with them or their aspirations—and maybe how to support them better
- Experts in social and organizational change like business leaders, educators, psychologists, and social scientists
- Change agents and early adopters who embrace what is coming early on, and help to build a consensus for it; those involved in visionary organizations or movements
- Cultural Creatives, a combination of social movements that is 80,000,000 strong

Attention to Visionary Thinking

As I wrote this book, my attention was on the visionary *process* and the individuals most enmeshed in it. By the time it was done, my focus had changed to visionary *thinking*. It is a quality not only of certain gifted or driven individuals, but of *all individuals*. Then the issue becomes, who reaches beyond their usual range of effort to make it happen? It is the impulse to stretch beyond the rational or easily attainable, to "go for it" in some way that defies customary limits.

It is that quality, the spark of inspired "what if?" this book addresses. I feel that urge arises much more often within each of us than we consciously recognize. That sublime impulse deserves to be encouraged, whether or not a person ever takes it very far. To the question "who can benefit from more visionary thinking?" the answer is increasingly: we all can.

To those who cannot get their bearings or decode the unfamiliar signals being encountered these days, the chapters ahead offer some clues and a few time-tested tricks. But I also urge readers to realize there are no bystanders who do not have a stake in these matters.

Everyone alive is being given a vote between a flailing *status quo* or something inspired we want bad enough to work hard to make it happen. Our individual wee small voices are working overtime to get us into position where our unique interests and abilities match up with the world's needs.

For anyone heading off to new frontiers, here is my stack of spare wheels, maps, and camping gear. For those readers who see any of their own issues and challenges described, it is my hope you will take renewed courage to stand strong.

For those who don't care to hang out over the edge, maybe a better understanding of what is involved will build compassion for those who do.

A Specific Visionary – Sam Houston

"Do Right and Risk the Consequences"

Distinct stages and trials test everyone who walks the visionary path—without regard for their personal skills, qualities, or form of contribution. Still, it is helpful to put a face on the progression of the visionary process, and how likely it is to encounter extreme highs and lows.

I chose Sam Houston, a political figure whose long life spanned a period of significant social change in the mid-1800s (1793-1863). As The Father of Texas, he influenced many of the large-scale changes of that period and embodied the visionary process for a generation.

His efforts significantly speeded up the western expansion of America. Houston was a rare historic figure whose actual exploits were even more remarkable and heroic than the fictionalized yarns that grew up about him.

Houston was an American statesman, soldier, and pioneer. He was a polarizing and controversial figure in his day, who was at some points widely popular, and at other points reviled and rejected. In whichever role he played, he was ardently outspoken for what he considered right.

His fortunes ebbed and flowed because of it. But he stuck to his principles, as befitted his slogan, "Do right and risk the consequences."

Although Houston had significant achievements, he also had significant failures. Even his confidantes were usually kept in the dark about his true intentions. He kept those who relied on him off balance with his vacillation and doubts. By swimming against the popular tide time and again, he amassed powerful enemies. He was a man of contradictions; historians still argue about what accounted for his inconsistent behavior.

Houston was Governor of Tennessee early in life, but turned his back on that relatively settled and respected life. After a personal disgrace, he withdrew to the Indian territories and lived among the Indians for a long time. He eventually ended up in Texas when it was fighting for its independence from Mexico.

He led the undisciplined ragtag army to victory over Mexico, and helped to found the Republic of Texas (its own country). Later he arranged for Texas to be annexed to the United States—a move which was highly unpopular among many Texans.

Historic Facts about Sam Houston:
- Lived among the Indians (truly off the beaten path); later he acted as an advocate for their fair treatment
- Successfully led the army in the War with Mexico which led to the establishment of the Republic of Texas
- First and third President of the Republic of Texas
- Negotiated the annexation of the Republic of Texas to the U.S.A.

- U.S. Senator from Texas
- Governor of the State of Texas (after it joined the USA); also Governor of Tennessee, much earlier
- Refused to swear loyalty to the Confederacy when Texas seceded from the U.S.A.
- Resigned from Texas governorship rather than lead Texas against the Union side in the Civil War (another unpopular stance)
- Died in poverty and relative disgrace

Those speak to his accomplishments in the public eye. But the visionary process is also about the inner journey and how a person matures to their full character. Houston's insistence on human values and doing the right thing reflect well on his inner stature.

Some of his public "failures" indicate his being torn between high ideals about democracy and the high-stakes pressure of leadership in such a polarized and combustible period.

Despite being demonized by his opponents, he did not choose to play in the mud. However, he displayed enough inconsistencies between opportunity and action to be considered a "flawed giant." Yet we can see that his life demonstrated the visionary process in many respects. (See list of visionary stages in Chapter 8.)

What We Can Learn from Sam Houston

- He was a high-profile agent of change at points where massive change happened—more than once
- He was a populist, a proponent of human dignity who never forgot his humble roots
- He took unpopular stands on principle, often at great personal cost because it was the right thing to do
- He fought for the big picture and long term, and refused to sacrifice it for his own gain, or to short-term but ill-advised political influences
- He was a true leader, not willing to bend to popular pressure or duck the hard questions
- He was a flawed person with some skeletons in his closet, who consistently held to certain standards, although frequently torn and immobilized by doubts
- He made hard choices and accepted the consequences for himself and his position
- Although maligned and misunderstood, history has shown him to be on the right side of many of the issues he espoused

Bringing It Home

Using a visionary as swashbuckling as Sam Houston as an example seems remote from today's concerns. He is a figure from a point in history with very different realities than our own period.

Yet he was very much ahead of his time, a frontiersman in every sense of the word. He lived in a time of revolutionary change and his activities altered history on a grand scale.

Houston was larger than life and a very polarizing figure even when alive. Most of his principled stands have stood the test of time. And now the myth of the man has overtaken the facts about his life or accomplishments.

You could well be asking, **but what about me?** My life and circumstances are not nearly as dramatic. I am not like that and never could be. But am I a visionary? Or could I be one if I want to?

I cannot give a 10-item quiz, after which you conclude "I guess I am a visionary." But you don't have to read very far to sense either an affinity with the visionary path, or not.

Your heart will quicken with the recognition of where you *already stand* on these matters. Some of you will sense those leanings within yourself, and know they have been present for a long time.

Embedded in the language of this book itself is an energetic field. There is plenty for the mind to digest. But there is also a subliminal message sent out on the channel accessed by your inner awareness—the one your mind cannot grok. (*Grok* means To have an intuitive understanding of; to know something without having to think about it; from *Stranger in a Strange Land* by Robert Heinlein)

That channel has been activated to a marked degree in those inclined to walk the visionary path. It resonates to the sound of the distant drummer, the tug of an inspired notion that refuses to fade into the background, the dream for a better tomorrow because of something you did "for real." That energy is experienced as the longing of the heart, the beckoning of the wee small voice, or the pull of one's destiny.

While that possibility exists in all people, for most it is the Door B that never gets opened—or just a crack. The visionaries open Door B and step through. If your heart beats faster and you feel those urges in yourself quicken as you read this you know: I am one! Or I'm leaning in that direction.

If a leaning forward does not happen as you read, you probably aren't (at this time, anyway). But anyone could do more to encourage their creative insights and invite the Muses. And once they are engaged, no telling…

Nobody is born a visionary. It results from wanting a bright and shiny notion enough to surrender to what the visionary process demands of those committed to it.

So the next question: "What should I do? Tell me what to do next." Here is what the visionaries come to understand: "Nobody can tell me that. Even if someone tried, I wouldn't listen. This is *my journey*, done *my way*. Perhaps some encouragement or lucky breaks would help, but lack of them won't stop me. *It's why I am here.*"

Besides, a large component of the visionary journey comes through self-discovery. So it speaks only to you—in ways that matter to you very specifically.

Insofar as this book is concerned, everything I have written can be likened to a rough trail through dense woods, marked by an X etched into the bark of a few trees. It indicates someone else has passed this way and left some clues.

The energy riding along between the words of the page is nourishing to the inquiring spirit. It assures those who share the visionary path that: "You are not by yourself. There is a larger purpose at work, that is not only personal to you."

For those readers who sense a pull toward an inspired summons, the renewed courage that comes with accepting what a vision of your own requires could help you accept your own "knowing."

It might spark a resolve to "follow where my inspiration leads me." That inner voice is the one you must heed in *taking steps to ground your vision*. With it comes a clear sense of a larger purpose.

I am also hoping the journey can be less arduous for future travelers because what I described helps them prepare for what lies ahead.

Chapter 2 - Tracking the Visionary Process

Trailblazers can expect no handy roadmap with duly marked hazards for where they are headed. Those who set out must be tenacious, courageous, and a bit "touched in the head."

The Unpredictable Dark Horse

The visionary path tends toward the unlikely outcome—the "crazy idea" that inexplicably caught on. The freshly minted notion starts with little likelihood of prevailing. Its urging toward change begins as a mere drip… drip, drip, possibly growing to a steady drip, then maybe a flow, or then a torrent.

But at no point early on could the magnitude of change it brings have been predicted. The notion was a long shot—right up until it wasn't.

The visionary path resembles a steeple chase. Out of the starting gate, each participant must clear certain hurdles before moving on to subsequent ones. Can someone make all the jumps? Will they go the distance? There is no finish line, no trophy, and the biggest winners (giants) might not come close to completing the course. Their individual performances will vary, but all are dark horses.

In *Making Ideas Happen*, Scott Belsky speaks to the long odds of any new idea living long enough to catch on or make a difference.

> Creativity is the catalyst for brilliant accomplishments, but it is also the greatest obstacle. If you examine the natural course of a new idea—from conception to execution—you'll see that nearly all new ideas die a premature death.… New ideas face an uphill battle from the moment they are conceived.[6]

How far a specific visionary goes to a large extent depends on factors he or she could not have anticipated or controlled. One is aware though of riding the dragon of unpredictability and they must hang on.

Even those who died unsung might have started a drumbeat that echoes over time—to undermine the forces allied against them. Their efforts might have dislodged the snow clump that launched an avalanche that never could be stopped, once it was set in motion.

No matter how carefully a particular visionary activity is planned and executed, the outcome will defy expectations. That much, at least, is predictable. Even the most optimistic visionary cannot help but be humbled by the way fate plays a hand.

Whether credit is given to God, destiny, the times being ripe, or the confluence of circumstances, the visionary succeeds (to the extent they do) despite being unlikely.

---

[6] Belsky, Scott, *Making Ideas Happen: Overcoming the obstacles between vision and reality* (New York: Portfolio, 2010), 8.

The Zeitgeist Sets the Stage

The world itself is a player in the visionary process. It is not a static backdrop that decorates the stage where the drama occurs. The time and place provide the nest that forms and informs all the actors—the arbiter of conventional standards and morals. The visionary's culture defines the *way people think* and express what they feel. What is valued? What is tolerated? What isn't?

The zeitgeist shapes the intellectual, cultural, ethical, and political climate of an era. (Zeitgeist is a German language expression literally translated: Zeit, time; Geist, spirit, meaning "the spirit of the age and its society.") It harbors the full range of human behavior styles and emotions expressed.

The zeitgeist determines the ways people develop and share their ideas. And to a more particular degree, it dictates sub-arenas for science, politics, and specific arts.

The social environment provides the pond out of which visionaries arise, and the water each of them must swim through. The pond is a collective mode that reflects prior history, as well as all the humans who share their same period and place. Visionaries attempt to change some aspect of the shared environment.

But the changes that forerunners promote will only occur when individuals actually alter their thinking or behavior in favor of the new idea. Anything less acts as a vote for the *status quo*.

The Destination Is Not Arbitrary

While the visionary process seems unpredictable as it is happening, it is not random. The path is marked by identifiable stages and rites of passage that lead somewhere. Progress traveling along it cannot be judged by worldly standards of success, for that is seldom the visionary's main motivation. Nor is that the only way they leave a lasting impact.

A visionary is someone who walks the visionary path

Despite the circular definition, it is that simple. All the words to come amplify that statement. People who willingly follow that path think and act differently than those who don't in some very specific ways.

It alters the frame of reference of those embarked on it. Its route leads travelers toward greater maturity and integration—not just for them personally, but in ways designed to benefit the larger community as well.

The visionary path is not normal—by definition, it cannot be. It represents a repudiation of at least some of the standards of the specific person's time, place, or field of interest. Its travelers produce something new and different, as yet untried, that defies the common perception and *status quo*.

Change agents succeed, in part, because they break free of some of the limiting bonds inherent in the prevailing mindset and values. In the process, they demonstrate what unfettered creative initiative can produce.

Such pioneers of fresh thinking add "something more" to the mix of possibilities. They are also few in number and burn with a passion that drives them on.

We are all (even visionaries) prisoners of our time and place. Each of us is tied to the values and prejudices of the world around us. It takes extraordinary effort even to sense the extent those influences have on our desires and thinking. Those who are most creative and visionary are the ones determined to escape those restrictions as much as possible. Their creative fruits show the rest of us how they used that freedom.

What drives some determined individuals to resist the pull of what is safe and familiar to pursue another calling without regard for conventional expectations? What do such determined non-conformists contribute that would not otherwise happen in the course of day-to-day concerns?

Visionaries of the past have often been tortured souls, estranged from their communities and forced to function in the margins. That built character, but the costs were too high—for the budding visionaries, as well as the larger society (or particular discipline).

The true value of their contributions exceeds the collective worth of their separate visions. Visionaries represent a different mode of functioning that upgrades the standard of what humans can be, or can accomplish.

Some visionaries stand out over time—the giants who redirect history. Yet each visionary could be seen as belonging to a sub-culture of "normal visionaries," which encompasses those who share certain defining characteristics.

How ironic that those who break away from the mainstream share so much common experience. Even trailblazing demonstrates an element of conformity since each pioneer treads a similar course into the unknown—leading who knows where.

It is in the movement away from the herd a person comes to know aspects of his or her identity that can only come into focus in isolation, or by disconnecting from social conventions.

Visionaries have been rare. Those who are able to bring about earth-shaking change are rarer still. Individuals who launch revolutions are later praised for their specialness—as though an ordinary person could not have done such a thing.

Yet for each visionary who was lauded in their time, there are many more who carried on with single-minded, even obsessive, doggedness without much encouragement or recognition. Yet some of them too ushered in important changes.

They, too, endured the hardships of the visionary path, without reaping many tangible rewards for their efforts. What of them? Are they any less visionary? These unknowns personify the visionary path as well. Surely, there needs to be something beyond the public's acceptance or recognition that defines the winners or giants.

Visionaries Leave the Beaten Path

Our world has been made and remade by such brave pioneers. The visionary journey requires that individuals head into uncharted territory for a time. When starting out, they have no way of knowing how difficult it is likely to be. Or how long it will take them. Or if what they're trying to do will work. But they go forth anyway.

A visionary is probably an average person until some over-riding event, discovery, or significant change in perspective turns his or her life upside-down. They head off in a new direction—or with added impetus if it is the course they have already chosen. To quote Joseph Campbell, who wrote about the power of myths, "We must be willing to get rid of the life we have planned, so we can have the life that is waiting for us."

Sometimes the impetus to grab hold of one's vision is abrupt. Sometimes it is gradual. Sometimes it develops through hot-and-cold stages. Sometimes it happens early in life; sometimes it is late.

But sooner or later, for some the force of a strong vision or whack of clarity is too powerful to be ignored, too insistent to be treated as merely optional, too disruptive for one to continue with business as usual.

Without regard for prior life circumstances or plans, a person might take a fork in the road, away from their previous expectations about where life was taking them. Past that point, the person will be pushed to his or her limits—and beyond.

In the process they, along with the driving vision, will be re-made until the two function symbiotically—each influencing and defining the other.

Thoreau wrote: "If a man loses pace with his companions, perhaps it is because he hears a different drummer. Let him step to the music which he hears, however measured, or far away."

Most people who hear a different drummer would not seriously consider marching after it—away from where they planned to go. Why do some take that drumbeat as a compelling summons, and not others?

A similar metaphor, about taking the less-trod path, away from the familiar, is Robert Frost's poem, "The Road Not Taken."

The Road Not Taken
Robert Frost (1915)

Two roads diverged in a yellow wood,
And sorry I could not travel both
And be one traveler, long I stood
And looked down one as far as I could
To where it bent in the undergrowth.

Then took the other, as just as fair,
And having perhaps the better claim,
Because it was grassy and wanted wear;
Though as for that the passing there
Had worn them really about the same.

And both that morning equally lay
In leaves no step had trodden black.
Oh, I kept the first for another day!
Yet knowing how way leads on to way,
I doubted if I should ever come back.

I shall be telling this with a sigh
Somewhere ages and ages hence:
Two roads diverged in a wood, and I—
I took the one less traveled by,
And that has made all the difference.

What Makes Some People Choose the Road Less Traveled?

- Do they have a greater sensitivity to the beckonings of inspired calls or visions?
- Do they notice almost-imperceptible early signs of what is coming before they are apparent to others?
- Are they trusting their creative imagination to show them where to go next?
- Are they driven by novelty? Curiosity? Rising to tricky challenges?
- Do they *feel they must*? They could not do otherwise.
- Are they acting from disenchantment with authority? Or an unwillingness to go along with the crowd?
- Or is it a combination of these qualities, or others still?

Once someone has been jerked away from a complacent view of life in a brush with "something more," he or she is no longer satisfied to plod along as one of the crowd. The person sets off in a new direction. Maybe it won't be right away, but it is not surprising if a veering off with life-altering consequences follows.

Every step along the visionary path takes travelers further away from the tried-and-true and into uncharted terrain. Their contemporaries would consider such a path irrelevant—a mistake, a dead-end, a wrong turn.

All true from one point of view, since this path does not lead to where everybody else is going. But the individuals who go that way are navigating a new course leading to a future they have yet to define.

How a particular visionary deals with the inevitable ups and downs of charting a course through unfamiliar territory characterizes the way he or she will eventually be perceived by history. And just as important, it could determine whether they leave a lasting legacy others can pick up, use, refine, and pass along.

What visionaries have in common is a determination to make things better. Most of them have little desire to destroy other than to improve on what is in place—in line with what they envision. Nor are they primarily motivated by animosity against the present circumstances or those in charge.

Since they see what is possible, they are willing to fight for that end if necessary. Slim odds be damned! They are betting the ranch on it.

The visionary process works in such a way that the person *and* their message are both being fine-tuned simultaneously. If the necessary tweaking is done as opportunities present themselves, the visionary and the message will be a perfect match for each other—totally congruent and tailored for those with a reason to care about it.

While visionaries are often change agents, they are quite specific about what they want to alter. Their determination to bring about the advances they argue for pits them against the way things are.

In order to stay in the game, visionaries are driven to figure out where their efforts have a snowball's chance of taking hold—and who their allies are.

The Visionary Path Is Strewn with Casualties

It is the nature of the visionary process that the person's best efforts can and will fail—often and sometimes dramatically. As T.S. Eliot reminds us, "Only those who risk going too far can possibly find out how far one can go."

Grounding an untried notion requires plenty of trial and error. Much of the testing happens in the leaping—then waiting to see if there is flight or a crash-and-burn outcome. Visionaries count either result as learning what works—then make adjustments for the next testing stages.

In *Changing Minds*, Howard Gardner, a pioneer in the area of multiple intelligences, described the disparity between the practitioners of a field who gain recognition and all the rest who never did.

> [Visions we know about] represent hard-won victories, gleaned from the plethora of creative misfirings. We remember and honor the handful of scientists and artists whose works have endured over time and have shaped

our consciousness. We forget the many thousands whose work made little impact, or whose own contributions are lost to history.[7]

Trailblazers can expect no handy roadmap with duly marked hazards for where they are headed. Those who set out must be tenacious, courageous, and a bit "touched in the head."

A levelheaded person would read the daunting signals and re-consider the venture. But the visionary is initially sustained by the clarity that propelled them on this sometimes excruciating, always novel, journey.

And the brighter that clarity continues to burn (or is susceptible to being rekindled), the less the world's rejection or intermittent crashes seems to matter. They seem to intuitively know what Michelangelo warns us about: "The greatest danger for most of us is not that our aim is too high and we miss it, but that it is too low and we reach it." Visionaries aim high.

Grounding involves a person embodying their vision in a variety of ways. Consider the word "embody": to take something abstract and incorporate it into a physical form—which includes their own flesh. Visionaries draw on every ability or resource they have, some of which only become evident in last ditch efforts. They put it all on the line.

When someone feels his or her primary commitment is at risk, they will be even more motivated. *Any practical steps* taken toward making what they see (or foresee) as concrete grounds it further. Mundane problem solving approaches do not inspire that totality of devotion. Nor are they likely to take on something earthshaking.

Like with youth, the visionaries need to be overeager rather than responsibly deliberate. If governed too much by caution, the head and fear of uncertainties dominate, instead of trusting the inventive optimism that drives them on. Once engaged, their urge to find out what is over the horizon tolerates no excuses or dissembling.

Visionaries Wonder:
- Can I deliver the invaluable notion blazing bright within me?
- Will people hear me or care enough to embrace what I discovered?
- Am I adequate? Can I survive the apparently endless challenges and delays?
- Will my vision and sacrifices make a positive difference in the long run?

If focusing on the challenges to be faced paints a rather dismal picture of the visionary experience, it is far from the whole story. There are some very real benefits and rewards to be had as well.

---

[7] Gardner, Howard, *Changing Minds: The art and science of changing our own and other people's minds* (Boston: Harvard Business School Press, 2004), 123.

Are the apparent downsides commensurate with the less-certain upsides? That is for each particular visionary to say, but their persistence seems to indicate they think so.

Most of the Immediate Rewards Are Inner Ones:
- Clarity and insights; a creative buzz, which can be very satisfying; exhilaration
- Compelling sense of purpose toward a worthwhile goal
- Thrill of discovery or creating something truly original
- Serving the big picture or greater good; sense of knowing the Truth
- Sense of drawing on the best one has to offer; living one's purpose
- Personal growth and greater knowledge about the true nature of things

The tangible rewards that come with success or public acclaim are less certain or predictable. While some visionaries get them, more do not. But most feel driven to carry on the best they can and leave the eventual outcome to fate or factors they recognize as beyond their control.

Further Out on the Limb

Although the path they have chosen is precarious, visionaries do not parse out their choices mainly to minimize their risks. They have already taken the leap of faith and passed the point (probably several) where they second-guess the wisdom of proceeding. The decisions made are less and less constrained by what is typical, socially acceptable, or economically viable.

When it comes to caution, many visionaries seem determined to discount warnings and tempt fate. Somehow, they realize predictability does not necessarily determine how things turn out. Such individuals count on being the long shot that defied the odds—and won. An article in *Newsweek* (March 16, 2009) paints a picture of massive unpredictability,

> The mysteries of life—the passions, the envy, the greed and mischievous second hand undoing the supposedly careful work of the invisible hand of the market, the unpredictable everywhere scrambling those best-laid plans. All this has been playing out, leaving chaos in its wake, while the gods of fate and destiny bend over the table, sly smiles on their faces, utterly heedless of the predictions.[8]

The visionary path has very different inducements and rewards than everyday life offers—few of which would be considered desirable to the conventionally minded. Visionaries employ a different calculation of success and failure than most. That is why those in authority are prone to underestimate and dismiss the "idiot" who is so misguided and overmatched.

---

[8] Epstein, Joseph, "Past Their Prime (Rate)," *Newsweek*, March 16, 2009.

Entrenched power players cannot recognize the peril to a belief or system that has run out of steam. But making a case for what they see coming is the visionary's stock in trade.

Who would not bet that what is solidly in place will continue? Anything else would be an imprudent gamble. However, unpredictability is one of the defining differences between visionary change and gradual, slow-but-steady improvements. The establishment does not seem quite so invulnerable when a gutsy maverick turns the tide in unexpected ways.

Revolutionary change obliterates the gradual accretion of drift, the incremental tinkering with established trajectories. After the dust settles, the recently displaced murmur is "Never saw it coming."

But at the time a change begins (even if it becomes mammoth), it is much too early to be able to tell if it will have any impact at all. While the visionary zealously does everything possible to make it stick, what follows is seldom in his or her hands.

What they demonstrate is a willingness to go "all in" — without hesitation or reservation. Such fervor is rare — even fanatical. But as Frank Lloyd Wright said, "You have to go wholeheartedly into something in order to achieve anything worth having."

Or as I've said before:

Half-hearted is Half-assed

Moving Hearts and Minds

Visionary thinkers instigate debate about the worth of current ideas, values, and routine practices. Their new ideas come up in the give-and-take where people openly argue about their divergent points of view.

While individuals and groups disagree, they can also find points of agreement — points that could set off earthshaking developments. That is the essence of democracy; spirited debates playing out around the dinner table, in the workplace, or wherever people chew the fat.

Those ahead of the curve often play a key role in framing the issues and identifying the problems that cry out for resolution, or ideas worth considering. They argue that what they are proposing is more desirable than whatever exists already. Any voice for change could act as an entering wedge, the gadfly who shows what grass-roots changes can produce.

What is to come of a freshly minted notion will only appear in the gradual steps taken to ground it. And that brings in a variety of players and their attendant agendas

Admittedly, the degree of official (or unofficial) resistance that visionaries call forth will vary. But like the drip-drip-drip of erosion, even rock-solid opposition must eventually yield to an idea whose time has come.

And why is that? There is a confluence of factors, certainly, but individual persistence and repetition in the face of long odds play a greater role than is usually recognized. In almost any major change, there probably can be found a solitary fool or two who persisted in their folly. And they attract others…

As anthropologist Margaret Mead reminds us, "A small group of thoughtful people could change the world. Indeed, it's the only thing that ever has."

Spotting Budding Visionaries

Historical distance is usually required to sort out who is (or was) a significant visionary. It usually takes the clarity of hindsight to spot change agents who actually changed things in meaningful ways. So their promise is unlikely to be remarked upon while they are still developing their voice and unique message.

The public tends to recognize the movers and shakers only after the changes they proposed have taken hold to some extent. Time will tell if a particular person or core group left a lasting or worthwhile mark.

Was their impact transitional, presaging a trend on which others continue to build? Was their legacy largely positive, or was it marred by too many missed opportunities and unintended consequences?

Assessment of a person's influence can seldom be sorted out during the short period of their lifetime. Neither can it be judged accurately by only looking at their philosophy, works, and deeds. For instance, Nobel Prizes are routinely given for discoveries made thirty years prior.

It takes time for the truly revolutionary, groundbreaking discoveries to prove themselves and for the secondary, long-term impact to appear. And changing public perceptions about something new seldom happens overnight.

For any number of reasons, a person can be on the visionary path and reject it, or can abandon a fruitful line of thought early on. As a result, that person might never be acknowledged as a full-fledged visionary. I call such people "incipient visionaries" because in the fullness of time, what they developed could be recognized as visionary indeed.

Many on the visionary path do not leave an easy-to-identify influence—even when it was significant. Their legacy could be tangential, such as being a mentor to someone who unleashes a revolution, or as a member of a group (school) who together redefined their field, or by developing an analytic technique or tool which others used to map out whole new scientific specialties.

New ideas should not be considered to be *not visionary* simply because they died in the birthing stages or were too far ahead of their time. The best ideas are not always the ones that survive, that get traction. Sometimes it is a mediocre, yet palatable, notion that catches on. But it might initiate a cascade of better ideas from thinkers down the road.

Looking at the life's work of any particular visionary (no matter how significant and worthy) cannot reveal the full extent of their contribution. The benefits derived from those who undertake the journey are cumulative, shown by the countless ways humanity continues to grow and make evolutionary leaps. Every living person has a "dog in that fight."

Understanding the lawful nature of the journey they are embarked on could help more budding visionaries rise above the inevitable difficulties, so they can eventually contribute what their vision demands of them. Such a creative groundswell could bring no end of fresh solutions to the fore.

Widespread awareness about how much is at stake for budding visionaries to succeed in the long run could also encourage bystanders to lend them a hand, as they go about their challenging work.

The visionaries among us help us all—even if you and I don't know who they are, or specifically care about what they are trying to achieve. To the extent anyone stands up boldly to make a positive difference, they offer a model of what the rest of us can do as well.

Perhaps, through their example more people will be emboldened to speak up against injustice, cruelty, and unethical practices; wrangle against systemic stupidity and waste; develop a non-polluting fuel; take their art in a new direction, and on and on.

The Spectrum of Achievement

The visionary process reflects a spectrum, with any particular person's long-term influence ranging anywhere from trivial to earthshaking, from bringing forth insights that are merely useful or enjoyable, to movements that redirect the course of history.

A large proportion of visionaries never get their message to gel enough to be acknowledged by their contemporaries. Whereas some who receive acclaim while alive might be dismissed later as a passing fancy.

There is a wide range of proficiency encountered as well with respect to each participant. Certainly, there is increasing expertise for travelers regarding their field or discovery, but there is also added expertise acquired with respect to the nature of what they went through on the visionary path.

A vision might start as a profound, larger-than-life abstraction that needs to be repeatedly refined and grounded before it becomes sufficiently relevant for widespread acceptance. It is not enough for the core idea to be massaged into something comprehensible, however. Sufficient emotional intensity is needed in order for it to inspire trust or change behavior.

In *Switch*, Chip and Dan Heath explore how to get intellect and emotion to cooperate.

> Usually [discussions about change] are treated separately—there is 'change management advice for executives and 'self-help' advice for individuals and 'change the world' advice for activists. That's a shame because all change efforts have something in common. For anything to change, someone has to start acting differently. Your brother has got to stay out of the casino; your employees have got to start booking coach fares. Ultimately, all change efforts boil down to the same mission: can you get people to start behaving in a new way?[9]

Arguments to build consensus for a vision must be compelling without sour notes that could undermine wholehearted confidence in it. A new notion that is too complicated will sink under its own weight, rather than inspire total acceptance or enthusiasm for it.

The heart also needs to be involved since it is the heart that recognizes the "ring of truth" that encourages belief and action. Bare facts will not generate enough enthusiasm to make listeners eager to adopt the kind of changes a visionary message calls for. Rational acceptance alone cannot move people deeply enough for them to embrace the freshly minted notion without reservation—then bring it into their lives.

If people do not fully "get it," they file the new argument (or discovery) away among similar ideas, but that will not galvanize change in them. It also has to grab people in the gut, emotionally, before they act. Both head and heart need to buy in for the envisioned change to be meaningful enough to act on it.

A Recognition of What Is Evident

Those who follow the visionary path do so because it seems like their best hope to accomplish what they consider possible, but which is *inconceivable* to everyone else. A common quality of forerunners is a "trust in the inconceivable." Whether or not the person can pull it off is not the crucial difference between them and the larger society. It is their *belief* that they can.

Visionaries are gambling on what they see (foresee) as achievable. They *could* be right, but usually act well before that confidence can be verified. He or she commits in a way that does not hedge their bets—they go "all in." Why bother with lukewarm or half-way approaches?!

One effect of leaving the beaten path is to draw a line, an irreversible and notable marker. It demonstrates the movement from what is safe or "to be expected," *to* an alternative that is both less likely (but for their efforts) and more risky. Going past that point serves as their leap, their "crossing the Rubicon."

For visionaries, most of what is discussed here feels obvious because it resonates on the *heart-brain channel* that they increasingly rely on. Strengthening that

---

[9] Heath, Chip and Dan, *Switch: How to change things when change is hard* (New York: Broadway Books, 2010), 4.

linkage is a large component of the visionary path. Much of the explanation in this book dances around the heart-brain alliance. It points to something that seems illusive with metaphors as though it is hard to see.

For some it is opaque; for others it is not mysterious at all. The heart sees more than the unassisted brain can. But together, one gains a fuller comprehension because of what each approach can "see." Some elaboration is for the benefit of those who do not read "the signs" as unerringly as a neon sign.

Those who feel vision-driven themselves can easily spot "the signs" when they happen to be present. It includes seeing them in others, even if the person is a "covert leaper." A covert leaper may still "pass as normal," but is gaining a broader outlook that is not shared by the larger group.

It is that heart-brain alliance, more than any specific activity, which marks the visionary point of view and point of no return. However, that alliance characterizes an emerging and growing trend that influences more people than visionaries and creatives. It represents a more integrated way of thinking and making things happen. And for many people, that approach is already growing stronger.

What Becomes Stronger Off the Beaten Path:
- Sense of urgency—the need to "do something" (even if the person appears to be dreaming)
- Greater intensity and passion about their message
- A broadening perspective about their contribution
- Stimulation of the sense of discovery, along with a search for fresh insights
- Heart-mind-body alliance becoming more evident and effective
- Greater determination, desire, and discipline by the individual

Trees? Forest? Which Do You See?

In Praise of Trees

The visionary journey examines the entire forest, including the backdrop that can only be discerned from taking the broadest perspective. It even considers the terrain that encompasses the forest against a very long time span. The forest includes the overall patterns in play—large and small, personal and impersonal, short term and long.

A wider vantage point or vision shows the top-down view of the wide forest—above the trees is possible, drops back to normal life (among the trees). Grounding only happens at ground level, feet on the ground (how apt).

This book considers the forest itself, with little attention paid to individual trees. But make no mistake, the trees are important! Every one of them.

Each tree (vision-visionary dyad) had to struggle to take root in inhospitable soil. Each faced long odds of reaching maturity, of sending out seeds to take root elsewhere. Some seeds never germinated or grew. Of those that grew, some were lovingly tended; others were hacked down or paved over.

Some never got larger than a sapling, while others developed towering canopies. Some were short lived; others perennial. But despite their marked differences, each started from a person or group with an inspired insight. They saw a better answer, then committed to make that vision a reality.

Individuals who set out on the visionary journey will be remade by what happens to them. So will the vision. The "tree" that stands tall in the forest might be bent or broken by the elements. But still it grew. It left some marks of its being there. It put forth seeds.

This forest shows no lasting sign of the seeds that failed to take root. Yet we know there are many more of them than only those that germinated—that grew to be tall trees. The forest is benefited by those less fruitful efforts as well, for they were all woven into the living ecology.

To set out on a journey does not presage arriving at the destination. But it does indicate devotion—tangible efforts made toward reaching a desired goal. It shows signs that the vision is sending down roots and trying to take hold. The fleeting idea grew into a plan of action and moved one step closer to becoming a tall, mature tree.

Setting out defines a fork in the road—off the beaten path. Who knows how far the visionary will be able to go before stopping—for any reason? But that incipient path may mark an opening to someone who comes later, who extends it further. Those narrow trails may hint at the terrain yet to be explored that calls out to travelers still to come.

Every far-seer stands on the shoulders of those who came before. So those who may have left no identifiable "trees" still enriched the forest by stimulating other growth, even as it took root over them. Their existence helped to maintain the ecosystem while their presence supported the development of nearby trees.

For the forest to remain healthy, there must be new growth and a paring of weak and unhealthy wood. A forest is a combination of seeds, seedlings, saplings, mature trees, and dying ones. They reflect all the stages of the growth cycle, each competing for water, sun, and nutrients from the soil.

If there is insufficient sunshine or water, they all suffer. With severe enough conditions, the survivors become stunted and distorted, even while hanging on.

The metaphor of a forest is apt because it is alive—growing and continually changing. There is constant new growth, side by side with decline and death. Even the strongest oaks must re-seed or recede. The largest and oldest trees are in danger of becoming rigid, unresponsive, and riddled with wormy places.

There are different kinds of trees—not all elms or oaks or evergreens, which represent the diversity of artists, philosophers, scientists, and political leaders, and ordinary folks. It takes all kinds of trees (plus shrubs, molds, and flowers) to create an ecosystem—not just a tree farm. The wide diversity adds an element of uncontrolled growth to the forest.

Is one tree better than another? As it grew tall it may have seemed so. It got advantages others did not. It was able to push competing saplings aside, sucked up the resources for its growth to the detriment of younger or established trees. However, there is never a single tree (or several) in a forest. Their large numbers define the space. They protect each other, attract smaller plants, insects, birds, small animals, and microbes that live together symbiotically. And when the parts are out of balance, they all suffer.

Not Forest *Or* Trees

The forest represents the big picture and humanity's march toward our own maturity. Each visionary's (tree's) contribution reflects only a small segment of that grand progression. If this book does nothing more, it is to honor the interplay of the forest *and* the trees, of the different scales of participation, of general and particular—to recognize that no single organism can exist without the intermeshed influences of them working together. They survive together as a small world—an ecosystem where all parts influence all others.

Any distinction I have drawn between forest and trees is a false one because it is partial, designed simply for clarification. Recognize the forest as a mental box as well (a box where a tree is paradoxically both *in* and *not in*). But such distinctions are heir to all the "either-or" hair-splitting in the province of the rational mind.

Past the discussion of nuanced distinctions about the process, you must step back and look again at each element with critical detachment. Where do each fit in the larger view? Then step back yet again: Where do I and what I want to achieve fit into this framework?

The truer view is simultaneously forest *and* trees, and more, with the viewer (you) being a participant as well. A multi-layered view is also available, very much a part of the wider perception. It is there to be seen—if you are looking for it.

You need not choose one reality or perceptual mode to the exclusion of the others. In fact, *you must not*. To do so acquiesces to the very conceptual boxes that hold us hostage to a diminished view in an expansive universe.

In *The Intention Experiment*, Lynne, McTaggart makes the case for our thoughts having a critical influence on the world itself.

> We can no longer view ourselves as isolated from our environment, and our thoughts as the private, self-contained workings of an individual brain. Dozens of scientists have produced thousands of papers in the scientific literature offering sound evidence that thoughts are capable of profoundly affecting all aspects of our lives. As observers and creators, we are constantly remaking our world at every instant. Every thought we have, every judgment we hold,

however unconscious, is having an effect. With every moment that it notices, the conscious mind is sending an intention.[10]

I was recently criticized for being hung up on forests and trees, which are visible, and my emphasis on the overview. My critic claimed I failed to mention the sharply focused narrower and deeper view—looking at the small particulars and *beneath the surface*. That's a valid point. A comprehensive view also requires noticing the cellular and sub-cellular realities, on which the mid-scale and the larger scale rest.

The broader scope should be capable of going granular—down to the leaves and pine needles. The aim is to see the forest and trees, along with the smaller components—looking at the myriad relationships of all the elements.

It is not simply to see and understand them, but to further adjust one's perceptual lens to the widest view, without losing sight of the profusion of layers. Doing so makes us capable of sensing an implicit wholeness.

This speaks to one of the themes of this book. The visionary process moves us away from habitual thinking, in whatever form it takes, and toward a more integrative, less structured or limited view. This divergence from the limitations of the accepted mindset is very liberating. To disengage from the established view accounts for many of the difficulties encountered by visionary thinkers.

The Cosmic View

Let me push this metaphor further still, to engage a scope of perception several steps even further removed from your customary perspective. At some point of time, you can look back from a distant vantage point and put a "wiser you" in the picture, who is out of the forest and trees, and sees them both.

For there is a new *awareness of your place in all of it* that is also forming. That perspective brings out your own sense of a deep connection with what is being seen.

Over the stretch of the visionary journey (or your personal life), you have built that vantage point. It was not there at the outset. But once you can use it to see your broad span of efforts and contributions, the possibility exists to see how your part fits into an even larger context.

That awareness indicates touching the absolutes—the reality from which inspiration and vision come. This view transcends forest and trees, and everything else in the manifest world. Yet as a person grows into greater mastery and wisdom, those realities are understood to be less and less separate.

A person who has built those internal bridges in their understanding begins to see the inherent unity of every particular element.

---

[10] McTaggart, Lynne, *The Intention Experiment: Using your thoughts to change your life and the world* (New York: Free Press, 2007), 194.

The path that has been trod all along seems clear enough in retrospect. But it is the eye that was being trained to notice the markers: trees, forest, and the larger relationships of which they are but parts. Those on the visionary path learn to tread lightly — sensing our place in the larger flow — to respond to the energetic ebb and flow.

While visionaries are the forerunners, the march of humanity follows on the paths they define. So in one sense, where visionaries go influences everyone. And everybody has a stake in the best creative notions prevailing (Chapter 19).

Acting as Agents of Change

The Visionary Process as a Battering Ram

The visionary process is confrontational, going head-to-head with existing ideas and institutions. Advocates for a vision take on the powerful and well-established with seeming disregard for the odds against them.

When they champion that "best idea since sliced bread," they bump into resistance: some through indifference, some calculated, some intense.

Visionaries persevere against ridicule, against opposition, while weathering failure after failure. The person must find ways to confront the flavors of rejection and indifference, in order to demonstrate the new idea's merit and to build a compelling case for it.

If their notion is to prevail, it has to be better in some significant way than what it seeks to replace. Like a salesman countering objections, the visionary addresses people's concerns, whether expressed or implied, to get them to "buy it" or "try it."

Sometimes dramatic confrontations occur, pitched philosophical battles when the new guy argues with the establishment. Sometimes both camps will tangle — each defending their turf and looking for a decisive victory.

Such is the evolution of revolutionary ideas. They challenge the *status quo* on many fronts, until their vision supplants it — or fails in the attempt.

While most of those confrontations won't make the news, they become more and more public as the process proceeds — a gain here, a stand-off there. It adds up.

The Mantra of "Change Is Good"

Only in recent generations did the notion of change become a synonym for the better life offered by technology and expanded social opportunities. We accept accelerated change as the price of modern life because we want the plentiful comforts it promises.

Throughout human history, change happened gradually, except for an occasional war, revolution, or natural calamity. (See Chapter 9 about change.)

The Industrial Revolution and both World Wars set events in motion that accelerated change of all types—social, economic, agricultural, scientific, you name it. In modern times social standards have changed past knowing what is beneficial, past the warnings of good judgment or common sense, past moral constraints or a sense of fair play.

Indiscriminate change is not to be preferred to the *status quo*. Visionaries are change agents, but change itself is not their goal. A better future that includes their big-picture vision is what they seek. It is also worth noting what is being changed, both intentionally and unintentionally.

Change agents are like merchants out hawking their wares. Mostly the public responds with ho hum, who cares? Either they are satisfied with what they have already or they assume there will be something else better, smaller, cuter, or faster tomorrow. So they usually bide their time with what they have—or until an even better choice comes along.

But those ideas that are most revolutionary could have a much harder time getting traction with the public since what is most novel "scratches an itch" that people might not know they have. Revolutionary change trumps incremental change in the way it up-ends what is considered essential or desirable.

People often have trouble grasping the worth of using something truly original when it first appears. Who could have foreseen, let alone desired, many of the groundbreaking products that we cannot live without today (like laser surgery or the GPS)?

And that is just the stuff. Imagine how difficult it is to comprehend how life would be improved by galvanizing people to think boldly enough to take on the really tough questions, like eradicating systemic poverty or not feeling constrained to "color within the lines." The sky is the limit.

These days, we do not only have a surfeit of change that requires immediate attention, we are also getting new tools and approaches that expedite the change process itself. So, we are not dealing with one change at time, or one right after another, but have entered a milieu of steady change.

But there is no holding back the tides of change. That ship has sailed. It is driving secondary changes as well—in almost every sphere of life. For instance, we are seeing how quickly personal computers and the Internet are propelling widespread social adjustments and new economic models, seemingly overnight. And successive ripples of change continue to build upon each other.

In *Here Comes Everybody*, Clay Shirky describes how technology has fueled new forms of social interaction. These have changed how we form groups and relationships.

Communications tools don't get socially interesting until they get technologically boring. The invention of a tool doesn't create change; it has to have been around long enough that most of society is using it. It's when a technology becomes normal, then ubiquitous, and finally so pervasive as to be invisible, that the really profound changes happen, and for young people today, our new social tools have passed normal and are heading to ubiquitous, and invisible is coming.[11]

What would it take for something that seems like science fiction when introduced to become commonplace? Those ahead of the curve keep blurring the distinctions between what is fiction and what is fact, between what is possible and our next leap forward. And they are taking new forms.

Not only that, according to Daniel Pink, who chronicles such matters: "We are moving from an economy and a society built on the logical, linear, computerlike capabilities of the Information Age to an economy and a society built on the inventive, empathic, big-picture capabilities of what is rising in its place, the Conceptual Age."

Don't Discount Spontaneous Events

Never overlook the power of little things to redirect the course of history. The visionary may frame the issues or lead the charge, but the tipping point of earthshaking change cannot be foreseen or controlled. Any overt act might reflect a change of attitude—a new receptivity that moves events away from the tried and true.

New York Times columnist David Brooks points to the micro-influences that signal a shift in the social climate. We cannot quantify them, but they swing the balance in a new direction.

> The fate of nations is determined by glances and chance encounters: by the looks policemen give one another as a protesting crowd approaches down a boulevard; by the presence of a spontaneous leader who sets off a chant or a song and with it an emotional contagion; by a captain who either decides to kill his countrymen or not; by a shy woman who emerges from a throng to throw herself on the thugs who are pummelling a kid prone on the sidewalk.

> The most important changes happen invisibly inside peoples' heads. A nation that had seemed apathetic suddenly mobilizes. People lost in private life suddenly feel their public dignity has been grievously insulted. Webs of authority that had gone unquestioned instantly dissolve, or do not. New social customs spontaneously emerge.[12]

---

[11] Shirky, Clay, *Here Comes Everybody: The power of organizing without organizations* (New York: Penguin Press, 2008), 105.
[12] Brooks, David, "Fragile at the Core," *New York Times*, June 19, 2009.

A Time of Changing Gears

Here in the U.S.A., our trust in the future is badly shaken. Failed financial systems, governmental incompetence, corporate irresponsibility, educational ineptitude that hobbles our youth, and numerous forms of social breakdown bear witness that too many modern institutions have lost their way. Those priorities have taken us as far as they can go.

Many of today's widely-accepted standards and practices represent dying dinosaurs. They are collapsing under their own weight. They are incapable of changing their ways. Some institutional priorities are not sustainable in their present form—nor do they deserve to be.

They *will* be replaced. The still-to-be-resolved questions are, replaced by what? And is what comes next an improvement?

In *Nonzero: The logic of human destiny*, Robert Wright describes cultural lag.

> The early-twentieth-century sociologist William Ogburn attributed many of the world's problems to 'cultural lag.' Cultural lag happens when material culture (including governance and social norms) has trouble catching up. In short, the disruptive part of culture gets out ahead of what Ogburn called the 'adaptive' part of culture.[13]

If we want to counter the considerable costs of cultural lag, along with other serious maladies of modern life, fundamentally different approaches must be found pronto. Continuing to tinker around the edges of so much dysfunction cannot make the messes go away.

Einstein is often quoted as saying, "We can't solve problems by using the same kind of thinking we used when we created them." What is needed is a *different level of thinking on a widespread basis*. The visionary process is uniquely able to develop individuals capable of that quality of thinking. Nothing less can prevent our sinking deeper in the quagmire.

It takes farsighted judgment to unlock the solutions adequate to modern life's complex challenges. The current changing of the guard should be toward those who thrive on creative energy, and have learned to use it in imaginative and constructive ways. If our society wants those benefits, we must allow those who can see ahead of the curve to help lead the way.

I propose a slogan for what is needed that will be a recurring theme throughout this book:

More Vision - Less Division

---

[13] Wright, Robert, *Nonzero: The logic of human destiny* (New York: Vintage Books, 2000), 232.

The Energy that Drives Creative Thinking

In my opinion, humanity is in the midst of an energetic revolution as well—not the kind that heats our homes or runs our cars, but rather a refined form of energy that drives innovative thinking. It is incumbent upon us to more effectively draw on the infinite reserves of creative energy that has been held back for too long.

This insufficiently tapped resource fuels the capacity to resolve intractable problems by developing fresh approaches to them. It also supplies the power for one to make their original ideas work. *That* is the form of energy our world needs the most.

Individuals skilled in drawing on high concentrations of creative energy should be trusted to instigate innovative ideas and desirable social progress.

I am confident that as more of the factors supporting the visionary process become better understood, people will increasingly choose to *tap into it* to drive their own inventiveness. And all of us will benefit from the fruits of such undertakings.

Most modern institutions operate at a very low creative energy level, devoid of much vision or sufficient desires for fresh approaches. However, the widespread waning of strong leadership and proficiency on a large scale is opening pockets of opportunity—areas where new and better ideas can take root and thrive.

While not making light of the suffering experienced by many people during the transition, it is necessary to replace, or significantly alter, rigid and unresponsive institutions. What replaces them should support our society (and individuals) in ways that are not held hostage by the self-serving, short-sighted, and well-connected.

Unbridled expediency is blind to the worth of integrity, human dignity, and the kinds of values that do not show as line items on the balance sheet. But ethical values need to be considered in the calculation of what choices organizations are making.

If the changes afoot are to be beneficial and sustainable, they must rest on solid values that factor in the full scope of their likely impact.

Yet America's current widespread difficulties should not be blamed on a few corrupt ideas or rogue institutions, so much as on a pervasive worldview that is too mired in material concerns.

Most decisions being made seek short-term rewards and answers, without regard for the long-term and widespread costs. The quality of needed solutions should also address the imbalance between our internal and external states.

Answers attuned to the future have to move beyond "every man for himself" to a recognition that "we are all in the same boat." As Marshall McLuhan said, "There are no passengers on spaceship earth. We are all crew." That shift in attitudes is required on an individual basis, by each of us, as well as by those in positions of leadership and broad social reach.

Send in the Visionaries

Periods of great creativity can flourish in the wake of social turmoil or disintegration. After the Dark Ages, the Renaissance nourished immense expansion in the arts, science, and social institutions. The current breakdown of social structures and values acts as the bugle call to summon those most capable of reforming the fabric of society.

To quote Victor Hugo, "There is nothing more powerful than an idea whose time has come." Now is such a time—a time of evolutionary change. The combination of social and economic unrest, coupled with a vacuum of effective leadership in every sphere of life, assures there *will* be change.

The question is whether insightful influences can prevail over calamitous ones. That depends on the strength of our individual or collective will, and how intelligently each of us places our bets for the future.

Dinosaurs gave way to nimble mammals. We are facing such a period now. Old methods are being supplanted by fresh ways of defining, confronting, and solving our problems. The changing of priorities already started is in the direction of new kinds of answers—as well as toward those able to conceptualize and accomplish them.

The next wave of visionary thinkers will use these destabilized conditions to launch a groundswell of inventive solutions.

Part of the cause of collapse results from the inadequacy of today's short-term, profits-above-all-else, and winner-take-all strategies. The old guard is bogged down in outdated assumptions and values about what is important. Such power-hungry methods cannot deal with the needs of today—let alone capably anticipate what is on the horizon.

The world has occasionally turned to visionary thinkers at times of massive change. But more often, forward-thinking individuals were unable to gain the public's ear early on, when the need for what they proposed was most acute.

Today's demanding conditions argue against waiting for the gradual pace of attrition and validation of fresh approaches to work themselves through. We must be open to untried ideas with merit, without fear or vested interests to prevent them from being put to the test.

Those capable of visionary thinking need to be at the forefront of significant change. Individuals with the needed skills and judgment can no longer sit quietly in the back seat to those in power. They are not willing to continue being waved off as out of touch with reality, when they have carefully-developed notions that are capable of being both possible and enduring.

The best efforts of many far-sighted problem solvers and change agents will be required to reconstruct the breakdown evident in every aspect of modern life. Always before, visionaries had to win over, or knock down, "the establishment" and prevalent notions in order to get a hearing.

Now, much of that structure is riddled with cracks, leading to a rabid hunger for trustworthy solutions. A cascade of significant change, starting at the grass roots, is gathering momentum.

The direction of so much growth need not be left to chance, however — if the spirit of cooperation and the greater good are included among the priorities. Skilled and creative individuals are preparing to step out of the margins.

No single wave of visionary thinkers could re-seed so much newly barren soil. These emerging voices will find alliances with others with the will to see and do what is possible. Efforts by single visionaries are still welcome, but collaborative highly motivated teams are forming as well.

As creative and determined individuals step forward, we must avoid the errors of the past that ignored and rejected freshly minted approaches. It is up to all of us to blow on the sparks of inspiration so they blaze bright.

The far-seeing visionary spirit provides humanity's best hope to drive a steady stream of useful advances. It bodes well, not just for our material existence, but for our quality of life as well.

A New Model for Visionary Participation

Legendary tales about the giants make them seem larger than life, more capable than the rest of us. But much of what we know about them is the mythology surrounding them — heroic stories about what they endured on the road to greatness.

But no man is an island. The abilities that forerunners demonstrate in spades are not unique to them, but can show up anywhere, in anyone. Those that take root are largely a matter of will, coupled with opportunity.

We all have a stake in encouraging determined individuals who are eager to share their visions. But each of us also has an even more immediate stake in letting *our own visions* flower to a greater extent in our personal lives. Increased clarity from doing so enriches the way we live individually, as well as the lives we touch.

It is time to support the signs of new visions capable of remaking our reality. Let us cheer on inspired voices struggling to be heard above the mumbling of mediocrity or the thoughtless repetitions of the past. Together, we can redefine the direction of the future.

We are presented with the opportunity to create the kind of world we want to live in, or to leave the outcome to chance. My advice: **Seize the spark**. Or carry a banner:

SEIZE THE SPARK

That would be a worthy movement—opening untold doors on every scale. Anyone and everyone can play!

New forms of collaborative efforts, on many fronts, are using ingenuity and communities of interested individuals to tackle mammoth challenges. The Internet and shared, self-defined networks are rewriting the concept of collaboration. Millions of happy-to-be-involved people are mobilizing in ways that are truly revolutionary and visionary.

A secondary, but no less important, effect is unleashing a larger, more inclusive worldview that is not defined by where we have been. Possibilities flower because more people can see beyond what is wrong, and are willing to participate in taking the next step—or leap to "something more."

As the visionary spirit is recognized as not being the bailiwick of only a few giants or mavericks, we will recognize its presence in many more individuals and in many more forms.

In doing so, we can see the need for removing stumbling blocks that keep innovative thinking from taking root. New approaches will also show themselves in the way troublesome problems come to be resolved.

Supporting the Heavy Lifters

While the call goes out to visionaries to step up to the plate, a comparable charge is laid on the rest of us. The world has long been hesitant to accept ideas from those who challenge conventional thinking. But we cannot afford to systematically thwart the very individuals and creative approaches that are needed.

On the visionary side of the equation, I see no shortage of motivation or great ideas. But I do see a dearth of encouragement for them. Forerunners should not be dismissed without a fair hearing for what they have discovered.

And they could use allies. Well-meaning bystanders can do more to give encouragement or hands-on help, when it is likely to do them the most good.

To mention a single concern of mine, one has to wonder what is wrong with the way we raise and educate our young? So much of their unique and positive capabilities remain undeveloped. Why do we routinely stifle their native creativity?

Why limit opportunities for them to express their full promise? These could be the much-needed visionaries of tomorrow—if given the right encouragement.

Chapter 3 - Stripping Down to Essentials

Being naked refers to systematic and sustained efforts to get in touch with that deeper level of awareness. It helps us get our conscious fingers on those interior levers.

Build a Better Mousetrap *Maker*

Ralph Waldo Emerson sounded the rallying cry for innovators: "Build a better mousetrap, and the world will beat a path to your door." To the sorrow of many who developed their own form of a better mousetrap, it usually does not work out that way—certainly not as smoothly as they expected. The world shrugs, and those eager to launch "the next big thing" feel misled.

Emerson's essays encourage us to act on our flickers of genius, and many on the visionary path attest to his motivating influence on them. His abiding gift is urging us to roll up our sleeves and do something about our inspired visions. If Emerson's advice is to serve as more than glib rhetoric, however, there better be a mousetrap produced sooner or later.

The Sayings of Ralph Waldo Emerson

- An ounce of action is worth a ton of theory.
- What lies behind us and what lies before us are small matters compared to what lies within us.
- To be yourself in a world that is constantly trying to make you something else is the greatest accomplishment.
- Genius always finds itself a century too early.
- You must not worry about your success or failure. It does not concern you. Your duty is to work each day, quietly, to accept the failures which are inevitable and to leave to others the care or measuring of the applause.
- The high, contemplative, all-consuming vision, the sense of right and wrong, is alike in all. Its attributes are self-existence, eternity, intuition, and command. It is the mind of the mind.
- Men love to wonder, and that is the seed of science.
  - Once you make a decision, the universe conspires to make it happen.
- Our chief want is someone who will inspire us to be what we know we could be.
- Our greatest glory is not in never failing, but in rising up every time we fail.
- The man of genius inspires us with a boundless confidence in our own powers.
- The reward of a thing well done is having done it.
- The sum of wisdom is that time is never lost that is devoted to work.
- The world is all gates, all opportunities, strings of tension waiting to be struck.
- To be great is to be misunderstood

At a point in my life when I was launching an invention of my own, I had a friend who was a venture capitalist (though not an investor). He told me that before moneymen like him decide whether to back a new product or project, they are especially concerned about *the quality of the person behind it*.

An invention or untried idea cannot stand on its own without the driving force of a committed and capable champion. Investors are placing their money bet on the person as much as their idea.

They will not risk their money without considering the advocate's track record: Does the person have the needed skills? Are they capable of working out the nuts and bolts of the endeavor all the way to the payoff? Is this their first mousetrap? As with first love, an upstart creator cannot imagine the world won't want and embrace what they have done—once the word gets out about how great it is.

Has he or she survived the disappointments of that naïve phase (sadder but wiser), then taken an idea through the stages to follow? In sum, how likely is the person to pull it off? Bernard Girard even has the figures to show how important it is to have prior experience in *The Google Way*.

> In a 2006 study titled Skill vs Luck in Entrepreneurship and Venture Capital: Evidence from Serial Entrepreneurs, Paul Gompers and colleagues at Harvard University calculated that 'entrepreneurs who succeeded in a prior venture (i.e., started a company that went public) have a 30% chance of succeeding in their next venture. By contrast, first-time entrepreneurs have only an 18% chance of succeeding and entrepreneurs who previously failed have a 20% chance of succeeding.' In a market fraught with high risk, this sort of expertise is invaluable.[14]

But there is a larger view to notice as well, beyond the practical outcome of the undertaking. While the innovator developed and launched what they assumed was the next eagerly awaited "mousetrap," they had also been remaking the mousetrap maker (himself or herself).

They were becoming more vision-focused than before. What the person went through in devoted service to their over-riding mission refined their discernment and proficiency. It also expanded their perceptual lens, to bring more kinds of know-how and judgment to bear in any future undertaking.

Less apparent, the person was not simply more capable but was a step removed from their prior frame of reference. They had disengaged from where they started, to some extent, and thereby changed their long-term trajectory.

To paraphrase Emerson, "Build a better *mousetrap maker*, and the world will beat a pathway to your door." The world desires and needs *better mousetrap makers*

---

[14] Girard, Bernard, *The Google Way: How one company is revolutionizing management as we know it* (San Francisco: No Starch Press, 2009), 17.

much more than a larger selection of mousetraps. Anyone who can find original and ingenious solutions to what people want, as well as reinvent who they are in the bargain, is sure to make waves.

Being "Naked" Serves the Visionary Process

Becoming naked is both a metaphor and an accurate description of what occurs on the visionary path. The process strips away layers of cultural training and misinterpreted life experience, assumptions, and accepted philosophical verities. No matter how much has been removed voluntarily, more stripping is required as the process goes forward.

Getting naked involves deep and profound change within the individual. Visionaries encounter many degrees of nakedness because the visionary path is one of disrobing. First it happens without the person realizing it, later it is done willingly but with some trepidation.

But as the entire experience ripens, increased nakedness assures anything out of harmony with their grand vision recedes in influence.

It is a journey toward self-discovery and self-mastery—at the very same time one must tackle the practical challenges of finding words for the vision and persuading an indifferent world. It also colors how they see their world. As their customary perception is pushed aside, whole new worlds might swim into view.

Henry Miller said, "The moment one gives close attention to anything, even a blade of grass, it becomes a mysterious, awesome, indescribably magnificent world in itself." And that also applies to noticing ourselves.

The visionary path provides an extended period of testing—of the person, of their unique message, of the value of the changes they espouse, and of individuals and organizations who encounter or embrace the new notion.

The visionary's journey grows more demanding when it moves them from abstract vision to developing concrete principles and practices—as it goes from pristine idea to the practical reality of followers, budgets, and Do Lists. The visionary must sort out the never-ending "means versus ends" trade-offs on a day-by-day basis.

Their degree of nakedness influences *how the devoted visionary looks at the world*, along with the determination to make a significant contribution to it. Being naked removes many distortions that color normal perception.

Visionary thinking entails them *seeing with fewer of the limiting assumptions and perceptions*. Getting stripped down is necessary to get where they are trying to go.

Their willingness to drop so many social expectations and protections sets visionaries apart from those still fully clothed in the common values and mindset of their community. Admittedly, those on the visionary path do not know at the outset how much disrobing will be required. But it is the price of admission for reaching later phases of the journey.

Most of those comfortably settled in the mainstream are not inclined toward so much self-exposure and its attendant risks. They might take off a garment now and then, maybe hang around with some naked people, but they are not driven to risk it all or leave the protective cover of the conventional world.

How Many Ways to Get Naked?

Taking off clothing would seem to be unrelated to the visionary experience. Yet other meanings of "naked" go to the heart of it. Nakedness is not so much about the clothing one wears—or doesn't, but *what lies underneath*. It involves the internals more than the externals; what is unseen more than what can be seen.

Also, there are degrees of nakedness, so becoming more naked is a gradual process—the value of which becomes more evident over time and because of disrobing.

Naked Implies:
- Exposed; uncovered
- Innocent; newborn
- Unprotected; vulnerable
- Unadorned; unpretentious
- Stark; simple

Each of these concepts relates to a person's *inner states and approach to life*. Most of the nakedness indispensable for inner maturity involves developing greater intuitive awareness. One must dig deep down inside to find the essential message that could fire up the world. Being grounded within is tough to accomplish, but it is essential for greater self-knowledge about oneself, or for being perceived as trustworthy by others.

The meanings of being "naked," as used in this book, coincide with the primary goals of the visionary path. It is about removing culturally acceptable protections that confine our inherent self-determination and scope of vision. Nakedness dismantles our illusions and self-serving behaviors that obstruct accurate self-awareness and big-picture judgment.

Travelers gradually become more adept at bringing their external world and their inner landscape into alignment, so they operate more as a unit. Neither the inner nor the outer realm is better than the other, but both play a vital role in forming an all-embracing view. As the collaboration between them develops, one grounds the unseen in what is seen with greater finesse.

With more nakedness comes an increased capacity for clarity. His or her degree of nakedness shows itself in the visionary's uncommon preferences and decisions. It shows in their inclination to let go of attitudes, desires, and goals no longer shared with their peers—or that inhibit their insight.

Nakedness relates to the person's most basic identity. It shows more aspects of his or her underlying nature, and which they choose to express, and a clearer sense of "who I am." As one strips down, many of their false starts and sour notes gradually fade away.

Going within for answers points the way to a reality beyond the senses. This added clarity is the pay-off for each layer of discarded clothing and for digging down deep inside. Nakedness aids vision but it also increases our enjoyment of its fruits.

Getting naked exposes pretext of all kinds—most not previously suspected by the person clothed in them. It reveals how much vulnerability and self-exposure they can tolerate. Nakedness relates to character and values, the philosophical underpinning of their motivation. Its endgame is inner maturity.

That aspect of the visionary process moves travelers toward greater precision in the way he or she relates to what happens to them—both on the inside and the outside. This chapter explores how increased nakedness (removing layers and distortions) supports the entire visionary process.

The Inner Journey

Modern life largely ignores the inner world—pretending what is going on around us is most important. Inner states are not much spoken of in polite company—treated as though they are much too private or erratic to trust. Except for acquiring enough self-control to keep our inner life from acting up in public, it is barely trained, acknowledged, or understood by the vast majority of us.

Becoming naked refers to systematic and sustained efforts to get in touch with that deeper level of awareness. It helps us get our conscious fingers on those interior levers. However, diligent pursuit of those largely subjective experiences is often at odds with getting on with accepted measures of success.

David Brooks speaks to those frequently-ignored influences in *The Social Animal*.

> We are living in the middle of a revolution in consciousness. Over the past few years, geneticists, neuroscientists, psychologists, sociologists, economists, anthropologists, and others have made great strides in understanding the building blocks of human flourishing. And a core finding of their work is that we are not primarily the products of our conscious thinking. We are primarily the products of thinking that happens below the level of awareness.[15]

---

[15] Brooks, David, *The Social Animal: The hidden sources of love, character, and achievement* (New York: Random House, 2011), x.

The inner realm is illuminated by science, but it is not a dry, mechanistic place. It is an emotional and an enchanted place. If the study of the conscious mind highlights the importance of reason and analysis, study of the unconscious mind highlights the importance of passions and perception. If the outer mind highlights the power of the individual, the inner mind highlights the power of relationships and the invisible bonds between people. If the outer mind hungers for status, money, and applause, the inner mind hungers for harmony and connection—those moments when self-consciousness fades away and a person is lost in a challenge, a cause, the love of another or the love of God.[16]

If the concept of being a visionary means anything at all, it is about someone acting on a compelling vision. And those inspired impulses can only be accessed from within. No matter how many practical challenges might come with bringing a vision to life, clarifying our internal landscape is every bit as vital to making the vision real.

Translating that elusive meaning into concrete results in the everyday world is the real work that visionaries do.

The Visionary Path Leads to Increased Levels of Mastery

Humans live internally and externally simultaneously. Each of us responds to events with our thoughts and emotions, as well as through our senses and physical reactions. Our related but unseen assumptions and principles also chime in. But people don't really have two separate lives—an inner life and an outer life.

Either alone is but a fractional aspect of being a whole person. The two are designed to work together. Our inner and outer awarenesses are both crucial and need to operate in tandem.

Operating in our external world is the stuff of daily life—never really avoided. Nor should it be. But by training and innate inclination, we are much less adept at controlling the levers of our inner states. The mind gets educated, but emotions, one's sense of identity, values, and spiritual awareness that operate out of sight, are a mish-mash that is much harder to sort out. And there are no words for much of it, anyway. Yet these unseen influences run the show from behind the curtain.

Mastery reflects the degree to which a person's inner and outer worldviews work together. It involves someone effectively combining his or her inner and outer states, so each is permitted to perform its optimal role. As one's internal and external ways of knowing cease their tug of war, they bolster each other. Even better, they stop pulling in opposite directions.

Mastery signifies that level of integration. However, it cannot be accurately understood as only one side of the coin. It is the *whole coin*. Even high-level

---

[16] *Ibid.*, xi.

accomplishments in the practical world prove to be insufficient unless a person has also developed some degree of self-knowledge and personal growth.

The rewards for inner development differ significantly from those gained in the everyday world. A wide imbalance between inner and outer awareness hampers access to the field of all possibilities—the realm of vision and inspiration. For instance, someone who has all the perks of success could still feel flat and empty.

Without a corresponding level of accomplishment in the person's inner life, experiences are shorn of a dimension of fullness. By the same token, even the greatest adept of the inner realms must find a way to function as a citizen of Earth.

Mastery is a door that swings both ways—connecting the realms of one's inner awareness and one's outer awareness. Although reference may be made to subject-matter mastery, or self-mastery, or inner mastery, they are each subsets of integrated mastery. And that is one of the destinations toward which the visionary path leads—although certainly not the only way to get there.

Naked Simplicity

Greater integration enhances our ability to navigate life circumstances with confidence and integrity. It dramatically broadens our scope of possibilities since our otherwise competing priorities are finally pulling together in the same direction.

The visionary puts his or her creative stamp on some aspect of their world, but the impulse to do so arises from within. It seems those who become visionaries are more responsive than their peers to such prodding from the wee small voice within. So being in tune with those urges becomes increasingly pressing for them.

Nakedness is simple. Not simple-minded, but discerning. It does not get lost in the buzz of details. Those who accept the need for nakedness are less afraid of complexity. As their perceptual distortions diminish, there is less confusion between first things and second things—between what is in the foreground and what is in the background.

Getting stripped down adjusts that lens of discernment toward elegant simplicity. Increased nakedness counters some of the influences of narcissism and makes us more adept at responding sensitively to the people we encounter. *Making Ideas Happen* by Scott Belsky speaks of the downsides that can easily constrict the creative flow.

> The process of creation is deeply consuming and lined with narcissism. We fall in love with our ideas and become both certain and protective. We forget to spend time on articulation (and marketing) our ideas, we become less receptive

to criticism, and our ideas stagnate in isolation. As we dig deep within ourselves, we lose the ability to tune into the needs and sensitivities of others—an awareness that is required for our ideas to thrive.[17]

The Purpose of the Visionary Path

The visionary process is much more than a problem-solving or product-development strategy. Besides making the vision tangible and real, it also makes the visionary *even more real* than before.

That results from allowing the vision to take root in its host so it influences his or her behavior. As the process continues, the inner self takes a firmer hold on the concrete outer identity.

One purpose of nakedness is to minimize the distance between our various unconnected ways of knowing "who I am." The distance between one's inner awareness and outer awareness is the source of all sorts of misperceptions about our fundamental identity. Getting all these views of self in sync comes only with learning to navigate our inner landscape as capably as the external one.

We have usually looked at what a specific person has done (be they visionary or not) as their measure of achievement. But that view dismisses other significant accomplishments that can be even more enduring: building a life—building a worthy life, being the best the person can be. These are not slogans but guiding principles for those on the visionary path. Heck, for anybody.

Walking the visionary path alters those who walk it, certainly. But it also expands the worldview and consciousness available for all of us. Disrobing is done as Everyman as well—whose next step toward self-discovery demonstrates what is possible when vision and a person's uniqueness can work together to achieve a worthy end.

Another purpose of the visionary process is for the person to make of themselves, as Nathaniel Hawthorne describes it, a place "where the Actual and Imaginary may meet." One acts as a citizen of both realms and can function in concert with them both. In that sense, those who relate to their visions are the ambassadors who can speak of those otherworldly concerns to the normal world.

Building a "Naked" Mousetrap Maker

The capacity to bring an idea to fruition is even more valuable than the specific mousetrap that is produced. There could be many of those developed when our creative juices flow.

Changing the visionary's inner states is a primary purpose of the journey, not an incidental by-product of it. What is being created could be considered the by-

---

[17] Belsky, Scott, *Making Ideas Happen: Overcoming the obstacles between vision and reality* (New York: Portfolio, 2010), 112.

product of the journey. But this distinction is not about which is more important. They happen *together*, and both deserve notice. Their growth and fruits are complementary outcomes for a person grounding what shines bright for them.

Getting their inner world and outer world to operate in harmony is one of the requirements for anyone reaching the later stages of mastery. That alignment can also enhance the *quality* of their mousetraps.

Getting naked is less about stripping for the view of others than to see our own undistorted self with access to the full range of our abilities. The visionary path leads its travelers toward greater self-knowledge, even while each undertakes their practical pursuits. And learning how to get naked helps the *better mousetrap maker* happen.

My Life as a Nudist

Since I have been using nakedness as a metaphor, I need to come clean about my experience as a nudist, and what I learned from it. I grew up in Alaska, which is not conducive to running around naked. When I was about 16, my mother (a model of defying social convention) decided my siblings and I needed to be more open-minded about our bodies (I think the word "prude" came up).

Somehow, she thought joining the local nudist group would be the solution. She found out about their next monthly meeting—a potluck at someone's house (outdoor gatherings were unthinkable). The five of us arrived with a casserole and our clothes on. We kids had no intention of getting naked, and my mother did not consider doing it herself since she was there for our benefit. We spent the evening at a rather pleasant social gathering of about 25 people—talking about everything but nudity.

Such was our dampening influence, all the regular members felt constrained to leave their clothes on as well. I never saw even one naked adult at those gatherings. By the time we got home, Mother summed up the experience as, "They are such lovely people." She counted our evening a hit and was looking forward to the next meeting. Who were we kids to argue? A month later we went back, with identical results. And the following month. And the one after that. And the one after that...

My mother's delight in getting to know such lovely people blinded her to the fact that we had single-handedly destroyed their group. Nobody got to be naked—and they did not know how to get rid of us, being such lovely people.

I suspect they started having gatherings besides the regularly scheduled ones we were faithful to attend. Forever clothed. At some point, Mother considered her experiment a success—much to our relief, but especially for the nudists.

The point: my family went through the motions of being nudists—except for taking our clothes off. And there was no pretending we did—or ever intended to. Nobody was fooled—especially the real nudists, whose goals were being held hostage by our interference. So just going through the motions of inner growth or a changed outlook without any disrobing won't get a person very far.

The Social Environment that Provokes Change

The Times Being Ready for Change

Some new ideas flourish because they are on the pulse of history. When events conspire to weaken or remove obstacles that have outlived their usefulness, bold measures and untried ideas are less likely to fall on deaf ears.

Visionaries who rise out of destabilized conditions encounter less resistance, so they have an easier time out of the starting gate (though still not a slam dunk).

It is the natural order for things to decay and vanish to make new growth possible. Ideas and social structures are no different. Destabilization due to chaos, ineffectiveness, and social ferment eliminates the inherent advantage of what already exists. After massive change, sitting tight until things return to normal is a losing approach because there is no normal to which to return.

Visualize gradual change as a sidewalk paved with concrete. Not much grows except in the cracks where a few blades of grass spring up. With revolutionary change, the whole sidewalk is buckled, so any seed that comes along has a good chance of taking root. Then weeds and flowers alike compete among themselves as to which of them survive or dominate.

Which seedlings push others aside and grow strong at their expense? Which of those seeds of change will survive or define the evolving spirit of the times (zeitgeist)? Will those who are the most farsighted and creative help to chart the new course? Which changes represent evolutionary improvements, rather than regression?

Historically, unstable circumstances have been a breeding ground for change agents. The chances of a new idea being adopted in such a receptive environment are greatly improved. People are more likely to respond positively to untested or visionary ideas than they would in stable times.

The destabilized social conditions create receptivity for change and a need for resolution. But without a person or electrifying idea to set off a spark, that receptivity won't ever catch fire. According to Denis Diderot, a French philosopher from the 1700s, "Genius is present in every age, but the men carrying it within them remain benumbed unless extraordinary events occur to heat up and melt the mass so that it flows forth."

Ideas or institutions that don't work and offend our sense of decency or fundamental fairness are unlikely to last indefinitely. Monuments to power, ego, privilege, or greed become less and less able to function when the spotlight of public disapproval points to them.

Widespread outrage or disillusionment can quickly turn up the heat and pressure for change—whether people are voting with dollars (purchases), active revolt, or with mobilized public opinion. The public does not willingly tolerate repressive or unsustainable conditions for long.

Today's instant communications can galvanize public opinion to act against them via mainstream media or social networks. (Recall what happened in the grassroots uprising in the Arab Spring). Democratic mechanisms further such grassroots participation.

When decay or corruption makes it rotten from within, seemingly impervious institutions can collapse with relatively little direct confrontation. An example is the fall of the Berlin Wall that divided East and West Germany twenty years ago, the symbol of the Cold War. That is described by Margaret J. Wheatley in *Leadership and the New Science*.

> Before the event, there were many small changes going on throughout East Germany, most of which were not visible to anyone beyond their immediate neighborhood. But each small act of defiance or new way of behaving occurred within a whole fabric. Each small act was connected invisibly to all others. The global impact suddenly became visible in those few days when people tore the Wall down. The fall of the Berlin Wall demonstrates the power of 'think globally, act locally.' It proves that local actions can have enormous influence on a monstrous system that had resisted all other political attempts to change it. Germany could not be reunited by traditional power politics, or by high-level leaders from powerful nations. It was local actions within the system, combined with many other influences globally, that coalesced into a moment of profound change.[18]

Conditions Ready for Change:
- Institutions or rules out of step with the needs of the public (or a specific field)
- Inefficiency; incompetency; riddled with contradictions and hubris
- Corrupt; abuse of power or resources; lack of legitimacy; competing fiefdoms
- Controlling or inflexible leadership; rules are too burdensome or bureaucratic
- Outlived its usefulness; lost its way or sense of purpose; morally bankrupt; destructive to human dignity or decency; malevolent
- Obsolete; requires too much time, manpower or money to maintain; better choices are available
- Hodgepodge of burdensome and inconsistent viewpoints, rules, and structures

---

[18] Wheatley, Margaret J., *Leadership and the New Science: Discovering order in a chaotic world* (San Francisco: Berrett-Koehler Publishers, 1999), 44.

Revolutionary change need not be political or attempt to persuade the entire community in order for it to alter the prevailing mindset in a meaningful way. As William James explained, "All the higher, more penetrating ideals are revolutionary. They present themselves far less in the guise of effects of past experience than in that of probable causes of future experience, factors to which the environment and the lesson it has so far taught us must learn to bend."

New Ideas Compete for Public Acceptance

There is an invisible competition among ideas. Those already in place have the home court advantage, poised to pick off rookie challengers as they appear. But the competition is not just between the new guy and the old guard, but also among the slew of new guys jockeying among themselves.

Which of their competing versions of progress can gain the advantage? The various new solutions they advocate might be similar enough that victory could easily turn on how well the idea is packaged, or upon the advocate's charisma.

The world is not ready for change—even when it is badly needed. It is human nature to protect what we have, to be suspicious of calls for change, to play wait-and-see, to fear the unknown, to put things off, or to avoid something that is likely to be difficult or risky.

Even widespread grumbling about how bad things are is not enough to counter "better the devil you know than the devil you don't" that argues for sticking with what is in place. **There also must be a catalyzing event or outspoken advocate in order for change to capture public attention.**

Defining What Must Be Different

Each vision puts forth a specific proposed change to the predominant belief system or practices. Some provide a novel elaboration of what is in place; whereas, a major break replaces what is already there, ushering in something uniquely and significantly different.

Each shift alters the existing frame of reference—be it large or small. But even the best new ideas have to deal with inertia—the inherent inclination to leave things the way they are. As Howard Aiken, a computer pioneer, quipped, "Don't worry about people stealing your ideas. If your ideas are any good, you'll have to ram them down people's throats."

A vision needs to resolve real problems or to answer questions that matter if it hopes for any chance to motivate change. The advocate must find a way to express what the vision offers in a way that allows listeners to imagine results *they already desire* in some regard. To persuade people to take action sooner rather than later, the new idea must be framed in core issues they care deeply about.

Frances Moore Lappé is a pioneer in sustainable living and grassroots organizing. She writes about the need to change the context in *Getting a Grip*.

> [People implicitly rely on] the power of 'frame,' the lens through which we interpret our world. But what creates our frame? Largely, it's language—the words and metaphors we use every day.... A big piece of the challenge is disciplining ourselves to find and use words that convey a new frame, one that spreads a sense of possibility and helps people see emerging signs of living democracy that fuel the spiral of empowerment.[19]

In order to change hearts and minds, the message must seem so attractive people prefer it to what they already have. They can see a way to use it because the benefits are easy to grasp and achieve. And they have to be able to get its promised benefits without too much effort (although what "too much" means will be dictated by the circumstances).

The visionary message provides a context of assumptions and philosophical principles that taps into areas of doubt or dissatisfaction that are not being satisfactorily dealt with already. It should relieve some pain, frustration, or ignorance (as in a scientific discovery).

On the other hand, enjoyment is a powerful motivator, so if the vision relates to that, people are less likely to think twice before checking it out. Here is where the arts thrive.

A Soapbox that Spans the Globe

Part of the zeitgeist of our time includes the power of individuals to openly express what they think. Through the marvels of technology, an idea can be quickly communicated to almost anyone who would find it compelling.

The Internet, blogs, social media (like Twitter and YouTube), and alternative media make it easy for someone to reach almost anybody with similar interests. And such methods can be interactive as well so real-time sharing and feedback are possible—with results building on themselves.

Geographic proximity to each other is no longer necessary to develop affinity with like-minded people. The ease of instant communication without face-to-face contact is redefining the nature of what being a community means.

Grass roots participation is integral to today's shift toward worldwide interdependence. It is not just commerce that has gone global. Any new voice or notion has a chance to gain public attention, perhaps a following beyond its allotted 15 minutes of fame.

The soapbox is global and almost immediate. Established media gatekeepers (newspapers, print magazines, radio, TV, publishers, institutional pundits) no longer dominate the information delivery channels. Nor do they decide which voices are worthy—the public gets to help determine that.

---

[19] Lappé, Frances Moore, *Getting a Grip: Clarity, creativity, and courage in a world gone mad* (Cambridge, MA: Small Planet Media, 2007), 47-48.

Small pockets of individual voices (or niches) are placing their votes as to what is considered valuable through the degree of their interest or involvement. As traditional barriers to participation have been breached, fresh ideas can gain traction almost overnight.

That ease of entry continues to redefine the nature of the obstacle course—as well as revealing innovative ways people find to get through it.

Naked On the Inside—The Naked Messenger

Getting Even More Naked

Nakedness takes a person down to the bare essentials: simplicity, authenticity, innocence, and his or her core identity. Many layers must be peeled away before one can be sufficiently refined (and redefined) to be true to their highest potential or avowed undertaking.

Each gradation of nakedness cuts closer to their essential nature. This process is going on *within* the visionary at the same time they are "birthing" their message, and finding support for it in the big world.

"Naked" serves as a metaphor for simplicity or a lack of distortion. It can reveal the extent of an individual's inner and outer maturity. How pronounced any of these qualities may be for a particular individual reflects their combination of personal characteristics and where they happen to be along the visionary journey.

Just to be clear, people can and do become naked in any of the ways mentioned here *without being a visionary or highly creative*. The inner states that accompany greater emotional or spiritual maturity coincide with further nakedness. However, only the motivations most relevant to visionaries are the focus of this chapter.

Through the process of living, each of us acquires layers of habits and perceptual filters that build up over our fundamental consciousness. Most of that accumulation is unconscious, and runs on autopilot. A life goal for being a mature human is to become more conscious, or at least less controlled by those unconscious influencers.

That calls for us to take a more active role in noticing and removing that buildup. It clouds our ability to make conscious choices. Many unconscious influencers are not only unnecessary but harmful. As our distortions decrease, our creative powers can shine through more frequently.

These are increasingly difficult to spot or counter as Edward T. Hall, a cross-cultural researcher explains in *Beyond Culture*.

> Everything man is and does is modified by learning and is therefore malleable. But once learned, these behavior patterns, these habitual responses, these ways of interacting gradually sink below the surface of the mind and, like the admiral of a submerged submarine fleet, control from the depths. The hidden controls are usually experienced as though they are innate simply because they are not only ubiquitous but habitual as well. What makes it doubly hard to differentiate the innate from the acquired is the fact that, as people grow up, everyone around them shares the same patterns.[20]

When a person discovers the extent their behavior and emotions are controlled by the unconscious influences, they take a big step toward reclaiming volitional control. At that point more of our consciousness can step in and actually take charge.

We need our unconscious machinery to function in life. But much of it needs *supervision* at the conscious level. When a person can develop such awareness by cleaning out their old stuff, they could gain Super Vision. That is one of the perks of integrated mastery.

Travelers Drop Their Excess Baggage

Travelers on the visionary path are embarked on an arduous journey. They must pare down to essentials—not once but again and again. Each cuts closer to the bone, with ever greater subtlety and precision.

Numerous layers of distortion or old thinking must be peeled away before the visionary can be true to what this journey demands of them.

Each visionary's contribution is only partly defined by their igniting vision. Others who tried to share their inspired discoveries trod the same path with uneven results—sometimes favorable, sometimes disastrous. While history records countless tales about such pioneers, many more left no lasting mark, their grueling efforts lost among the clamoring voices of their time. Yet even they served the forces of progress.

Another way to think of nakedness is being "without baggage." This meaning relates to flying with inspiration or reaching top-of-the-mountain views. Naked in this sense means not being so weighted down with stuff from the past that it is impossible to take flight. A related term is "earthbound," locked into conventional thinking so no alternate approach is deemed possible.

We all have some baggage, along with an accumulation of innumerable habits and assumptions, most of which we no longer track. How much of it is outgrown or counter-productive? The aim argued for here is not to eliminate all luggage (what is lugged along), but for someone to know what they are bringing along because they want to.

---

[20] Hall, Edward T., *Beyond Culture* (New York: Doubleday, 1976), 42.

This path puts a premium on traveling light. Too much baggage means staying earthbound. On the other hand, not enough means you become spacey because you've lost your grounding.

The visionary path is thorny and demanding since those who walk it tread new ground, far from the comforts of established roadways. Never doubt that by the time the journey is complete, the traveler will be significantly changed. There is no disparagement of those who do not complete the journey or whom the world ignores. Any steps taken along the visionary path are demanding and deserve encouragement—irrespective of how much of the path is navigated.

Along the way, the visionary must also correct weak spots in how their message is packaged and delivered: assumptions that are not well thought through, gaps in application, or the lucidity of their delivery. The message improves and becomes more coherent precisely *because it responds to resistance*.

Like a politician on the stump, those interactions spell out the notion (or invention) as it starts to gain currency in the public awareness. Who is "buying it?" What features and arguments ring their bell? Where do they hold their nose?

In the same vein, the visionary must also confront their personal weaknesses and limitations. Such fine-tuning addresses their resilience, personality, skills, and ethical priorities. The visionary must "walk the talk" as a modeler of the message, as well as a proponent. As Einstein said, "Example isn't another way to teach, it is the only way to teach."

Visionaries push for novelty with an intensity that makes his or her normal life concerns secondary. But those secondaries are not gone or irrelevant. Making the two competing realities coexist is tricky—another reason a visionary's life can be so arduous. That difficulty alone explains why some people turn their back on their visionary impulses.

Why *Not* Get Naked?

Reluctance to slipping off our well-developed protections is natural. It is disrobing that is unnatural. So, some of the earliest tests along the visionary path are about how willingly a person will strip. Where are the points of refusal or hesitation? How readily does a budding visionary build on the ensuing gains that come from losing a "protection" (rather than mourning the loss of it)?

Many of the layers, firmly in place, protect us from vulnerability—to avoid being at the mercy of risky people and circumstances. But they also blind us to many other possibilities and tie us to the cold hand of our past experience. Lessons already learned could be worse than useless to us when novelty beckons. Plus, creative expression and fresh thinking cannot flourish when they are not given free rein.

Protective Layers Are Normal when They:
- Make us feel safe and secure; to fit in
- Maintain a sense of our sense of uniqueness (although in truth, our core identity only appears when naked)
- Achieve desires built on long-held and widely accepted goals
- Achieve our being liked or respected; to sustain relationships
- Maintain habits or illusions that have not been recognized yet

The traits listed below are clustered into three categories. Each of these qualities would not apply equally for each visionary. Each describes a spectrum—from a small degree to fully developed. How intense and multi-faceted it might be is an individual matter. Anyone on the visionary path is becoming more sensitive to such nuanced distinctions. See more in Appendix A, "50 Ways to Get Naked."

"Naked" as Personal Qualities of the Visionary
- Newborn and innocent
- Exposed and vulnerable
- Trusting and naïve
- Not fearful or defensive
- Humble and free of hubris

"Naked" as Ways the Visionary Is Perceived
- Unorthodox and eccentric
- Gadfly
- Daring
- Outsider
- Cutting edge; *avant garde*
- Out of step; clueless

"Naked" as the Visionary's Impact
- Revolutionary or rebellious
- Activist
- Forerunner, explorer, or pioneer

These traits are not totally different from each other; many of them overlap or are subsets of others. However, each points to meaningful distinctions that would be lost if they were to be lumped together. Bear in mind, no single visionary displays all these traits, even over a long lifetime. Also, people can become "naked" in any of these ways without ever acting as a visionary.

Each Step Produces Further Polishing

Those on the visionary path are often required to leave behind many of their "favorite things" that would inhibit their forward progress. That loss may be temporary or permanent.

It could be debated whether what goes was given up, outgrown, or taken away. Regardless, a person's normal life and possessions are "placed on the altar," demoted relative to the person's primary concerns—which includes their vision and a surer sense of what is enduring.

Such sacrifices may include social standing, creature comforts, habits of all sorts, friendships, and material possessions. Even if such things do not need to be jettisoned, they will not matter nearly as much to travelers the farther they proceed. Objects lose their power to dictate the visionary's priorities and choices because their attention is focused elsewhere—on the horizon and bigger-picture discoveries at hand.

However, such tangible sacrifices pale compared to the pain of letting go of the assumptions and mental practices they never questioned before (like being in control or knowing what is trustworthy when everything falls apart). In the process, the visionary's sense of identity goes through a tumbler, as it gets polished up as well. Distortions inherent in a small, self-centered worldview are being buffed away.

Increased nakedness fundamentally alters someone's point of view, so it is possible to see the world, and one's role in it, very differently. An expanding clarity allows one to see anew and at a grander scale. According to a Sufi aphorism, "When the heart weeps for what is lost, the spirit laughs for what it has found."

To Be Congruent, the Incompatible Must Go

Unsuitable clothing (egotistical preening, self-serving priorities, unbecoming poses) at odds with the traveler's big-picture goals must fall away. Anyone determined to keep their fig leaves in place is stalled out of the starting gate.

Trust is crucial and essential. People cannot believe in one's cause if they don't trust the messenger. *The Speed of Trust* by Stephen M. R. Covey makes the point about congruence.

> A person has integrity when there is no gap between intent and behavior … when he or she is whole, seamless, the same—inside and out. I call this 'congruence.' And it is congruence—not compliance—that will ultimately create credibility and trust.… When you consistently demonstrate inner congruence to your belief system and to principles, you inspire trust in both professional and personal relationships. People feel you are strong, solid, and dependable, and that you are committed to live in ways that are certain to bring positive results and validate their confidence in you.[21]

Those who are struggling to strip down can easily tell who is fully clothed (or what garments are still in place) to the extent they have removed their own. To proceed very far along the visionary path, getting naked is not optional. But the extent of the benefits that came with disrobing is only apparent to the unclothed.

---

[21] Covey, Stephen M. R., *The Speed of Trust: The one thing that changes everything* (New York: Free Press, 2006), 62-3.

Make no mistake, the visionary process won't make a person into a nice guy—if he or she is not one already. This path does not change the personality very much. And all that criticism and rejection could make someone withdrawn or prickly.

Each individual still has to work out their personality kinks and shortcomings, and to deal with their relationships and life choices. But the process prevents those on the visionary path from being interested in the raft of less consequential concerns they used to care about.

The visionary's need to find their authentic voice is pressing and ongoing. Being in the public eye invites scrutiny. Observers are not just deciding whether to pay attention to the message for which they beat the drum, but people are also judging the visionary personally. Authenticity is crucial—for both the visionary and their message.

Enthusiastic followers might form unrealistic expectations of what the visionary can deliver, but the visionary should not encourage it. Nor should they try to live on a pedestal. Only disappointment can come of that.

> The human resource of vision (the internal archetype of the visionary) opens the creative spirit and pulls our voice and authenticity into the world.... The Visionary archetype—the relentless power within us that constantly extends an invitation to be who we are—requires the expression of authenticity, vision and creativity. Writer Gertrude Stein tapped this archetype when she told emerging writers of her time, 'You have to know what you want to get. But when you know that, let it take you. And if it seems to take you off the track, don't hold back, because perhaps that is instinctively where you want to be. And if you hold back and try to be always where you have been before, you will go dry.'[22]

Surface beauty (attractiveness) might begin as skin deep, but as a person becomes more *congruent all the way through*, their inner beauty can shine forth as well. While nakedness is perceived at the surface layer, *it is mainly indicative of what lies beneath it.*

Ultimately, once enough distorting layers and low-energy influences are removed, it is possible to reach our underlying essence. Only at that point are inner vision and outer expression pretty much the same.

Just as the visionary should take pains to be authentic and congruent, those traits are every bit as important in the support organization. There, it needs to be expressed and demonstrated by many different people in their respective roles. The same core values inherent in the vision should be clear and the bright-line standard for everyone involved in promoting it.

---

[22] Arrien, Angeles, *The Four-fold Way: Walking the paths of the warrior, teacher, healer and visionary* (San Francisco: HarperSanFrancisco, 1993), 84.

Visionaries Turn From Too Many Distractions

Many visionaries are not overly concerned with possessions or money since getting, having, or using stuff distracts from what is primary to them. While some visionaries were notorious spendthrifts, even more experienced wretched poverty. (Entrepreneurs, high-tech visionaries, and an occasional artist would be exceptions to this.)

In many cases, being on the visionary path has already led to a significant drop in income (or its attendant rewards as they stepped away from their prior responsibilities). However, visionaries are sensitive to the need for sufficient resources to bring their vision into reality. So they cannot disregard money pressures entirely.

The person usually delegates financial responsibilities so they can maintain their focus on the visionary spark that started it all. Their vision may sustain the visionary personally, but what can sustain the growing movement or organization? Revenue demands exert a steady, competing pressure on the priorities of the visionary and core group.

On-going operations, research, outreach, and housing the operation can be pricey. So growth usually depends on finding ways to pay for it. There is likely to be an ongoing tension between the inspired dream and dealing with the practical reality of covering expenses.

Dealing with the practical aspects of grounding one's dream fully engages the visionary's heart, mind, physical energy, time, and most of their resources. However, over a lifetime a single visionary might give life to numerous visions or enterprises (serial entrepreneurs). That is not because they are fickle, but they are attuned to what is on the horizon. Someone on the leading edge could be ideally positioned to catch the next wave. And the next...

Getting to the Heart

Digging Deep Inside—To the Heart

The visionary perspective won't do anyone much good until they get the "heart" piece correct. The new paradigm we are moving into is more heart-centric, rather than being mainly mind-based (our current predominant mode). Trying to engage inspiration and vision without the heart's full participation cannot fly.

Being in touch with the heart gets to the core of who a person really is. But talking about it puts us into a mushy area, where logic and objectivity lose their grip. Sometimes, we stumble over too much romantic wishful thinking, as perpetuated by novels and movies. One's over-reliance on it can lead to "magical thinking," in which we fully expect our wishes to be granted.

It is quite different than the visionary approach that couples fantastic hopes and dreams with extended roll-up-the-sleeves effort. For each of us, the crucial choice should not be between whether to trust our heart, *or* our intellect, *or* our gut feeling. But how can we allow heart, mind, and body to each perform its proper function—so the sum of the parts becomes greater than each on their own?

> Each of us is a physical being, an intellectual being, an intuitive being, and an emotional being; therefore, we must bring all parts of ourselves to this process, or indeed to any important process. When we can stand balanced and upright at the center of our lives—at the center of our well-considered thoughts, our well-cared-for bodies, our honored emotions, and our far-reaching vision—we won't be merely intelligent about emotions, and we won't simply bring balance to our psyches. We will be ingenious, inquiring explorers who can bring new awareness to our deepest issues, new commitment to each of our relationships, and new dedication to a waiting world.[23]

I can cite no greater philosopher than *The Little Prince*, (by Antoine de Saint-Exupery) "It is only with the heart that one sees rightly; what is essential is invisible to the eyes." Staying attuned to that level of meaning involves tiptoeing with care, and setting one's attention to "high alert."

Few writers make it clear what they mean when they say "heart," or "feelings," or "intuition," or "emotions." The four terms are not, in fact, the same or interchangeable (even though often treated that way). It's a sloppy mess.

Gaining hard-to-acquire discernment about them allows a person to make sense of the wealth of overlapping and ill-defined sensations each of us has involving our inner reality. However, to learn how to make clear distinctions related to them within one's inner universe is crucial to achieve self-mastery.

Writing about anything so mushy is already tricky enough, and the popular lore about these concepts has utterly muddied the waters. Sorting out distinctions between emotions and feelings, or anything heart-oriented, would entail its own book. That degree of intricacy is not the goal here.

I am merely trying to set out fluorescent traffic cones in order to urge caution around any of these concepts. *Drive carefully! Make no assumptions. Proceed slowly.*

That said, a clearer understanding of the crucial role of the heart in the creative process is too essential for me to slip those terms in *without any* explanation. Scientific thinkers and stoically unemotional types might complain and dismiss this topic as diversionary fluff.

There is no question that matters of the heart can be distorted by blatant romanticizing and over-the-top drama. But clear-sighted understanding of our own heart-oriented nuances is vital to the creative process or to accessing the big picture.

---

[23] McLaren, Karla, *Language of Emotions: What your feelings are trying to tell you* (Boulder, CO: Sounds True, 2010), 22-3.

Progress along the visionary path requires the heart and mind to play nice and work together (and the body too). To do that involves developing a more nuanced appreciation of our deeper emotional states and to engage alternative ways of knowing (Chapter 7). We must not reject what each approach brings to the table.

Clarification about the Concept of "Heart"

The heart is one entity, one vessel. It is a physical organ, and it is also energy — a nexus where realities and levels intersect. A heart is unified, while having a wide variety of functions it can perform. The mystery is how to account for the enormous range of feelings it generates. How can the basest emotional impulses coexist with the most radiant of impulses?

The heart is like a piano that each person plays in their own way. It can perform an infinite variety of melodies and it responds to the full range of skill levels. People can either use it to make music or noise.

When a student is first learning, most of what they "play" sounds like noise. A period of banging on the keys without any subtlety is followed by a phase of learning about which notes go together, and how the full arrangement of keys work.

The heart constantly strives for harmony, which is not easy to achieve. The greatest musicians have mastered the keyboard (the heart) and have a grasp of all it is capable of expressing. But each person plays their instrument with varying degrees of talent and skill.

The instrument has an infinite capacity for creating harmony or noise. Whether it is played with banging hands or with finesse cannot be blamed on the piano. The music that comes out is unique to the person who plays it.

His or her inimitable energetic signature is being expressed through their heart as well. But the more a person practices and studies how it works, the more complex and nuanced their harmonics can become.

The visionary process accelerates coming to terms with one's feelings and heart-oriented awareness (along with what they might bring to light). As Carl Jung said, "Your vision will become clear only when you can look into your own heart. Who looks outside, dreams, who looks inside, awakes."

Chapter 18 goes into more detail about heart matters. For an insightful and revolutionary look at emotions, I recommend Karla McLaren's latest book, *Language of Emotions: What your feelings are trying to tell you.*

The heart urges us to take right action (act from timeless values). However, while it can discern the correct and ethical action to take, it is often unsure about the right timing. Visionaries get out of sync with 3-D time and want to leap/act too soon. A component of mastery is learning to judge the timing influences better.

Inspiration and vision energize us in the heart, mind, and body all at once. In such moments they all operate in an integrated way. The heart never gets lost in questions or doubts because it "knows," in an entirely non-rational way.

It takes a wise heart, a balanced and attentive heart, not to get caught by extreme emotions or mood swings. It has learned to differentiate between passion and compassion.

To complicate the topic further, the heart and emotions can correspond to humanity's higher-order needs or lower order needs. Some of what it expresses comes from natural physical processes engaged on the survival level. (See Maslow, Chapter 11.) But some of the heart's impact arises via the exercise of higher-order needs (self-actualization) or through pursuing creative activities that generate psychic energy. The resulting energy is not simply physical in nature, but has some ineffable and highly charged qualities as well (Chapter 13).

In addition, our emotions and feelings each have a different source and capacity. Most emotions are related to the everyday 3-D world. Whereas, feelings are related to our "knowing place," which have an otherworldly quality—and they're not much concerned with everyday matters. Those feelings can reflect the degree of our connection to inspired perceptions.

In a world where heart and mind are conceived of as separate and at odds with each other, those for whom heart and mind act as a unit appear out of step. But that is closer to the truth, and beginning to change for many people.

The visionary path is largely about strengthening the collaborative bond between heart and mind, and between inner and outer awareness. It furthers a gradual movement away from feeling the need to *choose between* them, or to maintain a preference for one of them.

This newfound cooperation between them also characterizes the paradigm coming into focus (Chapter 19). At some point in the future, many of the visionary qualities treated as suspect in the larger culture of today will be both widespread and acceptable. Once the onus of social rejection is less severe, the nature and quality of the challenges visionaries face can decline in some regard.

In the process of growing up, each of us develops and learns to satisfy our most basic and pressing needs first. As we mature and gain more inner awareness, more upbeat and creative energy becomes available to us (Chapter 13). However, too often people do not grow up with regard for their heart-based abilities.

We all recognize situations where the emotional responses of the heart are overwrought, dissonant, or shockingly intense without obvious provocation. But we do a tragic disservice to the heart by concluding it has done something "bad." It is important to acknowledge that the heart's feelings are always authentic and true.

They are simply the keys on our piano and will always make the same sound when struck. It is the responsibility of the piano player to make harmony or noise, not the job of the piano itself.

When the player's thoughts, beliefs, or assumptions are distorted, untrue, or misguided, the piano will respond accordingly. So when the output of one's heart turns into unattractive, downright painful, noise, the rule of thumb is to stop playing and examine what the player is thinking. The sour notes happen in the mind and conclusions of the player long before the heart plays them back.

Individuals who trust mind-over-heart and those who trust heart-over-mind must both make adjustments so they can operate in ways that heart, mind, and body shine.

The visionary process leads to a form of heart-brain-body intelligence that gains access to enhanced perceptual abilities and wisdom. The amalgam is where mastery begins to hold sway. And what it creates can be truly remarkable.

Vision Drives Beliefs and Change

Authentic on the Inside *and* the Outside

Most people are not very discerning about the significance of what they routinely observe. Too many of the details of information received are ignored and presumed to be irrelevant. So they are filtered out and treated as background noise.

But changing our way of looking *while it is occurring* reveals many important messages that would usually be missed. Many of those details give evidence of a larger context that is actually quite influential.

People are inclined to look at something's external appearance and assume it accurately reveals its true nature. However, its appearance, underlying substance, and larger context could bear little relation to each other, for a variety of reasons. Acquiring greater mastery increases the ability to see and understand more of those peripheral, yet instrumental, messages.

It is amazing how becoming more naked improves someone's ability to see. As we strip away our layers of distortion, we become increasingly aware of the presence of those layers operating in others too (but not in a judgmental way). We start to *see beneath the surface appearance* of what is going on as well.

What was hidden becomes more visible, and some of what was puzzling ceases to be so. Awareness dawns—and in the darndest places.

Like an optical illusion that has been figured out, a person cannot look at the situation again without the solution popping out, unbidden. New faculties seem to be at our beck and call because the true significance of what is being experienced shines through.

As Zen master Shunryu Suzuki once wrote, "In the beginner's mind there are many possibilities, but in the expert's mind there are few."

Getting Down to Work

Greater nakedness alters how each of us sees "who I am" as well. It reveals hard-to-endure truths about where we are congruent (or not) and areas where we are under-developed. It becomes starkly evident where we have been fudging.

Such discoveries about our own behavior need not be perceived as self-criticism, so much as a collapse of illusions. Our inner work reveals whatever interferes with us being able to operate from our full capacity.

Authenticity exists to the extent one's inner and outer states mesh together and act in unison. Getting that to happen does not occur without diligent effort and ongoing vigilance to eliminate whatever could interfere with that happening.

~ Inner Work ~
A BonBon ~ Faith Lynella

Inner work is hard work.
- It is not daydreaming.
- It is not introspection.
- It is not wishful thinking.
- It is not dogma or beliefs.
- It is not creative visualization.
- It is not self-judgment or criticism.

Inner work is learning about yourself from the *inside*. It reveals to you what works for you and what doesn't. You begin to see your limits with candor and acceptance. You find and repair damaged and hurt places. You discover strengths and virtues you didn't know you had. Your goal is not to change, but to truly understand yourself, as you *already* are.

Too often, people are not satisfied with themselves and spend considerable effort trying to change into being someone they would like better. Those efforts to change are very different from what is required to know yourself. Yet, attempts to change are doomed unless they include an awareness of what is already in operation. The better way to grow is to value those qualities which are already functioning and enhance them. Then you are building on your strengths, using your resources to greater advantage.

Inner work is the difficult but solitary effort to "take your invisible mental clothes off" and see yourself naked and undistorted. As you eliminate all pretense, all muddled thinking, all preconceptions, you see your own real self—honestly and with love. The combination of courage, vulnerability, trust, and gentleness necessary to "Know yourself" is hard to achieve. But inner work cannot occur without them.

From *BonBons to Sweeten Your Daily Life*. Or from *More BonBons*

The Naked Message—The Vision as Blueprint

Crafting the Package for the Vision

The message and messenger mirror each other in myriad ways. The message that comes to be known to the world at large as "the vision" is an amalgam of the initiating insight(s) and the qualities of its proponent. The need for nakedness and authenticity is every bit as important for the espoused vision (message) as it is for the person beating the drum for it.

For a visionary message to be compelling, it must be much more than another good idea. It needs to spell out the related changes of opinion and behavior that go with it. Chapter 6 explores the nature of visions and Chapter 10 explores their packaging.

So far as the public response to it, a vision or invention is not just another brand of toothpaste being bought and sold. When people grasp the worth of a significant new idea, its impact depends on whether using it changes their habits, as well as their opinion about it.

How consistently do those who like it put the brand-new idea (or invention) into practice? Too many new-fangled notions and products get bought but not "taken out of the box."

Some visionaries are narrow in scope or relate to a specific audience (i.e., scientists or sculptors), whereas, others could impact a culture or epoch. But each group member needs to feel it "speaks to me" if they are to take the next step, and embrace what is being offered.

More than Superficial Appearance

Refinement in the expression of the message continues well past honing its *apparent meaning*, which is only a small part of the vision's emerging message. Polishing a visionary idea increases its relevance and usability. People feel moved to put it to use more and more.

Such tinkering clarifies the arguments, along with the secondary implications that were not even considered initially. Also, much of the movement toward greater fluency is happening *within the visionary,* as well as in the developing organization as followers or employees get involved.

Qualities of the Message

1. The Naked Message Is Uncomplicated and Elegant

- Easy to grasp
- Easy to gain the significant benefits
- Easy to put into practice; flexible applications
- Easy buy-in initially; few barriers to getting the advantages offered; inclusive
- Simple enough for a beginner to participate (or if a specialized field, relevant for its members)
- Delivers what is promised
- Presents a compelling "story"; it satisfies
- Elegant simplicity; pleasing or satisfying, with something "extra"

In spheres where considerable training and expertise are necessary, the new message must also be sophisticated enough to stand analytical scrutiny among insiders. Yet it adds a beneficial enhancement to that field.

2. The Naked Message Rings True Emotionally

It delivers a believable and relevant message for receivers. It is sent to the right audience for it. The concept is clear, simple, meaningful, and graspable. It combines logical precision with emotional resonance. The core idea is more than a mental construct since it transcends practicalities alone—but it also does not ignore them.

3. The Naked Message Is Original, Creative, and Germinal

The innovative idea (or invention) brings something new and different. It is easy to adopt and adapt to real-life situations. What it delivers is not locked into the limitations of past thinking. Nor does it merely recycle what already exists in a new wrapper. It is flexible enough to grow and shift functionality as it is put into action.

Each realm of interest has its own way of expressing originality. For example in the arts: "Each poet, musician, or artist who leaves a mark must find a way to write, compose, or paint like no one has done before. So while the role of artist is an old one, the substance of what they do is unprecedented."[24]

4. The Naked Message Is Common

The message that changes a culture speaks to Everyman. It connects with our intrinsic awareness, touching deep threads all of us share. It deals in universalities and principles that are broader and deeper than everyone's personal or provincial concerns.

---

[24] Csikszentmihalyi, Mihaly, *Creativity: Flow and the psychology of discovery and invention* (New York: HarperCollins, 1996), 193.

On the other hand, some messages are meant only for a few because of the specialized domain of expertise involved. Such messages can be comprehended only by those who share a long, well-defined training, like performing musicians and highly specialized scientists. Participants communicate with a shared vocabulary that is both inclusive (difficult to learn but usable by anyone who knows it) and exclusive (outsiders cannot make sense of what insiders are talking about).

5. The Naked Message Is Virtuous

Because it is rooted in inspiration, the vision adheres to high principles and ideals. It is fundamentally ethical and offers a model of desirable behavior to be imitated. Such upright standards should never be casually sacrificed to expediency. When respected, such transcendent values bring forth the best in the visionary or core group.

6. The Naked Message Is Plain and Humble

The message can stand up to scrutiny without resorting to glitz and glamour. Rather than putting on a show, it allows its clarity to shine through to those with the eyes to recognize it. It promotes actual change, rather than superficial adjustments or fiddling for appearance's sake. All aspects of it fit together smoothly, without contradictions.

Chapter 4 - Bridging Between Vision and the World

One certainty visionaries share is that they have something to say or demonstrate that has not been done before. There is a creative embellishment all their own that must see the light of day.

Unlikely Qualities are Very Likely

Visionaries are all over the map regarding their personal qualities. Mihaly Csikszentmihalyi studied personality traits of extremely creative individuals and details those findings in *Creativity, flow and the psychology of discovery and invention*.

> If I had to express in one word what makes their personalities different from others it would be complexity. By this I mean that they show tendencies of thought and action that in most people are segregated. They contain contradictory extremes—instead of being an 'individual,' each of them is a 'multitude.' Like the color white that includes all the hues of the spectrum, they tend to bring together the entire range of human possibilities within themselves.[25]

Each of us has a full array of these traits within our individual make-up. However, by training and personal preference, most of us develop certain sides of our nature, while rejecting others we do not like, or struggle with. A complex personality is akin to what Carl Jung considered a *mature personality*—where the expressed and suppressed (unacknowledged) parts of a person's nature are embraced at the same time. It involves the whole person—warts and all.

Such a person is not constrained much by the expectations of others, but freely moves from one extreme to the other, responding to the situation. They feel little or no inner conflict about it.

Individuals who have a complex personality are at home with the contradictory extremes of a trait and experience either end (and points between) with equal intensity. Nor are they surprised to encounter that flexibility in others. That's part of what makes creative types such a mystery to those around them, who assume that holding one position precludes holding the opposite (a characteristic of linear and either-or thinking).

This corresponds to Emerson's saying, "A foolish consistency is the hobgoblin of little minds." It is satisfied with a single point of view. Those who see the world that way treat what they see as the truth—the whole truth and nothing but the truth. But that misses a lot.

Creativity always seeks a broader, more expansive and integrated perspective. it accommodates not only black and white, but shades of gray as essential parts of the picture. however, that openness to multiple interpretation does not mean they are wishy-washy or without values.

---

[25]Csikszentmihalyi, Mihaly, *Creativity: Flow and the psychology of discovery and invention* (New York: HarperCollins, 1996), 57.

Having a complex personality means being able to express the full range of traits that are potentially present in the human repertoire but usually atrophy because we think that one or the other pole is 'good,' whereas the other extreme is 'bad.'[26]

Paradoxical Combinations Found in Very Creative People

Csikszentmihalyi illustrates this capability to embrace extremes through ten traits he studied that are usually presumed to be opposites. These traits tend to become integrated in creatives and visionary individuals. So the full range of characteristics could show up in whatever they are doing.

Paradoxical Traits:
1. Have an abundance of physical energy, but are also quiet and restful
2. Smart but naïve at the same time; the ability to combine wisdom and childishness
3. Playfulness with discipline; responsibility with irresponsibility; lightheartedness with dogged perseverance
4. Imagination and fantasy combined with a "rooted sense of reality"
5. Extroversion and introversion at the same time
6. Remarkably humble and proud simultaneously; ambition along with selflessness; both competitive and cooperative
7. Masculine and feminine qualities intermixed; aggressive toughness coupled with emotional sensitivity
8. Rebellious and independent coupled with paying one's dues in a field of knowledge; traditional or conservative along with breaking rules and taking chances
9. Passionate about their work while being very objective about it
10. Openness and enhanced sensitivity make them feel great suffering, along with great enjoyment[27]

Such paradoxical juxtapositions would be impossible were it not for the degree of self-awareness the person is acquiring via the creative process. And that does not come overnight or without considerable soul searching.

Part of what has been happening to them on the visionary path is a dismantling of conceptual and emotional boundaries that are at odds with pursuing their sparks of genius. These restrictive boundaries continue to diminish throughout the process.

Far-sighted Visionary Strategists

When such individuals are examined closely, what stands out is their wide diversity. They show up in all areas of endeavor—championing their causes and urging the world to pay attention. They could get noticed as much for their

---

[26] *Ibid.*, 57.
[27] *Ibid.*, 58-76.

idiosyncrasies as for the merit of their vision. However, it is likely they will be ignored or rejected on both counts.

Visionaries usually have a rich inner life and are not bored with their own company. They seem to come alive when they are fully engaged with their primary passion—drinking from their own creative spring.

He or she may appear to be idle or lazy to outsiders since it sometimes "doesn't look like they are doing anything." Temporarily, the world's concerns are pushed to back burner so their inner life can be front and center. And the creative juices are flowing.

Disapproval toward those who prefer their creative inner world to what are considered normal pursuits can carry a high social cost. It is not unusual for them to become isolated or outcasts.

In *Tribes*, Seth Godin reminds us why being a being a visionary can be a high-risk occupation.

> Our culture works hard to prevent change. We have long had systems and organizations and standards designed to dissuade people from challenging the status quo. We enforce our systems and call whoever is crazy enough to challenge them a heretic. And society enforces the standards by burning its heretics at the stake, either literally or figuratively.[28]

Vision implies the ability to see beyond the present—to focus on the long term and big picture, without getting too bogged down with immediate and nitpicky concerns. Visionaries see with the inner eye of possibility. Sometimes it is in other realms, like an ideal or future state.

Their focus goes from *what is* to *what could be*. But they are not satisfied with holding only one view *or* the other, but are busy building bridges between them—grounding what they imagine in the "here and now."

The visionary has his or her eye on the horizon, while planting a seed (maybe many) that could take root and grow as they envision. What they foresee does not yet exist—except in their imagined world. But like a farmer, planting seeds gives way to caring for tender shoots, until an eventual harvest.

Strategies they employ to realize their vision are inextricably linked with their long-range view. Forerunners attempt to ground future outcomes in today's practicalities, in both large ways and small. So even simple day-to-day decisions are attuned to that desired future.

They know they are on board for the long haul. That calls for stamina and persistence. However, as Walter Elliot, a writer in the 1800s points out, "Perseverance is not a long race; it is many short races, one after another."

---

[28] Godin, Seth, *Tribes: We need you to lead us* (New York: Penguin Group, 2008), 71.

Knitting together the abstract realm of ideas and the world of concrete substance depends on a steady back and forth between them—inspired moments followed by hands-on time in the trenches. One lives with the flip-flop progression between them. It is slow and prone to error—even without the interference of the "who needs it?" crowd.

The proffered concept or invention comes alive as it is expressed through the visionary's point of view and energy. The intangibles must come to be translated into the kind of changes people can relate to and believe in—or nothing is going to happen. Bear in mind, as Peter Senge points out, "People don't resist change. They resist being changed."

A visionary is willing to stand up for unpopular (or not yet popular) ideas. They are ready to make sacrifices and suffer for their cause, if necessary. Their confidence in a vision can be infectious.

The visionary often acts as a real-live example of someone who believes what they propose. People can sense such totality of devotion, so they sometimes respond as much to the emotional tenor as to the notion's merits.

> To change minds effectively, leaders make particular use of two tools: the stories that they tell and the lives that they lead. In terms of our levers of change, the 'resonance that exists—or doesn't—between those stories and those lives proves of tell-tale importance.[29]

Making a Unique Statement

Early on, every visionary is challenged to create something akin to their "brand"—an original notion in a unique package. Yet every original vision contains some of the same philosophical verities that have been discovered time and again.

What makes theirs new and relevant is the visionary's unique personality and enthusiasms, coupled with their time and place in history. Those add the one-of-a-kind flavor to their discovery and message.

Daniel Goleman, author of *Working with Emotional Intelligence*, addresses the range of impulses that arise through creative pursuits.

> The creative mind is, by its very nature, a bit unruly. There is a natural tension between orderly self-control and the innovative urge. It's not that people who are creative are out-of-control emotionally; rather, they are willing to entertain a wider range of impulse and action than do less adventurous spirits. That is, after all, what creates new possibilities.[30]

---

[29] Gardner, Howard, *Changing Minds: The art and science of changing our own and other people's minds* (Boston: Harvard Business School Press, 2004), 69.
[30] Ibid., 100.

One certainty visionaries share is that they have something to say or demonstrate that has not been done before. There is a creative embellishment all their own that must see the light of day.

Romantic artist Eugene Delacroix observed, "What moves men of genius, or rather what inspires their work, is not new ideas, but their obsession with the idea that what has already been said is still not enough."

This chapter and the next look at the qualities most likely to apply to visionaries as individuals. When speaking of vision as a singular event or a lifelong commitment, that is for simplicity's sake in my writing about it. It does not distinguish between them.

Many on this path are serial visionaries — who commit to more than one significant vision at different points in life, or according to new interests. For those on the leading edge, the nature of what is new is forever changing.

The visionary process leads every traveler toward a similar destination, but it exudes a different appeal for each. Everyone charts their own inimitable course, encountering unique adventures along the way. And the form their journey takes is informed by the inter-meshing of inspiration and practicalities, of the impetus to act followed by the consolidation of gains. These do not have separate realities.

Where Is the Person Along the Visionary Cycle?

Historically, major visionaries didn't come along very often. The first who come to mind are the towering giants, so they are assumed to be rare and unlikely (Black Swans). Such bright lights are unique as to their personality, message, and how their story unfolded. But in ways related to the visionary process they are not unique at all.

Geoff Colvin discusses the amount of devoted preparation required to get ready for "spontaneous" creativity in *Talent is Overrated:*

> The greatest innovators in a wide range of fields — business, science, painting, music — all have at least one characteristic in common: They spend many years in intensive preparation before making any kind of creative breakthrough. Creative achievement never came suddenly, even in those cases in which the creator later claimed that it did.[31]

Even the giants played out the same script used by most visionaries. Far from being random flukes, they prove, yet again and in many ways, the lawful nature of the visionary process. Most visionaries have a long period of preparation, acquiring the requisite skills and knowledge of their field of interest.

---

[31] Colvin, Geoff, *Talent is Overrated: What really separates world-class performance from everybody else* (New York: Penguin Group, 2008), 151.

Once the person gains sufficient subject-matter mastery, he or she is equipped to see past the shared and accepted view, so they might introduce something original.

In most regards, a process is the same for all who share it. Most stages are necessary for proceeding on to later ones, as the steps play out a preset sequence. Some travelers on the visionary path bloom early, some late. Some are skilled at riding the forces of change that supercharge their efforts, while others struggle in obscurity. The process accommodates them all.

Usually a stage cannot be skipped. When crucial stages are not completed in ordered progression, a person is likely to be blocked from reaching later stages of the cycle. Also, successful achievement of a stage is preparation for subsequent ones.

For instance, those who are just setting out face somewhat different obstacles (survival and self-doubt) than those which must be confronted at the rapid-growth period.

In order to be useful, descriptions of visionaries and the process must be precise enough to identify and tweak apart the nuanced personal qualities of participants. They must make sense of how individuals come to be altered along the way—from their initial vision to its fruition.

They should acknowledge the unseen influences that make a vision something more than just another good idea in the marketplace of ideas.

That points to one of the dilemmas inherent in discussing the visionary path. It is a long-term process and a person keeps changing throughout. That is why it is nearly impossible to compare where different visionaries are relative to each other at a specific point in time—or even to compare a particular person at different phases of their process.

Visionaries Differ Greatly in Their Scale of Impact

Major visionaries herald a scale shift—to something that would not have been expected considering what already existed. It acts as a break from the *status quo*—along with a break*through* in the way people perceive or apply a concept later. Over time, related ideas and conduct change for many people, so it increasingly corresponds to the new frame of mind (or invention).

Change on the largest scale alters fundamental assumptions. It shifts behavior enough to impact society (or individual lives) in a wide variety of ways. It also triggers a ripple of concomitant changes, as many people (both visionary and skilled) step forward to re-weave the emerging fabric. They will, together and individually, ground and express the next up-and-coming mindset.

Change begets more change. Quieter revolutions could arise around the margins. Smaller-scale discoveries fill in the gaps—logical and intuitive enlargements of the body of what is known. Most inventions and scientific experiments are incremental gap-fillers. While useful and necessary, their impact is quite different from the creative output of someone who changes the prevailing paradigm.

Another way to assess the scale of the visionary's influence is by asking whether their contribution could have been accomplished without encountering significant resistance from the establishment. Incremental change can; revolutionary change cannot. Also, how far did the person need to move away from the protective arms of their community or discipline before they could gain traction for their discovery?

A common challenge to accomplishing projects is "mission creep." That is the gradual expansion of a project beyond its original intent and goals. It keeps creeping larger and larger with one more thing...

Visionary projects could have an even riskier variation, which I dub "mission leap." The driving force of a vision pushes its proponent ahead of the curve. That coupled with the non-linear qualities of creative thinking and spontaneity could easily lead to leaping way ahead of existing preparation.

Mission leap takes visionary activities out to the edge of possibilities, where existing boundaries get pushed further still. Such projects are likely to outrun the original intent or the available resources — all of which increases their unpredictability and riskiness.

Each of us has access to the realm of possibilities. What we choose to make of them reflects the scope of our unique lens of perception. And as the visionaries demonstrate, that scope is infinitely elastic. To the extent we stretch our limits, they have less ability to hold us back.

Rosamund Stone Zander and Benjamin Zander speak of the "university of possibility" in *The Art of Possibility*.

> Let us suppose, now, that a universe of possibility stretches beyond the world of measurement to include all worlds: infinite, generative, and abundant. Unimpeded on a daily basis by the concern for survival, free from the generalized assumption of scarcity, a person stands in the great space of possibility in a posture of openness, with an unfettered imagination for what can be....
>
> The action in a universe of possibility may be characterized as generative, or giving, in all senses of that word — producing new life, creating new ideas, consciously endowing with meaning, contributing, yielding to the power of contexts. The relationship between people and environments is highlighted, not the people and things themselves. Emotions that are often relegated to the special category of spirituality are abundant here: joy, grace, awe, wholeness, passion, and compassion.[32]

---

[32] Zander, Rosamund Stone and Zander, Benjamin, *The Art of Possibility: Transforming professional and personal life* (New York: Penguin Books, 2000), 19-20.

Holding a Broad Perspective

Takes a Long View

The visionary path is infinitely flexible and novel. There is a defining vision or there isn't. It could be a single occurrence or ongoing ones. Its impact can be short-lived or lifelong, hard going or relatively easy. It might be experienced after long preparation or in a flash, without warning.

All combinations could be true and equally possible since visionaries represent the exceptions — the ones who manage to carry on in the margins and out of the mainstream.

Too many die unsung. Visionaries are commonly described as "being before their time." Yet their work might live on, carried on by devoted followers who adhere to their playbook, or by those who find a way to use their ideas without knowing the source.

On the other hand, history also records some visionaries who succeeded in the short term, but lacked staying power.

Visionaries and their creative endeavors change and grow. Time passes. Social conditions give way to new ones. So the milieu the visionary interacts with is constantly being altered — possibly in response to his or her efforts.

As with any long journey, many more embark on the visionary path than reach their desired destination. But all travelers contribute to the march of progress to some extent — as well as to furthering the specific communities to which they owe allegiance.

Travelers who only go a short way still feed the whirlwinds of change. Their actions reflect an underlying process that is not just about them personally.

While most starts do not ripen into a lifetime commitment or leave a discernible impact, everyone on the visionary path contributes to the ongoing dialog about what is important, or which changes are considered desirable.

Even those who do not stay the course alter the pathways they tread — making some of them more pronounced or accessible for those to come. While most visionaries play out their visions on a small stage, the determination and courage needed to hold steady against limitations and resistance from entrenched interests applies for all.

Nothing Is Wasted on the Visionary Path

The visionary's job is to make their inspired notion tangible, to bring it to life. Through sustained effort, the initial vision, the visionary, and the resulting message all merge into a coherent expression — a seamless embodiment of a transcendent idea made manifest.

The forces of novelty play out in innumerable ways in real life. How each visionary goes about making that happen is *their* story, possibly their life's work.

Nevertheless, the visionary's role does not end if or when the public accepts (or rejects) their gift of insight. That merely moves them to subsequent stages of the visionary journey—which is always larger than the fate of any particular vision.

Many new ideas never reach the critical mass of popular acceptance, but are adopted in a smaller niche or for a different application. Some are half-baked, containing first-rate and unformed elements jumbled together.

Yet a crumb of it could get noticed and embedded in the public awareness, so it flowers in unexpected ways. Such ideas can take on a life of their own, independent of whomever first stated them.

While the birthing and launch of an idea resembles a mother's role, any idea can grow past the early expectations for it. New ideas thrive where they're wanted, dry up when rejected, or might meld with compatible notions. It is often impossible to locate the source of a notion, once it catches on.

Even when a vision doesn't develop past the preliminary stages, sometimes the core ideas are picked up and incorporated into a very different theory or application—where they live on without attribution.

A budding visionary might shift gears, abandon an early enthusiasm, or prefer to pursue unrelated new interests. Some outgrow a pastime, only to return to it later in life—from a different vantage point. Others find their initial interest morph into something quite unconnected.

Such detours or delays do not signify the person left the visionary path (once they were on it) because indirect routes often provide the stuff of life that can make a vision germane. So it grows in unforeseen ways. The self-discipline, determination, and abilities someone develops for one pursuit could be equally useful when exploring other undertakings.

All such life-driven activities contribute to the visionary's cache of skills, personality traits, and scope of outlook. By the time they are working on master-level issues, *anything* the person subsequently does (even in dissimilar fields or as a rank beginner), will be approached in a masterful way. That is because the requisite abilities and comprehension are already in place.

A visionary must learn to be selective about where his or her time and attention goes. Not only are their resources limited but the person's efforts must be engaged where they will do their vision the most good. As Peter Drucker points out "Nothing is less productive than to make more efficient that which should not be done in the first place." Fledgling visionaries should be careful to choose to pursue visions that are not only engaging to them, but are worth the candle.

For some, being out of the mainstream or ahead of their time is too weighty to bear, and too heavy to endure. But their determination and resilience keep them going—even when the cause seems to be lost.

Their Stage Influences the Person's View and Key Roles

The visionary process requires participants to continually focus, and then refocus, on what is primary for them. At each phase, the visionary is compelled to adapt and grow, to rework the package for the vision in light of all they've discovered. Specific events or issues have a very different significance for them in the early stages than they might have later on because of all that is acquired along the way.

And it is not just an individual's own growth at stake, but a larger-scale process with a mammoth cast of characters. As science fiction writer Orson Scott Card noted: "Saving the human race is a frantic business. Or a tedious one. It all depends on what stage of the process you're taking part in."

Early decisions set the course for later ones. Successful moves (as well as failures) build on prior decisions and clarify the next steps to take. Events alter the visionary's level of self-confidence and expectations in ways that weren't foreseen. How adeptly can the visionary or team steer around the constantly changing obstacle course? The ability to learn and adapt quickly is at a premium.

There is plenty of discouraging and thankless work to be done, even while the enterprise requires a full measure of devotion. Dings to their self-confidence or expertise are disappointing. They sting. As old beliefs are shaken or replaced, it becomes increasingly difficult to find something trustworthy—within oneself, or out in the world.

In the early phase the visionary's function is largely disruptive, as they counter the *status quo*. If what is espoused takes off or grows into a movement, strong leadership and organizational skills are called for as well. The eventual success of a revolutionary idea often depends on the level and type of support the visionary can garner at the outset, and as additional responsibilities are demanded.

Walking the Visionary Path Takes Lots of Time

On a personal scale, many of the visionary's efforts are slow to reach a critical mass whereby the desired changes become evident. So the gradual buildup needed to shift the unbending calls for patience, determination, and courage. On a grand scale, the visionaries are ahead of the growth curve, and are thereby instrumental in directing the form it takes.

Arthur Koestler's germinal work, *The Act of Creation* explores the types of creativity, whether scientific, religious, or humorous.

> [In both art and ideas] the truly original geniuses are rare compared with the enormous number of talented practitioners; the former acting as spearheads, opening up new territories, which the latter will then diligently cultivate. In both fields there are periods of crises, of 'creative anarchy', leading to a breakthrough to new frontiers—followed by decades, or centuries of consolidation,

orthodoxy, stagnation, and decadence — until a new crisis arises, a holy discontent, which starts the cycle again. Other parallels could be drawn; 'multiple discoveries' — the simultaneous emergence of a new style, for which the time is ripe, independently in several places; collective discoveries' originating in a closely knit group, clique, school, or team; 'rediscoveries' — the periodic revivals of past and forgotten forms of art; lastly 'cross-fertilizations' between seemingly distant provinces of science and art.[33]

While our creative energies might serve our visions — they are simultaneously in service to each individual's sense of identity and purpose. A visionary's life involves much more than acting as a drudge for the vision — shackled to an endless Do List and battling the ranks of naysayers.

After all, any creative individual is likely to have many visions — innumerable sparks of genius. And the fate of any one of them cannot fully define the person who gives it an opportunity to take root.

The visionary path is long and thorny, often lonely and discouraging. What keeps someone going during the tough times often comes down to one's degree of passion about it. The intensity of their devotion warms travelers in the face of a cold, uncaring world; and in times of triumph, that devoted perseverance makes what comes to them all the sweeter.

These intrepid souls take an optimistic view of the outcome they seek. As Gandhi, himself a rather naked giant, said, "First they ignore you, then they ridicule you, then they fight you, then you win."

One of the telltale markers of the visionary process is being "ahead of one's time." The person who was dismissed as irrelevant or wrong during their lifetime may become greatly respected much later, or after they are dead. The world will be well served if that long-drawn-out time lag can be shrunk.

As each of us becomes more attuned to our own bright insights and willing to give them credence, we are also more receptive to those sparks arising in others. Even if such notions cannot be grounded in a practical way, the sheer recognition of their presence and silent appreciation of their inherent worth recharges our creative springs. That awareness permits a different kind of dialog and focus that is expansive and rich with possibilities.

More Attuned to Unconscious Influences

A Greater Respect for the Unconscious

One possible meaning of "off the beaten track" could be to move away from consciousness to some degree. One disengages from the logical mind in order to pursue the unconscious mind with greater intent (as consciously as possible).

---

[33] Koestler, Arthur, *The Act of Creation* (New York: The Macmillan Company, 1964), 335.

The unconscious plays a central role in how everyone lives and works, but it is largely unacknowledged by our ego or conscious faculties. Modern-day humans have a cultural bias to give credit to the logical mind and to treat our motivations as largely rational.

> *The Social Animal* by David Brooks sheds light on the role of the unconscious: The conscious mind writes the autobiography of our species. Unaware of what is going on deep down inside, the conscious mind assigns itself the starring role. It gives itself credit for performing all sorts of tasks it doesn't really control. It creates a view of the world that highlights those elements it can understand and ignores the rest.[34]

The visionary path is a journey inward while simultaneously dealing with hands-on practical matters. Much of what makes visionaries so puzzling to bystanders is their willingness to look "under the hood," at their own internal process. Directly or indirectly, these individuals grapple with access to their inner reality as a crucial means of bringing their visions to life. Brooks also said:

> The unconscious is a natural explorer. Whereas conscious thought tends to march step by step and converge on a few core facts or principles, unconscious thought tends to spread out through a process of associations, venturing into … the dark and dusty nooks and crannies of the mind. [The early part of the brain] therefore produces more creative links and unlikely parallels. Unconscious thought can take in many more factors. It naturally weighs the importance of various factors as they come into view. It restlessly scurries about—many parallel processes at a time—as the conscious mind is busy with other things, trying to match new situations with old models or trying to rearrange the pieces of a problem until they create a harmonious whole. It chases vibes and metaphors in search of connections, patterns, and similarities. It uses the whole panoply of psychological tools—emotions as well as physical sensations.[35]

Mentions of "vision" or "enhanced clarity" in this book largely reflect the functioning of the transcendent mind—one that operates from a larger frame or beyond the finite reality. It exists beyond our individual consciousness *or* unconscious states, being larger than either of them, and yet it cooperates with both. (See Chapter 6.) Still in another sense, it is not "out there" *or* "in here," but a core reflection of who each person is.

Opening the Door to What Is Hidden

The unconscious mind is integral to creative insight. Vision and the Muses point to ways our unconscious machinery interfaces with our conscious awareness. By giving credence to its role, the conscious faculties become further engaged in bringing about what is envisioned.

---

[34] Brooks, David, *The Social Animal: The hidden sources of love, character, and achievement* (New York: Random House, 2011), *xiii*.
[35] *Ibid.*, 244-5.

Once the person's conscious mind and unconscious mind start to respect what each does best, one gains the best of both. To a large extent, the visionary path reflects the ripening consequences of that alliance.

Erik Calonius, author of *10 Steps Ahead*, explains the brain's reliance on its unconscious functions, as well as rational ones.

> Scientists are discovering that the brain is a visionary device—that its primary function is to create pictures in our minds that can be used as blueprints for things that do not yet exist. They are also learning that our brains can work subconsciously to solve problems that we cannot crack through conscious reasoning, and that the brain is a relentless pattern seeker, constantly reinventing the world.[36]

Humans are equipped with multiple systems of knowledge and awareness. Accepting the need to integrate the various elements involved in our creative efforts is key. Integration occurs when each of the approaches cooperates with its appointed tasks, sphere of expertise, rules of operation, and ways of acting on what it understands.

These should not be competing or exclusive, but complementary modes of operation within ourselves. Treating the conscious mind, or rational thought, as the only respectable way to operate ends up in a very limited cul-de-sac.

We could strive to mimic the White Queen (of C.S. Lewis) who said, "Sometimes I've believed as many as six impossible things before breakfast." Visionaries sometimes manage to demonstrate the "impossible" is doable.

Growth, on any level or at any scale, is toward greater integration of as many functional elements as possible. A willingness to take seriously more of our largely-ignored unconscious influences goes a long way toward appreciating the "invisible" role the unconscious plays.

Not that it needs permission. It already pulls many strings without the logical side being cognizant of just how few rational choices are actually required in ordinary daily life.

What neither the conscious mind nor the unconscious mind can do on its own is to represent the whole of the individual. For that, they must develop a working partnership. These days there are abundant influences pushing each of us in that direction.

By definition, the word "unconscious" means not in our conscious awareness. The <u>sub</u>conscious is a subset of that. Within that amorphous category of the unconscious, some of it is beneath our notice, but could be perceived by the simple act of paying greater attention to certain specifics.

---

[36] Calonius, Erik, *10 Steps Ahead: What separates successful business visionaries from the rest of us* (New York: Portfolio/Penguin, 2011), 3.

Much of our habitual thinking and behavior would fall here and can benefit from at least occasional conscious oversight of our choices. (Without getting into a complicated side issue, this discussion does not conform to Freud's theory of the unconscious, and is not based on his definitions of the id, ego, or superego.)

"Vision" does not refer to the <u>sub</u>conscious mind (beneath consciousness) so much as to the expanded, transcendent mind (beyond consciousness). But they are both unconscious relative to our rational mind, which lacks a clear sense of how to relate to either of them. However, from the perspective of an integrated self (mastery), the <u>sub</u>conscious mind and the transcendent mind are active participants.

Another aspect of the unconscious includes the unorganized debris of living — trivia, lost or forgotten memories, no-longer-relevant facts, etc. Such information is not of much value. Retrieving something specific from there is a near impossibility and seldom worth the trouble. The unconscious also contains miscellaneous data that will never be made conscious because there is no way to access it.

Negative Connotations of Being a Visionary

To be called a "visionary" is not necessarily flattering. The term is often used to portray someone who is irresponsible and distracted, someone who cannot be relied on. However, such stereotypes fail to give credit to the wide range of competencies likely to be present in the person as well. Being able to bring a vision to flower demonstrates very real practical skills in the everyday world.

"Visionary" considered as a character flaw:
- Out of touch with reality; fanciful; spacey; crackpot; space cadet
- Malcontent; loner; weirdo; eccentric; trouble maker; meddler; iconoclast
- Dreamer or day-dreamer; unwilling to deal with practical matters
- One whose imagination overpowers reason; Don Quixote; quixotic
- Impractical; one who builds castles in the air; pie in the sky
- Unreliable; irresponsible; gadfly; dilettante; erratic
- Foreign; alien; not like us; does not fit in; madman

Because they are at odds with mainstream thinking, visionaries are routinely misquoted, misunderstood, maligned, and misrepresented. Their motives are questioned, and they are likely to face a daily diet of resistance or puzzlement.

Maurice Maeterlinck notes "Each progressive spirit is opposed by a thousand mediocre minds appointed to guard the past." Somehow, even that much disapproval is not enough to keep these intrepid souls in line. They have other fish to fry.

Extra criticism is meted out to late-blooming visionaries. Some individuals show great promise early on, so their careers take off while still young — the early bloomers. And in some fields, like mathematics, the age of major discoveries is relatively young. They are able to enjoy more fruits that result from their contributions, along with a following and various types of support.

Contrast that with the person who spent twenty years fine-tuning a quirky theory or style of painting that nobody wants. Their diligent efforts are unrewarded in the short term, and they are treated as failures because they have "nothing to show for it." In the fortunate circumstance when their undertaking is recognized in the public sphere, they are treated as "overnight successes."

There is no way to know in advance which of the apparent "losers" will be vindicated—or how long until it happens, if ever. And truth be told, most never will be. But public acceptance is only one measure of the visionary's success or contribution. Some bloom post-mortem, leaving signs of their genius behind. What a waste!

Visionaries Take Action

The Visionary and Vision Acting *Together* Behave as a Catalyst

The agitating presence of a visionary often sets events into motion, much like a catalyst.

Definitions of Catalyst:
- In chemistry—a substance that initiates or accelerates a reaction without itself being affected
- Something that causes an important event to happen

A catalyst initiates a complex process or sequence, and even if it is removed the sequence continues to play itself out. In chemistry and biology, such changes are easier to recognize than they are in social interactions, where causation is much less apparent or clear-cut.

Also, social change occurs over a much longer time span and involves many confounding influences. The visionary is likely to be unaware of his or her influence as a catalyst, preferring to give credit for any acceptance to the clarity and potency of their message.

Similarly, once the visionary tosses the pebble into the pond the ripples of change continue outward, without necessarily depending on what they do next. However, since the person usually remains involved in the very environment (field) being altered, they are likely to respond to what is set in motion too. And they will continue to throw pebbles…

The visionary is often driven to take a public stand at some point—even when it does not play to their strengths—or they risk unpleasant consequences. They feel strongly enough about the rightness of their position to go public in some way. Visionaries abandon any reluctance to rock the boat—and not just once. They persist in doing so.

That willingness to speak out and take the heat requires considerable courage and tenacity, further alienating them from their colleagues. Foolhardy? Maybe, but forerunners know they are not in this to win a popularity contest.

A Changed Sense of What Is Important

One of the most notable differences between visionaries and the larger community is what each group considers to be important. For those on the visionary path, as their vision becomes increasingly primary, many of their other concerns get demoted to the sidelines. Ignoring widely accepted priorities puts the visionary further at odds with what is considered normal behavior.

Long before taking the fork in the road, however, the visionary was probably driven by curiosity and unafraid of pushing limits to the point of annoying others. Many have a lifelong track record of taking risks, of challenging the rules or accepted limits.

Leading-edge Thinkers Repeatedly and Tacitly Imply:
- What you all think so important really isn't; there is more…
- What I am doing *is* important
- You should pay attention to me, my view, or discovery; it has value

That insistence alone defies the dominant mindset. Walking the visionary path further fires them up about there being something more worthy of their time than mundane concerns. This change in emphasis could be happening long before the person found their defining vision.

It also points to a shift in the direction of greater integrity. Choices that might seem minor by themselves are considered significant because of the larger principles involved. One makes the honorable choice because it *does matter*.

Author, Brenda Ueland said, "In true courage there is always an element of choice, of an ethical choice, and of anguish, and also of action and deed. There is always a flame of spirit in it, a vision of some necessity higher than oneself."

Life Goes On

The person's devotion to their vision or field of expertise cannot eliminate the rest of their daily concerns, however. Living makes competing demands on them—they still must eat, pay the bills, and deal with the people in their lives. And those concerns may take precedence for long periods, during which their vision might have to wait for attention and energy.

When one's eye is on the horizon, it is easy to stumble over pebbles. The far-sighted visionary often struggles to deal with the minutiae of daily life. To do so involves taking their eye off the ball, off the beckoning goal. Besides, visionaries have less and less tolerance for what they consider secondary matters.

Being able to be true to a driving vision is fully engaging. It disdains distractions. It is crucial for individuals to stay focused on what is coming together for them. Those on the visionary path keep simplifying their lifestyle and priorities. They are increasingly willing to jettison whatever does not further their sense of purpose, or that takes time away from their primary interest.

Losing interest in routine responsibilities has consequences on the home front. Such disregard for everyday practicalities creates friction with family and friends, who feel obligated to make endless adjustments, to pick up the routine balls the visionary dropped. That argues for fledgling visionaries to get a sidekick or support circle willing to deal with such concerns as the demands of their vision grow.

Prior relationships and commitments are inevitably strained or redefined (unless those individuals eagerly support the thrust of the vision). And new affiliations develop around the visionary's new primary interest.

The ups and downs along the visionary path tend to make a person split hairs so they can be more discerning. Travelers are finding a tolerable and intuitive balance between their inner and outer states of awareness, and each of them is involved in the hair splitting.

Learning to redirect material desires toward what is beautiful and nourishing to the spirit feeds their creative force. Artists and visionaries have always worked to strip away whatever is nonessential in order to see and celebrate what is lovely and true. Their example encourages the rest of us to do so as well.

Visionaries Engage the Public

The visionary process is largely about persuasion. The visionary offers his or her vision of the future. Some people like it, some do not. Some welcome the proposed changes, others reject them. Success for a new idea often comes down to people deciding "this works for me" — or not.

A battle ensues among competing ideas; but when the dust settles, it will be people's preferences that determine whether or not the new concept or invention takes hold. Even science, which considers itself objective in such matters, is rooted in consensus building among scientists.

People vote through their degree of interest or indifference; by how quickly or passionately they adopt a new-fangled practice or concept; by whether they are moved to be advocates involved in spreading the word.

A visionary's people skills matter a great deal because the vision needs to be packaged and sold to the public (or to members of a niche). Who the visionary engages and how they go about doing so reflect their domain of interest: audience members for performing arts; professional journals for scientific or theoretical research; talk shows for social change agents, etc.

The term for gaining wholehearted acceptance is "enrolling," whereby people "buy the vision." At its best, it is both expansive and passionate. That is explained by the Zanders in *The Art of Possibility*.

> Enrolling is not about forcing, cajoling, tricking, bargaining, pressuring, or guilt-tripping someone into doing something your way. Enrolment is the art and practice of generating a spark of possibility for others to share.... Our universe is alive with sparks. We have at our fingertips an infinite capacity to light a spark of possibility. Passion rather than fear is the igniting force. Abundance, rather than scarcity, is the context.[37]

How large their target group needs to be to shift the existing mindset depends on whether the vision is for the masses or for a circle of exotic specialists. The same approach will not work across the board, but there are established methods related to the various specific domains of interest. Howard Gardner also said:

> Political leaders seek to change minds directly through face-to-face encounters. Artists, thinkers, inventors, policy makers, and scientists are also keen on changing mental representations ... indirectly, through the works or products that they create in various media or symbol systems. The next axis [of influence] ... has to do with the composition of an audience: its uniformity or diversity. Political leaders and those who seek to institute policy changes work with diverse or heterogeneous populations. Their messages do not presuppose any kind of specialized knowledge or membership.... Or they work [with] groups where members are alike or have a degree of expertise in a content area, a homogeneous audience.[38]

Visionary Qualities

Visionaries Ask Questions and Argue with Those in Authority

They question everything and everyone, unsatisfied to blindly accept what they are told. A visionary can easily offend those in authority and is likely to be the one who boldly announces, "The emperor has no clothes."

Those on the visionary path are predisposed to question—unwilling to settle for canned or simplistic answers. They are curious about what is *not being said* or what is being hidden from them (intentionally or not). They search for the "how come?" behind the common wisdom, to find the further and likely implications of the array of possible choices.

These independent-minded voices for change wrestle with ideas and the institutions that espouse them. They are inclined to repeatedly question and assess, then badger some more. They wring out an idea's secondary meanings— never fully satisfied the subject at hand has yielded all its secrets.

---

[37] *Op. cit.*, Zander, 125-6.
[38] *Op. cit.*, Gardner, 130-1.

Visionaries cannot be controlled by a quiet shushing. "If you would be a real seeker after truth, it is necessary at least once in your life you doubt, as far as possible, all things," said Descartes. But beyond doubting, they also insist: There *is* a better answer. I have the answer, or I'll find it.

Visionaries Confound Expectations and the Powerful

Visionaries offend. They not only refuse to go along quietly with "something rotten in Denmark," they point accusing fingers at what smells. They gore sacred cows in public — heedless of possible retribution. No wonder they make powerful enemies.

Visionaries are often garbed in the cloak of fairness or big T truth when stepping into the public arena. They speak out as Everyman for common values — some of which are unpopular. In that role, they feel they are giving voice to those who are ill-used or suffer because of the practices that they have chosen to challenge.

Whether the visionary is dismissed as a gadfly, or treated as a serious threat to those with something to lose by their interference, depends on how much is at stake. This tendency toward high-minded self-sacrifice often ends badly for the intrepid contrarian. But that is the price for gaining the public ear — and/or necessary to chisel a crack in a solid edifice.

The kind of challenge to authority they display often has a disorderly quality that messes up the carefully laid plans of those in authority. They refuse to "leave well enough alone." Science historian Jacob Bronkowski said, "It is important that students bring a certain ragamuffin, barefoot irreverence to their studies; they are not here to worship what is known, but to question it."

Such acts of apparent defiance are seen by visionaries as a service to their vision and the world at large. Any personal reluctance they might have to taking the heat is put aside for a greater good. It mobilizes them. Author Audre Lorde said "When I dare to be powerful, to use my strength in the service of my vision, then it becomes less and less important whether I am afraid."

Side-stepping Everyday Concerns

As Marshall McLuhan wrote, "The poet, the artist, the sleuth — whoever sharpens our perception tends to be antisocial; rarely "well-adjusted," he cannot go along with currents and trends."

They go "into the desert" to disconnect from the socially-structured world. Withdrawal, to some extent, leaves both their prior pleasures and responsibilities behind. During that phase the person feels the need to ignore distractions to what is quickening within them.

The degree of isolation can be apparent to others or not, depending on how abrupt or protracted it might be. But it is characterized as retreating from the accepted worldview (mentally and/or physically). And that disengagement provides the opening wedge where another vantage point can develop.

During that disconnected phase, the person struggles with his or her conflicting priorities, as well as any inner demons that need resolution. Very uncomfortable! Their customary thinking needs to be sorted out as their developing point of view ripens. What he or she discovers can move them from having an unusual experience (their vision) to a lifestyle change in service to it. That includes the far-off doors to which the commitment leads.

Initially, the person proceeds without any notion of how much of his or her daily life is going to be affected by the emerging frame of reference. By the time they realize the extent to which it takes over, there is no going back. They have outgrown much of what was casually left behind. Where they go next will become their unique story.

It is not without risks, as Denise Shekerjian points out in *Uncommon Genius*.

> If you're trying to do creative work, by definition you have stepped out of the normal channels for things and into the cracks—if not the void. [There is a] dilemma of yearning on the one hand to go beyond the culture with some new idea or discovery or accomplishment but at the same time realizing that if the creative person leaps too far, the culture will probably crucify him.[39]

Image courtesy of Doug Johnson
http://www.doug-johnson.com

---

[39] Shekerjian, Denise, *Uncommon Genius: How great ideas are born* (New York: Viking, 1990), 54.

Visionaries Defy the Common Wisdom

While rooted in the values and assumptions of their community, these individuals are not locked into them. They want more, insist on finding more. They are willing to pay the price for achieving something unprecedented.

Visionaries are disrupters who seem unpredictable to their contemporaries. Their motives seem so at odds with the common mindset that even friends and family, who want to encourage them, are likely to be flummoxed by their behavior.

Creative types push for the excitement that comes with finding a novel answer with an intensity that makes most of their other concerns secondary. What sets visionaries and boundary pushers apart from the norm are differences of degree.

Many creative types are bunched up at the unpredictable end of a continuum between being totally conventional, and being downright incomprehensible. Is what they are doing crazy? Inspired? It depends who you ask.

For some, taking the visionary path can be likened to a game of chicken that flirts with insanity. It certainly demands steely nerves, courage, and stamina. The path can be summed up by the bumper sticker: That which does not kill us makes us *stranger*. Stronger, too.

As long as the dangling carrot remains fresh before their "eyes," visionaries are not put off by the problems encountered while bringing their creative notion into form. They are unwilling to give up because they have already tasted the triumph of their vision in their imagination.

Often that degree of determination does not take into account whether anyone else will actually embrace the result. The visionary artist is a particularly grand example of this state of mind.

While it is nearly impossible to list what characterizes those on the visionary path, it is much easier to describe those indifferent to it. Those are the vast majority, who never got the irresistible itch to change the way things are in a big way—or if they did, certainly not enough to risk all to do something meaningful about it. Peers of visionaries cannot fathom why they insist on acting so rash and "inappropriately."

The seemingly weird behavior attributed to them is not at all puzzling to others who share that expansive, vision-driven perspective. In fact, what seems quirky to most people acts much like a mating call, recognized instantly by those who are similarly inclined.

Another visionary can often spot the signs without hesitation because they understand the significance of particular non-conforming activities. It is like the childhood taunt, "It takes one to know one."

Such fellow travelers make valuable friends and mentors for those out of the mainstream because they alone realize how much that journey exacts from those who go that route. It is a beautiful thing when visionaries can find ways to support each other on their journeys.

While each person has their own work that needs doing (within their field of interest), the challenges after leaving the beaten path do not feel so lonely or futile.

Visionaries Step Out and Leap

No pussyfooting for this crowd! The visionary is a leaper by nature. The saying, "Look before you leap," cautions people against acting prematurely or unwisely. Visionaries don't get unduly hung up on delaying tactics or fears of crashing. They do not dwell on the tough challenges to come or they might never take the next step.

They are nourished by the excitement of the vision. Sometimes such impetuosity is considered a failing—but to be too sensible would stall the enterprise.

Leaping into uncertainty is a recurring aspect of the visionary process. To quote Agnes de Mille, an American choreographer: "Living is a form of not being sure, not knowing what next or how. The moment you know how, you begin to die a little. The artist never entirely knows. We guess. We may be wrong, but we take leap after leap in the dark."

There are at least two places of leaping early on: (1) during the period of commitment, and (2) when the person feels ready to act. However, the visionary finds the need to keep leaping and recommitting throughout the process: after setbacks, to chart a change in direction, and upon reaching desired goals. At such times the person might feel ready to leap further still.

If the visionary senses the hand of God or destiny upon them, the usually protective functions of fear and caution are largely dismissed. People who give much credence to the obvious risks do not leap. They are not even tempted. But most visionaries are leapers, who accept there will be consequences of leaping—not all of them pleasant.

They are likely to leap when the impulse is at its most intense—before the passion has cooled. It is usually not premeditated in the sense of getting adequate preparation or "thinking it through." Some follow Ray Bradbury's advice: "Go to the edge of the cliff and jump off. Build your wings on the way down."
Visionaries have to be optimistic enough to think some good is sure to come from throwing caution to the wind. They expect pleasant surprises; they expect to win in the end. Those who sense destiny or divine guidance urging them forward do not bother to develop an extensive safety net or Plan B. To the

contrary, they are inclined to think a fallback plan indicates a lack of commitment.

However, that does not mean they are so out of touch they expect water to run up hill. To the extent possible, they do assess and prepare for what is ahead.

At some point a visionary needs to realize that being dismissed and having their contributions devalued is not some cosmic error. Their separateness from the mainstream at the outset prepares them to "stand on their own shoulders," to be a thought leader later. Rejection and isolation are often essential in becoming a mature way shower—the carrier of some inventive wrinkle that flowers down the road.

Visionaries Are Resilient and Persistent

Their uncanny ability to bounce back, despite whatever is thrown at them, is legendary. They tend to outlast the obstacles and emerge as survivors— eventually. "Patience and tenacity are worth more than twice their weight in cleverness," Thomas Huxley reminds us.

Resilience is the quality of character that makes a person (or group of people) rebound from misfortune, hardships, and traumas. It permits us to work with adversity in such a way we are even *better off* because of what was endured. It allows us to face life's difficulties with courage and patience—refusing to give up.

Persistence and resilience grow out of a tenacity of spirit—the determination to embrace all that makes life worth living, despite overwhelming odds. When coupled with a clear sense of identity and a guiding vision, we can hang on. It builds our determination to hold fast for a vision of a better future.

Such breakthrough creativity is most likely to appear when one's back is against the wall, when it seems all options have been exhausted. It is do-or-die time. Resilience is also referred to as hustle, brazen nerve, resourcefulness, or chutzpah.

Persistence
President Calvin Coolidge

> Nothing in the world can take the place of persistence. Talent will not; nothing is more common than unsuccessful men with talent. Genius will not; unrewarded genius is almost a proverb. Education will not; the world is full of educated derelicts. Persistence, determination and hard work make the difference.

The Place of Passion

Visionaries Are Passionately and Deeply Involved

Many are remarkably intense and enthusiastic about what interests them. They're busting to share it. There is a penetrating focus that marks such individuals and their creative efforts. Visionaries are fired up, stoked, throwing off sparks of brilliance. As such, they're likely to be precipitous and overeager, too.

Lukewarm won't cut it. Unless they are somewhat fanatical, he or she will have trouble sustaining their vision during the dry spells where rewards are few. It helps to be extremist, adamant, uncompromising, dedicated, fixated, zealous, driven, fervent, and obsessive, as well as buzzing with creative energy.

The word "enthusiasm" comes from the Greek term "entheos" (en, from, + theos, god), "having the god within." Over time, the meaning of enthusiasm extended to a confident belief in being inspired by God or destiny. Those who feel they are on an inspired mission, or have seen "the truth," throw caution to the winds. They don't spare the horses.

Whether that degree of intensity is seen by others as rash or self-destructive could depend on whether the person develops sufficient staying power to outlast the critics. Too many visionaries flash bright and burn themselves out. Learning how to manage their energy or pick their battles goes a long way toward surviving long enough to leave an enduring influence.

However, for some individuals, expressive restraint in relating to others might have little to do with the authenticity or intensity they feel inside. They don't let it all hang out" because they recognize others could consider fiery enthusiasm a boundary-buster—something they did not invite or want to endure.

Such a person could be wildly passionate about something, but still adapt a lukewarm persona for others, so their zeal does not run them over like a steamroller. In that case, deciding to appear less enthusiastic doesn't affect the enduring intensity of their passion, dry spells or not.

Visionaries are zealous in pursuing their vision or principal area of devotion. Time spent doing what they love does not feel like work, but like pleasure. They find too much enjoyable in the creative process to tire of it—no matter how much it demands of them. Having a strong passion for something means you cannot *not* do it. To quote Stephen King from *On Writing*,

> Talent renders the whole idea of rehearsal meaningless; when you find something at which you are talented, you do it (whatever it is) until your fingers bleed or your eyes are ready to fall out of your head. Even when no one is listening (or reading, or watching), every outing is a bravura performance, because you as the creator are happy. Perhaps even ecstatic.[40]

Sometimes that joy found in discovery or creative expression is all the reward someone gets, when the world turns a deaf ear. By the same token, those who feel they're doing what they love feel fortunate. They are more willing to make mistakes and try again, without giving up because they are not only looking at the fruits or external consequences of what they do. They like it all, not just for

---

[40] King, Stephen, *On Writing: A memoir of the craft* (New York: Pocket Books, 2000), 150.

the "good parts." Setbacks don't feel so much like failure or reflect on the worth of what they are trying to do.

Passion Is Red Hot

Passion can be spotted by its intensity—it is hard to miss it. Passion refuses to sit quietly in the background or bide its time. It demands attention—pronto! Lacking that, a project is merely an interest, one among many, which is slipped in among the obligations of life.

Americans have a high opinion about the "pursuit of happiness"—getting to do what we are passionate about. It has been idealized as the brass ring that allows the rest of life to make sense. We assume that if only we could follow our passion, everything else would fall in place. A tad simplistic and seldom true— but it is what we want.

Still, we feel considerable conflict about passion as well—and rightly so. By its very nature, passion is excessive; it lacks moderation. Passion leads to extreme mood swings and outrageous behavior. So much unrestrained, fiery intensity released at once can (and often does) lead to negative consequences. Nor can it be sustained indefinitely, so there is a letdown.

One role of passion is to enflame us and carry us away. That energy cannot be controlled. It takes us over—heedless of the costs that might follow. Passion comes from the Latin word, "passio," which means to suffer. Such feelings are so intense they are painful. Unbridled passion is often associated with intense suffering, sooner or later. However, passion need not bring dreadful suffering, but joy and pleasure.

There is a sexual connotation to passion as well. By the manner in which humans are wired up, intense outbursts of creativity are linked up with sexual energy. Given how much intense pleasure can be generated with either one, they can be all-consuming.

Some creative types need that high intensity like a drug. They cannot handle a return to a commonplace state. Being passionate sometimes unleashes tendencies toward addictive behavior. This is only mentioned in the context of a warning.

Passion is not a gift without strings so much as a potent energy to be mastered. That is not the same as it being suppressed or stifled, however. It is possible to learn to channel its powerful force to our advantage, without being overwhelmed by it. It takes a mature person to handle passion well, which means not being subject to extreme mood swings or dramatic outbursts. Those skills, too, develop in the maturing process.

Finding Your Own Passion

The joy and satisfaction that comes with doing what we love most should not be treated as an afterthought or as lesser motivation, when making the big life choices. For that, more than any other factor, could determine whether someone sticks with it, or has a life they truly enjoy.

Howard Thurmond, the civil rights leader, said, "Don't ask yourself what the world needs; ask yourself what makes you come alive. And then go and do that. Because what the world needs is people who have come alive."

The height of passion is to feel, without a particle of doubt, that a specific activity is what you were born to do. Usually a person will be better at that than almost anything else they could be doing.

What makes someone pursue one vision or field of endeavor with passionate enthusiasm, rather than all the others? Whatever gets us excited, that stirs us deeply, could be leading us to precisely where we belong. Your wee small voice could be a passionate one, when it is heeded.

Many influences are at work in helping us to find our purpose—most without our conscious awareness. The choice to respect our deepest desires is reserved for each of us alone. What is *your* preference?

Falling into your passion is easy for the fortunate few who discover it serendipitously. Searching for your passion, on the other hand, is the challenge for the rest of us; and it is not easy. If you expect it to be, you will be frustrated. The two most common trip issues involve (1) searching in your head instead of your heart and (2) a misplaced focus on money.

When one pursues the question "what is your passion?" most people expect an immediate answer from within. When one doesn't appear, they begin to force the issue with their minds, searching every accessible memory bank and storage locker of past experience in the left-brain hemisphere. Options appear and the sorting begins.

The problem here is that the left brain wouldn't recognize original, unique, or inspiring if you beat it with a stick. We are looking for love in all the wrong places.

So when you are advised to "look deeper within yourself," what those advisors are really saying is pay attention *elsewhere* within. The right brain is a parallel processor (versus the left brain serial processor) and home to visions, inspirations, connectedness vs. separateness, and the chemistry of bliss. We receive its messages through feelings, often coming in whispers rather than shouts.

The only way to access it is to disengage from the chaos that dominates the left brain. Some people meditate. Some people garden. Some people interact with nature. Be still and you will eventually be gifted with the realization you seek, the yearning within that you *know* is the one for which you are uniquely motivated and equipped.

That discovery is yours and yours alone to creatively fashion to your heart's delight and the world will be better for it (although the world will surely argue with you at first).

The other issue involves trying to turn a passion into a business or livelihood, which can easily kill the excitement about it. Having to execute all the parts of a business model devoted to your prime interest that aren't much fun might start to feel like drudgery, sapping away the richer benefits of the creative experience. The risk is that you might stop enjoying what you used to love doing.

Once a passion is tied to financial survival, the motivations are totally altered. While some individuals manage to pull it off, that is not the only way to fully engage it. Nor is commerce suitable for many visions.

In all things, each of us should strive to be true to "who I am." It requires an honest and discerning eye, without aggrandizement or defensiveness. And true to life, the more attentively you choose to engage the experiences that come your way, the more accurately you can read the signals about yourself.

Visions about what we want to become are no different in that regard. We begin to see more of the implications about the interplay between foreground and background, between the central concern and the peripheral ones. We fine-tune our attention to the point of picking up the more subtle messages that are also present. That level of discernment is integral to expertise. Nadia Boulanger, a well-known music coach said:

> I have the impression that the more I try to think of the essentials of music, the more they seem to depend on general human values. It's all very well to be a musician, it's all very well to be a genius, but the intrinsic value which constitutes your mind, your heart, your sensibility, depends on who you are. You may have to lead a life in which no one understands who you are. Nevertheless I believe that everything depends on attention. I only see you if I pay attention. I only exist in my own eyes if I pay attention to myself.[41]

Pay more attention to what makes your heart sing, your eyes light up when you speak about it, and your ideas their most scintillating. That is tangible evidence of you being in focus. At such moments, your heart, mind, body, and spirit are united in a combined sense of passion that nourishes your deepest awareness. And each of these aspects of yourself responds avidly to that energetic charge in its own manner.

Seek out opportunities to feel that way since it is drawing you unerringly to where you are most potent—feels good, too. As Steve Jobs of Apple Computer said in the 2005 commencement address at Stanford:

> Your time is limited, so don't waste it living someone else's life. Don't be trapped by dogma—which is living with the results of other people's thinking.

---

[41] Bruno Monsaingeon, "The Cardinal Virtues, Conversations with Nadia Boulanger," *Knowledge of Reality Magazine*, Issue 17, http://www.sol.com.au/kor/17_02.htm

Don't let the noise of other's opinions drown out your own inner voice. And most important, have the courage to follow your heart and intuition. They somehow already know what you truly want to become. Everything else is secondary.

Where Is Mine?

On the other hand, passion can be problematic for those who are wondering: What is mine? Those whose passion is palpable have been able to identify what turns them on, so they are puzzled why others find it difficult to discover. It is one of our cultural assumptions (valid or not) that it is something everybody seeks or "deserves."

So, those who do not have a readily identifiable passion could feel something is missing, like they have failed somehow. Daniel Pink, who writes about the changing nature of work, spoke about finding one's passion.

> When we find ourselves in the midst of a career change or feel a dull sense that what we're doing now isn't what we should be doing forever, our friends and families—along with every mentor, advisor, and consultant—will smile knowingly, lean in tenderly, and pose this question: Tell me, what's your passion?
>
> The idea is that if we simply acknowledge what fires our soul, if we just pull out our metaphysical arthroscope and examine our hearts, the path will reveal itself.
> So—with a voice that quavers in expectation and an inflection that italicises the final word—they ask us again, 'What's your passion?'
>
> Ladies and gentlemen, I detest that question. When someone poses it to me, my innards tighten. My vocabulary becomes a palette of aahs and ums. My chest wells with the urge to flee.
>
> Oh my. The answer better be amazing—not some fumbling, feeble reply. But I know the responses I've formed in my head aren't especially good. Worse, they're probably not even accurate. And I'm not alone.[42]

For those in doubt about what their passion is, or who are deeply interested in too many things to have a favorite, this is not a failing. Passion… Doing… Which comes first? Does a person's passion drive their doing or vice versa? The dilemma could be a chicken-or-egg issue, where either could come first.

Those who have not yet found "it" could instead look for indications of what excites them in their current behavior.

Try tabling the issue and let what you *actually do* lead the way—pointing to where you are already headed. De-emphasize passion and re-emphasize the

---

[42] Pink, Daniel, "Ever Felt Like Your Job Isn't What You Were Born to Do? You're Not Alone," *The Telegraph*, February 26, 2011, http://www.telegraph.co.uk

hands-on of doing. It could be a timing issue, and you are still in the preparation phase. Do not try to hurry it. Keep preparing through a combination of learning and doing. Stay involved with *something you care about* (even if not passionately). Stay alert for a ripening within.

It is like the childhood game of Getting Hotter or Colder. Somebody hides an object. As the seeker moves around looking for it, they are only told if they are getting hotter (closer) or colder (farther away), until they hone in on it.

As you do what you do, pay attention to what is saying "hotter" or "colder" within yourself. It is your emotional sonar that beeps back. Steering toward various hotter inclinations gradually pulls you in the direction of your heart's desire.

The alignment of your skills, strengths, and passions can lead you to *doing your life's work*. For some people the passion comes first, for others it is later. But if a desire to "do something" leads the way, you still can end up living from your passion.

~ Ship Ahoy ~
A BonBon ~ Faith Lynella

It was always my greatest fear that when the time of severe testing or significant opportunity came, I would miss the boat. I feared that my own lack of attention, preparation or desire would waste the long-awaited opportunity. I have since come to realize that I am *already* doing my life's work and fulfilling my destiny. Instead of "missing the boat," I'm aboard and launched. I had doubted that I would be prepared, but my mission is already occurring.

How easily our fears can blind and mislead us. Mine compelled me to push myself relentlessly to cultivate my strengths and confront my weaknesses. Such efforts occupied me so fully, that I failed to notice that my initial fear was no longer valid. Nevertheless, it had served me as a worthy impetus for self-growth.

Fear is only good when you *use* it. Grab it and struggle against it. It will make you potent. Fears become stronger as you avoid them. But grappling with them strengthens you while weakening them. What an irony! What an obscured truth!

From *BonBons to Sweeten Your Daily Life*. Or from *More BonBons*

Chapter 5 - Going to Extremes

*The ability to figure things out is rational, where the mind shines.
Visionaries add to that skill by taking the conclusion past where
rationality is inclined to go. They keep pushing toward the "unthinkable."*

Now Hiring: Visionaries

Don't expect to find ads looking to hire visionaries. There is no job description for a visionary, no ideal preparation, no certification. The pay scale is likely to be non-existent or greatly delayed—except for a "lucky" few. And there is nothing resembling a retirement plan. The position can involve considerable inconvenience, rejection, and social criticism—some of it intensely personal.

Family and friends seldom approve of how disruptive following one's vision can be to other commitments. Working conditions can be squalid. The post has been known to effectively undermine a comfortable personal life or most recreational interests.

Tangible rewards can be minimal, sometimes deferred until well after someone dies (one of the possible marks of a visionary). Being misunderstood, misquoted, and underestimated are to be expected. Significant resistance and duplicities are the likely outcome of being noticed. Not too surprising, there are not a lot of people standing in line for that type of work.

Such a person would not say, "Hello, I am a visionary." It is a term more likely to be said *about them* or in reaction to their creative accomplishments. It is bestowed by others. Using the term to describe oneself is likely to ring as self-promotion. Besides, a visionary usually prefers to speak about their vision and cause rather than getting personal.

On a related note, these non-conformists tend to make their mark because of what they manage to pull off. They are not afraid to take chances in order to find out what works. Then they try something else, continuing to perfect their act. As author Louise Pierson said, "The next time you are in a meeting, look around and identify the yes-butters, the not-knowers, and the why-notters. Why-notters move the world."

Visionaries Are Extreme—And Not

Visionaries do not play it safe or hang out in the middle of the road. So does that make them riskier, or just likely to go in directions that are hard to define? They have an uncanny ability to confound expectations. Those who push the limits "swing for the fences." That involves taking risks, rather than thinking defensively most of the time.

Most visionaries are not junkies for novelty, however. While there are areas in which an individual gives their creative abilities free rein, in most areas of life they are content to be quite ordinary. Although comfortable with change, these creative types do not feel the need to prove it so at every opportunity.

It is sometimes said, that nothing is as boring as endless novelty. An easy-to-spot blunder of neophyte creatives is their need to make change for its own sake. For instance, *avant-garde* arts can be too heavy handed with discordant messages added for shock value. Discernment and judgment are advanced skills that accompany subject-matter mastery. Adepts understand the nuances, the fine distinctions, and add novelty with a delicate touch.

Some visionaries stay tightly focused within a narrow area of interest, while others are eclectic enough to scan widely or push the limits in a variety of directions. Some might shine in more than one field of interest at the same time. Some see with a broad lens through which they glimpse connections across the breadth of human knowledge. Broad, narrow, scatter-shot, all are equally valid ways of walking the visionary path.

Although these men and women have to be smart, the most intelligent people do not tend to become the visionaries. Those with the most invested in the *status quo* are seldom visionaries, either. As a group, visionary types do not perform very well on intelligence or personality tests. Such *standardized* tests cannot capture many of their inherently uncommon qualities. It is not surprising since they are less likely to behave in ways that can be easily categorized or measured.

What sets most visionaries apart from other folks is their single-minded curiosity and creative pursuits. Csikszentmihalyi points out the internal conflict between creativity and making the least effort.

> We are generally torn between two opposite sets of instructions programmed into the brain: the least-effort imperative on one side, and the claims of creativity on the other. In most individuals entropy seems to be stronger, and they enjoy comfort more than the challenge of discovery. But we all respond to both of these rewards; the tendencies toward conserving energy as well as using it constructively are part of our inheritance. Which one wins depends not only on our genetic makeup but also presumably on our early experiences.[43]

Visionaries as Mythic Characters

The life stories of towering visionaries are the stuff of legends. Their remarkable achievements in the face of long odds sound like fictional heroes. All the elements are there. It is not just the hero performing great deeds despite grueling obstacles, They felt destiny's hand on them.

In the hands of Hollywood or a good novelist/biographer, we know how those stories go:
1. Person has a wretched life; was treated badly or unfairly
2. Person has a passion or a brilliant idea, to which they devote all their energy
3. Person struggles to succeed, but receives only rejection and misery

---

[43] Csikszentmihalyi, Mihaly, *Creativity: Flow and the psychology of discovery and invention* (New York: HarperCollins, 1996), 110.

4. Person is at the verge of giving up — broken and discouraged
5. When it is *almost* too late, a breakthrough; their luck changes — triumph, a testament to the unquenchable human spirit
6. And suddenly it was all worthwhile, and everybody comes around — fame, respect, and money flow
7. The End

Hold on a minute. Even if we can hear the sound track in the background, these visionaries were real live people. Yet there is a temptation to fictionalize them, to make them two-dimensional. Those who became noteworthy for what they discovered do not need a Dickensian life story to make them interesting. Misery is not essential to their greatness.

The real-life personal backgrounds of visionaries are all over the map, and many are probably more engaging than the fake veneer of the fanciful stereotypes. And their story rarely ends with their discoveries or gaining public recognition for them.

If we look at the lives of giants, we should not just buy into the myths about them. They are not paragons or geniuses cut from different cloth than everybody else. These men and women struggled, made mistakes, hurt people they should not have, screwed up in ways that hindsight could have prevented. They were complex and very human. However, none of those concerns prevented them from leaving a significant and lasting contribution.

Tidy biography should not trump the truth about those pioneers or what made them tick. What meaning or inspiration can the rest of us find in their specific examples? How could we conduct our own pursuits to greater effect in light of what they did? Their stories can be instructive to us in many ways. But we do them, their discoveries, and their memories no service if we just see them through their tarted-up Hollywood versions.

To be honest, such "bright lights" seldom know their larger role — challenged as they are with the everyday requirements of living and establishing their new creative undertaking. They are doing what seems to be necessary at the time. Only in retrospect does it sometimes become evident how extraordinary their determination and achievements were.

Visionaries keep their eyes on the horizon, looking toward a future that is still to be realized. They take a step away from what their contemporaries consider most important. Philosopher Robert Grudin said, "Fast drivers can see no further than slow drivers, but they must look further down the road to time their reactions safely. Similarly, people with great projects afoot habitually look further and more clearly into the future than people who are mired in day-to-day concerns."

Riding the Ups and Downs

Reports about the early development of world-changing ideas are usually documented long after the fact—after the original conditions were changed in some decisive fashion. Subsequent books and interviews about the start-up period imply a sort of inevitability—as though events had to happen thus and so, culminating in a breakthrough or triumph.

Most of the wrong turns and dead ends are missing from such reports. Truth be told, such stories are mostly hindsight or by people who were not even involved. *Nudge* (by Richard Thaler and Cass Sunstein) points out the flaw of retroactive inevitability.

> In many domains people are tempted to think, after the fact, that an outcome was entirely predictable, and that the success of a musician, an actor, an author, or a politician was inevitable in light of his or her skills and characteristics. Beware of that temptation. Small interventions and even coincidences, at a key stage, can produce large variations in the outcome. Today's hot singer is probably indistinguishable from dozens and even hundreds of equally talented performers whose names you have never heard.[44]

Confidence was not consistently present on a day-to-day basis, when the visionary (or core group) toiled with the same practical and self-confidence issues we are all heir to—the personal stuff. For the vision, however clear and sublime it feels as it "clicks," does not come with a how-to manual. More likely than not, the visionary tosses out established directions and wings it (further evidence of leaving the beaten path). No wonder there is so much crash and burn.

If this paints an overly grim picture of the difficulties, it is also important to note that visionaries are not masochists or victims—far from it. Many feel honored to be the caretaker of so important a charge. The downsides cannot be ignored, but those who are not constrained by the difficulties or personal costs of their task also are responding to their higher angels.

There is a certain satisfaction that comes in staying the course as well as humanly possible—to follow where destiny leads.

Efforts to ground vision put what is good for humanity in the long-term into the mix of daily life. Visionaries seem to be particularly adept at finding the work-arounds that provide a path to the desired outcomes they advocate. These passionate individuals really believe they can make a difference—and that is a powerful and praiseworthy inducement. By and large, they respond to that calling as a service to us all (even if that realization comes much later).

---

[44] Thaler, Richard and Sunstein, Cass R., *Nudge: Improving decisions about health, wealth, and happiness* (New Haven, CT: Yale University Press, 2008), 56.

Context and Extraordinariness

Howard Gardner attempted to define a science of extraordinary minds. His analysis aimed to identify the ways in which all such individuals are similar. In order to identify who is extraordinary, he argued (and echoed Csikszentmihalyi) one must look to the dynamic interplay of three factors:

Factors that Influence Each Other:
- The **individual** who brings in novelty
- The particular **domain** or discipline in which they work—with its shared lore, standards, practices, and vocabulary
- The **field**—the set of experts, insiders, and institutions that validate the new idea

Their influence on each other corresponds to phases of the visionary path. In one way or another, every visionary struggles to find a way to express extraordinary and creative qualities that set their thinking apart. Of course, each of them differs in the quality and originality of their output, or in how effectively they build a case for it.

Forms of Creative Achievement:
- Producing original and creative works *within a discipline*, like Michelangelo or Edison
- Interpreting works already created, as in *performance art*, like Martha Graham and Caruso
- Solving *problems already recognized*, such as developing a flying machine or identifying the structure of DNA
- Theory building—*original conceptualizations* by identifying elements and processes, like Darwin and Einstein

It is impossible to assess any particular visionary's contribution by looking at their work alone, or at a single point in time. Their productive output gives only a limited view of the dynamic interplay that is unfolding as they and their mission develop. Nor can public recognition be the standard of a vision's worth since that tends to come later, if at all. Gardner's extensive research, detailed in *Changing Minds*, reached several conclusions.

Extraordinary Insights:
- Extraordinary individuals stand out in the extent to which they reflect—often explicitly—on the events of their lives, large as well as small.
- Extraordinary individuals are distinguished less by their impressive 'raw powers' than by their ability to identify their strengths and then to exploit them.

- Extraordinary individuals fail often and sometimes dramatically. Rather than giving up, however, they are challenged to learn from their setbacks and to convert defeats into opportunities.[45]

These Are Not Equivalent

Visionaries demonstrate countless ways to carry out their missions. They are a remarkably diverse group—a rather independent one. The roles that follow are not synonyms for "visionary," although there can be significant areas of overlap among their functions. And a person is likely to wear many of these hats in achieving their aims. Some roles are more prevalent at particular stages of the process.

A Visionary will *Not Necessarily* Be a:
- Rebel or revolutionary
- Innovator or entrepreneur
- Creator and creative types—as in artistic expression
- Guru, teacher, mentor
- Orator; public speaker; trainer; advocate
- Inventor, researcher
- Leader; long-range goal setter
- Philosopher, system builder
- Writer
- Idealist or altruist
- Futurist
- Genius, prodigy, or super smart
- Pioneer
- Zealot, activist

But they could be. While any person could operate in any of these roles while walking the visionary path, it is just as likely that someone can function in any of these roles *without being a full-fledged visionary*.

Visionaries Are Black Swans

Not so Impossible After All

The appearance of a rare or improbable event is called a Black Swan. When something is considered impossible or rare, it is treated as an exception to the general rule (all swans are white). But rareness does not mean something is impossible (or close to it). It is just as likely to indicate we had simply not noticed it before.

---

[45] Gardner, Howard, *Changing Minds: The art and science of changing our own and other people's minds* (Boston: Harvard Business School Press, 2004), 14-15.

Most human experience falls within a narrow range of what is considered "the norm." The Black Swans (whether events or individuals) fall outside of that range. Since our expectations are mostly within that scope, anything else comes as a surprise. By definition, surprises are unforeseen—except perhaps for the one who found it. That is the essence of innovative thinking.

In my opinion, most visionaries, and what they contribute, are Black Swans. Taleb's investigation of the phenomenon explains why history so often misses their presence or importance. Taleb also said:

> There are two varieties of rare events: a) the narrated Black Swans, those that are present in the current discourse and that you are likely to hear about on television, and b) those nobody talks about, since they escape models—those that you would feel ashamed of discussing in public because they do not seem plausible. I can safely say that it is entirely compatible with human nature that the incidences of Black Swans would be overestimated in the first case, but severely underestimated in the second one.[46]

Mostly, the public ignores visionary thinkers or those who contradict common knowledge. Or they overinflate the uniqueness of such individuals, as though such abilities are too special for the rest of us ordinary mortals.

Both approaches are misguided and reveal the observers' perceptual limitations. The ability to recognize Black Swans for what they are requires a different mentality and scope of attention.

There is more that each of us can do to be alert to such individuals and the innovations they bring. In the process, we just might notice some of that thinking that is closer to home. Hmm… maybe our own?

Taleb identifies several perceptual biases that make most people tune out anything that remotely resembles a Black Swan.

Blindness to Black Swans (according to Taleb):
  a) We focus on preselected segments of the seen and generalize from it to the unseen; the error of confirmation.
  b) We fool ourselves with stories that cater to our Platonic thirst for distinct patterns; the narrative fallacy.
  c) We behave as if the Black Swan does not exist: human nature is not programmed for Black Swans.
  d) What we see is not necessarily all that is there. History hides Black Swans from us and gives us a mistaken idea about the odds of these events: this is the distortion of silent evidence.
  e) We 'tunnel': that is, we focus on a few well-defined sources of uncertainty, on too specific a list of Black Swans (at the expense of the others that do not easily come to mind).[47]

---

[46] Taleb, Nassim Nicholas, Th*e Black Swan: The impact of the highly improbable* (New York: Random House, 2007), 77.
[47] *Ibid.*, 50.

Non-conformists have always had rough sledding in a world that is suspicious about what they are *really* up to. Their overt differences are too often considered a threat to what is normal or acceptable behavior. (And in some regards that is true—they do not march in lockstep or toe the party line.)

All of us can do more to appreciate or encourage genuine creative efforts and big-picture thinking when we encounter it—without undue rejection and adulation of it. I hope that as the world becomes a more receptive place for visionary thinking, more people with such qualities will be emboldened to bring those abilities into the open.

On the other hand, Black Swans have little difficulty recognizing the presence of other Black Swans, directly or through their fruits. They would be the best ones to encourage the fledgling visionaries they encounter. They can demonstrate Mark Twain's advice, "Keep away from people who try to belittle your ambitions. Small people always do that, but the really great make you feel that you, too, can become great."

With a greater understanding of the visionary process, I am hopeful many more latent visionaries will feel inclined to recognize their own unique voices and accept the mantle of their developing capabilities. Imagine a world where Black Swans do not stand out because lots of people feel free to act on their visions or to get ahead of the curve. A point to ponder: What would a recognized Black Swan be called?

A Different Take on Disappointment or Failure

The visionary path is often heartbreaking, yet transformative. Calamities and unexpected twists of fate are treated not as *failures on the path*, but *the nature of the path*. What would scare off most people is accepted as merely the next thing to deal with in service to the visionary's mission.

Most visionaries feel they must persist despite any foreseeable obstacles, rejection, duplicity, challenges to their self-worth, financial difficulties, and the unrelenting barrage of surprises. (What would you expect of a path away from predictability?)

Visionaries are neither blind nor indifferent to practical considerations. They just do not feel they can be ruled by them. Inventive pursuits function quite differently than project management with its precisely defined goals and predictable stages. The visionary's route away from the tried and true is not so tidy or anchored by reassuring benchmarks.

In a detached cost-benefit analysis, most visionary undertakings would not make the cut—jettisoned as too high risk and uncertain. What tips the balance in the notion's favor is likely to be the intensity of the visionary's unreserved devotion to it.

Failures are more likely to be seen as insufficiencies of the strategy or execution, rather than a flaw of the vision itself. So visionaries redouble efforts in the face of overwhelming obstacles, for as long as humanly possible. Their near-fanatical determination is often the only thing keeping someone from throwing in the towel, especially during the dark days.

Tharp identified several kinds of failure:

- **Failure of Skill** — 'You have an idea in mind but not the requisite skills to pull it off. This is the cruelest, crudest, most predictable form of failure. Your reach exceeds your grasp.'
- **Failure of Concept** — 'You have a weak idea that doesn't hold up under your daily ministrations. You torment the idea and instead of growing it shrivels up.'
- **Failure of Judgment** — 'You leave something in the piece that should have been discarded.... I'll say I'm sorry for being so ornery, but I'm not really apologizing. Neither should you when it's your judgment on the line.'
- **Failure of Nerve** — 'You have everything going for you except the guts to support your idea and explore the concept fully. The corrosive thought that you will look foolish holds you back from telling the truth."
- **Failure through Repetition** — 'Repetition is a problem if it forces us to cling to our past successes.'[48]

After a major setback, trust the visionary to resume — after a time-out for licking wounds and emotional regrouping. Groundbreakers usually feel there is something really important at stake in what they are doing. Crises of self-doubt are grudgingly accepted as essential since the person has already learned, though prior bouts of self-questioning, that that's where inspiration is clarified, renewed, and reaffirmed.

Serious flops are seldom treated as final, but simply as setbacks. Because the next step could be fueled by an unexpected insight, a helping hand, or a broader perspective, visionaries learn to take their victories when they can — and in any form they come.

Since the process encourages simplicity and fewer distractions, a wipeout might actually speed up the process. Of course, nobody wants that consciously. According to David Whyte, "For the personality, bankruptcy or failure may be a disaster. For the soul, it may be grist for its strangely joyful mill, and a condition it has been secretly engineering for years."

It goes along with the motto: Fail Faster. Not that failure is desired, but the flood of new insights likely to follow often opens new lines of inquiry. Failure permits

---

[48] Tharp, Twyla, *The Creative Habit: Learn it and use it for life* (New York: Simon & Shuster, 2003), 215-7.

a fresh start, built on all that has been learned so far. In *Where Good Ideas Come From*, Steven Johnson quotes William Stanley Devans, an economist in 1874.

> The errors of the great mind exceed in number those of the less vigorous one.' This is not merely statistics. It is not that the pioneering thinkers are simply more productive than less 'vigorous' ones, generating more ideas overall, both good and bad.... Error is not simply a phase you have to suffer through on the way to genius. Error often creates a path that leads you out of your comfortable assumptions.... He kept probing at the edge of error, until he hit upon something that was genuinely useful. Being right keeps you in place. Being wrong forces you to explore.[49]

Truth be told, dealing with disappointment and delay represent one type of common obstacle, while dealing with the irretrievable failure of the undertaking represents a different kind of difficulty. In the first, all it takes is one success to instantly erase weeks, maybe months or years, of disappointment and delay.

On the other hand, an outright failure could start a raft of consequences that set the visionary off course for a very long time. The person might retrench or act like a hibernating bear or a turtle playing dead indefinitely.

Depending upon when it occurs in the person's life, it might propel the visionary away from risky behavior permanently. Or they might eventually resurrect and create again. Sometimes, even if they pursue their visions, it is without any interest at all in whether anyone appreciates what they are doing.

The point is, those who pursue their vision with wholehearted devotion are not afraid of failure. They use what it teaches to keep fine-tuning their message and improving their strategies. Clay Shirky adds some perspective in *Here Comes Everybody*:

> The overall effect of failure is its likelihood times its cost. Most organizations attempt to reduce the effect of failure by reducing its likelihood.... The obvious problem is that no one knows for certain what will succeed and what will fail.... [A collaborative system like Open Source] doesn't reduce the likelihood of failure, it reduces the cost of failure; it essentially gets failure for free.... Cheap failure, valuable as it is on its own, is also a key part of a more complex advantage: the exploration of multiple possibilities.[50]

---

[49] Johnson, Steven, *Where Good Ideas Come From: The natural history of innovation* (New York: Riverhead Books, 2010), 137.
[50] Shirky, Clay, *Here Comes Everybody: The power of organizing without organizations* (New York: The Penguin Press, 2008), 245-7.

Common Visionary Qualities

Visionaries Need to Be Adaptable

Over the course of their creative development, the visionary relies heavily on certain abilities. There is a daunting array of roles they are called to play — some optional, some not. Any particular visionary will not demonstrate these to the same degree, but might pursue most of them sooner or later.

None of these abilities are unique to creative and visionary types. However, they do display them more often and in greater intensity than most. Robert and Michele , who wrote *Sparks of Genius*, point to the inextricable link between science and art.

> The absolute similarities between the thinking process of scientist and artist are true not only individually but on a social level, too. What the scientist perceives as common problem solving, the artist understands as shared inspirations — but the 'answer' springs from the same creative act.… French physician Armand Trousseau agreed: 'All science touches on art; all art has its scientific side. The worst scientist is he who is not an artist; the worst artist is he who is no scientist.[51]

Visionaries proceed from a sense of confidence there is a solution or answer — if only they can find it. They hope to find an ingenious answer others would not even consider, let alone attempt. They expect their resourcefulness and tenacity to help them outwit any dilemma or handicap that impedes them.

Not only are they unwilling to accept that something is impossible on its face, they have been known to figure out how to "spin straw into gold," now and again.

Visionaries Are Curious

Many have a nearly insatiable thirst for discovering something new or unexpected. There is a method to their non-stop inquisitiveness. Their search is not indiscriminate, though it may appear to be, given the diverse assortment of topics or tangents that catch their interest.

That trait was probably palpable from early childhood. In that sense, a visionary never outgrows the innate curiosity of childhood. They cultivate it. A visionary's mental radar often casts a wide net attuned to spot the dots that connect with those they already have. What sets the truly creative apart from others is their ability to spot the connections between *apparently disconnected ideas*. They feel driven to know more and more — insatiable regarding their areas of interest. Nothing is beneath their notice.

---

[51] Root-Bernstein, Robert and Michele, *Sparks of Genius: The thirteen thinking tools of the world's most creative people* (New York: Houghton Mifflin, 1999), 11.

Noticing has a cousin: curiosity. You can tell they are the same bloodlines because one is usually shadowing the other. Curiosity leads, noticing follows. Or perhaps it's the other way around, noticing coming first, spotting some wrinkle and insisting on a closer look; curiosity wondering how the wrinkle affects half a dozen other things. In time, a connection is made and a revelation discovered. If you didn't know any better, you'd call it blind luck.[52]

The focus is not so much on *what* they are curious about. They will always be able to find something of interest. Curiosity is a form of receptivity—an openness that grabs someone, that *fully engages* them. That is the operative term: fully engaged. There is nothing casual about it. Just ask Seth Godin, author of *Tribes*.

> Curious people count. Not because there are a lot of them, not because they're the ones who talk to people who are in a stupor. They're the ones who lead the masses in the middle who are stuck. The masses in the middle have brainwashed themselves into thinking it's safe to do nothing, which the curious can't abide.
>
> It's easy to underestimate how difficult it is for someone to become curious. For seven, ten, or even fifteen years of school, you are required to not be curious. Over and over and over again, the curious are punished.
>
> I don't think it's a matter of saying a magic word; boom and then suddenly something happens and you're curious. It's more about a five- or ten- or fifteen-year process where you start finding your voice, and finally you begin to realize that the safest thing you can do feels risky and the riskiest thing you can do is play it safe.
>
> Once organized, the quiet yet persistent voice of curiosity doesn't go away. Ever. And perhaps it's such curiosity that will lead us to distinguish our own greatness from the mediocrity that stares us in the face.[53]

Visionaries Figure Things Out

They are drawn to complicated or thorny problems—those that involve seeing the intricate connection of more and more dots. Their determination to know more and do even better is never fully satisfied. They just keep on polishing the twin skills of critical thinking and complex reasoning their act demands. With that preparation, they are primed to spot something new when it pops up.

Innovative thinkers look for ways to organize disparate information that can make sense of how all the elements fit together—ways that are not defined by, or limited to, their prior thinking on the topic. As Galileo said, "I do not feel

---

[52] Shekerjian, Denise, *Uncommon Genius: How great ideas are born* (New York: Viking, 1990), 153-4.
[53] Godin, Seth, *Tribes: We need you to lead us* (New York: Penguin Group, 2008), 64.

obligated to believe that the same God who endowed us with sense, reason, and intellect intended us to forgo their use."

By the same token, they don't allow pre-established categories of information prevent them from seeing relevant dots that fall outside of those boundaries. Many major discoveries bring with them a new way of organizing prior knowledge or data.

The ability to figure things out is rational, where the mind shines. Visionaries add to that skill by taking the conclusion past where rationality is inclined to take it. They keep pushing toward the "unthinkable"—the wrinkle beyond the rational conclusion. It is on the cusp of what we do not yet know—but we intend to find out. Rote thinking will not ever get there since this step "over the edge" requires an intuitive leap. The evidence is not yet in, but waiting for it won't stop them from proceeding.

By and large, such individuals are inclined to ruthlessly analyze ideas before accepting them. But they do not just analyze them mentally—their intuitive (gut level) input carries considerable weight, too. Even after adopting a new idea or mindset, the person is ever alert to how it matches, or contradicts, the rest of their thinking. So the fine-tuning keeps getting finer.

Visionaries doubt—not in the way of muddled thinking, but as an art form. They are inclined to take the same torchlight used to examine concepts and turn it inward on their own processes and ideas. They are not likely to be blind to their own self-doubts or personal flaws, but study them as well. Nor do they ignore the gaps in their own thinking or what does not ring true. That is why they stay fully engaged and willing to "turn on a dime."

Visionaries Take Risks

"Off the beaten path" can be construed as symbolic of making risky or dangerous choices. They leave what is safe and familiar and strike out for parts unknown. And that is just the beginning. Who knows where that road will lead? Taylor Clark makes the case for taking risks in *Nerve*.

> If there's one group of people who epitomize this upbeat view of perilous, highly demanding situations, it's the clan of unique individuals.... Risk-takers aren't mysterious head cases at all—they just see the world in a distinctive way. [Psychologist Frank] Farley has spent his entire forty-year academic career researching the differences between those who thrive on risky, demanding activities (whom he calls the Big T personality type, with the t standing for *thrill*) and those who veer toward the safer, more predictable end of the spectrum (whom he calls the small t type)....
> The question of why we might view life's risks so cheerfully, Farley says, boils down to how we interpret things like uncertainty, novelty, and change—factors that show up in all stressful activity. 'Small t's are very enamored of security, stability, predictability.' ... [Big T's] would love an ever-changing world. The small t's would love a never-changing world....

Farley's research shows that risk-takers associate chaos with 'excitement and opportunity.' They also tend to believe that they can handle whatever comes up, that their destiny lies in their own hands.… And they like to test their boundaries, even if it means occasionally crashing and burning.[54]

Visionaries resemble martial arts warriors. They are underdogs who look for ways to turn their opponent's superior strengths against them. Their efforts could shift the balance of power to bring down the adversary who appears to have all the advantages. Certainly, *status quo* is on their side. In the process, the established and powerful sometimes get caught off guard and flipped over.

A visionary commits to a course of action that takes him or her away from the herd, which is often a lonely road. By reducing distractions and external influences, they can stay on task. But they do so convinced, that on some level, the choice to pursue the vision is not only about them or their personal desires. There is something more at stake.

On one hand, they are following in the footsteps of their heroes, mentors, or giants in their field. On the other hand, they are setting a new trail for those who may follow them. Whether or not the individuals involved (across time) know of each other, they are making that path more evident for those to come.

The person's withdrawal from social involvement is not just further evidence of their weirdness. They need the alone time to reflect and somehow they know that others who were ahead of their time also faced similar challenges. They are gambling on their vision being deemed a benefit to humanity in the long run. But first, they need to give it space to grow.

What they are doing specifically is less important than that they are respecting those inner-focused urges, as Julia Cameron said in *The Artist's Way*.

> Many of the peculiarities attributed to creative persons are really just ways to protect the focus of concentration so that they may lose themselves in the creative process. Distractions interrupt flow, and it may take hours to recover the peace of mind one needs to get on with the work. The more ambitious the task, the longer it takes to lose oneself in it, and the easier it is to get distracted.[55]

Visionaries Maintain a Sense of Purpose

Vision cannot be understood in isolation from the concept of someone's purpose. But the two notions are not the same, as Peter Senge explains in *The Fifth Discipline*.

> People with a high level of personal mastery share several basic characteristics. They have a special sense of purpose that lies behind their visions and goals.

---

[54] Clark, Taylor, *Nerve: Poise under pressure, serenity under stress, and the brave new science of fear and cool* (New York: Little, Brown and Company, 2011), 112-3.
[55] *Op cit.*, Csikszentmihalyi, 120.

For such a person, a vision is a calling rather than simply a good idea. They see "current reality" as an ally, not an enemy. They have learned how to perceive and work with forces of change rather than resist those forces.

They are deeply inquisitive, committed to continually seeing reality more and more accurately. They feel connected to others and to life itself. Yet they sacrifice none of their uniqueness. They feel as if they are part of a larger creative process, which they can influence but cannot unilaterally control.[56]

This tracks with moving away from an ego-oriented, structure-bound worldview, to a more encompassing one. Devotion to a vision engages an ever-expanding worldview that is also larger than the person's particular vision.

Visionaries Respect Those Who Led the Way

Even the most original idea owes a debt to prior knowledge in its subject area. "If I have been able to see farther than others, it was because I stood on the shoulders of giants," said Sir Isaac Newton. An idea, even a radical one, must exist within a domain of knowledge, with its own abstract symbols, vocabulary, and a contextual frame of reference.

Each visionary must pay their dues by acquiring the knowledge base and skills of their discipline before they can set out to alter it. That includes becoming familiar with the history and contributions of the pioneers who blazed the trail they are on. Such forerunners were not satisfied with minor tinkering, but pushed the limits, taking their field or art in unexplored directions.

With greater subject-matter mastery, someone acquires a more comprehensive view of their field and where, or how, their own inventive wrinkle fits. They come to recognize the larger *value of their own vantage point.*

They see how much their inspired ideas resemble the insights and philosophy of the greatly respected giants, whose views were heretofore seen as so far beyond (or different than) their own. But in the world of vision, we are all equals.

Visionaries Are Devoted Advocates

Having a vision opens the door for developing something original and ingenious. But if it is never turned into action or grounded in a tangible way, it was a mere possibility, a pipe dream. For our purposes, someone is not considered a visionary unless they not only have some form of motivating vision but they actually *take concrete steps to express and ground it.*

The public's reaction to the vision is secondary and subsequent to the actual visionary's realization of its value. But the visionary must at least make an

---

[56] Senge, Peter, *The Fifth Discipline: The art and practice of the learning organization* (New York: Broadway Books, 1990), 142.

attempt to overtly express the spark that arose within. Finding a suitable media or package for what they can see (and others do not) is a monumental hurdle.

It is not only about communicating ideas, but finding ways to engage the mind, heart, and senses in the process—each in its own manner. In *Sparks of Genius*, the Root-Bernsteins discuss the range of sensory input involved in imagination.

> Artists, designers and engineers share an age-old problem, how to move facts and ideas from one mind to another: how are these mental transfusions achieved? Through the use of images—not just in the form of pictures and diagrams but with words, demonstrations, even music and dance.' We not only see with the mind's eye, we hear with the mind's ear, imagine smells and tastes and body feelings—and any or all of these sensation pictures may be involved in the imagination and communication of images. To put it another way, if we observe with our eyes, we form a visual image. If we observe with our hands, we form a tactile as well as a hand position, hand-movement image. If we observe with our nose, we form a smell image that may play a major role in scientific or artistic invention. What we can observe, we can imagine, what we imagine, we image.[57]

People who exhibit visionary tendencies are likely to have more than one primary vision, or to be willing to commit to expressing numerous grand insights (over time). Also, they are unafraid of holding multiple points of view simultaneously—some of them contradictory. That is because a visionary's wide-angle perspective is not limited to the narrow 3-D worldview.

It includes *what could be*. This ability to tolerate protracted ambiguity is an unmistakable quality of growing into a broader, more inclusive frame of reference.

Clarity Ebbs and Flows

When someone places complete trust in their inspiration, in the value of a vision, he or she needs to be prepared to discover that the undeniable certainty that motivates them comes and goes. What seems obvious and leads them to leaping at one point can be hard to find or explain later, even to oneself.

The unshakable certainty that arises in creative bursts cannot be commanded or controlled, no matter how hard we try. One of the hardest parts of the visionary journey regards the rise and fall of certainty. The certitude available in high-energy creative or inspired moments is not a steady state. Finding only confusion where total clarity held sway is worse than uncomfortable.

How can someone deal with the fuzzy headed times, where certainty only flickers, without resorting to self-doubt or false bravado? He or she needs to understand they have not lost their faith or resolve. That sense of loss is not due

---

[57] *Op. cit.*, Root-Bernstein, 56-7.

to their lack of will or devotion. While we cannot command it, we can be faithful and alert for signs of its return. Then grab it!

This is where the "99% perspiration" come in — carrying on with the practical tasks, nonetheless. One stays engaged and ready, attentive for any pings of clarity in the peripheral vision. Some comfort might also be found in what Bertrand Russell said: "The trouble with the world is that the stupid are cocksure and the intelligent are full of doubt."

The down times are not evidence of personal failings but of larger cycles. They may be beyond our control, but not always beyond our notice. This is where integration of gains (both inner and outer) happens — without much glamor or applause. But it is also an opportunity to deal with humdrum tasks (like mending fences, sowing, and tending the crop) that keep the endeavor on track.

A related discovery is that there is nothing one can do about it. The ego is powerless to make insights happen (that "1% inspiration" part). So, one is humbled and forced to accept that true creativity comes from outside our abilities or preparation, and always has an element of grace when it does.

That already tricky balancing act becomes trickier once someone goes public with their vision since people are watching and judging them. It is hard to learn, and then remember, that reliance on rational certainty is one of the things that must give way to "innocence of perception," which is vital to the creative process. That is what holds the space for "I don't know," where originality is welcome.

The Collaborative Visionary

A visionary need not be a lone actor. Nowadays, much of the groundswell in scientific and technological fields is coming from teams, R & D investments, and new forms of cooperative interaction. Shirky also said:

> We are so natively good at group effort that we often factor groups out of our thinking about the world. Many jobs that we regard as the province of a single mind actually require a crowd. Michelangelo had assistants paint part of the Sistine Chapel ceiling. Thomas Edison, who had over a thousand patents in his name, managed a staff of two dozen.… The centrality of group effort to human life means that anything that changes the way groups function will have profound ramifications for everything from commerce and government to media and religion.[58]

A visionary's outsider status could be compensated by creating a core group until their idea gains traction. In addition, the creative cycle itself is often streamlined or shortened as the combined strengths of a devoted group work toward a common goal. Point to ponder — is a group of outsiders outside, or have they become their own "insiders?"

---

[58] *Op. cit.*, Shirky, 16.

Once a visionary launches his or her vision into the world, they may also develop an organization to protect and spread it. Or they might join forces with organizations that have similar goals. Some visionaries even thrive within larger institutions, or may become involved with the kinds of unstructured grassroots affiliations that are becoming so prevalent.

New forms of collaborative innovation allow individuals to pool their inventive ideas and skills—without being in close proximity or within the same organization. The Internet and recent technological developments permit those with novel ideas to find each other. They can work together on projects in ways that have proven to be fruitful, enjoyable, and in some cases lucrative.

These avenues for innovation are dramatically speeding up various aspects of the problem-solving process. This form of participation is a rapidly building wave of the future. In *Wikinomics,* Tapscott and Williams "read the tea leaves" on where collaborative is leading us all.

> The new promise of collaboration is that with peer production we will harness human skill, ingenuity, and intelligence more efficiently and effectively than anything we have witnessed previously. Sounds like a tall order. But the collective knowledge, capability, and resources embodied within broad horizontal networks of participants can be mobilized to accomplish much more than one firm acting alone.... The ability to integrate the talent of dispersed individuals and organizations is becoming the defining competency for managers and firms. And in the years to come, this new mode of peer production will displace traditional corporation hierarchies as the key engine of wealth creation in the economy.[59]

Because of the Internet and convenient access to information from so many sources, a person can live and work wherever they choose. A visionary need not be isolated from society—but only from the influences they find objectionable or a waste of their time. Someone can still interact with others on their wavelength, or with those pursuing similar interests, via online media.

Belsky cites a study that shows that those with strong online networks are more productive.

> An article in the February 2009 issue of the Harvard Business Review cited a recent MIT study showing that employees with the most extensive personal online networks were 7 percent more productive than their colleagues, and those with the most cohesive face-to-face networks were 30 percent more productive. Clearly, our respective communities—both online and offline—play a critical role in helping us refine our ideas, stay focused, and execute to completion.[60]

---

[59] Tapscott, Don and Williams, Anthony D., *Wikinomics: How mass collaboration changes everything* (New York: Portfolio, 2006), 18.
[60] *Op. cit.*, Belsky, 112.

Visionaries Get Burned for Their Unconventional Thinking

Visionaries are often labeled as eccentric or weird. (They do not see themselves this way but have to bear the pejorative misinterpretation of others.) Many of the traits that led them toward the visionary path are naturally ingrained—evident since childhood and at the core of the person's sense of identity. Their parents and community institutions probably did their best to mold them into "good citizens," so did everything they could to curb early signs of non-conformity.

Like a cowlick, the unusual ideas of a creative type just kept popping up. So the caretaker's grooming efforts were likely to be redoubled. It never occurred to most determined teachers that a cowlick could be a diamond to be cut and polished.

Of course, sometimes there was encouragement, but lack of it did not deter the person from eventually marching toward that distant drummer.

It is not surprising that many fledgling visionaries feel they might be flawed because of their independent or quirky take on things, thinking it a bad habit in need of purging. Yet they also know it is a fundamental part of who they are, and it feels so right when they heed it. These persons really cannot give up their non-conforming ways—even when they try.

The budding visionary qualities that have earned them little but correction (and maybe severe punishment) sometimes go underground. When the young person fails at eliminating what others find offensive or inappropriate, they are likely to adapt by thinking about such matters alone and in secret.

Though some might attempt to fit back in and act like everybody else, their inability to "pass muster" could force them to go their own way. This could display as social maladaptation, whereby they become socially stunted.

The Following Adjustments Are Common:
- They **withdraw** into themselves to avoid exposure. Realizing they are seldom understood, they stop trying to connect and take defensive measures to protect their unconventional ideas. They might hide their true value under a basket.
- They flaunt their difference and **confront authority** with an "in your face" rebelliousness. They force polarization in order to keep their boundaries up and strong. They do not let people in, knowing they are likely to be judged and misinterpreted.
- They ignore their desires or gifts in the name of **service or responsibility**. They try to fill the needs of those around them in order to feel valued and accepted. Their frustration comes with the discovery that the recognition or appreciation they desire is given (if at all) for *what they do*, not for "who they are" or what they consider most important.

Of course, some visionaries do not have to go through such rejection in their formative years. For many, the issues about being rejected do not get severe until they push their new-fangled notions. How well the person adjusts to being treated as different and wrong reflects the broad range of strategies.

Some individuals grow strong enough to stand tall despite their lack of encouragement. Or a sense of purpose may burn brightly enough within to nourish them despite lack of support from those around them. Still others do not take to the visionary path until late in life, after their personality and coping skills are formed.

Regardless of their degree of resilience, the unappreciated visionaries are likely to bear at least some psychological scars into their adulthood. They assume that if they work hard enough to develop something the larger community values, then they might eventually be embraced as brilliant and worthy of acclaim.

But whether or not that ever happens for a particular person, he or she must look for most of their companionship and rewards out of the mainstream. And the freedom inherent in the visionary path holds a special attraction for them.

While many individuals do suffer for their inspiration, Csikszentmihalyi debunks the stereotype of the tortured genius. And in our more enlightened times, it might become less so. But we are not there yet.

> But after several years of intensive listening and reading, I have come to the conclusion that the reigning stereotype of the tortured genius is to a large extent a myth created by Romantic ideology and supported by evidence from isolated and — one hopes — atypical historical periods. In other words, if Dostoyevsky and Tolstoy showed more than their share of pathology it was due less to the requirements of their creative work than to the personal sufferings caused by the unhealthy conditions of a Russian society nearing collapse. If so many American poets and playwrights committed suicide or ended up addicted to drugs and alcohol, it was not their creativity that did it but an artistic scene that promised much, gave few rewards, and left nine out of ten artists neglected if not ignored.[61]

Resentment as a Psychological Marker

The visionary path plays by different rules than those used in ordinary life. Taking the fork in the road brings with it an awareness of "not being in Kansas anymore." It takes a while on the visionary path for someone to discover many of the new rules or freedoms that characterize it. Noticing one's resentments (or the reduction of them) can serve as a marker of a maturing outlook.

By and large, visionaries are not resentful. One seldom noted characteristic for those on the visionary path is the absence of the slow death by pervasive resentment that infects some of their peers. They have made their choice to take action about something and are now taking responsibility for seeing it through.

---

[61] *Op. cit.*, Csikszentmihalyi, 19.

Pioneers accept the reactions of critics, who sit on the sidelines and throw stones, as the price they must pay to follow their dream. The hard work of grounding may be physically tiring, but it is not soul deadening in the way negative emotions can be.

Resentment is the antithesis of inspiration. Resentment is common in the everyday world, but has no place in the expansive worldview of creativity. So instead of only looking at what's being done (or not), notice, too, whether it is being done with or without resentment.

Similar negative emotions, like projecting blame on others, or seeking revenge, are not much in evidence among visionary types, either. Being treated badly does not reflexively bring out those reactions since they do not see rejection as a reflection on their identity or the true value of their work.

Author Nigel Richmond said, "You can choose to be part of the forces that govern you, or to be resentfully governed by them." A more encompassing view brings greater awareness of those broader forces at work, both in oneself and in the world. Then someone must choose to align with the big-picture team, or not. Visionary thinkers give the edge to the larger view.

Leaping into the unknown is not a calculated risk. It is imbued with inspired certainty, coupled with a sense that one *must* do so. There is not much fretting about the risks of taking action, or where the chips might fall just then. It simply is not possible to fully commit to one's vision or to leap when resentful. Someone would balk. Game over.

Breaking Down the We-Versus-Them Approach
Everybody Can Do More to Cultivate Their Own Sparks of Brilliance

Let me backpedal a bit. In my efforts to point out noteworthy qualities of visionaries, this book accentuates how these individuals differ from their contemporaries. But that disregards the underlying similarities we all have in common. Each of us carries the visionary gene. To quote Buckminster Fuller, "Everyone is born a genius, but the process of living de-geniuses them."

What sets visionaries and boundary-pushers apart from the norm are differences of degree. These individuals reside on the leading edge of a continuum between being totally predictable and so over-the-top as to be flirting with crazy. Almost everyone has an occasional moment of inspired vision.

Those most committed to the visionary path are willing to throw caution to the winds in pursuing it. But everybody falls somewhere along the vision continuum. And most people act on their own mini-visions from time to time.

Among the visions each of us carry is an image of "*who I could be.*" That embryonic vision is specific and unique for every individual. We get a whole lifetime to get it into focus. As the deaf and blind Helen Keller said, "It is never too late to be what you might have been."

> [According to Csikszentmihalyi] Each of us is born with two contradictory sets of instructions: a conservative tendency made up of instincts for self-preservation, self-aggrandizement, and saving energy, and an expansive tendency made up of instincts for exploring, for enjoying novelty and risk—the curiosity that leads to creativity belongs to this set. We need both of these programs. But whereas the first tendency requires little encouragement or support from outside to motivate behavior, the second can wilt if it is not cultivated. If too few opportunities for curiosity are available, if too many obstacles are placed in the way of risk and exploration, the motivation to engage in creative behavior is easily extinguished.[62]

A double bind arises within each of us: our urges toward being curious and creative, countered by all the reasons why we do not act on them. The vast majority feels committed to stick with what they know. The visionaries, who push the limits, are at the skinny leading end of the bell-shaped curve. (How interesting that it is called "the normal curve.") Anything at the extremes is not considered normal. Developing your affinity for insights, then to act on those impulses, might not make you a visionary. But it could greatly enrich your life experience.

Not So Different

Most people think of the visionaries as only being the giants (like Edison, Michelangelo, Newton, and Mozart) who blazed bright and left an inarguable impact. However, even those who left a clearly recognized legacy did not know if history would treat them kindly. They persisted *anyway*.

We cannot know which of our sparks of inspiration will have an historic impact. But it is still worth giving ours a fighting chance.

There is no precondition of specialness about those who eventually join the ranks of the widely acclaimed visionaries. Any of us is able to draw on those same abilities *when the urge is great enough*. The capability lies latent within each of us. Visionaries are not remarkable because they are different or smarter than everyone else. Their main distinction comes from their unstoppable determination and total devotion to an over-arching idea. They refuse to quit, come hell or high water.

However, the present we versus them view of visionaries must loosen up if the larger culture can ever be expected to respect early signs of original thinking before it is forced underground. On a personal level, the denial of our still-forming notions could be *foisted on us* by others, or be *done by and to ourselves*, by rejecting the fresh ideas arising in our own thinking.

---

[62] *Ibid.*, 11.

Each of us has no shortage of naysayers around us, eager to squelch what they consider too risky, weird, or scary. Those cautionary voices are external, however. Of greater consequence to our scope of possibilities is our own internal naysayer. We should not so willingly let our critical side stifle and ignore our creative urges when they awaken within us.

Trusting our inspired impulses more coincides with our recognition of our reflexive tendency to tune them out. Such habitual thinking makes us kill our bright ideas while they are still in the cradle.

Stop it! Then watch for what develops.

Styles of Reactions by Creative Types

In *Making Ideas Happen*, Belsky identified three broad categories of creative individuals:

- **Dreamers** — always generating new ideas, but often jump from one new idea to another. They're likely to become engaged in new projects at the expense of completing current ones.
- **Doers** — obsessively focused on the logistics of execution. Doers often love new ideas, but their tendency is to immerse themselves in the next steps needed to truly actualize an idea.
- **Incrementalists** — have the ability to shift between distinct phases of dreaming and doing. They have the tendency to conceive and execute too many ideas simply because they can. This rare capability can lead to an overwhelming set of responsibilities to maintain multiple projects at the expense of ever making one particular project an extraordinary success.

> There is no ideal category. The Doers, Dreamers, and Incrementalists all have their own strengths and limitations. However, once you consider which type you might be, you can leverage the forces around you — potential partnerships, organizational tools, and other resources — that can make all the difference ... [to take] the first step to establishing lasting partnerships and collaborations.[63]

To that list I would add a parallel category: **Occasional or Accidental Creatives**. People who fall into this category do not consider themselves particularly innovative. They don't divorce their creative activities from the rest of what they do, and it isn't a lifestyle choice.

Such a person gets briefly inspired, does something about it, but they never made a serious or intense commitment toward it. Even though he or she stumbled onto (made) something novel or worthwhile, they did not stay engaged with it. Whatever follows from it does not become a big deal for them. Something lucky could come from it — or not.

---

[63] *Op. cit.*, Belsky, 16.

Those in this amorphous group do not see what they did as inspired or out of the ordinary, even if it proves to be fruitful. These are not the strident haranguers for a cause or boundary pushers. But they are more receptive to knitting their insights into something tangible than most.

Some who are in this pool could be fledgling visionaries. But all of them are building muscles that allow him or her to be comfortable as a visionary thinker.

I see this as a growing trend as more people feel free to look for previously unexplored ways to navigate life's choices. I predict such openness will be even more in evidence in the new paradigm discussed in Chapter 19.

Engaging Your Personal Vision and Life Purpose

Everybody is occasionally given dreams and visions—exactly his or her cup of tea. Each vision comes with a query, an invitation: What can you make of this? Our "higher angels" wait and watch without interfering, amazed by our response of indifference or ingenuity.

Although the choice about what to do with our own vision may be personal, the effect of it (on some level) is made for us all.

Who wouldn't want to make their visions real? And like ripples on a pond we have no idea how far those influences will extend. Energetically... Over time... On people we will never know... The reach of a grounded vision has the potential to be world-changing—and not just in the here-and-now. Our intuitive abilities get stronger when they are allowed to be expressed and acted upon.

It is easy to confuse your visions with the desired outcomes tied to your preferences. Which is primary *in this moment*, and which is secondary? The next moment could call forth a different answer. You must learn to engage both your vision and sense of purpose in navigating life's challenges because it provides the widest frame of reference.

It is not so much about choosing between a vision *or* your bundle of skills and circumstances, but for you to find a way to keep each worthwhile component engaged and reinforcing the others. Peter Senge explains the difference between vision and purpose. They are not synonyms.

> Personal vision comes from within.... Most adults have little sense of real vision. We have goals and objectives, but these are not visions. When asked what they want, many adults will say what they want to get rid of. They'd like a better job—that is, they'd like to get rid of the boring job they have. They'd like to live in a better neighborhood, or not have to worry about crime, or about putting their kids through school. They'd like it if their mother-in-law returned to her own house, or if their back stopped hurting. Such litanies of 'negative visions' are sadly commonplace, even among very successful people. They are the byproduct of a lifetime of fitting in, of coping, of problem solving. As a

teenager in one of our programs once said, 'We shouldn't call them 'grown ups' we should call them 'given ups.'[64]

> Vision is different from purpose. Purpose is similar to a direction, a general heading. Vision is a specific destination, a picture of a desired future. Purpose is abstract. Vision is concrete. Purpose is 'advancing man's capability to explore the heavens. 'Vision is 'a man on the moon by the end of the 1960s.' Purpose is 'being the best I can be,' 'excellence.' Vision is breaking four minutes in the mile.
>
> It can truly be said that nothing happens until there is a vision. But it is equally true that a vision with no underlying sense of purpose, no calling, is just a good idea—all 'sound and fury, signifying nothing.' Conversely, purpose without vision has no sense of appropriate scale.[65]

What is your vision but the heart's desire to create a unique and relevant presence in the world? Making your visions come alive is one way of "making a difference." Isn't that an inalienable human right? Something deep within each of us hopes so, and wants it to be true. And what is life but a daily opportunity to make it so?

In *The Startup of You*, Reid Hoffman and Ben Casnocha argue that one's identity is not something solid and waiting to be discovered.

> Contrary to what many bestselling authors and motivational gurus would have you believe, there is not a 'true self' deep within that you can uncover via introspection and that will point you in the right direction. Yes, your aspirations shape what you do. But your aspirations are themselves shaped by your actions and experiences. You remake yourself as you grow and as the world changes. Your identity doesn't get found. It emerges.[66]

To the extent you attend to your inspired urgings, your capacity to live up to them will grow—as they become more clear and pressing. Then your next challenge is to bring them into tangible reality.

Make Your Vision Tangible:
- Give it words; talk it up; share the passion
- Give it precision of imagery and emotion imbued with rich and telling detail; look at it from 360°
- Give it a place of respect among your most pressing priorities; take time for it
- Give it steps and a progression toward a clear goal—via your feet planted on the ground

---

[64] *Op. cit.*, Senge, 147.
[65] *Ibid.*, 148-149.
[66] Hoffman, Reid and Casnocha, Ben, *The Start-up of You: Adapt to the future, invest in yourself, and transform your career* (New York: Crown Business, 2012), 35.

- Give it daydream time so you can fill in the details; but do more than that, keep learning and becoming more capable in knowledge and skills about it
- Give it your best—no shirking, no shrinking, no reneging, no excuses

It is worth noting that our change in priorities alters both our immediate behavior and our long-range trajectory. The greater the person's level of self-awareness, the more they mesh and work together. Jonathan Haidt discusses the shifting relationship between short-term and long-term goals in *The Happiness Hypothesis*.

> The psychologists Ken Sheldon and Tim Kasser have found that people who are mentally healthy and happy have a higher degree of 'vertical coherence' among their goals—that is, higher-level (long term) goals and lower-level (immediate) goals all fit together well so that pursuing one's short-term goals advances the pursuit of long-term goals.[67]

We set things in motion that will move us away from some of what is familiar and toward what we want more. But even when the commitment is clear, the nature of development and cycles assure that we grow into the expanded identity bit by bit. Over time the work goes deeper, to our very core, as Herminina Ibarra describes it in *Working Identity*.

> Most of us know what we are trying to escape: the lockstep of a narrowly defined career, inauthentic or unstimulating work, numbing corporate politics, a lack of time for life outside work. But finding an alternative that truly fits, like finding our mission in life, is not a problem that can be solved overnight. It takes time. Whatever the first step, the process gradually changes the nature of what we know and what we seek to learn. Learning happens in cycles. Early cycles focus on the most immediate (or surface) problems. Later cycles provoke the bigger questions: How do I put it all together? What other facets of my life do I need to adjust?[68]

---

[67] Haidt, Jonathan, *The Happiness Hypothesis: Finding modern truth in ancient wisdom* (New York: Basic Books, 2006), 145.
[68] Ibarra, Herminina, *Working Identity: Unconventional strategies for reinventing your career* (Boston: Harvard Business School Press, 2003), 87.

Chapter 6 - Finding a Paramount Vision

The power of the vision, coupled with the totality of the visionary's devotion to it, establish the sense of urgency and intensity needed to express what they've seen.

A Light in the Dark

A light bulb is a common symbol of an insight, a vision, or a moment of blinding clarity. Such a moment feels like a high-watt light bulb went on, making it possible to "see" so much more. What could be seen exceeded what the physical eyes are capable of perceiving. Also, details and intermeshed connections become more apparent.

A light bulb similarly signifies being able to see in the dark, into the previously unknown, the unexplored, or that which was feared. Intensity can range between a candle-size spark of blazing display. What makes the greater difference is whether that the light is on or off — present or absent.

Humanity has been led forward by sporadic insights and discoveries of farsighted pioneers. Imagine human history as a dark background speckled with the lights of inspiration, rather like stars in the night sky. Some stars shine brighter than others; some seem to cluster, while others shine alone. The panoramic scope of the heavens is inspiring, especially since such bright lights made much of modern life possible.

The energy unleashed in moments of inspiration imparts a sense of wholeness — a realization that the self is part of something far grander than it is by itself. Sometimes there is a recognition that "who I am" and the "vision" are inextricably linked on some plane that flits in and out of awareness.

What is glimpsed is sometimes recognized as a flickering indication *of "who I really am,"* as well as a possibility of *"who I am becoming."*

In a blink, the proper order of things appears obvious. How could I have missed it before?? This broadened scope of vision shows how all the elements connect in perfect harmony: (1) the particular person who experiences it, (2) what is seen — the vision, (3) the otherworldly reality from which it arises, and (4) the tangible everyday world in which it actually manifests.

It all fits! Everything about such experiences is sensed as miraculous and extraordinary. Normal life pales by comparison. Hugh I'Anson Fausset describes the sense of unity in *The Flame and the Light*.

> The realization of this undividedness, when it comes, is immediate and beyond all arguments or theory. It happens in us when certain conditions are fulfilled and certain barriers removed. One condition is that we should reject all

attempts to define it. Since any positive definition excludes its opposite, while [the experience] is all-inclusive.[69] [italics mine]

A vision might include sudden feelings of intense clarity, happiness, well-being, wonder, inspiration, and awe. Such moments of illumination often release a person's creative energies—coupled with an unquenchable devotion to what has been discovered.

Moments of blissful freedom and wholeness come with a related and deflating discovery, one that melts like snow on a sunny day. Awareness of that state of being is not permanent. What can be experienced is always there. It is available, but I am the one who goes *away from it*. There is a shock of remembrance at each return.

This chapter and the next focus on the vision itself. We'll investigate first the qualities of the experience, and then look to how we animate the vision, bringing it to life. Of course, it is neither possible, nor advisable, to consider any vision without referring to the one who brings it forth.

They come to define and refine each other, partly as an identity issue, partly as how they are perceived by the world.

The Transcendent Experience Defies Description

Visions puncture the humdrum of ordinary experience, allowing our sense of a larger purpose to dominate once again. An overarching vision delivers a recharge of what is known to be true and abiding, deep down in our "knowing place." There's a prod to cherish all life as significant and imbued with meaning. At its core, nothing is trivial—nothing.

Vision is much more than a logical culmination of ideas since it has little in common with ordinary thinking. The experience acts as a temporary break from our rational mindset and the demands of everyday life.

Like a tall, majestic mountain often shrouded by clouds, mortals do not see the pinnacle very often. But there is no mistaking the shock of recognition when even a glimpse of it appears once more. It is out of this world! The highly charged resonance we feel in those sublime moments is reawakened. What has seemed so remote and inaccessible is present again.

Anyone deeply involved in creative activities encounters dilemmas in expressing what they have seen or sensed. The person's determination to share their message compels them to keep refining and demonstrating it. But their efforts seem so paltry and limited, given how grand the vision.

---

[69] Fausset, Hugh I'Anson, *The Flame and the Light: Meanings in Vedanta and Buddhism* (New York: Greenwood Press, 1958), 60.

Those who act on their visions are devoting themselves to expressing something that is unique and original—even while feeling it is what's seen in the mind's eye.

Robert and Michele Root-Bernstein speak to the universality of the creative process. It transcends specialties or specific expertise.

> It is too easy to look at the diverse things people produce and to describe their difference. Obviously a poem is not a mathematical formula, and a novel is not an experiment in genetics. Composers clearly use a different language from that of visual artists, and chemists combine very different things than do playwrights. But neither is all scientific thinking monolithic (physics is not biology) or all art the same (a sculpture is not a collage or a photograph). To characterize people by the different things they make is to miss the universality of how they create. For at the level of the creative process, scientists, artists, mathematicians, composers, writers, and sculptors use a common set of what we call 'tools for thinking,' including emotional feelings, visual images, bodily sensations, reproducible patterns and analogies. And all imaginative thinkers learn to translate ideas generated by these subjective thinking tools into public languages to express their insights, which can then give rise to new ideas in others' minds.[70]

Visions Are Cryptic

A touch of the profound is always difficult to describe. During the experience, words are both inadequate and unnecessary. The sense of overriding clarity and wonder allow seeing beyond the frame of rational understanding. That fullness of knowing is much more complete than is receiving a single bright and shiny message. Afterward, one cannot forget the experience—or replicate it either.

Gossamer will-o-wisps vanish with any attempt to hang onto them. What seemed so obvious and unforgettable in an inspired state is simply not available while in normal life. What is captured is unlikely to be as comprehensible or as tidy as a fortune cookie slogan.

More than likely, the message brought back is not concise enough to guide one's steps except in a general way. Does it set a goal tantalizingly out of reach? Or might it leave a feel-good memory too vague to describe?

The words and images associated with the instigating vision are bound to generate multiple interpretations. Over time, the vision's meaning will change, not because memory fails, but because the mind was never adequate to unlock or grasp its fully expanded meaning. With increasing maturity, the initial meaning, along with the importance of the entire vision experience, takes on other interpretations—and further significance.

---

[70] Root-Bernstein, Robert and Michele, *Sparks of Genius: The thirteen thinking tools of the world's most creative people* (New York: Houghton Mifflin, 1999), 10-11.

The vision is not static, but organically complex—revealing further nuances with each encounter or recollection of it. The vision ripens and discloses further layers of meaning while it is being executed.

Like the fabled predictions by an oracle, in retrospect the message will be seen to have been true all along—but not in the way it was interpreted. Comprehending the richness of what the vision discloses must await the fullness of time and events.

Peter Senge *et al* warns us to be open to our vision changing form in *The Fifth Discipline Fieldbook*.

> Keep the vision fluid. Don't have the words printed in a full-color brochure or etched in stone in the corner of the building. Visions are always evolving; they are an expression of our hearts' desire. As we work toward our vision, we learn more about ourselves and other possibilities become clearer.[71]

Taking notes during the time of maximum clarity is out of the question. A person cannot imagine not being able to remember anything so unforgettable. Besides, efforts to write down the vision while it is fresh and obvious turn out to be no more comprehensible than chicken scratches after the fact. "Hmmm… what did I mean by that?" The right side of the brain in its resplendent glory will not tolerate the mechanistic interruptions of the left.

The stream of creative novelty will flow freely as long as there are brave souls willing to embrace their calling visions. A worldview that values innovation encourages more of them—and allows original ideas to emerge in more areas of life. Our collective future will be auspiciously altered in the bargain.

Visions build on each other. Repeated visits to the realm of visions improve one's ability to hold onto something comprehensible upon return. Consequently, a change occurs in the visionary's expectations, along with improved powers of observation. Each new transcendent insight becomes integrated with those that preceded it.

However, the nature of the experience is such that it is out of the range of the normal mind's operations. Attempts to talk about it at all encounter a great divide that's mainly defined by its incommensurateness to normal experience.

David R. Hawkins describes enlightenment as being something that is "only awareness"—but even that says either too much or too little.

> Ultimately, there is neither duality nor non-duality; there is only awareness. Those who have reached this state of awareness report that it cannot be

---

[71] Senge, Peter, Kleiner, Art, *et al.*, *The Fifth Discipline Fieldbook: Strategies and tools for building a learning organization* (New York: Doubleday, 1994), 305.

described and can have no meaning for anyone without the experience of that context. Such a recognition of awareness is the essence of enlightenment.[72]

The Stuff of Vision

Almost everybody has visions from time to time. It is a jolt out of the everyday mindset, an inspiration, a trip to "another place," a surge of upbeat energy. What makes visionaries different than everyone else in that regard is their determination to act on what they discovered in some decisive manner.

They feel they *must* give it a primary place in their lives. The vision ignites a determination to making what was seen actually exist. While their visions might not be much different than anybody else's, their way of responding to them is.

Visions Are Variously Called:
- A brush with God, the Universe, divine guidance, Truth, All that Is, Unity, Source
- The Muses—particularly in the creative arts
- The "aha!" moment; eureka experiences; peak experiences; in the flow
- Waking up—coming out of a fog, confusion, or sleep
- Moments of illumination or en*light*enment (note the "light" of inspiration)
- A new possibility, Perfection, utopia, the ideal Future
- View from the top of the mountain; the perfect place or space; out of this world
- My calling, my destiny, I saw! And I knew! (on the most intimate level; about myself and my purpose)

People have tried to describe such experiences in countless ways; these are just suggestive. What they have in common is specialness, an otherness that make them stand out from everyday existence. These experiences are also energizing, briefly adding a vibrancy and buoyancy to one's way of being. It is sometimes called a creative high or rush.

Some people avoid the term "vision," and instead use phrases like "insight," or "creative intuition," or "sixth sense" for how they know without it coming through their ordinary ways of knowing. These terms all work—particularly if the people who experienced it took subsequent steps to bring it to life, and into tangible form.

Visionaries value elevated experiences that evoke the enhanced clarity that fuels their inventive activities. In *Uncommon Genius*, Denise Shekerjian speaks of the "fragile potential" that can become concrete.

---

[72] Hawkins, David R., *Power vs Force: The hidden determinants of human behavior* (Sedona AZ: Veritas Publishing, 2000), 189.

> Freshly conceived, innocent, and untested ideas, no matter one's field, hold certain characteristics in common. They are, for the most part, ephemeral in nature—which is to say, timid, indecisive, fluid, and unstable. When we first think of them we experience the held breath of anticipation, and when we talk about them the hot flush of uncertain promise. These are characteristics that will endure until an assault has taken place in an effort to claim dominion. Without the attack, a new idea is nothing but fragile potential. Owning it is something else again. In the cold hard business of giving it form and setting the parameters and running it through its proofs, what was once lively and airborne turns as heavy and as obstinate as dour stone—this is where drive and concentration figure into the creative process.[73]

How they go about manifesting the vision afterwards reflects the intersection of the specific person's unique abilities and interests, coupled with their particular circumstances or opportunities. A fortuitous outcome for the vision could well depend less upon their efforts than on how malleable they are to being stretched and reformed by the visionary process.

Creative types learn how to let the vision take precedence over other concerns and "speak for itself."

The Clarity Reconciles Lesser Truths

An inspired state can be achieved via meditation, lucid dreams, daydreams, as well as communing with nature or art. Or it can come unbidden—out of the blue. One disengages from the known world and enters another space that is not so limited. But any breakout moment seems random unless one can find a way to develop their capacity to access that state more easily. Becoming able to do so is one of the secondary aims of the visionary process.

The moment of heightened awareness (flying, top-of-the-mountain) is not mainly about *what is seen*, or even the *seeing itself*—wonderful as that might be. ("Moment" does not connote duration since visions are out of time.) Higher-order visions also bring the unassailable *certainty that one knows*. One knows with "every fiber of one's being."

The visionary is neither limited by what is known to be possible or desirable, nor by their prior or normal life experiences—or obstacles. That partly explains why they refuse to steer clear of problems because the problems seem less real than the vision. In that transcendent state, the highest order of truth seems obvious—revealing the unique and inherent worth of every moment.

A profound insight is often called a flash of genius. "Genius" is from the Latin word, "gignere," which translates "to beget, cause, make happen." Genius actually refers to the *force of creative energy* that seeks to bring about some tangible expression or action. It generates; it produces; it causes. Such a force has power and might—something not to be taken lightly or for granted.

---

[73] Shekerjian, Denise, *Uncommon Genius: How great ideas are born* (New York: Viking, 1990), 129.

The word "genius" has devolved in its common usage to describe a really smart person—but the original emphasis on brilliance and inspiration to act should not be lost.

The total certainty evoked during a vision does not arise rationally. Rather, every cell in the person's body, every emotional resonance, every physical sense is united in rejoicing because the fog of doubt is lifted.

Previous confusions are understood to be illusions, without power to mystify—for the moment. The sense of a new dawn after a long dark night is likely to be palpable.

Visions can magnify even the most ordinary existence by expanding one's customary frame of reference. As the vision takes greater hold over time, one might begin acting in ways that seem "larger than life" because living is no longer so self-centered or limited.

When the world eventually starts to take notice of these individuals, people sense there is "something more than meets the eye." (Sometimes it is felt as charismatic.)

Having visions can also be perplexing by the very nature of their unnaturalness—their remoteness from one's usual outlook. But with the embrace of a larger perspective, those illusions of being off in the future shrink somewhat. One senses greater immediacy in the vision experience—it *could* happen!

To some small extent, the visions are starting to have a presence already—through you and your interest in them. They are not so much an alien experience as a reminder of a view in which that, too, is "who I am."

Being able to see beyond the "here and now" is in our human DNA, and bringing our insightful clarity into tangible reality is the essence of creativity. It is what the visionaries have long felt driven to accomplish—ahead of all else. And the form it takes is what each of us must discover for ourselves, in our forging of a meaningful life.

Gaining a Broader Perspective

Grand visions do not file neatly in memory since what is known with absolute certainty during the experience is more than the rational mind can grasp. But the *sensation* of it is held in the cells themselves.

The physical body is permanently stamped with the sublime sensation of unassailable certainty. It wants more of it! Later, what comes to be called "the vision" is never far from awareness since it "colors" all of the person's ordinary experiences.

Creative energy (which is feminine, as in "to give birth to") is combined with the drive to make things happen (which is masculine "can-do" energy). That combination has the power to craft something concrete that did not exist before. Creativity embodies energies that represent the strengths of both genders.

What is created would not occur without the participation of both. So using birth metaphors for inventive results is quite apt. Together, the immaterial *and* the material, the abstract ideal *and* the numerous practicalities come to work as one in order to make something tangible and lasting. That is the essence of the creative process. It is also why the vision and visionary are required to meld into a functional unit so something original can develop. What the world chooses to do with what is made manifest is an entirely different matter.

Efforts to capture a profound experience conceptually resemble dipping into the ocean with a bucket. While the ocean is enormous and undivided, the bucket can hold only the tiniest amount of it. Wet certainly, but what the bucket holds fails to convey the true nature of its immensity or oceanic qualities.

Likewise, the ability to retain a conscious awareness of the immensity and universal wholeness associated with a transcendent experience generally improves with practice over time. But there is always some sense of newness about recurring visions as well.

Sequential visions build on each other, with realizations coming from multiple perspectives that knit the pieces together. Tesla's electrical inventions were so far ahead of his time (early 1900's) that scientists still have not been able to figure out all that he understood about electricity. He is unambiguous in crediting his visions for his inspiration and what he invented.

In his biography, Nikola Tesla speaks of the extraordinary capabilities he could employ in heightened states.

> It was a mental state of happiness about as complete as I have ever known in life. Ideas came in an uninterrupted stream and the only difficulty I had was to hold them fast. The pieces of apparatus I conceived were to me absolutely real and tangible in every detail, even to the minutest marks and signs of wear.... When natural inclination develops into a passionate desire, one advances towards his goal in seven-league boots.[74]

Regarding how I refer to "vision" in this book, it might apply to single or multiple experiences—the central, primary vision, as well as secondary or subsequent ones, a singular experience or their combined summation. My admitted bias will be toward expressing the term's infinite elasticity.

I have come to believe, as a result of my studies and my own experiences, that visionary faculties develop over time and with greater discernment; and that the more the visionary attempts to communicate the qualities and properties of the vision (even to oneself), the meaning of the vision will coalesce even further.

---

[74] Tesla, Nikola, from his autobiography, *My Inventions: The Autobiography of Nikola Tesla,* date and publisher unknown.

No attempt is made here to distinguish the whole of what is seen from the person's limited perception of it—or to assess someone's skill at expressing what precisely they saw.

The Profound Vision Experience

From Whence Came the Life-defining Experience?

Visionaries can be roughly differentiated according to how they received their dominant vision. At one end of the spectrum is the "burning bush" variety, i.e. the Bible account of Moses receiving directly divine instructions to facilitate the liberation of the Hebrews from the enslavement of the Egyptians.

In such rare cases, the vision occurs without any prior warning—even without the person's willing acquiescence. At the other end of the spectrum, the vision might develop incrementally and without remarkable drama. It might not even be recognized as a vision until later, or perhaps not at all.

Frequency of Visions:
- Once in a lifetime and apparently random
- Infrequent—occasional insights that build upon each other
- Recurring experience—might be related to rituals or systematic preparation
- Waiting expectantly for inspiration to come back—calling the Muses
- Spiritual or creative practice; intentionally maintain a receptive state
- Freely accessed altered state, but still flip-flop between it and normal worldview
- Steady state of being in both dimensions simultaneously and continuously—called enlightenment—where 3-D and other dimensions are seen to be in unison; those who can do so are rare but prove it is possible

Abrupt

In an abrupt vision experience, the person's reality is literally shaken so absolutely they are obligated to make sense of the divine or unexpected intrusion. Or they might deny it happened at all. Attempts to ignore or forget such a profound encounter cannot be trusted to keep it blanked out since any trigger can reignite it.

Heaven-sent visions, like angelic messages or visitations, seem to be more prevalent (although still rare) for visionaries on a spiritual path. Even those cases are more likely to happen at a tipping point where a critical mass of readiness has been acquired. It might include knowing what steps are necessary, but visions are usually not that specific.

Being "called" or given a detailed mission dictates a specific course of action. However, a calling is often a vocational or emotional urging, and it might not have a bearing on other parts of the person's life. Such instructions must be specific, clear, and intense enough to instigate a break from life's prior trajectory. Or it could reinforce it with the added mandate: Act now!

The basis for "being chosen" is seldom or ever known. In fact, initially, a person is likely to feel certain there has been a mistake—I am not qualified or the best choice! Those who proceed *anyway* despite feeling inadequate to the charge are placing inordinate trust in the vision.

Redefining Moments (may be abrupt or incremental):
- Awe as discovered through art, nature, beauty, solving a daunting puzzle
- Wipe-out of identification with one's prior and limited self—a major crash
- Brush with death—whether one's own or someone close
- Experience someone else's suffering up close and intensely
- Near-death experience—and being sent back to complete something
- Major mental, emotional, or spiritual breakthrough (or combo of them)
- Surrender or remorse, when one's lesser truth or customary worldview are abandoned
- Profound visions and a sense of unity with All That Is

Gradual

It might be impossible for someone to identify a single, particular vision or event when things changed for them, but the person's subsequent behavior points to there being a marked divergence from their prior frame of reference. Rather than a single life-defining vision, a person might find himself or herself engaged in activities that grow to be more and more central to how they live—and away from the concerns of those about them.

In retrospect, it is often apparent the budding visionary was growing into their vision for some time, before the whack of clarity. Such cases are likely to illustrate a smooth wedding of the individual's divine purpose with their personal skills and desires. For them, the leap of faith to take action did not require faith, but they went directly to marching.

I have also found a person might claim that "I never had a vision," only to admit on questioning that there was, indeed, an experience where their point of view and priorities changed irrevocably. It might not have seemed a big deal at the time, but the igniting event was a "last straw" or "tipping point."

The Slow Hunch
Steven Johnson identified a particular kind of gradual insight development that he called the "slow hunch." He wrote about it in *Where Good Ideas Come From*.

Keeping a slow hunch alive poses challenges on multiple scales. For starters, you have to preserve the hunch in your own memory, in the dense network of your neurons. Most slow hunches never last long enough to turn into something useful, because they pass in and out of our memory too quickly, precisely because they possess a certain murkiness. You get a feeling that there's an interesting avenue to explore, a problem that might someday lead you to a solution, but then you get distracted by more pressing matters and the hunch disappears. So part of the secret of hunch cultivation is simple. Write everything down.[75]

… He needed a work environment that carved out a space for slow hunches, cordoned off from all the immediate dictates of the day's agenda. And he needed information networks that let those hunches travel to other minds, where they can be augmented and polished.[76]

… A slow hunch can't readily find its way to another hunch that might complete it if there's a tariff to be paid every time it tries to make a new serendipitous connection; exaptations can't readily occur in another disciplinary line if there are sentries guarding those borders. In open environments, however, those patterns of innovation can easily take hold and multiply.[77]
[Note: Exaptation means the utilization of a structure or feature for a function other than that for which it was developed through natural selection]

This speaks to the issue of preparation. As a person becomes increasingly involved in an area of interest, they spend more time thinking about their insights and arranging conditions to cultivate and capture them. They learned what Nietzsche pointed out, "Ideas come when they want, not when I want."

Quiet Visions Emerge From a Person's Core

Rarely does the vision come in one brilliant moment of realization. More likely, it builds upon many small insights of quiet clarity, when the person *knows* they are doing "what I am here to do." Even if the *why* or *how* of making it take root remains unclear, the heart beats faster each time someone touches that certainty about their vision in some fashion.

Such still moments might not be commented upon to others, though they are probably noted and cherished by the person who experiences them as they occur. Based on his extensive research on the topic, Csikszentmihalyi states, "A genuinely creative accomplishment is almost never the result of a sudden insight, a light bulb flashing on in the dark, but comes after years of hard work."

---

[75] Johnson, Steven, *Where Good Ideas Come From: The natural history of innovation* (New York: Riverhead Books, 2010), 83.
[76] *Ibid.*, 91.
[77] *Ibid.*, 232.

Because there are no trumpets or cherubs singing in the gradual build-up, it is easy to overlook their cumulative significance in the reordering of one's priorities for a long time. But at some point, quiet visions can add up to the same realization of undeniable purpose that might follow top-of-the-mountain moments. Such gentle certainties are of the same stuff, every bit as real.

In one sense, they are *even more* valuable because they are already being grounded in the normal world. They are becoming evident in the visionary's life as an ongoing embodiment of their life's purpose and beckoning vision.

For some, single-minded devotion might develop through years of intense involvement with their primary concern(s), without any expectations beyond that. It is what they do for the sheer satisfaction of doing it. What was considered a passion grew, along with the requisite skills, until it attained significance beyond a hobby or a career.

That is more likely to occur in creative arenas with long and demanding training—as the person masters the craft of violin playing, or sculpture, or dance. Having attained mastery in their field, the person is now poised to stretch or remake it.

It is not unusual for visions to occur after a person experiences intense or total loss—when they cry out in anguish "Why?" The wipeout of certainty opens an unexpected vantage point. When forced to face the inadequacy of their belief system, a person is less wedded to it and could surrender to a more all-embracing view.

That route to blinding clarity is not as pleasant as the top-of-the-mountain variety, but the resulting lucidity that comes can achieve the same purpose—driving someone to act on what they have seen. And, at least temporarily, all restraints are disabled.

Those in the creative and performing arts may be less inclined to think in terms of having a vision, but they feel committed to art or beauty (or a specialty within a discipline) that represents something of a higher order for them.

While the person serves that fickle mistress with varying degrees of devotion, artists hunger for the elusive visits of the Muses, who elicit their finest creative outpouring.

In still other cases, a person can point back to an inspired experience of indisputable *knowing* in early childhood. The foretaste marked them in a permanent way and acted as a life-defining thread they were able to follow as they developed.

A youthful experience of that caliber could be considered a vision even though the child lacked the language or judgment to comprehend it. (But then, who does?) I put myself in this category.

Accepting the Visionary Mantle

When the vision occurs as the burning bush or "calling" type, the person can't help but wonder, why me? The shock of receiving the unexpected mandate is likely to stir up considerable personal resistance.

Getting past the reluctance to be drafted is crucial for them to commit to what's being asked of them. This dilemma is less of an issue for those whose vision developed gradually.

Along with that sense of being singled out for a special mission, there may also be a sense of destiny. Destiny delivers a message: "This is what I was born to do!" How can anyone argue with that? By comparison, most ordinary choices seem drab indeed.

Reluctance:
- I am not worthy or adequate; I do not have what it takes
- Why me? — surely there is someone who would be better
- Why hasn't someone else already done it or seen it?
- I am busy; let George do it; I do not want to bother
- I'm already doing _____ (whatever, prior expectations and responsibilities)

If any personal argument serves as a sufficient deterrent, then no commitment will be made — or, at best, only a tepid one. It is no small matter to trust the "call" enough to take it on. And that is just the stepping off place — what follows is the leap.

Peaks and Plateaus

In *One Taste*, Ken Wilber subdivides the direct vision experience into two distinctly different phases: peak experiences and plateau experiences.

> Peak experiences are relatively brief, usually intense, often unbidden and frequently life changing. They are actually 'peek experiences' into the transpersonal, supramental levels of one's own higher potentials.... The higher the level of the peak experience, the rarer it is.... Plateau experiences are more constant and enduring, verging on becoming a permanent adaptation. Whereas peak experiences can, and usually do, come spontaneously, in order to sustain them and turn them from a peak into a plateau — from a brief altered state into a more enduring trait — prolonged practice is required. Plateau experiences, like peak experiences, can be of the psychic subtle, causal, or nondual domains.[78]

The permanent growth that comes with plateau experiences permits a person to have a more frequent access to higher states. Their level of consciousness has expanded. And they have developed the requisite skills to relate to what feels like an unnatural perception.

---

[78] Wilber, Ken, *One Taste: The journals of Ken Wilber* (Boston: Shambhala, 1999), 314-6.

This type of transformation relies on acquiring considerable self-awareness, whether it is emotional, spiritual, physical, or with regard to one's higher centers.

Such abilities are achieved gradually. They develop as the person makes sustained efforts to integrate that rarified awareness into their everyday life. Past the initial stages, most on the visionary path feel a need to rearrange their lives in such a way as to accommodate those urges. That level of devotion builds mastery.

Visionaries *See* Something

A "visionary" is defined as a seer, one who "sees." It usually indicates seeing something with significant clarity or it is imbued with overarching truth. That ability involves grasping meaning through sight—whether eye*sight* or in*sights*.

The word "visionary" exposes a conceptual bias toward the ability to see, whether with inner or outer eyes. But humans are equipped with five senses (as well as other ways to "sense" the world). Each of our senses is capable of an array of perceptions. And during transcendent states, we seem to have even more ways to access what is being shown to us.

Truth experienced through *any* of the five senses shares many of the same qualities attributed to visions via the eyes. Intense perceptions of beauty or awe correspond with being transported to an enhanced frame of reference— irrespective of which of the physical senses are involved. Similarly, a person can be a visionary without it mattering which senses played a role in their "vision."

Auditory guidance with a perception of being "spoken to" or "called" is cited, especially among mystical or religious visionaries. Sound plays an important role in many forms of inspiration—vocal or instrumental music, chanting, and repeated rhythms, such as drumming.

Movement and kinesthetic awareness as engaged through dance and other rhythmic and repetitive physical activities bring participants into an uplifting experience. More often than not, touch, taste, sound, and smell are also involved in ancillary ways.

The most complete visions involve all the senses engaged at once—integrated as an out-of-the-normal-world experience. In truth, the senses are not distinct and separate from each other. Each acts as a narrow window into a comprehensive occurrence that's larger and more integrated than any single sense can capture.

This book treats vision as *what is apprehended*—whichever senses were involved. And some kinds of visions do not involve any physical senses at all.

Lest it be forgotten, the senses are physical, organs of living flesh. Each is quite specific about the range of stimuli it can perceive. In addition, the sensory inputs integrate with one's complementary mental and emotional awareness during any experience. However, in heightened states, those modes are not separate from each other—they operate as one.

The Whack of Vision Redefines What Is "Real"

Everyday life, previously understood to be the real world (small "r") seems diminished compared to the big "R" reality of the vision state. During the transcendent episode, the person understands, beyond the limits of language, the meaning of what happens in either realm.

An upsurge of gratitude and awe magnifies such moments. All visions are equally exalted because each partakes of the same numinous qualities of divinity, truth, or perfection. They differ from ordinary perceptions because the veil of not knowing is briefly lifted. Such a sense of certainty fades in the everyday business of living, but could beam forth again whenever the animating vision is touched.

Notice the word "animating"—to add more life force and energy. Those experiences recharge the creative faculties and energize us. Keeping those fires kindled is a primary inducement for going within. That access taps into our underused strengths and reveals fresh ways of approaching the challenges life presents.

While the wisp of vision is insubstantial, it sometimes instigates a sequence of practical steps that give it tangibility. It is interesting to note the word "realization," which can refer to the vision experience itself as well as the eventual accomplishment of it—to make something real and tangible.

In *The Poetics of Music*, Igor Stravinsky splits the hair about creative imagination.

> Invention presupposes imagination but should not be confused with it. For the act of invention implies the necessity of a lucky find and of achieving full realization of this find. What we imagine does not necessarily take on a concrete form and may remain in a state of virtuality, whereas invention is not conceivable apart from its actually being worked out. Thus, what concerns us here is not imagination itself, but rather creative imagination: the faculty that helps us pass from the level of conception to the level of realization.[79]

The vision surpasses outside challenges and personal self-doubts. During the lucidity of vision, logical analysis and self-criticism are absent. The steady background noise of the mind searching after rational explanations is quieted.

Someone in an inspired state inhabits an inner place where absolute clarity and virtue reside. They know—without even needing to know what's known or how it comes to be known. Deciding what to do about it comes later—in the reflective aftermath. Subsequent bouts of self-doubt might actually be less about having specific doubts and more about feeling estranged from that sense of total clarity. The following is from Evelyn Underhill.

---

[79] Igor Stravinsky, *The Poetics of Music*, publisher and date unknown.

> This utter transformation of the soul in God continues only for an instant: yet while it continues no faculty of the soul is aware of it, or knows what is passing there. Nor can it be understood.... I knew it by experience.[80]

The "Fortuitous Accident" Is Not Accidental

Out of the blue discoveries (and related visions) are probably more than mere coincidence. "Chance favors the prepared mind," said Louis Pasteur. While it is nearly impossible to predict a particular discovery, it is very likely that the prepared mind will discover *something*.

One has been watching for it, so probably will not miss the signs of something truly unprecedented if it shows up.

Creativity is conceptually broken into four stages: (1) preparation, (2) incubation, (3) illumination (the vision), and (4) verification. Notice, the vision usually doesn't come first, though it can. When unforeseen discoveries seem to come from nowhere, they could well arise during the incubation phase—after extensive effort and while an idea has been simmering.

The fortuitous discovery is unlikely to happen without any prior preparation. Without enough general knowledge about a topic, something new, perplexing, or unusual that comes up probably would not have been noticed. Accounts of stumbling upon the unexpected answer usually disregard that there was a previous question in search of a solution.

Csikszentmihalyi argues that the psychic energy that comes with a puzzle or acute need is critical in order to persist until a new answer is found.

> The creative process starts with a sense that there is a puzzle somewhere, or a task to be accomplished. Perhaps something is not right, somewhere there is a conflict, a tension, a need to be satisfied. The problematic issue can be triggered by a personal experience, by a lack of fit in the symbolic system, by the stimulation of colleagues, or by public needs. In any case, without such a felt tension that attracts the psychic energy of the person, there is no need for a new response. Therefore, without a stimulus of this sort, the creative process is unlikely to start.[81]

Those with a curious turn of mind are likely to be on the alert for an unusual piece of the puzzle that connects with the pieces they have already assembled. They can see a new dot of information fitting with related dots they previously collected. That is how the person has the wherewithal to recognize where an "odd" piece fits—and the possible implications of it.

As with Fleming discovering penicillin in bread mold, he was not the first person to see the mold-killing action, but he was the first to recognize its

---

[80] Underhill, Evelyn, *Mysticism* (New York: E.P. Dutton & Co., 1961), [quoting St. Theresa] 371.
[81] Csikszentmihalyi, Mihaly, *Creativity: Flow and the psychology of discovery and invention* (New York: HarperCollins, 1996), 94.

possibilities. Choreographer Twyla Tharp said (in *The Creative Habit*) she uses everything that happens to inform her art.

> My daily routines are transactional. Everything that happens in my day is a transaction between the external world and my internal world. Everything is raw material. Everything is relevant. Everything is usable. Everything feeds into my creative. But without proper preparation, I cannot see it, retain it, and use it. Without the time and effort invested in getting ready to create, you can be hit by the thunderbolt and it'll just leave you stunned.[82]

Spiritual Visionaries Mapped the Route

Mystics develop their facility to sustain a connection with otherworldly states through meditation and spiritual practices. No group has worked harder to explain what visions are (and are not) than the mystics since visions have long been a powerful component of the spiritual tradition. Yet great care has been taken by them to distinguish God-given communications from the merely fanciful ones that resemble them.

The acronym, RSME, is sometimes used by writers rather than struggling to make distinctions among the similar experiences. RSME stands for Religious, Spiritual or Mystical Experiences. While the terms are not synonymous, what they signify can and do overlap in numerous ways. Tweaking their meanings apart is not necessary for our purposes, and any of these terms may be used here without indicating their equivalency.

RSMEs alarm the rational mind since they seem to defy logic or undercut a comprehensible view of reality. Actually, they are about a different reality—the big "R" one. However, I feel strongly that spiritual topics can be explored with the same degree of care and precision required for scientific investigations. The amount of rigor applied by spiritual masters could be considered on a par with any other demanding domain of theoretical knowledge.

The precision of language required to describe visions is most clearly demonstrated by Evelyn Underhill, author of *Mysticism* and related works, who explored the writings of the great mystics and saints in describing their inner journeys. She noted coherent patterns related to these uncommon (and private) visions.

> 'Vision,' that vaguest of words, has been used by the friends and enemies of the mystics to describe or obscure a wide range of experience: from formless intuition, through crude optical hallucination, to the voluntary visualizations common to the artistic mind. In it we must include that personal and secret vision which is the lover's glimpse of Perfect Love, and the great pictures seen by a clairvoyant prophet acting in their capacity as eyes of the race.... Vision, then, is recognized by the true contemplative as at best an imperfect, oblique, and untrustworthy method of apprehension: it is ungovernable, capricious,

---

[82] Tharp, Twyla, *The Creative Habit: Learn it and use it for life* (New York: Simon & Shuster, 2003), 10.

liable to deception, and the greater its accompanying hallucination the more suspicious it becomes.[83]

Underhill distinguished between intellectual visions and imaginary visions, which function very differently.

> The Intellectual Vision … seems to be a something not sought but put before the mind, and seen or perceived by the whole self by means of a sense which is neither sight nor feeling, but partakes of the character of both. It is intimate but indescribable: definite yet impossible to define…. Consciousness is at its highest, and hallucination at its lowest point. Nothing is seen, even with the eyes of the mind…. In Imaginary Vision … there is again no sensorial hallucination. The self sees sharply and clearly, it is true: but is perfectly aware that it does so in virtue of [the inward eye]…. Imaginary Vision is the spontaneous and automatic activity of a power which all artists, all imaginative people possess….
>
> In the mystics [it takes] two main forms: (a) symbolic, (b) personal.
> (a) In the symbolic form there is no mental deception: the self is aware that it is being shown truth 'under an image'…
>
> (b) The symbolic and artistic character of the visions is obvious…. [Another is the imagery seized on by the subliminal powers]. The life-enhancing quality of such an abrupt apprehension, however, the profound sense of reality which it brings, permit of its being classed not among vivid dreams, but amongst those genuine mystic states in which 'the immanent God, formless, but capable of assuming all forms, expresses Himself in vision as He had expressed Himself in words.[84]

Intense Feelings Magnify the Vision's Potency Later

The power of the vision, coupled with the totality of the visionary's devotion to it, establish the sense of urgency and intensity needed to express what they saw. The more potent the experience, the more likely it is to sustain him or her during the long and lonely patches to come.

Taking some decisive action to solidify that undeniable, though brief, clarity in some manner is crucial. In themselves, such overt actions can fail or seem futile, but just in the making of them the person affirms a commitment to their vision's reality. It demonstrates their initial effort to ground what was experienced. Later activities build upon those baby steps.

The visionary experience is rooted in an amplified emotional state. This fullness of feeling is not like the sentimentality of everyday emotions, however. The uplifting emotional states are fully integrated with knowing in the realm of visions. That total clarity and certainty will not fit in the more structured 3-D

---

[83] *Op. cit.*, Underhill, 279-281.
[84] *Ibid.*, 282-289.

mindset. Accessing heightened states of awareness involves an entirely different skill—the willingness to shift out of our familiar reality.

An uncomfortable tension exists between the vision and the workaday environment, and resolving that discomfort can be very motivating. Peter Senge speaks of gaps as the source of creative tension in *The Fifth Discipline*.

> People often have great difficulty talking about their visions, even when the visions are clear. Why? Because we are acutely aware of the gaps between our visions and reality…. These gaps can make a vision seem unrealistic or fanciful. They can discourage us or make us feel hopeless. But the gap between vision and current reality is also a source of energy. If there was no gap, there would be no need for any action to move toward the vision. Indeed the gap is *the* source of creative energy. We call this gap creative tension….
>
> There are only two possible ways for the tension to resolve itself: pull reality toward the vision or pull the vision toward reality. Which occurs will depend on whether we hold steady to the vision.[85]

When Words Fail

There is a word for when words are woefully inadequate, as when trying to describe with language something like love's longing—that word is ineffable.

Ineffable Means:
- Too sacred to be uttered
- Cannot or should not be expressed in spoken words; unspeakable
- Beyond expression in words
- Forbidden to be uttered; taboo

Using words to explain what is beyond words sets up a dilemma I wrestled with in writing this book. Whatever I write must be as true as possible for the unseen realm as it is in our everyday one. And the language should strive to conceptually tie them closer together.

It is not possible by relying on words or symbols alone. But our feelings can help (yours and mine) to bridge that gulf. That is one of the reasons people respond so readily to analogies or stories. They can see it and sense the point directly. Resonant stories may trigger a visceral reaction in the reader's prior experience: "I know what she means!" That kind of insight leaps the gap where words cannot go.

Better yet, emotionally charged symbols help a person to mine their own depths of experience more fully. "Oh, that's what that meant!"

Add to the inherent limitations of language, most people seldom give words to what they consider obvious.

---

[85] Senge, Peter, *The Fifth Discipline: The art and practice of the learning organization* (New York: Broadway Books, 1990), 150.

Anthropologist Edward T. Hall explains why cultural influences are so difficult to describe.

> People avoid verbalizing what they take for granted—their basic modes of interacting with each other. One reason for this is that much of the truly integrative behavior that falls under the rubric of culture is under the control of those parts of the brain that are not concerned with speech.... What we are
>
> discussing are super gestalts, so important and so centrally located in the scheme of things that they are almost impossible for us to formulate verbally. This is because much behavior is not experienced on the verbal level but on the emotional.[86]

In attempting to describe their vision people can encounter several barriers:
1. Can I find a way to express it? The emphasis is on *what message is sent*.
2. Can other people receive it? Or what do they get instead? The emphasis is on *what message actually gets through*.
3. Another dilemma relates mostly to artists and creatives who attempt to transmit an experience through various senses and largely without using words.

That difficulty highlights the impressive achievement by anyone who found a way to express the "something more" without relying on language or logic. This is not just a concern in the arts. Each domain of interest specializes in a way of resolving this dilemma.

Artistic forms sidestep the mind by communicating directly with the senses (physical), as well as at gut and emotional levels.

All those who want to share their inspired insights come up against this communication hurdle, and they must find their own way to deal with it. It is impressive how often the hard-to-express message actually gets through.

What kept me trying to describe what is beyond words throughout this book is my sincere trust that your emotional resonance to this material can span the gaps and "get it." Then, you and I can connect in a space of common understanding. An "Ah, I get it!" somehow leaps across that unbridgeable chasm. My mind and heart are both fully engaged in the writing, so I hope either, or both, meanings get through.

Vision Is Fluid

Even when a single concept from a vision can be expressed with precision, it will be filtered through the receiver's assumptions and conceptual framework. They will interpret its meaning according to *their existing perspective*, having no doubt that their interpretation is what the words mean.

---

[86] Hall, Edward T., *Beyond Culture* (New York: Doubleday, 1976), 153.

Compound that with the Telephone Game, where successive repetitions of a message by different people over time garble it further. Meanings that can be conveyed without relying totally on language stand a better chance of getting through without distortion. Artists largely dispense with words in favor of other symbols, as Howard Gardner describes.

> When it comes to artists, it makes little sense to describe their ideas in words.... Artists work in their respective media or métiers, and are appropriately understood in terms of how they convey their personal visions using light and color, sound and rhythm, metaphor and rhyme, bodily movement and facial expression. [Visions of] artists can be apprehended only by those who understand the nature of the media or symbolic system — the artistic forms — in which these creative giants worked and who are able to appreciate the breakthroughs that these artists respectively fashion.[87]

Time Conundrums

Time acts strangely during and afterward because visions occur out of time — out of the rational mind that relates to time. Timelessness is one of the ways to differentiate a vision from a good idea. Being in another perceptual mode really is timeless — time simply does not carry much weight. It is not about having unlimited time — even infinity itself is still a concept *within* time.

Without the backdrop of time, cause and effect, before and after, fast and slow — all gone. *Temporarily.* Organizing principles that the mind imposes on events, and how we relate to them, do not apply either. It takes another perceptual frame to be able to operate in that unnatural space — one without the rational limitations we usually take for granted.

Time reasserts itself as soon as someone pops back into their normal mindset. But the body never leaves the material, time-based world; it is our unfailing anchor in the physical reality. When an otherworldly traveler returns home, everything that was left behind, including time, is back — along with linear thinking and related mental habits.

However, one of the signs of escaping our everyday mindset more often is the increasing incidence of serendipity, synchronicity, and apparent coincidences that occur for us. These are not synonyms, but tend to show up together, as the grip of the logical mind yields to the unfathomable.

Signs of Added Significance:
- **Serendipity**: Accidentally discovering something fortunate, especially while looking for something else entirely

- **Synchronicity**: Experience when two or more events that are not causally related occur together in a supposedly meaningful manner

---

[87] Gardner, Howard, *Changing Minds: The art and science of changing our own and other people's minds* (Boston: Harvard Business School Press, 2004), 122.

- **Coincidence**: An event that might have been arranged although it was really accidental. It can be persuasively argued that there is no such thing as a coincidence *or* that *everything is a coincidence*. Your choice. The trick about coincidences is whether anybody is noticing

In *The Stuff of Thought*, Steven Pinker points out how we can't ever avoid a concern for time and space.

> People assume that the world has a causal texture—that its events can be explained by the world's very nature, rather than being just one damn thing after another. They also assume that things are laid out in space and time. 'Time is nature's way to keep everything from happening at once,' according to a graffito, and 'Space is nature's way to keep everything from happening to me.' But in people's minds, time and space are much more than that. They seem to have an existence even when there are no events to keep apart; they are media in which the objects and events of our experience must be situated—and not just real objects and events, but imagined ones, too.[88]

This causal texture is disrupted by visions, by visits outside of one's customary time and place. As a person opens to more of such experiences, it is nearly impossible to find relevant anchors or boundaries. Learning to navigate through this topsy-turvy shift of realities is one of the trickiest aspects of the visionary path.

Many visionaries operate on a different time line than everyone else. By not staying rooted in linear time, they are engaged in actively creating what is forming. That could put them "ahead of the curve" or "before their time." Some of those effects arise more often for those who repeatedly enter the realm of vision.

Consider the providence of when someone has a vision. According to Barry Jones, "If you have the same ideas as everybody else but have them one week earlier than everyone else then you will be hailed as a visionary. But if you have them five years earlier you will be named a lunatic."

Visions Are Not Simply Personal

In our normal reality, we cannot help but take things personally—to consider how everything we encounter relates to me. That is the small "r" reality of human nature—*it's all personal*. In the realm of visions, however, things are not seen through the ego's small lens. The verities are universal—equally valid for everyone, part of the big "R" reality.

As someone spends more time in the intrapersonal, impersonal realm in which visions arise, that enhanced quality of experience starts to bleed over into their everyday personal life. One becomes aware of shifting back and forth between

---

[88] Pinker, Steven, *The Stuff of Thought: Language as a window into human nature* (New York: Viking, 2007), 154.

their lifelong personal view and an increasingly impersonal one. And at some point, he or she can choose between them as need be.

The vision and the visionary develop a symbiotic relationship. Many seeds of vision are planted — probably in everybody, and more all the time. The visionaries are the devoted gardeners who tend their seeds, determined to make them bear fruit — and not just fruit for themselves alone.

The "Grand Scheme of Things:"

1. Vision or a seed of inspiration that comes from "elsewhere," more than me, larger than life — the big "R" reality

2. It takes root in an individual, then is expressed and incorporated into their goals and creative efforts, which it imbues with an element of inspiration

3. *Together* the person and their vision mature into something both personal and impersonal; yet through "who they are" and what they create, the vision is made tangible in normal life; they bridge the material and immaterial realms

In another sense, the person could occasionally lose his or her sense of a separate or limited self, so deeply do they become engaged in the overarching purpose of their journey. This could be described as a journey to somewhere — with different qualities than normal life — or within — or to one's core. Underhill describes the intermeshing of the inner and outer journeys.

> [A seeker may be described] in two apparently contradictory, yet really mutual explanatory ways. First he may see it as an outgoing journey from the world of illusion to the real or transcendental world: a leaving of the visible for the invisible. Secondly, it may appear to him as an inward alteration, remaking or regeneration, by which his personality or character is so changed as to be able to enter into communion with … the indwelling God, who is the fount of his spiritual life.[89]

Visions Are Humbling

Visions surpass the reach of rational comprehension. So we do not get to grasp, know, and remember them in our usual way. A wise friend once explained the difference between having a concept and a vision. It turns on where its source is. "A vision comes *through* me (from somewhere else or deep within), but an idea comes *from* me."

One distinction between the two considers the amount of ownership of the notion. A vision is attributed to other powers — treated as a wondrous gift, without someone taking credit for creating it. It arises from one's "knowing place" or from a greater wisdom.

---

[89] *Op. cit.*, Underhill, 127.

When an idea comes *from me* as a rational concept, it tends to get entangled with my ego identifications. That sets up a personal defensiveness about how the notion will be received by others.

Each of us is challenged to find the proper degree of detachment to allow the creative process to rumble through us — without it being shanghaied by the ego's limited agenda about where the credit goes.

Genuine humility is a perspective that is only possible when one is disengaged from their personal identification with what is created or accomplished. It plays by rules that ego cannot understand and is unable to turn to its own advantage. Humility is not the opposite of pride, where the ego reigns and preens, "Notice me."

Humility is inconceivable from the either-or mind except as feeling "lesser than." Being humbled is not a demotion, it is the removal of a false perception of "who I am," without its highly-charged self-centeredness.

Genuine humility permits us to take our rightful place in the big picture. And that is not trivial. There is not much need to reject egoistical tendencies when in a humble state since they simply do not arise much.

What those who are genuinely humble come to know is that what they're doing *is important* on a broader stage (different scale) than they realized before. Humility evokes the paradoxical discovery of simultaneously being elevated to see the added meaning of our efforts, while also seeing how insignificant our prior self-centered notions were in the larger scheme of things.

Humility offers an additional benefit that becomes increasingly evident along the visionary path. It permits us to hold unfilled the "I don't know" space, which is where true creativity thrives. When we are in the "I already know" mind, we close doors to whole avenues of what is still unknown and available.

Getting Too Practical

It should be noted that transcendent visions are quite different than the way vision is usually conceived or discussed within organizational settings. There, "vision" refers to a future practical goal, and the emphasis is on outcomes. By contrast, inspired visions are beyond time, with a numinous quality. That has little in common with corporate vision statements or the leader's declaration of a vision for the enterprise that mostly express strategies and tactics.

Business visions are not about being guided by something beyond the everyday world, but are mainly about *this* world. They are logical constructs that deal with accomplishing practical matters.

These are about *how* — whereas inspired vision is usually about *what* — and leaves the visionary to fill in the *how to do it*. They are similar, but fundamentally different.

Corporate visions predict or direct future business possibilities, using profits and statistics as the measuring sticks of success. That meaning of a vision serves the organization's priorities, rather than superseding them. David Hawkins, a researcher about consciousness, said "Society need visionaries of means, not dreamers of ends. Once we have the means, the ends will reveal themselves."

Defining Your Personal Vision

Finding Your Unique Voice

Every human is programmed with an inborn urge to find his or her own sense of identity and purpose. Part of that drive is to find your own unique voice. Finding your voice sets off the fortuitous merging of your heart's desire with your ability to make the ideals that burn within you real in the world.

Expressing yourself through your voice and personality means that whatever you do demonstrates an inimitable flavor of your own — an amalgam of inner and outer characteristics and quirks. And when wedded to a worthwhile vision, that drive is powerful! But its form is yours alone and must be claimed, and then asserted to give force and focus to your ideals.

Psychologist, Dr. Robert Firestone said "You are not going to find the meaning of life hidden under a rock written by someone else. You will only find it by giving meaning to life from inside yourself."

With finding your voice comes the shock of also finding out you are *"more than you thought,"* rather than *"less than you feared."* That is a very personal discovery that comes once in a while. It reflects our sense of alignment with our larger purpose. It shines through us and in whatever comes out of us. But we tend to lose sight of it when life dings us.

One of the hardest tasks in life for virtually everyone is to identify our most distinctive and essential qualities. This is inherently difficult but essential to the visionary path. Each person's core traits are so deeply entrenched and omnipresent, it is super hard for any of us to spot our own. Even when we see them and own them, there tends to be an assumption that others have them too; ours are not *that* unique. So we fail to accurately judge our own specialness.

Finding your fundamental uniqueness requires unearthing what is glaringly distinctive about your identity — a sense that no one embodies the confluence of certain traits as totally as you do. Your distinctive voice cannot be found by imitating someone else's.

As writer Hugh Macleod points out, "Part of being a master is learning how to sing in nobody else's voice but your own.… Put your whole self into it, and you will find your true voice. Hold back and you won't. It is that simple."

Being able to identify your voice amounts to claiming your distinctive, special advantages *intentionally*. Until a person discovers what their unique point of view is, they will muddle along with mediocre moves—even while hold winning cards he or she undervalue.

Those in the arts, particularly performers, often work with existing material (plays, concertos, choreographed dances), yet their measure of excellence shows in their extra degree of passion or meaning given to the performance. Those individuals move their audience with such an emotional intensity that viewers feel the performance deeply.

An artist's consistent ability to communicate at a deeper emotional level represents *their distinctive style*—readily identifiable by connoisseurs of their medium. When someone has a distinctive voice, the public can recognize it, appreciate it, and seek it out. His or her creative outpouring is sought for that definitive quality.

Each vision is custom made for and by a particular person—a combination of one's specific worldview and actions taken. It fits you perfectly, just like a suit tailored to fit looks quite different than one picked off the rack. A person aware of their uniqueness and purpose signals that as well.

Sometimes, what a person calls their vision seems generic, like "feed the poor" or similar sound-good ideas. Half-baked and unfocused notions describe a worthwhile desire rather than a personal vision. Ask yourself, what makes a particular idea *your vision*, done *your way*? Where is the passion, the sense of needing to get started? Right now! Personal vision coalesces in a way that would not fit anyone else as well as it does you.

One way to escape limbo or a generic goal is to jump in. Take action, even while it is not clear where it is headed, as yet. In committing to *do something* and taking the next step, circumstances are invited in and allowed to grab you. So they lead you step by step, building in ardor and clarity.

At some point, you could look back and see a path you have made (and are making)—and a vision expressed that is yours alone. Don't worry about how to add your distinctive style and flavor as you do so. It would be nearly impossible to keep them out.

Implicit in the visionary's desire to accomplish a worthy goal is the need to do it *in their inimitable way*. Incorporating one's distinctive personal qualities and skills into what is motivating them makes his or her vision their own.

According to Hugh MacLeod, "Your idea doesn't have to be big. It just has to be yours alone. The more the idea is yours alone, the more freedom you have to do something really amazing. The more amazing, the more people will click with your idea. The more people click with your idea, the more it will change the world."

What each of us chooses to make of ourselves over a lifetime reflects our expectation about what's considered possible. In defining "who I am" or what I think I am capable of doing, each of us makes the raw material of our lives correspond with that hoped-for future for myself. In that regard, everybody must invent themselves. Just being alive calls forth the creative energy for the job. Taking pains with it could make it a work of art.

Finding Yours

What if I do not have a vision, even a hint of one, you might ask. Maybe it is like dating more than one person, and not wanting to settle down with just one. If the level of interest in a notion doesn't feel like "the one," better to keep trying out a variety until something rings your bell. (See Chapter 4.)

Is a particular interest desired more intensely than the competing enticements (some would say distractions) of modern life? One could be your vision waiting in the wings—if there is a strong enough passion behind it. Every human heart has at least one.

Your larger purpose is nudging you toward discovering your own. When someone attends to those murmurs, the meaning becomes clearer to them.

Maybe it will not come as a top-of-the-mountain variety, but any efforts to trust, express, and ground that inspired insight will build the muscles that can serve whatever vision your drummer hears. Even reading this book and thinking about visionary concerns is a response to those urges. You have already begun to take those impulses to heart.

For those who have a vision simmering on back burner, allow it to come more alive *in* you and *through* you. Ferret out the ligatures of resistance that keep it on back burner, and you're off to the races.

Also, don't worry about it being the "right one." There is no reason a person cannot fulfill a variety of important and engaging visions over time. You are equipped to spot the beckoning of possibilities that turn you on. Now draw on the confidence to take them on.

Passing It On

One not-to-be-overlooked aspect of grounding is sharing what we discover on a more intimate and particular level. It is also an integral component of the visionary process. We cannot help but leave our creative "fingerprints" on what we make or the way we deliver it. And that includes our relationships.

A vision is much more than a great idea generator. It has a life force all its own. The abstract notion can be made to exist in practical and tangible ways. But it is also important to find ways to bring the vision's spark and energy into the lives of people we encounter individually. It does not only help and inspire them, but it makes your own creative spark brighter still.

~ Beyond Knowledge ~
A BonBon ~ Faith Lynella

What you discover from your own experience is more true than anything you can learn from a book (including this one). And that knowledge will become even truer for you if you share the discoveries with other people.

You graduate from intelligence to judgment to wisdom, but there is something beyond wisdom.

> **The bridge from intelligence to judgment is experience.**
> **The bridge from judgment to wisdom is character.**

Yet wisdom is solitary. Beyond wisdom is generosity of spirit, where wisdom is coupled with the fundamental human need to share and apply what has been learned.

From *BonBons to Sweeten Your Daily Life*. Or from *More BonBons*

Each of us influences those we encounter in ways great and small; in ways we intend and in ways we do not intend; in ways we know about and in ways we never imagined. While a visionary sets out to change the *status quo*, activities they set in motion can also change people, and change lives on a rather personal level.

These seldom-commented-upon influences that happen on a one-to-one basis could well eclipse the larger-scale contribution the forerunner sets out to make.

The truest influencers, who leave the deepest impact, are those who inspire others on a personal level through their wisdom, knowledge, motivation, encouragement, and sheer example. What he or she shares is *the force of their vision and their real-life example*—not just their message or practical benefits.

There are those whom each of us admire and wish to emulate. But as we follow in that person's footsteps, we take on some of their admired qualities, too. Who can ever know how many we touch by our example, or what effects flow from it? That is a personal legacy, quite aside from the fruits of the vision itself. Helen Hayes said it well: "We relish news of our heroes, forgetting that we are extraordinary to somebody too."

Chapter 7 - Bringing a Vision to Life

What they are attempting might well be foolhardy – time will tell. But a vision's worth cannot be judged solely by worldly measures of success, or even by its practical results.

Warning—Painstaking Work Ahead

With the vision conceptually packaged and launched, the visionary moves forward into the growth phase, more often long and uphill than not. This stage evokes the caretaker to nursemaid the undeveloped vision into viability. It's a slippery course that demands mindfulness, lest crucial missteps occur.

Of course, tricky choices exist for everyone, but the path is already precarious so blunders here could compromise or curtail the vision itself.

Visionaries face the challenge of keeping the long-term plan on track, with constant fine-tuning along the way. They must deal with personal frustrations, along with social and organizational traps of all sorts. The near-giddy excitement of taking up the challenge gives way to the tedium of working out the bugs and building support for it.

Intrinsic Hazards of the Visionary Process:
- Visionary's personal limitations and vulnerabilities
- Trying to do things that have not been attempted or successful before
- Social and organizational indifference or resistance
- Finding a way through uncharted territory; building the wheel
- Outright opposition
- Insufficient energy, time, money, resources

A driving vision is insistent, and like a bawling baby demands day-in, day-out care. With all it requires, grounding a vision is usually a job for more than one person. Some of the skills required are difficult for many creative types. They tend to be better originators than managers, more attentive to the global view than the minutiae of execution, more adept at adventurous discovery than minding the store.

For example, most writers, musicians, and painters would rather crank out new works than deal with getting them to market. Running the business side involves routine like handling orders, correspondence, promotions, and money management. While necessary, such tasks are seen as distractions from more creative pursuits.

Growth Occurs on Several Fronts:
1. The visionary's knowledge base, personal growth, along with developing the focus of the vision and support structure for it

2. The receptivity of public and institutional structures encountered — with their competing priorities and opposition
3. Getting the job done
4. Their legacy — building something of lasting value, without their continued presence

Sidestepping Traps and Potholes

Efforts to bring a vision to life start small — sometimes with little more than a fleeting vision and a determined visionary. As the undertaking grows, the difficulties common to any type of start-up arise. Most are no different for visionaries. *Except*, the challenge for a visionary might be an abrupt change from where they were prepared to go.

In addition, the urgent pace or order of steps is seldom optimal by planning standards. Visionaries leap and are likely to be "in over their heads" for portions of the process. Plus, visionary goals have a greater risk of failure than more mundane projects designed to develop according to established and predictable methods.

Visionaries are trying to do things that have not been done before. Thus the sheer possibility of success is persistently questioned and subject to doubt by others.

It could be argued that the visionary had no choice; *the vision chose them*. Many who are following their vision say those very words. In any case, such earnest and determined souls proceed as dutifully as possible — irrespective of the risks, ignoring whether they have enough of what they need to actually get the job done. Their weakest links will be tested until they break or become strong.

Visionaries tend to encounter certain kinds of risks and traps more often than others. While any particular difficulty might have minimal impact, another could prove fatal to the undertaking. Some kinds of challenges are more likely to arise at one stage than another, and will certainly appear once certain milestones have been reached. Also, various fields of interest offer their own brand of foibles and trials.

Some trials are intensely personal, played out amongst the person's competing desires and priorities. Some are organizational. Some involve finding ways to proceed without sacrificing long-term goals to short-term pressures.

Some are just about dealing with insufficient time, hands, or resources; while others are social and political, involving large groups. All of them require one to walk and chew gum at the same time.

Those on the visionary path are developing an added measure of personal maturity. The demands are great and much more than just project planning and team building skills. The person must weave the competing aims of inspiration and practical tactics together so *the combination* works harmoniously—while getting the job done. Peter Senge speaks further about creative tension.

> The juxtaposition of vision (what we want) and a clear picture of current reality (where we are relative to what we want) generates what we call 'creative tension': a force to bring them together caused by the natural tendency of tension to seek resolution. The essence of personal mastery is **learning how to generate and sustain creative tension in our lives.**[90] [his emphasis]

> People with high levels of personal mastery do not set out to integrate reason and intuition. Rather they achieve it naturally—as a by-product of their commitment to use all resources at their disposal. They cannot afford to choose between reason and intuition, or head and heart, any more than they would choose to walk on one leg or see with one eye.[91]

Making the Vision Manifest

The vision is a blueprint of what a visionary tries to bring into tangible existence. Execution entails choices about materials, measurements, the sequence of steps, and construction methods, until the elements fit. The structure is built step by step until the vision is real.

Grounding what was envisioned involves unending learning curves and practicalities that arise as one nurses the fragile vision. Their milieu and sphere of expertise establish the context for what is produced. The degree of mastery the person attained largely determines its quality.

> It takes skill to bring something you've imagined into the world.... No one is born with that skill. It is developed through exercise, through repetition, through a blend of learning and reflection that is both painstaking and rewarding. And it takes time.... If art is the bridge between what you see in your mind and what the world sees, then skill is how you build that bridge.[92]

Although bringing about meaningful change takes considerable effort, a visionary probably won't consider what they do as work in the usual sense. Devotion to their driving passion can be a labor of love, rewarding them with the thrill of discovery and a sense of purpose.

For some, their enthusiasm can be so vivifying that doing what's required is not seen as tedious, but as *the only thing they want to do*. They cannot *not* do it. As Scott Belsky said in *Making Ideas Happen*, "Passion yields tolerance—tolerance for all of the frustration and hardship that come your way as you seek to make your ideas happen."

---

[90] Senge, Peter, *The Fifth Discipline: The art and practice of the learning organization* (New York: Broadway Books, 1990), 141.
[91] *Ibid.*, 168.
[92] Tharp, Twyla, *The Creative Habit: Learn it and use it for life* (New York: Simon & Shuster, 2003), 9.

Creating a Unique and Supportive Place to Shine

The first and most pressing task for a highly creative person should be to create a context in which to flower. What best suited a forerunner is seldom readymade. Often it is necessary for a person to design and build their own "vehicle," since nothing else would as fully accommodate their distinctive strengths—and accomplish what they intend.

Whatever form it takes, a person needs a quiet and private place to disengage and think deep thoughts. "Others inspire us, information feeds us, practice improves our performance, but we need quiet time to figure things out, to emerge with new discoveries, to unearth original answers," according to Esther Buchholz, an expert on solitude.

The "disengage, then re-engage" pattern is crucial to the visionary process. What appears to be idle time is *exactly* where the shifts occur. It is then that the person re-engages progressively, a step beyond where they were before.

It is important for them to maintain some control of personal time and priorities, or the necessary creative part of the enterprise ends up taking a back seat to anything that comes along. Author Hugh MacLeod reminds us, "You have to find a way of working that makes it dead easy to take full advantage of your inspired moments. They never hit at a convenient time, nor do they last long."

Figuring out how to best express the message, and to whom, are crucial to leaving an enduring mark. Trying to be all things to all people is a formula for failure. Precisely identify the proper audience (or end user) in order to craft a relevant message focused for them. If there are multiple audiences, each deserves a tailored version. A connection is forged when people sense: "That speaks to me. They understand my needs and what I'm looking for."

We cannot predict which of our efforts will be home runs. So we must make the most of each opportunity or project. Wildly successful artists are likely to admit they did not see their biggest hits ahead of time. But they managed to keep up their creative output. They hold an "as long as it takes" mentality that views the failed attempts as the road to eventual success.

One of the difficulties in writing about the visionary process involves dealing fairly with the wide spectrum of expertise across so many domains of knowledge. All reflect creative expression to some degree, but a scientist laboring in the lab to collect data operates with very different methods and mindset than a mystic, painter, or philosopher.

Trailblazers feel committed to understanding something that appears incomprehensible until it "clicks" for them—revealing a larger, more integrated picture than they began with. It connects more elements and layers of relevance. In their own way, each is trying to make sense of what is being discovered, to convey something meaningful about it, and to shed more light upon the field of endeavor involved. The next step: how do they best share what they have found?

As a person moves ever further away from conventional thinking (and the assumptions related to it), they became more attuned to their own perspective. The more a person disengages from the community's (or niche's) shared outlook (vanilla pudding), the more their unique flavor starts to become apparent to onlookers. Their uniqueness starts to come to the fore — expressed as *their* voice, *their* style, *their* knack.

That is not to say that the visionary's unconventional approach is more important than routine responsibilities, or that practical concerns are unnecessary. It is just different. And someone *does* have to "mind the store." The ability of a visionary to stay on task regarding their vision often depends on somebody else picking up the slack, whether it means financially or doing the devilish details.

Those who assist in the mundane tasks are also supporting the vision, and they deserve more appreciation than they usually get for its survival. Many visionaries languish for want of someone (or a small circle) to assist them emotionally or practically.

Unreasonable Expectations

Visionaries are sometimes criticized because their expectations are not realistic. Of course they're not realistic! That's the nature of a visionary with a vision! In this case, it's actually the *critic* that is not being realistic. Caution and conformity simply cannot muster the fervent devotion required to stay the course.

Being over the top is a given, not a miscalculation. As George Bernard Shaw said, "The reasonable man adapts himself to the world; the unreasonable one persists in trying to adapt the world to himself. Therefore all progress depends on the unreasonable man."

"Realistic" is etymological kin to "normal," "responsible," and "sensible." They are value byproducts of the conventional mindset that was largely abandoned when the visionary took the fork in the road. For those on the visionary path, tidy predictability is also among the casualties. Their vision compels them to push the envelope into regions where such criteria do not apply.

What they are attempting might well be foolhardy — time will tell. But a vision's worth cannot be judged solely by worldly measures of success, or even by its practical results. Visionaries know what those in the mainstream say about what they are doing, but cannot give much credence to their criticisms and warnings.

Besides the person's own "inner Mom" who nags about what is expected of them, plenty of well-meaning bystanders offer cautionary advice every step of the way.

Burt Nanus explores the kinds of surprises in *Visionary Leadership*.

> Don't be overly idealistic. A vision should represent a worthwhile challenge, but it loses its force if people think it too ambitious or unrealistic.... In the end, however, as long as the vision appears attainable — even if it requires

extraordinary efforts and some lucky breaks for it to be achieved—don't be afraid to stretch a little and go for it.

Reduce the possibility of unpleasant surprises. There are three sources of surprises: something you expect to happen and doesn't, something you don't expect to happen does, and something you never even thought about happens, with unfortunate consequences for your vision. Obviously, by definition, there will always be surprises, but the domain of surprise can be reduced and the negative effects of surprises can be ameliorated.[93]

To be a visionary often means to have fantastic expectations—if not personally, then at least for one's creations. They have seen (foreseen) immeasurable value in their vision, and expect the world to recognize it too (sooner or later). Part of embracing a vision is working toward its acceptance as a step forward for the larger community. These pioneers do not expect it to be easy, but they do expect to prevail—eventually.

Susan B. Anthony, the Suffragette said,

> Cautious, careful people, always casting about to preserve their reputation and social standing, never can bring about a reform. Those who are really in earnest must be willing to be anything or nothing in the world's estimation, and publicly and privately, in season and out, avow their sympathy with despised and persecuted ideas and their advocates and bear the consequences.

~Ode to Being "Had"~
A BonBon ~ Faith Lynella

TOO GOOD TO BE TRUE! What do those words mean to you? Not true? Unable to be trusted? Counterfeit? Naïve? Con game?

Most people will lose interest in something that appears to be "too good to be true." It doesn't make sense; in fact, it offends your good sense. You'd be a fool to trust it, downright gullible. Besides, down deep you feel you ought to know better.

"Too good to be true" is a tug-of-war between hope and logic. It is the conflict between what you would like to happen (indeed a fragile, often forlorn hope) and all the reasons it won't or couldn't happen. Logic can be 100% true, yet in such cases I prefer to discount it. Reason can only deal in probabilities, not certainties.

There is a slender window of opportunity where logic can be skirted. A crack of possibilities through the impenetrable (impossible) exists and can be found. As

---

[93] Nanus, Burt, *Visionary Leadership: Creating a compelling sense of direction for your organization* (San Francisco: Jossey-Bass, 1992), 168-9.

long as you place your trust in hope, desire, or determination it is not closed to you. To accept the voice of logic means the attempt isn't even made.

I know the value of intellect, but it is not wise and cannot comprehend vain hope or the human drama from which it arises. It will disregard the improbable in favor of the likely. If I am to err, it will always be for the dream, the wish, the hope, the long shot. When nourished and acted on with determination, such notions can have greater power than the forces that impede them. Logic does not and cannot understand this—but I do.

Too good to be true? Yes, but that need not mean unattainable. It IS possible, though reaching that goal is far from reliable or effortless. Sometimes you get to discover that what you pursued with such single-minded determination is both good (actually wonderful) and true. That is the victory of personal vision over reason. That is the rare and elusive reward for persisting in your folly.

BEWARE: Watch out for con men; they love people like us. Caution is advised.

From *BonBons to Sweeten Your Daily Life*. Or from *More BonBons*

Visionaries expect what they are attempting to be hard work, and are seldom disappointed. Heading off to points unknown also means going back to the basics. It is not so much that conditions are primitive, but they might have to physically build their vision from scratch.

What the person can also count on is plenty of trial and error, as the details get worked out. But in most cases, they are committed to stick with it for the long haul. In *Crossing the Chasm*, Geoffrey Moore shows how hard it is for really innovative products to get launched.

> Visionaries are building systems from the ground up. They are incarnating their visions. They do not expect to find components for these systems lying around. They do not expect standards to have been established. They do not expect support groups to be in place, procedures to have been established, or third parties to be available to share in the workload and the responsibility.[94]

Visions that Bear Fruit

When all is said and done, the vision must pass the "But will it fly?" test. Does their new-fangled mousetrap actually catch mice? Leaving aside the questions of acceptance or whether others have done it better, did the visionary's creation live up to what they wanted it to do?

Of course, getting something to fly is greatly to be desired. But almost any outcome will send the visionary back to the drawing board in order to make it better, or to dig even deeper. They implicitly know there is more work to be

---

[94] Moore, Geoffrey A., *Crossing the Chasm: Marketing and selling disruptive products to mainstream customers* (New York: Collins Business Essentials, 1999), 58.

done. So they proceed with endless tweaks and improvements. And if the activity is a labor of love, why would anyone want to stop?

Once something proves it can fly, however, it is time for a well-deserved and long-awaited bow to acknowledge such a milestone. Other battles can wait another day. And as Henry J. Kaiser, the American industrialist, instructs, "When your work speaks for itself, don't interrupt."

> The love you have for what you're doing is actually the most important thing.... Love is the only thing that's going to pull you through and get you to finish.... But there is also a paradoxical and interesting fact: The thing you actually end up making is going to be such a failure compared to the original feeling that you had, the original vision that you had. If you finish and you find out it's not a failure, it means that you didn't try hard enough, because when you really fall in love with something, you idealize it, and you develop a vision of it that's actually unattainable in reality. The feeling of it is so pure that you can't make a real thing that has that feeling and so you're inevitably going to be disappointed by it. And in some way, the depth of that disappointment is in direct correlation to how beautiful the vision was to begin with.[95]

Progress cannot be judged primarily by the end results however. Various answers are interspersed throughout the undertaking. These act as emotional rewards and fuel the next cycle of adjustments. Csikszentmihalyi said:

> The fifth and last component of the [creative] process is elaboration. It is probably the one that takes up the most time and involves the hardest work. This was what Edison was referring to when he said that creativity consists of 1 percent inspiration and 99 percent perspiration.... A person who makes a creative contribution never just slogs through the long last stage of elaboration. This part of the process is constantly interrupted by periods of incubation and is punctuated by small epiphanies. Many fresh insights emerge as one is presumably just putting finishing touches on the initial insight.[96]

A vision's thrust is expansive, much like a stream where clarity flows easily and naturally. Occasionally, it is worth noting where its development is not free to flow. Where are efforts being held to a trickle in some ways, while being a surging torrent in others? On the other hand, where is the new notion finding its own channels and exceeding expectations?

Downstream and later, how is the notion actually being used in people's lives? The most genuine acceptance is demonstrated by those several steps removed, who have fully adopted the visionary idea as natural. They do not recall what was there before, or they don't miss what it replaced.

---

[95] Belsky, Scott, *Making Ideas Happen: Overcoming the obstacles between vision and reality* (New York: Portfolio, 2010), 217-8.
[96] Csikszentmihalyi, Mihaly, *Creativity: Flow and the psychology of discovery and invention* (New York: HarperCollins, 1996), 80.

A significant vision touches many people as it ripples out. The visionary should take pains to ensure its influence is worthy of all the energies invested in bringing it to life. It should also have a positive effect on those it touches. The talent, passion, and wisdom required to give a vision life are too precious to be wasted on trivial or base undertakings.

Dealing with Practicalities and Optimistic Biases

Visionaries are not impractical, not at all. They care very much about practical matters, but only as secondary considerations. The vision arrives with almost no blueprint or assembly guide. It is the visionary's responsibility to figure that out. Starting with something that *could happen* at some future point, he or she takes the baby steps *for it to happen* in the everyday world.

The visionary is often working from a larger scale or a future timeline very out of sync with the present reality. No wonder they run into communication problems and confound onlookers. In one sense, forerunners see the future stages or completed project as a *fait accompli*, without the intervening specifics. In promoting the vision to others, they are describing something only they can see — so far.

The person is confident in their vision's full possibility, even if there are many steps before that point, any of which might be hard or impossible in their own right.

To the visionary, the goal that motivates them is just around the corner. On one level that's true, but in everyday reality they face infinite opportunities to slip up. The clearer the visionary sees their vision, or the longer they've been intimately living with it, the harder it is for them to realize their judgment about it is distorted.

Fundamentally different scales of appraisal exist for them and everyone else. For instance, while the person knows what they foresee is in the future, they're likely to significantly miscalculate how long it will take — often not even during their lifetime.

Various scale distortions are so common that they can serve as defining markers of visionary thinking. These are not mistakes, although they usually appear to be so (unless a successful outcome compels a reappraisal). It is not just the public who is confounded by the discrepancies.

The visionary keeps going back to the drawing board again and again, trying to figure out why what they see and the real world do not mesh, despite their unflagging diligence. For those deeply enmeshed in the visionary process, this list could act as a checklist for making adjustments.

Realizing he or she is subject to systematic biases gives a hint about where the person's focus might be "off." But it also provides an assurance that their "equipment," theory, or judgment is not broken. It might simply need adjustment.

Common Visionary Distortions:
- Confusion about **scale** — they see a grown-up version of the vision, but it is still in diapers; they pursue a long-term mission, involving many kinds of growth curves and factors inherent in the situation, which are themselves in flux
- Confusion about **scalability** — they may be dealing with a model or prototype without thinking about how, or whether, it can apply to other contexts
- Confusion about **timing** — they are ahead of the time curve, so any notion they have about how soon something will manifest is likely to be way off
- Confusion about **resistance** — although they expect the path to be uphill, they seldom have an inkling of all the iterations of resistance and inertia they are stirring up
- Confusion about **completeness** — their image is of an integrated whole; they may have no idea about how the interim or composite parts fit together
- Confusion about **flexibility** — they see the benefits of certain changes, but discount the extent of structural factors maintaining the *status quo*
- Confusion about **identity** — by participating in the world of vision and otherworldly awareness (even a little bit), one is torn between the conventional assumption that we are only a body/mind/heart, and the realization we are spiritual beings too
- Confusion about **efficiency, trade-offs, and costs** — in a world of limited resources, how much is possible or "worth the candle"? What is reasonable or doable regarding the tangible and intangible costs?
- Failure to see **partial answers being used** — they see how something could be done "right," so dismiss the abundance of Rube Goldberg solutions people are already using — which results in people's inability to feel a need for the visionary's much-better version
- Failure to consider the **amount of learning/complexity/change** involved for users — people are not willing to subject themselves to these, unless the notion is compelling, or the alternatives have failed dismally
- Failure to recognize the **extent of their own changed perspective** — they too grow and change during the undertaking

Specialized Visions Are Not for Everybody

Many visions are not for wide distribution because they do not lend themselves to being popularized. They would only be of interest to those who have mastered a challenging discipline — like an artistic field or some exotic scientific specialty.

To communicate a vision requires a domain that permits capturing and translating information in some reproducible form — in language, musical notation, mathematical symbols, dance steps, etc. No doubt, there are many other conceptual frameworks possible—just waiting for an advocate able to articulate the hardly explored perceptual field.

Sometimes, there may hardly be anyone around who is equipped to respond to their message—not so unlikely for a person or discovery ahead of their time. So an idea might languish, possibly to be discovered anew by audiences yet unborn.

How useful is the new-fangled notion? Is the vision a single-purpose tool, good at what it does but with limited application? Or is it a Swiss Army Knife, adaptable for any and all circumstances? How readily does it become indispensable because people cannot imagine ever going back to living without it?

After the Igniting Vision

Seize the Spark and Run with It

An inspiring vision beckons a person out onto a limb—with nudges to go out further still. He or she sticks their neck out—maybe too far. As the vision takes on greater centrality for them, the "solid" ground they used to stand on seems less important.

Visions inspire action—pursuing it is too tempting to ignore. Alfred North Whitehead said "The vitality of thought is in adventure. Ideas won't keep. Something must be done about them."

Although it blazes forth from within, a vision is really *external*. It shows the person a conceptually perfect example of *what is possible for the world*. One's *life purpose is internal* and about him or her personally. However, on the visionary journey the individual's life purpose and their responsibility to the larger vision merge to the point they are one and the same.

Metanoia means to make an abrupt change of direction, a conversion from a prior state. The word comes from the Greek, "meta," beyond the normal mind. Visions lead to a fundamental change of orientation—from restraint to greater clarity and resolve. According to Jung, *metanoia* indicates a process of self-healing, which includes the person embracing thoughts beyond his or her prior limitations. The ensuing change of direction need not be religious, although in a religious context *metanoia* is considered a sign of repentance.

Making a Commitment

The vision can be dramatic and sudden, or it might build over time. Similarly, a person's commitment to it can be immediate or by degrees. (Remember, we are not including those who did not feel compelled to act on their visions.) For some, it has been niggling at them for a long time—until they feel they must do something about it.

Sometimes the commitment phase takes years because so much of what is changing for the budding visionary is happening beneath his or her conscious awareness.

The vision's intensity in large measure determines how much impetus there is to "do something." Someone who commits is likely to experience a sense of rebirth—along with a bright and shining sense of purpose. Thereafter, they change how they use their time and what they anticipate.

When a commitment occurs, it often carries a wholehearted, "must be" quality about it. The visionary's commitment is the confluence of his or her unique talents, character, degree of determination, and courage, along with the prevailing circumstances. Those taken *together* formulate their specific story.

Taking that step alters the person's life trajectory. Having their vision might not be their turning point, but committing to follow it draws a line. (Disclosure— Being vision-driven myself, I'll admit to being tone deaf regarding the motivations of those who are disinclined to act on what they've been shown.

> Once you accept that it is natural to create, you can begin to accept a second idea—that the creator will hand you whatever you need for the project. The minute you are willing to accept the help of this collaborator, you will see useful bits of help everywhere in your life. Be alert: there is a second voice, a higher harmonic, adding to and augmenting your inner creative voice. This voice frequently shows itself in synchronicity.[97]

Part of the commitment stage involves solidifying an intention to bringing the vision to flower. The person accepts the obligations and difficulties sure to flow from the decision. It includes releasing some control of how things unfold and accepting a larger purpose than they had before. This might not only lead to them acting individually, but to mobilizing others to get aboard as well.

In *The Corporate Mystic*, Gay Hendricks and Kate Ludeman speak to the role of intention in giving a vision life.

> Intention precedes and inspires vision. Intention lives in the zone between potential and action, organizing the diffuse energy of potential and bringing it toward reality. Intention is also the ability to hold a visionary context in which all of your specific visions are organized. Inspired leadership is the ability to work from the zone of intention, so that your very being brings forth visionary thinking in your colleagues.[98]

The visionary path leads a person to seek a measure of wholeness in their humdrum world—through any available means. When someone follows their inspiration in a "never say die" way, he or she forges a bridge across the

---

[97] Cameron, Julia, *The Artist's Way: A course in discovering and recovering your creative self* (London: Pan Books, 1994), 119.
[98] Hendricks, Gay and Ludeman, Kate, *The Corporate Mystic: A guidebook for visionaries with their feet on the ground* (New York: Bantam Books, 1996), 61.

otherwise irreconcilable gap between abstract ideas and material substance (with all its limitations and practicalities).

Setting Forth Where Destiny Leads

Commitment sometimes resembles preparing for a quest—the person feels they *must* go forth, determined to give their all to what lies ahead. As in the legends of yore, it greatly matters how devotedly and promptly one sets out (without foot-dragging).

The visionary who has committed feels nobody else can be the bearer of this particular undertaking, the caretaker for its beckoning reality. Others may have equally palpable destinies, but this one has their name on it.

Making a decisive gesture serves as a stepping-off place, where the possibilities shine the brightest. Despite foreseeable difficulties, the vision (mandate) is perceived as essential and pressing. Fears and doubts have no potency for the moment.

The mindset is imbued with confidence—eager to take on whatever is demanded. The task is viewed less a burden than a gift—one uniquely forged for them.

A good idea cannot ignite that much drive, but an inspired one can. Goethe speaks to how the dynamics change: "The moment one definitely commits oneself, then Providence moves too. All sorts of things occur to help one that would never otherwise have occurred... unforeseen incidents, meetings, and material assistance, which no man could have dreamed would have come his way."

The person has been changed, and is ready to act. Commitment is one of the turning points of the visionary path. It binds the person to the process in a way that cannot be lost. To be perfectly clear, whether their vision lives or dies cannot alter that.

The person is moving forward to the next stage of their own growth—toward increased mastery. The mousetraps (even wonderful ones) do not define the *mousetrap maker*.

The Day After...

Volunteering to go forth is most likely while the vision's pull is strongest and unassailable. But then what? In the light of day, back in the familiar frame of mind, one cannot help but see what was not apparent (or relevant) when taking the plunge.

Someone is still who they have always been, and they have no clue about how to bridge the gap between the grand vision and the freshly launched mission. They wonder, How on earth is it going to happen?

Such a sobering realization requires a re-dedication—the first serious challenge of the visionary path. The practical side needs to sign on also. That establishes the point when the person *really* gets aboard. For those who have made the leap or walk their talk, any signs of success are treated as verification of their choice. Nice, certainly, but not why they did it.

They're determined to stay the course, successful or not. But, truth be told, something about their vision foretold a successful outcome.

The visionary might devote a lifetime to expressing the truth of what was seen—and many visionaries have reported they still count all their efforts as too brief. How strong was the whack? How long did it last? How often did it occur? Such questions are not the point; never were. It is the acquiescence between the inspired self and the practical self, *functioning as a team*, that probably determines whether the quest is undertaken—or might eventually succeed.

The Decision to Set Out:
- Cannot be explained rationally (although the attempt is made)
- Cannot be justified
- Cannot be made to seem normal
- Cannot be compelled or done from fear or other people's desires
- Cannot be risk-free

Those who go forth feel they *must*—because any other choice is unthinkable. The difficult decision is not only for or against committing to the enterprise, or about the importance of the vision itself. But it reflects on their acceptance of its *primacy* among their competing interests. Henceforth, most other considerations start to arrange themselves around the requirements of the vision.

Making that degree of commitment, despite all pressures to the contrary, is what marks a visionary. As Seneca, the ancient Roman philosopher said, "It is not because things are difficult that we do not dare; it is because we do not dare that they are difficult."

Committing can act like a re-birth, a fresh start in which one's prior life is seen as prologue—a phase of preparation for this opportunity. What happens next leads to a progressive detachment from limiting structures—one by one—more and more nakedness.

In some ways, the initial commitment relates more to stepping onto the visionary path than about grounding the specific vision itself. Such insights come later, from a wider vantage point.

Another change involves becoming more at home with holding multiple perspectives simultaneously. Individuals who do so cannot be tied down to a single view as "the truth." But rather they recognize any single view as only a partial truth.

In a fundamental way, they are committing to a more encompassing view. They can tolerate more ambiguity—and see it as beneficial. In *Making Ideas Happen,* Scott Belsky said:

> With greater self-awareness comes a greater tolerance for uncertainty. Patience in the face of ambiguity helps us avoid brash decisions driven by our emotions instead of our intellects. We must use time to our advantage and temper our tendency to act too quickly....
>
> The best leaders have a high tolerance for ambiguity. They don't go nuts over the unknown, and they don't lose patience when dealing with disappointments. They are able to work with what they know, identify what they don't know, and make decisions accordingly.[99]

Vision as Touchstone

It is said a person can never step into a stream more than once. That is because the water is not the same as it was before—nor the surroundings. But neither is the person who steps. They have been changed by the prior "stepping into" and by all experiences since. Their former worldview has expanded as well.

The same is true of a vision, as it is being expressed through effort. The igniting vision cannot be revisited for the first time again because both the vision and person have changed through their influence on each other. They have become yoked together to some extent—no longer having a separate existence.

The initial vision (or culmination of several) is held in memory, from which it might occasionally be retrieved and cherished as something precious. And it is. But the recalled version is no longer the vision being served. Each encounter with one's vision and each step toward making it tangible have moved it a bit out of the world of abstraction.

Also, it is no longer the visionary's vision alone, but in some measure it has been claimed by those who accept and adopt it. They, in turn, adapt it for their own purposes. This is how a new idea gains traction, as it becomes increasingly influential in practical ways.

Each vision-visionary dyad represents a point of connectedness, which adds another pixel to the larger picture of what is known.

The visionary individual is being altered on multiple levels. Some of the changes are practical and apparent, but the person's degree of consciousness is changing as well. *States of consciousness* are temporary (top-of-the-mountain, breakthroughs), while *stages of consciousness* are permanent (milestones of mastery). Living through the visionary process is building on those gains— reflected in increasing levels of inner and outer mastery.

---

[99] *Op. cit.,* Belsky, pp. 204-5.

When the vision is made concrete, it ceases to be a vision for everyone except the visionary. It doesn't appear to others as a vision, but rather a new reality. Then, and only then, does the new reality exert its influence in an external fashion which more resembles a good idea. Most people have no clue that it's going to change the world... Until it does.

The visionary is the only one who ever glimpses the vision and gets to experience it in its pristine state. They might describe it before it has actually achieved some sort of measurable form, but what they're up to is *transforming* the vision into an opportunity in 3-D reality.

A Broadened Sense of "Who I Am"

Another aspect of growth is toward an expanded sense of identity. It is less and less personal or self-centered. This coincides with seeing from a more encompassing scope of awareness.

Ken Wilber's Integral Theory describes a three-step sequence of moral development:

- Egocentric — immature, largely self-absorbed; about "me"
- Ethnocentric — conventional stage of morals; centers on their group, tribe, nation; about "we"
- Worldcentric — individual's identity expands to include a concern for all people; about "us"

At each increasing level of conscious development one acquires, transcends, and includes the previous stage. But each level has slightly different orienting values about them. And the person's scope of possibilities widens further. These stages are not mutually exclusive and a person may find different ones more influential for different areas of his or her life.

During this progression, there is also a refinement in the person's relationship between head and heart. Each of them becomes more compatible with the other, and can take the lead as required.

In *First Things First,* Stephen R. Covey *et al.* address the collaborative nature of heart and mind as the vision progresses.

> Wisdom is a marriage — a synergy of heart and mind. Many times what our conscience tells us to do will seem familiar or 'common sense.' It's something we've read about, thought about, or experienced, so it's part of our rational framework. In these cases, conscience pinpoints or highlights the appropriate application of the knowledge.
>
> At other times, the wisdom of the heart transcends the wisdom of the mind. We may have no direct knowledge or experience in doing what we feel we should do, but somehow we know it's right. We know it will work. As we learn to listen to and live by our conscience, many of the things it teaches us are transferred through our own experience into our rational framework of

knowledge. We learn to reason things out in our minds, but not to get lost in reason.[100]

The body's role is just as important, and crucial to making abstractions tangible. Our physical side is too often left out of the debate, or treated as unworthy of otherworldly pursuits. At the same time, it's taken for granted. But the visionary process leads to a greater respect for the flesh, as we move to an integration in which heart, mind, and body all work together.

Coming Back Home

Early on, those who take the visionary path diverge from conventional thinking. Travelers no longer consider normal life or "home" all there is. The new route requires pioneers to find their way in unfamiliar circumstances, with few supports beyond their own resourcefulness.

As they proceed beyond accepted boundaries, they gain a measure of wisdom and judgment. It reveals they are growing inwardly and outwardly at the same time.

While the visionary path is a journey, it is more about the experience than the destination. Where it leads is left vague — or the tantalizing bright and shiny thing being reached for. But it will not ruin the adventure to also say the end is the same as the beginning, because we bring home what we have discovered along the way.

The person who returns is different than the same person who set out. That the adventurer grew in capability is not in dispute. But they have also gained a degree of self-mastery that honors their inner journey.

As T. S. Eliot famously wrote, "We shall not cease from exploration. And the end of all our exploring will be to arrive where we started and know the place for the first time."

At some point upon acquiring sufficient experience and mastery, the visionary path changes from heading *away from* the familiar world, to bringing back what was found — *converging* with the familiar once again. Thereafter, travelers can re-enter the normal world without losing the inner compass that keeps the person connected to a larger view. He or she gained a solid foothold in the all-embracing context, as well as in 3-D reality.

The person learns to establish a space in which to ground a larger-than-life view in very tangible ways. To the extent they become complete, so too, are their usually competing realities (the inner and outer realms) reconciled. Those who step forth with resolve to honor both spheres reinforce the possibilities each perspective represents.

---

[100] Covey, Stephen R., Merrill, A. Roger, Merrill, Rebecca R., *First Things First: To live, to love, to learn, to leave a legacy* (New York: Simon & Shuster, 1994), 175.

Energy Management for the Long Haul

Do Not Run Out of Gas

As any athlete knows, going the distance means learning how to pace one's self. The visionary path can be likened to a marathon. It is not a sprint, but requires long-distance endurance. "Stamina is utterly important. And stamina is only possible if it is managed well. People think all they need to do is endure one crazy, intense, job-free creative burst and their dreams will come true. They are wrong, they are stupidly wrong," insists Hugh MacLeod.

Energy management is the ability to sustain a consistent and ready energy supply for the entire venture. While creativity requires extra-large reserves of energy to ignite, it also throws off large bursts of vivifying energy. However, until someone learns to handle those extra bursts of energy efficiently, they gain little advantage from them.

The ebb and flow of creative energy leads to the mood swings and start-and-stop progress so commonly experienced by creative individuals.

The visionary process swings between the highs of inspiration and the lows of failure, tedium, and social rejection—rather like a roller coaster ride. And for long stretches of time, the downs seem to greatly outnumber the highs. The highs most valued are in the visionary's heart of hearts, where the truth of the igniting inspiration still shines. As Csikszentmihalyi said:

> The important thing to remember is that creative energy like any other form of psychic energy, only works over time. It takes a certain minimum amount of time to write a sonnet or to invent a new machine. People vary in the speed they work—Mozart wrote concerti much faster than Beethoven did—but even Mozart could not escape the tyranny of time. Therefore, every hour saved from drudgery and routine is an hour added to creativity.[101]

The intensity and passion visionaries sustain consume vast quantities of physical and psychic energy. They often go flat out until the body quits. It calls for super-human endurance—with few respites in the near term. It is vital for those devoted to creative pursuits to recharge often, and at every opportunity.

One must learn how to pick their battles and issues carefully. Creative energy is too valuable to fritter away on frivolities or negative thinking.

That is not the same as avoiding play or recreational activity, since those have the power to restore depleted energy reserves. It is wise to watch where energy is spent—or if one is spending more than is warranted.

Also, adequate sleep, regular exercise, and a healthy diet work wonders for restoration. (See more about high-octane energy in Chapter 13.) All efforts made to build one's resiliency will certainly help to keep the mission on track.

---

[101] *Op. cit.*, Csikszentmihalyi, *Creativity*, 353.

When Denise Shekerjian interviewed MacArthur Fellowship recipients for *Uncommon Genius*, she found they relied on a variety of methods to sustain high levels of creative output, even into their later years. Any of us would be wise to stay curious and resilient since those qualities continue to be enriching, regardless of age.

> The clues for building resiliency are everywhere you look: maintain a variety of projects; choose your friends wisely; embrace your errors and disappointments to see what you can learn; when a problem seems intractable, leave it, come back to it, leave it again, and again return; invest yourself in the vision, focusing not just on the goal but on the process; be accepting of the rhythms of pleasure and pain; retain a plasticity and curiosity about the potential of your field; learn to see the advantage in a hardship; develop a philosophy that allows you to accept defeat on the same terms as you would welcome a victory; make an effort to know yourself and determine what works for you.[102]

~ Energy Policies ~
A BonBon ~ Faith Lynella

Politicians have it all wrong. They think that the country needs energy use and conservation policies dealing with oil, gas, and nuclear energy. The energy policy that it needs most is the one each of us develops for ourselves. Where do we get our energy and how can we get more of it, so we can face each day with enthusiasm and force?

Next, notice where the energy goes. What saps our spirit leaving us drained and discouraged? Energy can leak away, like water draining through holes in the plumbing. Then, no matter how much we start with, it is soon gone. We end up feeling stranded and depleted. Those leaks are the places where we need to make repairs.

As we work on our personal energy priorities, we discover ways to make adjustments, much like a well-trained mechanic. Soon we have our lives running like a tuned-up automobile. Then we can go wherever we want — with energy to spare.

From *BonBons to Sweeten Your Daily Life*. Or from *More BonBons*

Inspiration is not a steady state — it flashes bright, then fades away. It is up and down. It does not take long to learn to "make hay while the sun shines." Paying attention to our energy helps us notice where it goes, and how quickly it goes. Staying attentive could, at least, slow down the inevitable decline.

Greater awareness to sustaining both physical and psychic energy is, to some extent, a learned skill, which I call Energetic Intelligence. (See Chapter 13.) It is

---

[102] Shekerjian, Denise, *Uncommon Genius: How great ideas are born* (New York: Viking, 1990), 209.

important to notice how we consume our energy reserves. We also need to look for ways to replenish our energetic springs.

The biggest boosts to gaining and feeling high-octane energy are: love and joy, being creative, and being in situations where we feel awe, gratitude, or inspiration.

Reduce Energy Wasters:
- Negative emotions—worry, stress, and anger
- Spinning one's wheels in indecision
- Repetitious and unproductive activities
- Letting the expectations of others call one's tune
- Ambivalence, marching in place
- Trivial or shallow pursuits that consume lots of time or energy without going anywhere

Energy management should also include a resolve to expend energy wisely. And that goes beyond the merely personal. The visionary should also respect the energy needs of all people they touch: customers, employees, investors, followers, etc.

Energy Costs of Crash-and-burn:
- Loss of momentum
- Actual costs of repairs and to replace what is lost or broken
- Lost time to get back in place to resume; opportunity costs because of the delay
- Psychological wounds: second-guessing oneself, disappointment, self-criticism
- Slower pace upon resuming
- Healing and rebuilding on numerous levels

Something valuable may be learned in the process, but it does not come cheap—energy-wise. Over time, a person gets smarter about when to withdraw and regroup, when to watch "which way the wind is blowing." He or she gains skills at riding the currents, rather than plowing full speed ahead, or slamming into easily-avoided obstacles.

Advocates for their cause discover which delivery methods work best for their particular niche or mission. What makes people respond favorably? It helps to use both splashes and ripples, so the influence of one's idea builds up and gains staying power.

As Mitch Joel explains in *Six Pixels of Separation*:

> Splashes do work (when done right), but only for a very limited time. Think about it. You drop a rock in the water, and the splash comes up high and fast, but fades just as quickly. The only way to keep your momentum is to keep

making splashes, which … gets messy and confusing super quickly. … Splashes are also expensive to start, execute and then repeat.

Ripples work in an entirely different way. With less energy, you can toss a small pebble (your ideas) into a big lake and let the ripple effect take hold. True, it is not as dramatic as a splash, but it sustains itself for a longer period, covering a much wider area.

In the digital world it's actually easier and less expensive to create a ripple than a splash. Ripples are the power conversations that are generated when you share your content (text, audio, video, images) online.[103]

Considering the visionary path as a marathon, with a combination of splashes and ripples, makes sense and adds staying power. Not only do the messages build on each other, the variety of methods appeals to different types of problems or people.

Banish Burnout

Many visionaries fail because they burn bright but lack sufficient endurance. They take for granted that there will be a desire for what they know and it will be considered to have value. Or they are sure they can outwait or out-argue detractors.

But most visions have an unusually long germination period before taking root. It is like a start-up business, which is seldom profitable for years. How many expect to work tirelessly for so long for so little before success arrives?

The inherent risks of the visionary process are both psychological and practical. Will the individual be able to keep reaching down deep, while acquiring enough resources to avoid discouragement or burnout?

> Burnout happens for a variety of reasons, but it is caused most frequently by working too many hours for too long, expecting too much too soon, and forgetting to create enough space between an organizer's work and her life outside that work.… We sometimes feel we have to tackle everything at once. If our efforts don't instantly achieve dramatic results, we are quick to criticize ourselves, and doubt that our efforts can matter.… The question of burnout, then, can usually be solved by taking time off, making an effort to create some healthy space between the personal and professional, remembering that organizing [a vision] is an endurance activity, accepting (even celebrating) our own imperfection, and honestly acknowledging the many doubts we have.[104]

---

[103] Joel, Mitch, *Six Pixels of Separation: Everyone is connected. Connect your business to everyone* (New York: Hatchette Book Group, 2009), 76-7.
[104] Thompson, Gabriel, *Calling All Radicals: How grassroots organizers can save our democracy* (New York: Nation Books, 2007), 168-170.

Burnout can also be an issue at any stretch of the visionary path. For instance, it will take a different form in the neophyte than the battle-weary veteran who is beginning to question their whole life as a "wrong turn." This is another argument for a team or circle of supporters. No one can maintain sufficient energy for the whole trek without encouragement.

It is an error to think one can or should go it alone. Sometimes it is necessary — but not all the time, or at every challenge. Every single one of us needs each other in various ways. Being able to draw on each other's energetic boost and different points of view (in healthy ways) are some of them. How to trust and rely on others to cover our short suits is one of those hard lessons to be learned by the "loners" on the visionary path.

Between the Knowing and What Is Known

Opening Up to Open Questions

My relationship to knowledge forever changed during a college philosophy lecture, when I first learned about "open questions." From that hour, I no longer considered knowledge about accumulating information or treated my comprehension as the measure of what I knew.

That shift in awareness also moved my scope from gathering endless facts to seeking the connections, the characteristic patterns at work.

Later and slowly, I learned to disengage from what I know in order to see anew. Embracing the *mystery of not knowing* leaves the mind unfilled — while avoiding the temptation of quick or apparent answers. It feels rather like holding an "unoccupied space" for some other answer to form — despite the pressing urge to fill it with what is already known.

To resist the desire to pull something out of memory requires quieting the mind and its relentless spinning of facts. I imagine myself being the reclining cat that does not need to chase every mouse (idea) that runs by.

Such an unnatural and unfamiliar frame of mind requires a tolerance for uncertainty and ambiguity. It must be cultivated or it will not happen. Rather than treating the lack of an answer as a failing or a stuck place, *avoiding the immediate answer* requires great skill and persistence. Holding that space unfilled (disengaged) invites something more original. What comes instead yields revealing insights the more resolutely it is practiced. (See Chapter 12.)

Openness to new perspectives requires us to remain in the uncertain, open-question mode until "something else" forms. It arises out of the jumble of ideas — clearing the fog of confusion in hitherto unexpected ways. Until the fresh insight arises, it is necessary to hold back the flood of thoughts pushing to rush into the unfilled space in our attention.

Remaining in ambiguity feels awful—awkward and unresolved. Paul Tillich, the theologian, said "The awareness of the ambiguity of one's highest achievements (as well as their deepest failures) is a definite symptom of maturity."

Immaturity cannot stand to wait. Yet the fruits of inspiration are worth waiting for, even if sometimes they are slow to arrive.

Holding that state sounds easier to accomplish than it actually is—and it's most unnerving, too. It puts the brake on a lifetime of wanting to know—the smart kid with their arm held up high for the teacher's nod. The mind refuses to go along with "pretending" not to know when it thinks there is a perfectly good answer already filed in memory.

But even the antsy mind is likely to be occasionally pleased with insights that might come bubbling up—the surprising ingenuity of finding something truly new. Refusing to settle for the most immediate answers opens up the opportunity to see more, as yet unfamiliar, elements as they begin to arrange themselves and change the resulting image.

Resolution might come as a blinding flash or as an accumulation of little perceptual shifts. It sometimes comes with a rush of energy—one's creative force in full throttle. It might take a while to put the dawning clarity into words, but the lens of perception is no longer quite what it was.

Poet John Keats coined the phrase "negative capability," describing it thus: "When man is capable of being in uncertainties, mysteries, doubts without any irritable reaching after fact and reason." He believed the greats (especially poets) have the ability to accept that not everything can be understood or resolved.

Negative capability is a state of *intentional open-mindedness*. It revels in open questions, and in the mystery of not knowing. Sometimes, the desire for direct and easy answers makes us chaff at such a circular approach—irritably "reaching after fact and reason." But we are truly in the mystery of our creative powers when we can embrace negative capability.

Jonah Lehrer is describing the value of that state in How We Decide:

> Embrace uncertainty. Hard problems rarely have easy solutions. There is no single way to win a poker hand, and there is no guaranteed path to making money in the stock market. Pretending that the mystery has been erased results in the dangerous trap of certainty. You are so confident you're right that you neglect all the evidence that contradicts your conclusion....
>
> There are two simple tricks to help ensure that you never let certainty interfere with your judgment. First, always entertain competing hypotheses. When you force yourself to interpret the facts through a different, perhaps uncomfortable lens, you often discover that your beliefs rest on a rather shaky foundation....
>
> Second, continually remind yourself of what you *don't* know. Even the best models and theories can be undone by utterly unpredictable events.... You

know more than you know. One of the enduring paradoxes of the human mind is that it doesn't know itself very well. The conscious brain is ignorant of its own underpinnings, blind to all that neural activity taking place outside the prefrontal cortex. This is why people have emotions: they are windows into the unconscious, visceral representations of all the information we process but don't perceive.

For most of human history, the emotions have been disparaged because they're so difficult to analyse—they don't come with reasons, justifications, or explanations. But now, thanks to the tools of modern neuroscience, we can see that emotions have a logic all their own.[105]

Holding a Space for "Not Knowing" in the Usual Way

Intellectual analysis is only one avenue for finding new ideas. The heart and emotions (as well as one's body sense) are quite capable of contributing relevant perceptions the mind has no clue about. As Chesterton pointed out, "There is a road from the eye to heart that does not go through the intellect."

All these dissimilar ways of understanding our reality have a part to play in the creative process. A person cannot be highly creative by relying upon rational thinking alone. Inventiveness shuns recycled thinking, so it can never be fully satisfied with what is already known. It stays curious.

Holding the conceptual frame open and unfilled until something novel appears is a form of divergent thinking. Someone gathers more and more bits of information and bides their time—waiting for just the right moment. It involves spreading the perceptual net wider and wider, receptive for something unknown to tiptoe in.

The more patiently someone allows a matter to keep expanding and remain unresolved, the larger the scope of what will be "caught" when the dynamics shift. That's the divergence. The clarity of vision or insight triggers the convergence. The crucial tipping point is described by Roy H. Williams, the Wizard of Ads.

> **When Divergence Becomes Convergence—And It All Comes Together**
> We love that moment when a divergent anomaly becomes the missing piece of the puzzle.
>
> The key that unlocks a mystery.
> The "Eureka!" of an inventor.
> The punch line of a joke.
> We hunger to see disparate elements resolve into a coherent pattern.
>
> Tedious teachers tell us the answers. Astounding teachers make us see the answers for ourselves; Click! Snap! The light comes on and we are filled with the electricity of life.

---

[105] Lehrer, Jonah, *How We Decide* (New York: Houghton Mifflin Harcourt 2009), 247-8.

Divergence: How much does it not belong?
Convergence: How well does it fit?
Divergence X Convergence = Fascination

Most people do what obviously makes sense. This is why most people are boring. The key to holding the attention of the world is to do what indirectly makes sense. This is a simple, yet practical application of Chaos Theory. (Chaos, in science, does not speak of randomness, but rather the opposite. Chaos is a higher level of organization than is immediately apparent.)

There can be no delight without an element of surprise. We notice the disparate element and think, "This doesn't make any sense. I must be missing something." Wait for it... Wait for it... Wait for it... Then it all comes together in an implosion of understanding and we are submerged in a new reality.

Three elements are all it takes. But each of the three must be sufficiently divergent from the other two. If the divergence is insufficient, there will be no surprise when they come together.

You must also have an explicit moment of convergence. If your three divergent elements fail to converge into a clearly coherent pattern, you will have merely created randomness....

Randomness is irritating.
Chaos is thrilling.
Be chaotic. (Or be boring. It's your choice.)[106]

Another Way of Knowing—*Fingerspitzengefühl*

The German language has an unwieldy word for a slightly different way of knowing something. *Fingerspitzengefühl* means "keeping one's finger on the pulse." It combines hands-on contact with an integrated overview that is poised to act. This kind of knowledge is not quite the same as rational thinking or gut level intuition, but incorporates them both (and more).

Because this 19-letter word it is nearly impossible for any English-language speaker to say or remember, I call the concept Fingertip Smarts. In Germany, this concept was demonstrated in the role of the General, constantly adjusting the military strategy in response to the changing developments on the front lines.

Fingertip Smarts points to the importance of current, *unfiltered* input. It brings together our primary modes of knowing, our sense of timeliness, authority, and a readiness to proceed. Trustworthy communication channels are key.

---

[106] Williams, Roy H., "When Divergence Becomes Convergence — And It All Comes Together," http://www.mondaymorningmemo.com/newsletters/read/1898, November 8, 2010.

\multicolumn{2}{c}{**Fingertip Smarts** - *Fingerspitzengefühl*}
Head	Rational
Body	All the physical senses, not just touch
Heart	Emotional and intuitive awareness
The combination	The integration of ways to know and take action

Fingertip Smarts describes having a sure instinct about something, an integrated understanding that relies on the accuracy of the particular input (as opposed to already interpreted bits of information).

The quality and precision of input is likened to the gentle touch of the fingertips, which are organs of exquisitely refined sensation. Fingers can distinguish very subtle gradations.

This capacity is a combination of intuition and judgment based on *direct experience*. Emphasis is on "direct" because it does not have many layers of distortion or interpretation by others (as in a hierarchical organization). It presumes one has also developed the judgment with which to assess specific facts in preparation for taking decisive action.

Fingertip Smarts describes *integrated knowing*, a knitting together of the full array of sensory input. But it does not just merge all the relevant information into a stew, since the individual elements that went into it remain accessible, too. The usefulness of the separate elements is valued and recognized as useful in its own right.

Fingertip Smarts merges the overt intellectually-processed information (the mind) with the covert sensory-processed information that is picked up nonverbally from the more abstract, sensual, and intuitive realms. It relies on having enough of each to exercise especially effective decision making. This values full sensory acuity as integral to making decisions and taking action.

Rational knowing mainly relates to static knowledge and competence. By comparison, Fingertip Smarts is more experiential, fluid and less verbal. It is responsive to events *as they are happening*, attuned to constantly shifting dynamics in real time. It entails a more encompassing awareness of all the circumstances in order to devise the most critically updated response.

An apt description of how Fingertip Smarts weaves conscious and unconscious knowledge together seamlessly comes from David Brooks in *The Social Animal*:

> If the conscious mind is like a general atop a platform, who sees the world from a distance and analyses things linearly and linguistically, the unconscious mind is like a million little scouts. The scouts careen across the landscape, sending back a constant flow of signals and generating instant responses. They maintain

no distance from the environment around them, but are immersed in it. They scurry about, interpenetrating other minds, landscapes, and ideas. These scouts coat things with emotional significance.[107]

Fingertip Smarts involves an integration of multiple perspectives and levels of information, each adding to comprehension. Making sense of such integrated input is a leadership function that permits a synthesis of the whole picture, without loss of the granular specifics. The information is also more reliable due to its timeliness. Stale information is not much good since what was true yesterday might no longer be relevant or reliable.

Cultivate the Art of Knowing in Multiple Ways

Usually the tug-of-war regarding knowledge is between rational and emotional, or between conscious and unconscious, or between old (established and well-known) and new (untested). You'll notice they are usually framed as "either-or" choices, but there are many, many other ways to know.

The truth is, we can employ all the approaches we care to use, not just one. I just laid out the case for Fingertip Smarts, which is rather sophisticated. But it is not the best approach all the time, either.

No single approach is the best one to use in every occasion, or is more true or reliable than the others. They are simply different. It is their *combination* and our practice with each that matures our decision making capability. That builds trust in the quality of the information we gather to direct our activities, our resources, and ourselves.

Each of the slightly different approaches needs to be recognized as a relevant and valid method to understand our reality better. And each of them should be respected as having something useful to offer that is not provided by the others. I would argue that relying on any single one of them alone misses the mark.

Each has its strengths and weaknesses, but disparate ways of knowing can reinforce each other in order to yield a higher-order view, drawing on the broadest possible input. Until one can move smoothly from one approach to the next, as need be, the scope of comprehension will be somewhat compromised.

Not to be overlooked, we could attempt the counter-intuitive approach that poet Dean Young suggests: "Let's get better at *not* knowing what we're doing." This argues for an innocence of perception that leaves us open to something else entirely.

Perhaps it could be called the Art of Not Knowing. How long can a person endure that level of uncertainty? It is possible to remain that disengaged only as long as one's attention doesn't waver. To be overeager for it to be resolved ends "what might have been."

---

[107] Brooks, David, *The Social Animal: The hidden sources of love, character, and achievement* (New York: Random House, 2011), p. *xi*.

Jonathan Fields advocates riding those butterflies in the gut that come with uncertainty.

> Snuffing out uncertainty leads to a sea of prematurely terminated mediocre output, when 'sweet mother of God' was just over the hump if only we'd had the will to embrace uncertainty, risk, and judgment and hang on a bit longer. If only we'd learned how to harness and ride rather than hunt and kill the butterflies that live in the gut of every person who strives to create something extraordinary from nothing.[108]

"Not Knowing" Shifts Our Customary Perceptual Lens

With a wider lens of perception, prior confusion or misperceptions stand out for what they are—shorn of the power to muddy the waters of our understanding. As either-or, us-versus-them, good-or-bad thinking become less accepted as the dominant, or only, way of looking at our world, many illusions dissipate like fog in the sunlight. In its place, more clarity shines through.

While I occasionally criticize the rational mind or logical thinking, it is because they are so limited—even while insisting on being the only acceptable way to know "the truth." Unfortunately, the mind is often co-opted by the person's ego and displays signs of pomposity or self-centeredness. Worse yet, the ego harbors its own agendas that we might not endorse consciously, and it cares little about ethics or other people.

Inner growth is largely about learning how to govern one's ego so it serves in its rightful place. Since the non-rational ways of knowing are not as attractive or accessible to the ego, the combination of these approaches blunts the ego's influence on our choices somewhat.

While the heart can get shanghaied by the ego (as in a diva or "god complex"), excessive ego coupled with emotion is so blaring, it does not pass unnoticed (as it can with rational approaches).

The various ways of knowing can be treated as developmental stages. Black-and-white thinking comes first and is easiest to accomplish. Children function that way. More nuanced conceptual thinking comes later, and involves learning to distinguish shades of gray. As with other areas of physical and emotional growth, developing a skill permits moving on to subsequent, more complex, and challenging ones. But the earlier stages remain available too.

Thinking is itself a skill that can become more refined through practice. As a person becomes more accomplished in splitting hairs, they still continue to use all their prior capabilities, as need be. Mastery and inner maturity are mentioned here as life goals or later phases of the visionary path. Those stages rely on us to develop and fine-tune the multiple ways of knowing.

---

[108] Fields, Jonathan, "Ride the Butterflies," http://www.jonathanfields.com/blog

Respecting the other ways of knowing as valid would also help individuals to communicate with those who are reliant on approaches unlike their own. It allows one to listen to others without their opinions being suspect. But just as important, each of us can accept more of *our own* unclaimed knowledge without partiality against it.

I foresee our numerous and varied ways of knowing heading toward a measure of convergence. In my opinion, one of the coming major paradigm shifts of our times will be a reconciliation of these competing ways of knowing (Chapter 18).

To be open to fresh answers, we must not limit ourselves to a single, one-sided way of knowing and understanding the world. We really need not, and *must not*, choose just one and foreswear the rest. The various approaches must be engaged more effectively. Fausset describes the progression in *The Flame and the Light*.

> Life proceeds from the unseen to the seen, from mystery to meaning. It is, therefore, right that we should begin our new journey [inward], as we began our natural life, in an ignorance which is an act of faith, not involuntary as with the infant, or doctrinally determined as in the acceptance of a creed, but in a willing suspension of the kind of knowing, with its attendant beliefs and unbeliefs, which we have acquired as we grew up.[109]

Digging Even Deeper

Vision always reveals a measure of truth, the stretch-for-it kind, not the I-already-know-it kind. We *almost know* because those discoveries of "something more" are not simply rational knowing. On an individual level, our discoveries of our own untapped knowledge do not have to be treated as rare peak (or peek) experiences.

One's "knowing place" is rooted in the heart, in a place where the rational mind is a foreigner—it can't speak the language. As we grasp and ground a worldview that includes the mutual involvement of head, heart, and flesh, what we *can do* becomes both known and actualized in the material reality. It is right here, right now.

Grounding takes what we visualized out of the realm of theory, dream, or possibility, by making it concrete. What is added in the process has the visionary's unique signature all over it.

There is a saying: "We do not know what we do not know." When we use multiple ways of knowing, we come at the shapeless mass of what is unknown from a variety of directions. Each of the approaches yields something we never knew about (and probably would have been quite satisfied to never know). But as we claim new inroads we hone our burrowing abilities.

---

[109] Fausset, Hugh I'Anson, *The Flame and the Light, Meanings in Vedanta and Buddhism* (New York: Greenwood Press, 1958), 61.

Most people would insist there is quite enough known about above ground, thank you. But think of some kinds of visionaries resembling coal miners who descend into the pit. They go deep underground (within) and mine what is buried or accumulated there. It indicates yet another way to go off the beaten path, while pointing to unlimited and beckoning new frontiers.

This form of exploration and discovery extracts nuggets amenable to precise analysis. Some artists have built their careers upon such spelunking. They were not satisfied to dig close to the surface, but rather tunneled down deep—where almost all of what is there is unknown.

It is not what we know, but *how we know* that defines the scope of our individual perceptual lens. To function effectively in the world, we gain by being open to alternate inputs and strategies. Each of us can become more adept at switching gears and digging down even further.

Common sense and good judgment argue for having as wide and undistorted a lens as possible. And that means being proficient at engaging more ways of knowing. In *Reinventing the Sacred,* Stuart Kauffman makes the case for bringing our long-held ways of knowing into alliance.

> If both natural law and ceaseless creativity partially beyond natural law are necessary for understanding our world, and if we as whole human beings live in this real world of law and unknowable creativity, these two ancient strands of Western civilization can reunite in ways we cannot foresee.
>
> Out of this union can arise a healing of the long split between science and the humanities, and the schism between pure reason and practical life, both subjects of interest to Immanuel Kant. Science is not, as Galileo claimed, the only path to truth. History, the situated richness of the humanities, and the law are true as well.… This potential union invites a fuller understanding of ourselves creating our histories and our sacred, as we create our lives.[110]

---

[110] Kauffman, Stuart A., *Reinventing the Sacred: A new view of science, reason, and religion* (New York: Basic Books, 2009), *xii*.

Part II - Grounding Insight in Practical Ways

Grounding a vision demonstrates the interaction of imagination and doing—inspiration made tangible. The idea bears fruit. It worked! We did it! Hooray! It is easy to get excited about the achievement—particularly once what had been foreseen actually exists.

Getting people to embrace the tangible is much easier than persuading them of the value of something only yet imagined. It is far from effortless, of course. Like a pregnant woman, the visionary has nourished the fragile seed from conception to delivery.

And now something that was only a possibility has been born. The moment of birth elicits a sense of the miraculous and is a one-of-a-kind experience to fully savor.

Soon enough though, the realization of our responsibility for nurturing our creation begins to dawn. Now come the challenges of parenting, of providing an environment where our fragile notion can flourish. Many visionaries are better at the concept-birthing phase than they are at the day-in-day-out caretaking that follows.

So that stage often requires more help: employees, members, expert advisors, volunteers, sub-contractors, buyers, and devotees. Our wiser forbears understood that it takes a village to nourish new life properly. Also, this growing vision support team often needs some form of organization.

Part II explores the feet-on-the ground concerns that arise when what was only an abstraction before begins to exist in tangible ways. This stage is both demanding and precarious.

Peter Drucker, an organizational expert, points out how tricky it is to choose the right problem on which to focus: "Defining the problem may be the most important element in making effective decisions.… A wrong answer to the right problem can, as a rule, be repaired and salvaged. But the right answer to the wrong problem, that is very difficult to fix, if only because it is so difficult to diagnose."

Section II Contents

Chapter 8   Tackling the Challenges
Chapter 9   Identifying the Spectrum of Change
Chapter 10 Packaging a Vision that Resonates
Chapter 11 Engaging the Visionary Drive
Chapter 12 Seeing "Outside the Box"
Chapter 13 Developing Our Energetic Intelligence
Chapter 14 Practicing Visionary Leadership
Chapter 15 Building Supportive Environments

Chapter 8 - Tackling the Challenges

Walking the visionary path is a delicate balancing act, where each step can be tricky or fatal. Such halting steps require balancing paradoxical and metaphysical influences – to which normal life is largely blind.

A Pair of Giants—Galileo and Van Gogh

Galileo and Van Gogh occupied very different fields of expertise, yet both were soundly rejected during their lifetimes. Galileo was publicly discredited by the church and scientists of his day. Van Gogh's work was so unconventional he was totally ignored by the public.

These days, we recognize both men as visionaries, acknowledge their enormous contributions, and respect their accomplishments.

Science and painting both require very long periods of training before a person becomes proficient. Neither man can be faulted for their competence, but both were ostracized by their peers because they "went too far." Fortunately, each left a significant body of work that could speak for them to future generations.

Galileo was an Italian mathematician, astronomer, and physicist in the early 1600s. He played a major role in the Scientific Revolution that gave birth to modern science. Galileo's significant scientific discoveries are largely forgotten compared to his stance that science must not bow to social conventions and pressures.

Using a telescope improved by his modifications, Galileo made many important discoveries, like the moons of Jupiter. But he is best remembered for his defiance of the church and secular authorities. The conflict was quite political, forcing fellow scientists to take sides on the issue.

Galileo challenged the common assumption (and church doctrine) that placed the Earth at the center of the universe. He insisted that the Earth and other planets revolve around the Sun. He was found guilty of heresy in the Catholic Inquisition in 1633. Subsequently he was held under house arrest until his death about ten years later.

Van Gogh was a Dutch painter whose works display vibrant colors and bold brush strokes. His artwork is now appreciated for its strong emotional impact. Yet in today's culture, Van Gogh is more widely known for his insanity and cutting off his ear than for the artistic qualities of his paintings.

He was an alienated outsider, who did some of his best work while institutionalized for mental illness. He died by his own hand at age 37.

Van Gogh never sold any of his 2,000 paintings and drawings during his lifetime. Now his paintings are among the most widely recognized and expensive works of art worldwide, and he had a noticeable impact on the style of later artists. As Hugh Macleod notes however, "People are fond of spouting out the old cliché about how Van Gogh never sold a painting in his lifetime.

Somehow this example serves to justify to us, decades later, that there is somehow merit in utter failure. Perhaps, but the man did commit suicide."

These two men illustrate that even the giants cannot know if their efforts will survive or be appreciated later while they're pursuing their driving ambitions. Yet they kept working at their endeavors. Mostly, they are remembered more for their story than for what they actually accomplished.

It is easy for us, many years later, and from a different vantage point, to look at their contemporaries and wonder, how come everybody failed to notice their brilliance? But visionary leaps are nearly always out of phase with their times.

It is worth wondering about the extent to which we are making the same mistake with the not-yet-recognized giants in our midst today.

Sequential Stages in the Visionary Process

As in starting a business, grounding a vision proceeds through recognized stages: preparation, launch, reach out and sell the idea, growth, consolidation of gains, and succession.

If any enterprise or mass movement is to remain alive, it must find a way to stay fresh and relevant throughout the process. The notion needs to respond to changes in the marketplace of ideas, the larger society, and in the priorities of its supporters. Sooner or later, the original idea needs to evolve or it withers.

While an endeavor is getting launched, there is not much documentation being done. So the record of a movement's early history is usually constructed well after the fact. By then, the early tentative steps, dry holes, and rough course corrections have been forgotten or varnished over.

The full progression from hazy idea to mass movement is unlikely to be seen until looked at from the vantage point of history. By that time, the vision that prevails represents a mix of historic facts and myth that add a false patina of inevitability.

Stages of the Visionary Process:
Roughly in this order, although a specific idea may not reach the later stages

1. Period of preparation (or within a domain of interest) includes developing the requisite personal qualities and skills
2. The vision experience itself, abrupt or gradual
3. Commitment to the vision or mandate
4. Leave the beaten path; withdraw and disengage from prior worldview; can be early or late, brief or long term
5. Finding one's unique voice; can be early or late
6. Initial efforts to package the vision and develop a coherent message
7. Inner circle of supporters forms; early adopters get involved
8. Missionary phase—selling the notion; manage growth

9. Encounter mix of acceptance and resistance in the larger arena
10. Challenges of grounding the undertaking; ebb and flow of clarity and progress; encounter backlash
11. Refining the message and organization (ongoing)
12. Early stages of structure and organization develop—followers, proponents, adversaries
13. Popular acceptance, growth, and expansion; reaches wider audience or secondary applications; spin-offs
14. Reinvention or factional splits (optional); abandon undertaking; can be early or late
15. Stories about the founder and early movement develop; myth and popular lore
16. Master level concerns of the visionary or core group members (optional)
17. Decline, replaced, outgrown (possible)

Are there exceptions to this order? Of course. But this sequence is fairly predictable for the life cycle of a vision, however short or long that may be. Skipped stages usually have to be worked out at some point, or they could lead to insurmountable roadblocks later. Bear in mind that the visionary path is also likely to be a lifestyle choice, influencing all of the person's decisions, not just those related to a specific vision.

The progression is not always apparent in the short term since this sequence can play out over a very long time frame. Also, the person who launched the idea has often moved on to other visions or creative endeavors before the fate of their original vision was known. There could be a cast of characters left behind who continue to carry the ball.

Eric Hoffer describes this progression in *The True Believer*.

> A movement is pioneered by men of words, materialized by fanatics and consolidated by men of action. It is usually an advantage to a movement, and perhaps a prerequisite for its endurance that these roles should be played by different men succeeding each other as conditions require. When the same person or persons (or the same type of person) leads a movement from its inception to maturity, it usually ends in disaster.[111]

Most of these stages follow a natural progression and act as markers or turning points for a particular person's journey. It bears repeating that the visionary path is a lifelong journey; so specific visions or missions can, and do, come and go. Some are brief, whereas others can involve huge support teams, extending over multiple lifetimes.

As the visionary progresses along the path, the fate of any particular vision rarely defines their movement, choices, or overall contribution.

---

[111] Hoffer, Eric, *The True Believer: Thoughts on the nature of mass movements* (New York: Harper & Row, 1951), 146.

The visionary path is a maturing process, so each stage or step forward indicates growth. Grounding and building activities represent the middle phase, when both the notion and the visionary are growing up. In this process of growth and change, elements build on each other.

Prior components are not gone, but gradually evolve into something which incorporates the old into what is developing. It often requires a sense of history to reveal many of the factors in play. The sequence builds on and incorporates prior stages as it moves toward wholeness. Ken Wilber describes the process in *The Simple Feeling of Being*.

In this developmental or evolutionary unfolding, each successive level does not jettison or deny the previous level, but rather includes and embraces it, just as atoms are included in molecules, which are included in cells, which are included in organisms. Each level is a whole that is part of a larger whole (each level or structure is a whole/part or holon). In other words, each evolutionary unfolding transcends but includes its predecessor(s), with Spirit transcending and including absolutely everything.[112]

Every Stage Is Part of a Cycle

The visionary path is a lawful process because it corresponds to mechanisms already in place—like brain physiology or the pull of the tides. Each participant experiences roughly the same progression through the stages, without regard for the subject matter involved.

For example, a young child rolls over before crawling, crawls before walking, and walks before running. Successive stages may go faster or slower in a specific case, but their order is, by and large, fixed. Those on the visionary path pass through some stages at a different rate than others—and with greater or lesser ease of execution.

However, on careful examination, even the "overnight successes" probably were plodding through the stages long before the world noticed them.

Something that is necessary or accurate during one stage is just as likely to be untrue or irrelevant at another. Even well-meaning advice could easily steer travelers wrong. Each of these trailblazers must discern from their own sensibilities *what works for their* situation.

The span between the initial vision experience and its being accepted could take many years, so the thrust of the visionary's contribution inevitably evolves over time. At what point is it possible to nail down the definitive version? How soon is it apparent what the contribution can truly mean? Or whether the idea prevailed?

---

[112] Wilber, Ken, *The Simple Feeling of Being: Embracing your true nature* (Boston: Shambhala, 2004), 69.

A clever way of acknowledging the evolution of his theories is demonstrated by Ken Wilber, whose books span more than 30 years. His later writings refer to himself as "early Wilber" to distinguish what he wrote previously on a topic from his current position about it. He counters his early opinions the same way he would argue with a third party.

The Visionary Path Is Future Oriented

Forerunners look ahead, not in the way a fortune teller or oracle would, but as an architect would. They see what "could be." Visionary thinkers are the architects of the future. Unlike idle dreamers, they set to work constructing the possibilities they see.

Any type of thinking ahead of the curve is trying to influence the future. But Hoffer points out a distinction between the way different philosophical positions look at both the present and what lies ahead. Either of these styles could be found within the ranks of visionaries.

> The radical and the reactionary loathe the present. They see it as an aberration and a deformity. Both are ready to proceed ruthlessly and recklessly with the present, and both are hospitable to the idea of self-sacrifice. Wherein do they differ? Primarily in their view of the malleability of man's nature. The radical has a passionate faith in the infinite perfectibility of human nature. He believes that by changing man's environment and by perfecting a technique of soul forming, a society can be wrought that is wholly new and unprecedented. The reactionary does not believe that man has unfathomed potentialities for good in him. If a stable and healthy society is to be established, it must be patterned after the proved models of the past. He sees the future as a glorious restoration rather than an unprecedented innovation.[113]

I would argue there is yet another approach, which is spelled out in these pages. By building on the force of inspiration and our ability to learn and modify strategies as we go, it is possible to transcend some of the limitations of human nature.

Our innate sense of purpose can guide us forward. This approach is based on the infusion of insight and its gradual integration into how we operate.

Tightrope Walking with No Clothes On

Walking the visionary path is a delicate balancing act, where each step can be tricky or fatal. Any misstep could disrupt the forward trajectory or bring the embryonic endeavor crashing down. It is not simply about solving the practical concerns.

Such halting steps require balancing paradoxical and metaphysical influences — to which normal life is largely blind.

---

[113] *Op. cit.*, Hoffer, 73.

Maintain a Balance Between:
- Certainty *and* self-doubt—between "I know" *and* "I don't know"
- The vision's requirements *and* society's expectations or needs
- One's inner states, which are abstract, *and* the external practicalities
- The freedom the mission requires *and* the existing rules and standards
- Being engaged with the undertaking *and* disengaged enough to be receptive to abrupt shifts and surprises
- Short-term choices *and* the big-picture, long-term implications
- Normal reasoning *and* an expanded view of what is real or possibilities that are not yet shared by many
- One's solitary self-interest *and* the needs of other people (or as part of humanity)
- What is foreseeable and what is doable—considering costs, resources, available time, and alternatives

Gradually someone's prior and normal way of thinking gives way to a more integrated approach. The individual comes to see how all the disparate elements of the broader view are necessary and can work together. It includes accepting the mix of success and failure as essential for grounding the vision.

The visionary path makes no secret of being high risk or of its staggering attrition rate. It is not unusual for leading-edge explorers to get lost or overwhelmed when moving very far off the beaten path.

Many of life's supports previously taken for granted are no longer available: resources, small comforts of home, encouragement, breaks from the ongoing and grueling demands.

A forerunner cannot pop over to the shopping center and restock. However, they get considerable satisfaction from finding what is needed to survive through their ingenuity and resourcefulness. Concepts like efficiency or self-sufficiency take on a new meaning on some level, as the person starts to think and feel like a pioneer.

Finding Solutions that Work

The number of thorny issues to work out that weren't evident during the vision is sobering. Albert Einstein said, "In theory, theory and practice are the same. In practice, they are not."

To make the abstract tangible calls for a daunting series of untried steps that were not apparent at the outset. And each step involves taking a closer look at how the vision and real life can be meshed.

Atul Gawande breaks problems into three categories in *The Checklist Manifesto*. The visionary path encounters all three.

> [Scientists have noted] three different kinds of problems in the world: the simple, the complicated, and the complex. Simple problems are ones like

> baking a cake from a mix. There is a recipe. Sometimes there are a few basic techniques to learn, but once these are mastered, following the recipe brings a high likelihood of success.
>
> Complicated problems are ones like sending a rocket to the moon. They can sometimes be broken down into a series of simple problems. But there is no straightforward recipe. Success frequently requires multiple people, often multiple teams, and specialized expertise. ...
>
> Complex problems are ones like raising a child. Once you learn how to send a rocket to the moon, you can repeat the process with other rockets and perfect it. One rocket is like another rocket. But not so with raising a child....
>
> Every child is unique. Although raising one child may provide experience, it does not guarantee success with the next child.... And this brings up another feature of complex problems: their outcomes remain highly uncertain.[114]

Taking the visionary path is not so much about changing particular habits, or finding novel answers, as shifting one's overall perspective. Those on that path are not satisfied simply to find a solution to a particular problem. But they also feel the need to understand events in a more comprehensive way.

At some point, the person's labors move outside the scope of the zeitgeist—pointing to a future iteration of what exists already. (Or it could be tied to some small pocket of it.) Doing so taps into a larger scale, with fewer limitations but also many more unknowns.

That development trumps the visionary's prior loyalties. By taking steps to realize his or her vision, the person has been growing into a larger vision, a more universal and less personal vision. They have embodied it, and the process as well.

Supporting the Venture

When matters related to the vision are primary, other concerns are pushed to the side. But issues about money cannot be avoided. While they are secondary, they refuse to stay in the background. There are always bills to pay and choices that depend on financial resources.

To complicate matters, money is so entangled with our reward systems that it often triggers deep-seated emotional reactions, as well as fiscal ones. Promoting a vision requires dealing with financial realities in many different forms. It is easy to get caught up in them and find the tail wagging the dog.

The biblical quote by Jesus "Render to Caesar the things that are Caesar's, and to God the things that are God's"[115] can be interpreted as dealing fairly with the

---

[114] Gawande, Atul, *The Checklist Manifesto: How to get things right* (New York: Henry Holt and Company, 2011), 49.

conflicts between matters of inspiration (the vision and inner life) and the pressures of everyday life (external and material demands). It is a tricky balancing act, but they must both receive their due. Csikszentmihalyi speaks to this recurring tension.

> As powerful as poetry is, it does not resolve all one's problems. Mastering a symbolic style—be it poetry or physics—does not guarantee one will also bring order to those events that lie outside the rules of the domain. Poets and physicists may bask in the beautiful order of their craft as long as they are working at it, but they are as vulnerable as the rest of us when they step back into everyday life and have to confront family problems, time pressures, illness and poverty. This is why it becomes so tempting to invest more and more energy in one's work and forget everyday life.[116]

The lengthy time necessary for many visions to coalesce and gain widespread acceptance creates a dilemma for the visionary. How can one support one's self and their commitments while trying to get traction?

Often the person's prior career and money-making sources dry up as launching their vision becomes more time-consuming. There simply is not enough time and energy to pursue prior obligations while serving the vision.

Many of life's demands recede in influence as the vision comes to dominate the visionary's time and attention. Some prior pursuits fall away because they are seen as distracting.

And like a growing child, those vision-based demands will increase—and must be met. Being obliged to spend too much effort chasing money distracts from their higher concerns. Many a noble vision has foundered in these stormy seas.

Being able to create and be true to one's vision is fully engaging. It disdains distractions. Making a living usually competes with spontaneous creativity—divergent priorities. It is crucial from the outset to stay focused on what is coming together through fresh insights.

Then one must act on the impetus without delay. Having to chase dollars at the same time can easily compromise the main event.

The visionary process tends toward simplicity and a sharpened focus. However, the field of interest dictates what the bare minimum or optimal resources might be.

A philosopher or mathematician might only require a pen and paper; whereas a scientist needs a laboratory with sophisticated equipment; or an artist requires supplies used for their art form—and maybe the right light.

---

[115] Mark 12:17, *Bible*, English Standard Version, quoted from Jesus.
[116] *Op. cit.*, Csikszentmihalyi, *Creativity*, 252.

Securing Needed Revenue:
- Visionary's resources—usually the first consumed; earnings through paid employment; speaking, writing, teaching
- Debt—borrowing against future revenue that must be repaid
- Resources of friends and family (whether given or borrowed)
- Charity—whether begged or it is offered without being asked; passing the hat
- Bystanders, patrons, members, fans and benefactors; fund-raising and donations
- Chicanery or selling snake oil—fleecing followers or the public
- Establish an organization (possibly a non-profit or arm of another organization) for fund-raising and to promote the cause
- Grants or loans to the organization, although most will not conform to established lending practices since might not be profit-based
- Investors and angels—mostly for business start-ups or innovations with commercial potential

Until a visionary has reached some level of success, getting funding is almost impossible. Society at large, including foundations and philanthropists, needs to do a better job of embracing and supporting the originators of new ideas earlier in the process.

The most truly creative and promising individuals, and their ideas, are usually discarded precisely because they are too weird or deviant to fit into the mold.

Even if the visionary has access to abundant resources, the "velvet handcuffs" that too often come with them are likely to inhibit the visionary process. More than likely, a relatively comfortable lifestyle has to be left behind (temporarily or permanently) in order to totally cement the visionary's change of perspective and priorities.

Later, with sufficient acceptance, the distractions of money and assets take a different form—too much instead of too little. Managing one's stuff competes with keeping primary attention on the mission. How to handle the organization's resources is a defining challenge of any developing enterprise.

Even if the visionary might not be tempted or sucked in by their earthly goods, others among the followers are likely to be. So its hypnotic influence will always remain an issue for the mission.

Hanging onto Outdated Thinking and Assumptions

When our focus is on going forward, it is easy to overlook whatever is holding us back. Part of the task is not just to challenge the *status quo* but to demonstrate the new idea in action. The visionary must throw overboard whatever smells of discredited assumptions or prior habits that do not serve their larger view.

A visionary cannot be stuck in the past—part of what they serve is a brighter future. Much of the difficulty in grounding the vision comes from trying to supplant the prior frame of reference.

Visionary thinkers are the voice of change, of new ideas, so must be particularly vigilant about preventing seeds of inertia and old thinking from creeping into their own approach.

The visionary must commit to ruthlessly examining his or her ideas and assumptions in light of what is coming into focus via the vision. Those unconscious or unrecognized influences from the past that "call one's tune" need to be recognized for what they are.

As Lana J. Ford said, "In each moment of confusion, we have the opportunity to let go of old habits, prejudices, outdated belief patterns and conceptions of the past and the future. In this way, we set in motion the possibility of getting in touch with the magic that gave us birth."

More precisely, emptying the old stuff out of the mental and emotional closets creates more room for what is coming in fresh. Besides, on the visionary path too much baggage is a liability (How much luggage can you lug?). Wise counsel comes from Mark Twain, "What gets us into trouble is not what we do not know. It is what we know for sure that just ain't so."

When a person disengages from superficial levels of awareness, the clarity that is glimpsed literally changes their brain patterns. Such experiences move a person out of their customary neural pathways—their embedded ruts. And they establish new connections. Those new neural pathways permit, dare say demand, one's behavior to change.

~ Ligatures of Devotion ~
A BonBon ~ Faith Lynella

Inspiring!... Powerful!... Life changing!... Motivating!... A moving call to action!...

The speech was a knockout. Everyone in the audience was touched, moved, and challenged. To a person, they got the message and vowed to follow the call. They were persuaded, willing to make the necessary and desired changes.

Then, to a person... nothing happened. Nothing at all!

While it is important to kindle the vision and muster the resolve, that is the easy part. All of that motivation achieves nothing unless you also cut your ligatures of devotion. They bind you and blind you to achieving heartfelt desires, challenging goals, or a greater vision.

These strands may be small, but there are many of them:
- Habits, those things you do routinely without thinking or attention
- Cold slogans and clichés that have long served you, but which have lost their relevance
- Relationships, along with their related expectations, that have ceased to grow and nurture
- Unexamined assumptions
- Dogmatic and slavish devotion to the past and the familiar
- Ways you regularly waste your time, energy, money, and opportunities
- Causes and commitments that no longer suit you or serve you
- Short-sighted values and priorities
- Passivity, indifference, and inertia
- Self-defeating behaviors that repeatedly lead to unintended, yet predictable, consequences
- Irresponsible desires and activities
- Early childhood programming that you're never examined or outgrown

Each of these ties can be changed or broken in a moment's effort—once you pay heed to their restrictive pull. But you must first notice their presence, their negative influences. They are your *status quo*. Each of them asserts a powerful drag that keeps everything (and you) just the same. Their tendrils hold you, tied like a prisoner of your own past and unexamined habits.

Whenever you break those ligatures of faded devotion, you are like Gulliver, severing his puny bonds. After you're freed from those many small ties, you can move forward—toward your beckoning goals.

Your devotion to many of the old and cold connections doesn't serve you. Inquire, "Does this link bind me to strengths or to limitations?" Sever those restrictive ligatures. Each snip acts as a liberation! Finally, your resolves and desires can move you forward decisively! At last, whatever has inspired you is within your grasp.

From *BonBons to Sweeten Your Daily Life*. Or from *More BonBons*

Prior failures and disappointment need not short-circuit our efforts to move toward our desires. Colin Wilson cautions, "Human beings do not realize the extent to which their own sense of defeat prevents them from doing things they could do perfectly well. The peak experience induces the recognition that your own powers are far greater than you imagined them."

A particular warning relates to the Van Gogh Fallacy. It is an invalid argument to say because Van Gogh lived his life in obscurity, yet was later recognized as a great artist, that other artists who are also living in obscurity are also likely to be recognized as great artists later. Obscurity and rejection are not indications of eventual success.

This trap does not just catch artists, however. Its lapse of logic could ensnare anyone who is struggling for recognition, and expects the future to prove them right. Such misguided optimism can interfere with sufficient roll-up-the-sleeves efforts in the short term.

Grounding a Vision Is Tough

Get Ready for the Slings and Arrows

Visionaries are accustomed to rejection. Being spurned goes with the territory. They usually take an unpopular stand (or at least an untested one). Since the old order seldom sees any use for what they bring to the party, he or she needs a tough skin to deal with being rebuffed, without taking it personally.

As Jonathan Swift wryly put it, "When a true genius appears in this world, you may know him by this sign, that the dunces are all in confederacy against him."

On a similar note, George Bernard Shaw said, "All great truths begin as blasphemies." So the greater the level of truth, the more likely it is to ruffle the feathers of those who truly believe in what is being challenged. Firm resistance and retaliation are to be expected from those who are most invested in what is being challenged.

The visionary sometimes triggers fear or outright opposition in those holding power. When authorities feel questioned or threatened, they can be formidable enemies. The truth in the pioneer's heart will sustain them when the *status quo* army gathers momentum and starts harping with epithets and labels.

But the visionary needs their own regiment of advocates, too. (And these are not the same as followers, who like the new idea but are not in the cross hairs.)

If at all possible, visionaries should avoid going it alone. They need to find at least one tried-and-true kindred visionary spirit (or a supportive inner circle) who can prop them up with love and appreciation when the rest of the 3-D world is clucking to each other about the resident nut case. This will almost never be a professional therapist. Many widely recognized visionaries have some "crazy" skeletons in their closets.

Clarity of Expression

If a vision is to catch on, it must be communicated in such a way that it makes sense to listeners. And for it to even be heard or considered, the visionary needs to find those who are open to it.

Peoples with closed hearts or minds are highly resistant to change of any sort. So, advocates should carefully craft their message in order for it to open minds and engage interest—well before making their pitch.

William Harmon said, "A belief system may be defined as open to the extent that new data can enter and affect existing beliefs. A person will be open to information insofar as possible, but will unconsciously reject it, screen it out, or alter it insofar as is necessary to ward off threat and anxiety. The closed mind can distort the world and narrow it down to whatever extent is needed to serve these protective goals and still preserve the illusion of understanding it."

Creators toil tirelessly to solve a problem or to make a breakthrough, assuming all the while that what they're currently addressing is the tough part. But "making it fly" is often just an escalator to a whole new set of challenges. The breakthrough is not the moment of triumph they expected.

It actually ushers in the next phase when they discover the world is neither ready, nor eagerly waiting, for what they've so painstakingly brought to the fore. Worse yet, the next challenges will certainly include the *status quo* protecting itself from intrusion.

As a literal example, consider the Wright Brothers. Figuring out how to make the first flying machine was easy compared with the years of wrangling and jumping through bureaucratic hoops that followed. For a long time, they could not get patents, despite the undeniable originality of their invention.

Many years of litigation and character assassination resulted in their creative energies being almost totally consumed by non-productive rear-actions.

Visionaries Are a Hardy Breed

As careers go, life as a visionary can be counted as high risk and high stress. As with any group, some individuals handle the difficulties better than others. But to the extent these non-conformists fail in what they are trying to achieve, they are unlikely to blame it on the stress. Such individuals are not surprised that it is difficult. They are geared up for it to bring out their best efforts.

Psychologist Salvatore Maddi studied the long-term effect of stress. Based on twelve years of data and a large subject pool, he was able to identify three key traits of those who thrived despite high-stress conditions. It is not a stretch to point out that that by Maddi's measures, visionaries are hardy indeed. Maddi's research is described by Taylor Clark in *Nerve*.

> What was the difference between those who crumbled and those who flourished? Maddi found three common themes, a trio of attitudes about stress that he has dubbed the 'Three C's.'… All displayed commitment; instead of running away as stress mounted, they remained involved with the world around them, actively pursuing goals no matter how tough things got. Second, they showed a strong sense of control; they recognized that even in the roughest circumstances, they were never helpless. And finally, these resilient workers saw challenge in their ever-changing world; they could mentally

transform a crisis from a threat into an opportunity for growth.... Maddi has grouped his Three C's of commitment, control, and challenge under a single umbrella term: hardiness.[117]

Looking for the Balance in Execution

The broad-scoped vision is innately connected to the heart and emotions, as well as to the intellect, because it comes from a realm where heart, mind, and emotions function as one — in integrated balance. There is essentially no physical component during a vision, but it becomes an essential component later as a person grounds the vision.

The heart perspective is expansive by nature, tending toward the largest, most inclusive, scope possible (feminine, yin energy). Whereas the rational mind is more reductive and analytical as it narrows focus in order to act (masculine, yang energy).

The tension between them provides the fullness — which will collapse if the complementary tension cannot be maintained. The interplay of these expansive and contractive forces plays out in the visionary's efforts to give life to the abstract notion.

Each of us customarily prefers one of the three modes over the others: action (physical), ideas (mental), or emotions (feeling). In addition, modern culture is biased toward the rational perspective and has rigged the reward system in that direction. Yet grounding a vision requires that each and all of the modes be brought into concrete expression.

Much of the interaction comes into focus while the package for the vision is being created and launched. It continues to be a factor over the life of the mission. The body's role in grounding cannot be exaggerated for it supplies the hands-on approach to manipulate material reality.

The post-vision, "make it happen" phase puts a premium on the interaction of the three abilities. A sincere heart tempers the drift toward unbridled practicality and furthers the "innocence of perception" that keeps ideas fresh.

Tensions among the mental, physical, and emotional components sustain a dynamic balance — the dance of active give-and-take that prevents settling into an overconfident rut. Keeping creative freshness alive is key because it (in part) distinguishes visionary undertakings from mundane ones.

Over time, the visionary's personality style or circumstances inevitably favor one mode over the others. So the other modes could drift to back burner, though maybe not intentionally. Many of the common challenges that arise are a result of the mental-emotional-physical equilibrium having been compromised.

---

[117] Clark, Taylor, *Nerve: Poise under pressure, serenity under stress, and the brave new science of fear and cool*, (New York: Little, Brown and Company, 2011), 115.

To bring them back into balance again takes substantial and sustained effort. But for the same reasons it got off kilter, the resulting problems are likely to pass unnoticed until they are serious.

It is worth noting we are likely to give ourselves credit for being logical, even when the emotions are determining our choices. Rational behavior may be more of a figment than a reality in determining what we do. The dynamics of the brain's role in reaching non-rational answers is described by Russell H. Granger in *7 Triggers to Yes*.

> [In studies using brain imaging, Dr. Dean] Shibata discovered that people use the emotional parts of the brain to make what they believe to be rational decisions. He found that the emotional context helps you make the best choice, often in a split second—long before the rational centers of the brain seem able to come into play. Researchers recently made another stunning discovery. When the emotional center of the brain, the amygdala, is damaged, people are incapable of making most decisions, even though their rational brain sites are fully functional.[118]

Resistance to Change

The Latin phrase, *status quo* means "the way things stand now" or "the existing state of affairs." For change to happen, there has to be considerable energy applied to move the unmoving.

The *status quo* has inertia on its side. "Inertia" is defined as the resistance to change, and it includes the dampening effects of both apathy and stagnation.

Resistance to change is a serious problem that shows up in all manner of forms. Change agents need to figure out how to get over it, or around, or through it, or it will hold any new ideas hostage.

Common Sources of Resistance:

- **Inertia**. Guy's law of enchantment: People at rest will remain at rest, and people in motion will remain moving in the same direction unless an outside enchanter acts upon them. Existing relationships, satisfaction with the *status quo*, laziness, and busyness hinder change.

- **Hesitation to reduce options**. People like, or at least think they like, the ability to make free choices and the availability of a breadth of choices.... Thus making a decision results in the reduction of options, and the prospect of this outcome can scare people.

- **Fear of making a mistake**. People may think that as long as they haven't made a choice, they **haven't made a mistake**. Once they make a choice, they're either right or wrong. The fear of finding out can make people

---

[118] Granger, Russell H., *7 Triggers to Yes: The new science behind influencing people's decisions*, (New York: McGraw Hill, 2008), 48.

reluctant to make a choice—although not making a choice is itself a choice.

- **Lack of role models**. If there are no role models, people don't have a behavior to copy. So they hesitate to give your cause a try. This is why early adopters are so important....
- **Your cause sucks!** There is no other way to put this: You or your cause may suck. Then people are right to be reluctant. God forbid that this is true, but it's sometimes the case.[119]

Entropy and Confusion

The counterweight to growth and progress is entropy, the natural tendency of energy to run down. To inject new ideas into a system requires a significant amount of additional energy to be subsequently added. Unless there is enough fresh energy added to maintain it, any idea or project defaults to inertia.

The more innovative efforts actively being pursued (or permitted), the greater the vitality of the entire culture or field. That is why visionaries exert an impact disproportionate to their numbers. Visionaries are energized! They are passionate! The degree of dynamic force offsets some of the forces of decline and stagnation.

If change agents expect people to go along with their new idea, they must be crystal clear about the direction the public should go with it. If there is any confusion whatsoever about what to do or why to do it, nobody is going to bother to do anywhere with the new idea (or product).

The visionary's message must be forthright and clear to himself or herself first, so they can make it clear to would-be beneficiaries. *What looks like resistance is often a lack of clarity by the receiver*. People don't "get it."

It is up to the visionary to keep refining the communication and the delivery about its value until certain kinds of resistance hardly come up any more.

Backlash Is Inevitable

Even when progress is the order of the day, don't be surprised by the backlash that follows any gains. Clear sailing is likely to be temporary. The most significant changes visionaries introduce go beyond superficial matters, often touching upon deeply-held values or beliefs.

These cut across personal choices, even if they are not often thought about consciously. Core values and widely shared cultural norms are remarkably difficult to change.

---

[119] Kawasaki, Guy, *Enchantment: The art of changing hearts, minds, and actions* (New York: Portfolio/Penguin, 2011), 71-2.

Even when basic agreement is reached, it takes some time for the new notion to trickle down and become wholehearted acceptance, or for it to reflect a new way of behaving. Until a shift happens, the prior, "natural," and familiar ways keep reasserting themselves. Also, there is a pendulum-like movement, during which the change in flux swings back and forth between old and new — until one prevails.

Of course, various forms of active backlash can arise as well. Those who have the most invested in the *status quo* will fight back if they feel threatened by the new notion. Contrary forces place a barrage of obstacles in the way of change agents.

It is a mistake to think those who resist change are not motivated; they are just not motivated *to change*. In most cases, they do not see the need for something different than what exists already.

Also, they might be unwilling to deal with the likely secondary costs, learning curves, disruptions, and readjustments the proposed change would bring with it.

Let's be honest. Change *is* risky and Seth Godin is correct to say so (in *Tribes*). But the balance of forces is shifting, and that can serve the change agents.

> Our culture works hard to prevent change. We have long had systems and organizations and standards designed to dissuade people from challenging the *status quo*. We enforce our systems and call whoever is crazy enough to challenge them a heretic. And society enforces the standards by burning its heretics at the stake, either literally or figuratively.
>
> But the world has changed a lot. There are heretics everywhere you look. It's so asymmetrical that burning heretics isn't particularly effective any longer. As a result, more and more people — good people, people on a mission, people with ideas that matter — are stepping forward and making a difference.
> Just about every system, whether it's political, financial, or even religious, has become asymmetrical. The process has turned upside down: scale isn't the same as power; in fact, scale can hurt.[120]

Discomfort about possible complications is a factor in the public willingness to acquire the latest whiz-bang gadgets, no matter how wonderful they seem. For some, "new" is a plus factor; but for others it is a minus factor — regardless of what is being offered. People tend to stick with their style of reaction. (See Innovation, Chapter 9.)

Sticking with what is in place has familiarity and habit on its side. So, those who have no reason to care about the new notion tend to be reactive — against anything that disturbs what they consider the natural order of things.

---

[120] Godin, Seth, *Tribes; We need you to lead us* (New York: Penguin Group, 2008), 71-2.

> Why, during radical revolutions, do some people rapidly discard their old, erroneous ways of thinking, whereas others hold tenaciously to the prevailing dogma? Historians, sociologists, philosophers, and psychologists have all proposed answers to the question.... In spite of numerous hypotheses, and
>
>> considerable empirical research, there is no satisfactory answer to the question of why some people rebel and why others, just as zealously defend the status quo.[121]

Even if people do not specifically dislike the new notion, many are likely to block it because they fear the disruption or confusion it might cause in the solid future they expect.

The Flame and the Vessel

Vision resembles fire. There is a *spark*. It *burns* bright or low, can *ignite* devotion and long-term efforts, can be *lit* in others, can *burn out* and grow cold. It gives off light to see by. Fire sometimes gets out of control—to the point of being a destructive force. If not handled carefully, someone can get *burned*, or their fruits could turn to *ashes*.

The spark of inspiration that resembles fire points to an eternal conundrum—the Flame and the Vessel Paradox. Someone can share their bright light directly with others. But if their light is to exist for a larger circle or after the person dies, there must also be a vessel to hold the flame and keep it lit. An inspired person could also be considered a flame, as the voice of a powerful idea.

Flame inspires, vessel preserves. Vessel acts as a lamp, protecting the flame and giving it staying power. Vessel provides the structure for the flame, which can include an organization or individuals in various supportive roles. Vessel can take a variety of forms: writings, teachings, stories, practices, ceremonies, programs, and facilities. Some are tangible, others are not.

All flame, no vessel, is vulnerable. All vessel, no flame, is merely doctrine. Both, together with appropriate boundaries, is the ideal.

The functions of flame and vessel are fundamentally different, but complement each other. Flame can be shared so it ignites further insights in more people. Vessel does what is required to ground and protect the light, the flame. Each plays an important interdependent role that keeps the vision influential.

In the case of spiritual leaders, vessel takes the form of a religion or sect. The form the vessel takes is known as its dogma.

Vessel cannot create new flame or insights. It simply maintains them; and in a variety of forms. But the vessel should never be mistaken for the flame itself. Vessel is almost entirely engaged with the normal everyday world. Flame burns

---

[121] Sulloway, Frank J., *Born to Rebel: Birth order, family dynamics and creative lives* (New York: Vintage Books, 1997), xi.

with the spark of big T truth, but flame is very hard to explain. However, watering it down too much would essentially change its nature and could easily put the truth of it out.

The solid nature of the vessel competes with the flickery nature of what is otherworldly. Vessel's role is to make the flame somewhat intelligible and accessible, no matter how much the amorphous quality of inspiration makes such a translation difficult.

There is an unavoidable tension between them—like mixing oil and water. If vessel (structure) becomes too dominant, it ends up being all edifice and rules— at the expense of any flame that remains.

Over time, a vessel can become quite unbending and crush out signs of flame (even by the founder) that are not officially sanctioned. Keepers of the flame might feel that defending "the truth" requires them to fight for it, taking intolerance to the extreme with anything that doesn't comport with the official version.

What starts with a desire to be of service often morphs into dogmatic tactics to stamp out heresies and to maintain doctrinal purity. While many vessels take on the trappings of self-righteousness, not all do so.

The best vessels permit and encourage people to take a spark of the flame and make it *live within themselves*. When believers are encouraged to become more flame-like, they model the original inspiration through *their own* dynamic and responsive words and deeds.

They, too, are able to share and interpret the spark in ways they find meaningful. It keeps the notion organic, alive, and more pertinent than a static belief. It avoids idolatry, while keeping the flame growing and relevant.

As with any type of paradox, the resolution is not to choose one side *or* the other (or to split the difference). One must aim for a broader, more encompassing view, where each side is a component and necessary part of something larger still.

Flame does, indeed, need some protection or it will go out. The vessel also provides the visionary with practical support and protection that grounds the vision. In that way, flame gives vessel its purpose and meaning.

The Flame versus Vessel Paradox is not just an issue for religious fields (Chapter 18). It could develop among politicians, artists, philosophers, or anyone with followers who think they have a corner on what is true.

As we look for ways to nourish visionary and unorthodox thinking, we must also be attentive for the weeds of rigid dogma that so often sprout up nearby.

Mental and Emotional Challenges

Looks Kinda Crazy

Visionaries are often stereotyped as the mad scientist or the idle dreamer who is vague and forgetful. However, such stereotypes are wildly off the mark in most cases. Still, it has to be admitted that this process exacts a heavy psychological toll on almost everyone who is called to it. What they committed to could push someone to the breaking point — and maybe beyond.

Sooner or later, the visionary questions his or her own sanity or ability to cope — just as those around them, who have been puzzled by their choices, have been doing all along.

Well-meaning but clueless advice is likely to confuse the fledgling visionary, prolong their distress, or result in aimless wandering. Sometimes, this process "plays with your head." Many of the signs of nakedness (and there are lots of them; see Appendix A) could be viewed as pathological by medical or mental health professionals.

It is not the specific behavior that seems "off," but the extreme versions that set off their alarms. Visionaries not only go to extremes, but they embrace contradictory extremes. Efforts to assist an individual to become "well adjusted" are usually at odds with time-honored stages of the visionary process. And the more "progress" a person has made to disengage from convention, the more it reinforces the professional's certainty there is a problem.

Also, we know too many stories of creative types who went over the edge, like Hemmingway, Van Gogh, or Plath. So this route is suspect. Besides, "it is not what normal people do."

Forms of "Maladjustment:"
- Neurotic and exaggerated emotional states
- Physical illnesses, worn down
- Anger at injustice; confrontations with authority in highly visible ways; acting out
- Unpredictable; loss of interest in "normal" concerns; irresponsible
- Psychotic breaks; out of touch with reality
- Hot and cold periods with wide mood swings; manic-depressive stages
- Withdrawal from everyday life — disengaged and involved with intense preoccupations
- Abrupt changes of priorities; renounces various responsibilities; high-risk or self-destructive behavior
- Disregard for rules and "appropriate" behavior
- Exhibitionism

NOTICE: I do not advocate these as ideals or proof of progress on the visionary path. I wish to point out, however, these behaviors are *not necessarily* pathologies. They can be and are interpreted differently when the context is acknowledged and "normal" is not the only standard being pursued.

More importantly, this is not intended as an effort to excuse bad behavior under the guise of creative license. It is imperative that visionaries take responsibility for his or her behavior and its impact on those around them. Failures in that regard are regrettable and do harm to everyone involved. Never should others suffer due to the visionary's obstinacy, irresponsibility to their own obligations, or driven behavior.

When someone sacrifices the goodwill and trust of others in service to their own vision, something has gone very, very wrong. Outbursts are not evidence of mastery, but rather show where more inner work still needs to be done.

All persons on the visionary path need to attend to maintaining his or her mental, physical, and emotional stability. However, I urge caution about whom to rely on for such assistance. It is my sincere desire that a better understanding of the visionary process will develop more effective systems of support for possible side-effects of the creative process.

Remaining Virtuous Is Vital

The visionary has a special responsibility to represent the vision entrusted to him or her honorably. Visions arise in a space where integrity is an inherent quality of what's seen. So bringing it into our commonly-shared reality comes with the responsibility to keep the transcendent qualities intact (to the extent possible). To treat ideals as secondary or inconsequential is anathema!

The visionary can and will occasionally fall short through weaknesses and carelessness. However, failing in execution is very different than putting expediency or self-centric goals ahead of the integrity of the mission.

Intentional lapses of integrity there are indefensible because they destroy trust and the link to inspiration. Integrity is always a priority and never up for debate. Honesty and credibility should be the standard in all dealings with the public.

It is as unfair for the public to expect perfection as it is for the visionary (as a public figure) to imply that he or she never fails or makes mistakes. We are all human, and as such, we understand having trouble pushing back from the dinner table without a second slice of pie, or failing to keep the garage uncluttered. These are not on a par with moral lapses.

The Crucible of Mastery

Visionaries who reach an advanced stage of achievement can often point back to a darkest hour, when everything in the outer world seemed most against them. They tasted defeat. They doubted they could prevail—to the point of giving up.

But in desperate straits when everything seemed lost, the person found additional strength of character or discovered a decisive new voice within.

The person was reduced to their essence—a state of near-total nakedness. By reaching inner bedrock they found something solid and unaffected by life's difficulties. When they come out the other side, the newfound fluency continued to grow within them.

Afterwards, compared to that monumental wipe-out, other obstacles lose their ability to strike fear in them. "Only to the extent we expose ourselves over and over to annihilation can that which is indestructible in us be found," Pema Chodron reminds us. She is a Tibetan Buddhist.

This coincides with a closure of a prior stage and a start of a new one. It is not a breakthrough, which occurs *within* a stage.

After a major defeat or rejection one feels alone—stripped and solitary (dare I say "soul-itary"). An individual encounters their core identity, which is seldom available in the hubbub of life's concerns. It is a humbling that has less to do with defeat than with surrendering to a higher wisdom. Totally letting go brings the quiet certitude, "I am meant to do this and will find another way."

Mystics actually seek such a wipeout of their worldly identity. It is called "purgation," an essential mid-phase of the mystical path. However, everybody else would put the experience in the failure column. It hurts; it is lonely, a setback to one's confidence and expectations.

In reading the life stories of major visionaries, it is impossible to miss that the turning point in their creative life is often forged in the pit of anguish.

What survives? The person is compelled to see, in the face of what was lost, that which remains is more than enough. It is the kernel shorn of the chaff. It is the "who I *really* am." Those Dark Nights of the Soul engender a collapse of previous certitude, and represent key turning points in the visionary process. But there is a fundamental misperception about them.

A Dark Night of the Soul is not a one-time experience. Periods of intense despair reappear at various points along the visionary process (or in serious inner work). It is a necessary aspect of being refined and renewed. Someone could get caught in such anguish for a very long time. But there is no mistaking the tipping point of release and transformative energy when the darkness becomes light.

While few seek out such horrific experiences, one senses a solid finality about growth acquired that way. It represents a stage completed that draws a line. It presages new faculties and a greater fluency *that cannot be lost or forgotten*, no matter what follows.

Something within the individual crystalizes, which adds a gravitas and refinement to their voice. This development is independent of their success or failure in life, or of their particular vision. This is about character.

Facing Ego Issues

Dealing with one's ego is a challenge for everybody: too much, too little, just right. To be human means to have an ego and the need to find a workable balance between wimpy and arrogant. Ego does a decent job of making things go as we planned. The threat comes when it operates without the supervision of conscious attention, or it tries to run the show.

Many a worthy mission has failed because egotistical posturing, self-righteousness, or spiritual pride got in the way. Self-centered, me-centered, and egotistical are roughly the same—assessing what is happening simply in terms of what is good for me, above other considerations.

Those on the visionary path have been steadily moving away from such a self-serving point of view, and closer to functioning with a more inclusive perspective.

Nakedness and Ego

Ego represents a false face each of us shows to the world—which is also assumed to be "who I am." But like Frankenstein's creation, an ego puts together a mishmash of parts it likes, or thinks it needs, to build an identity. These were gathered and tacked together over time, and in the process the authentic self got buried underneath.

Chesterton said, "One may understand the cosmos, but never the ego; the self is more distant than any star." It takes considerable self-awareness to operate from our authentic power rather than egotistical bravado. The task is made more challenging because for most people the mind does the ego's bidding, without even realizing it.

> The most common ego identifications have to do with possessions, the work you do, social status and recognition, knowledge and education, physical appearance, special abilities, relationships, personal and family history, belief systems, and often also political, nationalistic, racial, religious, and other collective identifications. None of these is you.[122]

A person needs to develop a high degree of self-awareness (both internal and external) in order to keep his or her ego in check—or even to want to do so. The ego is remarkably skilled at achieving our goals in practical ways. It should be respected for that.

However, the objective is not to eliminate the ego, but to arrange for it to function *appropriately*. It must serve rather than govern. As the saying goes: Ego makes a terrible general (or king) but a great sergeant.

---

[122] Tolle, Eckhart, *The Power of Now: A guide to spiritual enlightenment* (Novato, CA: New World Library, 1999), 37.

According to spiritual writer Gary Zukav, "If you are not conscious of all of the different parts of yourself, the part of yourself that is the strongest will win out over the other parts. Its intention will be the one that the personality uses to create its reality." For most people that is the ego. And it is seldom challenged for running the show in a preemptory way.

Each of us is much more than our ego-based self can fathom, and we should not allow our boundaries to be so small. Were it not for the disrobing and added discernment that takes place through our inner growth, the ego would take credit for all the positive outcomes that flow from the creative process.

It grabs any acclaim or rewards at any opportunity. However, as one's self-absorption diminishes, interest in taking credit and control diminish as well.

Emotions Have Their Place

Most of us need to develop a greater fluency regarding our emotional signals. As we permit our heart, mind, and body to work in a more integrated way, that also means we cannot ignore very relevant ways our emotional states override our intentions or rational interpretation of what we do.

It is yet another form of self-knowledge and mastery that helps us bridge our inner and outer states. And there are economic consequences, as shown in a *Newsweek* article by Jean Chatzky:

> Harvard University professor Jennifer Lerner says anger makes people optimistic and risk seeking, while fear makes them pessimistic and risk-averse. Sadness makes people eager to buy things; disgust makes them unlikely to want to buy anything at all; both make them likely to sell on the cheap things they already have. 'When you're sad, you're trying to change your circumstances,' says Lerner. 'When you're disgusted, you're trying to cleanse.'[123]

A key to staying involved and growing is to find ways to gain frequent reinforcement along the way, rather than pinning one's hopes on achieving the long-term goals. An integral aspect of energy management is getting recharged at every opportunity. A lot of this depends on how we structure our expectations and rewards, as explained by Kerry Patterson *et al.* in *Change Anything*:

> The now proven tactic of using many small goals rather than one huge goal is especially important when it's applied to incentives. Never make the mistake of attaching rewards to achieving your *ultimate* goal.... After all, your biggest risk with any long-term change project is not that you'll fail but that you'll drop out *at the beginning*.
>
> As you reward yourself frequently and in small increments, also take care to reward the right thing. Reward your actions, not your results. Results are often

---

[123] Chatzky, Jean, "Emotion-Free Investing," *Newsweek*, October 3, 2011.

out of your control (at least in the moment), so link your incentives to something you can control—your vital behaviors. Reward what you do, not what you achieve.[124]

The Public Face

Building Trust and Credibility for a Vision

Nothing is more important than the visionary walking their talk. Lapses pull them off course, muddy their message, confuse the public, and make close insiders feel betrayed. A mission melds the individual with a larger purpose. To quote Grande, "My life is an indivisible whole, and all my activities run into one another.… My life is my message."

The success of a vision depends on people "buying it." Before people buy anything, it must appear to be worthy of their trust. Building trust is necessary to persuasion and inspiration. For without that, all other efforts are for naught.

Our ability to trust is governed by the limbic part of the brain that developed prior to humanity's rational facilities. But it is still fully operational. It reacts faster than logic or verbal explanations do. The limbic system controls our fight-or-flight reactions and the logical side yields to it.

If something "smells fishy" or confusing, people stop being open to it. They get suspicious and disconnect.

Integrity is vital, since any discrepancy or mixed messages trigger the limbic flight (reject) responses toward them. In a sense, a confusing message gets rejected, with no second chances. It is nearly impossible to undo that rejection later, or repair it with more facts. Eric Hoffer points out the power of words that people can believe in.

> We know that words cannot move mountains, but they can move the multitude; and men are more ready to fight and die for a word than for anything else. Words shape thought, stir feeling, and beget action; they kill and revive, corrupt and cure. The 'men of words'—priests, prophets, intellectuals—have played a more decisive role in history than military leadership, statesmen, and businessmen.
>
> Words and magic are particularly crucial in time of crisis when old forms of life are in dissolution and man must grapple with the unknown. Normal motives and incentives lose their efficacy. Man does not plunge into the unknown in search of the prosaic and matter-of-fact. His soul has to be stretched by a reaching out for the fabulous and unprecedented.[125]

---

[124] Patterson, Kerry, Grenny, Joseph *et al.*, *Change Anything: The new science of personal success* (New York: Business Plus, 2011), 110.
[125] *Op. cit.*, Hoffer, 107.

A person's ability to persuade is largely at the mercy of the public perception about them. Do they come across as "one who knows?" Do they speak with authority? People have fewer doubts about someone who appears to have their act together.

Finding the balance between over-confidence and timidity, between being clear and believable or boastful, is crucial to attracting followers. The public withholds trust about anything they do not understand. Also, their feelings about the messenger will be interpreted as reflecting on the value of the message itself.

He Who Knows
Arab Proverb

He who knows not and knows not he knows not: he is a fool — shun him.
He who knows not and knows he knows not: he is simple — teach him.
He who knows and knows not he knows: he is asleep — wake him.
He who knows and knows he knows: he is wise — follow him.

Earliest followers rely on their own scrutiny and gut reactions. But as the idea or movement grows, people are also attracted by the implied validation of those already aboard. Those who get on the bandwagon later are influenced by those who have already chosen to do so — signs of a trend in which they would like to take part.

At some critical point, a notion could take off, become popular, garner respect, or be anointed the "next great discovery."

How the World Sees the Visionary and the Vision:
- Insiders and supporters — those who like the champion and/or the message
- Detractors — those who dislike or reject the champion and/or the message
- The public who knows nothing (or only a sound bite) about it

The upstart visionary must consider their level of credibility with each of these factions. What, if anything, can be done to sharpen the message in order to relate to their needs or expectations? Which is the right audience or forum for what I am offering?

Personal Qualities Constantly Being Tested:
- Authenticity — being real and sincere
- Honesty, integrity, and trustworthiness
- Courage and tenacity
- Humility and appropriate self-regard
- Flexibility and resourcefulness
- Patience — attuned to the flow of events and a long timeframe
- Stamina — hanging on, no matter what

Maintaining the same high degree of integrity throughout the project can be more difficult than it is to ground the more tangible parts of the vision. Expediency may argue for treating such considerations as side issues. But if that connection with principle is broken, or tossed aside casually, the mission loses its legitimacy.

The world is awash in derelict organizations that drift on without their original moral compass, purpose, or vision engaged. Financial considerations alone cannot obscure the fact that values still matter.

In a *New York Times* article, Thomas Friedman quotes Seidman about the crucial role of values in leadership (March 22, 2009).

> 'There is nothing more powerful than inspirational leadership that unleashes principled behavior for a great cause,' said Dov Seidman, the CEO of LRN, which helps companies build ethical cultures and the author of the book 'How.' What makes a company or a government 'sustainable,' he added, is not when it adds more coercive rules and regulations to control behaviors. 'It is when its employees or citizens are propelled by values and principles to do the right things, no matter how difficult the situation,' said Seidman. 'Laws tell you what you can do. Values inspire in you what you should do. It's a leader's job to inspire in us those values.'[126]

Moving People from Listeners to Believers

Understanding, even accepting, an idea is nice but not enough. That is the rational mind signing on. For belief in an idea, the heart and emotions must sign on as well—once they *sense the truth in it*.

Persuasion need not rest on words alone, or on rational argument. Accepting is little more than an entry door to knowing about something or trusting it. The ideal communication also delivers a non-verbal message that carries quiet certainty, along with the overt message.

The receiver knows from the gut (limbic resonance). It is like the body language leaps—from the "knowing place" of the visionary to the "knowing place" of the listener. They're in essential agreement, without needing to explain.

Persuasion has gotten a deservedly bad rap because it is a frequent tool of manipulators. People fear being "had" yet again, and keep their guard up. Hoffer points out the limits of persuasion.

> We tend today to exaggerate the effectiveness of persuasion as a means of inculcating opinion and shaping behavior. We see in propaganda a formidable instrument. To its skillful use we attribute many of the startling successes of mass movements of our time, and we have come to fear the word as much as the sword....

---

[126] Freidman, Thomas L., "Are We Home Alone?," *New York Times*, March 22, 2009.

The truth seems to be that propaganda on its own cannot force its way into unwilling minds; neither can it inculcate something wholly new; nor can it keep people persuaded once they have ceased to believe. It penetrates only into minds already open, and rather than instil opinion it articulates and justifies opinions already present in the minds of its recipients. The gifted propagandist brings to a boil ideas and passions already simmering in the minds of the hearers. He echoes their innermost feelings. Where opinion is not coerced, people can be made to believe only in what they already 'know.'

Propaganda by itself succeeds mainly with the frustrated. Their throbbing fears, hopes and passions crowd at the portals of their senses and get between them and the outside world.[127]

Getting Caught by Fame and Glory

Consider the illusive nature of celebrity. Is the person basking in the spotlight truly a gifted artist or thought leader? Do they offer something really groundbreaking and valuable? Or have they simply made the most of their 15 minutes of fame? Is their handiwork truly art (or a significant discovery) with staying power? Or is it merely a craze, soon to fade?

Too often, the term "visionary" has been casually demoted from the farsighted pioneer, who may have the power to change the world, to a synonym for the latest whiz-bang fad inventor.

Fame (or the desire for it) has been the downfall of many, especially if it comes too fast or to someone who has not yet developed the character to handle it. It's a beast that must be fed, with a voracious public watching and judging.

Those who get seduced by fame and hero worship must struggle to maintain their public image—a treadmill with relatively little creativity in evidence. Equally distracting as the longing for fame is the grieving for the glory days of the past (if it has come and gone).

Sometimes, a person becomes a slave to their widespread success—particularly in the arts, or where there is public adulation. Sometimes, a person cannot let their creative expression be freely demonstrated anymore because their public only wants more of the same of what they did before. He or she is locked into creating nearly repetitious works, becoming a caricature of their public face.

Some giants were able to totally reinvent themselves and avoid that pitfall. Picasso and Alfred North Whitehead come to mind. So this is a word of caution for neophyte visionaries. Fame is not the end, but another challenge or risk in the creative process. Tread carefully and realize why fame is sometimes called "a pact with the devil."

---

[127] *Op. cit.*, Hoffer, 102-3.

Ideas Rise and Fall

The creative process generates an abundance of ideas. Not all are valuable or deserve the effort that would be required to fully develop them. A person must pick and choose among those notions that are not only inspired but possible — those that stand a snowball's chance of happening.

They know they must cull their ideas to avoid being pulled in too many directions — even while knowing they are likely to be torn. Other considerations like the availability of adequate resources, a feasible time frame, and collaborative assistance are often decisive.

The long period of testing of something further refines the fresh notion. Part of that is beneficial, but shouldn't be an end in itself, as Scott Belsky explains in *Making Ideas Happen*:

> The natural immune system that extinguishes new ideas in big companies is essential. After all, fresh ideas have the potential to take us off course; they are seldom economical (at first) and introduce tremendous risk to a finely tuned system. So it is with good reason that every new idea faces a battery of external obstacles before it even has a chance of materializing. Sadly, these obstacles don't discriminate between good and bad ideas.[128]

The complicated obstacle course facing almost every new idea assures that very few of them will survive. Many of the casualties have merit, however. What can be done differently so the most worthy ideas get better treatment? This is not as much about individual notions so much as there being a timely reconsideration of what would work better. We need to find more effective mechanisms to support the forces of cultural progress.

An idea whose time has come can also go. Wonderful notions, too, can outlive their usefulness, or the conditions that spawned them. A visionary sometimes needs to detach from his or her vision and catch the next wave.

However, if someone is too identified with their vision and its short-term implications, they could easily miss the next iterations of it to come.

Even after an idea is accepted, it can be short lived. That could be a good thing if it furthers the march of progress. Ideas wax, wane, and evolve in order to reflect the needs of their time and place. Further elaboration or modification of the idea will follow as circumstances require.

Arthur Koestler speaks about the signs of a fading new notion in *The Act of Creation*.

> Yesterday's discoveries are today's commonplaces; a daringly fresh image soon becomes stale by repetition, degenerates into a cliché, and loses its emotive appeal. The newborn day or the piercing cry are no longer even perceived as

---

[128] Belsky, Scott, *Making Ideas Happen: Overcoming the obstacles between vision and reality* (New York: Portfolio, 2010), 8-9.

metaphorical; the once separate contexts of birth and dawn have merged, there is no juxtaposition—reverting to jargon, bisociative dynamism has been converted into associative routine.[129]

Originality must stay true to its nature. It deviates from the norm and appears in a variety of forms that were not currently being expressed. Creative ideas combine destructive and constructive influences that assure the forms they take stay dynamic. Then those new revolutions develop, fade, and the process continues with the next creative wrinkle. As Arthur Koestler also said:

> The measure of an artist's originality, put into the simplest terms, is the extent to which his selective emphasis deviates from the conventional norm and establishes new standards of relevance. All great innovations, which inaugurate a new era, movement,

> or school, consist in such sudden shifts of attention and displacements of emphasis into some previously neglected aspect of experience, some blacked-out range of the existential spectrum. The decisive turning points in the history of every art-form are discoveries which show the characteristic features: they uncover what has always been there; they are 'revolutionary,' that is, destructive and constructive; they compel us to revalue and impose a new set of rules on the eternal game.[130]

The End of a Vision

Every vision has a life cycle. When it commences, it is an insubstantial idea that might catch on or produce results. Even if it comes to flower, it eventually becomes another idea taking its place in the zeitgeist. At some point the originator is no longer pushing it as something novel. And people may consider it a unique idea less and less. That does not mean it was forgotten, but that it mostly turned into a 3-D manifestation.

How Accepted Visions End:
- Absorbed into the larger culture or context—becomes the common wisdom
- Fad that flashes and quickly fades
- Cannot deliver on its promise; discredited
- Snuffed out by resistance or factions already in place
- Overtaken by better ideas
- Major developments push it into irrelevancy (war, scientific discoveries, economic collapse)
- Becomes so widely accepted it becomes common knowledge (or it represents the new consensus within a particular domain)
- Forgotten or eventual success through adoption

---

[129] Koestler, Arthur, *The Act of Creation* (New York: The Macmillan Company, 1964), 335.
[130] *Ibid.*, 334-5.

Chapter 9 - Identifying the Spectrum of Change
*One of the new mindsets that must be developed for a workable
future is finding a way that change can occur without creating such
a cleavage between those who gain by it and those who lose out.*

Change Happens

Change is like the air we breathe—ubiquitous. In the same way nature abhors a vacuum so air rushes in, life abhors being static and change rushes in (or trickles). Change is the norm; it is but an illusion that things stay the same. The amount of change reflects a continuum—from minuscule or beneath notice *to* massive. Change is irreversible and cumulative, but it is not stoppable.

Change can come along so gradually it seems to not be happening at all. But it is. "To exist is to change, to change is to mature, to mature is to go on creating oneself endlessly," according to Henri Bergson. It can come fast or slow. But that is totally relative.

Change. Is there any word more dividing? It draws a line between before and after—separating what came already from that which follows. (Notice I didn't say cause—causation is something different.)

There is no turning back the clock. Even if we try to go back to something earlier, we have been changed somehow and cannot manage the innocence of "not having peeked."

Considerations about change should factor in the scale of change involved—over how much time or how many people affected. My rearranging my living room furniture is no big deal compared to the same furniture being moved by a tornado.

Some change involves only a small segment of a person's life (or just occurs in a specific activity), while other changes involve generations and alter historic trends.

According to Peter Drucker, "We no longer can even understand the question whether change is by itself good or bad.... We start out with the axiom that it is the norm. We do not see change as altering the order.... We see change as being order itself—indeed the only order we can comprehend today is a dynamic, a moving, a changing one."

Our culture loves the fun stuff technology delivers, but turns a blind eye to some of the downsides that tag along. There is a price to be paid for either welcoming or resisting change—though not the same price. Much more is at stake than producing a steady supply of new gadgets or labor-saving devices. Seth Godin (*Tribes*) reminds us how much modern life is geared to change.

> Here's what's changed: some people admire the new and the stylish far more than they respect the proven state of affairs. And more often than not, these fad-focused early adopters are the people who buy and the people who talk. As

a result, new ways of doing things, new jobs, new opportunities, and new faces become ever more important.

> Marketing, the verb, changed the market. The market is now a lot less impressed with average stuff for average people, and the market is a lot less impressed with loud and flashy and expensive advertising. Today, the market wants change.[131]

While this chapter focuses on change, it is a mix of broad brushstrokes and finer impressionistic detail. It all relates to what is being altered by the forces of change in play. I liken functioning during times of gradual change to steering a ship on calm seas, whereas, revolutionary change calls forth the requisite skill to steer a ship during a typhoon.

Everything Changes with Time

A culture or field of knowledge usually changes like a glacier moves—a little at a time and more pronounced around the edges. A glacier looks immobile, composed of ice from eons ago. But lo! It moves! Its leading edge melts and shifts ever so slightly ahead. The immense mass of ice follows along in its own good time.

Stop-action photography reveals the encroaching movement. Little by little, the glacier creeps forward—its stationary appearance an illusion.

The collective work of change agents melts apparently solid institutions and cultural "givens" as new thinking prevails. Over time, such overall movement comes to be called progress. But credit cannot be given to any particular person, philosophy, or vision, as necessary as they might be to melt the frozen and unyielding mass.

Massive change can occur through incredibly tiny increments or choices. Even change on the scale of cultures or paradigm shifts includes an infinite number of personal decisions, with more and more of them tilting in the direction of what actually develops. But times of revolutionary change certainly confound any predictability about what will be next.

Visionaries are sometimes accused of causing indiscriminate or irresponsible change. As change agents, they often hang out in the space where the gears are changing. Their presence and influence lubricate the stuck places of what is already established, introducing novelty at every opportunity.

To the extent the pioneering individual succeeds in grounding their vision, there will be consequences. Some could be monumental. While many factors that contribute to the outcome are beyond their control, change agents should try to be sensitive about what they are setting in motion—on an individual scale, as well as in the large-scale context.

---

[131] Godin, Seth, *Tribes: We need you to lead us* (New York: Penguin Group, 2008), 16-17.

The Fallacy of Tidy Change

Almost everyone who encourages change only wants a little bit of it, so it stays manageable. They do not want it to mess things up much, or destroy predictability and control enough to be painful. That is certainly the case in organizational settings—just enough change to season the roast, not enough to serve up a whole different meal.

Throughout the book, the phrase "revolutionary change" comes up a lot. Change on *that* scale is very disruptive and unpredictable. It cannot be controlled even by (or especially by) those who set it in motion.

Revolutionary change flirts with anarchy. It will not play out according to any existing rules and it is apt to upend stability on a massive scale.

Of course, the zeitgeist is a major factor by providing the unstable circumstances or requisite unrest for revolution. Whether revolutionary change takes the relatively genteel form described by Kuhn's paradigm shift, *or* the French Revolution, an extreme in class warfare, subsequent events could play themselves out in dramatic and uncontrolled ways. Nobody can put the genie back in the bottle—once it is set loose.

Revolutionary change unleashes creative destruction, which is necessary for rebirth and new growth. The three are complementary aspects of recurring cycles. It has a Shiva energy that sweeps away anything in its way. The Indian Hindu trinity is Brahma (the creator), Vishnu (the preserver), and Shiva (the destroyer). The three act as a unit, each having an essential role to maintain the continuity of life.

We in the West are uncomfortable with the idea of necessary or chaotic destruction. We treat it as a surprise—an unanticipated flaw in the plan or our inability to factor in enough variables. But it is not. We cannot impose our will on many of the forces that influence us and our world. But it is human nature to be vain enough to think it can be done.

However, we can do a better job of broadening our perceptual lens in order to attend to many influences we now ignore—not so they can be controlled, but to work more effectively with them.

Unless we are prepared to accept the results of substantial change as random fate, we must learn how to read the signals—and take our cues from what they are telling us.

Drawing a Line

Large-scale change is not just disruptive and messy, it creates a demarcation: Before X *and* After X. People on the Before X side look at certain issues in a fundamentally different way than people do After X.

Notice it can be a very fat line between them. During that span between Before X and when After X settles in, there is a war zone.

Blood (both actual and symbolic) is being spilled. There will be no shortage of betrayals, double-agents, and traitors to the cause as individuals and organizations choose up sides — then fight to the death. By the time it is over (After X), there will have been death or decline for both sides — the *status quo* and the challenger.

It is probably not total obliteration of either stance, but it is apparent which position prevailed. Making peace demands a great degree of accommodation amongst the survivors.

There are no unaffected bystanders in a revolution. Those who take sides know which side they are on. Those who avoid taking sides or shrink into the corners are likely to be cannon fodder for the *status quo* team. Some players fight dirty because each side thinks it is fighting for the right to decide the future. And as the saying goes, "the winners write the history books."

But even the victors cannot control what is coming, more than a few moves ahead. The aftermath is also like war, in that peace requires all parties to clean up the devastation and heal the scars in order to go forward. People's lives *will* change. There will be winners, losers, and collateral damage to deal with.

Whichever side prevails will re-stabilize somewhat as it sets about establishing the next *status quo* — which will invite its own challengers in due course.

Long in advance of a specific revolutionary change, there are probably many early warning signs of disharmony, of things not working, of subordinate elements shifting. Such usually misread disruptions set the stage for large-scale movement. Increased discordant behavior (both individual and institutional) could relieve pressure points — pending a large enough change that renders them irrelevant.

Before and during the transition, more and more gray areas creep in where it is hard to tell what is true from hubris or outright lies. Some ethical standards get muddled. As more of these muddy areas become the norm, people accept the resulting moral ambiguity as though it is the natural human condition. When a true visionary bearing fire from the gods appears, it is a galvanizing event. "Oh my gosh! Something to believe in!" *or* "Oh my gosh! This is trouble; get rid of it."

Revolutionary Change Changes Everything

Widespread disaffection or unstable conditions are ripe for dramatic change or mass movements. In *The True Believer*, Eric Hoffer described many of the factors that contribute to revolutionary change.

> There is a period of waiting in the wings — often a very long period — for all the great leaders whose entrance on the scene seems to us a most crucial point in the course of a mass movement.... Once the stage is set, the presence of an outstanding leader is indispensable. Without him, there will be no movement.

The ripeness of the time does not automatically produce a mass movement, nor can elections, laws and administrative bureaus hatch one.[132]

Discontent by itself does not invariably create a desire for change. Other factors have to be present before discontent turns into disaffection. One of these is a sense of power. Those who are awed by their surroundings do not think of change, no matter how miserable their condition. When our mode of life is so precarious as to make it patent that we cannot control the circumstances of our existence, we tend to stick to the proved and the familiar.[133]

Those who would transform a nation or the world cannot do so by breeding and captaining discontent or by demonstrating the reasonableness and desirability of the intended changes or by coercing people into a new way of life. They must know how to kindle and fan an extravagant hope. It matters not whether it be hope of a heavenly kingdom, of heaven on earth, of plunder and untold riches, of fabulous achievement or world domination.[134]

For men to plunge headlong into an undertaking of vast change, they must be intensely discontented yet not destitute, and they must have the feeling that by the possession of some potent doctrine, infallible leader or some new technique they have access to a source of irresistible power. They must also have an extravagant conception of the prospects and potentialities of the future. Finally, they must be wholly ignorant of the difficulties involved in their vast undertaking. Experience is a handicap.[135]

When people are ripe for a mass movement, they are usually ripe for any effective movement, and not solely for one with a particular doctrine or program.[136]

Change and Integration Lag

Change, whether gradual or breakneck, requires concomitant adjustments throughout the system—whatever the scale. What is new has to be integrated with what is in place, and that takes time.

"Innovation arrives more rapidly than does change in culture and values," said Joel Garreau. Technological developments can catch on much faster than the necessary adjustments to it that ripple throughout the larger community. The discrepancy shows up as considerably more cultural lag to be dealt with.

These days the pace of technological change has been speeding up faster than the rest of the culture can absorb it. For instance, we want the benefits of atomic energy, without dealing with radioactive wastes; or the benefits of global trade,

---

[132] Hoffer, Eric, *The True Believer: Thoughts on the nature of mass movements* (New York, Harper & Row, 1951), 110.
[133] *Ibid.*, 7.
[134] *Ibid.*, 9.
[135] *Ibid.*, 11.
[136] *Ibid.*, 16.

without dealing with human-rights inequities and exploitation that accompany it.

Modern life seems to be driven by an insatiable hunger for new ideas and fresh directions. And technology makes it easy to jump aboard the next big thing. Steven Johnson shows the growing receptivity of the public to the next new thing in *Where Good Ideas Come From*.

> It is one of the great truisms of our time that we live in an age of technological acceleration; the new paradigms keep rolling in, and the intervals between them keep shortening. This acceleration reflects not only the flood of new products, but also our growing willingness to embrace these strange new devices, and put them to use. The waves roll in at ever-increasing frequencies, and more and more of us are becoming trained surfers, paddling out to meet them the second they start to crest.[137]

Very real dilemmas come with all the gifts of technology. Initiators must be sensitive to what the likely implications are well in advance of their trail of unintended consequences. Those who lead the charge should consider the full range of tangible and intangible costs implicit in the decisions being made.

The human costs of such massive shifts have been very high — to communities and our way of life. Neither individuals nor organizations have been able to keep pace. So they exhibit increasing signs of maladaptive behavior. Too often, so much change has destabilized norms without putting something better in their place.

Those adept at riding change spring ahead and leave the rest further behind. While some groups or individuals can and do adapt quickly, many more become stuck or dysfunctional. The resulting winners and losers (economically, socially, educationally) can find little common ground for deciding on what is desirable — or what is in their mutual interests for the long term.

One of the new mindsets that needs to be developed for a workable future is finding a way that change can occur without creating such a cleavage between those who gain by it and those who lose out. The social implications riding on resolving this are enormous.

Visionary Change Needs to Remain Flexible

Visionaries break structures and expectations. Unpredictability is one of the tools they wield — sometimes with devastating effect. They must remain adaptable to changing circumstances, or they will fall heir to the same issues they have already rejected and are supplanting.

Not only do they usher in their version of change, these individuals must also stay on the pulse of the emerging zeitgeist and be willing to ride those forces.

---

[137] Johnson, Steven, *Where Good Ideas Come From: The natural history of innovation* (New York: Riverhead Books, 2010), 13.

Grounding the vision is not a one-time deal. It grows and evolves over time, and as it is put into action. Adaptation over time keeps the notion timely and broadens its usefulness. Efforts to "cast it in stone" or to keep the vision pristine are misguided and counter-productive. That could hew too closely to the very practices visionary thinkers are trying to change.

Inflexibility and dinosaur thinking will creep in unless there is vigilance about it. It is the human default setting. Some things do not really change but claim to—continuing to maintain the *status quo* behind a new veneer.

Likewise, in the midst of changing circumstances, it is important for each of us to resist the reflexive urge to hang on even tighter to what is fading. Even our relationship toward what we consider true or moral bedrock needs to be reconsidered so it stays germane. We maintain the flexibility of truth through our action, and the way we let it guide our choices.

As important as a commitment to our highest truth may be, it can only be kept relevant through daily practice. We honor truth not by casting our ideals into stone, but by living them.

~ Fresh Truth ~
A BonBon ~ Faith Lynella

Truth can too easily become a cliché. The old truths degrade into dogma. As it eventually becomes rigid, it is less capable of discerning or responding to subtle nuances. Such truth is wielded like a sword—stiff, unbending, heavy-handed. Certainly, the words are still true, but much of the force that made them relevant has been lost. The effort to sustain such heavy truth stifles both you and the truth you value.

Despite our most sincere efforts, such truths cannot inspire or be living forces to animate the way we make decisions. We need to discover truth and continually rediscover truth for it to remain living and relevant to us. The desire to find and then to express the truth is ACTIVE. It demands much more than a passive parroting of slogans. We do not acknowledge truth simply by our acceptance or acquiescence, but through our unceasing discovery and application of it.

The awareness of freshly rediscovered truth has force. It animates. It uplifts. It resonates through whatever we are doing. Newfound truth is not simply true, but through us it becomes alive and true. In such ways we can renew truth and make it a vital force. Truth cannot exist in a static state. Unless it is renewed, it hardens or withers. When it is not fresh truth, it becomes less than true.

From *BonBons to Sweeten Your Daily Life*. Or from *More BonBons*

The Appropriate Role of Rules

The tug of war between non-conforming thinking or behavior and the widely accepted mindset is often framed as conflict between rules and individual rights—as though choosing one negates the other. But the issue is better framed as the peril from creating rules that supersede our ability to exercise wise judgment that is attuned to the particular situation.

We live and work in communities in which many people have competing priorities and rights. So some rules act as the lubricant for getting along. Those are mostly social conventions people go along with because they help us set appropriate and agreed-upon boundaries. Rules usually reflect an official statement of what is, and is not, permitted.

There is likely to be an "or else" if one breaks them. Modern life has gotten quite top-heavy, with the proliferation of so many rules and regulations. In my opinion, every rule is an assault on judgment.

Modern life requires a mix of common sense, individual responsibility, and reasonable regulation. If we are to correct the abuses of the past, each of us needs to find a way to balance these competing forces throughout our various activities. These days the dialog about the appropriate scope of each is being renegotiated in a zillion contexts.

I am willing to predict that once the dust settles due to so much institutional breakdown, what replaces it will reflect a new consensus about the role of regulations. It will also consider how much of it is beneficial or acceptable.

Zero Tolerance Equals Zero Sense

I have an intense aversion to a type of thinking that is quite popular these days—Zero Tolerance Policies. Proponents treat them as so objective, so fair and reasonable, so unbiased and evenhanded. They are none of those things!

Such policies should be called "Zero Judgment Policies" or "Cover Your Ass and Avoid the Hard Choices Policies."

There is no proportionality in their enforcement, and any hair-trigger event could bring down the full force of retribution without warning. Rather than "one size fits all," it gives us "one size fits nobody." Not only is the punishment unlikely to fit the offense, it can easily deliver a penalty without there being an actual offense. Authorities wedded to such policies are not showing leadership, but an abuse of their authority, along with an abdication of judgment or responsibility.

How else could anyone account for the absurd consequences such policies deliver? They lead to "consequences" that almost never suit the circumstances. In what universe does it make sense to arrest a preschooler as a sexual predator because he kissed a classmate? In my opinion, anyone in a position of power who endorses, or hides behind, Zero Tolerance Policies deserves to be tarred and feathered.

Besides, these inflexible approaches do not work. They produce too many negative results and unintended consequences. The American Psychological Association reviewed the data about the impact of zero tolerance policies in education. Quoting from the final report of the task force:

> Concern has been raised in the literature that zero tolerance policies may create, enhance, or accelerate negative mental health outcomes for youth by creating increases in student alienation, anxiety, rejection, and breaking of healthy adult bonds.... The overwhelming majority of findings from the available research on zero tolerance and exclusionary discipline tend to contradict the assumptions of that philosophy.[138]

Some confusion about the value of unbending objectives arises because virtues themselves are absolutes. Ideals like Truth, Honesty, and Integrity are non-relative. They transcend the everyday world. However, for the world we live in, everything is relative. And it is our responsibility to do the best job we can to make our behavior and ideals correspond.

Human judgment is the tool that makes discernment and adjustment possible. It permits us to respond appropriately to each specific circumstance. Nothing good can come from official policies that insist our best judgment has no place.

Complexity Yields Confusion

People often feel overwhelmed by our imponderably complicated society, with change speeding up in every area of life. All our choices seem to be more complex than they used to be. And when someone gets caught up in the particulars, it can feel like too, too much.

So, disengagement is needed occasionally to find a more encompassing view — wherein what is forest and what is trees becomes apparent.

For example, technology sounds intricate and sophisticated, but its role in modern life should be simple. It should serve human priorities, not the other way around. Our computer-based machines should make things easier for us to do. How did we manage to get that turned around?

High tech environments (and we are living in one) are something more than gee-whiz gadgets. They color our decision-making process in numerous ways.

In a *New York Times* article (May 27, 2010), David Brooks describes the inherent problems when technology meets psychology.

> The real issue has to do with risk assessment. It has to do with the bloody crossroads where complex technical systems meet human psychology. Over the

---

[138] American Psychological Association Zero Tolerance Task Force, "Are Zero Tolerance Policies Effective in the Schools?" *American Psychologist*, December, 2008.

past decades, we have come to depend on an ever-expanding array of intricate high-tech systems. These hardware and software systems are the guts of financial markets, energy exploration, space exploration, air travel, defines programs and modern production plants.

These systems, which allow us to live as well as we do, are too complex for any single person to understand. Yet every day, individuals are asked to monitor the health of these networks, weigh the risks of a system failure and take appropriate measures to reduce those risks. If there is one thing we have learned, it is that humans are not great at measuring and responding to risk when placed in situations too complicated to understand.

In the first place, people have trouble imagining how small failings can combine to lead to catastrophic disasters.... Second, people have a tendency to get acclimated to risk.... Third, people have a tendency to place elaborate faith in backup systems and safety devices.... Fourth, people have a tendency to match complicated technical systems with complicated governing structures.... Fifth, people tend to spread good news and hide bad news. Everybody wants to be part of a project that comes in under budget and nobody wants to be responsible for the reverse.... Finally, people in the same field begin to think alike, whether they are in oversight roles or not.[139]

The Adjacent Possible

Stuart Kauffman, a biologist, developed a concept called "the adjacent possible" that explains why the changes that actually occur are not likely to be random, out of an infinity of choices. All future paths are not equally available at any point in time. Some events or choices can only arise after others occur because opening one door gives access to related ones. Steven Johnson discusses the adjacent possible in *Where Good Ideas Come From*.

> The phrase captures both the limits and the creative potential of change and innovation.... The adjacent possible is a kind of shadow future, hovering on the edge of the present state of things, a map of all the ways in which the present can reinvent itself. Yet is it not an infinite space, or a totally open playing field. The number of potential first-order reactions is vast, but it is a finite number, and it excludes most of the forms that now populate the biosphere. What the adjacent possible tells us is that at any moment the world is capable of extraordinary change, but only certain changes can happen.[140]

> When we are wrong, we do have to challenge our assumptions, adopt new strategies. Being wrong on its own doesn't unlock new doors in the adjacent possible, but it does force us to look for them.[141]

---

[139] Brooks, David, "Drilling for Certainty," *New York Times*, May 27, 2010.
[140] *Op. cit.*, Johnson, Steven, 31.
[141] *Ibid.*, 138.

You can see the fingerprints of the adjacent possible in one of the most remarkable patterns in all of intellectual history, what scholars call "the multiple": a brilliant idea occurs to a scientist or inventor somewhere in the world, and he goes public with his remarkable finding, only to discover that three other minds had independently come up with the same idea in the past year.[142]

The adjacent possible is as much about limits as it is about openings. At every moment in the timeline of an expanding biosphere, there are doors that cannot be unlocked yet. In human culture, we like to think breakthrough ideas are sudden accelerations on the timeline, where a genius jumps ahead fifty years and invents something that normal minds, trapped in the present moment, couldn't possibly have come up with. But the truth is that technological (and scientific) advances rarely break out of the adjacent possible; the history of cultural progress is, almost without exception, a story of one door leading to another door, exploring the palace one room at a time.[143]

Getting Clear about Possibilities

Visionaries function in the realm of possibilities, but there are various types of possibilities, and they should not be confused. Better to ask, *what is possible right now?*

Types of Possibilities:

Latent Potential—the possibility exists, at some point; it *could* happen

- Actual Potential—circumstances exist so it's possible for it to happen right away

- Logical Possibility—a philosophical concept; something *could be true* because it is not rationally impossible

Possibility and actuality are two fundamental, dyadic elements that permeate every facet of our existence in this world. They have teased our imagination and tortured our psyches for millennia and probably will for as long as we are living, thinking beings. They surface in the deepest of our thoughts about the divine to the smallest thoughts of trivialities of our days. They are like the air; we are so immersed in them that we don't realize they're there.

But they're there, nonetheless—and **understanding them is possibly one of the best things we can actually do to flourish in this world.**[144]

---

[142] *Ibid.*, 34.
[143] *Ibid.*, 36.
[144] Gilkey, Charlie, "*How to Think About Possibility – And why it matters,*" http://www.productiveflourishing.com

The important point is, all possibilities are not the same and should not be treated as if they are. Possibility does not indicate probability, the likelihood of something specific happening. So, another way of framing an issue considers *how likely* it is to happen.

That outcome depends on a dollop of motivation and action. Here is where conventional thinking and the visionary approach seem to rely on very different calculations.

~ Beware of Potential ~
A BonBon ~ Faith Lynella

"But Dad…, he has so much potential!"
"This business has a lot of potential…"

The word "potential" paints a beautiful unmarred picture. It suggests unmixed images of success, achievement, and delightful possibilities, off there on the horizon, just waiting for you to claim them. And it's all yours—because you have the foresight to make a commitment now. Just act now, sign here, pay now, commit. After all, opportunities like that don't come along every day…

Sure they do.

Potential is nothing but a dream, a possibility. Yet it is presented and "sold" with an element of inevitability that misleads all too often. I'm all for promoting the dream, nurturing the undeveloped talent, and reaching out for the grand vision. They are vital for a full and vibrant life. They justify whatever risks and hard work are necessary to bring them to reality.

There is the key phrase "hard work." Between the conception and the reality exists a long path filled with diligent effort, struggle, frustration, and self-doubt—without any certainty that there will be a rewarding outcome.

Yes, there is an important role for potential and whatever it promises is, indeed, possible. But an emphasis on the activity's potential often disregards the prolonged efforts or commitment necessary to achieve it. It has to be nurtured.

Reach for that vision—want it so badly you're willing to pay any price necessary to get there. But walk into the picture with your eyes open to the full significance of your commitment. Choose it, knowing that it will cost every bit that you expect—and more. In that way, you aren't being surprised or misled by the glamorous possibility dangling like a carrot ahead of the donkey.

Then you'll gear up, calling on all your inner and outer resources—knowing every one of them will be required and tested—to the limit. Only then does your buy-in contain enough reality to exist as more than a dream.

There is latent potential in every seed. But thank heaven there's a farmer willing to toil from planting through harvest. The seed is important, vital in fact, but it is only the first stage of a long, arduous, and complicated series of stages—whether that be growth or transformation.

Seeds, like dreams, need to be nurtured, and cultivated, and pruned before they're ready to yield their potential. But recognize that to reach your dreams you must be the farmer. A seed starts to grow when it is placed in the ground. And your dreams start to become reality only after they are grounded and put into action—by you!

From *BonBons to Sweeten Your Daily Life*. Or from *More BonBons*

Change Can Sever Connections Too

Change is not just about adopting what is new or moving into an ever-expanding future. It often breaks continuity with what previously existed. And some of those secondary effects can have far-reaching consequences in their own right. The old does not go away just because a person or culture moves on. Completion is required too. Even when something new is started, there is still a need to support smooth closure and arrange for an easy transition. Lacking that, people keep re-fighting the old battles.

One way to look at change is with the concept of action chains. Too much change, or when it happens too rapidly, breaks action chains. The kinds of maladaptive behaviors that result could overlap with cultural lag and other instabilities of modern life. Too much, too fast gives change a bad name.

Anthropologist Edward T. Hall introduces the concept of action chains, that become too distorted when change comes too quickly.

> An action chain is a set sequence of events in which usually two or more individuals participate. It is reminiscent of a dance that is used as a means of reaching a common goal that can be reached only after, and not before, each link in the chain has been forged. Like frames, action chains can be simple, complex, or derived. Every action within a frame has a beginning, a climax, and an end, and comprises a number of intermediate stages. If any of the basic acts are left out or are too greatly distorted, the action must be started all over again.... I seriously doubt if man does anything of a social nature that does not involve action chains. Some action chains are incredibly long, requiring more than a lifetime to be played out, while others last only a few seconds.[145]

> Rene Spitz, the Swiss psychiatrist, developed a theory about distorting action chains: If human beings (or other animals) are put in the position of having to cope with the consequences of too many broken chains, they will compensate. The compensations will ultimately become so numerous as to block or prohibit

---

[145] Hall, Edward T., *Beyond Culture* (New York, Doubleday, 1976), 141-3.

normal behavior. The culmination of this process, he calls 'derailment of dialogue,' a term that indicates not only words but actions as well. To such derailment, he attributes many of the ills of our overcrowded cities, including juvenile delinquency, sadistic teen-age crimes, neuroses, and psychoses.[146]

Revolutionary Times Call Forth Mighty Change

The world has come to the place where the immensity of its problems exceed any single organization's or nation's ability to resolve them: destruction of the ocean ecosystems, widespread human rights abuses, illnesses that travel easily beyond national borders, etc.

Traditional organizations and governments seem paralyzed, not just by the scope and number of such problems, but also by too many unknowns or the infighting of political factions. Resolving such large-scale challenges (many with a global impact) exceeds the current capacities of the top-down organizational model.

Institutions are usually slow to respond to early warning signals of danger, or to shift gears in a decisive way—except for their own protection. They downplay or resist the steady rumblings that presage a new direction. Launching truly revolutionary developments is usually left for the upstarts and outsiders—the Black Swans.

> The problem for a market leader in the old technology is not necessarily that it lacks the capacity to innovate, but that it lacks the will. When a disruptive technology appears, it may confound an existing player because the technology itself is so radically different. More often the problem was not technological but psychological and organizational: it is hard for a major organization to pay much attention to a piddling new idea that makes little money and invites a yawn or a blank stare from important customers.[147]

History teaches that change comes in cycles, which reflect larger patterns in play. They stir the mix of possibilities and permit new and untried ideas to gain a toehold. Progress builds on the ruins of what came before, spurred on by imagination and some measure of hopeful confidence. The march of progress may gallop here or dawdle there, and sometimes it takes a few steps back. But it never stands still. In *Adapt: Why success always starts with failure*, Tim Harford said:

> [In crises of the past] for every institution that failed, or every business model that outlived its usefulness, new and better ones rushed in to fill the void. Past periods of crisis eventually gave rise to new epochs of great ingenuity and inventiveness. They were the times when new technologies

---

[146] *Ibid.*, 148.
[147] Harford, Tim, *Adapt: Why success always starts with failure* (New York: Farrar, Straus and Giroux, 2011), 242.

and new business models were forged, and they were also the eras that ushered in new economic and social models and whole new ways of living and working.[148]

Survival in stormy seas depends on being able to leverage the waves of change with minimal non-productive effort or negative consequences. It is important not to resist those forces in play, nor to deny their threat either. When we understand the full range of the forces involved, we can adapt more intelligently and quickly.

Fixed strategies will not cut it; they are almost always behind the curve and slow to catch up. Those who become the survivors of major disruptions employ three traits identified by psychologists Suzanne Kobosa and Salvadore Maddi (*Strategy of the Dolphin* by Dudley Lynch and Paul Kordis).

Traits of Survivors:
- A clear focus on what it is they want to achieve in their work and career

- An ability to experience surprises as challenges and setbacks as valuable learning experiences, refusing to be immobilized by change

- A firm sense that most of the time they are in control of their actions and the meanings they assign to events, and not in the control of the events themselves[149]

Technology Delivers Change on Steroids

Change or Die

Not only is change coming faster, in some regards it is getting less risky, and sometimes even cheaper. Business and social institutions are being compelled to keep changing in order to stay relevant.

Whole industries are rising and falling on the ever-changing whims of the buying public or the hard-to-gauge economic trends. And everyone is finding it extraordinarily difficult to relate to the scope of changes required of us.

In an environment continually changing, companies that keep doing what brought them success in the past, under previous conditions, are probably going to slide further and further away from the success they enjoyed before. And competing ideas and methods that are more nimble and inventive will gain the advantage.

---

[148] Florida, Richard, *The Great Reset: How new ways of living and working drive post-crash prosperity* (New York: Harper, 2010), x.
[149] Lynch, Dudley and Kordis, Paul L., *Strategy of the Dolphin: Scoring a win in a chaotic world* (New York: Balantine, 1990), 78.

Forget one-size-fits-all products or services. The marketplace doesn't respond to it anymore. There really isn't any viable, long-term choice that doesn't involve: reinventing oneself, focusing on what is coming, and embracing brilliant but untried possibilities. This is, and has always been, the key to creating something better. It helps us stay on the pulse of change.

Richard Florida has documented the cultural change to a creativity-based economy. In *The Great Reset*, he addresses environmental factors that support such a shift.

> Our own collapse, in the early years of the twenty-first century is the crisis of the latest economic revolution—the rise of an idea-driven knowledge economy that runs more on brains than brawn. It reflects the limits of the suburban model of development to channel the full innovation and productive capabilities of the creative economy. The places that thrive today are those with the highest velocity of ideas, the highest density of talented and creative people, and the highest rate of metabolism.[150]

Companies and industries that always operated profitably according to large economies of scale are scrambling. Buyers have gotten used to a wider array of choices that are exactly what they want—and they know how to find them. They must respond to industry-wide and culture-wide trends.

In *Built to Last*, James Collins and Jerry Porras describe the shifting trends and the need for companies to reinvent themselves or fail.

> Our key framework concept, preserving the core/stimulating progress will also become increasingly important in the twenty-first century. Look at the trends of business organization: flatter, more decentralized, more geographically dispersed, greater individual autonomy, more knowledge workers, and so on. More than at any time in the past, companies will not be able to hold themselves together with the traditional methods of control: hierarchy, systems, budgets, and the like. Even going into the office will become less relevant as technology enables people to work from remote sites. The corporate bonding glue will increasingly become *ideological*. People still have a fundamental human need for guiding values and sense of purpose that gives their life and work meaning. They have a fundamental need for connection with other people, sharing with them the common bond of beliefs and aspirations. More than any time in the past, employees will demand operating autonomy while also demanding that the organizations they're connected to *stand* for some something....
>
> And look at the trends of the outer world: fragmentation, segmentation, chaotic change, unpredictability, increased entrepreneurship, and so on. Only those companies particularly adept at stimulating progress will be able to thrive. Companies will need to continually renew themselves, perhaps through awesome BHAGs [Big Hairy Audacious Goals], in order to remain exciting

---

[150] *Op. cit.*, Florida, 46.

places to work. Companies in search of greatness will need to relentlessly push themselves for *self*-stimulated change and improvement *before* the world demands change and improvement.[151]

Success rests on anticipating and pursuing those kinds of changes as highly desirable ways to stand out. That is the arena where leaders must prove their mettle.

Plotting a Winning Strategy

Such concerns make one ask what an enterprise is attempting to achieve beyond survival. Most traditional management strategies do not fit the new reality — let alone indicate what is over the horizon. When protecting one's turf is the first order of business, it is easy to fail to foresee a future where those factors do not matter so much — let alone keep rooting for it.

In *Six Pixels of Separation*, Mitch Joel speaks of ways the Internet has altered commerce — and will continue to do so.

> We're still shipping tons of stuff, but we've shifted from crates and barrels into bits and bytes now.... The pace of change continues to increase and all of us have to get much better at spotting these trends or, at the very least, doing our best to stay informed and connected. We also have to accept another very real concept: It is going to shift from bits and bytes into something else as well and we are not (and cannot be) prepared for that, either.[152]

The business world has been of two minds about how to treat what technology has dumped in its lap. Technology has proven to be a two-edged sword — both extraordinarily helpful in increasing efficiencies and cutting labor costs, while being calamitous because of the way it has destroyed predictability.

Chapters 14 and 15 explore the impact on the workplace. But it is not technology itself that determines whether those gifts are a godsend or a misadventure. Technology is an amoral tool. Although powerful in its impact, it serves the values and goals of those who employ it. And it cannot fully compensate for lack of judgment — just accelerates the outcome.

Jim Collins address the proper way for technology to serve the organization's needs in *Good to Great*.

> Good-to-great companies think differently about the role of technology. They never use technology as the primary means of igniting a transformation. Yet, paradoxically, they are pioneers in the application of carefully selected

---

[151] Collins, James C.V. and Porras, Jerry I., *Built to Last: Successful habits of visionary companies* (New York: Harper Collins, 1997), 247-8.
[152] Joel, Mitch, *Six Pixels of Separation: Everyone is connected. Connect your business to everyone* (New York: Hatchette Book Group, 2009), 257.

technologies. We learned that technology by itself is never a primary, root cause of either greatness or decline.[153]

Integrating Waves of Change

Individuals and organizations position themselves as to whether they are on the leading edge of change or further back in the pack. And being out front is not determined by their specific type of profession or industry, but by their eagerness to introduce or embrace what is new and still in the process of coming together.

Each phase (or group of consumers, below) has developed its own sense of which pace of change works for them, and which does not.

Those who introduce new products or systems need to be clear about how new products will meet the needs of those in their market (ideal users). People go through a process when deciding to adopt, or reject, a new invention/idea. Even after they accept/buy it, they might just as easily discontinue its use — if it doesn't measure up.

The easier it is for someone to adapt the new product or idea to suit their needs, the more likely it will be accepted and catch on.

Decision Stages to Adopt an Innovation:
1. Knowledge of the innovation — information gathering
2. Persuasion — forming a favorable (or unfavorable) attitude toward it
3. Decision is made to accept or reject it
4. Implementation of the innovation — putting it to use
5. Confirmation — seeking reinforcement of decision from others as to its value

Everett Rogers wrote the oft-cited 1962 classic work about the spread of new ideas, in which he identified five distinct groups. Members of each group have fundamentally different ways of relating to acceptance of new products, each with distinctive characteristics. Therefore, it does not work well to treat all groups of potential customers/clients or users the same.

Each of the five groups represents a different market, with its own specific needs and expectations. That is not to say each of them is equally lucrative or worth courting. Companies learned the hard way about introducing products that represent positive or negative discontinuities.

Geoffrey A. Moor discussed the special challenges of discontinuous innovations in *Crossing the Chasm*.

---

[153] Collins, Jim, *Good to Great: Why some companies make the leap… and others don't* (New York: Harper Business, 2001), 13-14.

> [Our attitude about learning curves is significant] any time we are introduced to products that require us to change our current mode of behavior or to modify other products and services we rely on. In academic terms, such change-sensitive products are called discontinuous innovations. The contrasting term, continuous innovations, refers to the normal upgrading of products that does not require us to change our behavior.... Whereas other industries introduce discontinuous innovations only occasionally and with much trepidation, high-tech enterprises do so routinely and as confidently as a born-again Christian holding four aces.[154]

Diffusion of Innovations:
- First there are the *Innovators*. These are the geeks for whom venturesomeness is an obsession.... [They] always want to be first with anything. They love to be rash, daring and risky.... They add up to 2.5 percent of the population....

- *Early Adopters* are just slightly ahead of the crowd. But they are much more connected to the social fabric.... [They] constitute a seventh of the population.

- The *Early Majority* follows. They are numerous—a third of the population. They never lead, but they don't want to be stick-in-the-muds.

- The *Late Majority* then kicks in. For them, change has become inevitable, usually because sticking to their old ways is killing them economically.... [This group] is another third of the population....

- Finally come *The Laggards*. They tend to be suspicious of any change and stick to other people like themselves.[155]

Fifty years later, this pattern still applies, but new products and societal changes are coming so quickly anymore the time lag that used to separate these groups keeps shrinking. The issue might not be how receptive people are, but how constant and insistent change is.

I question those percentages, which I think are much higher now, at least in the two fastest categories. These figures are from 1962, when an interest in innovation was not as widespread as it is today.

Due to the many ways technological developments impact our lives, a person can occupy more than one of the categories, depending on the specific topic. One could be an Early Adopter, an Early Majority, and a Late Majority responder at the same time, depending on other practical factors that are not acknowledged by these broad distinctions.

---

[154] Moore, Geoffrey A., *Crossing the Chasm: Marketing and selling disruptive products to mainstream customers* (New York: Collins Business Essentials, 1999), 10-11.
[155] Garreau, Joel, *Radical Evolution: The promise and peril of enhancing our minds, our bodies – and what it means to be human* (New York: Broadway Books, 2005), 60-1.

In my own case, as a writer I stay on top of new developments in the fields of publishing and communications. But as a "homesteader," who spends some of my time off the grid and without electricity, I steadfastly resist the intrusion of modern conveniences inclined to complicate a simpler life.

Technological change has become increasingly pervasive in modern life. The computerization of everything has delivered ever-greater efficiencies and speed. But some of what it brings bears little relationship to how people are accustomed to doing things—or how it coincides with their preferences.

Often these secondary factors carry more weight in the decision to say "yes" to something new than the product's desirability.

Completely new products or services that are unlike anything the customer has yet seen involve major learning experiences for them. Truly novel discoveries in technology can be contrasted with the steady tinkering and upgrades that characterize most advances in those fields. But, just as the speed of innovation has accelerated, so has the speed of obsolescence. We are losing some things so quickly we don't even notice before they are gone.

As an example, consider the book and the ways we communicate with language. Technological developments have turned words into bits and bytes. And in the process we must reinvent our relationship to them. Robert Darnton, the Director of Harvard's libraries, argues for the value of books and libraries in *The Case for Books*.

> Already we are witnessing the disappearance of familiar objects: the typewriter, now consigned to antique shops; the postcard, a curiosity; the handwritten letter, beyond the capacity of most young people, who cannot write in cursive script; the daily newspaper, extinct in many cities; the local bookshop, replaced by chains, which themselves are threatened by Internet distributors like Amazon. And the library?
>
> It can look like the most archaic institution of all. Yet its past bodes well for its future, because libraries were never warehouses of books. They have always been and always will be centers of learning. Their central position in the world of learning makes them ideally suited to mediate between the printed and the digital modes of communication. Books, too, can accommodate both modes. Whether printed on paper or stored in servers, they embody knowledge, and their authority derives from a great deal more than the technology that went into them. They owe some of their authority to authors.... By selecting texts, editing them, designing them to be readable, and bringing them to the attention of readers, book professionals provide services that will outlast all changes in technology.[156]

---

[156] Darnton, Robert, *The Case for Books: Past, present and future* (New York: Public Affairs, 2009), *xv-xvi*.

Collaborative Innovation Is Rapid and Widely Disbursed

Several factors in particular drive the runaway speed of change. One factor is the role of Moore's Law, which describes how the costs of computing hardware keep going down. (But even Moore's Law is already being surpassed.) The other is the major and increasing influence of the Internet—how people find answers and communicate with each other. Simply speeding up the product development cycle leads to a variety of problems of its own.

As technological developments accelerate the change process, it sends ripples across the entire culture. Technology grows (in part) and expands at an ever-accelerating rate. It is tricky for even the most determined to keep up, and information overload is impossible to avoid. But it is also altering how people work together, whether as employees or outside of structured organizations.

The lone inventor could yield to large impersonal teams, as G. Pascal Zachary argues in a *New York Times* article, "Genius and Misfit Aren't Synonyms, or Are They?" (June 5, 2007).

Technological innovation—not to mention new scientific knowledge—is increasing as a result of large teams, working in routine, predictable ways. Individuals matter, but their contributions often can no longer be measured, nor can credit be accurately apportioned—even by the people working closest with them.[157]

A new era of collaboration has developed on a worldwide scale. For young people who grew up on computers and email, this way of relating is as natural as using a telephone used to be. And participants continue pushing the capacity of interactive tools like text messages or social media.

With the advent of even better devices, there seems to be no end in sight. More about the influence of collaborative innovation and technology is covered in Chapters 14 and 15.

> In Wikinomics, Don Tapscott and Anthony D. Williams explain how the organizational structure itself is being restructured. Though it is unlikely that hierarchies will disappear in the foreseeable future, a new form of horizontal organization is emerging that rivals the hierarchical firm in its capacity to create information-based products and services, and in some cases, physical things. This new form of organization is known as peering.[158]
>
> To innovate and succeed, the new mass collaboration must become part of every leader's playbook and lexicon. Learning how to engage and cocreate with

---

[157] Zachary, G. Pascal, "Genius and Misfit Aren't Synonyms, or Are They?" *New York Times*, June 5, 2007.
[158] Tapscott, Don and Williams, Anthony D., *Wikinomics: How mass collaboration changes everything* (New York: Portfolio, 2006), 23.

a shifting set of self-organized partners is becoming an essential skill, as important as budgeting, R&D, and planning.[159]

Exponential growth is being generated by the emergence of whole new industries and players. And the trend toward self-directed teams is just warming up. These new forms of commerce and collaboration are not simply derivative or the result of tinkering with existing technology. Florida argues that our very lifestyle will also be restructured.

> For the Great Reset to become a bona fide recovery, society needs to come full circle to harness not only emergent and shifting values but also to generate new technologies, new economic systems, and new patterns of consumption. The next Great Reset must ultimately do for our times what suburbanization did for the postwar era—take shape as a new lifestyle and a new economic landscape that can ultimately power new kinds of demand and undergird a new round of growth.
>
> Pundits talk about how change happens at the speed of light in the digital age, but the current Reset will be anything but automatic.[160]

Grounding Large-scale Revolutionary Breakthroughs

There is considerable flux and shifting gears evident in every field and arena of life these days because many advantages that worked before are becoming handicaps. Large, dominant companies are out of step with current needs and opportunities—with too much inertia or old baggage for them to fly.

The costs to work out the nuts and bolts of building the products and the training of specialists are formidable. The more innovative, the longer the lead time needed for getting those elements in place. That is besides finding buyers who would like to acquire it.

The roots of significant innovative progress always reflect a wider historical context. They encompass much more than the specific technologies involved. Alex Steffen addresses the interplay of relationships necessary for bold changes .

> Changing the world today is all about the network. It's about playing well with others. Certainly one needs boldness and inspired leadership to undertake any world changing mission. But one also needs new models, new visions, willing allies and ready resources. And I would submit that these things far more often emerge from collaboration and networks than they spring from the foreheads of Fountainhead-style visionaries. When doing social change work, the strength and quality of the connections matters at least as much as the leadership zeal of any particular node.

---

[159] *Ibid.*, 19-20.
[160] *Op. cit.*, Florida, 106.

That being the case, business (at least business as it functioned in the 20th Century) is in fact exactly the wrong model for leadership development. You don't want to train a whole mess of egotists who excel at making funding pitches to boards. What you want to do is train people to collaborate effectively, to build networks of innovation and communication, to spread tools and swarm problems and maximize the impact of available resources. Nourish the network!

That doesn't mean that the idea of trying various approaches and supporting those which prove effective is a bad idea — of course it's not — but framing this as competition for 'performance' can quite often be poisonous.

Competition has its uses. But it's important to distinguish competition within a framework of collaboration from a war of all against all. Open source programmers compete fiercely for prestige, but they do so within a context in which all are made more effective.

And because the most important aspects of any truly innovative approach to social change are almost always intangible, almost always about relationships, trust, morale and the kind of conversations that foster genuinely insightful thinking and action, an obsession with performance metrics (and anything which means funding or its lack quickly will become an obsession) distorts the entire project, since the most important parts of it are only tangentially measurable at best.[161]

There Is No Going Back to the Way Things Were

"How ya gonna keep 'em down on the farm (after they've seen Gay Paree)?" That WWI song is about the soldiers who fought in Europe and got to go see what's beyond the farm. After they returned home, their former life on the farm was not enough.

They experienced a larger world, along with gaining an expanded sense of what was possible. Can a person who has been away relate to home as though nothing is different? Not likely.

A vision is like Paree (Paris) — showing there is more to life than was previously imagined. Now what? Once a person *sees* "something more," some want to *be something more* and *do something more.* They are open to new possibilities and less willing to accept their prior worldview or limitations.

The farm represents their familiar home and practical circumstances. Those don't go away. One of the challenges after returning from elsewhere is deciding how to relate to homebodies who never left the farm. How much of the unfamiliar can be spoken about? How much do those who stayed home want to know about that stuff they didn't share? How much can they understand the resulting changes in the one who left?

---

[161] Steffen, Alex, "How to Change the World," May 16, 2004, http://www.worldchanging.com

A single dramatic vision might not fundamentally change a person's life right away, but it is starting. And sooner or later new possibilities arise in them that could lead away from the former, smaller frame of reference. Will they hang out with the old crowd or with the guys who have also been abroad?

Do family ties and expectations curb their desires to further expand their horizons? There are strong pulls in both directions.

Even when a traveler comes back to the farm to stay, they will look for ways to alter the confining structures to fit their wider view better. They have grown and now must make the kind of adjustments that reflect the larger worldview. What kinds of choices do they make? Will they stay home or heed the distant drummer?

While there are infinite choices a person can make theoretically, they are not equivalent or equally worthy of pursuit. A significant aspect of heading into unexplored territory involves the person changing their priorities in line with a broader view. As with the adjacent possible, a person is only able to make certain decisions after others decisions are in place.

When someone grows in competence and judgment, his or her range of possibilities also expands. That is why being curious and a lifelong learner continue to pay off in an expanded range of novel possibilities. Home could become Paree.

~ Getting All You Pay For ~
A BonBon ~ Faith Lynella

Some of life's most valuable and precious lessons can only be learned by failure. If we then sink too deeply into disappointment or embrace self-pity, we fail to get the message that we have paid such a high price to receive. Insist not just that the suffering stop, but that a lesson is received for each setback. Most people are satisfied just to have the difficulty go away, even at the risk that it will return.

Unless we insist that we learn the meaningful message that comes through suffering, we haven't gotten the benefit we "paid" so dearly for. It is not possible to prevent some of life's upsets, but we can demand that we get an understanding from them. Hold on until you can say, with sincerity (you have to really mean it): "Painful as it was, I'm glad it happened, or I wouldn't have learned *_____." Whatever you say to fill in the blank is a trophy you can use forever—you've earned it, and it is valuable beyond price. That is the way wisdom is achieved.

We have the right to hold the universe accountable for the lessons it sends us, and it will give us a valuable answer—but only when we insist.

*It's for you to decide; fill in your own blank.

From *BonBons to Sweeten Your Daily Life*. Or from *More BonBons*

Welcoming Change to Our Personal Way of Life

We need to take an active role in destroying our auto-pilot comfort zones that lull us into passivity and habitual thinking. That approach thinks defensively, rather than expansively and imaginatively. In their place, we could be heeding the attractive enthusiasm of curiosity and the young-at-heart emotional urges that revel in play.

Enjoy all the sensuous pleasures to be had of the "stop and smell the flowers" variety. Let's stop being too busy and instead embrace the abundance of life that is happening all around us—leaving the door open to who knows what.

Along the way, people will have to entertain new bases on which to make choices. These go way beyond where to live or which amenities are most important, as Florida makes clear.

> It is hard for most people to imagine making sudden and radical changes to the way they live. Committed urbanites thrive on the cultural amenities cities have to offer and feed off the hustle and bustle of city life. Happy suburbanites would not think of leaving their comfortable homes with spacious yards and double garages full of minivans or SUVs. Both fall into the trap of thinking about future lifestyles as a choice between one or the other, as some sort of conflict between urban versus suburban living.... This is no black-or-white, city-versus-suburb, winner-takes-all battle. Cities and suburbs alike are part of the new spatial mix.[162]

But the real difference is less about geography or physical space than about emotional space. Our new way of relating must allow each aspect of "who I am" to have a place. The real choices, the hard choices, are not between the specifics, but in preferring the overall flexibility of choices that satisfy all aspects of our unique identity.

It is not just what we do at work or at home, but is an inseparable aspect of one's frame of reference. It comes with learning to feel "at home" in any environment.

Greater self-awareness opens us to a much larger array of options. When we feel confident enough to step out of what is familiar, we find new ways to use more of the often-ignored information available to us. And that degree of flexibility permeates the message, with extra impact on the audience.

In *The Art of Woo*, Robert G. Shell and Mario Moussa explain why being more self-aware leads to a positive reception of your message.

> Self-awareness is an internal thermometer that tells you whether you are happy, sad, insecure, or confident. In a persuasion encounter, the more self-awareness you bring to the table, the more you can monitor your own feelings and measure the reactions your audience is feeding back to you. Persuaders with a lack of confidence, a bout of nerves, or a fear of failure often tend to

---

[162] *Op. cit.*, Florida, 144.

focus almost exclusively on the content of their message. They are listening to what they are saying and thinking about what they will say next.

> By contrast, people who know their message cold can deliver it while simultaneously monitoring the moment-to-moment reactions of listeners as they experience the persuasion process.... By monitoring your audience and adjusting your pitch, you can keep everyone's attention and stay in the game. When you fail to adjust, you end up speaking in what amounts to a 'foreign' language.[163]

While that is true about persuading others to accept your point of view, it is even more important for you to be able to fully persuade yourself. The part of yourself that wants to change, that is ready for something new, must convince the parts of yourself that don't feel that way. Building that level of internal consensus can fundamentally alter your behavior or support desired change.

Embracing the Resolve to Change

A flood of insights, or reading a book like this, sets off a desire to make personal changes. If anything, the carrot is bigger, more alluring, and all the things we don't like act as battering sticks.

But hold on a minute... That's how it has been going on all along. The push to make changes shoves up against our personal *status quo*, and before long it has petered out. Herminina Ibarra addresses some of those issues relative to one's professional identity in Working Identity.

> The difference between a job change and a career reinvention lies in a depth of personal transformation that is largely invisible to an outside observer.... One of the reasons it is so hard to change careers—or why we change, only to end up in the same boat—is that we can so fully internalize our institutional identities, relying on them to convey our worth and accomplishments to the outside world.[164]

> A prolonged exploratory phase can be a defense mechanism against changing, and it can signal to others that we are not serious about making change. A true experimental method almost always leads to formulating new goals and new means to achieve them. As we learn from experience, we have to be willing to close avenues of exploration, to accept that what we thought we knew was wrong and that what we were hoping to find no longer suits us.[165]

The counter-weights to actually changing oneself are even more insidious when we get into our personality issues. Revisit the BonBon, "Ligatures of Devotion" in Chapter 8. At the point of resolve, consider those influences relative to what

---

[163] Shell, G. Richard and Moussa, Mario, *The Art of Woo: Using strategic persuasion to sell your ideas* (New York: Portfolio, 2007), 116-7.
[164] Ibarra, Herminina, *Working Identity: Unconventional strategies for reinventing your career* (Boston: Harvard Business School Press, 2003), 81-4.
[165] *Ibid.*, 100.

you want to be different. Spend at least as much effort considering what must be jettisoned as on the beckoning goals that sing to you.

Having done that, stay on the alert for signs of ligatures showing up — because they will. The insidiousness of the familiar and habitual acts as the natural default state. Do not expect it to retreat or yield just because you want something new. This is a battle of attrition — where your attention is the most powerful (perhaps the only) tool you have.

Many years ago, I joined a spiritual community devoted to inner work (where I stayed for 18 years). There were only a few firm rules a person had to accept at the point of getting aboard:

- Do not express negative emotions — which is not possible, but the attempt needs to be made
- Give up your causes — they put the emphasis on *fixing the world* instead of the more difficult task of inner work
- Do not try to change anything about yourself — at least at the outset

The third item focuses on how eager we try to "fix oneself," ahead of really seeing oneself dispassionately (and without self-judgment). Instead, we were urged to *just observe* our behavior. With that detachment, a person cannot help but see the tug-of-war between their intensions and their mindless habits. Now comes the tricky part, NOT acting on the discrepancy.

It hurts to see the amount of internal gamesmanship each of us has built up over a lifetime of trying to be "an even better person." The problem is, we were trying to create a false self. It was sincere on one level, but misguided on others.

Only after a month or two of sitting in that uncomfortable stew is a person prepared to see what's called "the horror of the situation." Individuals cannot control their attention or resolve — and it is an illusion for us to think we do. For the first time, one sees the immensity of our auto-pilot internal life — that has no intention of being any different.

Once the "horror" of that realization is seen, it trumps all other carrots or sticks. The person is now ready to really begin their inner work.

Chapter 10 - Packaging a Vision That Resonates

The package needs to make it obvious why people have a stake in the newer, better idea — and quickly, too. Unless the proposed notion is considered the "greatest thing since sliced bread," it is easy for people to leave it on the shelf.

Vision Demands Expression

Having a significant vision can change someone in numerous ways. Simply having a vision does not distinguish visionaries from their contemporaries, however. Creative flashes are common and most people have them occasionally. But they are more likely to treat such insights as a pleasant holiday from the routines of life. What form does their reaction take? Does it inspire action?

Ideally, such moments of clarity can and should improve the way someone relates to life in general so they desire to do something with what blazed so brightly for them. Ken Wilber insists (in *One Taste*) that those who have been given a significant vision are obligated to communicate it. There is a price for being permitted to see — one must speak out with all the passion and courage the person can muster. No excuses.

> All of those for whom authentic transformation has deeply unseated their souls must, I believe, wrestle with the profound moral obligation to shout from the heart — perhaps quietly and gently with tears of reluctance; perhaps with fierce fire and angry wisdom; perhaps with slow and careful analysis; perhaps by unshakable public example — but *authenticity* always and absolutely carries a *demand* and *duty*; you must speak out, to the best of your ability, and shake the spiritual tree, and shine your headlights into the eyes of the complacent. You must let that radical realization rumble through your veins and rattle those around you....
>
> Any realization of depth carries a terrible burden: Those who are allowed to see are simultaneously saddled with the obligation to communicate that vision in no uncertain terms: that is the bargain. You are allowed to see the truth under the agreement that you would communicate it to others ... and therefore, if you have seen, you simply must speak out. Speak out with compassion, or speak out with angry wisdom, or speak out with skilful means, but speak out you must.[166]

Visionaries have taken this obligation to heart to varying degrees. Although differing in their methods or loudness, they refuse to bury their light. Those committed to a vision use whatever means they can call upon to keep their flame alive, as well as to pass it along.

It is not surprising for someone to have difficulty expressing even a very clear vision. And visionaries are acutely aware of the wide gap between what they envision and the current state of affairs. They feel humbled by the immensity of

---

[166] Wilber, Ken, *One Taste: The journals of Ken Wilber* (Boston: Shambhala, 1999), 35.

what they have seen, especially compared to their keenly felt limitations—or ability to do it justice.

However, if that were a sufficient deterrent to taking the leap or to speaking out, they would merely be dreamers. Visionaries seem to be singularly energized by those discrepancies and are moved to take persistent action to bridge the gap.

Creating the Defining Story and Symbolism

The pristine vision is not achievable because it exists in the world of ideas. But the mission related to grounding it can be achieved—once it can be translated into a course of action. Grounding a vision requires developing a way for it to exist in a form that can be explained and acted upon.

The visionary has the igniting vision, but unless he or she can find a way to explain or demonstrate what they realized, that original clarity ends with them. The message needs form—in most cases that means words. However, those in the arts turn to other means of communication, with verbal explanations likely to be counter-productive.

Artistic types demonstrate their craft through new forms of expression which people are invited to experience directly (later this chapter).

Simply put, the package is about communication—deciding what to say, to whom, and how to express it, so that the audience might grasp and appreciate, even a little, the promise that the vision is offering. *What is actually said* is likely to be less compelling than *the way it is delivered.*

Delivery has a powerful influence on the *way people receive it and respond to it*. The emotional intensity and body language that attend a message are miles ahead of spoken or written words in their persuasive power.

At any point in time, some people will probably be receptive to the visionary's new idea. But they are not the majority. Many more will be indifferent, and others downright hostile. Even those ideas that prevail without major resistance took a while to get there.

A visionary expects some segment of the public (or target population) to be more than ready for the fresh idea or product they propose—ready enough to embrace it. He or she needs to garner supporters and allies as early as possible. They need to tailor the message to speak to their requirements and desires, before trying too hard to justify the message to detractors.

The visionary should craft their message from the outset to speak to those most amenable to its significance. Too many bright ideas foundered because they burned themselves out in head-to-head confrontations with opposing interests. The visionary must first learn how to manage their energy and pick their fights. It is usually wiser to focus attention on the positive responders right out of the starting gate, so momentum can gather with the support of allies.

Getting People to Care

The package needs to express a mix of mental, emotional, and physical components so people can respond to it from their own listening style. When hearers can fully resonate with the message's truth, it ceases to be some dry theory or hyperbolic pie in the sky to them. An absence of any of the preferential expression modes in the package could be disquieting or unlikely to ring true for certain listeners.

Of course, there has to be an emotional connection—on the personal level. Profound truth is too remote to galvanize enthusiastic action. The visionary must take an idea from abstract principle to solid ground by illustrating and defining it in specifics, so that it might begin to show signs of life.

In *Made to Stick*, the Heath brothers described how to get emotional buy-in for our ideas.

> How can we make people care about our ideas? We get them to take off their Analytical Hats. We create empathy for specific individuals. We know how our ideas are associated with things that people already care about. We appeal to their self-interest, but we also appeal to their identities—not only to the people they are right now but also to the people they would like to be.[167]

The package spells out (or demonstrates) the new idea's benefits, including what must change for it to happen. It combines carrot and stick—to get X (the promised advantage), you must give up Y (something familiar), or start doing Z (a new behavior or belief). It must somehow integrate a novel notion with the compatible assumptions of the larger culture (such as the value of efficiency).

A package must also be clear about how the new notion differs from what is in place—why it is distinctly advantageous. While the goal is to alter behavior, that generally occurs in stages, if at all. Guy Kawasaki lays out those stages in *Enchantment*.

Stages of Internalizing Values:
- **Conformity**. People join because of peer pressure, coercion, trickery, or a desire to belong to a group. Conformity isn't enchantment and won't last long without undue force unless you move to identification and internalization.

- **Identification**. When people identify with members of a group, they see commonality and shared interests. No one is forcing them to conform. At this stage the attractiveness of the enchanter and others in the group is important because people want the enchanter's approval.

- **Internalization**. This is the highest level. It means people have gone beyond identifying to believing. Their belief is not at odds with their feelings. There

---

[167] Heath, Chip and Dan, *Made to Stick: Why some ideas survive and others die* (New York: Random House, 2010), 263.

is no coercion, and they are not trying to please anyone. This is enchantment.

Internalization is the hardest level to achieve, but the one that will last the longest.[168]

Defining the Message

Each package introduces its own conceptual language and jargon. The language and imagery used provide the visionary's rationale for the new creative wrinkle. It includes the implicit expectation that listeners should accept it as well. Eric Hoffer said:

> The effectiveness of a doctrine does not come from its meaning but from its certitude. No doctrine however profound and sublime will be effective unless it is presented as the embodiment of the one and only truth.[169]

The package needs to make it obvious why people have a stake in the newer, better idea (or invention) — and quickly, too. Unless the proposed notion is considered the greatest thing since sliced bread it is easy for people to leave it on the shelf. The visionary's message should engage people in as many ways as possible — while striving to keep sour notes from creeping in.

Congruency, clarity, and authenticity must be the standards for presentation, for *they will be* the standards by which people judge it (albeit on a gut or intuitive level). Just as important is the manner in which the package is delivered to the waiting world, so those qualities do not get lost in the shuffle.

And over time, further tweaking is required to assure those authentic qualities still shine through.

The more fully all five senses can be engaged, the more ways people can find a way to relate to the new notion — by sound, taste, vision, touch, smell, and imagination. Such sensuous experience connects powerfully with the body memory and emotions that anchor beliefs. They *feel good*, so there is more enthusiasm engendered.

Sensory input gets past the habitual, logical gatekeepers and their objections. Actually, both intellect and belief need to be involved for long-term commitment to stick.

Ideal Qualities of the Package:
- Identifies and elaborates the message or goal
- Clear, concise, and comprehensible

---

[168] Kawasaki, Guy, *Enchantment: The art of changing hearts, minds, and actions* (New York: Portfolio/Penguin, 2011), 96.
[169] Hoffer, Eric, *The True Believer: Thoughts on the nature of mass movements* (New York: Harper & Row, 1951), 70.

- Coherent—the parts hang together
- Doable steps, practices, and procedures
- Relevant and beneficial to the person or reference group
- Emotional components people can relate to
- Resonates with integrity and plausibility; rings true
- Designed to win over both hearts and minds
- Not too strange, abhorrent, or offensive to core values

A Good Story Connects

We never outgrow the enjoyment of a good story, one that becomes familiar in the retelling—with interesting characters and challenges to be overcome. People find ways to relate to the same themes in their own lives. The combination of wonder and suspended belief in a story takes us to a place that taps into heartfelt beliefs, unhampered by feasibility.

The stories shared by a culture express the values interwoven into the social fabric. These are the threads people of the same time and place have in common, use in rearing their children, and to convey norms of behavior. They relate to the social sanctions and rites of passage.

Similarly, any new idea needs to incorporate its own stories and practices that resonate with their deepest values.

As Joseph Campbell points out, "Myth is the secret opening through which the inexhaustible energies of the cosmos pour into human manifestation." And a vision that can ride on stories that resonate with listeners will both move them and be remembered. Suitable stories add the credibility for the more logical elements in the package.

While the package can convey both a practical and an emotional message, it should also appeal to the listener's unquestioning openness that builds belief. Stories that move us deeply touch what is basic and at the core of each of us.

The emotional pull of the visionary story needs to feel desirable and ring true before people give it credence. Any perceived hype or manipulation could be deal breakers. Dan and Chip Heath said:

> Mental simulation is not as good as actually doing something, but it's the next best thing.… The right kind of story is, effectively, a simulation. Stories are like flight simulators for the brain.… This is the role that stories play—putting knowledge into a framework that is more lifelike, more true to our day-to-day existence. More like a flight simulator. Being the audience for a story isn't so passive, after all. Inside, we're getting ready to act.[170]

---

[170] *Op. cit.*, Heath, 213-4.

Ways of Transmitting Shared Cultural Values:
- Stories, fairy tales, fables, histories, myths (how we got here)
- Songs, music, dance, chants
- Parables, metaphors and symbols with agreed-upon underlying meaning
- Images that represent the key concepts, like a logo with a slogan
- Plays, performances, acting out a story or process
- Training, demonstrations, how-to, morality plays
- Human interest stories, testimonials, bearing witness
- Any of the arts; also using various media like audio, animation, video
- Rituals or ceremonies people perform either together or alone
- Learning exercises or ethical puzzles like, what would you do if…?

More specifically, the field of interest dictates the appropriate form of the package. For example, scientific packages involve research and statistical proof; composing involves musical notation. Publications, public media, or performances are employed as suitable for the specific genre where a person operates.

Of course, packages vary greatly as to the importance of its dogma, rituals, traditions, and the way it is to be carried on (as in specialized training or child rearing practices). Its form also depends on whether it is a concept for everybody or only for specialists. Or it could be for everybody, but only expressed and delivered via insiders or a "priest" class.

The visionary, core group, detractors, and the general public all see the vision from different perspectives. The package needs to be broad enough to have something to say to each of their diverse concerns and frames of reference.

> No matter what point of departure one uses, symbols inevitably have both a shared and an individual component. No two people ever use the same word in exactly the same way, and the more abstract the symbol, the greater the likelihood of a sizeable individual component.[171]

Deeply felt messages have staying power. Great care needs to be taken that the symbols and language used can be clearly understood and be felt intuitively, as well as grasped logically.

Tell the Visionary's Personal Story

Part of the package people especially like relating to is the visionary's personal history: their roots and how they came by their mandate. It tells the back story, with early hints of greatness and what influenced them—before and early into their mission. For example, Darwin's theory is a lot more interesting when it includes the voyage of the Beagle.

---

[171] *Op. cit.*, Hall, 241-2.

Another modern example is teenagers Steve Jobs and Steve Wozniak geeking around in their parents' garage with the ridiculous notion that anyone could have and use their own personal computer at home.

The visionary gambles his or her worldly status and comfortable life on the value of their discovery. They are banking on acceptance coming sooner or later. Proponents need to be enthusiastic about introducing the change they hope the public will embrace.

It is not enough to explain the concepts. People also want to know how it came about, or how it has made a difference in the visionary's life. All that backstory helps to make the message believable, real, and personal for them.

Every vision-visionary dyad has a tale to tell. That story may convey the reassurance: I am like you (in some regard)… I used to believe or do… You can too… (follow my example, benefit from what I have discovered). Or it could describe the trials and dead ends, which communicate "It was difficult to get the answer, but worth it because ____."

Such is the stuff of myth making—every bit as important for people to hang onto as the main message.

Using Ceremonies and Rituals

Experiences of shared knowing provide a powerful way to communicate both the essential and implicit message. It lets participants put themselves in the picture, providing a desire for it to come about. It is easy to sense the fervor in a revival tent or charged-up meeting.

People get on the same wavelength and act in concert. Their habitual resistance could also fall away.

Even when an authentic experience can be shared and accepted, as in rites of passage or inspired moments, that awareness fades. People easily forget, even when they believe. There needs to be ways to maintain and rekindle that connection, so it is not a passing fancy.

Long-term agreement involves changing the assumptions people use to assess their own experiences. Providing a new frame of reference and vocabulary help them relate to the idea in a fresh way. Social reinforcement with other participants further solidifies belief in the new idea. Widespread support develops as more people tell their experiences and stories about how the message helped them.

There Needs to Be a Buy-in Mechanism

The package should make getting involved easy enough for people to act while the urge is upon them. They want to get on the bandwagon when it seems like the right thing to do, and people they respect are doing it too.

When the vision being offered is seen as something they wouldn't want to miss out on, more joiners (or buyers) build the momentum. Sometimes a critical mass forms that drives the change, while sweeping away the impediments.

An idea or technological development is not adopted until it "feels right" mentally, emotionally and physically. That is what needs to click before the person solidifies their *belief in the message*. How steep is the level of buy-in required for listeners to join up or use the innovation?

Is it enough they buy a product or show up at an event? Is acceptance easy and gradual, or does it require total devotion, or repudiation of their former point of view? How susceptible is acceptance to buyer's remorse once the ardor fades?

There is nothing like taking a stand for someone to signal their being aboard. But is the listener expected to make a decisive and overt show of acceptance? What action (or philosophical change) cements their change of heart or mind? Or is it enough for people to accept it as *true enough* or *useful enough* to add to their bag of tricks?

Of course, the level of commitment is very different for the core group than for the general population. Calls to action mobilize interest. Whether it is to sign a petition, volunteer, or march to war, the person is asked to take a definite action. But embracing an idea might not be obvious only from behavior. Dropping resistance to an idea that one formerly opposed is no small matter either.

Once again, the nature of buy-in depends on the specific area of interest. It also depends on the type of action or role the motivated person takes. Eric Hoffer said, "Action is a unifier. There is less individual distinctness in a genuine man of action — the builder, soldier, sportsman and even the scientist — than in the thinker or in one whose creativeness flows from communion with the self."[172]

The package must also explain why the person has a stake in the newer, better idea — and quickly, too. This probably won't be considered "the greatest thing since sliced bread" (even for bread fanatics), unless it is framed in a way people think is important.

Something has to stand out besides being different or "New!" or "Improved!" Whatever is in place has inertia on its side, so people are inclined to leave well enough alone, or to only accept a minor upgrade. And to quote Dorothy Parker, "You cannot teach an old dogma new tricks."

Carving Out a Public Identity that Resonates

Modern life provides an incredible scope of information for everybody. It is not just from the established media like TV and newspapers but from Internet sources, cable channels, talk radio and so on.

---

[172] *Op. cit.*, Hoffer, 117.

Anyone with an opinion can find an audience. Also, people are sophisticated in using technology's tools to locate precisely the information they desire.

It has got to be simple or people won't "get it." So many features can get in the way of seeing its core benefits. Piling on extra value at the outset confuses. Peter Drucker said "An innovation, to be effective, has to be simple and it has to be focused. It should do only one thing, otherwise, it confuses. If it is not simple, it won't work."

The challenge for today's idea protagonists is to employ a variety of channels of communication to establish their own space in the public perception. While they are making a name for themselves and building a following for their message, they have to sustain their credibility with the audience.

Further, if it is a specialized and narrow group, the message must be packaged in ways members recognize and respect. Dan and Chip Heath address the emotional associations relevant to persuading the public.

> The good news is that to make people care about our ideas we don't have to produce emotion from an absence of emotion. In fact, many ideas use a sort of piggybacking strategy, associating themselves with emotions that already exist.... Exploiting terms and concepts for their emotional associations is a common characteristic of communication. People tend to overuse any idea or concept that delivers an emotional kick. The research labelled this overuse "semantic stretch.[173]

Who Even Cares and Why?

Listeners will hear the message with their normal way of listening — WIIFM (What's in it for me?). Being lukewarm to an idea equals rejecting it. People need a reason to care enough about something different for it to stand out from the hubbub of "notice me" messages that permeate daily life.

Does the proposed change call forth an "if it 'ain't broke don't fix it" reaction? Does it touch on what is central to the person's life? Or is it seen as just a positive, but optional, upgrade?

Howard Gardner describes the conditions that make it easier to change opinions in *Changing Minds*.

> It is more difficult to change the mind when perspectives are held strongly, and publicly, and by individuals of rigid temperament. It is easier to change minds when individuals find themselves in a new environment, surrounded by peers of a different persuasion ... or when individuals undergo shattering experiences ... or encounter luminous personalities.... It's easier to talk about

---

[173] *Op. cit.*, Heath, 171-4.

changing minds in general than to effect enduring changes in any particular mind.[174]

As far as the interest of the public, does the notion seem significantly better or more desirable than what they have already? Or are existing concepts and activities working just fine, thank you? Do people hang on to what they have got because it is too much trouble to think about changing—or because it would bring a raft of learning curves or hiccups? How much of a stake do people have in sticking with what is familiar? Are they satisfied because it is "good enough?"

Among those who do care, is it because they are ardently for or against the new idea? There is a huge difference between passive resistance or lack of interest and someone feeling threatened enough to fight back. It is not just indifference, but active opposition. The intensity of the visionary's ardor is often what carries the day.

Seth Godin said in *Tribes*:

> I've encountered thousands (it might be tens of thousands) of people walking around with great ideas. Some of the ideas really are great; some are merely pretty good. There doesn't seem to be a shortage of ideas. Ordinary folks can dream up remarkable stuff fairly easily.
>
> What's missing is the will to make the ideas happen.
>
> In a battle between two ideas, the best one doesn't necessarily win. No, the idea that wins is the one with the most fearless heretic behind it.[175]

Accelerating Development of the "Next Big Thing"

Sometimes the distinction between being the idea creator and end-users gets fuzzy because the buyers are in a hurry to have it. So they assist a company in developing exactly what they want. They are participating early in the product development cycle. This trend will become even more evident as voluntary visionary teams continue to proliferate.

This is described by Tapscott and Williams in *Wikinomics*:

> They [the Net Generation] are awash in options for information and entertainment.... As they navigate the hubbub, it is not surprising that the opinions of people they know (or feel they know) strongly influence their buying decision. Michael Furdyk says, 'Our generation really doesn't trust the media and advertising as much as we trust peer-to-peer opinion and social networks.... Net-Generationers are not content to be passive consumers, and

---

[174] Gardner, Howard, *Changing Minds: The art and science of changing our own and other people's minds* (Boston, MA: Harvard Business School Press, 2004), 6.
[175] Godin, Seth, *Tribes: We need you to lead us* (New York: Penguin Group, 2008), 42.

increasingly satisfy their desire for choice, convenience, customization, and control by designing, producing, and distributing products themselves.[176]

A related concept is crowdsourcing, as described by Jeff Howe in *Crowdsourcing*.

> Four developments created a fertile ground in which crowdsourcing could emerge. The rise of an amateur class was accompanied by the emergence of a mode of production—open source software—that provides inspiration and practical direction. The proliferation of the Internet and cheap tools gave
>
> consumers a power once restricted to companies endowed with vast capital resources. But it was the evolution of online communities.[177]

Going Forth with Missionary Zeal

The visionary has the vision but also needs a missionary mindset to gain a toehold with the larger community, or within the specialized field of interest. "Missionary" will be used here as a mid-stage of the visionary path—when it is launched into the world but before widespread acceptance. That phase requires taking the idea on the road.

The missionary stage involves those who initially package and spread the word, including, but not limited to, the visionary. Advocates must fire people up through their enthusiasm for the newly minted idea or innovation. As people are drawn to support it, buy it, or try it, some align primarily with the visionary personally, while others could be more attracted by the message or creative wrinkle.

That's why it is so important for all the elements of the package and visionary's story to reinforce each other. And that appeals to our human nature, as Robert Wright describes in *Nonzero*.

> Humans not only generate cultural innovations; they pass judgment on them. You can write any song you want, but other people will have to find it appealing if it is to spread. Your brain may give birth to any technology, but other brains will decide whether the technology thrives. The number of possible technologies is infinite, and only a few pass this test of affinity with human nature.[178]

This is also the verification stage—testing reactions to the message and package. As more people try it out, the notion develops more applications, buy-in, testimonials, endorsements, and sound bites. Early supporters help to show *it works* and *how it works*. Since people care about whom else might be aboard, this social and hands-on validation drives the desired change from the bottom up.

---

[176] Tapscott, Don and Williams, Anthony D., *Wikinomics – How Mass Collaboration Changes Everything* (New York: Portfolio, 2006), 52.
[177] Howe, Jeff, *Crowdsourcing: Why the power of the crowd is driving the future of business* (New York: Crown Business, 2008), 99.
[178] Wright, Robert, *Nonzero: The logic of human destiny* (New York: Vintage Books, 2000), 27.

The message needs to be precisely tuned to language that addresses where audiences are open or engaged as Shell and Moussa describe in *The Art of Woo*.

> The basic persuasion languages people speak parallel the six channels of persuasion.... These are the languages of authority, rationality, vision, interests, politics, and relationships. Your success as a persuader depends on your ability to find the channel—or channels—your audience is tuned to and then communicate using appropriate language.[179]

When the visionary is starting out, they are not ready for what is around the corner—though they do not yet grasp how true it is. If it were fully realized, there would be too much paralysis or indecision. The missionary phase further grounds the vision and the visionary's devotion to it, as the kinks are worked out. It is a bit like a play starting off-Broadway and being tweaked with each performance.

An ongoing task during this phase involves the visionary becoming an effective proponent: a skilled and persuasive public speaker, teacher, writer, public relations expert, marketer, trainer, etc. They are the human face for what they have developed. And it helps if the message can be delivered in a variety of methods and settings: through lectures, audio and video formats, multi-media, online, classes, retreats, or whatever is appropriate for the field so it has the best chance to find its audience or market.

Even though the visionary might not be skilled in all those roles, someone in the core group, or hired hands, will need to deal with those kinds of concerns. Another name for this phase is getting the word out.

There will always be a social component required in bringing a vision to life. Whether they encounter clear sailing or ill winds, the visionary must learn to navigate in the social seas. One form of that includes critics and arbiters, who pass judgment on the value of the vision or creation. Denise Shekerjian describes that role in *Uncommon Genius*.

> There are institutions and people who make decisions about what is going to get noticed and what is not. You don't have creativity unless you have a certain mind engaged in a certain domain of practice with other people looking in at it and saying, 'This makes sense, this doesn't, this is good, this is not, this is original, this is not.' But there is no statute of limitations on these judgments—they can occur immediately or two hundred years later.[180]

Avoid the inclination to incessantly polish the message or gussy up the package instead of getting it in front of those who react to it. A related snag is spending too much time and effort figuring out every detail before making a start. Obsessive planning can easily be a way to avoid action or risking failure.

---

[179] Shell, G. Richard and Moussa, Mario, *The Art of Woo: Using strategic persuasion to sell your ideas* (New York: Portfolio, 2007), 115.
[180] Shekerjian, Denise, *Uncommon Genius: How great ideas are born* (New York: Viking, 1990), 52.

Besides, it places entirely too much confidence in the rational processes to anticipate every eventuality.

On the other hand, an equally insidious temptation also exists to short-cut package refinements and careful planning. That's especially the case for those who disdain the devil in the details and are especially anxious to get their ideas in front of audiences and on the road. Like just about every other evolutionary step on the visionary journey, the wisest counsel is the one that advises balance.

Planning is largely a rational exercise, whereas, the measures of acceptance are largely emotional—which can be gauged by the way people respond to it. Einstein, no slouch in the intellect department himself, said "We should take care not to make the intellect our god; it has, of course, powerful muscles, but no personality. It cannot lead; it can only serve."

This concern is closely tied to being able to tell what is important from what is less important. The main activity should be toward getting the vision launched and grounded. If the vision starts to get fuzzy, it is too easy to get caught up in bailing the boat rather than making sure it stays on course.

From a Solo Act to a Team

Assembling a Full Deck

A visionary cannot be equally good at everything that needs doing, and there is always a strong temptation to spread oneself too thin. Ideally, the visionary needs at least two other people for support—having different skills and working styles.

Sometimes the forerunner builds an organization to accomplish the long-range mission. It could remain a very small or informal group or one that starts a mass movement that grows and grows.

The visionary is often thrust into the leadership role as soon as he or she moves from being a lone actor. Eric Hoffer points to the tricky balancing act required: "The leader has to be practical and a realist, yet must talk the language of the visionary and the idealist."

No matter how many skills the visionary brings to the task (their strong suits), they will be called to do many things in which they are not accomplished. The team that is assembled should build on the person's existing strengths and fill in those gaps.

It usually requires more than a single person and style of leadership to bring a vision to reality. Inevitably, the organization reflects the visionary's priorities, values, and personality. No doubt, the person relies on their strengths, but also keeps learning as the project goes along. Even so, the visionary struggles with personal shortcomings in their short and void suits.

Scott Belsky speaks to the impossible-to-avoid attrition of visionary activities.

> Whether you work alone or with a team, you will become mired in the challenges of staying productive, accountable, and in control. These journeys are physically and psychologically exhausting, and the road is littered with the carcasses of half-baked ideas that were abandoned or surrendered along the way. It is a tragic truth that most new ideas, despite their quality and importance, will never see the light of day.[181]

The organization compensates for the visionary's personal limitations and adds productive hours to their day. While nobody else will care as totally as they do, the visionary must inspire others who are on board and then *trust them* to work devotedly toward the vision's success. The team tries out ideas, tests strategies, and starts functioning as a coordinated unit.

Not all visionaries go through the team building phase. Some, like poets or philosophers, can spend their entire creative life as a solitary player. That depends as much on their field as their personal preferences. For instance, while an artist can create out of the public gaze, a performing artist or social change advocate cannot.

Visionaries are usually better at initiation and the break-away phase than the long slog. They're likely to be poor administrators because they do not care to stay submerged in the minutiae of management. Even when someone already has proficiency for those tasks, they find a steady diet of details deadening compared with the enlivening big-picture canvas on which they are painting.

The visionary should delegate routine details to the extent possible or the vision could languish. Sharing the necessary work means they'll have more time and energy to pursue the creative aspects of their mission. Besides their functional abilities, core supporters broaden the perspective and provide emotional support.

Can You Hear Me?

A visionary needs to be heard—somebody able to listen past the words who can "see" or "hear" what the visionary is trying to accomplish. This helps the advocate sharpen their focus. It is often the earliest listeners who believe in the message who build the person's courage to go public.

Listening garners crucial insights in every phase of the visionary path. But it's just as important to be listened to. Kay Lindahl makes that clear in *The Art of Listening*.

> Listening is a creative force. Something quite wonderful occurs when we are listened to fully. We expand, ideas come to life and grow, we remember who we are. Some speak of this voice as a creative fountain within us that springs forth; others call it the inner spirit, intelligence, true self. Whatever this force is called, it shrivels up when we are not listened to and it thrives when we are …

---

[181] Belsky, Scott, *Making Ideas Happen: Overcoming the obstacles between vision and reality* (New York: Portfolio, 2010), 9.

> Listening well takes time, skill, and a readiness to slow down, to let go of expectations, judgments, boredom, self-assertiveness, defensiveness. I have noticed that when people experience the depth of being listened to like this, they also begin to listen to others in the same way.[182]

Core group members are devoted to the person or the vision, or both. This initial group is likely to be very tight-knit and determined to spread the word. Their combined efforts anchor the vision in practical ways. These supporters are not merely employees chosen for their complementary skills, even if they are paid a salary. It is probably more than a job to them, but also a matter of conviction.

> [Hoffer said:] Imitation is an essential unifying agent. The development of a close-knit group is inconceivable without a diffusion of uniformity ... obedience itself consists as much in the imitation of an example as in the following of a precept.[183]

While these chapters address a visionary's personal risks, weaknesses, and lapses, these concerns apply to the nucleus of early supporters as well. Any of their individual biases or shortcomings could unduly influence the visionary or pull the endeavor off track. Core team members must all get off on the same foot, a common foot, the right foot, or they will not get anywhere.

Some of the earliest issues in starting an organization involve responsibility and delegation. The visionary must sort out which responsibilities can be entrusted to others, versus which should remain his or hers alone. How can the group avoid (or quickly resolve) power struggles and conflicts over priorities or interpretation?

The survival of the vision might well depend on how well participants can rise above their differences in order to pull together for a larger goal—putting the vision's requirements ahead of personal concerns.

Leaving a Long-Term Package and Legacy

Once the venture has been launched, the visionary is increasingly involved in organizational matters that involve other people and highly visible long-term goals. That brings up the need for leadership and management skills. Related concerns arise in gaining wider public awareness about the undertaking.

Organizational Concerns:
- Internal growth—the organization developed to support the vision (even if only the closest circle of supporters)
- External growth—whereby the vision comes to influence the world or specialized arena

---

[182] Lindahl, Kay, *The Art of Listening* (Woodstock, VT: Skylight Paths Publishing, 2008), 11-12.
[183] *Op. cit.*, Hoffer, 99.

- Establishing the visionary's own specialized niche within a larger context or field of interest

In creating a package and organization to solidify their notion, the visionary has to permit others devoted to the message to interpret and expand it to various degrees. Those elaborations allow it to grow and stay relevant. In some cases, the structure will outlast the visionary or core group.

Some visionaries give considerable thought to developing a successor or team to carry on for them, who will spread the word once they are out of the picture (or dead). Is the package clear enough and complete enough to exist without the visionary's active participation? Matters of succession become even more important when there is a large and growing organization or movement.

There is another continuum on which to compare visionaries: how much they anticipated or prepared for the vision's survival without their guiding hand. Does the person have a plan or do they leave what happens next to fate? Preparation can fall between none at all (a pile of dusty, obscure theories or unpublished manuscripts) and a well-developed system and organization, with trained lieutenants and all the eventualities mapped out.

It is worth mentioning that even the best notions have their limits. Ideas are dynamic; they must keep growing or they lose force. Those that hang around are no longer novel. What good is a stale vision? And nobody knows that risk better than the visionaries who see the need to pursue the next iteration of what they serve. So the measure of a vision's true benefit comes not just from it being accepted, but from its adaptability to changing circumstances.

Chapter 11 - Engaging the Visionary Drive
At first blush, a vision reveals an unbridled possibility – running free and unrestrained. In making the effort to understand its nature, and to ground it, the initial vision is no longer a "wild thing." It has been tamed and bridled – reflecting the desires of whoever tames it.

What they do can be so satisfying as to become an end in itself (intrinsic motivation). They intuitively seem to know, as Einstein said, "The true sign of intelligence is not knowledge but imagination."

Innumerable factors influence whether a person becomes a visionary, or whether a particular vision takes root; most are beyond the person's control. Realizing how much depends on unmanageable influences, the individual making the most of their strengths, and doing whatever possible to keep the developing notion on track.

That much singular drive could show up early in life, or late. Gender is not a handicap, any more than social status or income would be, as long as the person is operating above survival level. The particular field of interest cannot account for so much intense drive since so many fields have a percentage of participants willing and able to take their field in new directions.

Such vision-driven individuals are not greatly motivated by external coercion. They are not so much *pushing away from* what is disliked, but being *pulled toward* a beckoning possibility of their own making. Taking the visionary path indicates turning from what has been in the past (whether it was liked or disliked) and taking steps in the direction of an alternate future.

Only time will tell if the new direction promises success. But by the very attempt, they have already broken the pattern of sticking with what is familiar or safe.

The interplay of their family, cultural norms, and chance events makes their inventive contribution unique for each forerunner, and for each undertaking. There will be a combination of motivating influences, which interact with each other. Their relative importance will change as the mission goes along.

This chapter looks at factors that drive their motivation – or inhibit it. Although the motivations are discussed individually, what moves someone to act is complex. It is unlikely someone's behavior (or success) can be attributed to any single influence.

In our culture, we consider drive and persistence as evidence of one's personal will (or lack of it). So those who "make it" or stick with their aspirations are assumed to have more will than others. But drive is influenced by many more factors than one's personal will or desire. What may set visionaries apart could be their capacity to keep a desired outcome front and center, and to avoid or ignore distractions.

In *Change Anything,* Patterson and Kerry split the hair between skill and will.

> Many of the toughest challenges you face are difficult because they test your willpower. Everyone knows this. But what far too few people know is that will is a skill, not a character trait. Willpower can be learned and strengthened like anything else, and (no surprise here) it is best learned through deliberate practice.[184]

> Many of our personal problems are partially rooted in our inability to do what's required, and rarely do we think about this, because our lack of skill or knowledge sits in our blind spot. When this is the case, simply enhancing your personal ability can make a huge difference. When you learn how to do what you can't (by either adding behavioral skill or becoming aware of what's happening to you), change comes faster and easier.[185]

Talent, Strengths, Diligence, and Lucky Breaks

Beating the Odds

Picasso said "Every child is an artist. The problem is how to remain an artist once we grow up." How indeed? While a Picasso is rare, raw artistic ability is not; and it can be formed in many ways in the maturing individual. But Picasso's degree of dedication and ability to reinvent himself and his art multiple times is rare indeed. And doing that is a matter of motivation.

Many voices have weighed in about whether innate talent (a genetic gift) *or* diligent effort gets the credit for somebody's eventual success. In my opinion, both are required and each completes the other. It is a false choice to frame the issue as needing to choose one or to prize one over the other.

Individuals will differ as to which influence is more prominent for them. But these two factors interact with each other and with subsequent influences each step of the way.

Stories abound of heroes and visionaries who succeeded despite every possible handicap—armed only with their dogged determination. In fact, the more obstacles in their way the harder they soldier on—for the long haul. Whether those limitations are genetic, upbringing, oppressive social conditions, financial hardship, or insufficient learning, they do not seem to block them for long.

We love to hear about some person considered the least likely to succeed, who seizes the advantage and does the impossible—the underdog. When someone's vision has become all-consuming, they are in overdrive. Joan of Arc, the Warrior Maiden, was an improbable military leader by any objective measure. Yet she motivated the troops and won battles. She was inspired! She had drive!

---

[184] Patterson, Kerry, Grenny, Joseph *et al., Change Anything: The new science of personal success* (New York: Business Plus, 2011), 76.
[185] *Ibid.,* 68.

Although her story ends badly, that cannot be blamed on insufficient motivation.

Start Small

Finding workable new answers relies on trying out a variety of possible solutions, then testing them to see which actually deliver. The creative process involves plenty of blood, sweat, and tears to develop the best of the lot. Peter Sims makes the case for us learning by making small incremental steps in *Little Bets*.

> Starting soon after birth, experimenting and making mistakes are primary ways children learn and discover how things work. That tendency doesn't vanish when we become adults. As many researchers and observers have described, that innate curiosity which is the basis for so much creativity routinely gets squelched. Perfection is rewarded, while making mistakes is often penalized. The term 'failure' has taken on a deeply personal meaning, something to be avoided at nearly all costs…. Invention and discovery emanate from being able to try seemingly wild possibilities and work in the unknown; to be comfortable being wrong before being right; to live in the work as a keen observer, with an openness to experiences and ideas; to play with ideas without censoring oneself or others; to persist through dark alleys with a growth mind-set; to improvise ideas in collaboration and conversation with others; and, to have a willingness to be misunderstood, sometimes for long periods of time, despite conventional wisdom.[186]

The key is to experiment with low-risk trials, testing out a variety of approaches—without there being much at stake. That small-scale strategy avoids getting stymied by perfectionism, risk-aversion, or excessive planning. It also won't trigger the kind of resistance that arises when the *status quo* feels threatened.

Physical Capabilities Are Adaptable

Of course, genetics play a role to some extent—like having the ideal body type to be a ballerina or a sumo wrestler, or the long fingers of a piano virtuoso. But except for such highly specialized pursuits, an average mind or body is quite adequate for most visionary undertakings. Certainly, being average is not itself a disqualification.

Certain tools can amplify the acuity of most senses or expand other physical capabilities. The noteworthy differences of the driven are traceable less to inborn traits than to the extent of their training, honing, and unwavering hands-on effort. Howard Gardner found:

---

[186] Sims, Peter, *Little Bets: How breakthrough ideas emerge from small discoveries* (New York: Free Press, 2011), 160-1.

> Extraordinary persons must indeed be constructed out of the same building blocks as the rest of us but by the time they are formed, they are no longer indistinguishable from the proverbial man (or woman) on the street.[187]

For everybody, polishing their act starts really young. Normal infants are born with the capacity for all the strengths. Then the combination of the person's preferences and enthusiasms, coupled with what their world reinforces for them, leads each to choose some strengths over others.

In *Happiness*, Martin Seligman sheds light on which of the strengths take root.

> 'Strengthening drift' sets in over the first six years of life. As the young child finds the niches that bring praise, love, and attention, he sculpts his strengths. His chisel is the interplay of his talents, interests, and strengths, and as he discovers what works and what fails in his little world, he will carve in greater detail the face of several strengths. At the same time, he will chip others out, discarding the excess granite on the art-room floor.[188]

Usually physiology or inborn traits are not a handicap to someone realizing their full potential. In most cases, an ordinary individual's raw material can be molded enough to accomplish their desires. So, again the obvious differences in results often reflect the person's level of drive, plus the ability to be flexible and stay on target as they go along.

Our human physiology develops with its own timetable, roughly the same for everybody. It includes the related emotional development and skills that rely on interactive relationships. Except for conditions of extreme physical, emotional, or intellectual pressures, each individual is preparing for a life that suits them precisely.

Physician Jane Healy describes how the brain circuitry itself is altered as the child grows in *Different Learners*.

> Each brain comes equipped with a built-in developmental timetable for mastery of different types of skills. Brains mature in cycles that begin before birth and last until around age twenty-five or even later. Trying to force or accelerate mental development risks creating learning problems.[189]

> The brain's ability to respond, change, and either build or lose circuitry is called neuroplasticity. Brain plasticity is easy to understand if you liken brain circuits to muscles, which become larger and stronger after training and use. On the other hand, muscles can become weak and even atrophy if they don't get any exercise—and so can brain networks for unexercised skills. Thus, 'brain power' depends in large part on the environment.

---

[187] Gardner, Howard, *Extraordinary Minds: Portraits of exceptional individuals and an examination of our extraordinariness* (New York: Harper Collins, 1997), 4.
[188] Seligman, Martin E.P., *Authentic Happiness: Using the new positive psychology to realize your potential for lasting fulfillment* (New York: The Free Press, 2002), 244-5.
[189] Healy, Jane M., *Different Learners: Identifying, preventing and treating your child's learning problems* (New York: Simon & Shuster, 2010), 125.

If important brain circuits are not used at the proper age, they may be lost. Fortunately, these developmental windows are quite long for human brains.[190]

Einstein summed it up in the famous quote: 'Imagination is more important than knowledge.' Neuroscience confirms that a child's [or anybody's] imagination builds far more than castles in the sky — it builds functional connectivity to make his brain more powerful.[191]

Edmund Hillary, the first man to climb Mt. Everest said, "You don't have to be a fantastic hero to do certain things — to compete. You can be just an ordinary chap, sufficiently motivated." However, there can be considerable confusion on a personal level as to what our unique strengths might be, or how much control can be exercised over them.

The Readiness Factor

Readiness can be likened to collecting an enormous pile of logs and kindling. It only takes a few creative sparks to set it afire, so it burns and burns. But no matter how big the pile, without any sparks there won't ever be a bonfire. Readiness brings a prepared and motivated individual together with igniting circumstances. But there will always be elements of timing and luck at work.

Planning and acquiring enough skills are only part of a person's preparation. How fully have they integrated their prior training and experience? Equally important for them is discovering where to plug their contribution into the larger context (or specific field).

On the other hand, it is human nature for someone to think they're ready to do what they aspire to sooner than they actually are.

Often the only way to know if one is ready is by jumping in, then finding out exactly what one still needs to learn, and quickly, too. That's known as the Sink-or-Swim Strategy. And there are gradual variations — trying out one variable after another.

How to Look at Readiness:
- Are you adequately prepared? Have you developed the necessary knowledge base and skills? Are you ready to deliver a message? This can be gauged by objective measures in some respects

- Are you ready inside? This reflects your level of maturity, emotional resilience, and judgment; all of your faculties are at the ready and engaged; the assessment is totally subjective

- Is the world ready for your message? Or what can be done to get them in sync?

---

[190] *Ibid.*, 126.
[191] *Ibid.*, 119.

Apparently it also takes longer to get ready because of an increasing amount of subject-matter knowledge that needs to be acquired in many fields. And its sheer volume continues to grow (even within a narrow discipline). A *Newsweek* article (August 24, 2009) by Tony Jokoupil explained:

> Earlier generations of scientists didn't have to wade through quite as much preexisting work before making an original contribution. Now innovators are establishing themselves much later in life. Over the last century and a half, the average age of a Nobel Prize winner at the moment of his great breakthrough has risen more than five years, from 34 to 39 years old. Run-of-the-mill inventors are also older: the average for registering first major patents has jumped seven months per decade.[192]

If the vision is to succeed, readiness must be coupled with an earnest desire to take action if it is to move beyond being a fleeting possibility. The person must be alert for ways to grab the ball and run.

Hugh Macleod points out, "People who are 'ready' give off a different vibe than people who are not. Animals can smell fear; maybe that's it. The minute you become ready is the minute you stop dreaming. Suddenly it's no longer about 'becoming.' Suddenly it's about 'doing.'"

Additionally, curiosity serves the developing individual by leading him or her to search out what they need to know, assuring they will develop the necessary skills for their circumstances. Even a baby step devoted to hard work anchors a starting point from which to take the next steps. Concrete action signals a readiness to proceed and creates an opening to helpful opportunities.

By the same token, until both the person and surrounding conditions are ready for change, nothing much happens. In that light, the visionary is usually ready sooner than the conditions they encounter. However, all the contrariness they directed at the *status quo* might be nudging them toward readiness, too.

As motivational author H. Jackson Brown reminds us, "Opportunity dances with those who are already on the dance floor."

~ Opportunity Knocks ~
A BonBon ~ Faith Lynella

Opportunity knocks—but not the way you expect. It doesn't come up to your door like a well-bred guest, asking for admittance. *Opportunity knocks you down.* As you lie there, feeling beaten, you have several choices:

- Fume and grumble—maybe even get angry
- Move on as quickly as possible and dismiss the whole thing
- Feel really bad about how this could have happened to you
- Try to figure out if it might be an opportunity being offered (actually, shoved at you)

---

[192] Jokoupil, Tony, "Old People Are More Innovative," *Newsweek*, August 24, 2009.

When ambushed by adversity and disappointment, you are forced to see yourself and everything around you a little bit differently than usual. You get a chance to make a fresh start, set off in a new direction—coupled with the motivation to try it.

By knocking you down, something is trying very hard to get your attention. And the harder the whack, the more urgent the message. Pay attention! You've been stopped, derailed, disconnected from your familiar routine. Pause a moment before moving on again. Take a good look at the people involved, the less-than-welcome situation, and the way it all relates to you. Notice intensely, giving attention to *all* the pieces. It just might be opportunity knocking.

From *BonBons to Sweeten Your Daily Life*. Or from *More BonBons*

The sheer difficulty of the visionary path keeps travelers humble—and nimble. Despite any of our grumbling about setbacks, in the fullness of time, it is possible to look back and see how beneficial the stumbles were to opening our eyes to untried avenues.

~ Opportunity Knocks—Again ~
A BonBon ~ Faith Lynella

One way opportunity knocks is to knock you down to get your attention. Opportunity also knocks in a muffled and thumpy way. It keeps niggling at you, for a little while, just out of earshot, an intermittent ka-bump. It flirts with you, only to vanish as you attempt to listen harder. But it returns—alluring but illusive.

If you ask someone else about it, they will strain and hear nothing. This is a summons just for you. It is for you alone to answer its beckoning—or dismiss it. It is as individual as a key to a lock. Actually, it is a key for your lock, but you won't know that unless you respond and pursue it.

Logic, good sense, and your existing commitments will feel no patience with such a wild goose chase. But if something in your nature is compelled to respond, you just might be able to grasp it.

At that moment, *opportunity becomes destiny!*

From *BonBons to Sweeten Your Daily Life*. Or from *More BonBons*

Making It Stick Together

One reason acquiring subject-matter mastery takes so long is the need to integrate what is acquired. One is moving from collecting disparate pieces and skills, to forging them into something functionally coherent. Coherence is a mark of mastery because its presence is likely to pass unnoticed. But its absence is characterized by jarring notes.

The relevant concept is coherence. Jonathan Haidt discusses how it works in *The Happiness Hypothesis*.

> The word 'coherence' literally means holding or sticking together, but it is usually used to refer to a system, an idea, or a worldview whose parts fit together in a consistent and efficient way. Coherent things work well. A coherent worldview can explain almost anything, while an incoherent worldview is hobbled by internal contradictions.... Whenever a system can be analysed at multiple levels, a special kind of coherence occurs when the levels mesh and mutually interlock.
>
> We saw this cross-level coherence in the analysis of personality; if your lower level traits match up with your coping mechanisms, which in turn are consistent with your life story, your personality is well integrated and you can get on with the business of living. When these levels do not cohere, you are likely to be torn by internal contradictions and neurotic conflicts. You might need adversity to knock yourself into alignment. And if you do achieve coherence, the moment when things come together may be one of the most profound of your life.[193]

Use Different Strategies for Strengths or Talents

Although strengths and talents are often treated as synonyms, Martin Seligman points out important conceptual differences between them. In addition, most of us have some degree of confusion about what constitutes our individual strengths, or how much control we can exercise over them. Ideally they will reinforce each other.

> While they have many similarities, one clear difference is that strengths are moral traits, while talents are nonmoral. In addition, although the line is fuzzy, talents generally are not as buildable as strengths.... Valor, originality, fairness, and kindness, in contrast, can be built on even frail foundations, and I believe that with enough practice, persistence, good teaching, and dedication, they can take root and flourish. Talents are more innate. For the most part, you either have a talent or you don't.... Talents, in contrast to strengths, are relatively automatic, whereas strengths are usually more voluntary....
>
> A talent involves some choices, but only those of whether to burnish it and where to deploy it; there is no choice about possessing it in the first place....

---

[193] Haidt, Jonathan, *The Happiness Hypothesis: Finding modern truth in ancient wisdom* (New York: Basic Books, 2006) 226-7.

> A strength involves choices about when to use it and whether to keep building it, but also whether to acquire it in the first place. With enough time, effort, and determination, [strengths] can be acquired by almost any ordinary person. The talents, however, cannot be acquired merely by dint of will.[194]

No amount of readiness can make a talent appear, but it can influence whether someone does something worthwhile with it, if it is there. However, the ability to build upon and reinforce our strengths does exist for everybody. And we would all be wise to enhance them in order to support whatever talents we do choose to develop.

Competence and Mastery Cannot Be Rushed

Acquiring subject-matter mastery in an area of knowledge demonstrates a daunting level of commitment. Research by neurologist Daniel Levitin, and others in the fields of brain and physiological research, have found it takes at least 10,000 hours of devoted effort to a person's field of interest to achieve mastery. Malcolm Gladwell discussed that concept in *Outliers*.

> The emerging picture from such studies is that ten thousand hours of practice is required to achieve the level of mastery associated with being a world-class expert—in anything,' writes the neurologist Daniel Levitin. 'In writers, ice skaters, concert pianists, chess players, master criminals, and what have you, this number comes up again and again. Of course, this doesn't address why some people get more out of their practice sessions than others do. But no one has yet found a case in which true world-class expertise was accomplished in less time. It seems that it takes the brain that long to assimilate all that it needs to know to achieve true mastery.[195]

The need for such a massive investment of time and effort even seems to hold true for those who are termed gifted, or prodigies like Mozart. In addition, a person who has achieved mastery (or gotten close to it) in one field will find it easier to move rapidly beyond the basic tasks of subsequent areas of interest due to transfer of skills. But even more importantly, *how they relate to learning* itself has advanced considerably.

What experienced people bring to each new endeavor is a refined discrimination or an integrated overview unavailable to a neophyte. Also, they know how to make the most of the confidence that comes from a history of prior successes (and failures survived). Still, a person cannot do justice to more than a few domains of interest in a lifetime.

---

[194] *Op. cit.*, Seligman, 134-5.
[195] Gladwell, Malcolm, *Outliers: The story of success* (New York: Little Brown and Company, 2008), 40.

Actions Speak Louder than Words

Getting It Done

Vision and developing an idea conceptually represent one side of the coin; doing something about it represents the other side. Visionaries are known for having active imaginations in which they foresee a future where their idea has a prominent place. The scope of their notion might be very detailed and specific, or it might only indicate broad strokes, without the "clockworks" figured out.

Someone could spend years in this visualization phase. Observers are likely to write such individuals off as dreamers—if they take it no farther. What sets visionaries apart from idle dreamers may not be apparent at the outset, or from the outside. But at some point they *attempt to ground it*—not just fantasize about it.

So much rumination was not an escape for them as much as a preparation to act. Leonardo DaVinci urges action, "I have been impressed with the urgency of doing. Knowing is not enough; we must apply. Being willing is not enough; we must do."

Visionaries leap, unsatisfied just to perch on the edge. Maybe they seem to be perched for a really long time, but there is an *intention to leap*. And at some point they do. Whatever follows, they make adjustments and leap again. Lots of factors influence when the time is right, but at some tipping point the person acts on what has been coming together for them.

The Man in the Arena
President Theodore Roosevelt

> It is not the critic who counts; not the man who points out how the strong man stumbles, or where the doer of deeds could have done them better. The credit belongs to the man who is actually in the arena, whose face is marred by dust and sweat and blood; who strives valiantly; who errs, and comes short again and again, because there is no effort without error and shortcoming; but who does actually strive to do the deeds; who knows the great enthusiasms, the great devotions; who spends himself in a worthy cause; who at the best knows in the end the triumph of high achievement, and who at the worst, if he fails, at least fails while daring greatly, so that his place shall never be with those cold and timid souls who know neither victory nor defeat.

Those on the leading edge of change sometimes prevail because popular opinion catches up with where they stand during their period of inaction. Their stick-to-itiveness paid off, as the broader thinking starts to move in their direction.

Since grounding builds from an abstraction, the amount of concrete activity actually accomplished usually reflects the phase of the visionary process—starting out or as the undertaking ripens. But at some point after enough preparation, the bread needs to come out of the oven.

The public gets to taste it and to react to it. And the visionary adjusts the recipe accordingly. So the interactive elements of vision and tweaking continue to be essential in bringing a vision to tangible form. Daniel Pink describes how the workplace stifles the kind of inquiry that leads to new ideas in *Drive*.

> Solving complex problems requires an inquiring mind and the willingness to experiment one's way to a fresh solution.... Only engagement can produce mastery. And the pursuit of mastery, an important but often dormant part of our third drive [intrinsic motivation], has become essential in making one's way in today's economy.
>
> Unfortunately, despite sweet-smelling words like 'empowerment' that waft through corporate corridors, the modern workplace's most notable feature may be its lack of engagement and its disregard for mastery.[196]

We also need to take into account the mind's capacity when pursuing tasks. While intellect can handle a great many tasks and do them well, there tends to be slippage when shifting back and forth to unrelated information. Short-term memory and long-term memory operate differently.

Our short-term memories can hang onto only between five and nine things, max, at one time. If you try to store ten things in short-term memory, something will be dropped. This is made clear by Douglas C. Merrill in *Getting Organized in the Google Era*.

> The more you shift contexts and the more unrelated those contexts are, the harder your brain works to transfer, store, and flush information out of short-term memory to make room for more. And it doesn't just drop the things you no longer need; it drops things that are crucial to your ability to function.[197] Multitasking is something we all do these days. The problem is, our brains just aren't cut out for it. When you multitask, you're interfering with your brain's efforts to put information into short-term memory—a process that's fragile enough to begin with. And if the information doesn't make it into short-term memory, you won't be able to recall it later.... Multitasking—especially when you're trying to accomplish two dissimilar tasks, each requiring some level of thought and attention—makes it difficult to encode information into long-term memory.... *Multitasking usually makes you less efficient.*[198] [italics are his]

Give Some Credit to Overlooked Circumstances

Even with every possible advantage or ample preparation, mastering a field is daunting. Nevertheless, Malcolm Gladwell argues against any person taking too much of the credit for what they accomplish. An "outlier" is a person who is

---

[196] Pink, Daniel H., *Drive: The surprising truth about what motivates us* (New York: Riverhead Books, 2009), 111.
[197] Merrill, Douglas C., *Getting Organized in the Google Era* (New York: Broadway Books, 2010), 128.
[198] *Ibid.*, p. 9.

markedly different from the others of the sample. And many visionaries could be characterized as outliers.

> People don't arise from nothing. We do owe something to parentage and patronage. The people who stand before kings may look like they did it all by themselves. But in fact they are invariably the beneficiaries of hidden advantages and extraordinary opportunities and cultural legacies that allow them to learn and work hard and make more sense of the world in ways others cannot.
>
> It makes a difference where and when we grew up. The culture we belong to and the legacies passed down by our forebears shape the patterns of our achievement in ways we cannot begin to imagine. It's not enough to ask what successful people are like, in other words. It is only by asking where they are *from* that we can unravel the logic behind who succeeds and who doesn't.[199]

By Gladwell's reasoning, a person's success cannot be credited just to their good decisions or hard work. Nor should it be chalked up to luck. More appreciation should be given to supportive circumstances that are almost invariably unnoticed.

Birth order is an example of a usually overlooked factor that can exert a major influence on who is inclined to become a visionary. Traits which are rewarded or discouraged for a particular child reflect the family dynamics in which they grew up. Frank J. Sullaway's studies (described in *Born to Rebel*) show that firstborn children are more likely to become conservative, and later born children are more inclined to become the free thinkers.

> Most individual differences in personality, including those that underlie the propensity to rebel, arise within the family. The question of why some people rebel, including why a few particularly far-sighted individuals initiate radical revolutions, is synonymous with the question of why siblings are so different.[200]

Firstborns tend to identify with established tradition more than their siblings do. As latecomers to the family, later born children have to find an unoccupied niche, and their openness to a unique way to shine makes them more imaginative and creative. Sulloway also said:

> It is natural for firstborns to identify more strongly with power and authority. They arrive first within the family and employ their superior size and strength to defend their special status. Relative to their younger siblings, firstborns are more assertive, socially dominant, ambitious, jealous of their status and defensive. As underdogs within the family system, younger siblings are inclined to question the status quo and in some cases to develop a

---

[199] *Op. cit.*, Gladwell, 19.
[200] Sulloway, Frank J., *Born to Rebel: Birth order, family dynamics and creative lives* (New York: Vintage Books, 1997), *xiii*.

'revolutionary personality.' In the name of revolution, laterborns have repeatedly challenged the time-honored assumptions of their day. From their ranks have come the bold explorers, the iconoclasts, and the heretics of history.[201]

Satisfying Our Personal Motivations

Maslow's Pyramid of Needs

Research by Abraham Maslow, a humanistic psychologist, in the 1940s, established that people are motivated by more than survival concerns. He organized motivations according to a hierarchy of needs, moving from survival through "higher order needs," which are growth oriented. According to Maslow, until one's most basic physical needs are met, one does not move on to the higher order needs further up the pyramid.

While a person is unable to care about higher order concerns when faced with sheer survival, such self-development is more vital than it may appear. There is plenty of evidence showing that a sense of integrated wholeness cannot be achieved without satisfying needs at every level of one's being. Quoting Maslow:

> Human life will never be understood unless its highest aspirations are taken into account. Growth, self-actualization, the striving toward health, the quest for identity and autonomy, the yearning for excellence (and other ways of phrasing the striving 'upward') must by now be accepted beyond question as a widespread and perhaps universal human tendency.
>
> And yet there are also other regressive, fearful, self-diminishing tendencies as well, and it is very easy to forget them in our intoxication with 'personal growth,' especially for inexperienced youngsters....We must appreciate that many people choose the worse rather than the better, that growth is often a painful process.[202]

Many of these higher-order needs can be satisfied communally, as individuals engage in personal relationships and public ceremonies. For example, even a hungry beggar can participate in a religious ceremony that resonates with the highest human aspirations, which transports him to a place of beauty and inspiration.

Maslow's Hierarchy of Needs: (in this order)
- **Physiological Needs** — These are biological requirements, consisting of needs for oxygen, food, water, and a relatively constant body temperature. They are the strongest needs because if a person were

---

[201] *Ibid., xiv.*
[202] Maslow, Abraham, *Motivation and Personality* (New York: Harper Collins, 1987)

deprived of all needs, these would come first in the person's search for satisfaction—or survival.

- **Safety Needs**—When all physiological needs are satisfied, the needs for security can become active. Adults have little awareness of their security needs except in times of emergency or disorganization. It includes personal security, financial security, health and well-being,

- **Needs for Love, Affection, and Belongingness**—When the needs for safety and for physiological well-being are satisfied, the needs for love, affection and belongingness can emerge. Without these elements, many people become susceptible to loneliness, social anxiety, and other emotional distress.

- **Needs for Esteem**—When the first three classes of needs are satisfied, the needs for esteem can become dominant. Esteem presents the normal human desire to be accepted and valued by others, but it also includes self-acceptance and self-confidence.

- **Needs for Self-Actualization**—When all of the foregoing needs are satisfied, then and only then, are the needs for self-actualization brought to bear. Maslow describes self-actualization as what a person feels they need to be and to do—what the person was "born to do." It is the instinctive need to make the most of our unique abilities.

- **Self-Transcendence** was added later by Maslow as a specialized form of self-actualization. Those who become self-actualized sometimes become aware not only of achieving their own fullest potential, but also the fullest potential of human beings at large. He likened self-transcendence to peak experiences, but he also noted it's not always transitory and/or momentary. Certain individuals have ready access to it and spend more time in this state.

Creative types are junkies for self-actualization, as they pursue activities that expand their horizons. They are in the business of developing new creative wrinkles. The drive for self-actualization is central to the visionary process. If a person is hungry, feels unsafe, unloved, or lacking self-esteem, it is relatively easy to know what needs to be satisfied.

It is unclear what a person requires when there is a need for self-actualization. Besides, what would work for any specific individual is highly customized. Each person must discover what rings their bell.

Maslow was unsure how to handle spiritual needs, but felt they must be included too. A person can access them when they are at any level in the hierarchy. He put spiritual needs on top in order to represent their importance; he considered them the source of goodness. (See "B-Values," later in this chapter.)

Down in Maslow's Basement

The concept of Maslow's Basement was introduced by the Heath brothers in *Made to Stick: Why some ideas survive and others die*. They lumped the lower-order needs in the basement; their studies found a common irrational bias.

Most of us think we are being motivated by the higher-order needs (in Maslow's penthouse), but are inclined to think everyone else is motivated from the basement, even if we are doing the same thing they are doing. Our assessment as to what is driving our behavior is not accurate — either for ourselves or for others.

Framing choices as though some are higher or lower than others (on the pyramid) makes the higher ones seem more desirable or worthy of aspiration. However, all of the needs, at every level, are necessary and beneficial in their appointed role. And there is no reason to think, for example, that safety needs must be met before someone can care about their self-esteem or inspiration.

Most people are able to move freely between the various levels of needs as appropriate. Only in dire circumstances do the bottom-level needs prevent the higher-order needs from asserting themselves. If there really were a hierarchy among the various needs there would be no such thing as a starving artist. What could account for the ability to move most freely between levels might not be needs, but the type and quality of energy the person has available (Chapter 13).

Words from an Ex Turnip

I recall a period in my life when I suffered a severe health problem. My intellectual abilities and emotional responses dried up because there was not enough energy for running anything but essential physical processes. I could not even focus enough to read or sit up more than 15 minutes a day.

Only autonomic functions were keeping the lights on. I later described myself as having the brain power of a turnip, capable of nothing more than a lizard sunning itself on a rock.

Medical science couldn't help me at that stage. (There was no question about my diagnosis or that I would survive in the end, but I couldn't tolerate any medications, most foods, tastes, or any smells. Everything hurt and even sleep was beyond me for more than an hour a day.) Imagine having only 20% of the energy you usually have.

There was not even enough functional awareness for me to feel bad about it — let alone learn from the experience. I was stuck in bare survival mode, with minimal sensory awareness or rational activity.

Months later, at a point when I was starting to re-engage with the world around me, a friend commented, "You've been exploring the other end of Maslow's Hierarchy of Needs." That changed the perspective! Having spent a lifetime pushing the limits of self-actualization, I finally had a clue about what it means to live bereft of such interests or motivations.

That eight months as a turnip was the most unprecedented and "off the map" experience of my life. What that taught me was that until then I had absolutely no idea what "simple" or "doing nothing" meant. The contrast between being shut-down (hanging onto the bottom of the bottom rung of Maslow's pyramid) and the richness of my inner and outer life since fills me with gratitude—another upside to a wipe-out.

Intrinsic Motivation—Just for the Joy of It

Intrinsic motivation is doing something for the sheer pleasure of doing it. "The desire to do something because you find it deeply satisfying and personally challenging inspires the highest levels of creativity whether it is in the arts, sciences, or business" said Theresa Amible. Csikszentmihalyi said:

> Creative persons differ from one another in a variety of ways, but in one respect they are unanimous. They all love what they do. It is not the hope of achieving fame or making money that drives them; rather it is the opportunity to do the work that they enjoy doing.[203]

The true worth of such activities cannot be justified in a cost-versus-benefit way, or by only considering what it produces. Its value is totally subjective and immediate. The payoff in satisfaction comes right now—not eventually.

If someone enjoys doing "whatever" at the time, it does not matter much what anybody else thinks. It also does not matter if there is something to show for it.

Intrinsic motivations are contrasted with extrinsic motivations that come from outside. Extrinsic motivations are a mix of carrots and sticks used to reward or control behavior: money, desirable possessions, fame, social approval, power, threat of punishment, and coercion.

Our responsible side is likely to treat something done just for fun like getting an extra dessert—not something for every day. Or it might be treated as a reward for our "eating the yucky stuff" that we had to do. Of course, what anybody does for pleasure is a matter of taste: from puzzles, to gardening, to climbing mountains.

In that sense, there is no difference between making real pies or mud pies. But make no mistake, taking time to play and be joyful without needing concrete rewards is an important driving force of our behavior—no matter what our age. Peter Senge clarifies the relationship between intrinsic motivation and vision.

---

[203] Csikszentmihalyi, Mihaly, *Creativity: Flow and the psychology of discovery and invention* (New York: HarperCollins, 1996), 107.

Ultimately, vision is intrinsic not relative. It's something you desire for its intrinsic value, not because of where it stands you relative to another. Relative visions may be appropriate in the interim, but they will rarely lead to greatness. Nor is there anything wrong with competition. Competition is one of the best structures yet invented by mankind to allow each of us to bring out the best in each other. But after the competition is over, after the vision has (or has not) been achieved, it is one's sense of purpose that draws you further, and compels you to set a new vision. This, again, is why personal mastery must be a discipline. It is a process of continually focusing and refocusing on what one truly wants, on one's visions.[204]

Some visionaries are known for their playfulness and humor—sometimes downright silly. Everyone likes the fun stuff, but creative types have figured out that some form of break from work is essential for them to sustain their creative prowess. A person cannot go too far wrong playing more, and with greater abandon. That's the spontaneous play of flowing with life that young children know so well.

Additional and tangible benefits often result as well—like having something beautiful to look at afterwards, or getting paid real money for what it produced. Those are bonuses, and usually, by themselves, cannot fully replace that rush of satisfaction from doing a thing for its own sake.

Providing rewards beyond the intrinsic satisfaction of doing a thing can undermine enjoying it. It becomes a commodity As an example, efforts to encourage children to read for pleasure by paying them to read more books results in them *doing less recreational reading*. Reading for fun has its own rewards—in the reading itself. Adding a financial inducement reduced children's intrinsic motivation by putting reading in the same category as chores or work.

Curiosity is a highly valued intrinsic motivator. None of that "bird in the hand is worth two in the bush" reasoning for this crew. They have already seen the bird in the hand and are chasing the two (or who knows how many more) that have never been seen yet. To be candid, it is sometimes a wild goose chase. But not always... The fun is in the pursuit.

Acting on Values and Beliefs

Values reflect our most important life priorities. They determine what we actually do, desire, and want to become. Many values are shared by the broader culture or sub-group in which people are raised, while others are unique to each person. Values are not rational constructs, and much of their influence exists below rational thought.

---

[204] Senge, Peter, *The Fifth Discipline: The art and practice of the learning organization* (New York: Broadway Books, 1990), 150.

Our values underlie our rational ideas about the important matters of life and they influence our behavior across a broad swatch of personal choices. They inform our worldview. Values are deeply felt and slow to change, especially compared to opinions or choices made on a conscious level. It is intimately related to meaning and our core life purpose. "We are born for meaning, not pleasure, unless it is pleasure that is steeped in meaning," Jacob Needleman said.

For a person to change his or her values reflects something as significant as a paradigm shift or *metanoia*. If they resolve to act in a different way in the future, that is unlikely to happen unless such an intention corresponds to their deeply-held values. Daniel Goleman, author of *Emotional Intelligence*, speaks to how meaning fits in.

> The silence about values skews the collective sense of what motivates people. Making money alone seems to loom much larger than it actually is for many of us.... Except for the financially desperate, people do not work for money alone. What also fuels their passion for work is a larger sense of purpose or passion. Given the opportunity, people gravitate to what gives them meaning, to what engages to the fullest their commitment, talent, energy, and skill.[205]

Pablo Casals said that each person has worthy values at the core; the challenge comes in translating them to action. "Each person has inside a basic decency and goodness. If he listens to it and acts on it, he is giving a great deal of what it is the world needs most. It is not complicated but it takes courage. It takes courage for a person to listen to his own goodness and act on it."

Frances Moore Lappé also addresses our deep-seated drive for meaning in *Getting a Grip2*.

> More than simply being doers, we want our doings to have significance way beyond ensuring our own survival. Fromm called it simply the human need to "make a dent" in the wider world. It makes sense then, that when we act on our deepest values for causes we hold dear, we're measurably happier.... We humans have long met our need for transcendent meaning through religion, but also by striving to be good ancestors, ensuring our children's and their children's futures. So, to me, it feels only natural that we'd want to quench part of our deeply rooted thirst for meaning by contributing to the rescue of our threatened planet and, along the way, enhance qualities deep inside us—empathy, leadership, and courage—that this journey brings forth, if we can see the way.[206]

Our values reflect our judgment and help us sort out what's important in life. Maslow described what he considered important values that defined one's

---

[205] Goleman, Daniel, *Working with Emotional Intelligence* (New York: Bantam Books, 1998), 58.
[206] Lappé, Frances Moore, *Getting a Grip2: Clarity, creativity, and courage for the world we really want* (Cambridge, MA: Small Planet Media, 2007 and 2010), 18-19.

being (which he called B-values). These important values are meta-motivations, which are specific virtues of self-actualized people. He found that those who were self-actualized tended to incorporate more B-values than individuals focused on other needs.

Understanding which of these B-values is most important to you is essential to finding your calling. Developing them is likely to provide a highly gratifying quality of life. Notice that these are all about inner development and, as such, reflect the same qualities being polished via the visionary process.

Maslow's B-Values:
- Wholeness/Unity/Oneness
- Perfection/Just-so-ness
- Completion/Finality/Ending
- Justice/Fairness
- Aliveness/Full-Functioning
- Richness/Intricacy
- Simplicity/Essential/Honesty
- Beauty/Form/Richness
- Goodness/Oughtness
- Uniqueness/Idiosyncrasy/Novelty
- Effortlessness/Ease/Perfect
- Playfulness/Joy/Humor
- Truth/Reality/Beauty/Pure
- Self-Sufficiency/Independence

Satisfying the Urge to Laugh and Play

Visionaries do not take themselves too seriously, although they are quite serious about what they are trying to accomplish. They like games and playing in the way children do—as light-hearted fun. They seek situations that engage their curiosity or surprise them. Unfortunately, such apparently idle play reinforces their off-in-the-clouds stereotype.

The visionary path is an intense way of life, but it is not all a matter of slaying dragons. Creative types need to disengage from their primary pursuit, even if it is their vision, in order to recharge. Forerunners need to pursue recreational activities for their intrinsic rewards. Who does not long for down time—the peaceful chance to reflect, play, and enjoy their family?

That is especially important with creative activities because the Eureka! moment is likely to occur during times when the person is in the incubation phase of creativity. They are disengaged from the strenuous fact-gathering period.

But the subconscious mind has been carrying on, sifting and resifting data. And then, when the attention is on something rather minor the picture or insight pops into view.

Recreational play is a form of letting go. Unplugging from one's usual responsibilities shifts a person's perspective. Playful and humorous pursuits allow him or her to return not only refreshed, but able to see their creative endeavors with fresh eyes. Denise Shekerjian cites Koestler's insight about creative expression.

> Koestler, among others, saw the parallel between the broad sweep of creativity and a good joke, citing humor as one of the most basic forms of bisociative thinking. In his often-quoted essay 'The Three Domains of Creativity' he noted the similarity between various kinds of creative expression: artistic originality giving rise to the ha! reaction, scientific discovery leading to the aha! reaction, and comic inspiration resulting in the haha! reaction. With all three reactions, two different frames of reference collide to produce the surprising result.[207]

As a specific example, nobody disputes Einstein's mental brilliance or monumental contributions to physics. Yet, it is easy to find as many tales about his dreaminess and playing around as of his scientific proficiency. Perhaps one of his most useful contributions was to publicly demonstrate through his example that both qualities can work together to further innovative thinking.

Each of us can become more capable by making a practice of taking time for delightful activities that feed our creative side. The operative word is "delightful" since such pursuits satisfy our deepest longing and make us smile inside. Here is one of my recreations—a little different take on "playing God."

Cloudside Chats for Wit and Whimsy

Years ago, I amused myself by wondering what life would be like without any of the usual limits. It gave me a certain escape from my own problems to think about what an infinite being would do for amusement.

What developed for me grew out of the question: What would an unlimited, all-knowing, infinite being do with "free time?" I cannot imagine an infinite being who would not enjoy levity, but what form could that take? Of course, the concept is absurd because being unlimited negates boundaries or any customary human motivations.

I conceived and wrote hundreds of captions for a cartoon character who "never *made* a man he didn't like." I called it Cloudside Chats, and worked with an artist for half a year to create a whimsical character (who is neither religious nor anti-religious, simply curious and playful).

Although our efforts at syndication did not come to pass, this sweetly enjoyable project has recently come back to life for me. I am turning the concept and images into a graphic novel.

---

[207] Shekerjian, Denise, *Uncommon Genius: How great ideas are born* (New York: Viking, 1990), 7.

I Never <u>made</u> a man I didn't like

Money and the Stuff It Can Buy[208]

Creativity-driven individuals are happy to have money or economic comforts, but such rewards alone are not enough. In fact, many recognize that money and possessions can too often distract from what brings them greater joy.

The issue is not to be anti-money or to accept financial struggles as the price of staying uncompromised. The real issue comes down to the extent to which money is their master.

They spurn achieving the "good life" if it does not also include the palpable presence of inspiration and emotional freedom. The contrast between being money-driven or vision-driven is not just another either-or choice for them. It is better framed as: What is in service to what? Which is primary and which is subordinate in a particular situation?

Some on the visionary path consider putting material stuff ahead of their avowed purpose as "settling" or selling out. They are disinclined to chase after what most people consider "the good stuff." Having lots of possessions cannot compete with the feeling that they are "doing what they are here to do."

In negotiations, they often seem to get the short stick. But they feel that is O.K., so long as they are not compelled to settle. They try to hold the line for what they think matters in the big picture, relatively unconcerned about "giving away

---

208

the store" on material things. Here is a perfect place for creative types to allow a more practical advisor to participate in any horse trading.

Oprah is one of the richest and most recognized people in the world. In 2005, she took part in an extended case study with Harvard Business School, and later spoke to the students:

> If you only desire to make money, you can do that.... But what I will tell you—and I know this for sure too—that the money only lasts for a while in terms of making you feel great about yourself. In the beginning, the money is to get nice things. And once you've gotten those nice things, I think some of the most unhappy people I know are the people who've acquired all the things and now they feel like, 'What else is there?' What else is there? What else is there? And that feeling of 'what else is there' is the calling—is the calling trying to say to you [that] there is more than this. There is more than this.[209]

A Worthy Challenge—Because It Is There

Mallory answered "Because it is there" when asked why he wanted to climbed Mt. Everest. That phrase suggests that the challenge already exists, ready for somebody to take it on.

Many kinds of puzzles or questions are already framed—just waiting until someone breaks the code, or can explain it from a different direction. Science and math have plenty of these "Everests" to climb. And many fields of interest have various limits that nobody has breached—as yet.

But more forerunners find they prefer to stake out entirely new terrain that was never before contemplated. Only by them successfully climbing (solving) such a hitherto unsuspected mountain do the rest of us find out that it is there. In doing so, the person also gets to define the form it takes.

Thriving on Freedom

Freedom Is Relative

Those of a visionary bent prize freedom *to create* and freedom *from* too many expectations by others. The desire to be free motivates many of them to leave the beaten path, which symbolizes conformity and diminished freedoms. Speaking about freedom implies a related orientation: *free from* or *free to*—away from something or toward something else. Which is carrot? Which is stick?

Stephen Covey said, "People who exercise their embryonic freedom day after day, little by little, expand that freedom. People who do not will find that it withers until they are literally being lived. They are acting out scripts written by parents, associates, and society."

---

[209] Lagace, Martha, "Oprah: A Case Study Comes Alive," *Working Knowledge*, Harvard Business School, February 20, 2006.

Becoming emotionally mature involves learning about the constructive use of freedom. One learns how to use one's freedom wisely, to invest it judiciously. Freedom is not just about choosing from the possibilities, but is bounded by how many of our prior decisions inhibit our ability to take advantage of something new.

Another way to consider freedom is in terms of what it makes possible. What doors will be opened by freedom that would otherwise remain blocked by circumstances or what other people want? Harriet Rubin said, "Freedom is actually a bigger game than power. Power is about what you can control. Freedom is about what you can unleash."

At first blush, a vision reveals an unbridled possibility — running free and unrestrained. In making the effort to understand its nature, and to ground it, the initial vision is no longer a "wild thing." It has been tamed and bridled — reflecting the desires of its tamer. And the person and notion are changed in the process.

Once that impulse to be free has been bridled, it can be ridden — off to the horizon or wherever else we want. That is yet another way that skills mastered on the visionary path can take us where we are destined to go.

I do not agree with the sentiment that "Freedom's just another word for nothing left to lose" (from "Me and Bobby McGee" penned by Kris Kristofferson). Instead, I see freedom as a state of maximum possibilities.

There is a concept in statistics called "degrees of freedom." Every variable that is already known about the sample or data reduces the number of "degrees of freedom" that would be available for later choices. In other words, once some parameter is defined, there is less flexibility available in the next choice, and the next…

On a personal level, our current commitments limit our freedom in making subsequent choices. Hanging on to too much personal baggage restricts our options. Whether it is mental stuff or physical stuff, the effect is the same.

At the very least, freedom should permit one to have some control of one's living and working circumstances. For a creative person, this is vital to the creative juices flowing, as Twyla Tharp describes in *The Creative Habit*.

> When I look back on my best work, it was inevitably created in what I call The Bubble. I eliminated every distraction, sacrificed almost everything that gave me pleasure, placed myself in a single-minded isolation chamber, and structured my life so that everything was not only feeding the work but subordinated to it. It is not a particularly sociable way to operate. It's actively antisocial. On the other hand, it is pro-creative … being in the bubble does not have to mean exiling yourself from people and the world. It is more a state of

mind, a willingness to subtract anything that disconnects you from your work. It doesn't have to be antisocial.[210]

Within our distracted existence, we have to cultivate a version of a bubble if we want to work freely and with maximum fluency in making connections and harnessing our memory—and to maintain all this as a habit. The bubble gives you that chance. It is the ideal state where nothing is wasted, where every detail feeds your art because it has nowhere else to go.[211]

Freedom *From* Conformity

Freedom really is not free. Nor does it come without strings attached. It comes with responsibilities, even though the popular perception treats freedom as an escape from them. Rather it offers an *opportunity to choose something different*, something the person is quite willing to commit to.

The visionary path is not without responsibilities. They are just different ones than the majority care about. So in turning toward the visionary path, someone turns their back on many prior-life obligations and toward a different scope of possibilities. It is more about them *intentionally taking responsibility* for their choices, rather than letting what is expected or socially accepted be treated as their only course.

In *Nation of Rebels*, Joseph Heath and Andrew Potter speak about the roots of conformity in contemporary culture. So much of the autonomy of freedom has been bartered away for consumer trinkets.

> Mass society is indelibly associated, in the popular imagination, with the United States of the 1950s. It is a world of perfect families, white picket fences, shiny new Buicks and teenagers 'going steady,' yet it is also a world of complete conformity, where happiness is achieved at the expense of individuality, creativity, and freedom. It is a world in which, as the dead Kennedys put it, the comfort you have demanded is not mandatory.... What people need to be liberated from is not a specific class that oppresses them or a system of exploitation that imposes poverty upon them. People have become trapped in a gilded cage, and have been taught to love their own enslavement. 'Society' controls them by limiting the imagination and suppressing their deepest needs. What they need to escape from is conformity.[212]

Conformity always comes at the expense of greater diversity or originality. People differ greatly as to how much of that they are willing to tolerate, and at what cost.

Being free also points to the role revolutionaries play in a culture. Those intrepid souls challenge accepted restrictions and stand up for different (or more)

---

[210] Tharp, Twyla, *The Creative Habit* (New York: Simon & Shuster, 2003), 237-8.
[211] *Ibid.*, 239.
[212] Heath, Joseph and Potter, Andrew, *Nation of Rebels: Why counterculture became consumer culture* (New York: HarperBusiness, 2004), 30-31.

choices. They argue not just for their own personal freedom, but fight for what they feel everyone is entitled to as well. As Americans, we consider that right to be free a birthright, part of our national philosophy and character.

Visionaries are the ones most likely to argue in the public interest, or for the disadvantaged. They are outspoken opponents of the *status quo*, the powerful, and well-connected. They prize what freedom means because they paid the price for it. It is only those who have broken free who are likely to speak about the cage.

Being able to take advantage of what freedom offers requires considerable self-knowledge and courage. As Epictetus (himself a former slave) said two thousand years ago, "No man is free who is not a master of himself."

~ Jailbreak ~
A BonBon ~ Faith Lynella

Logic is a jailer. It keeps us functioning with preset limits and punishes us for escaping. It constructs restrictive and confining mental structures more solid than brick and mortar. Try spending a little bit of time every day eluding it. Carve out time and areas in your life where the "right way" or the rational way have no influence. Find lots of "wrong," awkward, silly, irrational ways to do the most familiar things.

Logic is over-rated. There are a zillion things in which it is not helpful at all. And it is so seldom fun. Abandoning it is often fun and fraught with surprises. So take a holiday from your intellect, first in small doses or activities. Then let the freedom creep into more and more of what you do. Break out of your own routine. Sure, you'll be "back to normal" soon enough.

Fear not, you can always get back and reclaim your briefly abandoned mental structure. But like any holiday, you return with fresh insights, a renewed and broadened awareness. You return with added flexibility, aware of more choices, even within your familiar limitations.

Back to jail maybe, but is it really a prison when you hold the key? Or does it become a prison only because you fail to use your key?

From *BonBons to Sweeten Your Daily Life*. Or from *More BonBons*

Freedom *To* Create and Live Responsibly

The challenge to each of us today is not to get stuck in being anti, against, or rebellious in the name of protecting our freedom. That puts primary emphasis on what is stuck or in the past. But rather, we should, individually and collectively, demonstrate our freedom in action.

That represents *movement to something even better*. Creative and engaged living draws on our unique perceptions and desires, tailoring them to the situation at hand.

The most important act of a creative person is to create a context in which they can exist and do their work. But it should also include a place where it is O.K. to fail without undue fear. As Gandhi said, "Freedom is not worth having if it does not include the freedom to make mistakes."

> [Lappé also said] Just mentioning the word 'values' unnerves many Americans; they believe we're hopelessly divided, so best not go there. In truth, we're hopefully united on some essential policies reflecting deeply shared values.... It seems likely that there is common ground to be developed, reflecting values that fuel the dynamics of effective democracy: fairness, inclusion, and mutual accountability. By 'mutual accountability,' I mean simply all sides shouldering responsibility—the opposite of the blame game. It is recognition that just pointing fingers at those up there—the president, wealthy CEOs—and bemoaning our victimhood leads nowhere.[213]

Motivated for the Longest Term

Retirement Is Not a Carrot

Creative types do not look forward to retirement—unless that means stepping out of a job (and other obligations) and finally devoting their time to projects they really care about. It is not uncommon for those who have been nursing their visions for a long time to launch second careers late in life. Or they feel they earned the right to head off in fresh directions that bear no relation to prior interests.

Research has found that senior citizens who stay mentally stimulated into old age tend to live longer. George Bernard Shaw described the desire to grab life with both hands:

> I want to be thoroughly used up when I die, for the harder I work the more I live. I rejoice in life for its own sake. Life is no 'brief candle' for me. It is a sort of splendid torch which I have got hold of for the moment, and I want to make it burn as brightly as possible before handing it on to future generations.
> This is the true joy in life, being used for a purpose recognized by yourself as a mighty one; being a force of nature instead of a feverish, selfish little clod of ailments and grievances complaining that the world will not devote itself to making you happy.

Some seniors thrive on innovative ideas and stay up on new trends well into old age. Even while their bodies and energy levels are fading, there is plenty that they still can do rather well. Contrary to popular opinion, the kind of memory

---

[213] *Op. cit.*, Lappé, *Grip2*, 65-6.

that involves integration and spotting connections does not go away, so long as the individual keeps mentally sharp.

Twyla Tharp makes a persuasive case that creativity doesn't dry up because we age in *The Creative Habit.*

> What's wrong with getting better as you get more work under your belt? The libraries and archives and museums are packed with early bloomers and one-trick ponies who said everything they had to say in their first novel, who could only compose one good tune, whose canvas kept repeating the same dogged theme. My respect has always gone to those who are in it for the long haul. When people who have demonstrated talent fizzle out or disappear after early creative success, it's not because their gifts, that famous 'one percent inspiration,' abandoned them; more likely they abandoned their gift through a failure of perspiration.[214]

> As we age, it's hard to recapture the recklessness of youth, when new ideas flew off us as if from a pinwheel sparkler. But we more than compensate for this with the ideas we do generate, and our hard-earned wisdom about how to capture and, more importantly, *connect* those ideas.[215]

Although many skills decline with advancing age, some become even more refined. This also tracks with various forms of mastery that ripen during the later stages of the process. In *Practical Wisdom*, Barry Schwartz and Kenneth Sharpe cite research about seniors increasing certain cognitive functions as they get older.

> Neuropsychologist Elkhonon Goldberg has written about the power and importance of pattern recognition in The Wisdom Paradox. Goldberg's focus is on how the brain and mental function change as we age. The straight news isn't good: brain cells die, memory gets worse, mental operations become slower and more effortful, we tire out more quickly. It seems as though the story of our mental life is a stage of slow and inexorable decline.... Even though our raw materials have ever-diminishing capacity, our experience in the world is making us ever better at recognizing patterns. The mature mind and brain can make good decisions with much less effort than the inexperienced mind and brain. The result, Goldberg suggests, is that we do more with less. A rich ability to recognize patterns, shaped by experience, makes us wiser.[216]

Whether or not creative thinking makes a person live longer, they are probably going to enjoy life more. Such individuals are unlikely to be depressed or nonproductive because they love doing what they do. And they truly enjoy the way doing that makes them feel.

---

[214] *Op. cit.*, Tharp, 232-3.
[215] *Ibid.*, 236.
[216] Schwartz, Barry and Sharpe, Kenneth, *Practical Wisdom: The right way to do the right thing* (New York: Riverhead Books, 2010), 86-7.

One reason people sustain a high level of interest and stay engaged into their later years can be credited to their resiliency. They have "been there, done that" enough to have developed confidence in what they can do. It is a good time to take Emerson to heart:

> Finish each day and be done with it. You have done what you could. Some blunders and absurdities no doubt crept in; forget them as soon as you can. Tomorrow is a new day; begin it well and serenely and with too high a spirit to be encumbered with your old nonsense.

They have entered into a time of harvest. With age and wisdom come perspective. It's possible to see the fruits of a lifetime of planting seeds and working from the ground up. There is still time to influence the lasting legacy of a long-served vision, or to hand off its care to those who want it to continue. Teilhard de Chardin said:

> Every person in the course of his life must build — starting with the natural territory of his own life — a work, an opus, into which something enters from all the elements of the earth. He makes his own soul throughout all his earthly days; and at the same time he collaborates in another work, in another opus, which infinitely transcends, while at the same time it narrowly determines, the perspectives of his individual achievement: the completing of the world.

Chapter 12 - Seeing "Outside the Box"

An expanded capacity to remain attuned to the grand view coincides with escaping one's customary expectations and preconceptions. It comes with a price — being less able to fit into the "smaller," normal worldview afterward.

Boxed in by Unseen Limits

What we think is colored by what we already know and take for granted. We see what we expect to see, and consider it real and true. Yet we simultaneously sift out whatever does not fit that perception of reality — without even noticing. Neither do we question our viewpoint very often. It constitutes our perceptual world — the box we live in.

The box symbolizes conventional thinking — with all our beliefs, assumptions, and biases in place. Each of us inhabits multiple boxes: our personal ones, and others we share — each having its defining qualities and limitations. For example, the perceptual box of kindergarteners does not have much in common with that of rocket scientists.

Unfortunately, each box constitutes an accumulated mishmash of truth and distortions which are anything but coherent. Yet our various boxes influence our behavior in every possible way.

The box metaphor also indicates fish cannot see the water they swim in (their unnoticed milieu). Only from *outside* our fish bowl (the box) can the water be perceived. A person cannot reason themselves out of its logical constraints. Those rare occasions when we briefly pop outside of it are the only times we are even aware it exists.

Humans are blind to whatever boxes we inhabit. Our relationship with them are beneath the level of our conscious awareness, so if pressed we would swear they do not exist or affect us at all. To even be aware of those influences on the self requires more than average discernment and detachment. The ideal, however, is not to escape the box entirely, but to stop being unaware of its influence on us.

On a similar note, we tend to be unable to recognize our customary mental biases and conceptual limitations — particularly those that are widely held. As a person moves further away from conventional life, those shared mindsets have less and less influence on them.

We are blind to our omnipresent context, as Heath and Potter describe in *Nation of Rebels*:

> If you asked the fishes to describe what it's like to live in the bottom of the sea, they would probably neglect to mention that it's extremely wet. Sometimes the most important features of our environment escape our attention simply because they are so ubiquitous. Our mental environment is much the same.

Some theories are so universal, so taken-for-granted, that we fail to notice that they are even theories.[217]

Problems with the Box Metaphor

"Outside of the box" is a popular phrase used to describe finding a more creative way to solve problems—by changing one's perceptions about the problem. Its use as a synonym for unconventional thinking has become a business cliché.

In almost every case, what is called "thinking outside the box" is really just moving to a bigger box—equally undefined but limiting. Although the larger box is more encompassing, its boundaries are still not abandoned. Usually the shift only lasts until the person's normal mindset returns, since their default state remains the same.

Each box is limited by time and space, both of which are inescapable with the normal 3-D mind. "Three dimensional" even describes how a box is measured: length times width, times height ($l \times w \times h$ = volume).

"Out of the box" also suggests we have gotten out of our comfort zone, which is really a smaller, cozy sub-set of our usual box. It is the one with which we are most identified. But that is defining "comfort" as being familiar, predictable, safe, and making us feel in control. Those concerns are missing and irrelevant during a vision or in states of enhanced perception, when the limits of box-ness are temporarily absent.

Almost every significant long-term change of behavior is really about someone changing the nature of their box, perspective, or mindset. The only true escape from box-ness is the way artists, mystics, and those in the grip of inspiration do it—by going outside of time and space, as in the vision experience. The person is briefly aware of the transcendent part of himself or herself that is out of 3-D entirely.

As customarily used, to "think outside the box" attempts to eliminate false constraints when solving practical problems. However, visions are something else entirely. The shift during a vision is not about being *inside* or *outside* anything because even that frame of reference is rooted in "either-or" thinking—either inside *or* outside of the box. The dimensions from which visions arise are holistic and out of time, which are also "larger than life."

"Out of the box" is supposedly contrasted with ordinary linear or logical thinking. However, the contrast is misleading because logic cannot function without a box—a context that is *within* time and space. Moving to even larger or different boxes cannot change that. Intellect, by itself, has no power to apprehend other states of awareness that are not spatially limited and defined.

---

[217] Heath, Joseph and Potter, Andrew, *Nation of Rebels: Why counterculture became consumer culture* (New York: HarperBusiness, 2004), 36.

Changing Boxes

We live in a time of run-away change. It is coming so fast, and from all directions we don't have time for something new to settle in before more change is upon us. Even the bedrock seems to be shifting, presaging long-term secondary shifts. However, unless a change brings a fundamental scale shift as well, it is still a change *within the existing framework* (or box).

A breakthrough is not the same as a level shift (or change of state), although any of them happen on an individual basis. **Breakthroughs are into a larger box**, but they are still on the same level and scale — within the 3-D frame of reference. A **level shift**, however, **involves movement** *out of any box* (out of 3-D itself). That temporarily alters the scope of what is perceived.

Both breakthroughs and level shifts tend to be of limited duration until someone has developed the ability to ground that altered perception. Doing so depends on the person's degree of self-mastery, which also reflects a shift to a **new default state**.

Our box represents our default state, where we are anchored. It is our home base and where we settle back to as "normal life." Through self-mastery and what I call

Straddle-span (Chapter 13), a person can have one foot out of the box. The creative process is another way for a person to get one foot out.

People sometimes transcend the box through artistry and creative acts — rising beyond the limitations of technique or box-ness. As an example, the reason a poem itself is never really the same as a paraphrase of it is that a paraphrase is not able to *operate on both a temporal and atemporal level.*

To quote Emily Dickinson, "If I feel physically as if the top of my head were taken off, I know that is poetry," (i.e., it pops her out of her rational mind). The reason for reading a lyric poem, moving through it temporally, word by word, is to arrive at that epiphanic moment that could lift the reader temporarily into an atemporal realm. Any of the arts are capable of doing that — something which sets them apart from everyday thinking and practical concerns.

Building a Different Default State

"Normal" is the universal human default state — totally grounded in the 3-D reality of our time and place. Each culture or community has its own conventions, but they all operate the same. It is the collective standard of behavior for most people of their shared social environment. What is considered normal reflects the social standard we are born and raised into. It acts like gravity, holding an object in a static place/state unless considerable effort is made for it to act differently. Even when one escapes (inspired experiences) the time is brief before returning to home base again. That can lead to a flip-flop between the two states. But mostly one resides in "normal."

One way to change our default state requires building a new base camp to ground one's top-of-the-mountain trips (out of the box experiences). For a long time, someone might shift between up there (top and out) and back to normal (flat and foot-of-the-mountain). However, with greater self-awareness it is possible to gradually begin to ground more of our enhanced perceptual awareness in daily life, after we briefly shift up and out.

Unknown to any of us at the time, we are building a base camp part way up the mountain. Once a base camp is established, it gives us a slightly different default state. It starts small, but becomes more substantial as we develop our greater inner faculties.

When someone falls from the peak of clarity, he or she does not return to where they started any more (all the way to the bottom). They return to the base camp that is anchored further up the slope. This is their new default state. Upward progress (growth) can resume from the base camp, rather than square one.

The basecamp acts as a toehold that is neither defined by, nor contained within, someone's perceptual box. It provides an anchor point that can be re-visited as needed. Over time and with sufficient inner development, other base camps are established higher up the side of the mountain. Each in turn anchors a more developed default state. It is all preparatory work for handling mastery-level issues.

Your base camp represents your growth and knowledge that cannot be lost through setbacks or forgetting. It is fully integrated because you have *fully embodied* that level. These represent stages achieved or turning point overcome. A basecamp is only seen in retrospect, when after a wipeout one stands with confidence in a place that was not wiped out.

It is a mistake to judge one's long-term inner growth by pointing to top-of-the-mountain experiences. Those are a gift and out of life—desirable but not necessarily a reflection of how far a person has grown (or has still to go). However, moving the default state reflects intentional inner work, achieved through dogged persistence and integrity. It is evidence of greater self-awareness.

The true measure of one's progress is between the base, where the person began, and their current default state. It becomes their new floor. As one is able to anchor more of their enhanced awareness and wisdom in everyday life, their default state (base camp) goes up the mountain another notch. Thereafter, he or she doesn't revert to the bottom but rather retains more of the peak (peek) experience. This is another approach to Straddle-span (Chapter 13) that signals increasing integration and mastery.

Seeing "Outside the Cosmic Box"

There is much we don't know about the actual capacity of human consciousness, the part or parts that can either travel to or possibly exist in nonphysical dimensions beyond our rational understanding. What we do know is that with the widespread advent (some would say a renewal) of metaphysics into Western Civilization during the 20th century, more and more humans worldwide are having and reporting experiences that our neurosciences simply cannot explain.

Most people who have not had such experiences find the descriptive narrative by those who have as far-fetched and implausible. And many of those who have had such experiences withhold sharing them for fear of the highly critical and too often cruel dismissive reactions they encounter.

Nonetheless, a far greater body of scientists, psychologists, humanities scholars, theologians, and others are beginning to recognize on an impressive scale that the nature of human consciousness is far more expansive than ever imagined and cannot be fully understood or observed yet, even with our most sophisticated imaging technology.

Given that scientists cannot yet explain the mysteries of subconscious dreaming in the sleep state, or the ability of many to experience parallel realities while under hypnosis, they are even further mystified by persons who experience visions while fully awake.

That said, I'm going to explore this topic as it relates to visionaries. I will be referring to general theories about how consciousness is perceived to operate outside of the boundaries of our current understanding of reality—theories that were derived from some science but nearly all from case studies, personal accounts, and informed speculation.

Human Consciousness Exists in Multiple Dimensions

As humans, our state as organic physical matter is dependent on this dimension from birth to death, anyway. But parallel to it and intersecting it are innumerable other dimensions which our human senses cannot directly perceive. Like *Alice Through the Looking Glass*, it is possible to enter other planes of reality when the circumstances are right, when our normal limits of perception are temporarily suspended.

The challenge upon returning to everyday reality is how to hang onto something from that extraordinary experience without blocking it out just because it does not fit into our original mindset.

Visions are ventures out of the box. True, but they are also outside of the customary time and space reality even while someone is still rooted in their body in this dimension. The bridge between parallel realities exists briefly within the visionary while in a vision or creative state, between big "R" and little "r" reality. Since time and distance are suspended for the duration, the trans-dimensional traveler feels the awe of newness and shock of fresh discovery on every trip.

During a transcendent experience the person is out of their everyday mind — and is in no hurry to return. They are no longer confined by the physical reality to which they are accustomed — or their mental or emotional realities either.

So much of the craziness that abounds these days is nudging us toward using the higher awareness available to us in order to make some sense of life. Coming and going between those states is less and less in the realm of science fiction. We all visit them unconsciously in dreams and occasional inspired states. But most of us are unable to ground the newfound awareness and hang on to it afterwards. With increasing inner maturity those insights can begin to make a palpable impact in the ordinary world.

Refined attention opens us to increased trans-dimensional perception. Our ongoing task is to incorporate and ground such luminous moments in daily life. An inspired experience (vision) can reveal the entire palate of possibilities. As a matter of fact, quantum physicists describe this field of energy as a matrix where all things appear connected — they actually call it "the field of all possibilities."

Imagine the quandary faced by trans-dimensional consciousness travelers (particularly those in the arts, the expressives) who experience the "full box of crayons" — then must make do with this dimension's seven primary colors, once back to their normal frame of mind.

Although humans operate primarily in this dimension by virtue of their physical bodies, our internal capacities are not so constrained. The proposition has gained considerable traction that every person exists as a multi-dimensional being, *capable of being aware of more than a single dimension at a time* (even though we are seldom conscious of them).

The intermittent disorientation all of us are sensing of late probably results from more frequent and abrupt shifting in and out of our customary dimensional mode (our box). And many more people are having these experiences more often.

The boundaries between dimensions appear to be more permeable than was originally thought — suggesting that the whole of humanity and the Earth are moving toward a more harmonious alignment. In the meantime, we flip-flop between the states like an inebriated sailor on shore leave. (Note: This is the topic of my prior book, *How to Survive a Spiritual Hangover: Practical Guide to Holding Steady in a Wobbly World*, © 2007.

Intense or prolonged experiences of passion, emotion, creativity, or spiritual awareness establish a stronger link between dimensions. Mystics and artists of all sorts have long been able to tap into higher-dimension energies to fuel their creative output. Gifted composers, painters, poets, and writers can occasionally capture and express their transcendent experiences in a form others can feel an immediate resonance with — without mediation through logic or language.

An expanded capacity to remain attuned to the grand view coincides with escaping one's customary expectations and preconceptions. It comes with a price—being less able to fit into the "smaller," normal worldview afterward. Many whose creative force is fed by excursions to higher-energy states face significant challenges in order to maintain a toehold in the everyday world the rest of the time.

They struggle to reconcile their transcendent experience with the diminished state they used to consider adequate. That includes figuring out how to deal with people unaware of the expanded view who lack the ears to hear or a willingness to believe there is more to life than that which can be seen or measured. The visionary's difficulty in coping with this lesser reality also contributes to the misfit stereotype that gets attached to them.

It is now gaining wider acceptance that children are born with an open connection to higher dimensions already in place but that innate linkage is usually severed in the course of being socialized and formally educated. Greater awareness by adults of the inherent value of multi-dimensional awareness may lead us to respect and nurture it.

It is no longer acceptable to violate and destroy that innate capacity as an unavoidable stage of growing up.

The Art of Seeing Uses Fresh Eyes

Vision Driven Creativity

Visionaries are constantly seeking connections—the readily noticeable, as well as the underlying, largely invisible ones. Such a tendency reflects one definition of genius—the ability to see the connections between *apparently unconnected* things. Anyone able to see and make these connections gets to glimpse more facets of the big picture—the holistic view.

It is possible for us to cultivate what I call the Art of Seeing. The astute eye scans broadly across the span of knowledge to spot connections that are not apparent through casual observation or habitual assumptions. Subtle patterns and relationships can and do become apparent when *seen without preconception*. Such a method of seeing seeks more for understanding than to identify things or reach conclusions.

This chapter describes things that anybody can do while in the box that can break us out of our limited awareness (our customary mindset). Besides, as Tesla said, "Our senses enable us to perceive only a minute portion of the outside world." Imagine what more is available when we "see anew."

To "see with fresh eyes," it is necessary to *avoid looking at anything in the usual way* – both physically and mentally. There needs to be an "innocence of perception," unmediated by prior experience or expectations. Unless someone looks with the intention to disconnect from what they already know, they reflexively use customary ways of looking. Or they rely on prior experiences to make sense of what could have been novel. That defeats the point, doesn't it?

Broad scanning ignores categorical distinctions that escape the too-narrow focus of seeing only what is expected. "Seeing with fresh eyes" also pulls a person out of their niche and into yet-unexplored fields where "innocence of perception" is more likely to occur.

The Art of Seeing should be cultivated and appreciated for the grace and nuance it brings to light. The word "art" underscores that it cannot be done from habit, but instead by breaking out of it. Paul Gauguin said "I shut my eyes in order to see."

Such an approach sensitizes someone to notice the ebb and flow of less-apparent influences that are routinely overlooked. It uncovers new combinations and permutations of data so that more of the underlying patterns can reveal themselves.

The Art of Seeing is a life skill that can work in every experience. And in the process it can direct us into unsuspected fruitful avenues of response. Developing the Art of Seeing can achieve more effective results than any amount of diligence alone. "The eye of the master will do more work than both his hands" said Benjamin Franklin.

Quantum physics demonstrated that how someone observes objects changes them—altering the relationship between the observer and the observed. The Art of Seeing adds another dimension to your role as observer. You *intentionally* put more of yourself into what is ordinarily the habitual activity of seeing. By being more fully present in the experience, you perceive significantly more connections and implications. You *intentionally* participate in changing yourself—along with what is being seen.

I hereby coin a term, "Naked Vision," as what someone can see by means of "innocence of perception" coupled with their own congruency. As Anaïs Nin said, "We don't see things as they are, we see things as we are." We become more aware as we earnestly engage in the everyday act of seeing. Naked Vision grounds that fuller awareness in the here and now.

Michael McKinney explains how we see in "The Persistence of Vision:"

I Think, Therefore I See

Biologists tell us that the eye does not function to replicate the world we come in contact with it but instead to sense, process and encode the motion, patterns and colors of the light we see into something our mind will interpret. We process this data in connection with information coming from all the other organs that respond to our environment, thus combining the new data with similar information already stored in our memory. As a result, no two people see anything exactly alike.

The mind's default setting operates in much the same way. We develop patterns of thought or mental models that shape what we see or perceive and thus what we think, as well as how we will choose to think about new

> information that comes our way. We persist in or hold on to thinking that connects with the mental pictures or models we have already formed. So as we go from scene to scene in our lives, our mind fills in the gaps between our experiences using the same old familiar thinking. It connects our thoughts and experiences in such a way as to keep them as consistent and uniform as possible with what we already think.
>
> Call it a persistence of thought. We see what makes sense to us. We develop beliefs and opinions consistent with what is already in our heads. Anything that is inconsistent with that image or contrary to our current ideas goes unnoticed or is ignored, so that we may maintain that continuous, uninterrupted picture of our world. Just as what we see is governed by what we think, so what we perceive as real—our feelings, thoughts and assumptions—is based on what we think is real.[218]

A person needs "innocence of perception" to get around "persistence of thought," no small task. It is a great challenge to consider it desirable to abandon their familiar way of seeing. That is the default, after all. Is attempting to go against nature worth the significant effort and repeated frustrations involved?

Someone would have to see great value in developing Naked Vision in order to undertake the requisite disengagement. Just a commitment to act on that desire requires a big step out of their comfort zone.

Our original ideas are biased by our existing concepts, categories, preferences, and stereotypes. To quote Dee Hock, the founder of Visa, "The problem is never how to get new, innovative thoughts into your mind, but how to get old ones out. Every mind is a building filled with archaic furniture. Clean out a corner of your mind and creativity will instantly fill it."

It is possible to observe in such a disengaged way that our prior experiences or assumptions do not leap to mind. Attention can be trained to hold them back—to look at objects and ideas as though they have never been encountered before. Poet Baudelaire must have been speaking of this capacity when he said, "Genius is nothing more nor less than childhood recovered at will."

Try to sense with the inquisitiveness of a child: *expectant without expectations.* That is an optimal default state. Doing that would give a chance for another first impression each time. It is not true that there is only one chance for a first impression—not if memory and reflexive perceptual habits can be held at bay.

Use your senses in different ways, breaking out of habitual modes of perception whenever possible. Gertrude Stein suggests: "A writer should write with his eyes and a painter paint with his ears."

---

[218] McKinney, Michael, "The Persistence of Vision," LeadershipNow.com. [Article originally appeared in the Fall 2005 issue of VISION]

One way of "seeing with fresh eyes" is to look (actually and symbolically) at something from as many different perspectives as possible. Doing so prevents being identified with any single one of them—and in particular a person's customary one(s). In the process, it is possible to gain a broader, more encompassing view.

However, even multiple perspectives are still subject to the constraints of boxness. The more readily someone is able to go "outside the box" (as many visionaries increasingly do), the more someone becomes aware of its presence. And the less willing they are to let those limitations fully define their world.

Visual Seeing Changes the View

Better answers can be found through Visual Seeing. In *The Back of the Napkin*, Dan Roam spells out a four-step process: Look, See, Imagine, Show. The key is to maintain conscious attention.

While we may do these steps in looking intuitively, this requires an additional awareness of doing so. No multi-tasking allowed. Each step captures the entire perceptual field. That alone can account for its effectiveness.

In *The Back of the Napkin*, Dan Roam breaks the act of "seeing" into distinct activities.

> **Looking** = collecting and screening.
> Looking involves scanning the environment in order to build an initial big picture sense of things, while simultaneously asking the rapid-fire questions that help our minds make a first-pass assessment of what is in front of us.
>
> **Seeing** = selecting and clumping
> While we are just looking we are scanning the whole scene and collecting initial inputs. Now that we're seeing, we are selecting which inputs are worth more detailed inspection. This is based on recognizing patterns—sometimes consciously, oftentimes not.
>
> **Imagining** = seeing what isn't there
> Imagining is what happens after the visuals have been collected and selected, and the time comes to start manipulating them.
>
> **Showing** = making it all clear
> Once we've found patterns, made sense of them, and figured out a way to manipulate them to discover something new, we've got to show it all to others.[219]

The challenge for us is to find a way to ground the fuller view through action. Showing is about sharing, communicating, and doing. It takes the next step to

---

[219] Roam Dan, *The Back of the Napkin: Solving problems and selling ideas with pictures* (New York: Penguin Books, 2008), 37-42.

make the process of seeing tangible. Plus it is done from your uniqueness, so it is always done *your way*.

As with other skills, someone gets more capable with practice. The artist and choreographer Oskar Schlemmer described the rewards of skilled observation late in his life, "I am experiencing with unfamiliar intensity the mystic effects of nature, and I observe that with the passing years one keeps learning to see in new and different ways."[220] One enters a world of possibilities that is without limit.

Possibilities
Søren Kierkegaard

> If I were to wish for anything I should not wish for wealth and power, but for the passionate sense of what can be, for the eye, which, ever young and ardent, sees the possible. Pleasure disappoints, possibility never. And what wine is so sparkling, what so fragrant, what so intoxicating as possibility?

Limits on Imagination

While the mind and imagination are not as constrained as the physical body, they still cannot be totally unfettered. The conceptual limits are described by Steven Pinker in *The Stuff of Thought:*

> The human imagination is a wondrous concocter. We can visualize unicorns and centaurs, people who are faster than a speeding bullet, and a brotherhood of man sharing all the world. But there are many things we can't imagine, at least not in the form of a mental image. It's impossible to visualize an apple next to a lemon with neither one to the right.... We know that elephants are big and gray, take up space, and are in a particular location at any given time. But while I can imagine an elephant that isn't big and isn't gray, I cannot imagine an elephant that doesn't take up space or isn't located somewhere (even if I have it floating around in my mind's eye, it is somewhere at every moment)…

> Our mind's eye is also sentenced to live in a world of time. Just as we can imagine an empty space devoid of objects but cannot imagine a set of objects that aren't located in space, we can imagine a stretch of time in which nothing happens but cannot imagine an event that doesn't unfold in time or take place at a given time.[221]

Looking Past the Obvious

To be creative means to prefer to innovate, to combine elements in original ways, to consider "what could be," rather than simply relate to what everyone

---

[220] Root-Bernstein, Robert and Michele, *Sparks of Genius: The thirteen thinking tools of the world's most creative people* (New York: Houghton Mifflin, 1999), 49.
[221] Pinker, Steven, *The Stuff of Thought: Language as a window into human nature* (New York: Viking, 2007), 154-5.

else sees. Quoting Alfred North Whitehead, "It requires a very unusual mind to undertake the analysis of the obvious."

Most of what a person registers (far less than all that's present or available to be seen) will be colored by their preconceptions and expectations. Settling for "obvious" answers is at the expense of *what else* could be discovered. Csikszentmihalyi says:

> Creative people are constantly surprised. They don't assume that they understand what is happening around them, and they don't assume that anybody else does either. They question the obvious—not out of contrariness but because they see the shortcomings of accepted explanations before the rest of us do. They sense problems before they are generally perceived and are defined as what they are.[222]
>
> The initial way we look at a problem is influenced by our usual way of seeing. Our unacknowledged preconceptions and desires inevitably influence what answers are found. We have to trick ourselves into not letting that "persistence of thought" close off alternate avenues of discovery. "Once we have settled on a perspective we shut down all but one line of thought. Certain kinds of ideas occur to us, but only those kinds and no others."[223]

Just rethinking what is considered a problem can open worlds for exploration not noticed before. Some of them could make the need for an answer irrelevant—it dissolves the problem. Look beyond the problem itself—to the larger situation and what needs to occur. How else can the job get done? Most problem solving resembles trying to break down a locked door, without noticing all the adjacent doors standing open that could serve our purpose.

How we describe or define a problem limits its scope as well as what we are looking for. If a certain outcome or benefit is desired, it is better not to be too specific about which answers would work. That is summed up by the old saw, "Nobody ever wants to buy a drill. They want a hole a certain size." If someone is fixated on drills, other solutions will pass them by. Csikszentmihalyi also said:

> Language predisposes our mind to a certain way of thinking.... Notice how the tagging of a complex flower with a simple verbal description detours human curiosity by predisposing us along certain avenues of thought. It is as if the language we use draws a magic circle around us, a circle from which there is no escape save by stepping out of the circle (language) into another.[224]

Looking at an experience or problem in as many different ways as imaginable permits a wider range of possibilities. Starting over and shifting gears in order

---

[222] Csikszentmihalyi, Mihaly, *Creativity: Flow and the psychology of discovery and invention* (New York: HarperCollins, 1996), 363.
[223] Michalko, Michael, *Cracking Creativity: The secrets of creative genius* (Berkeley: Ten Speed Press, 1998), 19.
[224] *Ibid.*, 51.

to look again from other angles broadens it further. The click of fresh perception, when it comes, incorporates all those facets into something magnificent and unexpected.

It pays to be mindful about how much attention we pay to our thinking. We must distrust our own thought processes. It is less about questioning external authorities than being suspicious of those arising in our own heads—those that run on autopilot.

Ways to Restructure a Problem:

- Make it more global and specific.
- Separate the parts from the whole.
- Change the words in some fashion.
- Make positive action statements.
- Switch perspectives.
- Use multiple perspectives.
- Ask questions.[225] [bullets mine]

> Combine elements of unrelated and contradictory ideas. Ruminate on possibilities like what could you do with all the needed resources available? Or if you had none? Keep combining any of the pieces in illogical ways. Try blending the multiple perspectives themselves. "It's important to spend time rephrasing problems in both more global and more specific ways. More specific problem statements lead to quicker solutions but less conceptual creativity than general statements."[226]

Expand the Pool of Possibilities

The giants recommend generating lots of ideas, without worrying about which are the keepers until later. Edison said "To have a great idea, have a lot of them." He told a reporter, "I speak without exaggeration when I say that I have constructed three thousand different theories in connection with the electric light, each one of them reasonable and apparently likely to be true."

Edison was well known for the sheer quantity of inventive ideas he could generate. He said "The first requisite for success is the ability to apply your physical and mental energies to one problem incessantly without growing weary." Do not settle for the quick, easy, or singular answers that block other lines of thought. This stage should not be rushed and continues to be fruitful over the long term—even after the deed is done. It could expose the next creative wrinkle.

There are very real advantages to developing a variety of possible answers early in the creative process, as Tim Harford explains in *Adapt: Why success always starts with failure.*

---

[225] *Ibid.*, 23.
[226] *Ibid.*, 24.

> This idea of allowing several ideas to develop in parallel runs counter to our instincts: we naturally tend to ask, 'What is the best option?', and concentrate on that. But given that life is so unpredictable, what seemed initially like an inferior option may turn out to be exactly what we need. It's sensible in many
>
> areas of life to leave room for exploring parallel possibilities ... but it is particularly true in the area of innovation, where a single good idea or new technology can be so valuable. In an uncertain world, we need more than just Plan A; and that means finding safe havens for Plans B, C, D and beyond.[227]

Creative people do not worry much about failure. They are the ones who fail the most consistently—then learn from their mistakes before making later attempts. It is summed up by the slogan, "Fail Faster." Scott Adams points to the distinction, "Creativity is allowing yourself to make mistakes. Art is knowing which ones to keep."

In my own case, I find it useful to make up unusual words and phrases to explain concepts, like "thoughtful chicken" (seeing what cannot be seen while in the normal focus of attention). Doing so allows the expression of a notion without the undesired baggage that accompanies familiar language. New terms diminish "persistence of thought," while introducing additional precision of articulation.

Initial ideas are usually poorer in quality than later ideas. Resist the urge to rush the creative process or to press too hard for any specific results. Letting new ideas bubble up often leads one to where they have never gone before, never even suspected. As Michalko said:

> The longer you work to improve and modify ideas, the more likely it is that the solution will be original and appropriate.... Ask what can be substituted, combined, adapted, magnified, modified, put to some other use, eliminated, rearranged, or reversed in the existing ideas?[228]
>
> Later associations are much more original and unique than the earlier ones. The first responses are the common dominant associations you have for that word. By arranging to give responses that are not common or dominant, you experience an increase in originality and imaginativeness of the responses.[229]

Ignoring Customary Boundaries and Barriers Is Freeing

The logical mind draws lines, defines categories, and names things in order to make them conceptually manageable. It is good at dividing things into categorical chunks. And the way we are educated, we learn about those chunks and "color within the lines." To paraphrase the definition of an expert, we know more and more about less and less. What would it feel like to know less and less

---

[227] Harford, Tim, *Adapt: Why success always starts with failure* (New York: Farrar, Straus and Giroux, 2011), 86-7.
[228] *Op. cit.*, Michalko, 263.
[229] *Ibid.*, 91.

about more and more? In other words, imagine seeing without so many mental associations. That would be novelty indeed.

However, to "see with fresh eyes," allows a person to connect the dots that lie outside of a defined field or context. Eliminating the categories of ideas allows someone to shuffle all the gathered puzzle pieces in order to find unexpected affinities—a skill that is in increasing demand.

Daniel H. Pink speaks of the need for us to break out of customary boundaries in *A Whole New Mind*.

> Creativity generally involves crossing the boundaries of domains. The most creative among us see relationships the rest of us never notice. Such ability is at a premium in a world where specialized knowledge work can quickly become routinized work—and therefore be automated or outsourced away. Designer Clement Mok says, 'the next 10 years will require people to think and work across boundaries into new zones that are totally different from their areas of expertise. They will not only have to cross those boundaries, but they will also have to identify opportunities and make connections between them.'[230]

What we perceive and how we organize what we know mentally could be a handicap to knowing in different ways. Creativity requires us to understand our own perceptual habits enough to be open to breaking them sometimes. But the timing is crucial since we escape our perceptual limits by what we do physically at precisely the point of choice. Rollo May said, "Human freedom involves our capacity to pause between the stimulus and response and, in that pause, to choose." Failing that, other influences take over.

Problem Finding Is Itself an Art

A good problem galvanizes the mind. It kindles an excitement, an eagerness to find an explanation, an answer, a better way. It purges the sluggishness of drifting along in the same-o same-o. But not all problems or challenges are significant and many are not worth the candle. "The uncreative mind can spot wrong answers, but it takes a creative mind to spot wrong questions," said Antony Jay.

Worthy problems are likely to defy quick and easy answers—but they call forth a new conceptual framework and focused creative force. They demand we grow and become more flexible, less inhibited by the past. To quote Problem D'Solver Law Number 13, "You're not done until you're glad you had the problem." It opened up hitherto unexpected doors.

Eric Hoffer argues that man is driven to find ways to deal with our limitations, whether that means doing what our physical body is not designed to do or attaining desires that seem out of reach. Eric Hoffer said in *The Ordeal of Change*:

---

[230] Pink, Daniel H., *A Whole New Mind: Why right-brainers will rule the future* (New York: Riverhead Books, 2005), 135.

> Man is most peculiarly human when he cannot have his way. His momentous achievements are rarely the result of a clean forward thrust but rather of a soul intensity generated in front of an apparently insurmountable obstacle which
>
> bars his way to a cherished goal. It is here that potent words and explosive substitutes have their birth, and the endless quest, and the stretching of the soul which encompasses heaven and earth.[231]

Reason Has Its Place

The mind is perfectly suited for certain kinds of problems, as Johan Lehrer explains in *How We Decide*. We err when we assume rational thought is capable of dealing with the other types of problems as well. One of the kinds of knowledge being acquired on this journey is an awareness of which of our modes (mental, physical, or emotional) is best suited for the matter at hand.

> Simple problems require reason. There isn't a clear line separating easy questions from hard ones, or math problems from mysteries. Some scientists, such as Ap Dijksterhuis, believe that any problem with more than four distinct variables overwhelms the rational brain. Others believe that a person can consciously process somewhere between five and nine pieces of information at any given moment. With practice and experience, this range can be slightly expanded. But in general, the prefrontal cortex is a sharply constrained piece of machinery. If the emotional brain is a fancy laptop, stuffed full of microprocessors operating in parallel, the rational brain is an old-fashioned calculator....
>
> Novel problems also require reason. Before you entrust a mystery to the emotional brain, before deciding to let your instincts make a big bet in poker or fire a missile at a suspicious radar blip, as yourself a question: How does your past experience help solve this particular problem? Have you play poker hands like this before? Seen blips like this before? Are these feelings rooted in experience, or are they just haphazard impulses?
>
> If the problem really is unprecedented—if it's like a complete hydraulic failure in a Boeing 737—then emotions can't save you.... The only way out of a unique mess is to come up with a creative solution.... Such insights require the flexible neurons of the prefrontal cortex. However, this doesn't mean that our emotional state is irrelevant.... [Studies of the neuroscience of insight] have shown that people in good moods are significantly better at solving hard problems that require insight than people who are cranky and depressed.[232]

Creative Problem Solving Is but One Use of Fresh Eyes

Problem solving involves figuring out what caused (or could cause) a problem, then finding ways to fix it. The primary thrust is on making a problem go away.

---

[231] Hoffer, Eric, *The Ordeal of Change* (New York: Harper and Row, 1963), 101.
[232] Lehrer, Jonah, *How We Decide* (New York: Houghton Mifflin Harcourt 2009), 244-6.

By comparison, creative problem solving uses creativity to solve a problem in an indirect or unconventional manner—to find solutions that are not apparent to begin with. The principal focus is on the process and finding a multitude of plausible answers.

Creative problem solving engages a process to find a solution, resolve a challenge, make an improvement, or take advantage of an opportunity. It should involve creativity, rather than just applying what was previously learned or already done before. The eventual result will typically contain novel elements. But that does not mean that it has intrinsic value or will be appreciated by anyone.

If the objective is to create a useful new object or process, the solution could be an invention—a specific device or technique. Innovations and inventions usually are motivated by economic gain and practicality, so are likely to be pursued primarily for their financial rewards—and be valued accordingly.

Most problem solving places too much emphasis on problems and crises. Nearly all efforts are consumed by avoiding them or dealing with putting out fires. It responds to urgency instead of heading them off beforehand, or while quite small. Under pressure, it is easy to get stuck in the firefighter mentality, but that is a misplaced use of time and resources—doomed to forever playing catch up. Too little effort is directed toward resourcefully launching desired and long-range possibilities that circumvent those issues entirely.

A visionary needs to carefully maintain his or her focus on the expansive frame of reference, rather than getting consumed by never-ending problem solving. Staying clear of what is primary and what is subordinate is the only way to prevent creative forces from getting bogged down in practical concerns too quickly. It is not enough to find a solution, but to persist until you find the best one possible for all concerned, and for the long term—one that does not sacrifice the vision to expediency.

However, idea generation can be seductive if the person gets so caught up in it that they never take the next step, or forget to ground it. A visionary is more than an idle dreamer or escape artist precisely because they *can and do* combine the inspired dream and action.

Dissolving Problems is Even Better than Solving Them

Back when I was a professional speaker and trainer, I called myself "The Problem D'Solver." My slogan: "Every problem is an invitation to open your mind and heart." Everything I spoke about showed how to see a problem anew, so it ceased to be a stumbling block. It was "dissolved," rather than being solved rationally—transcended by the clarity and possibilities that came with a larger perspective.

I finally had to accept that most people considered "Problem D'Solver" simply as a clever take-off on problem solver—without realizing that problem solving and problem <u>dis</u>solving are entirely different approaches to finding solutions. My message was about escaping habitual restraints.

In the same sense, the Art of Seeing is more than a technique to make everyday life more comfortable. It provides a measure of freedom that accompanies having a less restricted worldview — or habitual ways of seeing. As Arthur Koestler tells us, "Habit is the denial of creativity and the negation of freedom; a self-imposed straitjacket of which the wearer is unaware."

The Problem D'Solver Laws
Every problem is an invitation to open your mind and heart
Faith Lynella

1. A problem is a terrible thing to waste. Each is tailor-made for you.
2. Problem D'Solving is a process. Finding solutions changes you *and* the problem.
3. How you define the problem determines the kinds of solutions you get.
4. Every problem is a failure to see; improve your vision and understanding and the solutions appear.
5. Einstein said, "A problem can't be solved at the same level it was created" — the trick is in finding another level.
6. Every problem is a demand for change. The answer must be more complex than the conditions that led to it.
7. No problem occurs in isolation. You have more resources at your command than you realize.
8. The answer can be found *within* the problem.
9. Answers come from knowing less — not knowing more. Disengage from what's already known and hold…
10. No answer works until you *use* it. Part of the answer is the action taken.
11. No answer is final or complete.
12. Go beyond ordinary, familiar answers to find extraordinary ones.
13. You aren't done until you're glad you had the problem.

© *Faith Lynella and Off the Page Press, 1990 and 2012*

Number 9 was where people were most likely to balk. It is counter-intuitive, an unacceptable concept. But that one is about stepping away from the knowing mind and the ingrained habits of perception. Someone must move into uncertainty by holding an unfilled space where novelty can emerge. Letting go of what has always been taken for granted is a learned skill, and this chapter explains several ways to accomplish that.

I eventually stopped calling myself "The Problem D'Solver" or offering that training because the methods I urged were mostly being *incorporated into listeners' existing boxes*. I still have to wonder if changing one's perception can even be taught — not the techniques (they can be), but the desire or gumption for it.

Perhaps my affinity for creative types and visionaries is due to their unflinching preference for that enhanced view. Individuals who already know the value of the Art of Seeing for their own selves need no further persuasion.

Steer Clear of Directness

Everyday cause-effect thinking searches out the shortest, most direct, easiest-to-accomplish solution. It connects the dots in the same old way at each opportunity. So people keep repeating the same moves over and over, even when they are a small subset of what could be done. It also is the prescription for dinosaur thinking—functional but never creative or expansive. It stays in a narrow track, the tried and true, without regard for the interplay of the dynamic influences that are available.

Innovations are more likely to be made by those who refuse to entertain what is known already. They lean into the next idea like a sailor leans into the wind. They find it necessary to go sideways in order to move forward. Visionaries have polished the "art of the work-around" to a fine art in itself.

Insistence on avoiding what is expected is another interpretation of "the path not taken"—albeit on a smaller scale.

Try visualizing two different ways of crossing a stream. Either way, you reach the other side, but the different methods by which you get there are worlds apart. The logical and familiar way is to not step off the bank until you see the route, then step from stone to stone until reaching the other side. But that only permits you to take the route seen at the outset—stepping where there are stones, putting your feet down in an established order.

The Naked Vision approach makes a point of avoiding the obvious rocks or stepping in a pre-set order. Instead, the step off the bank is taken onto the first rock *without knowing how or where the other foot will be going down*. You hold, balance on one foot, while events or insights arrange themselves in a way that indicates where you should step next.

Going forward without a route in mind feels counter-intuitive, but it makes us much more responsive to the fluidity of the process, the initially unnoticed choices. For, indeed, they were not apparent while standing on the bank— maybe did not exist yet. Other rocks only "appear" because you are quite literally committed to entering the middle of the stream. This unnatural way of proceeding yields more novelty per step.

This approach allows the way forward to present itself to you. Stepping into uncertainty permits the broader range of possibilities to present themselves. As unbalanced as it feels to stand on one wobbling foot, a resolution cannot be rushed. This can also be called "remaining in the unresolved ambiguity." And the moment you lose your concentration to *not* proceed in a habitual way, it will reassert itself.

~ Life Is But a Stream ~
A BonBon ~ Faith Lynella

Everybody starts life as a curious, creative, endlessly exploring bundle of energy. Gradually we are tamed—civilized to live in a home, a family, a risky world. Somewhere along the way the taming shuts down our abilities to explore and create spontaneously. Such impulses become dammed up behind the structures we create and that are imposed upon us, for our own good of course.

Like a free-running stream that is channeled and then piped, the water may still trickle out at the end—but it's not the same stream. It is still water, but what has become of the meadow, the birdsong, the rippling surface, the minnows, the bundle of energy that made the stream vibrant and sparkling? These count for nothing if you only measure the stream as gallons of water.

That dammed-up stream is like the gifted child that resides below the surface of our daily lives. Beauty, fun, a world of wonder are sacrificed within the "shoulds" and "should nots" that dictate our lives. Yes it may be the same stream, but in every way that relates to beauty, or fun, or a world of wonder for the little live and growing things, there is no comparison.

As adults we rarely question our confinements. We move freely it seems; but in reality it is from tank (home) to cistern (work) to holding tanks (our various activities) by pipelines (routes, decisions) established long ago.

Yes it is still life, our life—if measured by quantity. But what has become of the rest?

Take time every day to let loose the curious, creative, endlessly exploring child within. Read a book. Solve a mystery. Be creative—quilt, sew, build an engine, fly a kite, or just meander down a path or sit by a stream.

From *BonBons to Sweeten Your Daily Life*; Or from *More BonBons*

Naked Vision involves exposing oneself to *what is not immediately obvious* and to ideas that could not be obtained by relying on sequential logic. It values what can only be discerned "out of the corner of the eye." By looking obliquely, a person can *almost see* something else. It is more or less out of focus, making one wait for it to swim into clear focus.

That involves *not looking directly at what is in the foreground*—what is apparent. Ignoring the obvious lets you spot the creative and unexpected answers that conventional thinking seems to miss.

People arrive at the less apparent, but more profound, messages through *indirection*. Emily Dickinson said, "Tell all the Truth but tell it slant…. The Truth must dazzle gradually / Or every man be blind." Each visionary is challenged to tell their truth from their slant, their angle so it does not shine too bright to be seen. They need to circle, repeat, and then re-approach the matter from a new angle. Then, "Oh my gosh! Where did that come from?" *You see.*

Notice What Is Hidden in Plain Sight

I love to read a good mystery where the clues are scattered page after page but nobody sees their significance because they are looking at the "facts" a certain way. They are relying on ordinary logic and expectations, so quickly jump to unwarranted conclusions that it takes the rest of the book to unravel. The turning point never comes until much too late, when it is discovered there is another way to view the pieces that were added up wrong.

A "red herring" is a false scent that is intentionally dragged across the trail by the bad guy in order to confuse the blood hounds. I like to say, "The way to solve a mystery (or problem) is to spot the red herring, *and then don't follow it.*" For me, the ability to spot the red herring is much more than a knack used for writing or reading mysteries. It is a life skill that sensitizes someone to distinguish what is significant from the welter of facts that obscure it—to distinguish the signal from the noise.

What is germane or what is a distraction? What is accurate, and what is not to be believed? A person can learn a lot about himself or herself by considering where they are likely to misinterpret certain kinds of signals again and again.

How hard could it be to collect enough clues *without jumping to conclusions* until the dots connect in a big-picture, everything-fits way? The Art of Seeing holds the clues *without connecting them* until they connect themselves—in a way that was not previously apparent. As luck would have it, that avoids most red herrings and brings higher quality clues to attention.

Much of what someone wants to know is right there—hidden in plain sight. But to catch it means holding back and not reaching for the answer too quickly. Holding with an "innocence of perception" that is disengaged from practicality tempts the world to yield its secrets. As Richard Farson said in *Whoever Makes the Most Mistakes Wins*:

> The best ideas are not hidden in shadowy recesses. They're right in front of us, hidden in plain sight. Innovation seldom depends on discovering obscure or subtle elements but in seeing the obvious with fresh eyes. This is easier said than done because nothing is as hard to see as what's right before our eyes. We overlook what we take for granted. Billions of tea drinkers observed the force of steam escaping from water boiling in a kettle before James Watt realized that this vapor could be converted into energy.[233]

---

[233] Farson, Richard, *Whoever Makes the Most Mistakes Wins* (New York: Free Press, 2003), 75-76.

Reading a Business Card

What could be more ordinary, more straightforward? But that little rectangle of paper is encoded with many more messages than people realize, consciously anyway. Twenty years ago I developed something I called "the body language of printed materials." Those words and images on business cards, letterhead, and ads communicate about the business priorities and identity more quickly, directly, and reliably than words.

In the same way a doctor can assess a person's health from a blood sample, I could often assess the health of a business by reading nothing more than its business card. I could see the gaps and weaknesses in the enterprise from what was (or wasn't) on the card.

The mindset and choices the owner made when developing the enterprise are every bit as evident as the words printed on the card. Those subtle impressions and associations are registered in the midbrain (below consciousness), the place that determines whether someone (or something) is credible. Faster than the card can be read, the reader has decided whether to trust them enough to do business with them.

Anyone can tell that and more from the hitchhiking messages about the business, which the enterprise did not know it was revealing. How this works was spelled out in *The Business Card Book: What Your Business Card Reveals about You, and How to Fix It*. My motivation to write the book was to demonstrate the extent to which business owners inadvertently communicate much more information about their competency and priorities to the world at large than they realize.

It pointed out typical types of unintended messages on their cards, many of which negated what they were trying to express about their businesses. But my larger motivation was to show if we do not even see most of what is on a business card. How much more useful and relevant information are we turning out?

With sufficient attention, the usually-overlooked messages become blaringly clear. The point is not specifically about business cards, or designing them, or even what is being said on them. The same principles about hitchhiking messages and symbolism show up in all our forms of communication.

This example simply illustrates that all our senses provide us with much more information than we register or use effectively. But we base our decisions on them nonetheless. A business card may be a small thing, but once someone starts noticing all that can be read there, they start "reading" much more than they ever noticed before. And it doesn't stop with an organization's card.

Splitting of Attention

"Seeing with fresh eyes" considers changing *the way of looking* — without regard for what is being looked at. Another approach to escaping box-ness is by becoming conscious of the seeing itself. Split attention is a method of putting another pair of your eyes outside of the fish bowl. There is no escaping being a fish in water (a person in 3-D) but that does not mean you have to be unaware of the fact.

Splitting attention shifts from a single point of view, as the fish, to also establishing a small wedge of attention that is disengaged and held separately as the *observer outside the fishbowl*. You still go about your daily activities but all the while you are watching from a detached perspective. Of course, that adds a perspective that the single-focus fish lacks.

Someone should not attempt to make changes about what they are looking at within the "fish bowl" from that split perspective. That undercuts the role of detached observer. Being disengaged avoids the usual self-centered perspective that defines the reality of a person. Although the fish will never escape the water or fishbowl, splitting its attention allows it to actually recognize the water in which it swims. In that way, choices cease to be fully dictated by the lack of awareness about its presence.

Eckhart Tolle describes that focused attention in *The Power of Now*:

> Be present as the watcher of your mind—of your thoughts and emotions as well as your reactions in various situations. Be at least as interested in your reactions as in the situation or person that causes you to react. Notice also how often your attention is in the past or future. Don't judge or analyze what you observe. Watch the thought, feel the emotion, observe the reaction. Don't make a personal problem out of them. You will then feel something more powerful than any of those things that you observe: the still, observing presence itself behind the content of your mind, the silent watcher.[234]

Split attention is an exercise, as are many of the "seeing with fresh eyes" techniques. Their effectiveness derive from shifting out of habitual modes—to looking with mindfulness, prepared to embrace unfamiliar perspectives and insights. And they work. Although not ends in themselves, they are powerful reminders to stay engaged in Naked Seeing. The larger purpose is to develop these modes as a way to broaden the scope of perception.

Be on Guard for Any Refusal to See

People are repeatedly shocked when the abundantly foreseeable happens—it does not matter how clear the warnings might have been. The inevitable still comes as a surprise when it happens. Denial is a widespread coping strategy of modern life. Though we would deny that too (wink). Since knowing the wolf is at the door would lead to fear, we irrationally act like it is better not to know. That is not a new reaction—but has hit epidemic proportions.

---

[234] Tolle, Eckhart, *The Power of Now: A guide to spiritual enlightenment* (Novato, CA: New World Library, 1999), 45-6.

Safety does not lie in refusing to hear news about the wolf. A refusal to accept what is apparent is as blind as the ostrich's head in the sand. Removing our blinders allows whatever we prefer not to see to come in. Denial is the easiest form of ignorance to cure—just by noticing it.

Frank Rich raises the question of whether we really want to know in a *New York Times* editorial.

> The question may be whether we really want to know. One of the most persistent cultural tics of the early 21st century is America's reluctance to absorb, let alone prepare for, bad news. We are plugged into more information sources than anyone could have imagined 15 years ago.... Yet we are constantly shocked, shocked by the foreseeable.[235]

These Art of Seeing methods help to reveal more of what we are not accustomed to noticing. It is powerful stuff! The one thing *not to do* with what is discovered is to act like it is any old idea. Inspired perceptions must be given credence—treated as precious pearls of wisdom. To treat them like a pig would will dry up the supply.

Be Here Now, Already

Now experiences take us out of the box. That accounts for much of its supernatural and mind-bending character. Much is made of the remarkable "Now" moment—the point at which we are most fully alive. The past and future are figments of the mind, a residue in the body's tissues. Whereas, Now is the essence of balanced and receptive awareness.

Now is out of time because each Now moment and experience is undefined by the past or future. What should be the most natural thing in the world—being oneself fully—is an always available choice but for our habits of seeing (and thinking) as though past and future matter. Tolle also said:

> Being is not only beyond but also deep within every form as its innermost invisible and indestructible essence. This means that it is accessible to you now as your own deepest self, your true nature. But don't seek to grasp it with your mind. Don't try to understand it. You can know it only when the mind is still. When you are present, when your attention is fully and intensely in the Now, Being can be felt, but it can never be understood mentally. To regain awareness of Being and to abide in that state of "feeling-realization" is enlightenment.[236]

Like love, Now experiences can excite passion and inspire rhapsodies. Vast libraries have been written to and about them both. Yet Now and love can only be known by *direct experience*, in this moment, as they arise and within the whole of you. It is also the aim of total nakedness and full alignment—the point of Naked Vision.

---

[235] Rich, Frank, "What We Don't Know Will Hurt Us," *New York Times*, February 21, 2009.
[236] *Op. cit.*, Tolle, 10.

Living in the Now trumps the daily grind. Becoming more aware of the life-limiting restrictions of our boxes, and how to escape them is the "open sesame" to authentic freedom. By that token, anything less than being here Now feels like something is missing.

The crux of Now awareness, as with any inspired experience, is intensely personal—which cannot be described from a sense of limited identity. Routine identifications and interests are eclipsed by an unassailable awareness of one's larger identity. The continuing challenge is to reconcile our dual identities—to eliminate the duel where either captures the advantage (yes, they are dueling competitors). Naked Vision permits us to see through both eyes—with perfect focus.

Getting Personal

Each of us has a toolbox full of tools to use while in our 3-D boxes. Using them can bring a brief escape from their limitations. Picking the lock of ordinary thinking and conventional seeing brings a measure of freedom—for the Now moment, anyway.

The only thing lacking for most people is the will to make a break for where freedom might take them. The visionaries among us are showing us all how it is done—and what it is good for.

Chapter 13 - Developing Our Energetic Intelligence
*When you watch your day going by as the ebb and flow of
energy, you will understand more about what "makes you tick."*

The Invisible Influence We Absolutely Love

Here is the "secret sauce" that really makes the inspired difference in the creative process. What actually fuels the innovative urge is invisible, colorless, tasteless, odorless, and cannot be found in a vacuum. However, *its presence can be felt,* and its influence is powerful! It is the very lifeblood of novelty and inspiration—the force that motivates a person when a vision grabs them, then recharges them along the way.

The invisible factor that is of incomparable value is high-vibration consciousness energy. It defies easy description because its power draws upon forces that reach outside the scope of the logical mind or the five senses—where words and logic fumble. It is also out of time and material reality. We all experience this energy in happy or inspired moments—the ones we don't ever want to end. It is what the "pursuit of happiness" is searching for, available in innumerable forms. It is an underlying determinant of many of our choices—humanity's magnetic north.

Like the chemistry crucial to romantic love, it is the "IT" that makes us feel most alive, inspired, and unstoppable. We simply cannot get enough of it. An abundance of it sometimes leads us in surprising and unexplored directions— for the sheer joy of it.

Bouts of creativity consume very high concentrations of that evanescent energy—and on a far more frequent basis than daily life requires. This "secret sauce" is the fuel of inspiration that's sensed by every cell in the body. The sensation that accompanies a surge of it is felt as joy, awe, a breakthrough, or "walking off the ground." Whenever we feel "light hearted," we are sensing an extra measure of that buoyant energy.

What causes that sensation is not a by-product of such buoyant moments, but the very *fuel for them.* That is an important distinction, especially if one wants to experience such energized states regularly. One need not revisit special places and experiences where it was most intense in the hopes that "lightning will strike again." It is possible to tap into available sources almost anywhere.

Intense surges of upbeat energy accompany transcendent moments—leaving us feeling speechless, riveted, free, mesmerized, zizzed, or inspired. Afterward, we cannot forget what blazed bright for us—or fully recall it either. But there is a satisfied wistfulness that lingers, filed away at the cellular level. Similar experiences, that happen later, stir a deep longing, like a haunting memory that flits at the edge of recall. (Could it be a sibling of the wee small voice, perhaps?)

Words like "flash" or "spark" refer to a rush of intense energy that tingles through the body, mind, and emotions in an exhilarating way. It is even called "having a rush." Flashes of insight, inspiration, and the sense of amazement are imbued with it. But this highly charged energy can also be sensed as quiet and still, connoting a deep sense of peace and "rightness."

High-vibration consciousness energy fuels the creative process, yielding clearer, faster, and more coherent connections than normal thinking delivers. Those engaged in creative work who can sustain a ready supply of it gain a major advantage. Creative and insightful activities also produce large quantities of this energy—which is why such pursuits can be so fulfilling in their own right.

In The Art of Possibility, Rosamund Stone Zander and Benjamin Zander speak of the surprise of finding that energy. But imagine knowing it is available and being to ride it… What then?

> Suppose for a moment that vital, expressive energy flows everywhere, that it is the medium for the existence of life, and that any block to participating in that vitality lies within ourselves. Of course, our minds tell us a different story. The world comes to us sorted into parts: people are distinct entities, shapes have edges, and apples and oranges cannot be compared. Rarely do we come upon or experience this integrative energy, and sometimes only serendipitously, like Alice falling through the rabbit hole. This kind of vibrancy may take us by surprise when we find ourselves committing to doing something extraordinary or when we meet each other on a most personal, elemental level.[237]

The more of those transporting experiences we have, the greater our capacity grows to sustain the energetic level. We also get better at grounding it in our activities and relationships. When a person is imbued with an enhanced energy level, it can often be sensed second-hand through what he or she says, creates, or makes while in that state.

Such energy is dynamic and fluid, which prevents it from ever being nailed down conceptually. Each of our encounters with it feels fresh and virginal, for it is the essence of innocent newness.

It is uplifting both physically and emotionally. I call it lift-of energy because it serves our visions by fueling creative endeavors and virtuous quests. We come to know about this special energy by being open enough to flow with those surges—without trying to control where they take us (as if we could!).

Speckles of such brilliance can be woven through an individual's art, performances, inventions, and quality of thinking. And that reservoir of untapped energy can be quite apparent when that spark is missing, as their work seems "off." It becomes easier to spot when a person has created a large enough of body of work, where at least some of it is "masterful."

---

[237] Zander, Rosamund Stone and Zander, Benjamin, *The Art of Possibility: Transforming professional and personal life* (New York: Penguin Books, 2000), 113-4.

Attending to Our Energetic States

Being carried away by inspiration, or whatever moves us deeply, takes us to an inner place (or state) of abundant higher-octane energy. When we have lift-off energy, we feel adequate to any challenge. We sink into that vast energy that seems to be ours to enjoy and feel renewed.

That reconnection acts as a tuning fork for our full complement of faculties — to which we resonate without forethought. As someone harmonizes with that special energy; the cells of the body (together with the mind and emotions) are tuned and attuned.

The inner work we do increases our capability to use and maintain elevated levels of this lift-off fuel. When inspired energy is flowing, its force pushes us toward being ever-more creative, expansive, inclusive, and integrated — all signs of greater self-mastery and inner maturity.

When it is at its strongest, a person can feel super-human and invulnerable. Sad to say, it soon passes.

Its presence accounts for why a master's output will usually be more *masterful* than what a novice is capable of doing. An abundance of this highly-charged energy makes the visionary path much more intense and productive than an idle amble off the beaten track. I call this awareness of our energetic states Energetic Intelligence. This chapter is largely about coming to understand this special energy.

Talking about something so ephemeral and "under the hood" is quite different from how we usually think about what drives our behavior. So the first step to developing your energetic intelligence is to pay more attention to what your energy states *feel like* — then, what makes them go up or down.

This is not quite the same as observing our emotional states, but they do influence each other — and you. Changes in our energy level and emotional states both bear watching. Much of what was puzzling about the people around us makes more sense when seen as a reflection of our (and their) energy levels.

When things happen around us, we usually notice the specific event or the personalities involved more than consciously noting *the extent of our own resonating energies we're attending to.* — the "out there" rather than the "in here." But we should give some conscious attention to how something made us feel energy-wise — whether it lifted us, drained us, or left us somewhere in between.

We gain an added capacity to interpret what is going on for us with greater accuracy as we factor in those usually-ignored energetic influences on us. That's true whether they are in-coming or out-going. The presence (or absence) of buoyant energy is palpably felt by everyone to varying degrees.

At some visceral level, we are attracted or repelled by what we sense: too much, not enough, just right.

The amount and quality of our energy hums along all the time. But most people tune out highly-relevant information about it. We don't give our energetic fluctuations conscious credence except when they are really high (wow!) or really low (drained). The more subtle fluctuations are usually tuned out. But ignoring this energy is like never bothering to check the gas gauge, yet being surprised when the car runs out of gas.

Anyone can get better at responding to its presence—just as we can get more skilled at fanning our flames of brilliance when they first arise. When you watch your day going by as the ebb and flow of energy, you will understand more about what "makes you tick."

Flying High on the Proper Fuel

Lift-off energy is not rare, but it is fleeting. Maintaining sufficient reserves pushes those driven to follow creative or vision-based pursuits to seek circumstances where it is most available. In addition, a person generates large amounts of it during the creative process—sometimes explosively. But it has a short shelf life and a person burns through it quickly.

Creative thinking and inspired actions require a different type of fuel than routine activities. The availability of enough of it generally accounts for the hot-and-cold cycles of creative thinkers or projects. Anyone who figures out how to maintain their optimal energy levels can accomplish their goals more consistently—and with less *down* time.

Like an airplane at takeoff, more fuel is needed to get airborne (up) than to maintain flight. Once disengaged from the ground, additional energetic bursts push them higher, into the rarified air. But running out of gas when flying could mean crashing. By comparison, running out of gas while on the ground (without taking the leap) is not such a big deal.

Sustained vision, inspiration, and big-picture output depend on securing sufficient supplies of this fuel—then using it judiciously. Creative acts require sharply focused attention to the task, so one minimizes interest in everything else. When the game is afoot, our intensified energy is not permitted to flow to peripheral matters.

At their most intense, creative outbursts consume almost all available energy. That requires life-off energy. A mark of mastery includes an ability to acquire adequate supplies—along with having decreased drag and resistance that waste it.

It is impossible to get off the ground with low-octane energy. Using the wrong fuel would be like putting water in an airplane's gas tank. But with enough of the proper fuel, amazing things can happen.

Fuel as Motivation

Consider lift-off energy as "carrots" and low-energy states as "sticks." It could be argued that the desire to gain increased access to ordinary inspired energy is the impetus for people following their heart's desires, or for leaving the beaten path (away from inherently low-energy states).

Most people's everyday pursuits operate at a relatively low energetic level. But their lives are punctuated by highly charged moments (highs) from time to time. Although almost everyone occasionally pops in and out of higher-energy states (like top-of-the-mountain clarity), some individuals are unwilling to leave that happenstance totally to chance.

They *actively pursue* situations where more lift-off energy is available. Such efforts include seeking out others who are also engaged in high-energy activities so they can reinforce each other. So much of what seems perplexing about the behavior of non-conformists makes perfect sense when it is seen in terms of them marshaling and protecting their energy resources.

The overriding need for extra high-octane energy for visionary pursuits diminishes the person's interest in many low-energy pursuits. They consider mundane or frivolous activities as "empty calories" that merely drain the "highs" away without much return.

What attracts (or repels) creative types does not depend as much on the social or rational rewards as on the amount and type of energy available for them. As a side note, that's true for everybody. People unerringly seek out others and situations matching their energy level. But such affinity is more often geared to "everyday energy," rather than "flying energy."

The more someone is accustomed to flying or using this buoyant energy in inspired ways, the lower their tolerance becomes for anything devoid of it. It feels soul deadening. And such individuals are super-sensitive to being drained. They can detect even small particles of the "wrong stuff" in the mix, and it shuts them down. Energy-deficient situations are not just sensed as stifling but suffocating, and cannot be endured very long.

Sooner or later, people are likely to walk away from jobs, relationships, or social situations that make them feel like they're running on dry too often. Many other factors may be involved, but at the root, the energetic incompatibility could be the deal breaker.

Feels Kinda Like Love

Love could be considered a very special kind of energy (aside from its emotional and romantic sentiments) because it has the highest potency fuel of all. The sharing of such energy has far-reaching influences on our other motivations. In the case of one's spiritual life, it is sensed as sacred. In nature or masterful artistry or breakthroughs, it can be sensed as awe.

Love is the most refined energy that humans are able to experience. One meaning of the phrase "God is love" is "God is the energy of consciousness." The vibration of love is both uplifting and a reminder of our true identity with our Source.

Energy to Run the Three-story Human Factory

G.I. Gurdjieff was a 20th century spiritual teacher who asserted that people need to do inner work in order to wake up and function consciously. According to him, a person has no will unless it is developed through diligent and conscious effort. His approach involved the need to work on oneself mentally, emotionally and physically—all at the same time. It is called a Fourth Way School for that reason.

Gurdjieff described the human body as functioning like a three-story factory. The bottom two floors are physical processes that usually run on ordinary energy. The top floor, which represents higher mental and emotional processes, cannot operate on that fuel. It needs a very refined form of energy that comes from positive impressions. In addition, such higher functions cannot operate in the presence of negative emotions.

Gurdjieff argued that a great deal of this refined energy can be generated through struggling against our negative emotions. The aim is to *function consciously*, by being awake. Ongoing third-floor activities permit a person to sustain an enhanced state of awareness, no matter what the activity.

Some activities (like writing a poem) are not inherently better than others (like scrubbing floors). The true value of any undertaking should be judged according to whether or not it is done with conscious awareness, while awake. Gurdjieff's approach aspires to do every activity consciously.

The special fuel that operates the third-story activities can also be used for mundane activities, to run the bottom two floors. But it does not work the other way around. That is why it is unwise to fritter away inspired energy on negative or mindless activities that are lacking anything uplifting. But efforts to live fully awake create even more of the vital energy.

A Physics Lesson

By the accepted laws of physics, energy is neither created nor destroyed; it just changes form. Thus the total energy into a system is equal to the total energy out. Usually the transition is from one form (electricity, gas, wood) that is converted into something like heat and "useful work." Conservation of energy is a cornerstone of physics, and it is not my intention to challenge it.

However, that premise does not apply to higher-octane energy because some (or all) of it is not 3-D based. It arises from outside the closed system of the physical world and does not conform to Newtonian physics. The energy triggered by inspiration or love can exceed the amount of physical energy present.

Let me state out front that 3-D energy conforms to the laws of the natural world, but higher-octane energy does not need to. It is unlimited, which 3-D is not. It functions differently and according to its own laws, which exceed comprehension.

Whether you treat that statement as a fact or as a metaphor does not matter, as long as you accept that it is counter-productive to confuse the two forms of energy. The way humans are wired inside allows us to tell these different kinds of energy apart, and to respond to each form accordingly.

The physical body, being matter, can use either form of fuel, as do routine mental or emotional activities. But intense creativity and vision operate with the enhanced energy only. Also, *not all* the energy that comes during an uplifting experience or a surge leaves immediately. Some of it declines slowly, so one gently drifts back to an everyday frame of mind.

Increasing Our Energetic Capacity

Energy in itself is not good or bad; it is neutral. But what can be done with it depends on whether it is Newtonian (3-D) energy or whether it has high-octane qualities. There is a spectrum that reflects the amount of high-octane present: from "none" to "rocket fuel."

Our energetic level tracks with our emotional state. When our energy level rises, so do our spirits, and *vice versa*. For example, feeling inspired and grateful coincide with an energetic boost, whereas feelings of fear and shame reflect a reduced energetic state.

Increasing our capacity to handle more of these intense, buoyant energies opens the door for all parts of "who I am" to participate in the intensified awareness. That sensation leads to our feeling whole, complete, and unified — exactly right.

Higher-potency energy is a counterweight to the downward pull of entropy — the natural tendency of energy to dissipate. So, attention needs to be paid to finding ways to slow its decline, especially when our supplies are low.

Energy management includes vigilance about innumerable unintended ways our energy reserves leak away. Waste of energy can be greatly reduced simply by making the effort to notice how and where we use it. What a waste to use too much energy on things we do not care about. Finding and repairing our energy leaks is a key component of building our energy reserves.

"Inefficiency" in this sense does not simply mean non-productive effort, but there is no energetic lift gained from the activity. Time spent in play, daydreaming, and doing nothing can be quite productive because of their ability to recharge us.

That which functions at a much lower energetic level is sensed as drag. Drag wastes energy and prevents us from flowing naturally with the possibilities available in the moment. Drag could also manifest as strong negative emotions like outbursts of anger or faultfinding—whether directed at others or yourself.

Repeated experiences of flying and landing smoothly build our capability to hold and carry larger reserves of lift-off energy. Over time and with practice, a person raises their energetic capacity, so he or she functions at a slightly higher energy level than before. It also makes them increasingly receptive to finding or attracting highly-energized experiences.

Increasing our energetic capacity resembles rewiring a house built with 110 watt wiring. Functioning on enhanced fuel is like running 220 watt current through the wires. The capacity of the system (wires) must be upgraded to handle the increased flow on a regular basis. Otherwise it will short out the system—literally. That upgrade permits greater competency and efficiency. But also, less and less of that energy is lost through resistance or leaks.

As our energetic capacity goes higher, we are inclined to be more expansive and vocal about what we can see and do with it. There is an impossible-to-ignore urge for more spontaneity and fewer restrictions. Acting on those desires requires a certain confidence in what is ahead—as well as in our ability to handle whatever comes.

A Different View of Maslow's Hierarchy

Maslow's Hierarchy of Needs has been a standard for how we think about motivation (Chapter 11). For purposes of this chapter, focus on the influence of available lift-off energy to interpret where something falls on his hierarchy (and B-Values). Higher-order needs are like the three-story factory; to satisfy them. The special fuel is required.

Lower-order needs operate quite adequately on everyday fuel. If there is not enough available, those needs nearest the bottom (survival) use what they require first. Then each ascending level, in turn, takes what it requires from what remains. So when supplies are low, self-actualization urges are starved or remain idle.

But the highest level needs do not operate on the same fuel. So, even when there is only an ample supply of ordinary energy, those higher needs will go wanting (*a la* the three-story factory).

Creative and inspired energy can arise independently of high supplies of practical energetic resources. Monks or artists who live just above subsistence can still have rich inner and creative lives (at the top of the hierarchy). Hence, a struggling artist is very possible.

It is time for us to take a serious look at the kind of policies and priorities being pursued, where energy is concerned—both culturally and individually. Power struggles (energy again) and divisive confrontational stances without vision and good will are wasteful uses of energy.

So often today, such tactics result in stand-offs and paralysis, because high-octane clarity is not available. Additionally, without enough high-potency energy for the executive-level ability to find workable answers, the quality of leadership suffers. We coast, we drift—but that is a downward path.

Heart, Mind, and Body as Allies

Flying and staying aloft get easier as we develop the capacity to drop our resistance to whatever life brings that we don't like—while rejecting anything that *drags* us down. As we sharpen our ability to recognize and marshal more of this high-potency energy, we find more ways to acquire enough of it to accomplish what we desire.

That pays off for us emotionally, mentally, and physically—with no aspect of ourselves left unsatisfied. But of even greater overall value, all aspects of one's self begin to function as a more coherent unit, whereby they reinforce each other. That internal teamwork allows us to shift into a higher gear, in which we are closer to functioning at our full energetic capacity.

Although these energized states arise (at least in part) from somewhere outside of the humdrum concerns of everyday life, they can greatly influence how well each of us responds to everyday experience. An increased ability to flow with uplifting energy when it is available depends on body, head, and heart being at peace with each other—functioning as an integrated whole.

Once the mind can learn to stand aside and allow "innocence of perception" to lead (Chapter 12), the entire self reaps the rewards—such as scintillating conversation and feeling "just right." Heart and body awareness both respond to those frequencies with full resonance. However, the rational mind needs to trust them when it comes to "reading" this energy because intellect is largely tone deaf to it.

Although each person's overall energetic level is usually slow to change (compared to the up-and-down, short-term fluctuations), under the right conditions it is possible to make sizable jumps in their capacity. The visionary process (among others) gradually increases the energetic capacity of those who stay engaged in learning, developing new skills, and doing their inner work.

Upwardly Mobile

The heart, mind, and body always function as a unit during "flying" or inspiration. It is only in everyday life that they seem to operate independently of each other. The more unified the three are, the more opportunities a person has for transcendent experience—disengaged from the normal world.

At the same time, the inner journey removes impediments to enjoying the full force of such high-octane energy. Maintaining an elevated energy level requires shedding incompatible low-energy concerns, along with their associated drag. Being creative involves using the increased bursts of energy it generates effectively. It also helps to remove prior habits and assumptions that no longer apply since they are dead weight.

Having more energy also allows us to remove some of the limitations on our customary scope of possibilities. It is not so much a matter of improving specific projects as *permitting new types of connections* to develop with the rest of our knowledge and perceptions.

You might even "walk on air," seemingly disengaged from gravity. Another energetic gain comes from spending less of our energy reserves on self-protection. However, even if a person might feel bulletproof to problems, they really are not invulnerable. This can be a risky world and requires a balancing act—between openness and discriminating trust.

The movement of history is toward an increase in humanity's emotional intelligence and mental complexity. The broad scope of evolution also corresponds with an increased capacity to use enhanced energies in more nuanced ways. That developmental trend can be true on an individual scale as well.

In *Radical Evolution*, Joel Garreau explored the big ideas about the future of our species. As described here, "love" is not so much an emotional feeling as the capacity to experience and respond to much higher emotional and energetic levels.

> Part of the evolutionary process—and this has continued with our technological growth in human cultural and technological history—is an increase of those higher emotional, intelligent functions. We see exponentially greater love.... Our ability to appreciate arts and music and to have stable relationships is increasing. That was relatively difficult to do even 200 years ago, let alone thousands of years ago.[238]
>
> Evolution moves toward greater complexity, greater elegance, greater knowledge, greater intelligence, greater beauty, greater creativity, and more of other abstract and subtle attributes, such as love,' observes Ray Kurzweil. 'And God has been called all these things, only without any limitation: infinite knowledge, infinite intelligence, infinite beauty and so on. Of course, even the accelerating growth of evolution never achieves an infinite level, but as it explodes exponentially it moves rapidly in that direction. So evolution moves inexorably toward our conception of God, from the severe limitation of its biological form which may be regarded as an essential spiritual quest.'[239]

Lift-off Energy Moves Us Toward Greater:
- Congruence—all parts of self operating in harmony
- Integrity—acting according to one's loftiest values

---

[238] Garreau, Joel, *Radical Evolution: The promise and peril of enhancing our minds, our bodies – and what it means to be human* (New York: Broadway Books, 2005), 93.
[239] *Ibid.*, 262.

- Commitment—toward our highest goals or a sense of life purpose
- Creativity coupled with the ability to see with fresh eyes
- Diligence about avoiding what is toxic, negative, or rooted in fear
- Binkles—the energetic zizz felt from connecting with others, creativity and moments of inspiration (later this chapter)
- Unity and a sense of connection with the bigger picture
- Emotional richness coupled with clarity of perception
- Relationships rooted in shared vision, affinity, and collaboration
- Synchronicity and serendipity

Recharging through Our Creative Fountains

Energetic Fine Tuning

When we take steps to heed our bright insights, even more inspired energy becomes available to us. It pushes us on—in the face of both known and unknown perils. By contrast, fear and doubt sever that inner connection, so that special energy quickly fades. Starts and stops that break the flow diminish our personal power. That also prevents lift-off energy from accumulating.

Adapting to an increased energetic level is gradual because there are so many low-energy distractions that catch our attention. And they each need to be dealt with before we can get free of them. The "wee small voice" can seldom be heard above the competing noises in your busy head. Besides, the beckonings from within are easy to miss or too quickly forgotten.

Each individual's energetic signature reflects thousands of experiences and subsequent energetic adjustments. Building up our energetic capacity takes a long time. It involves letting go of untold old baggage or habits. These are later replaced by a more comprehensive and delightfully inclusive worldview.

Also, the ratcheting-up phase to handle more high-potency energy is confusing because many familiar things we have always done do not work very well anymore. And it is not clear for some time what is taking their place for you.

The period of growth necessary to maintain increased energy levels can be exhausting. Most of the gearing-up occurs beneath conscious awareness. Also, because these energies are intangible, they pass largely unnoticed by our mind and five senses, so it is nearly impossible to recognize interim growth.

A person operating at a very high consciousness-vibration sees the world through a vastly different perceptual lens than most people. They are energetic beacons of moral authority, whose roles in life define them less than their ability to ground multiple perceptions.

Truth (or any of the virtues) resonates with a much faster, more buoyant energy than everyday thinking can provide. The more we can demonstrate such virtues through our thoughts and deeds, the more our consciousness energy level increases. That argues for committing to operate with the utmost congruence and integrity.

As your own consciousness vibration increases, *how you look at everything also changes* in fundamental ways. You will find yourself understanding more of the previously undisclosed thinking and motives of those who seem so wise, including nuances that previously eluded you.

Since love and virtuous behavior reflect a very high energetic state, someone can leap far above their customary energetic level through acts of loving kindness, forgiveness, and generosity of spirit. Given that, energy-wise: "It *is* better to give than to receive."

On the other hand, when dishonesty, mistrust, or ethical compromises proliferate in a person's life, their energetic level drops significantly. In the same vein, the opinions of those who vibrate lower seem less meaningful or relevant for us. Dismissing their opinions is not done intentionally. It occurs because who we trust has changed—our affinity has changed.

In *Power vs Force*, David R. Hawkins explains why genius is not about personality. It can access different energies.

> Genius is by definition a style of consciousness characterized by the ability to access high energy attractor patterns. It is not a personality characteristic. It is not something that a person has, nor even something that someone is. Those in whom we recognize genius commonly disclaim it. A universal characteristic of genius is humility. The genius has always attributed his insights to some higher influence.[240]

A large component of acquiring Energetic Intelligence comes from consciously working with increased access to this form of energy. And those who have developed the capacity to use it well serve as living conduits between the spark of genius and material results.

Increase Your Energetic Level:
- Discard or ignore low-energy activities and relationships—those that leave you drained or empty
- Notice what *increases* your energy level, your sense of well-being and joy—seek out more of that whenever possible
- Notice what *decreases* your energy level, your sense of well-being and joy—avoid that whenever possible
- Seek out high-energy mentors, peers, thinkers (as in reading the classics); spend more time with them
- Seek out binkles; trust your krindle
- Act with kindness and caring at every opportunity; respect everyone
- Take time for joy, gratitude, and lighthearted fun

---

[240] Hawkins, David R., *Power vs Force; The hidden determinants of human behavior* (Sedona AZ: Veritas Publishing, 2000)

The higher vibrational rate of inspiration and vision is up-lifting. Whenever enhanced-energies come into play, they infuse us (or circumstances) with increased vitality. An individual's personal vibrational level is magnified by the quality of seeds (deeds) they "plant" in the world since they and their seeds have the same energetic signature.

For example, a person cannot write a book (or create anything for that matter) that vibrates much above their customary energetic level. That would not matter much in a car repair manual, but it matters a great deal when they write about philosophical concepts. David Hawkins developed a system for determining the consciousness vibration level for people and objects, as explained in *Power vs Force*. It is discussed in Chapter 20.

When walking their talk, there is more at stake for the visionary than promoting their specific message. What they are creating reflects a higher energy level than purely practical accomplishments do.

What appears to be resistance or rejection of a new notion often results from a clash of energy levels—high-vibrational ones (vision) colliding with slower, denser ones, represented by the *status quo*. The *status quo* almost inevitably represents a slowed down energy (entropy). Whereas, the influences of creativity or fresh thinking (in whatever form they appear) offer a counterweight to those slower, bogged down energies.

When expanding to a larger frame of reference, virtues like honesty and devotion supplant the more casual morality of the larger community. Our moral sense asserts itself because it is unwilling to function in the background or to be treated like more toothless precepts.

High-energy character traits that are rooted in caring and cooperation serve the larger community. Over the long view, qualities that support others are more likely to thrive in high-energy conditions as well as to raise the energetic level. And the world at large is better off because the fruits of their efforts are shared widely.

At the same time, lower-energy opportunities become less and less appealing. If they are chosen, they are not as satisfying as they once were. So, such interests eventually cease to be seductive. Hawkins also said:

> Simple kindness to one's self and all that lives is the most powerful transformational force of all. It increases one's true power without exacting a toll. But to reach maximum power, it can be practiced with no exceptions, nor with the expectation of some selfish reward. A kindness, a shift in motive or behavior acts on a field which then produces an increased likelihood of responding in a positive way. Our inner work is like building up a bank

account, but one from which we cannot draw at will. The disposition of the funds is determined by a subtle energy field which awaits a trigger to release this power back into our own lives.[241]

Signs of Energy Depletion

The heart, mind and body each have their own ways to signal when they are out of kilter. They complain and insist on attention as they have less and less energy. Each of these is a cry for something to change. Many of the maladies of life can be traced to insufficient or constricted energy, sensed as an all-over feeling of being "off." Any of them can make us feel irritated or out of focus.

Loss of Energy:
- Mental—stuck, negative, bored, distracted
- Emotional—dissatisfied, frustrated, depressed
- Physical body—stressed, exhausted, tense, irritable

When people exhaust their self-control, what they're exhausting are the mental muscles needed to think creatively, to focus, to inhibit their impulses, and to persist in the face of frustration or failure. In other words, they're exhausting precisely the mental muscles needed to make a big change.... Change is hard because people wear themselves out. And that's the second surprise about change. What looks like laziness is often exhaustion.[242]

The Dampening Effect of Fear

Fear generally signals movement toward a lower and slower energetic state. It is a feature of human design that works perfectly. When we encounter a threat, we slow down considerably and go into an extreme state of alertness, taking in environmental details that we previously dismissed as unimportant. Fear has a valid protective function because it sounds the alert of a possible danger.

All states of mind, previous to the moment of fear, disappear as we focus intently on surviving. The problem is that only about 1% of the time we feel fear is there a legitimate cause for that sort of dramatic contraction of the energy field. The other 99% is emanating from our memory (moments in our past when we felt hurt) or our imagination (moments in the unknown future). That is mostly why fear gets such a bad rap. It constricts the flow of energy and the hopefulness that makes a person willing to take chances or act kindly.

Yielding to remembered or imagined fear freezes individuals and organizations in indecision or helplessness—at the very time their best analytical skills are needed.

---

[241] *Ibid.*, 192.
[242] Heath, Chip and Heath, Dan, *Switch, How to change things when change is hard* (New York: Broadway Books, 2010), 12.

It bears noting that fear has a host of disguises. It often cloaks itself in justifications or elaborate protective strategies, but the underlying driver is some flavor of fear. That is the natural default state in situations where we do not know what to do, or what (or whom) to trust.

Visionaries take risks not so much because they are fearless, foolhardy, or heroic. But rather, they know that giving much credence to fears (even valid ones) makes what seems fearsome stronger and harder for them to rise above. They reason that as long as they do not allow their fears to shut down their confidence or diligent efforts, another answer or approach will present itself. And they keep trying until it does.

Many fears are rooted in the sub-verbal fight-or-flight reflexes of the mid-brain, which operate beneath conscious awareness or control. Any little thing can set the alarms off. There is no proportionality since it acts in an all-or-nothing fashion. Fear-based responses are prone to over-reaction and limit a person's capacity to learn from positive outcomes. It is only marginally influenced by our rational intelligence or social conventions.

The immediate dangers from being fearful are not so much "out there" from something that could hurt us, but in the way we allow fear to shrink our field of possibilities, to impair our judgment. A fearful orientation is defensive and distrustful, valuing safety over other choices. It is averse to taking chances. Once fear runs the show, we wind up ensnared in a web of self-imposed limitations.

While quick action is great for truly dangerous situations, reflexive behavior overreacts to the kind of threats prominent in modern life. There aren't any bloodthirsty predators around, and it does not do much to protect us from the con-man variety. In addition, the analytical mind is able to conjure up endless dangerous scenarios. Who can function with confidence when constantly barraged with more reasons to be afraid? Living in a state of high alert wears us out, so there is no energy left for more important concerns.

On the other hand, skepticism and cynicism are not better approaches. Such outlooks are jaded and a tad self-congratulatory ("I am too smart to fall for this"). Having seen the flaw in somebody's argument, or spotted a latent trap or danger, should not be cause for rejoicing. They should, instead, be treated as inducements to come up with something much better. *That* would be cause for rejoicing.

Even worse than the large volume of serious problems in the world today is the amount of fear being enflamed *on purpose*. Fear mongering has replaced genuine dialog or intelligent judgment on a dizzying array of problems. When people see the world as an unsafe place, they do not make their best choices, let alone proceed with an attitude that the difficulties can be resolved. Sad to say, there are those who gain an advantage by exploiting fears and indecisiveness.

Changing Gears Requires Extra Energy

The amount of available energy is proportionate to our brain's ability to keep a lot of balls in the air—which complex and creative activities require. Our ability to shift contexts permits us to deal with a variety of things as they arise. But there are inherent limits in how much the brain can grasp and hold in short-term memory.

Additional energy is required for repeatedly shifting contexts or moving things back and forth between short-term and long-term memory storage. Douglas C. Merrill explains that in *Getting Organized in the Google Era*.

> When you're focused on one particular type of information, challenge, or task, and then you switch to something different, you're shifting contexts. Sometimes the transitions are huge and jarring. Other times, you don't even notice.... Frequent context shifts can be extremely distracting and impair your ability to concentrate on the task at hand. And worse, over the course of the day, they can seriously drain your brain's reservoir.... Shifting between all the meetings, e-mails, voicemails, hallway conversations, phone calls, and tasks in your day has used up an enormous amount of brainpower, leaving you feeling depleted. And when you have no mental energy, you can't think clearly about your challenges, whether they're major or miniscule, immediate or long term, expected or unexpected.[243]

The need to protect our space includes removing things that pull us off course that drain our energy reserves. We can simplify our circumstances by reducing the volume and constancy of context shifts. Research has established that short-term memory can only hold between five and nine items at once. Trying to hold more than that is quite draining.

> The more you shift contexts and the more unrelated those contexts are, the harder your brain works to transfer, store, and flush information out of short-term memory to make room for more. And it doesn't just drop the things you no longer need; it drops things that are crucial to your ability to function.[244]

> In today's fast-paced, information-saturated world, we struggle to keep our heads above water. We use incredible amounts of mental energy to handle all the information, all the tasks, and all the challenges that confront us every day. Then, when the unexpected happens, we have nothing left in our reserves.... Your brain is incredibly powerful, but it isn't optimized to handle a world with so many contexts and so much information.[245]

---

[243] Merrill, Douglas C, *Getting Organized in the Google Era* (New York: Broadway Books, 2010), 180-1.
[244] *Ibid.*, 182.
[245] *Ibid.*, 217-8.

Increased Energetic Capacity Is Quiet and Deep

Our identity becomes more integrated as we allow ourselves to respond fully to higher-octane energies. Increasing alignment with them changes how each of us thinks and feels about the world (and our place in it). As our outlook changes, we are less self-absorbed and negative and low-energy events recede in their influence. Those shifts reduce our attachment to what repeatedly brought us pain and frustration earlier.

Being able to hold onto high-energy experiences (insights and visions) is a mid-phase of personal growth that can lead to finding conditions most conducive to inspired action. Hanging onto incompatible concerns feels like a rock in the shoe—increasingly painful until it is dealt with.

Amped-up energy can be used for inspired activities or for humdrum ones. When the fortuitous combination of special energy and insightful clarity coincide, a person can create something wonderfully original. Being receptive to enhanced energy acts like a pile of straw, where sparks of inspiration catch fire, allowing us to briefly operate with full power and clarity. In that regard, vision and lift-off energy act the same. Ray Smilor describes vision in terms of a very potent energy in *Daring Visionaries*.

> I am convinced that vision is more than a destination or a desired stage of development; that it is more than a picture of a preferred future; that is more than a dream of where one wants to be.
>
> Vision is the organizational sixth sense that tells us why we make a difference in this world. It is the real but unseen fabric of connections that nurture and sustain values. It is the pulse of the organizational body that reaffirms the relationships and directs behavior.... Vision, in this context, is the organizational energy that charges behavior, fuels direction, and catalyses change. For vision to be genuinely powerful in organizations, it must be personal, positive, emotional, and larger than ourselves. Vision thus impacts an organization when people buy into and act upon the invisible.[246]

~ Smash the Mid-Range ~
A BonBon ~ Faith Lynella

Awareness doesn't work like an off-on switch—it is a continuum. One end is dead or close to it, like sleep. The other end is heightened perception, filled with inexpressible joy. Between them we live—with our awareness fluctuating: noticing, distracted, drifting, day-dreaming, attentive, vague, focused. We shift; we drift.

Many days awareness comes, flits in and out, turned down like a pilot light ready to ignite when interest summons it. Attention is "On Call," waiting to be

---

[246] Smilor, Ray, *Daring Visionaries: How entrepreneurs build companies, inspire allegiance, and create wealth* (Holbrook, MA: Adams Media Corp., 2001), 12-13.

roused from its daydreams, so close to the sleep end of the scale. Habit runs the show, leaving little room for innovation or flexibility. We get through the day, sort of, without noticing all that happens to us. Aware, yes—but just barely. Could that possibly be enough? Awareness is such a wonderful tool it can deliver much much more, into our lives, into our days, into every minute.

Crank it up—push it to reveal the rich texture available in each event, each person, each day you encounter. Engage every one of your senses and your mind at the same time. Penetrate beyond superficial impressions. See, hear, feel, sense, notice what else is present—sensations more subtle, yet very real.

Pause to register and enjoy. Experience intently and intensely, basking in whatever you discover. All that you feel now can be even more enhanced. As awareness is sharpened, held, and focused on the details, it shifts. Then a bigger, more complete and complex picture forms. You can get better at it simply by practicing it and enjoying it. Your capacity to live fully is much greater than routinely used.

Mostly, we stay in the middle of the scale—aware, alert, but filtering out details we don't think we need. But the wonder and the fullness are not there. They are up the scale of awareness, where we become fully involved. Why not live there, since it takes no longer, and provides so much more?

From *BonBons to Sweeten Your Daily Life*. Or from *More BonBons*

Building a Straddle-span

Straddle-span and Grounding

Each of us is one among billions who share this planet. Both feet are planted in the physical world, for that is the only space in which to ground oneself and our material reality. The inner world of each of us is more personal, private, and subjective—holding our sense of "who I am," emotions, values, precious memories, and unvoiced fears. That is all real as well. But much of what is held inside must rely on conscious expression in order for us to be aware of it.

Initially, the external and tangible world is front burner, and the inner world is largely back burner. Straddle-span describes the process whereby both realms become engaged as a collaborative unit in a person's life. That achievement is quite different from constantly flip-flopping back and forth, with only one engaged at a time.

Our inner world connects us with a larger view—one that is beyond everyday time and space. Until you consciously engage your inner life with an intention to know it, both feet are solidly rooted in 3-D. Gradually, with sustained inner growth, one metaphorical "foot" can disengage from 3-D and move into that other realm. That is a toehold "out there," while the other foot stays solidly grounded.

"Straddle-span" is the word I coined to describe how well a person can anchor a connection to both inner and outer perceptual frames *simultaneously*. The Straddle-span is the distance between your feet-on-the-ground reality and the top-of-the-mountain states. Like the plateau state of a vision, a wide Straddle-span reflects considerable self-knowledge and self-mastery. The increasing range of a person's Straddle-span reflects their scope of capability.

Notice the word "span." First the distance between the two ends is relatively short and only held briefly. Eventually the distance gets wider and wider until each foot can stand in its own realm. Here is the neat part—you come to be engaged in both spaces *at the same time*. In the process, you have created a living bridge between "who you *really* are"—both inside and outside of your everyday reality

Many visionaries are better able than most to keep a foot in both worlds because they treat that access as a life-sustaining priority. Benefits of a wider Straddle-span are a more consistent perspective and high-energy state. Usually, your inner world lets you reenergize your creative springs by disengaging from practical reality.

Once your straddle develops solidly, you can draw on more of those energies *without that disengagement* from the 3-D side of the equation. Another way to recognize that the straddle is getting wider is by a reduction in the number of situations where certainty-versus-doubt is slugging it out within yourself.

We can develop the capacity to maintain a foot in both realms more and more of the time. A person approaching mastery has less of the flip-flop but can hold the door open for either form of awareness to be engaged as needed.

Until a person can maintain that tenuous toehold in the realm of inspiration, they continue to flip-flop between otherworldly experiences and everyday ones. This lack of groundedness makes them seem spacey and disengaged. But grounding can only occur physically, in matter and in time—*within* the ordinary 3-D world.

Every inspired traveler must come down to earth in order to ground their unsullied discoveries in the messiness of ordinary life. Integration is largely about dealing with that grounding phase, whereby the two realms become allies.

Most people have not spent much time pondering long and deeply over the big questions, like the meaning of life, or doing enough inner work to read the signals. This high-vibration energy magnifies such prior efforts—if there have been any. Anyone who has not undertaken such spadework will feel greater frustration and resistance than they like.

Usually a major wipeout sends a person back to the starting point—the bottom. A Straddle-span survives setbacks by building a safety net. The person is only wiped out back to the base camp.

Straddle-span and History

I have long thought of Straddle-span as a personal challenge, something that each person must accomplish on an individual basis. Developing Straddle-span alters one's default state. That determines how far an individual will fall psychologically and emotionally when there is a major crisis.

Straddle-span is developed by inner work and acts of principled living. It establishes a form of a safety net that is anchored by a person's degree of rigor and inner strength. But I recently came to see there is also an aspect of Straddle-span that is much different than individual achievement.

When we share our wisdom and mentor someone regarding their inner understanding, that person can sometimes *gain the lesson without all of the pain*, the skill without so much trial and error. A certain amount of Straddle-span can be acquired by learning from others who know, coupled with the individual's own application of what is shared between them. This not about knowing mentally, but as accepted belief. In that way, prevalent values can be passed to children, as part of raising them to live with high moral values.

This type of knowledge is exchanged through what is known as "oral tradition" — passed from someone who knows to someone who is both open and ready for the lesson. This is part of the unwritten work a teacher, guru, or maestro provides students committed to the process.

The most important lessons are transmitted through their one-to-one connection — total affinity in the moment. Others in the vicinity may hear the words, but unless they are ready, the essence of the training is not conveyed to them.

Some Straddle-span (but to a lesser extent) can be passed culturally, as a quality of civilization. Cultured or high-consciousness energy societies develop a philosophy and/or spiritual tradition that set a high ethical standard for individual behavior and group practices. Values-based principles support human dignity and individual rights. That contrasts sharply with the uncivilized default state, predominantly marked by aggressive behavior and the principle of "every man for himself."

Living with Higher Consciousness Energy

Energetic Affinity Attracts

The saying, "Birds of a feather flock together" reflects the tendency to seek out others on our wavelength. That is not just about finding other people who have similar ideas and values but who also operate at an energy level comparable to our own. So hanging around creative and energized individuals makes us resonate with some of those same energies.

Everyone alive is participating in a massive energetic upgrade — although most people are not consciously aware of it. The vibrational adjustments that are currently underway are bringing our formerly dormant capabilities online. How much one gains by it depends on individual efforts to cut down drag or realign functional parts. The task now is to find or attract those who share a perspective or energetic reality. That requires building our support communities based on our affinity and intermeshing skills. According to Hugh MacLeod:

> The old ways are dead. And you need people around you who concur. That means hanging out more with the creative people, the freaks, the real visionaries, than you're already doing. Thinking more about what their needs are, and responding accordingly. Avoid the dullards; avoid the folk who play it safe. They can't help you anymore. Their stability model no longer offers that much stability. They are extinct, they are extinction.[247]

Enjoy your life more. Take a moment to notice whether the time spent doing something leaves you feeling more alive and energized. Does it make you appreciate "who you are?" There is more to happiness and joy than as incidentals, as Sonja Lyubombirsky explains in *The How of Happiness*:

> The *source* of the happy moments does in fact matter, for it influences the ability of the experience to be self-sustaining. Although the bliss of a sinful pleasure can trigger the same kinds of intellectual, social, and physical benefits as the bliss of hard-earned effort, the sinful pleasure is over quickly and, what's more, can leave guilt or other negative feelings in its wake....
>
> One of the chief reasons for the durability of happiness activities is that unlike the guilty pleasures, they are hard won. You have devoted time and effort to meditating or avoiding overthinking or committing acts of kindness. You have made these practices happen, and you have the ability to make them happen again. This sense of capability and responsibility is a wonderful boost in and of itself. When the source of positive emotion is yourself ... it can continue to yield pleasure and make you happy. When the source of positive emotion is yourself, it is renewable.[248]

Best Places or Activities to Recharge High-potency Energy:
- Close to nature; growing plants and animals, running water
- Enjoying the arts, whether as a performer or audience; learning an artistic skill (beginner's mind)
- Making something just for the fun of it (from mud pies to real pies, to pie in the sky)
- Convivial social activities and close personal relationships
- Recreation and sports for the sheer fun of it (but caution about rules that bring out the competitive spirit that can trigger lower energies or aggression)

---

[247] MacLeod, Hugh, *Ignore Everybody* (New York: Portfolio, 2009), page unknown.
[248] Lyubombirsky, Sonja, *The How of Happiness: A scientific approach to getting the life you want* (New York: Penguin Group, 2007), 265-6.

- Peaceful and meditative activities; quiet time; disengaged from "doing"
- Fun and playfulness
- Your own favorite place or time that never fails to uplift you

Going uphill energy-wise does not need to be persistent tough going—when it is done playfully. Being lighthearted can be energizing, too. The journey need not be all drudgery and earnestness. There is much more to a creative lifestyle than slaying dragons and rescuing maidens. Good humor and silly stuff also water the roots of novelty. That's what Sonja Lyubombirsky argues:

> So don't pooh-pooh pleasure. You can find pleasure in a silly TV show or in being wholly absorbed in a lecture on astrophysics. Both types of pleasure contribute to a happy life, and both types of pleasure can give rise to the multiple benefits of positive emotions, like feeling more sociable, more energetic, and more resourceful. An avalanche of studies has shown that happy moods, no matter the source, lead people to be more productive, more likable, more active, more healthy, more friendly, more helpful, more resilient, and more creative. This means that positive emotions actually help us achieve our goals (reinforcing the feeling that we are working toward something important) as well as help us strive for meaning and purpose in life. Indeed, a series of intriguing studies at the University of Missouri found that happy moods lead people to perceive their lives as more meaningful; for example, the more positive emotion people experience during a particular day, the more meaningful they judge that day. That seriousness and greatness must be accompanied by grumpiness is a myth.[249]

Master of Your Own Dance

Doing something you love can carry you to a place of stillness—where serenity, joy, and focused self-awareness reside. It takes you to uncharted territories where you might unearth rare gems of insight about things that matter to you. It takes curiosity and courage to let those creative energies take you where they will. But hey, why not?

Mastery of various kinds represents the pinnacle of achievement. However, it must be understood that mastery, like wisdom (its sibling) is not simply about how much a person knows or how sophisticated their tastes are. That's cumulative, built from years of direct experience.

But mastery that is rooted in self-knowledge relates to a disjuncture from cumulative comprehension. It functions by one perceiving their identity, priorities, and beliefs from a more encompassing vantage point. That includes the awareness of the energies that play such a significant role. Mastery includes a polished lens of perception that informs all the person's activities.

---

[249] *Ibid.*, 265.

A Lifelong Riddle

I believe everybody is born with some common deep questions about life and meaning. And we each have precisely one lifetime to find satisfactory answers. Finding your own answer adds a measure of meaning that is yours alone. Grounding your answer in "who you are" and what you do *is* your life's work. It is as simple as that.

Finding Your Answers:

- How many aspects of yourself can you discover and encourage to bloom before you die? (self-knowledge and self-acceptance)

- How many parts of yourself can you use in ways they reinforce each other? (making the combination stronger and more effective)

- What can you make or contribute of lasting value?

Looking for those answers will deliver that which is both true for you and increasingly relevant along the way. And it need not be complete to be useful. But it should not obscure the fact that certain fruits will not ripen for a long time—and only then as a result of considerable *determined effort*. Wisdom and mastery represent a vantage point that is the work of a lifetime. It is more embracing and integrated than prior capacity would suggest.

Mastery signifies assimilation of all aspects of our knowledge and experience. Self-knowledge incorporates untold layers of self-discovery. And those gains are never lost. First the fragmented elements of self are found, then embraced, then integrated, so all of them can participate.

Anyone who has acquired those abilities really is dealing with master-level issues. Mastery integrates them all, so a person can be the captain of their ship, rather than a flotilla of rowboats skittering around as they please.

Harvest High-potency Binkles

Binkles Feel Really Good

> **Binkle** – *the energy created when you really connect with someone or something that inspires you (even yourself). It's a zizz! – the smallest bit of upbeat energy that you can sense or share with another person.*

A binkle delivers a zizz of highly-charged energy. Some are mildly pleasant ripples and others are head-to-toe zaps. Repeated binkles can build on each other in a delightful way. Delight coupled with energy; that's what you feel. How or why it happened is secondary to the sensation and the energy surge. A view that "takes your breath away" or sensing something real and abiding can be high binkle because of the feelings that result.

It is the same energy as love and caring emotions, but it does not require emotional associations or a prior relationship. Some of your finest binkles happen with strangers without a word exchanged—we lock eyes and connect in an immediacy of sensing we are on the same wavelength.

I conceived and coined the word "binkle" in 1992. "Binkle" can be a noun or a verb. I consider it the fuel of our creative impulses—as well as the reward for them. Its impact is immediate. You can, on occasion, feel energetic surges without having a clue as to why, but there is a feeling of "just right" about it. That sensation is either present or it isn't; it cannot be faked.

Notice *it is the energy that is experienced*—not the reason the binkle happened or the situation in which it occurred. Binkles are not the thoughts you have about how you feel. It is not about whether or not you like something. It is no more complicated than the sensation itself—the rush of buoyant energy. If you reflect back on your happiest times, you will probably recall that special sensation that was present.

The binkle is a measure of high-octane, lift-off energy—much like a watt or an ohm. Rather than its intensity being registered by an electronic device, *you sense it with your body*. Every binkle is actually a jolt of higher-than-normal energy that can be experienced by the cells. You feel its presence and intensity—from mildly pleasant to electrifying and world shaking.

Binkles Are the Wonder Fuel

Binkles are exactly the same energy that is available during a vision or inspiration. They are exactly the same energy that fuels your creative efforts. They are exactly the same energy that fills your heart with joy, or wonder or, dare I say—love. Each is brief and atomic, but they build on each other. They can gather momentum and push all other concerns aside.

Binkles are energy, the energy of *feeling alive and happy* inside. Look out for them, from the leap of your heart when you sense one, to the residual afterglow that "life is good." Binkles are sensed as bright spots sprinkled through a person's everyday life—each a "now moment" being felt.

If you question the need for a separate word for this special energy, ask yourself: when you have had a surge of uplifting energy or special moments, didn't you give credit to the circumstances or other people present? It is so easy to get caught by the attributes of specific contexts as though each is different, rather than noticing the presence of *the very same energy* in each case.

But there is another reason for a different word (or trio of words). Binkle energy has a high-octane vibration that coincides with our heart, mind, and body being in sync as an *unbroken* whole. No amount of mundane energy can bring about that sense of unity.

It is not your mind that recognizes binkles, or even your emotions, but *your whole self*. Each binkle experience provides a brief moment of sensing oneself altogether whole—with nothing lacking. Binkles are not about reconciling all parts of one's self or getting them back together. When that energy is felt, you somehow *know yourself to be whole and complete already*.

Since we are not used to thinking about our experiences in terms of our energetic levels, we do not have words for them. Or we judge them as good or bad. In my opinion, we need a much larger vocabulary related to our energy states, so we can identify meaningful distinctions as we notice them.

Certainly, Energetic Intelligence deserves as broad a vocabulary as concepts like "snow" or "sex" that have hundreds of terms to point out slight distinctions. I predict that will come on its own, as more of us start to direct greater attention toward understanding our energetic states.

Visionaries are able to stick with their vision, and all the difficulties involved, because there are frequent binkles for them in doing so. And they feel binkles each time they are engaged with it. Compared to that immediate satisfaction from doing what they love doing, the world's rejection does not seem so hard to bear.

Binkles start our creative juices flowing and provide a reminder that what you really care about *is* important. So even though this word "binkle" may be new, you are already sensitized to what "rings your bell." To sum it up: Life without binkles is zizzless.

High-binkle experiences are energetically different than humdrum interests and they provide a pinhole into the larger, over-arching reality, where that kind of energy is unlimited. But moment by moment, we can seek out opportunities that allow binkles to charge us up.

Binkle, Krindle, and Laphe Work Together

To the concept of binkles, add two related notions: krindle and laphe (also coined by me).

Monitoring Your Upbeat Energy:
- Binkle – the *energy* that is felt; the zizz, a moment of sensed perfection
- Krindle – the *meter* or battery that detects and holds the special energy, located within the physical body
- Laphe – (pronounced, "laugh") the sense of being full of binkles; acts as a balanced feeling that is centered within

Krindle—It has long been apparent to me that humans have a specialized gauge attuned to the availability of binkle energy located within our bodies. However, medical science has failed to detect the specific organ function. The krindle is a binkle energy meter and short-term battery. It detects signs of available binkle energy, rather like a Geiger counter registers radiation. If a person is binkle depleted for too long, the krindle ceases to function—hence, no binkles.

Laphe — It acts as a self-adjusting shock absorber attuned to binkle energy. It keeps one's upbeat energy level on an even keel. Laphe resembles the bubble in a level, indicating whether a person's energy is balanced — "on the level" *or* "off kilter." When energy is high and without stress, it brings a sense of fullness and happiness.

When we are properly aligned with respect to energy, there is a sense of being centered and very responsive to changes in our circumstances. To engage life with a laphe approach, first detach from the specifics but hold an attentive place within yourself, where you are ready to respond to the energetic flow.

Being on the alert for binkles is not like hoping for lightning to strike (a breakthrough out of the blue) or awaiting a visit from the Muses (random inspiration). Rather, it is *within our power* to seek out experiences where binkles proliferate. And that makes our creative juices flow.

Looking at what you do in terms of the binkles, or increased energy levels, shifts the incentives for creative activities away from the tangible things that are created to the immediate pay-offs that come with the activity itself. Binkles release our creative force. That energy is capable of putting other gears in motion which add even more leverage to your efforts — the energy released as you are engaged, not simply the creative products which result.

As you allow the binkle, krindle, and laphe to operate in response to whatever is going on, you flow with the energetic currents that eddy around you. Anyone who knows about binkles is part of the Binkle Movement. That includes you. Talk it up, share it, and watch for opportunities to make the world a binkler place.

Adopt The Binkle Standard

Forget about your "To Do" list or your "what I always do" approach. Instead, gauge how your day went using a different yardstick.

The Binkle Standard:
- Spend more time and attention with people or activities that give you binkles
- Spend less time and attention with people or activities that drain your binkle energy away
- Pass them around! Leave a trail of binkle energy wherever you go
- Pause to enjoy how good it makes you feel

Chapter 14 - Practicing Visionary Leadership

Like queen bees, the creative individuals or teams are expected to lay the eggs of innovation for the enterprise. There is a constant tension between nurturing the sparks of inventiveness and conforming to the ongoing institutional practices.

Can Visionary Thinking Thrive in Organizations?

Has the image of the brilliant inventor toiling away in his solitary lab (or garage) been replaced by research and development departments? Will armies of faceless workers discover the next breakthrough technologies, medical marvels, or must-have and useful consumer gadgets?

Businesses need innovation since staying profitable requires new products and services to satisfy the constantly changing needs and desires of the buying public. In *Talent is Overrated*, Geoff Colvin said:

> In a world of forces that push toward the commoditization of everything, creating something new and different is the only way to survive. A product unlike any other can't be commoditized. A service that reaches deep into the psyche of the buyer can never be purchased solely on price. Creating such products and services was always valuable; now it's essential.[250]

Once useful products and services are developed, the marketplace reveals the winners and losers based on what people buy. New ideas or methods are permitted in an organizational setting to the extent they increase profits, reduce costs, or raise efficiencies—that can be translated into dollars. Original thinking that is not easy to quantify, or likely to yield a return in the near term, is usually a non-starter.

Where Profitable New Ideas Come from:

- Lone inventor or core group, "in the garage"—always a long shot
- Academia, theoretical and pure research, government sponsored programs
- Serendipity—with or without prior incremental preparation
- Corporations and organizations with research and development investments
- New collaborative models (later this chapter)

These days, the bulk of new products (patents) are coming from corporate R & D investments. In the process of making something original and useful with what they envision, visionaries often need to put its requirements ahead of their own humdrum concerns. But in the business environment, where the top priority is making money, the priorities are unlikely to bend so far toward the demands of the creative process. To what extent can visions or substantial creativity survive in impersonal, profit-driven institutions?

---

[250] Colvin, Geoff, *Talent is Overrated: What really separates world-class performance from everybody else* (New York: Penguin Group, 2008), 146.

In describing the new creative class, Richard Florida said:

> Creative people require more than compensation for their time—a quid pro quo trade of time and effort for cash and other financial considerations.... The best people in any field are motivated by passion.... There is no one-size-fits-all answer. Passion varies because people are different.[251]

In 2012, Florida totally updated his ten-year-old ground-breaking book and supportive statistics. In it he argues for a notion with which I totally agree: key task of the future must be to fully engage the creative talents of all.

The type of organization where the vision is "hatched" or nurtured greatly influences the shape of a creative endeavor. This chapter deals mostly with substantial business corporations, but many of their issues apply to any large institution or governmental entity. Mature organizations are at a different phase of the growth cycle than the lone actor or the early stage of a start-up (launching the mission).

Since the corporate climate and operating practices are solidly in place, creative efforts are likely to be stifled—unless they are carefully protected. Prudent leaders watch over such vulnerable projects. This chapter and the next consider the uneasy relationship between creative thinking and institutional priorities—and what more leaders should do to make them coexist.

Leaders are on record as wanting more vision and creativity within their organizations, but structural factors in the corporate culture make it unlikely. *In Built to Last*, James C.V. Collins and Jerry I. Porras identify the difficulty with pinning it down.

> The word vision conjures up all kinds of images. We think of outstanding achievement. We think of deeply held values that bond people in a society together. We think of audacious, exhilarating goals that galvanize people. We think of something eternal—the underlying reasons for an organization's existence. We think of something that reaches inside us and pulls out our best efforts. We think of the dreams of what we want to be. And therein lies a problem. All of us know vision is important, but what exactly is it?[252]

Like queen bees, the creative individuals or teams are expected to lay the eggs of innovation for the enterprise. There is a constant tension between nurturing the sparks of inventiveness and conforming to the institutional practices.

Policies and practices used to slow action, protect hierarchies, defend turf, and avoid blame if things do not work out frustrate the process of innovation. Creative types constantly butt heads with the unbending systems that define the

---

[251] Florida, Richard, *The Rise of the Creative Class: And how it's transforming work, leisure, community and everyday life* (New York: Basic Books, 2002), 88.
[252] Collins, James C.V. and Porras, Jerry I., *Built to Last: Successful habits of visionary companies* (New York: Harper Collins, 1997), 219.

workplace. And they are not proficient at the power games, so are at a marked disadvantage.

By their very nature, visionaries struggle with conforming or being "good little soldiers." How well can creative energy thrive in an environment that is determined to tightly control it? Peter Drucker argues that organizations cannot do much in that regard. "Large organizations cannot be versatile. A large organization is effective through its mass rather than through its agility. Fleas can jump many times their own height, but not an elephant."

Typically, a corporate culture does not know how to coexist with something at odds with its precisely defined structure and priorities. Institutions rely on predictability and risk reduction—180° from the visionary style. What kind of organizations can be flexible enough to permit creative methods to thrive? While novelty and stimulation are needed, spontaneity scares the corporate rank-and-file who consider that approach chaotic.

Businesses are more comfortable with fine-tuning small improvements than dealing with large-scale change, which disrupts the predictability expected of smoothly running operations. Despite considerable praise for the benefits of innovative thinking, organizations really do not want change in large doses, and implicitly reject early signs of it within their midst.

Vision or Creativity as a Commodity

Vision is rightly praised for driving innovation, maintaining institutional vitality, and helping an organization stay competitive. Within the corporate framework, vision might denote an institution's principal philosophy or purpose. Business leaders see vision as expressing its core philosophy.

James Collins also said, "Core ideology provides the bonding glue that holds an organization together as it grows, decentralizes, diversifies, expands globally, and attains diversity within."[253]

Vision is also treated as a desirable capacity of leadership—the ability to see ahead and chart the long-term course of an enterprise. John P. Kotter speaks to the catalyzing power of vision in *Leading Change*.

> Vision plays a key role in producing useful change by helping to direct, align, and inspire actions on the part of large numbers of people. Without an appropriate vision, a transformation effort can easily dissolve into a list of confusing, incompatible, and time-consuming projects that go in the wrong direction or nowhere at all. Without a sound vision, the reengineering project in the accounting department, the new 360-degree performance appraisal from human resources, the plant's quality program, and the cultural change effort in the sales force either won't add up in a meaningful way or won't stir up the kind of energy needed to properly implement any of these initiatives.

---

[253] *Ibid.*, 221.

Sensing the difficulty in producing change, some people try to manipulate events quietly behind the scenes and purposefully avoid any public discussion of future direction. But without a vision to guide the decision-making, and every choice employees face, can dissolve into an interminable debate.[254]

But being desirable begs the question about how much unconventional thinking is permitted within an organization or industry. The visionary mindset and the corporate one simply do not understand each other very well, as illustrated by the following example.

Spike Jonze has a track record for massive novelty in his films and music, and apparently TriStar wanted him for that reason. However, the studio pulled out of making a movie with him after the executives considered Jonze's vision a bit too bold. In "Bringing 'Where the Wild Things Are' to the Screen," Saki Knafo wrote:

> [When I asked Jonze about that] he shrugged. 'They didn't like my ideas, and they thought it would cost too much.' The project's demise, Jonze told me, actually brought him an 'odd sense of relief.' TriStar had been pressuring him to make the script jokier, he said, and he'd given in to the point where he barely recognized his own work. 'I realized only then that it happens millimeter by millimeter,' he told me. 'If you compromise what you're trying to do just a little bit, you'll end up compromising a little more the next day or the next week, and when you lift your head you're suddenly really far away from where you're trying to go.'[255]

Vision and creative energy cannot exist in isolation, but reflect and influence the social setting in which they occur. While not as easy to define as an intellectual property, i.e. trademarks and copyrights, creative efforts often lead to them or to new profit centers. That is largely why highly creative efforts are valued and tolerated within businesses.

But contrary to what people prefer, originality cannot be turned on and off when it is convenient. Keeping creativity flowing requires some loosening of control. In *Where Good Ideas Come From*, Steven Johnson explores the factors involved.

> Some environments squelch new ideas; some environments seem to breed them effortlessly. The city and the Web have been such engines of innovation because, for complicated historical reasons, they are both environments that are powerfully suited for the creation, diffusion, and adoption of new ideas.[256]

---

[254] Kotter, John P., *Leading Change* (Boston: Harvard Business School Press, 1996), 7-8.
[255] Knafo, Saki, "Bringing 'Where the Wild Things Are' to the Screen," *New York Times*, September 6, 2009.
[256] Johnson, Steven, *Where Good Ideas Come From: The natural history of innovation* (New York, Riverhead Books, 2010), 16.

Original Thinking Meets Inflexible Structure

Two fundamentally different personality styles are in conflict: those who like the thrill of novelty and change, and those who want things to stay the way they are. Organizations are comprised mostly of the latter—those who dislike being forced into unknown waters. In a world where so much is changing, which approach represents the riskier course?

The risk-opportunity trade-off is spelled out by Peter Drucker. "All economic activity is by definition 'high risk.' And defending yesterday—that is, not innovating—is far more risky than making tomorrow."

Having an official vision statement and cheerleading for innovation do not make an organization a visionary operation. To be that in actuality requires re-engineering the typical corporate structure to the extent new thinking, *in any department and at every level,* has a fighting chance. So, it is not just the product development department in need of new ideas, but logistics and human resources as well.

Making far-reaching change work depends on sufficient motivation up and down the line to replace the way things have always operated, encouraging fresh notions to develop. Effective leaders must do more than articulate the goals, but must also find ways to redirect forces within the organization that would undermine them. It is, of course, their responsibility to hold forth the big-picture vision, but they must also be a detail-level remover of obstacles.

Tom Peters points at the small-scale obstacles that need to be removed in order for creative tasks to see the light of day in *Thriving on Chaos*.

> The accumulation of little items, each too 'trivial' to trouble the boss with, is a prime cause of miss-the-market delays. As boss, you must consciously seek out opportunities to help in little ways. You must view yourself as basher-in-chief of small barriers and facilitator-in-chief of trivial aids to action rather than 'the great planner.'[257]

Organizations are protective of their prerogatives and continuity. Maintaining the intricate power structures (along with the inherent rewards) diminishes the value of the unique individuals who work there. As a person climbs the corporate ladder, adherence to institutional norms is further reinforced.

In *Good to Great*, Jim Collins describes a "Culture of Discipline" as having the need for *fewer* controls, not more.

> **A Culture of Discipline**. All companies have a culture, some companies have discipline, but few companies have a culture of discipline. When you have disciplined people, you don't need hierarchy. When you have disciplined thoughts, you don't need bureaucracy. When you have disciplined action, you
>
> don't need excessive controls. When you combine a culture of discipline

---

[257] Peters, Tom, *Thriving on Chaos* (New York: Alfred A. Knopf, 1988), 265.

with an ethic of entrepreneurship, you get the magical alchemy of great performance.[258]

Traditional organizational structure routinely squelches signs of unconventional ideas, or the individuals who have them. With set policies and rules come the rewards and punishments for conforming… or not conforming. Those in control keep sifting people and behavior into that which is wanted, and that which is not, which leads to many unintended side effects. Most are at the expense of individual uniqueness or the kind of unfettered thinking where creative notions can develop.

Having an articulated vision statement to guide the course of the institution is not enough. There is plenty of evidence that visionary thinking is hard to come by in most large institutions—even when leaders advocate more innovative efforts in-house, even in industries devoted to being leading-edge innovators.

Since innovative strategies and products are the lifeblood of commerce, stifling such efforts could compromise long-term competitiveness or survival. Tom Peters also said:

> The very purpose of the vision is to provide the bedrock upon which constant evolutionary, opportunistic change can take place. However, it is all too easy for even the most compelling vision (initially) to become static, impeding the very change it is meant to induce.[259]

It is not just creative energy that tends to get lost. Other principles equally hard to quantify, but very important to the character and integrity of the enterprise, get diminished as well. That casualness about ethical standards can lead to lapses of judgment down the road—and down the organization. Ethics and compliance are fundamentally different .

> The problem in organizations is that many 'ethics' solutions focus on compliance. The compliance definition of 'ethics' is not one of integrity or integratedness; it is a watered-down, devalued definition that essentially means 'follow the rules.' Ethics training, therefore is often focused exclusively on conformity to [rules and regulations] and not to clarifying values and fostering integrity to those values and to enduring principles.[260]

---

[258] Collins, Jim, *Good to Great: Why some companies make the leap… and others don't* (New York: Harper Business, 2001), 13.
[259] *Op. cit.*, Peters, 407.
[260] Covey, Stephen M. R., *The Speed of Trust: The one thing that changes everything* (New York: Free Press, 2006), 61.

Leadership and Vision

Management and Leadership Are Not Synonymous

It is management's job to keep a complicated system of people and technology running smoothly, whereas leadership defines what the future should look like for the organization. Leaders align people with that vision, and inspire them to make it happen. John P. Kotter explains why in *Leading Change*

> Unfortunately for us today, this emphasis on management has often been institutionalized in corporate cultures that discourage employees from learning how to lead. Ironically, past success is usually the key ingredient in producing this outcome.... Success creates some degree of market dominance, which in turn produced much growth. After a while, keeping the ever-larger organization under control becomes the
>
> primary challenge. So attention turns inward, and managerial competencies are nurtured. With a strong emphasis on management, but not leadership, bureaucracy and an inward focus take over.[261]

The leader-as-manager deals mostly with routine or repetitious tasks. A management-focused leader is more concerned with building up and stabilizing the organization than in breaking new ground. Since eliminating unpredictability is considered a strong measure of success, it offers an inhospitable environment for ideas, or people, that rock the boat.

Traditional organizations consolidate power in a few leaders, with executives vying for power, eager to reach the top. So, those who become the leaders are the very ones most skillful at playing insider politics. The usual notions about talents are hard to apply in business, as Geoff Colvin said in *Talent is Overrated*.

> If the concept of specific talents turns out to be troublesome in music and sports, it's even more so in business. We all tend to assume that business giants must possess some special gift for what they do, but evidence turns out to be extremely elusive. In fact, the overwhelming impression that comes from examining the early lives of business greats is just the opposite — that they didn't seem to hold any identifiable gift or give any early indication of what they would become.[262]

What Makes Some Leaders Remarkable?

A "visionary leader" charts the organization's direction for the long term. Even when the leader is the company founder and devoted to its initial concept, balancing both interests (vision and routine practices) tends to make a thorny marriage. According to Kotter:

---

[261] *Op. cit.*, Kotter, 27.
[262] *Op. cit.*, Colvin, 31.

> [Effective leaders] take an architectural approach and concentrate on building the organizational traits of visionary companies. The primary output of their efforts is not the tangible implementation of a great idea, the expression of a charismatic personality, the gratification of their ego, or the accumulation of personal wealth. Their greatest creation is the company itself and what it stands for.[263]

An unacknowledged tug-of-war pits organizational practicalities against the forces of originality, which are always "flighty." It is a rare person who can live and function comfortably in both modes. Bob Metcalfe co-invented Ethernet, a standard for connecting computers over short distances. He founded 3Com and describes his humbling education in the company he started.

Metcalfe's experience resembles the fate of other business leaders who wore the visionary mantle in the corporate environment, as he described in a *Wired Magazine* article: "The Visionary Thing," (November, 1999).

> To my naïve delight, investors and colleagues started calling me a visionary. Intoxicated by the flattery, I didn't immediately realize I was being manipulated. I didn't know that nobody really wants visionaries running companies, that visionary is a code word used by investors and colleagues for an unruly guy who, through an accident of history, holds a huge chunk of stock in an otherwise promising company. It's an old story, I know, but I wanted to run the company I'd founded. Everybody else involved wanted me to sit down and shut up.
>
> I aspired to be both the visionary and the CEO. Where visionaries can be good at persuasion, CEOs are good at wielding authority. Visionaries transcend organizations, resources, and current realities, while CEOs master them. I wanted to do both: think deep thoughts and recruit the team; accumulate fame and direct corporate strategy; plus, ignore the chain of command, undermine day-to-day operations, and opine endlessly on matters of international importance that had nothing to do with the business at hand.
> So I started looking for professional managers to handle daily operations. I expected that they would do what I told them, filling in and handling the dirty details, which, as you'll recall, is where God is.
>
> But making the visionary-manager relationship work is like letting two bulls into a china shop. Your chosen managers will be winners, in which case you won't be tolerated for long. Or they won't be, in which case you won't be tolerated for long. Either way, there's all that broken china.[264]

Defining the Place of Change within an Organization

Businesses prefer to handle change by keeping it reined in. Large institutions are designed for consistency and predictability, so procedures assure efficiency and

---

[263] *Op. cit.*, Collins, *Built to Last*, 23.
[264] Metcalfe, Bob, "The Visionary Thing," *Wired Magazine*, Issue 7.11, Nov. 1999.

uniformity, to the extent possible. However, it is not so much the rules themselves but how they are implemented that encourages (or inhibits) innovation within the enterprise.

> Leaders articulate and define what has previously remained implicit or unsaid; then they invent images, metaphors, and models that provide a focus for new attention. By so doing, they consolidate or challenge prevailing wisdom. In short, an essential factor in leadership is the capacity to influence and organize meaning for the members of the organization.... Managers are people who do things right and leaders are people who do the right thing. The difference may be summarized as activities of vision and judgment—effectiveness versus activities of mastering routine—efficiency.[265]

Change-oriented organizations operate quite differently than those rooted in a traditional top-down structure. They are experimenting with new ways to engage employees and the innovation process itself.

Forward-looking leaders, wary of perpetuating old assumptions, need to stay poised to change often and smoothly. The trick is in knowing the difference between critical change and optional tinkering. In *Built to Last*, Jim Collins makes the case for an unchanging core ideology.

> The fundamental distinguishing characteristic of the most enduring and successful corporations is that they preserve a cherished core ideology while simultaneously stimulating progress and change in everything that is not part of their core ideology. Put another way, they distinguish their timeless core values and enduring core purpose (which should never change) from their operating practices and business strategies (which should be changing constantly in response to a changing world). In truly great companies, change is a constant, but not the only constant. They understand the differences between what should never change and what should be open for change, between what is truly sacred and what is not. And by being clear about what should never change, they are better able to stimulate change and progress in everything else.[266]

Once its guiding vision has been made clear, everyone who works there should be keenly aware of the organization's purpose, and how it applies to their work. Collins said, "An enduring great company decides for itself what values it holds to be core, largely independent of the current environment, competitive requirements, or management fads."[267]

The organization's core purpose is its fundamental reason for being. It is not just cooked up at a corporate retreat or framed in the boardroom, but it permeates all decisions up and down the company. Collins also said:

---

[265] *Op. cit.*, Peters, 399. [quoting from Bennis and Nanus in *Leaders: Strategies for taking charge*]
[266] *Op. cit.*, Collins, *Built to Last*, 220.
[267] *Ibid.*, 222.

> You do not 'create' or 'set' core ideology. You discover core ideology. It is not derived by looking to the external environment, you get at it by looking inside. It has to be authentic. You can't fake an ideology. Nor can you just 'intellectualize' it. Do not ask, 'what core values should we hold?' Ask instead: 'What core values do we actually hold?' Core values and purpose must be passionately-held on a gut level or they are not core.[268]

Efforts made by such companies to change, experiment, and improve are not undertaken merely to increase sales or market share. Leaders also aim to build the mechanisms within their organization that can perpetuate its primary objective and core values. These are so ingrained in the corporate culture they are a guiding influence in all decisions. The company's survival and growth are the over-riding priority. In that light, Tom Peters defines another form of failure.

> Failure today is failure to change. The leader's vision is at once the license to dare to be better and the beacon and 'control system' which keeps the process of mastering new worlds from deteriorating into directionless anarchy.[269]

In contrast to minor tinkering and gradual improvement, revolutionary change alters the course of the enterprise. It can come from within the organization or result from major economic or social shifts that influence whole industries. Such forces are largely beyond any leader's control: stifling government policies, sharp demographic shifts, economic upheavals, competing technologies that make what they do obsolete, or the maturing of their industry.

How soon does it become apparent a significant course correction is necessary? Then what form will adjustments take? The organization's changing needs are very different than routine management provides, as Daniel Goleman describes in *Primal Leadership*.

> The visionary style [of leadership] works well in many business situations. But it can be particularly effective when a business is adrift—during a turnabout or when it is in dire need of a fresh vision. Not surprisingly, the visionary mode comes naturally to 'transformational' leaders—those who seek to radically change an organization.[270]

Goal Setting and Strategies

Articulating goals, and setting the strategies to accomplish them, is an important role of leadership. That process defines the finish line and rallies team spirit in a way that unifies the efforts of everyone on the team. Tom Peters describes vision in *Thriving on Chaos*.

---

[268] *Ibid.*, 219-20.
[269] *Op. cit.*, Peters, 401.
[270] Goleman, Daniel, et al, *Primal Leadership: Realizing the power of emotional intelligence* (Boston: Harvard Business School Press, 2002), 59.

Qualities of Business Visions:
1. Effective visions are inspiring
2. Effective visions are clear and challenging—and about excellence
3. Effective visions make sense in the marketplace, and by stressing flexibility and execution, stand the test of time in a turbulent world
4. Effective visions must be stable but constantly challenged—and changed on the margin
5. Effective visions are beacons and controls when all else is up for grabs
6. Effective visions are aimed for empowering our own people first, customers second
7. Effective visions prepare for the future, but honor the past
8. Effective visions are lived in details, not broad strokes.[271]

Garden-variety strategic planning and goal setting are not the same as a grand vision, and they lead to very different strategies. Vision need not be the exclusive function of top leaders. How widely the planning process extends beyond the executive suite reflects the importance of hierarchy in that corporate culture.

A willingness to broaden participation in the planning process to those in the ranks can be a distinguishing factor of visionary companies. How else can "shared vision" be encouraged? Charles Sigismund adds this inner-directed component to the mix in *Champions of Silicon Valley*

> Although vision is not strategic planning, it can productively guide and profit from a strategic planning process. But for many practitioners, vision is a more lively, concentrated, and powerful replacement for traditional strategic planning....
>
> If everyone in an organization truly sees and is inspired by the same picture of where they're headed and the way they want to conduct themselves in getting there, they can largely know for themselves what they need to do; they don't need to be told.[272]

Methods of Setting Organizational Goals and Strategies:
- The exclusive creation of top leaders without consultation, then announced
- Developed through a systematic process involving various stakeholders: employees, suppliers, customers/clients, industry leaders
- Exploration of alternative scenarios or options proposed from outside the organization
- Trial and error, with intermittent course corrections

---

[271] *Op. cit.*, Peters, 401-4.
[272] Sigismund, Charles G., *Champions of Silicon Valley: Visionary thinking from today's technology pioneers* (New York: John Wiley & Sons, Inc., 2000), 3.

- Testing the waters with a prototype or a phased-in change sequence
- Outside consultants or experts brought in to fix specific problems
- Some combination of these approaches

An organization is comprised of many individuals at various levels of authority, any of whom have the potential to make its guiding principles work better—if there is encouragement for it. But companies differ widely in the amount of initiative rank-and-file employees are encouraged to take. Or in how much heed is given to input that is given. Daniel Goleman also said:

> Visionary leaders articulate where a group is going, but not how it will get there—setting people free to innovate, experiment, and take calculated risks. Knowing the big picture and how a given job fits in gives people clarity; they understand what's expected of them. And the sense that everyone is working toward shared goals builds team commitment: people feel pride in belonging to their organization....
>
> Moreover, by framing the collective task in terms of a grander vision, this approach defines a standard for performance feedback that revolves around that vision. Visionary leaders help people to see how their work fits into the big picture, lending people a clear sense not just that what they do matters, but also why.[273]

Leaders are wise to make extensive preparations before announcing a significant change of direction. Two-way communication is even more important at such times. To simply pronounce a grand vision or sweeping new policy out of the blue invites confusion—or worse.

The more drastic or far-reaching the proposed change, the more likely it is to engender fear or resistance by those expected to carry it out. The way new goals are communicated often foreordains their success (or failure). Nor can goal setting be treated as a "set it and forget it" approach. Allow ten to thirty years! That is long-term commitment.

Visions that Inspire Others

Articulating the grand goal, even a worthy one, is not itself a vision—although it can lead to a groundswell of acceptance and institutional growth. On the other hand, a clear statement of "what we are shooting for" sets the goal high. When *inspired* to do so, employees rise to solve the "how" to make it work.

A vision is so much bigger than setting goals, although it is easy to confuse the two. A clearly stated vision allows people to see in their mind's eye what it *looks like*, what it *feels like* when its impact has been fully realized. It provides an exquisitely clear picture for the team of what each of them is working toward.

---

[273] *Op. cit.*, Goleman, 57.

Vision provides the "why" behind what they are doing—the larger purpose that is bigger than the profit and loss statement. Beyond that, a clear vision helps each participant to see how his or her individual efforts fit into the overall vision. In *Built to Last*, Jim Collins said:

> Although organizations may have many BHAGs [Big Hairy Audacious Goals] at different levels operating all at the same time, vision requires a special type of BHAG—a 'vision-level' BHAG that applies to the entire organization and requires ten to thirty years of effort to complete.... Indeed, inventing such a goal forces an executive team to be visionary, rather than just strategic or tactical. A BHAG should not be a sure bet—perhaps only 50 to 70 percent probability of success—but the organization must believe 'we can do it anyway.'[274]

Within the business setting, the way "vision" is usually used is closer to long-term strategic planning than the transcendent visions discussed in other chapters. That is because business visions are focused on real-world objectives, and are never divorced from practicalities and profits.

Those are *extrinsic* motivations, done for their tangible benefits. But grand visions are rooted in "something more," and are largely oriented to *intrinsic* motivation, where things are done for their own sake. Visionary leaders balance both intrinsic and extrinsic rewards in their priorities—and for their employees. I see that as an increasingly important ability of leadership. (See Chapter 15.)

Setting bold goals requires unreasonable confidence—past the point where realistic expectations would balk. Collins also said: "BHAGs looked more audacious to outsiders than to insiders. The visionary companies didn't see their audacity as taunting the gods. It simply never occurred to them that they couldn't do what they set out to do."[275]

Inspiration relates to beliefs, core values, and principles. People may agree logically with big plans and goals, but that will not fire them up. Logical arguments alone cannot inspire. That takes passion and an emotional connection to the goal. It also reflects the extent to which employees feel emotionally invested in their company's primary purpose (assuming that is clear to them).

Unless the leader can express a vision, a big dream, an inspiring belief they share, people will not be touched deeply enough to generate passion. They will not be moved to march. That leadership skill supersedes management style, and goes to the heart of why people go the extra mile—willingly.

Guiding the Change Process

Large-scale change in major institutions, or across industries, resembles what happens with scientific revolutions (Chapter 17). Long periods of routine

---

[274] *Op. cit.*, Collins, *Built to Last*, 232.
[275] *Ibid.*, 105.

activities (with minimal change or disruption) are punctuated by periods of massive and irreversible change. Different leadership skills are needed for each of those periods. It is one thing to captain the ship on calm seas and another in a typhoon.

During smooth sailing, routine management is quite adequate—maybe preferable for fine-tuning operations. But for stormy seas, the organization requires additional leadership skills that are outside the scope of smooth operations.

For a leader to plot a course corresponding to the abrupt twists and turns of circumstance requires throwing excess baggage (and non-productive practices) overboard. Inventiveness dictates taking a zigzag course that responds to changing conditions as quickly as they occur. And that puts the kibosh on prior expectations.

These days, the rate of change is accelerating by almost every measure. More leaders who know how to ride the waves of change are needed—those who will not be blindsided by factors for which they should have been preparing. Visionary leaders have a knack for navigating those uncharted waters.

Leaders need to address the implicit barriers to effective company-wide cooperation early on, in addition to defining far-reaching policies that make innovative efforts more likely, rather than less likely. Unfortunately, the will to change entrenched stuckness is seldom found in the organizations most in need of being repaired. Tim Harford points out the requisite messiness in *Adapt: Why success always starts with failure.*

> If even the best leaders make mistakes, a good organization will need to have some way to correct those mistakes. Let's recall the features that make our idealized hierarchy an attractive machine for carrying out correct decisions: the refinement of information to produce a 'big picture'; the power of a team all pulling in the same direction; and the clear responsibilities producing a proper flow of information up and down the chain of command. Every one of these assets can become a liability if the task of the organization is to learn from mistakes. The big picture becomes a self-deluding propaganda poster, the unified team retreats into groupthink, and the chain of command becomes a hierarchy of wastebaskets, perfectly evolved to prevent feedback reaching the top. What works in reality is a far more unsightly, chaotic and rebellious organization altogether.[276]

Leaders with Flash and Flair

Business writers like to debate whether a company is better served by a charismatic, high-profile leader, or by a detail-oriented manager who does not call attention to him or herself. It is not hard to find evidence for either

---

[276] Harford, Tim, *Adapt: Why success always starts with failure* (New York: Farrar, Straus and Giroux, 2011), 42.

argument, but that is not the issue. How flexible can either style of leadership be when serious change is needed?

The slow-but-reliable growth favored in business corresponds with steady management skills rather than the unpredictability of a flamboyant leader. But that is also the calm seas model.

Research by Collins disagrees with two widely held assumptions about successful organizations and their leaders. He argues that building a successful visionary company does not require either a great idea or a visionary leader. Either could get in the way of its long-term growth.

Collins' team found that visionary companies were much *less likely* to begin with a great idea than other companies. He found "a high-profile, charismatic style is absolutely not required to successfully shape a visionary company."[277]

Attempts to define leadership by personality style fall into the same trap that entangles efforts to predict the future or to make choices based on probabilities. These approaches work much of the time, but they turn a blind eye to factors that do not conform to expectations, or are low probability but cause dramatic effects if they do occur.

Successful leadership is a matter of the person's *effectiveness*, which is based on their functional skills. There will always be a wide range of capabilities that can produce outstanding results. What matters more than whether the leader is high profile or low is how well their abilities can serve their company, their industry, and the larger community as changing conditions accelerate. That is impossible to know except in the heat of a major crisis.

A truly effective leader is no easier to describe than a visionary is—for many of the same reasons. Recognizing such individuals requires looking less at the person's credentials and personality traits than at their actual deliverables. And what works is likely to defy simplistic explanations.

Columnist David Brooks recommends a modest hybrid that is not personality based or management-style based. He calls it the Humble Hound, from a *New York Times* article of that name.

> Alongside the boardroom lion model of leadership, you can imagine a humble hound model. The humble hound leader thinks less about her mental strengths than about her weaknesses. She knows her performance slips when she has to handle more than one problem at a time, so she turns off her phone and e-mail while making decisions. She knows she has a bias for caution, so she writes a memo advocating the more daring option before writing another advocating the most safe. She knows she is bad at prediction, so she follows Peter Drucker's old advice: After each decision, she writes a memo about what she expects to happen. Nine months later, she'll read it to discover how far off she was.

---

[277] *Op. cit.*, Collins, *Built to Last*, 32.

In short, she spends a lot of time on metacognition—thinking about her thinking—and then building external scaffolding devices to compensate for her weaknesses. She believes we only progress through a series of regulated errors. Every move is a partial failure, to be corrected by the next one.... She knows the world is too complex and irregular to be known, so life is about navigating uncertainty. She understands she is too quick to grasp at pseudo-objective models and confident projections that give the illusion of control.

She spends more time seeing than analyzing. Analytic skills differ modestly from person to person, but perceptual skills vary enormously. Anybody can analyze, but the valuable people can pick out the impermanent but crucial elements of a moment or effectively grasp a context. This sort of perception takes modesty; strong personalities distort the information field around them.... Because of her limitations, she tries to construct thinking teams. In one study, groups and individuals were given a complicated card game called the Wason selection task. Seventy-five percent of the groups solved it, but only 14 percent of individuals did.[278]

Be Flexible with Strategies

The desire for a single all-purpose strategy needs to be thrown overboard. What is always needed is a *responsive strategy*. And that depends on staying flexible and informed about changing conditions as they occur. Fixed strategies risk being wedded to past (and passed) circumstances, and they fail to account for what is in play. Responsive strategies must be free to learn from gauging what works.

The distinction between deliberate strategies and emergent strategies is useful, if only to illustrate that a combination of approaches produces better results than either approach alone. Guy Kawasaki describes it in *The Art of the Start* This flexibility also brings in the advantages of engaging Fingertip Smarts.

> **Write Deliberate, Act Emergent**
> In The Innovator's Solution, coauthors Clayton Christensen and Michael E. Raynor explain the difference between a 'deliberate strategy-making process' and an 'emergent strategy-making process.' The former is 'conscious and analytical,' featuring rigorous use of historical data, technology road maps, and competitive analysis. It is useful for mature companies and operating histories.'
>
> By contrast, an emergent strategy-making process is influenced by the day-to-day realities experienced by middle managers and workers on the front line. It is ad hoc and can react quickly to problems and opportunities. This is the right process to use in situations where the future is murky, and it is therefore difficult to develop suitable strategies.... You should write them [business

---

[278] Brooks, David, "The Humble Hound," *New York Times*, April 9, 2010.

plans] in the 'deliberate' style, but you should be thinking and acting in the 'emergent' style.[279]

The Time Horizon of Elliott Jaques

A skill that differentiates effective leaders is their grasp of the long-term impact of their decisions. Elliott Jaques, a Canadian organizational psychologist, spent thirty years researching the relationship between a person's time awareness and their job competence.

Jaques was able to show that how a person relates to time determines the limits of his or her work capacity. He defined a person's "time horizon" as the farthest time frame that they can formulate goals and carry them to completion. The level of work in a stratum is defined by the target completion time of the *longest* task, project, or program assigned to that role or job.

A person's time horizon indicates how much complexity he or she is able to handle. It reflects their maximum time span for processing information about the future. Jaques discovered six strata/levels in a typical organization (irrespective of the number of job levels in that enterprise).

Those with the largest time horizon have the best ability to foresee the future and make preparations for the various possible eventualities. Such skills are integral to the overall planning process and necessary for capable leadership.

> Years of field work also revealed that people in organizations were remarkably unanimous about where the cut-off points should be between one stratum and another: three months for stratum 1, one year for stratum 2, two years for stratum 3, five years for stratum 4, and 10 and 20 years for strata 5 and 6. The perceived complexity of work within an organization, in other words, does not increase in a consistent way. It is *discontinuous*, just as water is discontinuous in its progression from solid to liquid to steam. The fact that so many people, in so many different cultures and situations, perceived the hierarchies of their organizations in the same way persuaded Jaques that he'd stumbled on something fundamental....
>
> The smarter we are at processing information, the farther we are able to project ourselves into the future. That's the fundamental difference between Archie Bunker and Henry Kissinger — not just intelligence or acquired knowledge, but a measurable, qualitative difference in the way each solves problems, and in the time horizons of the roles in which each feels most comfortable.... And what usually happens when a CEO's cognitive abilities fail to match the level of hierarchy he occupies is that he shrinks that company down to his own level.[280]

---

[279] Kawasaki, Guy, *The Art of the Start: The time-tested, battle-hardened guide for anyone starting anything* (New York: Penguin Group, 2004), 72-3.
[280] Ross, Alexander, "The Long View Of Leadership," *Canadian Business*, May, 1992.

The ability to ground a significant vision usually requires holding a long time horizon for it. The visionary holds the vision of what could develop, beyond the numerous short-term challenges being faced. This explains, in part, why visionaries are so often ahead of their time and engender so much resistance from those who cannot see very far ahead. The difference in their perceptual time frames might account for some of the friction creative types stir up within the institutional setting.

Controlling the Future

Institutions, like most individuals, tend to continue doing what they are already doing, and to measure progress or success by what is easy to measure. Maintaining predictability, control, and steady continuity are considered evidence of good management. Managers plan for the future based on what is already known, as though corralling enough data eliminates surprises.

Computer modeling and statistical projections are rather reliable as long as conditions do not change much. But even they ignore many of the relevant factors we do not know how to quantify. And some factors that are crucial don't get documented at all. David Brooks explains how institutional attention is focused on data, rather than trickier stuff in "The Sandra Bullock Trade," *New York Times* (March 30, 2010).

> Most governments release a ton of data on economic trends but not enough on trust and other social conditions. In short, modern societies have developed vast institutions oriented around the things that are easy to count, not around the things that matter most. They have an affinity for material concerns and a primordial fear of moral and social ones.... Governments keep initiating policies they think will produce prosperity, only to get sacked, time and again, from their spiritual blind side.[281]

Those who rely on future forecasts count on very little change to the prevailing conditions. However, forecasting usually fails to factor in the positive forces of creativity, innovation, and technological advance that propel significant change.

Predictions also fail to note how quickly new products can alter the public's expectations and behavior. Joel Garreau explains why predictions are fallible in *Radical Evolution*.

Types of Bad Predictions:
- *The enterprise turned out to be a lot more complicated than it sounded.* This is why we don't have robotic maids, or electricity from nuclear fusion, or an explanation for what causes cancer.

- *The cost/benefit ratio never worked out.* This is why we don't have vacation hotels in orbit.

---

[281] Brooks, David, "The Sandra Bullock Trade," *New York Times*, March 30, 2010.

- *The future was overtaken by new technologies.* This is why automotive standard equipment does not include CB radios.

- *Bad experience inoculated us against the plan.* This is why there are so few new nuclear fission power plants.

- And most important:

- *Inventors fundamentally misunderstood human behavior.* This is why we have so few paperless offices.[282]

Predictions systematically ignore the possibility of the improbable outcome. People assume that what is unpredictable can be prevented with enough planning. Also, the organizational mindset places its bets on assuming that what is in place will continue. The Black Swan phenomenon is detailed by Nassim Nicholas Taleb in a book of that name.

> Contrary to social-science wisdom, almost no discovery, no technologies of note, came from design and planning—they were just Black Swans. The strategy for the discoveries and entrepreneurs is to rely less on top-down planning and focus on maximum tinkering and recognizing opportunities when they present themselves.[283]

Institutional blindness to Black Swans (improbable events) or deviations from expectations explains how easily companies can miss major changes that directly affect them. Aside from events being rather unpredictable, we do not read the signals well about what is coming because of our widely-held mental habits.

Distortions that Throw Plans off Course: (Taleb, but italics are mine)
a) *The illusion of understanding,* or how everyone thinks he knows what is going on in a world that is more complicated (random) than they realize;

b) *The retrospective distortion,* or how we can assess matters only after the fact, as if they were in a rearview mirror (history seems clearer and more organized in history books than in empirical reality); and

c) *The overvaluation of factual information* and the handicap of authoritative and learned people when they create categories.[284]

---

[282] Garreau, Joel, *Radical Evolution: The promise and peril of enhancing our minds, our bodies – and what it means to be human* (New York: Broadway Books, 2005), 211-2.
[283] Taleb, Nassim Nicholas, *The Black Swan: The impact of the highly improbable* (New York: Random House, 2007), *xxi*.
[284] *Ibid.*, 8.

Hanging on for Dear Life in Stormy Seas

When tried-and-true management approaches prove inadequate, or when projections fail to materialize, leaders are more open to considering other options. When on stormy seas, a different style of decision-making process is demanded.

The best way to get everybody behind significant change is for leadership to skillfully build a broad consensus for it. Such efforts are especially critical when a company is struggling. Difficult times often evoke a search for a "silver bullet" that will make the massive problems go away.

Some could argue that reliance on visionary methods is just another type of silver bullet. The stages of decline are identified by Jim Collins in *How the Mighty Fall*.

> **Five Stages of Decline:**
> Stage 1: Hubris born of success
> Stage 2: Undisciplined pursuit of more
> Stage 3: Denial of risk and peril
> Stage 4: Grasping for salvation
> Stage 5: Capitulation to irrelevance or death
>
> The longer a company remains in Stage 4, repeatedly grasping for silver bullets, the more likely it will spiral downward.... It's possible to skip a stage, although our research suggests that companies are likely to move through them in sequence. Some companies move quickly through the stages, while others languish for years, or even decades.[285]

By the time an institution is in serious decline, it often looks for new leadership or it is ready for something significantly different. However, the fact that they waited so long to change direction is a sign of weak leadership. Problems that bring a company down (or close to it) are usually complex and developed gradually, but they usually reflect slow-to-respond leadership, too. *How the Might Fall* also said:

> Betting big on an unproven technology, pinning hopes on an untested strategy, relying upon the success of a splashy new product, seeking a 'game changing' acquisition, gambling on an image makeover, hiring consultants who promise salvation, seeking a savior CEO, expounding the rhetoric of 'revolution,' or in its very late stages, grasping for a financial rescue or buyout. The key point is that they go for a quick, big solution or bold stroke to jump-start a recovery, rather than embark on the more pedestrian, arduous process of rebuilding long-term momentum.[286]

---

[285] Collis, Jim, *How the Mighty Fall: And why some companies never give in* (New York: Harper Collins, 2009), 22-3.
[286] *Ibid.*, 89.

Shifting the Business Model

This chapter and the next explore whether visionary leaders or organizations are sustainable. I am inclined to answer—not in their present hierarchical form. The old guard is losing the race in the market, in the quest for creative talent, in riding the tides of change. Even the concept of a defined business model may be out of date and too inflexible to correspond to the revolutionary forces that are altering the nature of commerce these days.

Organizations that can thrive in these circumstances, and for the long term, must be forward-looking, instead of hanging on to what they have always done, so they can respond to changing realities. Those companies able to accommodate the changing realities gain a competitive advantage. As Hugh McLeod insists, "All existing business models are wrong. Find a new one."

In *The Rise of the Creative Class*, Richard Florida details the significant shift in the work world toward those who drive the "creative economy."

> Workplaces are changing because the emphasis today is on creative work. And in the quest to elicit creativity, the typical workplace tends to become both more stressful and more caring. Stress increases because the Creative Economy is predicated on change and speed. If a firm is to survive it must always top what it did yesterday. The employees must be constantly coming up with new ideas; constantly finding faster, cheaper or better ways to do things—and that's not easy. It's brutally stressful. At the same time, the smart firm will do its best to attract valuable creative workers and give them what they need to be creative. The result could be called a 'caring sweatshop.'[287]

Another significant change comes with the digital reality that is redefining almost every industry. The very nature of what constitutes a product is up for debate, along with how and where the business is conducted. Nicholas Carr describes it in *The Big Switch*:

> Products are shedding their physical embodiments and turning into pure information, from money to plane tickets, to newspapers, to X-rays to blueprints to greeting cards to three-dimensional models. What's happening to goods is also happening to place. Many of the everyday interactions that used to have to take place in physical spaces—bank branches, business offices, schools, stores, libraries, theaters, even playgrounds—can now take place more efficiently in virtual spaces.
>
> The melding of the world of real things and places with the world of simulated things and places will only accelerate as the World Wide Computer becomes more powerful and as more devices are hooked up to it.[288]

---

[287] *Op. cit.*, Florida, 132.
[288] Carr, Nicholas, *The Big Switch: Rewiring the world, from Edison to Google* (New York: W.W. Norton & Company, 2008), 122-3.

Doing More with Less Structure

Organizational advantages of large size, massive investment, scores of employees, and being well established are now becoming major disadvantages. Size and tradition inhibit flexibility—which is vital. As the dynamics shift, tried-and-true methods are too slow to react promptly enough. The "or else" argument for innovation is made by Tom Kelley, founder of Ideo, as quoted by Daniel H. Pink in *Drive*:

> The ultimate freedom for creative groups is the freedom to experiment with new ideas. Some skeptics insist that innovation is expensive. In the long run, innovation is not expensive. In the long run, innovation is cheap. Mediocrity is expensive—and autonomy can be the antidote.[289]

In these days of rapid change, many traditional methods used for finding answers are too slow—dooming the non-nimble to miss the boat. Ross Perot, a major, and dissatisfied, stockholder of General Motors (GM) summed up corporate inefficiency and policies that defy prompt and appropriate action:

> The first [person] to see a snake kills it. At GM, the first thing you do is organize a committee on snakes. Then you bring in a consultant who knows a lot about snakes. Third thing you do is talk about it for a year.

What ails foundering companies and industries cannot be solved by playing "wait and see." Companies are hobbled by the limitations inherent in top-down control, along with allowing short-term profits to dictate decisions sure to have long-term impact.

At the same time, unprecedented forms of commerce and methods of communication are tapping into considerable creative output. Many are coming from the grass roots or the bottom up. The following is from Geoff Colvin in *Talent is Overrated*.

> As products and services live shorter lives, so do the business models of the companies that sell them. Time was when you could turn the crank on a good business model for thirty or forty years, and sometimes much longer.... But now we hear the startling sound of CEOs admitting publicly that their business models don't work anymore.[290]

The social structure of an organization defines its gatekeepers, its roles, its complicated rules, and an elaborate pecking order. But those methods are not working well—either at the top or at the bottom. Bureaucratic leaders are not responsive to signals they fail to see, comprehend, or have never seen before.

The most robust economic growth is mostly coming in enterprises that are using very different methods or a mix of new methods. These have largely abandoned

---

[289] Pink, Daniel H., *Drive: The surprising truth about what motivates us* (New York: Riverhead Books, 2009)
[290] *Op. cit.*, Colvin, 147.

many traditional management verities. The changing dynamic is explained by Don Tapscott and Anthony D. Williams in *Wikinomics*.

> The pace of change and the evolving demand of customers are such that firms can no longer depend only on internal capabilities to meet external needs. Nor can they depend only on tightly coupled relationships with a handful of business partners to keep up with customer desires for speed, innovation, and control. Instead, firms must engage and cocreate in a dynamic fashion with everyone—partners, competitors, education, government, and, most of all, customers.[291]

Ideas for new products and techniques are coming from product users themselves, those in the industry, and through loosely formed groups that lack customary business structures or incentives. Those who define the emerging trends are less and less the official media and talking heads. The ability to launch new trends is now more democratic, speeded up, and ubiquitous.

The traditional roles re flipped on their heads, as Jeff Howe explains in *Crowdsourcing*.

> If the means of production and distribution are now within the grasp of the individual, if the line between producers and consumers is blurring, where does that leave the 'firm,' the organizational structure that has governed how people make and deliver goods and services for over one hundred years? What constitutes an 'employee' or a 'manager' or 'president' in a crowdsourcing environment?[292]

Entrepreneurs as Visionaries

Americans respect inventiveness and boldness, considering those traits part of our national character and can-do philosophy. In its early years, the unexplored new country was defined by the pioneering spirit that rewards people for pushing past practical limits. We did not just conquer the geographic frontier in the move westward, but some of us continue to throw that same energy and resolve at any seemingly intractable problem.

The entrepreneurial spirit defines something uniquely American. It combines "going for broke" and thinking like the underdog in order to exploit some unexpected advantage. It capitalizes on whatever the situation presents (no wonder the system is called capitalism). Inventiveness is treated as an inalienable right—the chance for anyone to become a self-made man (or woman), or a maverick genius.

Often what they lacked in resources they made up in hustle and frantic do-or-die determination.

---

[291] Tapscott, Don and Williams, Anthony D., *Wikinomics: How mass collaboration changes everything* (New York: Portfolio, 2006), 18.
[292] Howe, Jeff, *Crowdsourcing: Why the power of the crowd is driving the future of business* (New York: Crown Business, 2008), 98.

They lacked money. They lacked know-how. They lacked connections. They lacked employees, advisors, partners. But could these ostensibly negative constraints have actually enhanced their ability to generate killer opportunities? Potentially. When you have no resources, you create them. When you have no choice but to fight, you right hard. When you have no choice but to create, you create … if the start-up doesn't hustle, it's game over. If you want to find out how resourceful you can be, shrink your budget. Moved your deadlines up. See how you cope. This may make you more resilient to actual hardships that arise.[293]

An entrepreneur can be a form of visionary who has strong financial motivation. Please note: "Entrepreneur" is not meant here as a synonym for the typical self-employed person, shop keeper, or small business owner. As used here, entrepreneurs introduce significant newness in products, services, or methods. They are groundbreakers.

With possible riches as the dangling carrot, many who have their own creative wrinkle are willing to start new enterprises. Michael Gerber argues:

> The entrepreneur is our visionary, the creator in each of us. We're born with that quality and it defines our lives as we respond to what we see, hear, feel, and experience. It is developed, nurtured, and given space to flourish or is squelched, thwarted, without air or stimulation, and dies.

Our confidence that anybody could make something so useful or clever that people have to buy it, do it, or throw their money at it is part of the American Dream. It is a version of our collective personal success story. That mindset accounts for the millions of inventions, start-ups, and small businesses that largely drive new jobs and the economy.

Most of them fail, but that does not stop people from trying — or trying again. In the process, they are becoming better mousetrap *makers* as well. Ray Smilor points to the dynamic nature of entrepreneurial change in *Daring Visionaries*

> In the first major national study on leadership skills of entrepreneurs conducted by the Center for Creative Leadership, the key predictor of success in entrepreneurial ventures was found to be the vision of the entrepreneur. More important than money, more critical than management, more essential than markets, vision is the driving and sustaining force that determines the growth and viability — the very life — of an entrepreneurial venture across all stages of development. The reverse is also true. Companies without vision collapse.[294]

---

[293] Hoffman, Reid and Casnocha, Ben, *The Start-up of You: Adapt to the future, invest in yourself, and transform your career* (New York: Crown Business, 2012), 167.
[294] Smilor, Ray, *Daring Visionaries: How entrepreneurs build companies, inspire allegiance, and create wealth* (Holbrook, MS: Adams Media Corp., 2001), 11.

> Entrepreneurs are, in fact, necessary subversives. Their penchant for change and their knack for pursuing opportunities creatively destroy existing systems and markets. But with this destruction comes remarkable vitality. By innovating, entrepreneurs launch new products and services, open new markets, and create real value that are essential for economic and social well-being.[295]

The market rewards those able to feed the voracious appetites for solutions and products that make life easier, better, or more enjoyable. Consequently, our system delivers a never-ending supply of "new and improved" products, and ever-better ways to do absolutely everything.

> Visionaries drive the high-tech industry because they see the potential for an 'order-of-magnitude' return on investment and willingly take high risks to pursue that goal. They will work with vendors who have little or no funding, with products that start life as little more than a diagram on a whiteboard, and with technology gurus who bear a disconcerting resemblance to Rasputin. They know they are going outside the mainstream, and they accept that as part of the price you pay when trying to leapfrog the competition.... As a buying group, visionaries are easy to sell but very hard to please. This is because they are buying a dream — which, to some degree, will always be a dream.[296]

The entrepreneurial mindset is relentlessly driven to find the next "mousetrap" that will "change everything." (Chapter 3) Entrepreneurial types are ever on the alert for the solution nobody has thought of — before them. Seth Godin said:

> As an entrepreneur, I'm blessed with 100% autonomy over task, time, technique and team. Here's the thing: If I maintain that autonomy, I fail. I fail to ship. I fail to excel. I fail to focus. I inevitably end up either with no product or a product the market rejects. The art of the art is picking your limits. That's the autonomy I must cherish. The freedom to pick my boundaries.
>
> We like to think opportunities lurk around each corner — and they do, for those astute enough to recognize them. This spirit drives a steady stream of new enterprises and individuals who are eager to take the long shots. Who hasn't seen some wildly successful discovery that grew out of a "crackpot idea" and thought "I could have done that"?

Bernard Girard debunks the risk-taker stereotype in *The Google Way*.

> Entrepreneurs are often depicted as heroes or adventurers, more willing to take risks than the average executive. That sounds romantic, but the image is pretty far from reality. In fact, successful entrepreneurs tend to be risk-averse and to take only a few, calculated risks.[297]

---

[295] *Ibid.*, 132.
[296] Moore, Geoffrey A., *Crossing the Chasm: Marketing and selling disruptive products to mainstream customers* (New York: Collins Business Essentials, 1999), 35.
[297] Girard, Bernard, *The Google Way: How one company is revolutionizing management as we know it* (San Francisco: No Starch Press, 2009), 24.

Entrepreneurs, who actually survive their high-stakes gamble, have found a way to marry innovation and execution. *That* is their singular accomplishment. Grounding a novel idea is tricky; grounding an idea that makes money—quite an achievement, indeed. And the successful ones do so with a strategy that is both adaptable and quick to change directions when the circumstances shift.

Geoffrey A. Moore describes their rush in *Crossing the Chasm*.

> [Visionaries are] in a hurry. They see the future in terms of window of opportunity, and they see those windows closing. As a result, they tend to exert deadline pressures—the carrot of a big payment or the stick of a penalty clause—to drive the project faster. This plays into the classic weaknesses of entrepreneurs—lust after the big score and over-confidence in their ability to execute within any given time frame.[298]

Some of those values and assumptions about our nation's exceptionalism and promise are under siege these days, along with the question about whether the American Dream is still achievable. I anticipate that its form is simply being redefined by current events; that there will always be an American Dream. It is part of our make-up and vision, but it looks different to each generation.

This is yet another area where new types of visionary guidance will be required to chart a different course in the near future. The trend toward grass-roots participation in finding novel solutions will be very much a part of where commerce is headed.

---

[298] *Op. cit.*, Moore, 37.

Chapter 15 - Building Supportive Environments

Leaders who want to encourage innovative thinking need to run interference for it. It is important to protect those most involved in developing the cash cows from getting bogged down in trivial or distracting matters.

Leadership that Encourages New Ideas

An innovative company does not necessarily sell high-tech or new-fangled products. An innovative leader at the top won't make the difference either, unless a certain level of flexibility permeates the organization. Innovation in the institutional setting is demonstrated by an openness to fresh approaches and an inclusiveness culture inviting different voices.

In *The Art of the Start,* Guy Kawasaki points to a key leadership skill needed to gain the respect of employees reluctant to push for innovative ideas.

> **Give Hope to the Hopeful**. Inside every corporate cynic who thinks that 'this company is too big to innovate' is an idealist who would like to see it happen. Good people in big companies are tired of being ignored, forgotten, humiliated, and forced into submission. They may be trampled, but they are not dead. When you show them that you're driving a stake in the heart of the status quo, you will attract support and resources. Then your goal is to advocate to these people, from wanting to see innovation happen to helping you make it happen.[299]

Protective support should extend to everyone drawing a company paycheck, irrespective of their job title. The world of work is changing so much that the motivational and personal concerns of employees have taken on greater relevance. Unless there is active encouragement for the brightest thinking, there won't be much of it. Removing company speed bumps is not just to benefit a few creative types, but rather supports a climate of greater flexibility across the board.

Belsky speaks to the need for systems that can encourage more creativity.

> The reality is that creative environments — and the creative psyche itself — are not conducive to organization. We become intolerant of procedures, restrictions, and process. Nevertheless, organization is the guiding force of productivity. If you want to make any ideas happen, you need to have a process for doing so.[300]

So the issue hinges on finding the proper balance between structure and initiative. This chapter considers some ways to nurture free-wheeling fresh thinking within an organizational setting. Chapter 14 explored how visionary

---

[299] Kawasaki, Guy, *The Art of the Start: The time-tested, battle-hardened guide for anyone starting anything* (New York: Penguin Group, 2004), 21.
[300] Belsky, Scott, *Making Ideas Happen: Overcoming the obstacles between vision and reality* (New York: Portfolio, 2010), 24.

thinking fares within the corporate culture. This chapter looks at environmental factors that foster creative output.

Leaders who want to encourage more innovative thinking need to run interference for it. They must protect the workers most involved in developing the cash cows from getting bogged down in trivial or distracting matters. The size of the system roadblocks are not the issue. The harm comes when the creatives or new thought progenitors are, by necessity, so mired in routine activities that they have little attention or energy to put into inspirational endeavors.

That need for protection extends to workers who are outspoken about what needs changing. Openness to criticism is a crucial aspect of building a setting where innovative approaches are encouraged. In *Whoever Makes the Most Mistakes Wins*, Richard Farson speaks up for the risk takers within an organization.

> Those who see what's obvious aren't necessarily brighter than others. They're just more likely to observe that the emperor is naked. Like children, they see what's actually there. Their perceptions are less clouded by belief systems, taboos, habits of thought. One responsibility of management—an important one—is to call attention to the invisible obvious, pointing it out as a child does (sometimes to the embarrassment of adults). Doing so also requires supporting employees who take that risk, too, and other risks as well.[301]

Factors that Stall Change or Growth in Organizations
- Inwardly focused cultures
- Paralyzing bureaucracy
- Parochial politics
- Low level of trust
- Lack of teamwork
- Arrogant attitudes
- Lack of leadership in middle management
- Fear of the unknown[302]

Getting Past Lip Service

Effective leadership depends on clear communication to rally the troops. But as with any form of persuasion, the message (or policy being proposed) is often less important than *the way it is delivered*—and with what spirit. Top-down organizations are better at giving orders than inviting feedback about the merit of them.

People are more likely to be influenced by messages that are simple, concrete, and credible—while touching them personally. Painting clear and specific

---

[301] Farson, Richard, *Whoever Makes the Most Mistakes Wins* (New York: Free Press, 2003), 6.
[302] Kotter, John P., *Leading Change* (Boston: Harvard Business School Press, 1996), 20.

verbal pictures about what is coming makes proposed goals more vivid and memorable. Also, the body language and enthusiasm of the person who explains it can make the message much more meaningful than an email. That provides the emotional component so necessary for others to get aboard. Kotter also said:

> Major change is usually impossible unless most employees are willing to help, often to the point of making short-term sacrifices. But people will not make sacrifices, even if they are unhappy with the status quo, unless they think the potential benefits of change are attractive and unless they really believe that a transformation is possible. Without credible communication, and a lot of it, employees' hearts and minds are never captured.... Most people won't go on the long march unless they see compelling evidence within six to eighteen months that the journey is producing expected results. Without short-term wins, too many employees give up or actively join the resistance.[303]

Encouraging people to speak up and risk rocking the boat, as appropriate, could improve the company from within. But such policies have to be sincere, with respect for unpopular opinions as well. Everyone up and down the organization is watching to see if there is sufficient will for leaders to deal with the hard questions. Before speaking up, employees need to see that management has reduced the risks of sticking one's neck out.

Building shared vision internalizes the process significantly.

> When a shared vision effort starts with personal vision, the organization becomes a tool for people's self-realization, rather than a machine they're subjected to. People begin to stop thinking of the organization as a thing to which they are subservient. Only then can they wholeheartedly participate in guiding its direction.[304]

The leadership shift is moving from command and control to collaboration and teamwork. Most of the power and rewards go to those at the top. Wider participation brings in all the messiness of workers injecting their own opinions, private lives, and preferences. To what extent does everyone under the company umbrella participate to some degree in making decisions? Is meaningful feedback welcome?

An institution is kept alive by organizing the efforts of many people who represent many different priorities and points of view. That diversity of opinions has considerable value in the hands of a leader who treats a broad scope of perspectives as an asset. Dee Hock said, "It is essential to employ, trust, and reward those whose perspective, ability, and judgment are radically different from yours. It is also rare, for it requires uncommon humility, tolerance, and wisdom."

---

[303] *Ibid.*, 9-11.
[304] Senge, Peter, Kleiner, Art, *et al., The Fifth Discipline Fieldbook: Strategies and tools for building a learning organization* (New York: Doubleday, 1994), 323.

One way a business can distinguish itself from competitors is by how willingly it breaks down some of the traditional institutional barriers in order to support the needs of workers, or to broaden participation in decision-making. It can also be compared on the basis of how protective it is of the *status quo,* at the expense of other influences or values.

Few at the top leave their lofty perch to work alongside the rank and file, or to take pains to find out what their unmet concerns are. The reality at the employee-level view is usually where problems show up first. Small and timely adjustments at that stage can prevent big problems down the road. Effective leaders lead by example and interaction throughout the organization, rather than by edict. Doing so keeps them on the pulse of their organization, as well as their industry and the larger economy.

Leadership through Fingertip Smarts

Front-line workers know particulars about the operation that leaders need to be aware of in order to make effective decisions. Timely and specific information is integral to Fingerprint Smarts or *fingerspitzengefühl* (described in Chapter 7) — the concept developed in Germany, a country that used to be engaged in frequent wars, whereby the general "feels" the up-to-the-moment conditions on the battlefront. Although he was removed by scope and physical distance from the action, communication from front-line soldiers informed the leader's logistical decisions.

Elements of Fingertip Smarts:
- Engages multiple perspectives at the same time
- Organizes disparate pieces into an integrated view
- Involves input of head, heart, and physical perceptions
- Includes up-to-the-minute updates
- Integrates multiple of kinds of knowing
- Takes action based on the combined, and integrated, information
- Relies on both specific and global levels of information

Fingertip Smarts involves a combination of the rational executive functions (mental), physical sensitivity (body), with both emotions and intuition (heart). Making decisions this way relies on the widest possible scope of input to form an overview that is highly responsive to changing conditions.

It supports a variable strategy, with constant tweaks of the dynamic elements in play. Given enough time and opportunities to keep making corrections, a variable strategy will consistently out-perform a fixed strategy. That's why current feedback is at a premium.

Many organizations that rely on top-down leadership alone insulate management from badly needed information or the latest updates. To reverse that, leaders and managers must develop additional lines of two-way communication to support Fingertip Smarts within the organization. That approach works well for mid-management or company departments too.

A fundamental difference between top-down management and some more-flexible organizational structures relates to the ways in which information is shared. Bureaucratic (top-down) institutions treat the head/leader as the brains of the organization, with information flowing down/out from there. That is in contrast to a grassroots style of organization, which is open to new or better ideas from anyone in the organization—or in the larger community. Fingertip Smarts information flows simultaneously to whoever can use it.

Fingertip Smarts can be humbling because the leader does not presume to know it all—or even be certain about which facts are more important. Leaders, along with the rest of their team, should take it as an article of faith that their best decisions depend somewhat on the quality of input coming from those on the front lines.

The ideal form is neither top-down nor bottom up, but information flowing smoothly in all directions. Fingertip Smarts embraces a holistic approach because every element (person in the organization) is interdependent, with crucial and open communication moving freely. That also makes for a more responsive and effective workplace.

A Different Kind of Worker

Getting Everyone on Board

Top-down institutional structures maintain power through executive control. Employees closer to the bottom are virtually powerless and expected to follow orders as given. They are at the bottom of the pecking order as well. But that organizational model is losing ground because it is too cumbersome and does not compete as effectively as it used to in the current business climate.

Some of those core principles are no longer valid, particularly those about how to treat employees. Organizations increasingly see the wisdom of permitting a greater flow of communication and responses (both up and down) and using cross-departmental teams. Their employees are involved in developing policies that impact their work, and in building a broader range of skills.

> For virtually every company, the scarce resource today is human ability. That is why companies are under unprecedented pressure to make sure that every employee is as highly developed as possible—and no one knows what the limits of development are.[305]

---

[305] Colvin, Geoff, *Talent is Overrated: What really separates world-class performance from everybody else* (New York: Penguin Group, 2008), 12.

Employees have their own motivations for doing their jobs, so they respond to different kinds of inducements and rewards. For some, work can be considered a job or a calling, not merely a way to earn a living.

In *The How of Happiness,* Sonja Lyubombirsky clarifies the three ways workers look at what they do.

> One fascinating study of workers found that people tend to see their work in one of three ways, as a job, as a career, or as a calling. Those who place their work in the job category essentially perceive it as a necessary evil, a means to an end—the job is needed to support them—and not as something positive or rewarding. Accordingly, they labor in order to have the money to enjoy their time away from work. By contrast, the career category is essentially a job with advancement. People who report having careers may not see their work as a major positive part of their lives, but they have opportunities or ambition for promotion. They invest more time and energy in their work because the opportunities they create for themselves may bring the rewards of higher social status, power, and self-esteem. Finally, those who see their work as a calling report enjoying working and find what they do to be fulfilling and socially useful. They work not for the financial rewards or for advancement, but because they want to; it is inseparable from the rest of their lives.[306]

Those who treat work as a personal calling will always be few in number and vulnerable to the conflicting pressures from the "it's just a job" mentality around them (which they do not share).

From the employer's point of view, those in the third group are more likely to care enough about what they do to stretch themselves. A calling is a form of personal vision, and when their own vision can be allied with the company's vision or purpose, something special could be at work.

Leaders who are most capable of building a shared vision are most likely to be able to inspire their entire workforce. The ideal organization is flexible enough to encourage workers to create *their own* ways of finding answers, solving routine difficulties, and providing feedback about what works, and what doesn't. Engaged workers keep learning *on* the job and *from* the job.

Peter Senge indicate how important the individual's vision is in *The Fifth Discipline Fieldbook.*

> It is increasingly clear that learning does not occur in any enduring fashion unless it is sparked by people's own ardent interest and curiosity. When the spark is not present, people compliantly accept training in a subject—statistical process control, executive development, or planning for reengineering.... On the other hand, if learning is related to a person's own vision, then that person will do whatever he or she can to keep learning alive.[307]

---

[306] Lyubombirsky, Sonja, *The How of Happiness: A scientific approach to getting the life you want* (New York: Penguin Group, 2007), 188.
[307] *Op. cit.*, Senge, 193.

Focusing on pay and benefits alone is misleading since much of what motivates workers is intangible. Surveys found that nine of the ten highly valued job factors are intrinsic (rewarding in their own right). These factors can and frequently do overlap.

What Employees Want

This list is from *The Rise of the Creative Class* by Richard Florida:

- *Challenge and responsibility* — being able to contribute and have impact; knowing that one's work makes a difference.
- *Flexibility* — a flexible schedule and a flexible work environment; the ability to shape one's work to some degree.
- *A stable work environment and a relatively secure job* — not lifetime security with mind-numbing sameness, but not a daily diet of chaos and uncertainty either.
- *Compensation* — especially base pay and core benefits; money you can count on.
- *Professional development* — the chance to learn and grow, to expand one's horizon for the future.
- *Peer recognition* — the chance to win the esteem and recognition of others in the know.
- *Stimulating colleagues and managers* — creative people like to be around other creative people, and they prefer leaders who neither micromanage nor ignore them.
- *Exciting job content* — the chance to work on projects and technologies that break new ground or pose interesting intellectual problems.
- *Organizational culture* — an elusive term that can include some factors already mentioned, plus more; perhaps best put for now as simply a culture in which the person feels at home, valued and supported.
- *Location and community*.[308]

Treat 'Em Right

Richard Florida documented a growing group of workers he called the "creative class" in his 2002 book, *The Rise of the Creative Class*. Members of this group create new ideas, new technologies, and new creative content. Florida estimates their number at 38,000,000, constituting more than 30 percent of the U.S. workforce.

Those in the creative class share common characteristics, such as creativity, individuality, wide diversity, and merit. Their priorities are having a profound influence on work and lifestyle issues. Unlike traditional employees, these workers expect to be treated as distinct individuals. Florida also said:

---

[308] Florida, Richard, *The Rise of the Creative Class: And how it's transforming work, leisure, community and everyday life* (New York: Basic Books, 2002), 91-2.

Creative work cannot be tailorized like rote work in the old factory or office, for several reasons. First, creative work is not repetitive. Second, because a lot of it goes on inside people's heads, you literally cannot see it happening — and you can't tailorize what you can't see. Finally, creative people tend to rebel at efforts to manage them overly systematically....

Peter Drucker captured it best when he said that knowledge workers do not respond to financial incentives, orders or negative sanctions the way blue-collar workers are expected to. I particularly like Drucker's observation that the key to motivating creative people is to teach them as 'de facto volunteers,' tied to the firm by commitment to its aims and purposes, and often expecting to participate in its administration and its governance. 'What motivates knowledge workers,' writes Drucker, 'is what motivates volunteers. Volunteers, we know, have to get more satisfaction from their work than paid employees precisely because they do not get a paycheck.'[309]

A True Story

Years ago, when I was between careers, I had a low-level desk job with a large national company. I took my job seriously enough to apply myself to streamline each step of a paper-shuffling procedure that was a main job function. I was pleased with how efficient I was able to get the sequence of steps, especially compared with about twenty others doing a nearly identical job. I couldn't wait to be noticed and have a chance to explain how smoothly the procedure could be done.

I got noticed all right. Several weeks later, I was called into the supervisor's office. Without any preamble or pleasantries, she announced: "We can't figure out what you're doing wrong. But nobody would be able to complete the amount of work you do. So you must be doing something wrong. We are going to let you go."

I was shocked and surprised — not just to be fired, but the reason for it. Doing too much?! There was no desire to know how the level of performance, which they were obviously measuring, could be increased that significantly. To depart from the usual pace of output was evidence that my work must have been flawed. Even though my completed work was not subpar, in any way the supervisors could tell, I had deviated from the norm, so I had to go.

The experience was puzzling to me at the time because there was no discussion. The supervisor had no curiosity about anything I might have to say that might have been useful in saving time or money for the company, or in my defense. I was dismissed in both senses of the term.

As I left the building that day, one message blared loud and clear for me: "You do not belong here." As a professional who has proven myself in high-stakes

---

[309] *Ibid.*, 133.

arenas, this didn't make me doubt myself or my ability. But it did remind me that none of my "good stuff" was of value in such a workplace.

This is a small example of why it is so hard for creative or challenge-driven individuals to flourish in large, impersonal settings. While I have had some really good jobs and careers over my life, that experience further reminded me why I feel I must work for myself—in ways that capitalize on my talents.

Communication Goes Both Ways

Corporate communication about where the company is headed works best when accompanied by the kind of give-and-take discussion that could engender enthusiasm and encourage buy-in. Those who get to contribute to crafting a policy feel they have a greater stake in its success.

Building enthusiasm builds on the intangible energy of a person who also sends emotional signals. Charles G. Sigismund discusses that in *Champions of Silicon Valley*.

> Visions are best communicated and kept alive orally. Oral communication, rather than the fixed words of vision statements, matches the organic—living, breathing, changing, adapting—and the contextual nature of vision itself. Writing is a useful and often necessary exercise, but it can't take the place of face-to-face communication.[310]

Involving workers more fully can allow them to define the tactics that use their particular abilities most intelligently. This approach depends on seeing workers as complex individuals, not as interchangeable parts. Employees who feel included and respected might also feel a desire to take more responsibility for keeping goals they like on track. At the very least, unworkable methods show up *before* they doom the "best laid plans."

Of course, the form and intent of the communication is very different when the goal is compliance or to prompt workers to make judgment calls (applying their own wisdom). That distinction is fundamentally related to the way the organization views those who work for it. The difference is not so much about the skill level of the worker as the amount of respect given to him or her.

Genuine communication relies on respect. One of the fundamental changes afoot (Chapter 18) is in the ways people are standing up and demanding they be respected. This is not just a front-burner concern at work or in politics, but that desire is also altering every kind of organization or personal relationship.

Building Two-way Trust Is Smart

When employees feel their opinions are respected, they are more likely to involve their hands, hearts, and minds in achieving even more than the job

---

[310] Sigismund, Charles G., *Champions of Silicon Valley: Visionary thinking from today's technology pioneers* (New York: John Wiley & Sons, Inc., 2000), 4.

requires. When wide participation is encouraged, every member of the team gets to feel valued as a problem solver within his or her sphere.

How widely shared decision-making and authority permeate an organization reflect the amount of trust placed in those outside of the executive ranks. There is a smart way of extending trust, which serves the organization and all staff levels. Simply put, as Ernest Hemingway said, "The best way to find out if you can trust somebody is to trust them."

Trust, and mainly the lack of it, is communicated very clearly by the layers of controls and safeguards that make it clear to workers how little real authority they actually have. What types of decisions are employees permitted to exercise on their own without supervision? Is management there to assist employees to do a better job, or to tie their hands?

Smart Trust is described by Stephen M. R. Covey in *The Speed of Trust*. Learning how to extend 'Smart Trust' is a function of two factors—propensity to trust and analysis.

> Propensity to Trust is primarily a matter of the heart. It's the tendency, inclination, or predisposition to believe that people are worthy of trust and a desire to extend it to them freely.
>
> Analysis is primarily a matter of the mind. It's the ability to analyze, evaluate, theorize, consider implications and possibilities, and come up with logical decisions and solutions.[311]
>
> Trust brings out the best in people and literally changes the dynamics of interaction. While it is true that a few abuse this trust, the vast, vast majority of people do not abuse it, but respond amazingly well to it. And when they do, they don't need external supervision, control, or the 'carrot and stick' approach to motivation. They are inspired. They run with the trust they were extended. They want to live up to it. They want to give back.[312]

Many companies try to treat workers as though they're "fungible." That term means that similar things are mutually interchangeable, as a ton of iron is "fungible," no matter where it comes from. While that works for commodities, it does not work for people. Moreover, creative class workers refuse to stay in settings that treat them that way.

The various forms of communication within a company can be compared on the basis of how much of it leans toward Rules Talk or toward Wisdom Talk. The distinction is spelled out in *Practical Wisdom* by Barry Schwartz and Kenneth Sharpe.

---

[311] Covey, Stephen M. R., *The Speed of Trust: The one thing that changes everything* (New York: Free Press, 2006), 289.
[312] *Ibid.*, 319.

In a way it's not surprising that Ethics Talk is Rules Talk and not Wisdom Talk. Practical wisdom seems to be a slippery thing. It lives in a gray world, not a black-and-white one. It is context dependent. You can just hand someone a set

> of rules to follow, but wisdom must be nurtured by experience. And when people who are unwise are given the discretion to 'use their judgment,' the results can be disastrous.... But rules are never enough. We blind ourselves by locking our public conversation into Rules Talk. Rules Talk needs to be supplemented with Wisdom Talk.... Rules Talk sidelines, or even labels as dangerous, moral imagination and emotion. Wisdom Talk puts them at the center because they allow us to see and understand what needs to be seen and understood.... Rules Talk marginalizes the importance of character traits like courage, patience, determination, self-control, and kindness. Wisdom Talk puts them at the center.[313]

The Human Equation

Finding Solutions from Crossing Boundaries

Industries and organizations are being forced to change faster and more dramatically than anyone could have imagined. But demand for change is happening on the individual level as well. People are discovering they must develop additional ways to leverage their personal and professional skills to their best advantage in the work world—beyond fitting into a prescribed job description.

Daniel H. Pink has been writing about the evolving nature of work. In *A Whole New Mind*, he introduces the notion of boundary crossers.

> What's the most prevalent, and perhaps most important, prefix of our times? Multi. Our jobs require multitasking. Our communities are multicultural. Our entertainment is multimedia. While detailed knowledge of a single area once guaranteed success, today the top rewards go to those who can operate with equal aplomb in starkly different realms. I call these people 'boundary crossers.' They develop expertise in multiple spheres, they speak different languages, and they find joy in the rich variety of human experience. They live multi lives—because that's more interesting and, nowadays, more effective.[314]

The most motivated and flexible individuals are *making their own opportunities*. Doing only one thing well at work is not the golden ticket it once was. Also, more people are opting not to be employees for a host of reasons (not all of their choosing). Some are discovering imaginative new ways to employ their talents, and earn a living, outside of traditional employment.

---

[313] Schwartz, Barry and Sharpe, Kenneth, *Practical Wisdom: The right way to do the right thing* (New York: Riverhead Books, 2010), 44-5.
[314] Pink, Daniel H., *A Whole New Mind: Why right-brainers will rule the future* (New York: Riverhead Books, 2005), 134.

That is raising the bar about what skills are essential, like improved computer literacy. Even the concept of job skills points to the ever-increasing levels of performance required. Demand for job skills based on complex thinking and judgment are increasing, while those based on physical labor or repetitious activities are decreasing.

The abysmal unemployment level these days is expediting this trend away from static workplace abilities. Employed or unemployed, people are seeing they must take greater responsibility for staying informed about the changing need for what they might be able to offer. They must keep upgrading what they know and can do.

Even if the number of unemployed workers returns to "acceptable" levels, workers have less trust toward employers who treat them as "disposable," and more incentive to choose their work environments carefully. In a *New York Times* article (October 20, 2009), Thomas Friedman describes "The New Untouchables."

> Those who are waiting for this recession to end so someone can again hand them work could have a long wait. Those with the imagination to make themselves untouchables — to invent smarter ways to do old jobs, energy-saving ways to provide new services, new ways to attract old customers or new ways to combine existing technologies — will thrive.[315]

Cross-pollination of abilities has become more frequent within organizations of all sizes. But it is even more in evidence outside of corporate America. That approach is leveling the playing field — whether related to novel products, ideas, methods, or worker expectations.

The ability to surmount obstacles (including institutional ones) as a boundary crosser is a personal capacity, that someone takes with them wherever they work — or with whatever kind of "mousetrap" they build. Employers cannot retain such high-value employees unless they provide a workplace that includes what those workers desire.

Institutions that want to hire or retain the loyalty of individuals capable of crossing boundaries will have to allow them more creative license. Such workers have other professional choices — and more all the time. Pink also said:

> Boundary crossers reject either/or choices and seek multiple options and blended solutions. They lead hyphenated lives filled with hyphenated jobs and enlivened by hyphenated identities.... They help explain the growing ranks of college students with double majors — and the proliferation of academic departments that dub themselves 'interdisciplinary.'[316]

---

[315] Friedman, Thomas, "The New Untouchables," *New York Times*, October 20, 2009.
[316] *Op. cit.*, Pink, 36.

Welcoming the Human Side

People are equipped with two somewhat independent approaches that they use in making choices or in deciding what is important. One is rational; the other is gut level and emotional. When these two approaches are working together or toward a shared goal, change can come quickly and easily. When the two approaches are not able to pull in tandem, change (or any major decision), can be very hard to come by.

Rational approaches are thoughtful and logical, whereas emotional approaches are more impulsive and instinctual. The two really operate differently, but under ideal conditions they complement and reinforce each other. Environments that encourage cooperation between these approaches need to recognize they each bring valid aspects to operations and the change process. Ignoring either head or heart will not remove their influence, just make it more covert and strident.

It doesn't work to simply pick one approach, insist on it, and expect the other modes to knuckle under. The mental-only approach that has dominated the business world is not able to operate as before. More recently, collaborative methods are righting the balance between head and heart in the workplace. Combined approaches also produce better outcomes than previous one-size-fits-all strategies. Official plans and revenue generation matter, but they are not *all that matter*.

One of the challenges for anyone working within a large organization, whatever their role, is to find ways to avoid institutional pressures that reward inertia or dinosaur thinking. Job satisfaction is too important to emotional and physical health for a person to ignore company practices that are ineffective and draining.

Employers who provide greater respect and flexibility in the workplace tend to have a higher ratio of people who "give a damn." Their motivation is not solely about money or having a job. Forward-looking institutions are also paying more attention to heart-based or intuitive concerns that such individuals prefer.

Two examples of adaptation are Corporate Mystics and Canny Outlaws. Of course, these are but two strategies whereby those within the organization are able to serve a higher good despite the straightjacket of official policies.

Enter the Corporate Mystics
In *The Corporate Mystics*, Gay Hendricks and Kate Ludeman defined a style of business leadership that involves emotions and spiritual priorities as well as profits (and they are not alone in that). Corporate mystics live life from a spiritual base. "They are in business for their hearts and souls as well as their

wallets. They are in business to support the hearts and souls of the people with whom they work."[317]

> [Hendricks said] From working with eight hundred executives over the past twenty-five years we make a prediction: Successful corporate leaders of the twenty-first century will be spiritual leaders. They will be comfortable with their own spirituality, and they will know how to nurture spiritual development in others. The most successful leaders of today have already
>
> learned this secret. Corporate mystics know that an organization is a collective embodiment of spirit, the sum total of the spirits of the individuals who work there. Those who think spirituality has no place in business are selling themselves and those around them short.[318]

Corporate mystics are committed to self-knowledge, which they gain in three ways. "They acknowledge and appreciate their emotions without dramatizing their feelings. They understand their programming from the past and are less likely to be blindsided by it. They are open to feedback, even when expressed as criticism."[319]

Those Who Are Corporate Mystics Draw upon These Principles:
- Strong connection with their intuition and know how to use it when it counts
- Operate on a base of integrity
- Pursue their visions with passion and compassion
- Evoke the full potential of those with whom they come in contact

Hendricks also said:

> [They] have a gift for engaging people in big dreams. They can stand in a future that does not exist and map out the details of how to get there. At the same time they can look steadily at right-now reality. Many [of these] people have a grasp of the nuts-and-bolts reality of the moment. They can look at the way things are and not flinchingly. On the other end of the spectrum, there are also people who can see the possibilities on the horizon. But often these two skills—keen distant vision and equally keen up-close focus—do not come in the same package. In corporate mystics they do. One of the striking characteristics of the mystics we've met is their comfort with this two-fold vision.
>
> Two-fold vision also includes the ability to focus on the separateness and the way everything is woven together.... Decisions made from this sense of wholeness tend to be sound and fair.[320]

---

[317] Hendricks, Gay and Ludeman, Kate, *The Corporate Mystic: A guidebook for visionaries with their feet on the ground* (New York: Bantam Books, 1996), xix.
[318] *Ibid.*, xviii.
[319] *Ibid.*, 6-7.
[320] *Ibid.*, 17.

Canny Outlaws Subvert Unbending Structure

In *Practical Wisdom,* Barry Schwartz argues that the workplace routinely compromises the imagination, empathy and courage of those who work there. In many fields there has been a movement to institute more and more rules and incentives in order to improve performance and bolster the bottom line. This led to the undesirable unintended consequences of constraining decision-making and corrupting people who work in these fields.

Institutions structured around traditional incentives and punishments tend to prevent people from working with purpose, empathy, creativity, flexibility, and engagement. Schwartz identified a group of individuals who undermine official limitations that he called "canny outlaws." Such canny outlaws exercise a measure of wisdom within organizations known to actively discourage initiative.

When too many rules and counterintuitive restrictions get in the way, there is little opportunity for workers to exercise their best judgment. Bringing values to bear at work combines expertise and compassion, which leads to them using greater wisdom.

Schwartz and Sharp argue for combining autonomy, mastery and purpose, so the needs of all those who work in a company are supported.

> There are legions of 'canny outlaws' who struggle to find ways to exercise wisdom within organizations that actively discourage it. And there are growing ranks of system changers who have been able to reform the way institutions are run—how practitioners are trained and how they practice—in ways that nurture and sustain wisdom rather than destroy it.[321]

> We all benefit from canny outlaws who have the moral will and skill to practice well, despite the formidable pressures assembled against them: the stress of time restrictions; the constraints of rigid rules and standardized scripts; the impediments of specialization and efficiency that drain them of empathy; the pressure of incentives that lure them to do the wrong thing. It can take courage and a streak of obstinacy to be a canny outlaw. And it not only takes wisdom to do the right thing. It also takes wisdom, including a certain shrewdness, to know how to carve out a space that enables you to practice well without threatening your job. But being a canny outlaw is arduous, and sometimes precarious....

> A professional, no matter how dedicated, can't avoid the business of making money. Decisions have to be made within financial constraints. Even the canny outlaws are frequently challenged to balance dollars and devotion. They must balance matters of money and time with what's good for their patients or clients.... [Professionals] are challenged to find the balance between commitment to doing things that are true to the 'soul' of their profession and

---

[321] *Op. cit.*, Schwartz, 10-11.

willingness to do things that keep their institutions alive and afloat. The wisdom to find the right balance demands skill *and* will.[322]

Although we are grateful when we find them, canny outlaws are not enough. We cannot rely on people doing the right thing in spite of the institutional structures in which they work. What we want is institutions that encourage the skill and the will to do the right thing.... These system changers are building institutions that encourage practitioners to develop practical wisdom instead of draining it from them.... These system changers — or system builders — are not focused on serving individuals on one as many practitioners are; they are not trying to balance competing principles or to interpret a rule or to figure out how to craft an action in a particular case. They need the wisdom to craft organizations that encourage others to learn to act wisely; they need the wisdom to formulate new procedures, create new curricula, and teach teams of colleagues how to support one another. Their aim is to structure practices that give people wisdom-inducing instead of wisdom-draining experiences.[323]

The message is getting through to some organizations that workers are not faceless commodities. The workplace must respond to the human side and uniqueness of those who work there. Global trends toward outsourcing, distressing economic realities, and a steady stream of technological marvels have attempted to displace the importance of workers — or homogenize them.

As a culture, we cannot afford to treat people as a commodity, and to do so erases the real competitive advantage that any organization has. The real bottom line, that cannot be over-emphasized, is that organizations will get nowhere until human beings are more inspired by relating gracefully to other human beings. There is more to each person than what they do, or create, or achieve as individuals. The in-coming paradigm takes that into account more.

However, framing the issues as a conflict between individuals and the structure, or between workers and management, or even between creative types and the rest of the workforce represents old thinking (and is itself part of the problem). The structure of organizations may be slow to shift, but workers are migrating away from companies that do not catch on.

As the brightest move to the geographic areas and work environments that support what they are looking for, the potential advantages that flow from leading-edge thinking and products go with them.

---

[322] *Ibid.*, 197-8.
[323] *Ibid.*, 213.

Technology Changes the Game Plan
Collaboration and the Internet Collapse Structural Limits

A recent development that is making the world smaller for us all comes from us being connected up essentially all the time—whether by cell phone, email, text messages, or however we get our news or entertainment. Being so connected means a person is almost never functioning separately or out of touch.

That has effectively removed almost all demographic or geographic barriers to participation in numerous larger communities. That permits even the smallest, most marginalized point of view to get organized and "find its people." We are not just linked, but hyper-linked.

The nature of collaboration has been widening with the ever-increasing role the Internet plays in so many of our lives. Improved and instantaneous forms of communication are dismantling almost every barrier to group effort—or to finding world-shaking answers that were previously considered impossible. We are witnessing a change in the way individuals pool their skills for a common purpose.

In *Here Comes Everybody,* Clay Shirky points to how online developments permit more effective collaboration.

> The phones and computers, the e-mail and instant messages, and the webpages, are manifestations of a more fundamental shift. We now have communications tools that are flexible enough to match our social capabilities, and we are witnessing the rise of new ways of coordinating action that take advantage of that change. These communications tools have been given many names, all variations on a theme: 'social software,' 'social media,' 'social computing,' and so on. Though there are some distinctions between these labels, the core idea is the same: we are living in the middle of a remarkable increase in our ability to share, to cooperate with one another, and to make collective organizations. Though many of these social tools were first adopted by computer scientists and workers in high-tech industries, they have spread beyond academic and corporate settings. The effects are going to be far widespread and momentous....
>
> By making it easier for groups to self-assemble and for individuals to contribute to group effort without requiring formal management (and its attendant overhead), these tools have radically altered the old limits on the size, sophistication, and scope of unsupervised effort.[324]

Increasingly, novel developments are happening outside of corporate America, and many of the methods being used have little in common with traditional business practices. New kinds of groups and pioneering forms of interaction

---

[324] Shirky, Clay, *Here Comes Everybody: The power of organizing without organizations* (New York: Penguin Press, 2008), 20-21.

herald the emergence of the non-organization. Much of this pooling of talents, coupled with the serious interests of the participants, grows from self-directed individuals who voluntarily connect because of a shared vision or purpose.

The scope of individuals involved can span the globe—as Bernard Girard said in *The Google Way*.

> [As] the time between the release of new products and the appearance of direct competition has decreased dramatically, the cost of innovation, including research and development (R&D), has only increased. In fact, in the 30 years between 1958 and 1988, these costs increased sevenfold in the United States.[325]

These new interactive models are also collapsing many of the customary costs and timeframes in the product development process. At the same time, higher quality products are possible because corrections and upgrades happen so much faster.

Individuals are involving themselves in new forms of groups, with very different purposes and incentives than before. Voluntary group participation could be the most powerful tool or trend currently remaking organizations. And since some use capable volunteers (like open source projects), labor costs are minimal.

On profit-based projects, most of (or a significantly larger portion of) the gains are going to those individuals ahead of the curve. Nicholas Carr makes that case in *The Big Switch*.

> There's a natural tendency, and a natural desire, to see the Internet as a leveling force, one that creates a fairer, more democratic society, where economic opportunities and rewards are spread widely among the many rather than held narrowly by the few.... But the reality may be very different. [Quoting from Chris Anderson in The Long Tail] 'millions of ordinary people [now] have the tools and role models to become amateur producers. Some of them will also have talent and vision. Because the means of production have spread so widely and to so many people, the talented and visionary ones, even if they're a small fraction of the total, are becoming a force to be reckoned with.' This is not, as it might first appear, a vision of a world of economic egalitarianism. It's a vision of a world in which more and more of the wealth produced by markets is likely to be funneled to a 'small fraction' of particularly talented individuals.[326]

Money considerations are not decisive in choosing which ideas are supported or go forward, as was the norm in traditional businesses. Difficulties with funding, or speed of becoming profitable, do not necessarily pre-qualify which ones get a chance. Those who get involved are tackling some of the major problems like starvation and illiteracy.

---

[325] Girard, Bernard, *The Google Way: How one company is revolutionizing management as we know it* (San Francisco: No Starch Press, 2009), 76-7.
[326] Carr, Nicholas, *The Big Switch: Rewiring the world, from Edison to Google* (New York: W.W. Norton & Company, 2008), 146-7.

Aside from whether participants are paid in money or not, they enjoy the satisfaction of solving worthy problems of interest to them. That includes the secondary rewards from figuring out how to circumvent obstacles and finding additional ways to use their skills. The social reward that comes from involvement with like-minded individuals is an added bonus. It all hinges on new group dynamics, as Carr points out.

> Tools that provide simple ways of creating groups lead to new groups, lots of new groups, and not just more groups but more kinds of groups.... When desire is high and costs have collapsed, the number of such groups is skyrocketing, and the kinds of effects they are having on the world are spreading.... The difficulties that kept self-assembled groups from working together are shrinking, meaning that the number and kinds of things groups can get done without financial motivation or managerial oversight are growing. The current change, in one sentence, is this: most of the barriers to group action have collapsed, and without those barriers, we are free to explore new ways of gathering together and getting things done.[327]

Significant innovation is seldom a singular event by a single visionary. There is instead an intense and brief window of time when there occurs concomitant explosions by several visionaries, seemingly at once. They present a constellation of various strengths that permit the development phases from energy (idea) to matter (product or practice) to be condensed into what seems like an instant. And usually only one person gets the credit.

This was precisely the same phenomenon that occurred when television appeared on the scene. There is much debate to this day about who really "invented" it when in fact there were three inventor/scientists with different strengths and approaches who popped the theory into matter within one year of each other. And the truth is that television as we know it today would not exist without the contributions of all three.

Some of the uncertainty and economic unrest that is widespread in modern America has put the brakes on various business activities. The forces are regrouping and the trajectory of growth may shift, but these changes are reflecting the changing economic realities. Any equation about the future of the economy or what the workplace holds must reckon with the ways technology accelerates change. In *The Great Reset*, Richard Florida explains the apparent ebb and flow of creative solutions.

> Innovation [ideas or products] do not slow down during crises, but because the economy is depressed, they tend to accumulate and bunch up. They then come bursting forward as the economy recovers.... 'Entrepreneurs keep on waiting to produce new things [so] that there's an accumulation of as-yet-unexploited new ideas that keeps mounting up....

---

[327] *Op. cit.*, Shirky, 20-22.

> Things can get only so bad. People want to eat, so at some point they resist further cuts to their consumption—it's not a bottomless pit. There's a rocking stockpile, a mound of fuel developing, to power new projects and new investment activity.... A lot of new projects are being deferred because of uncertainty, but as the downward spiral peters out the uncertainty will wane.[328]

During this lull these days, which is much more extensive than the economy or commerce, a thinning out is occurring. The tried-and-true and just-hanging-on notions are dropping, being replaced by more farsighted practices and ideas. Bottom line: after this lull there are going to be many new and different faces and ideas in the forefront.

While the Internet has accelerated many of the trends regarding commerce and bringing people with shared interests and abilities together, it cannot account for many of the ways it is used. It is a tool, a vehicle without any guiding principles of its own. So it speeds up and simplifies tasks, but it is amoral. It is crucial that our best judgment and values be at the helm.

> The Internet turns everything from news-gathering to community-building, into a series of tiny transactions—expressed mainly through clicks on links—that are simple in isolation yet extraordinarily complicated in the aggregate. Each of us may make hundreds or even thousands of clicks a day, some deliberately, some impulsively, and with each one we are constructing our identity, shaping our influences, and creating our communities.... We're still a long way from knowing where our clicks will lead us. When it's clear that two of the hopes most dear to the Internet optimists—that the Web will create a more bountiful culture and that it will promote greater harmony and understanding—it should be treated with skepticism. Cultural impoverishment and social fragmentation seem equally likely outcomes.[329]

Trends and Meta Environments
Reading the Signals about What Is Forming

We are on the watch for what is around the corner and still unsure about what direction it will take. Some aspects of a developing paradigm shift are discussed in Chapter 18. Whatever is coming into focus is still only a very weak signal, so it is much too early to tell what the trends add up to. But it is *not* too early for each of us to act in accordance with what you *would like it to be*. That is one way to increase its likelihood to prevail.

Since so much of what is familiar has lost ground, most of us have less confidence in our interpretation of events. They must be constantly adjusted as the signals become increasingly coherent. Sorting out meaningful signal from

---

[328] Florida, Richard, *The Great Reset: How new ways of living and working drive post-crash prosperity* (New York: Harper, 2010), 12.
[329] *Op. cit.*, Carr, 166-7.

noise is tricky. Because people aren't sure, they have to ask others, "Do you see it too? Am I picking up something meaningful?" But gradually two things happen:

Signal and Noise:
- Certain signals get louder and we have less difficulty spotting them or making sense of them. They increasingly build on each other and reinforce a coherent pattern.
- The person becomes more adept at spotting the significant patterns and relationships across environments, so can begin to act on them.

Over time, each person begins developing their own multiple frames of reference and learns to shift among them as appropriate: (1) the close and individual view, (2) the context and wider-perspective view, and (3) the impersonal and cosmic view — almost godlike in scope.

And all of that broadening of scopes reflects an expanding faculty in reading increasingly meaningful signals. However, the individual view is the default, and the individual must make conscious effort to spend much time in the other two modes. There's a pay-off in greater judgment and effortlessness. Doing that also reflects more inner maturity.

Thinking Bigger than the Organizational Level

We are in need of different collaborative models and different ways of framing the most pressing issues. New developments must be integrated into the social fabric if they are to be helpful. Most organizations and institutions should take advantage of more creative, grassroots approaches as they assert themselves.

Somewhere in the mix of new solutions, we must also develop revenue models that can accommodate and reward participants, when appropriate. Now, much of the impetus to take action or toward change is volunteer-based. But if collaborative methods are replacing the business model, some different calculus of value-versus-rewards must develop.

One factor rushing to the forefront of change (and sometimes even driving it) is the lowly grassroots approach. Those often-underestimated efforts are asserting substantial strength as they take on the establishment from the bottom up, and from the outside. "Grassroots" efforts are the most basic level of organized activity.

Such activities are usually close to home, start small, and are local in scope. Grassroots efforts have long been the bottom of the political pyramid or power pecking order. But that is less the case as various grassroots ideas and groups are asserting their power.

Consider the contrast between blades of grass and large, sturdy trees. Grass is simple, small, and maximally flexible. When things are done at the grassroots level there is an economy of resources and effort. The term suggests being the opposite of "the establishment." It also refers to bottom-up change due to the shift in attitudes by many people. Organizations and governments may come to support those ideas in time, but they didn't start from there (or get imposed officially).

Grass Roots
William James

> I am done with great things and big plans, great institutions and big successes. I am for those tiny, invisible loving human forces that work from individual to individual, creeping through the crannies of the world like so many rootlets, or like the capillary oozing of water, yet which, if given time, will rend the hardest monuments of human pride.

If we consider the largest environment that affects each of us, that would be the whole world. Influences that make us act are no longer only those close to home. Through the 24-hour news cycle, online access, and interactive media, we are plugged into whatever happens anywhere. It is inescapable. (See Chapter 9.)

This "real time" connectedness means that things move faster and change is nonstop. A particular organization cannot be considered a separate entity within a separate industry, country, or marketplace. Even national boundaries or huge distances are little more than speed bumps in the pell-mell expansion of our connectedness. And similar acceleration is underway in every aspect of our lives.

Often, being able to accomplish something worthwhile is not merely a willingness to do what is required, but to grapple with the numerous obstacles that are blocking action. Those exist at different scales and in many different contexts. Major or minor, they all need attending to, as they assert themselves in our way.

That is a large component of grounding; and it is also a significant portion of the 99% perspiration part of the innovation process. Being plugged into the world also means being compelled to consider the obstacles from far-off places too.

Frances Moore Lappé has been a leading proponent of grass0roots activities to save our planet. She speaks to the vital mindset rooted in engaged passion in *Getting a Grip2*.

> Local versus national versus global—this frame gets us nowhere. Rules of our economy and of politics set nationally and globally, now divide and disempower people locally. Yet many of us will become convinced that these rules can be made fair only as we experience change right in our own communities. So there is no chicken or egg—all have to be happening at once.

And are. The real question is not about the level of our engagement, but whether our choices fire our passions and reverse the Spiral of Powerlessness for ourselves and others.[330]

John Doerr, a venture capitalist who backed Google, Amazon, and Netscape, does not see much being done on a big scale by solitary individuals. He said, "It requires whole ecosystems." That is beyond the range of a single individual or organization, but evokes better ways to work together. It calls for new companies, systems, and alliances — as well as whole new industries.

Looking at the quality of our supportive (or inhibiting) environments gets us one step closer to understanding how the ecosystems involved can be improved and grounded.

Even if radically new breakthroughs and technologies are discovered, it would still be an enormous task for all the related components in the ecosystem to match pace. Entire industries would have to commit to building the needed infrastructure, including new standards, or scaling up of manufacturing systems for "the next big thing."

In truth, the real "next really big thing" is the quality of life we are in the process of making — or remaking collectively. And in it, commerce plays a less dominant role.

Matching Grassroots Growth and Regulations

The hardest obstacles to resolve in developing grassroots projects or breakthrough technologies should not be the regulatory ones. One expects clear sailing once the planners, scientists, and engineers figure out how something groundbreaking can be done. Laws and governmental requirements inhibit many kinds of grassroots or truly original developments.

Old standards and regulations that have not kept pace can easily inflict a stranglehold on truly innovative approaches. What is newest is usually outside of what is permitted (or mandated), or is in a form that doesn't comply with existing methods. Organizations and bureaucratic agencies are slow to respond to fast-moving trends. The laws on the books often make many kinds of growth even more difficult.

Almost all laws and regulations were framed at a time when many of the current (let alone future) conditions were not yet thought of. They act as a drag on experimentation with new approaches in a wide variety of ways. Rules are usually reactive and backward looking, so they do not address the issues that progress brings until long after the fact.

---

[330] Lappé, Frances Moore, *Getting a Grip2: Clarity, creativity, and courage for the world we really want* (Cambridge, MA: Small Planet Media, 2007 and 2010), 113.

For instance, the regulatory framework does not provide for developments like electronic rights for books, or the bandwidth required for electronic devices. And such strangleholds are hurting us now.

As an example, patent laws to protect original discoveries today (and on a global scale) are woefully behind the times, as is the current thinking on many of these matters. Where is the balance between rewarding inventors for original discoveries and walling off vast fertile fields of exploration from possible discoveries yet to come?

> We are entering an age of innovative transactions, collaborative transactions, crowd transactions, micro-transactions, sharing transactions—transactions that the legal field hasn't caught up with, like: Bartering. Sharing. Cooperatives. Buying clubs. Community currencies. Time banks. Microlending. Crowdsourcing. Crowdfunding. Open source. Community supported agriculture. Fair trade. Consensus decision-making. Cohousing. Intentional Communities. Community Gardens. Copyleft. … Until we evolve a new set of legal definitions, we'll dance uncertainly around the lines between "income" and "gifts," between "own" and "rent," between "employees" and "volunteers," between "work" and "hobby," between "nonprofit" and "for-profit," between "invest" and "donate," and so on. Our clients may have outside-the-box livelihoods and organizations, but it'll still be the job of lawyers to help them fit into boxes that are traditional enough to comply with the law.[331]

High Energy and High Binkle Environments

A discussion of supportive environments would not be complete without a consideration of the emotional climate of each particular setting we occupy. As we move inexorably toward a more heart-oriented future, our emotions and feelings are going to play a more conscious role in the decisions we make.

This gets back to energy-management concerns (Chapter 13). A business does not have to be a sweatshop to be a toxic work environment. Dead end and soul-deadening lifestyle situations will increasingly be avoided in favor of enriched and pleasant ones. Worn-down and drained people are not happy—they are also less effective. There is a dawning awareness that we need not continue to endure intolerable situations. It's about time.

Factors considered in assessing the tolerability of any situation:
- Limiting the amount of exposure to negative and draining influences or people
- Increasing the amount and variation in the way one recharges physical and emotional energy levels

Seeking nurturing circumstances also coincides with a person satisfying their higher-order needs, *a la* Maslow's Hierarchy of Needs. As one engages in self-

---

[331] Orsi, Jannelle, "Cooperative Law for a Sharing Economy," *YES! Magazine*, Sept. 10, 2010.

actualizing and inspired pursuits, the survival-based interests simply are not so all-consuming. Bear in mind that one's job is about surviving—unless we can elevate it to a calling or opportunity to keep growing.

We need to assure that there are ample opportunities to experiment without the risks of failure dooming all attempts. Not only do we need the fooling-around time to recharge and regroup, we must totally disengage in order to come back fresh. There is a physiological basis for this, as Sims describes in *Little Bets*.

> Creating an atmosphere that allows for playfulness and improvisation is one of the most effective ways to inspire the experimentation that leads to the best ideas and insights. In fact some compelling research has revealed the neurological basis for how improvisation can unleash creativity.... As respected neuroscience expert and author Jonah Lehrer described the study, 'It was only
>
> by 'deactivating' this brain area—inhibiting their inhibitions, so to speak—that the musicians were able to spontaneously invent new melodies.'[332]

> A playful, lighthearted, and humorous environment is especially helpful when ideas are incubating and newly hatched, the phase when they are most vulnerable to being snuffed out or even expressed because of being judged or self-censored. The imagined possibilities become the basis for little bets, just as comedians improvise to develop new material. Plussing [to build upon and improve ideas without using judgmental language] then forms the basis on which to build ideas toward perfection.[333]

Play Is the Work of the Heart

Activities that inspire and feed the spirit will be recognized as valid priorities and non-negotiable—as essential to a healthy lifestyle as clean air and water. We need to recharge our creative springs and our spirit of cheerfulness.

That includes enjoying more high-octane and high-binkle activities. As the triad of binkle, krindle, and laphe are engaged, one finds that the proportion of upbeat energy in one's life increases, while the proportion of draining ones decline. "Inside everyone is a great shout of joy waiting to be born," said David Whyte. Let's have more shouting, please.

We need adequate opportunities and time for emotional and physical recharge, just to stay engaged with life. We need the enrichment of the arts, which feeds the senses and our deep sense of meaning. We need curiosity to nourish our sense of wonder and the childlike, unjaded mind. And we need play because it is the all-purpose tonic. As Ross Grant told me, "The natural state of man is joy, but the natural act of man is play."

Playfulness is a high-energy pick-me-up that revives the body, while adding a dose of lift-off energy. Of course, the ways each person finds to add lightness

---

[332] Sims, Peter, *Little Bets: How breakthrough ideas emerge from small discoveries* (New York: Free Press, 2011), 65-6.
[333] *Ibid.*, 75-6.

are very personal. "Common sense and a sense of humor are the same thing, moving at different speeds. A sense of humor is just common sense, dancing," William James said. That's what is needed, dancing with joy and upbeat energy.

Are you noticing a pattern here? Such buoyant activities are spontaneous, unstructured, joyful uses of our time, of our life force. That is what releases our creativity into action, and into almost any circumstance — at the expense of the ball-and-chain of fear or dread.

Once in a while, run as free as a child — the child you used to be, who does not get out too often. Too silly? Try playing with it.

Part III - Spheres Where Vision and Practice Meet

Most visionaries act within a defined field of interest, with its requisite skills and standards. A musician, a chemist, or a high-tech inventor have each spent many years acquiring the knowledge base of their profession. Until they have gained sufficient subject-matter mastery, a person is unlikely to put his or her innovative stamp on their discipline.

Part I of the book described the components of the visionary process: the vision, the visionary, and the journey. Part II focused on concerns related to grounding the notion and bringing it to life. Part III considers several of the arenas where visionaries operate: the arts, science, and spiritual matters. But there are countless others spheres where visions take root (and more to come).

Visionaries are uniquely skilled in carving out unforeseen niches where their original discoveries can thrive. Each of these niches defines a new frontier of knowledge to be explored. Dorothea Brande, a respected author and editor, said, "Where there is an open mind, there will always be a frontier."

Section III Table of Contents

Chapter 16   Opening to the Transformative Power of Art
Chapter 17   Following Science and the Route of the Mind
Chapter 18   Following the Spiritual Route of the Heart
Chapter 19   Shifting the Paradigm
Chapter 20   Creating an Incubator for Visionary Thinkers
Chapter 21   Taking the Next Step

Chapter 16 - Opening to the Transformative Power of Art

Originality resists any efforts to pigeonhole it — while endlessly revealing itself in novel and unpredictable ways. And artistic types are more at home with the creative mindset than most.

Vision as Artistic Expression

Artists strive to communicate directly to our sensory awareness. The various arts explore inventive expression through color, movement, sound, verbal imagery, and other stimuli that fully engage the senses. Some of them appeal primarily to one or another sense, but any of them also triggers an array of emotions. Works of art can be engaging enough to produce an energetic kick or warm glow as well.

Art is something more than a stack of paintings, or books, or CDs, or videos of performances. It is not so much about what is created as *what it evokes* — both in the artist and in the audience, both during the initial impression and later. Masterful works usually communicate with an extra measure of sophistication or subtlety that somehow expresses the inexpressible.

Art resonates at multiple levels — transmitting an energetic and emotional reverberation. Rosamund Zander, a leadership expert, said: "Performance is not about getting your act together, but about opening up to the energy of the audience and of the music, and letting it sing in your unique voice."

Symbolic meaning communicates directly at the heart and gut level. Artistic expressions touch our deepest levels of aspiration and intuitive understanding. By connecting with a work of art at the sensual level, *we feel it*. It "speaks" to us. Author Madeleine L'Engle said, "No matter how true I believe what I am writing to be, if the reader cannot also participate in that truth, then I have failed."

Making an artistic work is much more than a matter of taste or of catering to popular trends. The best of it startles and engages the listener, reader, or audience. There is something familiar we already like, but also something unfamiliar or unexpected we must attend to. There is a moment of "What can I make of this?" and then we see (hear, whatever) and feel a surge of "Oh, I get it!"

The "I get it!" experience involves (1) the creator (painter, dancer, composer, designer), (2) the work, and (3) the particular person who attends to it — all simultaneously in a state of energetic alignment. For the briefest of moments, all participate in a common energy.

A work that goes directly to visceral communication moves us beyond comprehension. That immediacy passes rationality and most cultural barriers, as well as the passage of time. That's why certain forms are timeless or can touch people on a common note.

There is no "why" about what we like, or how it makes us feel. Besides individual works, artists can also communicate and influence behavior on a meta-level. In *Changing Minds*, Gardner said:

> Artistic masters alter our minds in three ways. First, they expand our notion of what is possible in an artistic medium.... Second, artists change minds by employing themes that rarely if ever have been the subject of art.... Third, artists help us to understand, indeed help us to define, the spirit of an era.[334]

The artist is always seeking a new mode of expression that builds something distinctive and pleasing, while being different from what has been already communicated in their medium. Each seeks to add his or her creative spin in a way that identifies their style and delivers the "sweet spot" the audience is hoping for.

Koestler showed the large arc of artistic development in *The Act of Creation*.

> The history of art could be written in terms of the artist's struggle against the deadening cumulative effect of saturation. The way out of the cul-de-sac is either a revolutionary departure towards new horizons, or the rediscovery of past techniques, or a combination of both.... But in between these dramatic turning points one can observe a more gradual evolution of styles which seems to proceed in two opposite directions—both intended to counteract saturation. One is a trend toward more pointed emphasis; the other towards more economy or implicitness.[335]

A particular artist's level of skillfulness can often be identified as their distinctive style across his or her body of work—their unique "signature." Any single work of theirs can be recognized as another sample of its creator's style. They are doing more than creating a work, but building a body of work that has a unique flavor of their own. But that does not come early. It ripens over untold engagements in their chosen field. Koestler also said:

> [In both art and ideas] the truly original geniuses are rare compared with the enormous number of talented practitioners; the former acting as spearheads, opening up new territories, which the latter will then diligently cultivate. In both fields there are periods of crises, of 'creative anarchy', leading to a break-through to new frontiers—followed by decades, or centuries of consolidation, orthodoxy, stagnation, and decadence—until a new crisis arises, a holy discontent, which starts the cycle again.[336]

The Artistic Process Runs on Creative Energy

Artistic expression is a particular type of creative undertaking that reveals the full gamut of the inspiration-to-tangible-form process. As such, it defies being

---

[334] Gardener, Howard, *Changing Minds: The art and science of changing our own and other people's minds* (Boston: Harvard Business School Press, 2004), 122-3.
[335] Koestler, Arthur, *The Act of Creation* (New York: The Macmillan Company, 1964), 335-7.
[336] *Ibid.*, 335.

reduced to tidy categories or how-to formulas. Originality resists any efforts to pigeonhole it—while endlessly revealing itself in novel and unpredictable ways. And artistic types are more at home with the creative mindset than most.

Artists understand that creative energies are not a spigot to be turned on and off. They learn to maintain high levels of creative energy and to be ready to use it when it is flowing. There's a constant struggle to keep some of their time and space private in which to pursue their stimulating inner life. Such individuals avoid having to be at the beck and call of the daily grind that competes with their inspiration.

For many of them, art is not a hobby, a flirtation with creative media, a time-out from humdrum responsibilities, but a life style choice. They feel driven by a need to be engaged in creative pursuits. They need to be surrounded by others similarly motivated. Art becomes their daily diet, the taskmaster that keeps raising the bar higher.

In *Adapt*, Tim Harford contrasts the leaper-style creatives and the more measured creative kin.

> In life we tend to notice and idolize those who make the wild leap.... In the creative arts, likewise we celebrate the decisive moment after which nothing is the same again—Joyce's Ulysses, Picasso's Guernica, Eliot's The Love Song of J. Alfred Prufrock, or indeed Sgt. Pepper's Lonely Hearts Club Band by the Beatles. The economist David Galenson provides a different perspective. Galenson studies the creative life cycle, gathering data on when artists, architects, poets, songwriters and others produced their definitive works. He has discovered many examples that confirm our natural tendency to conflate the precocious young talent and the creative genius, but offers equally many counter-examples. For every artist who makes dramatic conceptual leaps—a Picasso, a T.S. Eliot—there is a tentative experimentalist such as Piet Mondrian or Robert Frost.... Galenson argues convincingly that this is because they were slowly but surely perfecting their craft, climbing a single mountain of achievement while Picasso (or Orson Welles, or Jasper Johns, or Bob Dylan) vaulted from one vantage point to another.[337]

One approach is not to be lauded over the other, but are alternative approaches to living an artistic lifestyle. As with any visionary undertaking, the emphasis cannot be too much on what is created, or the public's response to it. True mastery is also about the creative individual's growth curve and how coherently the person is able to express and share their vision.

The Creative Conundrum

In Csikszentmihalyi's studies of the creative process and the individuals most engaged in it (*Creativity*), he splits the application into three types of individuals.

---

[337] Harford, Tim, *Adapt: Why success always starts with failure* (New York: Farrar, Straus and Giroux, 2011), 260

> The term 'creativity' as commonly used covers too much ground. It refers to very different entities, thus causing a great deal of confusion. To clarify the issues I distinguish at least three different phenomena that can legitimately be called by that name.... The first usage, widespread in ordinary conversation, refers to persons who express unusual thoughts, who are interesting and stimulating—in short, to people who appear to be unusually bright.... Unless they also contribute something of permanent significance, I refer to people of this sort as brilliant rather than creative.
>
> The second way the term can be used is to refer to people who experience the world in novel and original ways. These are individuals whose perceptions are fresh, whose judgments are insightful, who may make important discoveries that only they know about. I refer to such people as personally creative.... The final use of the term designates individuals who, like Leonardo, Edison, Picasso, or Einstein have changed our culture in some important respect. They are the creative ones without qualifications.[338]

In my mind, his distinction between the ways people display their creative flair could reflect where a person is along the visionary path (assuming they have gotten on it). What Csikszentmihalyi calls the "creative ones" are the masters far enough in the past, or of significant impact, for history to have weighed in about them. The other forms of creativity he describes reflect possibilities still in play.

So it is not yet apparent how much that is original or significant will ripen in any particular person. Visionaries can fall into all three categories, and might progress from one category to the next during their career.

Also, the person's sense of identity and their role change along the way. They are becoming "living bridges" between their inner world of vision and the practical world of getting things done. Each person is both an actor and being acted upon by the process of bringing an inspired idea into reality. As a consequence, they are able to tap into additional comprehension and skill the further they proceed.

Daniel Goleman speaks of the interweaving of intellect and emotion in *Working with Emotional Intelligence*.

> The act of innovation is both cognitive and emotional. Coming up with a creative insight is a cognitive act—but realizing its value, nurturing it, and following through calls on emotional competencies such as self-confidence, initiative, persistence, and the ability to persuade. And throughout, creativity demands a variety of self-regulation competencies, so as to overcome the internal constraints posed by emotions themselves.[339]

---

[338] Csikszentmihalyi, Mihaly, *Creativity: Flow and the psychology of discovery and invention* (New York: HarperCollins, 1996), 25-6.
[339] Goleman, Daniel, *Working with Emotional Intelligence* (New York: Bantam Books, 1998), 100.

One reason people engage so passionately with the arts is the way they feel through them. They sense a wholeness, a completeness that is at odds with the fragmented sense of identity that is so common in modern life. One "knows" there is something beyond the details that is truly real, truly inspiring. And through art one can feel totally connected to that larger reality. It is about personal identity, true, but it is also what one discovers and "knows" as Everyman. That awareness is as close as human beings come to sensing perfection.

Author Daniel Pinchbeck said, "If art contains a saving power, it is not in the atomized artworks produced by individual subjects, but in a deeper collective vision that sees the world as a work of art, one that is already … perfect in its 'satisfying all-at-onceness.'"

The Limits of the Craft

Once the artist attempts to turn what is envisioned into a work of art, there will inevitably be a sense of falling short. The process contains two distorting lenses—the artist's mind and the medium of expression. Koestler also said:

> To start with, the medium: the space of the painter's canvas is smaller than the landscape to be copied, and his pigments are different from the colors he sees; the writer's ink cannot render a voice nor exhale the smell of a rose. The nature of the medium always excludes direct imitation. Some aspects of expertise cannot be reproduced at all; some only by gross oversimplification or distortion; and some only at the price of sacrificing others. The limitations and peculiarities of his medium force the artist at each step to make choices, consciously or unconsciously; to select for representation those features or aspects which he considers to be relevant, and to discard those which he considers irrelevant. Thus we meet again the trinity of selection, exaggeration, and simplification.[340]

The early stages of an artistic ability are in the learning about the media. Years are required to gain control of the tools, to master the basics. That is the price of admission—learning the language and tricks of the trade. One has to learn the rules before one is able to break them, to ignore them intentionally. Artistry comes in learning how to disregard the rules so they startle and amaze. Artists push their craft, and in the process add their creative wrinkle to their field.

The Arts Speak the Language of the Senses

Art Stirs the Emotions

The arts arise in response to our creative urges—a combination of curiosity coupled with a stretching to be moved at a deeper level. The emotional intensity might touch on themes close to our core, those things that really matter to us. Or

---

[340] *Op. cit.*, Koestler, 333.

it could touch us in reflective times when, as William Wordsworth said, "Art is emotion recollected in tranquility."

Artistic works speak to us by communicating beyond the limits of language. Poetry has a special magic, for it occupies the place where our mind and heart *almost touch*. It uses words, without being limited to their literal meaning. In *A General Theory of Love,* Thomas Lewis steps out of the customary physician role to speak of the lawfulness of love.

> Poetry transpires at the juncture between feeling and understanding — and so does the bulk of emotional life.... The neural systems responsible for emotional and intellect are separate, creating the chasm between them in human minds and lives. The same rift makes the mysteries of love difficult for people to penetrate, despite an earnest desire to do so. Because of the brain's design, emotional life defeats reason, much as a poem does. Both retreat from the approach of explication like a mirage on a summer day.... Because it is part of the physical universe, love has to be lawful. Like the rest of the world, it is governed and described by principles we can discover but cannot change. If we only know where and how to look, we should be able to find emotional laws whose actions a person could no more resist than he could the force of gravity if he fell off a cliff.[341]

Dean Young, himself a poet, describes a poem as a perpetual negotiation between communicating and baffling or deferring communication "between interior and exterior, between liberty and obligation, anarchy and order, self and community... between defamiliarized and recognizable rhetorics." For Young, poetry is a spirit, an invitation from many voices to invention, exuberance, and risk-taking.

Young said, "Some things must be made opaque to be seen." He also indicates that words then become something materialized, and the result is:

> A kind of contradiction that somehow, gratefully, does not lead to a cancelling out: beautiful because it is reckless. So, if somehow the poem's opacity leads to a new kind of seeing — one from the slashed apart, ruinous rubble — that is a poem's force: being in dialogue with what it resists. And holding ground there.[342]

Creative answers are more likely to be found when we don't think we already know the answer. It requires a kind of disengagement so the urge of discovery can kick in. In *Not-Knowing*, Kim Hertzinger said:

> Writing is a process of dealing with not-knowing, a forcing of what and how. We have all heard novelists testify to the fact that, beginning a new book, they are utterly baffled as to how to proceed, what should be written and how it

---

[341] Lewis, Thomas, Amini, Fari, and Lannon, Richard, *A General Theory of Love* (New York: Vintage Books, 2000), 4-5.
[342] Young, Dean, The Art of Recklessness: Poetry as assertive Force and contradiction (Minneapolis, MN: Graywolf Press, 2010).

might be written, even though they've done a dozen. At best there's a slender intuition, not much greater than an itch. The anxiety attached to this situation is not inconsiderable.... The not-knowing is not simple, because it's hedged about prohibitions, roads that may not be taken. The more serious the artist, the more problems he takes into account and the more considerations limit his possible initiative.[343]

Kudos for the Physical Skills Developed

And let's not overlook the hands-on role of the physical body. The body is the unassuming and unheeded "donkey" expected to perform the "99% perspiration" that creative efforts demand. As exciting as the vision and inspiration phase may be, it is the body's willingness to tote the load that deserves more appreciation than it gets. That aspect of the creative process is key to actually grounding what is envisioned.

The long period needed to acquire the technical skills of artistic endeavor are largely about getting them ingrained into the body and emotional apparatus. And most arts require some physical manipulation that requires a finely tuned combination of gross motor and fine motor skills.

One mark of advanced proficiency: "they make it look so easy." The body has developed a fluidity whereby each component is integrated, so they no longer act as separate parts. The emotions and physical body are better at this than the rational mind is. But authentic integration requires each to play a role.

> There are no shortcuts to this painstaking process; becoming an expert just takes time and practice. But once you've developed expertise in a particular area—once you've made the requisite mistakes—it's important to trust your emotions when making decisions in that domain. It is feelings, after all, and not the prefrontal cortex, that capture the wisdom of experience.[344]

The Creative Process Fires Up Imagination

Artists, in large measure, are judged by the effect they have on an audience (or receiver). Yet standards about what is valued change over time. That dilemma is described by Geoff Colvin in *Talent is Overrated*.

> We can measure quite precisely the achievements of athletes, chess players, and others whose work can be evaluated objectively.... Even scientists can be judged fairly objectively, if not too precisely, by the influence of their work in the years after it was done. But composers, painters, poets, and other creators are judged by standards that inevitably shift, so we must at least be careful in drawing conclusions based on their greatness.[345]

---

[343] Hertzinger, Kim, Ed., *Not-Knowing: The essays and interviews of Donald Barthelme* (New York: Random House, 1997), 12.
[344] Lehrer, Jonah, *How We Decide* (New York: Houghton Mifflin Harcourt, 2009), 248.
[345] Colvin, Geoff, *Talent is Overrated: What really separates world-class performance from everybody else* (New York: Penguin Group, 2008), 28.

Even if the artist lived long ago or in a very different milieu, those differences are momentarily irrelevant if what they tried to convey gets through to us now. There is an immediacy and an affinity that comes with feeling what the artist felt. Any work of art capable of doing that is somehow timeless.

The emotional expanse of an artistic work bypasses rational analysis or our usual way of responding to what is happening. We might feel a *visceral resonance* with the emotional state of the artist/creator at the time the work was made and let it take us on a sensuous adventure.

The vital importance of emotions is described by Daniel J. Levitin in *This Is Your Brain on Music*.

> What most of us turn to music for is an emotional experience. We aren't studying the performance for wrong notes, and so long as they don't jar us out of our reverie, most of us don't notice them. So much of the research on musical expertise has looked for accomplishment in the wrong place, in the facility of fingers rather than the expressiveness of emotion.... If music serves to convey feelings through the interaction of physical gestures and sound, the musician needs his brain state to match the emotional state he is trying to express.[346]

What is being communicated to observers through an artistic experience needs to leave room for people to respond to it in multiple ways that are meaningful specifically for them. They attach their own meaning to the media, and not everyone derives the same meaning from it. The ability to convey different levels of symbolism is no mean achievement, as Denise Shekerjian describes in *Uncommon Genius*.

> One of the key things that I think about innovation in modern art is that in order for innovation to survive and be valued it has to have the power to mean different things to different people and to set up very different and often conflicting agendas.... Society has to accept the new discovery or object for it to be valued at all. And acceptance ... comes from the creation of a situation where a wide range of people can identify with the work, or at least with some fragment of it.[347]

Speaking for myself, I adore the writers or performers who engage me so fully they open my perceptual lens to experience more than I noticed before. And their influence on what I attend to continues to operate in me long after the book is closed (or I leave the auditorium). Moreover, they show me *how* to see (hear, whatever) something more for myself—and that does not go away.

As an example, I read Agatha Christie's mysteries to sharpen my logical mind in tracking the ambiguous clues. But I read Chesterton's Father Brown mystery stories to *focus how I look*. This insight from Father Brown is as true and useful

---

[346] Levitin, Daniel J., *This Is Your Brain on Music: The science of a human obsession* (New York: Plume Books, 2006), 208-210.
[347] Shekerjian, Denise, *Uncommon Genius: How great ideas are born* (New York: Viking, 1990), 55.

for developing any real life interest, not just crime or art. Quoting Father Brown in "The Queer Feet":

> 'A crime,' he said slowly, 'is like any other work of art. Don't look surprised; crimes are by no means the only works of art that come from an infernal workshop. But every work of art, divine or diabolic, has one indispensable mark—I mean, that the center of it is simple, however much the fulfilment may be complicated.... Every clever crime is founded ultimately on some one quite simple fact—some fact that is not itself mysterious. The mystification comes in covering it up, in leading men's thoughts away from it. This large and subtle and most profitable crime was built on the plain fact that a gentleman's evening dress is the same as a waiter's. All the rest was acting, and thundering good acting, too.[348]

Art Fosters Simplicity, Beauty and Grace

The Holy Grail of artists is to reach the essence of their subject with elegant simplicity. As Leonardo DaVinci said, "Simplicity is the ultimate sophistication." Getting there requires a clarity that cuts through the superficial chaos, to see what is most essentially unchanging.

It's harder than it looks, but when done well every element is "exactly so," and contributes to the finished work. Christopher Johnson speaks to such simplicity in *Microstyle*.

> Expressive economy [is] a basic design principle that's not limited to verbal messages. Maximizing the communicative power of few and simple elements was an important aim of modernism in all the arts. Cubist painters created landscapes and portraits from geometric shapes. Picasso's drawings tried to capture the human figure with a few simple lines. William Carlos Williams wrote poems, such as "The Red Wheelbarrow," using few and simple words and spare images.[349]

> Microstyle is all about expressive economy in language: getting a lot of idea out of a little message. The tools that I discuss directly serve the purpose of expressive economy. Ambiguity gives us two meanings for the price of one.

> Metaphor creates complex ideas out of simpler ones. Metonymy evokes complex situations via simple details. Sound symbolism squeezes meaning out of non-meaningful aspects of sound.[350]

The measure of success, however, is not in the sparseness of execution, but also whether the meaning/sensation still gets through. Einstein argued for simplicity when he said, "Any intelligent fool can make things bigger, more complex, and

---

[348] Chesterton, G.K., "The Queer Feet," *The Father Brown Omnibus* (New York: Dodd, Mead & Company, 1951).
[349] Johnson, Christopher, *Microstyle: The art of writing little* (New York: W.W. Norton & Company, 2011), 10.
[350] *Ibid.*, 28.

more violent. It takes a touch of genius—and a lot of courage—to move in the opposite direction."

When inspiration is grounded in the material world it often appears as grace and beauty. (Point to ponder: are they different or aspects of the same thing?) Grace and beauty add an element of luxury, of "something special" wherever they appear. And that presence is at the heart of what makes artistic experiences fundamentally different and more enjoyable than more functional ones.

Practical expediency would consistently omit such concerns or treat that added sparkle as expendable. Grace and beauty are not merely a matter of appearance because there's also a sense of fullness and rightness in how they make us feel.

The Arts Speak *to* and *for* the Larger Culture

The arts are not divorced from everyday reality, to be saved for rare or special occasions. But they are fundamental to the nourishment of the human spirit on many levels. Artist Paul Klee said, "The art of mastering life is the prerequisite for all further forms of expression, whether they are paintings, sculptures, tragedies, or musical compositions." They speak to the inner and outer person, and often across time and culture. It is one way we tap into the universals.

Poet Adrienne Rich argued that poets and artists should be engaged in the discourse of public life, that it should not respect boundaries between private and public life, between private and public sides of oneself. Poetry can engage with the world, and not simply be a mirror of it.

> I hope never to idealize poetry—it has suffered enough from that. Poetry is not a healing lotion, an emotional massage, a kind of linguistic aromatherapy. Neither is it a blueprint, nor an instruction manual, nor a billboard. There is no universal Poetry anyway, only poetries and poetics, and the streaming, intertwining histories to which they belong.[351]

> There's actually an odd correlation between these ideas: poetry is either inadequate—even immoral, in the face of human suffering, or it's unprofitable, hence useless. Either way, poets are advised to hang our heads or fold our tents. Yet in fact, throughout the world, transfusions of poetic language can and do quite literally keep bodies and souls together—and more.[352]

Mugging the Liberal Arts

It is difficult for me to write a chapter like this lauding the value of art without cringing. Promoting the arts is less about extraordinary accomplishments by a gifted few than building the whole person, which is within the reach of anybody. To be a well-rounded person means there is a place for art or "the finer things of life"—which is not about expense or privilege. Unfortunately,

---

[351] Rich, Adrienne, *Poetry and Commitment* (New York: W.W. Norton & Company, 2007), 21.
[352] *Ibid.*, 26.

encouraging more art awareness has receded from contemporary consciousness for a lot of very practical reasons.

According to the liberal arts ideal, young people should be introduced to a variety of disciplines and ideas that they probably never encountered or considered. According to Professor Robert Harris, "Knowledge of many subject areas provides a cross fertilization of ideas, a fullness of mind that produces new ideas and better understanding."

Exploring a variety of disciplines forms the basis of creative and critical thought. The wide-ranging investigation of many different ideas and disciplines creates a balanced approach that puts people in a better position to make good decisions. But it also provides more variety and opportunities for discovery that add to the fullness of life.

Exposure to the arts and humanities encourages basic human values like empathy and critical thinking. The belief that both individuals and communities benefit from exposure to a broad education was behind universal schooling in the United States. It also develops "good citizens," who can tolerate points of view different from their own.

British literary critic Terry Eagleton said in *The Guardian*:

> What we have witnessed in our own time is the death of universities as centers of critique. Since Margaret Thatcher, the role of academia has been to service the status quo, not challenge it in the name of justice, tradition, imagination, human welfare, the free play of the mind or alternative visions of the future. We will not change this simply by increasing state funding of the humanities as opposed to slashing it to nothing. We will change it by insisting that a critical reflection on human values and principles should be central to everything that goes on in universities, not just to the study of Rembrandt or Rimbaud.[353]

Nowadays, the idea of a classical education is almost quaint. So the arts are not supported by the tenor of the times. In many circles, pursuing the arts is considered a luxury only for the elite. Art training has largely become a victim of factors pushing toward greater specialization and cost cutting at all levels of education. And it is treated by many as fluff, an optional extra we can't really afford.

On the platter of academic choices (or in elementary grades) the arts lose out to subjects that seem more relevant or functional. In the push to get a good career that pays well, the arts don't fare very well. Too many schools have accepted the notion that time and money spent on art education might be better spent on practical skills.

So many of those programs are being slashed and children are not being exposed to arts programs at the very time when they are developing a sense of what is possible. The arts are for the inner person more than the outer person,

---

[353] Eagleton, Terry, *The Guardian*, December 19, 2010.

nourishing one's essential core. How can children grow into rounded adults if the arts haven't been given a place in their worldview? If the transformative power of art is not available to them, we will all be the poorer for it.

Art as Lifeline

I can sense it now, just like the first time. I was seated in a large auditorium, the ceiling soaring at least 20 feet above me. It was big enough to seat 500 people, though I doubted there would be very many tonight. Around me, people were milling in small clusters, making low-pitched small talk as they edged toward their seats. I didn't know anybody there, and had already taken my seat, about six rows back, close to the center—chosen to be close enough to make out the faces on-stage.

The air was crackling with anticipation in a subdued sort of way—this was to be classical music, after all. We could hear the orchestra tuning up behind the heavy folds of the curtain. The lights were turned low, as cloaked as the sounds from backstage. There was barely enough light for me to read the print of my program. Several extra copies had been discreetly collected for family who couldn't be there in person. The crisp coolness of the card stock seemed the more tangible given how muted were the lights and surroundings.

My son was about to play the violin for the first time in a public performance. I'd already perused the program and found his name—in small print since he was a beginner. But there it was! My mother's heart swelled with pride. Deciding to play the violin at 15 had been his idea, and he had stuck with it with passionate determination.

Tonight was a triumph of his will and desire over some formidable obstacles, like the fact that we were homeless, staying with friends after a crash and burn of mine. Yet in the midst of that difficult time, the violin had become his lifeline. He once told me, "Mom, I'm always happy when I am playing the violin." He would sometimes practice four to six hours a day since he felt he was making up for lost time. So this concert was a big deal for him, and for me.

I sat in a reflective mode in my plush stuffed auditorium seat, waiting for the lights to go down and the program to begin. I was thinking about the power of art to raise us above life's difficulties. And then it hit me.

In a moment of clear certainty, I understood art as not so much a form of expression, a performance, or a work of art. It was as much about the ability to sense the beauty in *any* experience. The art resides as much in the reception as in the making of the object or performance… as much in the enjoyment as in the inventive act.

My being in the audience and feeling the music, and resonating to its emotional currents, was art too. My response was an integral part of the evening's performance. I, too, was in a creative mode by my unfiltered openness to the richness of the whole experience. I was a connected part of an exquisite harmony.

I grabbed my purse and pulled out a pen and pad of paper. While in the heat of that intense insight, I wrote the BonBon that follows. I knew the truth about art because it was welling up in me. I overflowed with the intensity of it, its absolute beauty. I also knew, and still realize, I can see, hear, feel, and sense such fullness when I choose to open myself to it.

The music listed on the program hadn't yet started, but I was feeling it already. And then the curtain went up and it got even better.

~ Art, Music and Beauty ~
A BonBon ~ Faith Lynella

Art and music are about beauty. They have to do with the way we experience our world—not as something isolated and set down by the masters in the great classics. We turn our attention to the colors of the evening sky, the subtle shades and shadows of a loved one's face, the silhouette of a bird perched on a light pole. We hear the music in the sounds and rhythms of the falling rain, the laughter and squeals from a playground, the chirping of a cricket.

Art is all around us, and yet it is not the things we experience. Art is in us—in our ability to notice. An eye or an ear tuned to lovely things will always be surrounded by them. The more we have the urge to notice, the more power beauty will have to touch our lives.

From *BonBons to Sweeten Your Daily Life*; Or from *More BonBons*.

Exercising Our Creative Muscles

Creative Expression Acts as a Conduit *from* Elsewhere

There's a totality of engagement during creative endeavors. It is often described by the artist not so much as doing or making something as *being the channel* through which the works of art became manifest. They are merely the agent—albeit a compliant one.

To that end, the artist's responsibility is to stay available to such moments when the creative act "comes through" them. Knowing the timing is not something within human control puts a premium on staying receptive and open. Madeleine L'Engle described that tension in the Perkins Lecture Series, Wichita Falls, 1996.

> It isn't easy, it does take an incredible amount of discipline, you don't just write just when you feel like it or you're not going to build up much of a body of work. Inspiration comes to you while you're writing rather than before.... For me the discipline of writing and the discipline of prayer are identical, in that I

have to let myself be got out of the way because that's not a do-it-yourself activity, and listen.... When you write, don't think, write. You think before, you think after, you don't think during. When I'm praying, when I'm truly praying, I'm not thinking, I'm not speaking, I'm shutting up, so perhaps if God has something to say I can hear it. So writing too is an act of listening, listening to what has to be said.[354]

In a sense, there will always be an element of mystery about when, or how, or why, or why me? And these devoted to the arts wish to participate in the mystery even more than to explain it. For some there is a sense of contact with divinity, not unlike what the mystics experience.

Philosopher Kenneth Smith said: "Art traffics with the divine, that is, the hidden or occult, the mythic, which is after all of the very essence of man, the stuff his character and even his life are ultimately woven from. A wise society knows to have contempt for egomaniacal poseurs playing onanistically with art supplies, and a foolish society imagines that 'art is whatever artists may do.'"

But most people have no difficulty at all accepting authorship of their creative outpourings. This issue is not so much where the credit goes as whether or not it feeds a level of egotism and self-promotion. The artistic temperament can be rather self-centered, and if not carefully reined in it could lead to egotistical preening (Chapter 8). Those in the creative arts need to wonder whether what they make serves the small self or the expanded self, their ego or something universal.

Ken Wilber, an authority on the phases of inner growth, puts it bluntly. "So artists have to ask themselves, 'Is my art just a way of affirming my mediocre whiney-ass self, or am I up to the challenge of spiritual transformation, reaching for the higher self and a deeper art?'"

Courting the Muses

The Muses, who are given credit for igniting the creative process in artists and performers, seem capricious about when choosing to appear—or to vanish. Those who seek their favor must lure them, much like befriending a wild animal. Watch for it out of the corner of the eye... Wait... Hold... Stay open and ready... Don't rush... Don't get distracted... Never pounce.

Courting inspiration requires leaving part of the brain unoccupied—totally empty and receptive to the Muses' timing. One learns to maintain a quiet and unfilled place within where new ideas arise—and to keep it emptied of distractions. *Intentional disengagement from thought* is quite different from the mind's role when figuring things out.

That stage of the creative process has been described as staring at the blank page or an empty canvas, waiting for the ideas to start flowing. Someone sits there,

---

[354] L'Engle, Madeleine, Perkins Lecture Series, Wichita Falls, 1996.

not necessarily patiently, and maybe with increasing frustration, because once in a while… As with fishing, there won't always be a catch. But as the saying goes: "A bad day fishing is better than a good day working."

If not sitting quietly and watching for the tug on the line, not much gets "caught." And the enjoyment that eventually comes once there is a "catch" is all the sweeter for the anticipation.

Holding back from the nearly reflexive impulse to think about what to do next is a trained practice. Sustaining the pregnant pause indefinitely stimulates one's creative receptivity. In one sense, an empty space is held in the foreground of attention, and the rest of the world's concerns are pushed to the periphery. Then the work of art takes form in the vacant foreground.

Inspiration (the Muses) enters the unfilled foreground, with the artist waiting for what it brings. Such carefully focused availability to the creative impulse gets easier with practice, but it is never at *our* beck and call. We can learn how to get on the pulse of the creative flow, which is not quite the same as turning it on. In *The Artist's Way*, Julia Cameron describes the flowing creative energies.

> [Allowing the creative impulse to arise] is often expressed as 'The brush takes the next stroke.' In dance, in composition, in sculpture, the experience is the same: we are more the conduit than the creator of what we express.
>
> Art is an act of tuning in and dropping down the well. It is as though all the stories, painting, music, performances in the world live just under the surface of our normal consciousness. Like an underground river, they flow through us as a stream of ideas that we can tap down into. As artists, we drop down the well into the stream. We hear what's down there and we act on it — more like taking dictation than anything fancy having to do with art.… Most writers have had the expertise of catching a poem or a paragraph or two of formed writing. We consider these finds to be small miracles. What we fail to realize is that they are, in fact, the norm. We are the instrument more than the author of our work.
>
> The same may be said of all art. If paintings and sculptures wait for us, then sonatas wait for us; books, plays, and poems wait for us, too. Our job is simply to get them down. To do that, we drop down the well.[355]

The more someone steps out of his or her everyday frame of mind and opens to the creative process, the more novel ideas are likely to arise. One also becomes increasingly attuned to an idea's *latent possibilities*, so more juice can be squeezed out of it.

---

[355] Cameron, Julia, *The Artist's Way: A course in discovering and recovering your creative self* (London: Pan Books, 1994), 118.

Protecting New Glimmerings

It is important not to pre-judge what arises as it is coming, or to assess which are the "keepers" right away. That discernment calls upon different skills, and should come later, in a cooler frame of mind. Assessment forecloses the dynamic elements still forming. It is better to hold the door open to allow creative juices to flow as long as possible—basking in the delicious richness of the experience. That also permits greater originality since the elements are more diverse.

The creative process requires peace and occasional withdrawal from the world—sometimes for renewal, sometimes to hear the murmurings of one's own clarity. It is easy for someone to neglect recharging their body and spirit when there is so much stress on them to bring their vision to life. But that is exactly when the break from the normal world is needed most.

The visionary path demands considerable endurance for extended periods, so there is also a need to develop a cadence. This is not a sprint, but a long march, mostly uphill, with occasional breaks for R&R (rest and recreation). That interruption also serves the unavoidable ebb and flow of the creative process.

Uninterrupted time to reflect and refresh is essential, but it is often squeezed out by too many pressing responsibilities. Creative types try to respect their need for solitude, taking time to disengage and drink deeply from their subterranean inner resources. Those who rely on their creative talents need to vigilantly protect their creative "alone time" from intrusions. Cameron also said:

> An artist must have downtime, time to do nothing. Defending any right to such time takes courage, conviction, and resiliency. Such time, space, and quiet will strike our family and friends as withdrawal from them. It is.
> For an artist, withdrawal is necessary. Without it, the artist in us feels vexed, angry, out of sorts. If such deprivation continues, our artist becomes sullen, depressed, hostile. We eventually become like cornered animals, snarling at our family and friends to leave us alone and stop making unreasonable demands.[356]

The Art that Is Made

Art Is Experiential

The artistry is felt first by the work's originator during the act of doing or making something creative. (That includes the ancillary activities like organizing the space and assembling the materials.) Second, it is experienced by an audience or observer, which could occur as the art is being created or performed, or afterwards.

---

[356] *Ibid.*, 96-7.

Third, the art is the work of art or product created. Some forms are tangible, like a sculpture, but other forms are transitory, like a dance, leaving only an impression, coupled with the observer's reaction.

One reason artistic activities are so widely pursued is that the product doesn't have to be "good" to be pleasurable. The immediate reward is in the creative endeavor itself—unending intrinsic motivation. It's fun! It's fully engaging! It's a shot of fulfillment that is invigorating. And sometimes there's a prize that comes with it—the work of art itself.

I once saw a slogan: "A woman can lose herself in art. A woman can find herself in art." One gets so caught up in the losing and finding that the world's woes seem very far away. The person's level of skill cannot account for that totality of engagement and satisfaction because it is as available to a neophyte or a child at play as it is to the well-trained expert.

While there is considerable intrinsic value to be found in the creative experience, there is extrinsic value as well. But putting a monetary value on art, or the artistic experience, brings a host of issues. On one level, the artist has already been repaid for their creative act—by the energetic burst of creativity he or she receives while engaged in it.

The tangible work of art that results, plus the audience's enjoyment, act as additional inducements. Not ignoring the fact that money is needed in life, the money part is subsequent, and not itself part of the creative act.

Some forms of art can be captured by mechanical means. But that value often depends on how faithfully it corresponds to the original creation. New technologies used in production and reproduction are starting to alter the very definition of art itself.

In *The Big Switch*, Nicholas Carr points out how fundamentally our modern culture is altering *how* we decide what is valuable—even in the arts.

> The major constraints on the supply of creative works—high costs and narrow distribution channels—are disappearing. Because most common cultural goods consist of words, images, or sounds, which all can be expressed in digital form, they are becoming as cheap to reproduce and distribute as any other information product.... Tasks that once required a lot of money and training ... can now be done by amateurs.... And all the new digital products, whether fashioned by professionals or amateurs, can find a place in the online marketplace. The virtual shelves of the Internet can expand to accommodate everything.
>
> The shift from scarcity to abundance in media means that, when it comes to deciding what to read, watch, and listen to, we have far more choices than our

parents or grandparents did. We are able to indulge our personal tastes as never before, to design and wrap ourselves in our own private cultures.[357]

But does the addition of technology to the creative process tend to turn art into just another commodity?

Even the Arts Get Artier

Technological tools provide an edge in almost any discipline. They have even altered the way artists create and relate to their craft. It might make us rethink what we mean by the creative process. Jeff Howe points out those influences in *Crowdsourcing*.

> Media—publishing, filmmaking, photography, and music—comprise the vanguard in this movement [erasing the line between marketers and consumers]. Suddenly given access to cheap equipment, user-friendly software, and cost-free distribution, an entire generation of aspiring musicians, filmmakers, writers, and other creatives is choosing to reinvent the way 'product' has historically been generated, marketed, and sold. And these same dynamics are beginning to affect other fields as well.... [People who make up the crowd] are eschewing the established route to success. People are creating new business models simply by virtue of following their instincts and their hearts.[358]

In some cases, those who create "original content" are going directly to their market—sometimes without the involvement of packagers or distributors who have dominated some artistic fields. Those developments are creating new synergies between artist and fan, or between creative event and the later experience of it.

Technology and Artistic Creativity

The age of mass production and mass distribution is causing massive re-examination in the world of the arts. The "star" mentality leads to a few super-successes, who get most of the visibility and financial rewards. But what becomes of the rest, the virtual "unknowns"?

The Internet, with its long tail broadens the audience and possible buyers of artistic wares, but it remains to be seen if most artistic individuals (even the most gifted) can make a living through their craft that way. Even if they could, those formats may lack the intimacy and immediacy inherent in some forms of artistic expression—so they really are not the same. Carr also said:

> Creative works are not like other consumer goods, and the economic efficiency that would be welcomed in most markets may have less salutary effects when

---

[357] Carr, Nicholas, *The Big Switch: Rewiring the world, from Edison to Google* (New York: W.W. Norton & Company, 2008), 150.
[358] Howe, Jeff, *Crowdsourcing: Why the power of the crowd is driving the future of business* (New York: Crown Business, 2008), 71-2.

applied to the building blocks of culture. It's worth remembering, as well, that the Internet is a very unusual marketplace, where information of all sorts tends to be given away and money is made through indirect means like advertising. Once you fragment both the audience and the advertising in such a market, large investments in the production of certain creative works become much harder for businesses to justify.[359]

We could argue all day about what makes an original work, and who or what comprises an artist. Devices can be programmed to replace the creative touch, or eye, or ear of a trained artist. Is what machines make still art? According to what standard? How about artistic works by elephants or other animals who paint or perform?

You can be sure such questions will not be resolved soon or to many people's satisfaction. But in some form or another, art will continue to matter because of the way it awakens and feeds the spirit. Alongside all the practical, financial, and aesthetic debates about it, art has its own redeeming features. There is joy in the *doing* of it, as well as in the *sensing* of it. That could be enough.

---

[359] *Op. cit.*, Carr, 157.

Chapter 17 - Following Science and the Route of the Mind

Scientific research is a form of puzzle solving that connects the dots (data) in a systematic way. A paradigm shift represents a change in the thinking about how the specific dots relate to each other, and what they indicate.

Scientists Figure Things Out

Science is a system for solving certain kinds of problems—those amenable to a methodical analysis of the physical world. Its foremost tools are a disciplined mind and a method—the scientific method. However, there are whole categories of questions science stays away from and is not equipped to answer (despite widespread expectations to the contrary).

Science organizes facts about the observable universe. To that end, it relies on rigorous rules of observation and measurement. "Facts are the air of scientists. Without them you can never fly," said Linus Pauling.

Most scientists pride themselves on trusting only what can be proven objectively. Nothing wrong with that, but it leaves them blind in areas that do not yield to rational analysis—like aesthetics and social interactions. Yet the scientific frame of mind is too often applied in these areas of life as though science can or should explain them as well.

In my opinion, the scientific community needs to acknowledge the areas where the scientific approach is tone-deaf and seek ways to collaborate with the "unscientific" approaches in order to arrive at a more accurate picture of the entire world.

By the same token, people who do not understand science need to stop assuming that science can or should be applied everywhere.

As a child, I was taught that science and spiritual concerns are like the two wings of a bird. Both are necessary for the bird to fly. Since I grew up, I have encountered all manner of one-winged birds—some relying on intellect above all else, others primarily trusting the dictates of feelings, emotions, and the heart.

But they share the same affliction—over-reliance on one mode of understanding, while being dismissive of the other. However, there is only so far a person or notion can fly without resolving that imbalance. To quote Einstein, who worked very hard to fly with both wings, "Science without religion is lame, religion without science is blind."

This chapter discusses scientific and rational approaches to knowing (the mind's work), and the next chapter focuses on mystical and spiritual approaches to knowing (the heart's work). But an integrated viewpoint demands that both complementary perceptual approaches be given their due. The visionary path compels those who travel very far to become proficient with both.

To the extent that an individual can find a way to bridge those disparate modes of relating to life personally, they became a "better mousetrap maker" and a model of how the trick is done. As that occurs on a larger scale, we are poised for some surprising discoveries.

The Paradigm Shift that Kuhn Wrought

The phrase "paradigm shift" was first used in 1962 by Thomas Kuhn in *The Structure of Scientific Revolutions*. His treatise altered the thinking about how significant change occurs in science. All subsequent debate about how scientific theories gain acceptance pay homage to Kuhn's work. Significant shifts within any scientific specialty (or theory) seem to demonstrate his model.

As an historian of science, Kuhn focused on changes in the long-term patterns within scientific disciplines. He examined how new theories and ways of thinking displace prior ones. The influence of his theory extends well beyond scientific fields, however, and represents an example of a paradigm shift—illustrating how the broader culture has altered its thinking about change.

Before Kuhn, it was assumed that scientific progress was linear and gradual, reflecting an unending progression of refinements to the accepted laws and theories. He showed that considering change as a linear progression is not accurate. Instead, major developments in science have mostly been abrupt and revolutionary.

In my own case, reading Kuhn's book while in my teens had a significant influence on the development of my analytical framework. It attuned me to look for the meta-patterns of change and the significance of what would prove to be revolutionary influences early on.

In some respects, my interest in visionaries can be traced to wondering how the individual contributes to the meta-change process (scientific or otherwise). What dynamics influence the *paradigm shifters*? — in other words, the visionaries. Who dares to butt heads with the prevailing wisdom and practices of their field or their larger community?

Those who manage to shift the paradigm of their discipline come to be the giants, like: Copernicus, Darwin, Mendel, Currie, Einstein, Tesla, and Fleming. But even their sizeable impact represents more than gaining recognition for what they discovered. Each of them toiled in service to their vision despite its initial rejection by their professional peers. They personify the visionary process as well.

In my opinion, behind humanity's leaps forward can be found inspired vision diligently tended, coupled with superhuman persistence. While it is unfair to give too much credit to creative and visionary types, they act as crucial catalysts in the ground-breaking phase of the change process.

The Scientific Paradigm

The concept of paradigm predates Kuhn, and it is used in other disciplines besides the sciences. "Paradigm" is from Latin and Greek roots, that translate "to compare" and "to show" (from Latin paradigm and Greek *paradeigma*).

Paradigm Means:
1. One that serves as a pattern or model
2. A set of assumptions, concepts, values, and practices that constitutes a way of viewing reality for the community that shares them, especially in an intellectual discipline

More Specifically, a Scientific Paradigm Is:
- What is to be observed and scrutinized
- The kind of questions that are supposed to be asked and probed for answers in relation to this subject
- How these questions are to be structured
- How the results of scientific investigations should be interpreted

In his later work, Kuhn came to prefer and use the terms "exemplar" and "normal science" instead of "paradigm," to which he gave more exact connotations. Kuhn's concept of "exemplar" denotes a well-known usage of a scientific theory. His concept of "normal science" refers to the routine work of scientists experimenting within the prevailing paradigm.

Kuhn argued that scientific practice alternates between periods of normal science and extraordinary or revolutionary science. In *Ideas that Matter*, A.C. Grayling explains why paradigms are so different from each other: "Crucially, old and new paradigms are 'incommensurable;' the new is not an improvement on the old, it is just different, and the two cannot be compared."[360]

Scientists subscribe to a large body of interconnecting knowledge, techniques, and assumptions that make up the reigning paradigm for their specific field (as well as for the larger arena of science itself). The scientific method defines the acceptable practices to collect and analyze data, and is itself a paradigm. So it, too, is amenable to change as the consensus about it shifts.

According to Margolis in *Paradigms and Barriers*, when discussing a paradigm it is important to notice the habits of mind that practitioners within a paradigm use.

> A paradigm is commonly taken to encompass what is found in a textbook, but also it is widely understood — and certainly so in Kuhn's account — to include what is between the lines of a textbook. What is between the lines of a textbook that is essential for the operation of the paradigm are critical habits of mind that

---

[360] Grayling, A. C., *Ideas that Matter: The concepts that shape the 21st century* (New York: Basic Books, 2010), 333.

tacitly guide key intuitions within the community. Such socially shared habits of mind facilitate communication and many other aspects of constructive work, but they also constrain what can be seen as making sense.[361]

All the theories and research within any discipline build upon each other. Scientists tackle questions and design research studies that are amenable to building a broad consensus for a particular theory. Friedman, Norman makes that case in *Bridging Science and Spirit*.

> A paradigm becomes a filter through which experiences are passed to determine their acceptability within the framework of the scientific discipline. If an experience cannot pass through the filter, it usually is discarded and considered nonfactual, not real.... Thus, any theory, any model, any discipline of study is built on a limited number of elements extracted from the totality of information. When anomalies arise, one does well to remember that only a part of the whole has been considered.[362]

Altering the Established Scientific Consensus

Change in science largely occurs through building a new consensus for some theory that is different than what scientists in a particular field already accept. But it's a gradual process since consensus reflects the collective judgment by the community of scientists within a specialty.

Consensus rests on a combination of scientific arguments and the accumulation of research findings that employed the scientific method. Consensus implies general agreement among scientists, though not necessarily unanimity.

Scientific Consensus Is Normally Achieved through:
- Publication in professional journals
- Replication of research procedures and results by other scientists
- Peer Review and spirited debate about the new theory or its implications
- Communication at conferences and among peers directly
- Further elaboration in research, philosophical debate, and by countering competing theories

Taken together, all the work scientists do fills in the gaps in our knowledge about the natural world. Scientific research is a form of puzzle solving that connects the dots (data) in a systematic way. A paradigm shift represents a change in the thinking about how the specific dots relate to each other, and what they indicate.

The concept of paradigm shift is reserved for the really big movements of the accepted knowledge. And only historical distance can judge whether a specific change of perception brought about a paradigm shift. Even if a discovery has

---

[361] Margolis, Howard, *Paradigms and Barriers: How habits of mind govern scientific beliefs* (Chicago: University of Chicago Press, 1993), 26.
[362] Friedman, Norman, *Bridging Science and Spirit* (St. Louis: Living Lake Books, 1994), 282.

radically new implications, it must still undergo the same rigorous experimental testing applied to the rest of the research conducted by that discipline. It takes more than a sequence of successful experiments for the new guy to challenge the habits of mind inherited from generations of prior researchers (or their findings).

Margolis argues that a paradigm shift is a special sort of change in the habits of mind. It signals greater receptivity for some new scientific idea.

> The arguments here might seem more genial if I spoke of 'point of view' rather than habits of mind. But there is a good reason not to do that. A person is ordinarily conscious of a point of view. But unless specifically and effectively prompted, a person is ordinarily unconscious of habits and indeed is to a large extent completely unaware that she has various habits. Similarly a person ordinarily can try a different point of view and certainly understands what is being asked when someone proposes a look at things from another point of view. But we can't try out a different habit.... People within a paradigm share a point of view.[363]

Such habits dictate how a scientist sees and interprets what they see. Practitioners are unaware of the extent to which their shared perception colors what they see. That is why significant change in what is known about a subject area also needs to reflect a change of the habits of mind about it.

It usually takes a much longer time to change such underlying thinking than for people to accept new knowledge about specific facts. Also, there sometimes are competing factions, each espousing a different paradigm, as a shift reaches critical mass. These play out even beyond the laboratory in matters like access to funds or public acceptance. Grayling said:

> Critics argue that Kuhn's picture of science is harmful, because it supports the way that the dominant social institutions which control science and its funding confer legitimacy on their own preferred science and scientists, while excluding people and ideas different from or opposed to them.[364]

Scientific visions (still-untested theories) must be conceptually defined in such a way they can be tested or measured objectively. That is the role of scientific research. While even scientific visions or theories start as abstractions, they become tangible through the laborious process of accumulating the data that can support it.

Scientific visionaries have sometimes needed to design new measurements or procedures that permitted them to "prove" their theory experimentally. In *Adventures of Ideas* Alfred North Whitehead describes what drives scientific progress.

---

[363] *Op. cit.*, Margolis, 25.
[364] *Op. cit.*, Grayling, 333-4.

> There is a moral to be drawn as to the method of science. All scientific progress depends on first framing a formula giving a general description of observed fact.... Certain branches of science halt for centuries in this stage.... There is however a motive of unrest which urges scientists beyond mere satisfaction with the simple description,
>
> beyond even the general description. It is the desire to obtain the explanatory description which may justify the speculative extension of Laws, beyond actual, particular instances of observation.[365]

In Kuhn's view, there is a long time frame during which proposed new theories are resisted, adjusted, or allowed to settle in. In that sense, the measured pace of science serves a useful function by giving new ideas time to prove themselves. That time lag weeds out half-baked notions that are unable to stand up to methodical testing and ongoing scrutiny.

> As the London-based writer Ziauddin Sardar has noted, in the popular mind, Kuhn reduced science to 'nothing more than long periods of boring conformist activity punctuated by outbreaks of irrational deviance.'...
>
> Does this mean the misfit is always worth betting on? Not really. The often-ignored side of the Kuhn theory is that for long stretches of time, the frontier of science and technology is ruled by diligent people who are quietly filling in the grand vision that spawned a new paradigm in the first place.[366]

The world of science thrives precisely because it can accommodate both kinds of scientists within their discipline—the steady researchers as well as the voices for a radically new interpretation or change on a very large scale. Enough research findings piling up that cannot be accounted for by existing theories could eventually lead to corrective adjustments—if not to an entirely different paradigm.

Those destined to become paradigm shifters are looking specifically for topics where their talents can potentially replace prevailing thought with something more useful. It happens because their new theory for interpreting the body of data does a better job of explaining it, including the irregularities the old theory cannot account for.

A paradigm shift alters the frame of reference whereby people who share a common worldview make sense of information. It is about them moving to a different conceptual framework than they used before. The mental box itself does not go away, however, but its properties are different. So, thereafter what is seen and measured will add up in a new way.

---

[365] Whitehead, Alfred North, *Adventures of Ideas* (New York: The Free Press, 1933), 128.
[366] Zachary, G. Pascal, "Genius and Misfit Aren't Synonyms, or Are They?" *New York Times*, June 5, 2007.

Kuhn's model about the change process is itself heir to influences that change with time. Like any widely accepted theory, some aspects of it have held up better than others in the long run. Since it was published 50 years ago, it is also been both refined and attacked by later theorists (like Popper). In addition, using the concept of paradigm shift outside of scientific fields has watered down its initial precision and conclusions.

The Method Provides Validation

The scientific method is designed to reduce uncertainty about what is known by very specifically directing the way studies are conducted. It defines the acceptable rules for both theoretical and applied research, and it dictates the objective standards that must be satisfied for results to be considered valid. Valid does not necessarily mean true, but following these procedures make that as likely as possible.

Even the most rigorous analysis cannot tell the whole story, however. We should heed Einstein's caution: "Not everything that can be counted counts, and not everything that counts can be counted." Vision and speculation also have a role to play in science, so the inherent order of the collected dots can be revealed.

Vision and speculation precede data collection and analysis. Why bother collecting data unless it is perceived to have a purpose? The standard final method of presentation is a shorthand way to present information concisely, which was especially important when printing costs were high for information with very low readership. Whitehead also said:

> New directions of thought arise from flashes of intuition bringing new material within the scope of scholarly learning. They commence as the sheer ventures of rash speculation. They may fortunately obtain quick acceptance, or they may initiate a quarrel of scholars from which all tinge of speculation has faded.... Pure speculation, undisciplined by the scholarship of detailed fact or the scholarship of exact logic, is on the whole more useless than pure scholarship, unrelieved by speculation. The proper balance of the two factors in progressive learning depends on the character of the epoch in question and on the capacities of particular individuals.[367]

Scientists slice and dice inanimate and living objects in order to better analyze them. This leads to endless fragmentation and specialization. But that method has greater difficulty dealing with realities of life or properties of thought and matter that cannot fit in the experimental mold. Scientists struggle with factors that are too difficult to define or measure — or ignore them altogether. Then along comes a new theory that can make sense of what was unintelligible.

---

[367] *Op. cit.,* Whitehead, 108.

Science Tends toward a Narrow Focus and Gradual Change

It is remarkably difficult to replace a theory in science since any lasting change involves altering the thinking of a large number of scientists and other authorities over a long time period. And those higher up the pecking order have a vested interest in supporting what has proven itself already.

Scrimmages between the established thinking and newer, untried theories tend to occur in the margins. Because of the intense specialization in tiny fractions of the real world, there often are only a few people who have the knowledge or interest.

There is not a single all-defining paradigm within science; many paradigms only relate to specific specialties or aspects of the natural world. Which of the accepted theories do the best job of explaining the facts as practitioners in the field know them? Which can effectively accommodate new discoveries as they occur? On the other hand, what types of questions do the prevailing theories have a hard time explaining? An original theory that can make sense of those perplexing areas is likely to be a revolutionary one.

However, enough clear victories in research and theoretical elaboration about it might foretell the broadening consensus that presages a paradigm shift for a particular subject area. There is a saying, "Progress in science proceeds one funeral at a time." Those most invested in the existing paradigm need to die or cede power as the new ones gain ground.

The gradual pace of acceptance can lead to some awkward effects. Waves of change can come so fast they crowd up on each other. So in some arenas two, three, or more theories on a single topic might be functioning at the same time. Further, several different paradigms related to the same subject can coexist, even in the same field.

We see this in Newtonian physics and quantum physics. They really are not in conflict, but have different spheres of application. Einstein's discoveries and the whole field of quantum physics would not have been anticipated by the accretion of gradual experiments relying on the laws of Newtonian physics.

These coexisting scientific models are suggesting a yet larger framework—perhaps the unified field that Einstein himself couldn't grok. (Grok means to have an intuitive understanding of something without having to think about it.)

Aside from the research standards of their field, the position any scientist takes on a specific issue is likely to be colored by his or her personal and professional interests and self-interests as well. And insider politics inevitably flavor the mix too. In *Kuhn vs Popper,* Steve Fuller said:

Now more than ever [knowledge is] preoccupied with face-saving exercises to shore up expertise, the elusive quest for what philosophers call 'credible testimony' and sociologists call, more brutally, 'boundary maintenance.'[368]

Boundary maintenance considers the ways in which groups maintain distinctions between themselves and others, who they consider to be unlike them in some regard. Those accepted norms for a group stand in contrast to the way a group defines its inherently ambiguous peripheral areas, its boundaries.

The distinction between what is acceptable and what is in the gray areas reveals what constitutes the cultural or specific discipline's values. Most of the change in theories occurs in the margins, where there is less formal resistance and the conceptual structures are not as rigid. Within science, the tendency toward ever-narrower specialization can easily get caught up in concerns around boundary maintenance. However, the generalist chooses to use a wider lens that looks at a larger-scale view across fields of interest.

Insisting on clearly-drawn boundaries between specialized fields keeps the focus on how practitioners or theories differ, rather than on the commonalities they share. It is contractive rather than integrative. The tendency toward ever-narrower specialization needs to be countered by the expansive and more integrated scope of the generalist. But both approaches must play a more collaborative role.

Paradigm Shift as a Cultural Cliché

Since Kuhn's first use in the 1960s, the term "paradigm shift" has assumed a life of its own outside of science. The concept is used so widely and casually as to have become a cliché. Popular usage of the phrase creeps up all over. An Internet search engine showed over three million references to it, and you can bet most of them do not relate to what Kuhn had in mind.

The term "paradigm shift" is often applied on a personal scale, to indicate someone's change of heart, a breakthrough, or an insight. People misuse the phrase to apply to changes as simple as modifying a behavior (which is closer to "metanoia," whereby someone acts on a newfound awareness). Yet those personal changes are at too small of a scale, involving an attitude change, rather than a change in a shared consensus.

Scale aside, a paradigm shift signals the established view about a matter has been replaced by a very different one—and people will henceforth behave accordingly toward it. While a paradigm shift does not eliminate their common box, it significantly redefines the parameters of their perceptual box to support the new collective point of view.

---

[368] Fuller, Steve, *Kuhn vs Popper: The struggle for the soul of science* (Cambridge, England: Icon Books, 2003), 6.

Learning More and More about Less and Less

The scientific method relies on mathematical and statistical analysis to make sense of experimental data. But the results they yield can never be any more reliable than the assumptions inherent in the formulas or models used to collect and analyze the data. As a particular consideration, scientists seek *significant results*. Significance is likely to be treated as though the information is important and accurate—maybe even true.

Looking for answers from collected data assume the results represent information worth knowing. Statistical results are not necessarily useful or important. Significant statistical conclusions are just as likely to be a by-product of other factors in the experimental design. It is easy to come up with significant results that do not prove or disprove any particular theory. In the end, the scientist must make sense of their research findings, so they actually further our knowledge—not merely fill in the gaps.

Scientists risk being so analytical or reductive they lose sight of the integrated wholeness of what they study, like the nature of life. It is important, once in a while, to adjust one's perceptual lens to include both the forest *and* the trees—as well as what unites them.

A scientist once advised me to stop talking about forest and trees, but to get smaller. Look at leaves and needles, or the cells and molecules. The needles of a tree may have more profound implications than the forest, I was told. Getting smaller may be where most of the startling answers are to be found. Like how a mind thinks and makes decisions. These answers may eventually be found on the molecular level.

One definition of an expert is someone who "knows more and more about less and less." That's a very different approach than the liberal arts model, which seeks to develop a wide-focus lens so the secondary connections can be seen as well. Analysis breaks ideas and objects into smaller and smaller pieces that can be more easily studied, measured, and compared. And that compounds the need for further clarification and research.

"Science is always wrong," George Bernard Shaw famously proclaimed in a toast to Einstein. "It never solves a problem without creating 10 more."

In pursuing an ever-narrowing focus, one risks losing sight of the unbroken wholeness. Scientists should heed the Gestalt maxim of life being more than the sum of its parts. And let's not overlook the relationships among wholes and component parts, and the meta-relationships, too.

A persistent problem with the scientific approach is compartmentalization. It is a natural outgrowth of specialization and the analytical way the scientific method structures measures of proof. Most specialists are not geared to notice or validate relationships of data outside of their narrowly defined specific field of science. Nor can the scientific method analyze information at different levels of specificity.

But even more significant, the role of the researcher is not an invisible one. What they think, assume and do accordingly has a very real influence on what they find. The inextricable link between observer and what is observed is explained by James P. Carse in *Breakfast at the Victory*.

> In modern thought the awareness that there is something out there that we are not yet awake enough to see is the engine that drives the investigative mind. Relentless and systematic questioning: this is the spirit of scientific intelligence. In this spirit we dissent to see what connects, we dismember to understand the whole, we kill to catch life in its act.... Once interpretation enters, an interpreter enters with it. With all wonder there is a wonderer. No longer can we separate the reality we are looking at from the reality of the looking. What we see depends partly on what is there and partly on who is looking.[369]

Scientists trust the mind's rational abilities, but looks askance at what the heart or body sense knows. They generally ignore the fact that heart, mind, and body each have specific capabilities that are intertwined in function. In a variety of ways, the three modes operate as a unit, and must compensate among themselves when any of them is underused or left out.

If rational analysis is treated as the only way to discover or prove the truth, any such partial, hobbled approach yields a limited view that systematically ignores present and *relevant* information.

Another risk of over-reliance on analysis is described by Alfred North Whitehead as the Fallacy of Misplaced Concreteness. Someone commits such a fallacy by mistaking an abstract belief, opinion or concept about the way things are for the concrete reality it refers to. To rely too heavily on analytical models leads to incorrect conclusions about what's being described.

That misperception could lead a researcher to confuse an abstract model of how people (or other subject populations) act under certain circumstances for their actual behavior. The risk is especially crucial when one relies on hypothetical theories or models for predicting the future.

Wedding a Pair of Paradigms

For me, the term "paradigm" always brings up two sets of associations, Kuhn's and Rene Daumal's as described in *Mount Analogue*. It is a novel about a journey taken by a party of visionaries, so in some regards their story describes the visionary process itself. Daumal's work predated Kuhn's, but his concept of "paradam" and Kuhn's "paradigm" and theories seem to me to share an underlying relatedness.

Kuhn deals with revolutionary change in institutions, whereas Daumal's use deals with fundamental and irreversible change within the individual.

---

[369] Carse, James P., *Breakfast at the Victory: The mysticism of ordinary experience* (New York: HarperCollins, 1994), 96-98.

Daumal's "paradam," (which I treat as a French spelling of the term) was a material symbol for a person's inner growth. It describes a symbolic lens of perception. By comparison, Kuhn's concept of paradigm applies to scientific fields or the larger society, rather than to the state of the individuals who launched the change.

Please note, the following excerpt is from a work of fiction, and is presented only as a metaphor. There is no physical place or such substance in nature.

> There is found here [on Mount Analogue], rarely on the lower slopes and more frequently as one ascends, a clear and extremely hard stone, spherical and of variable size. It is a true crystal and—an extraordinary instance entirely unknown elsewhere on this planet—a curved crystal. In the French spoken in Port 'o Monkeys, this stone is called paradam. Ivan Lapse [a character] is still puzzled by the formation and the root meaning of the word. It may mean, as he sees it, 'harder than diamond,' as is very much the case, or else 'father of diamond.' And some say that diamond is in reality the product of the disintegration of by a sort of squaring of the circle or, more exactly, cubing of the sphere. Or else the word may mean 'Adam's stone' and have had some secret and profound complicity with the original nature of man. This stone is so perfectly transparent and its index of refraction so close to that of air in spite of the crystal's great density that the inexperienced eye barely perceives it. But to any person who seeks it with sincerity and out of true need it reveals itself by a brilliant sparkle like that of a dewdrop. Paradam is the only substance, the only material thing whose value is recognized by the guides of Mount Analogue. Therefore, it remains the basis and standard of all currency, like gold in many countries.[370]
>
> [Pierre, the leader spoke] 'I have brought you this far, and I have been your leader. Right here I'll take off the cap of authority, which was a crown of thorns for the person I remember myself to be. Far within me, where the memory of what I am is still unclouded, a little child is waking up and making an old man's mask weep. A little child looking for mother and father, looking with you for protection and help—protection from his pleasures and his dreams, and help in order to become what he is without imitating anyone.'
>
> As he spoke, Pierre had been delving in the sand with the point of his stick. Suddenly his eyes froze; he bent down and picked something up—something that shone like a tiny dewdrop. It was a paradam, a small one, but the first for any of us.[371]

To my way of thinking, an amalgam of the two concepts (paradigm and paradam) brings the outer and impersonal view (scientific precision) together with the particular individual and their personal philosophy. They can thereby

---

[370] Daumal, René, *Mount Analogue* (Baltimore: Penguin Books, 1952), 90-91.
[371] *Ibid.*, 100.

coalesce into an effective focus — its own perceptual lens. Science searches for crystal-clear clarity. But it also requires the perception of the particular scientist be unclouded by personal biases — particularly those unconstrained by the scientific method.

Self-knowledge determines the way the lens is polished. Otherwise, what's been studied is unintentionally skewed by the scientist's own unrecognized perceptual habits and preferences. In my opinion, a "naked" and integrated scientist serves the scientific body of knowledge best. The need for finding the requisite balance is explained later this chapter.

Science and Human Values

It is easy to get swept up by the fruits of scientific discoveries and technology. But we also need to look at ethical and secondary impacts of what is being accomplished once they are applied. Just because science can figure out how to do a thing does not mean it should be done.

Science strives to be objective, but it is not neutral. Not all of what it discovers is benign. Science also needs the judgment and restraint of values. What the sciences are capable of doing requires the mediating influence of ethical considerations. As Martin Luther King said, "The means by which we live have outdistanced the ends for which we live. Our scientific power has outrun our spiritual power. We have guided missiles and misguided men."

The determination to reduce everything to objective measures does violence to integration. As a particular complaint against current methodology, I think what constitutes people's personal or inner life certainly deserves to be treated as something more than "contamination of objective data."

Amit Gotswami points out the dilemma in *Creative Evolution*:

> How do we study life without excluding living? Studying behavior is one way, to be sure, but that is only the outer aspect of living. There is also the inner aspect — feelings. These we can study only from the inside. Materialist biology, by ignoring the distinction of living and nonliving, also ignores the distinction of outer and inner in living, eventually ending up ignoring the inner aspect of living altogether.[372]

One of the dilemmas of our times is that humans are conscious beings, but there is no adequate scientific explanation for consciousness. While advances in the methods to study brain waves shed light on how the brain works, we cannot adequately explain consciousness as merely a physiological function. Nor can it explain a wide array of abstract and subtle mental or emotional functions (let alone life itself, or how it can emerge from insensate matter).

---

[372] Gotswami, Amit, *Creative Evolution: A physicists resolution between Darwinism and Intelligent Design* (Wheaton, IL: Quest Books, 2008), 221.

The Caring Dimension

People are much more complex, kindly, and warm-hearted than our biological traits can account for. We cannot simply look at the scientific and rational side of what it means to be human without acknowledging there are other valid sides of the human equation in play that are very influential.

Scientists sometimes claim expertise they do not have or that's beyond what science is designed to do. Or unrealistic public expectations arise about what science can and should accomplish. What the public considers acceptable solutions should not simply be "*can* we do it?" but "*should* we do it?"

The tension between technological advances and the softer human values is explained by Joel Garreau in *Radical Evolution*.

> Introducing compassion into the equation is at the core of meaning. 'Without more kindliness in the world, technological power would mainly serve to increase men's capacity to inflict harm on one another,' Bertrand Russell once wrote. Compassion may thus be at the core of successfully managing transcendence—of coming up with a practical way to prevail over the blind forces of change.[373]

For instance, it simply is not possible to understand a person's emotional response to something exquisitely beautiful or awe inspiring by measuring their brain waves. Art cannot be defined that way. We are capable of knowing more. But if scientists feel obligated to reject answers that are not amenable to the scientific method, such value-rich and emotion-laden information is discarded as irrelevant.

Preferring Two-Winged Birds

Ending the War between Science and the Humanities

Scientific fields deal with the external and physical world, whereas philosophy and metaphysics deal with consciousness and the inner world. Their approaches are quite different, but loyalty to either approach alone leaves too much of what exists out of the perceptual frame. They are complementary—two sides of the same coin.

Science studies the lawful nature of matter—that which can be observed and analyzed. Scientific progress has largely coincided with advances in technologies that extend our methods or scale of measurement. Philosophical study can be just as rigorous, although it lacks the measurable validation science employs. Intellectual rigor is still involved.

My scientist friend informed me, "Scientists are annoyed by people flying around in circles flapping one wing, and acting like they have better answers—but no way of proving that those answers are better." And that gets to the root

---

[373] Garreau, Joel, *Radical Evolution: The promise and peril of enhancing our minds, our bodies – and what it means to be human* (New York: Broadway Books, 2005), 262.

of it. Neither camp finds the other side's proof trustworthy or compelling. Surely, the stalemate cannot stand.

Alfred North Whitehead argues the two modes of acquiring knowledge are not separate but they complete each other. For him, science and philosophy (by which he means the understanding of abstract, non-material, ideas) must collaborate in order for intrinsic patterns to be evident above the "bare welter of facts."

> In one sense, Science and Philosophy are merely different aspects of one great enterprise of the human mind.... Science and Philosophy are both concerned with the understanding of individual facts as illustrations of general principles.... In the greater sense, in which it is here used, 'curiosity' means the craving of reason that the facts discriminated in experience be understood. It means the refusal to be satisfied with the bare welter of fact, or even with the bare habit of routine.[374]

These scientific and philosophical systems coincide with Kuhn's view of paradigms. But they can and do sometimes languish for long periods until a major revolutionary influence leads to the next paradigm. It is fair to say the sciences and humanities are stuck in an entrenched face-off that has kept both camps trapped in a limited frame of reference that prevents greater integration between them. Until or unless the impasse is broken, science and the humanities are both broken—themselves models of stuckness for their respective areas.

A Cessation of Rivalries

In 1959, C.P. Snow presented an influential speech describing the Two Cultures dividing the intellectuals of the West: The Left-Handed culture of the humanities and the Right-Handed culture of the natural sciences. They do not speak to each other; in fact they are at war. They are locked in perpetual battle to discredit the other.

Snow described the breakdown of communication between the Two Cultures of modern society as a major hindrance to solving the world's problems. The quality of education has suffered because of this gap, and well-educated professionals have too little awareness beyond their own arena of learning—certainly, most professionals are not well informed regarding the demonized territory.

In the last fifty years since Snow's sounding of the alarm, the gap has gotten wider and more sensitized. We cannot afford to go on like this. To the extent the estrangement is left unresolved, the full force of science is not available. I do not know how long it will take, but this is the point where a break with tradition is required. Snow said:

---

[374] *Op. cit.*, Whitehead, 140-1.

> I now believe that if I had asked a simple question [about physics] not more than one in ten of the highly educated would have felt that I was speaking the same language. So the great edifice of modern physics goes up, and the majority of the cleverest people in the western world have about as much insight into it as their Neolithic ancestors would have had.[375]

A new paradigm, that is larger and more inclusive than the scientific method, is needed, in which the Left-Handed culture, and the Right-Hand culture can work toward integration, so they can support each other in the larger human endeavor.

Before that can happen the strengths inherent in each approach must be appreciated by the other side. Only then can each side of the coin be incorporated into the larger context they already share.

Whatever form those discoveries take, they will themselves contribute to a fundamental shift of the current worldview of educated people, which is comprised of wedges of a sliced pie. The more integrated approach that is to come will need to be more *cognizant of the whole pie* itself. Integration demands the dismantling of barriers to understanding.

As with any revolutionary change, the consensus is usually slow to catch up to what frontrunners foresee and advocate. I sense the polarizations within the current knowledge base are serving as the birth pangs of the next phase of thinking.

Fundamental to healing the rift is changing the prevailing habits of thought, which are too constrictive to entertain the opposite perspective. The mind recoils. The scientific approach is partial to linear and incremental analysis. It is as though loyalty to science precludes a respect for anything that is outside of its framework.

Other perspectives are likely to be dismissed as "unscientific" — hence, without merit. But as already discussed, science is not equipped to deal with many areas of knowledge. The big world is heedless of our human efforts to understand it. It is larger and more complex than the systems we rely on to explain how the laws of nature work. For instance, simply developing a systems approach won't get us there. Ken Wilber says as much in *Integral Spirituality*.

> Using systems theory, because it seems inclusive or holistic, only gets half the necessary story, at best — it expands our models to cover all of the Right-Hand world, but does not expand the models to incorporate insights from the Left-Hand world.[376]

---

[375] Snow, C.P., "The Two Cultures", Rede Lecture, delivered 1959, Cambridge, and subsequently published as *The Two Cultures and the Scientific Revolution*.
[376] Wilber, Ken, *Integral Spirituality: A startling new role for religion and the modern and postmodern world* (Boston: Integral Books, 2007), 284.

Other ways to indicate this divide are: between reason and faith, between head and heart, between inner and outer, between idea and matter. Between. That's a significant clue; it speaks to getting beyond either-or thinking. It cannot escape those logical constraints. Yet those who follow the visionary path do not stop there since it entertains a greatly restricted scope of possibilities.

Have human beings come far enough to attempt to integrate science and the humanities? That is the great rift at our stage of history—with numerous sub-fractures within each camp. Building those bridges will require a broader, and more integrated scope, than currently exist in our polarized areas of specialization. But something is amiss. There are simply too many "facts" that do not fit and they are not about to go away quietly.

This also parallels the various ways of knowing (as described in Chapter 7). To the extent either approach to knowing attempts to be primary or exclusive, it fails to produce an all-embracing view. That undercuts our ability to get an integrated understanding of that which is already integrated.

Time to Integrate Across the Rift

To the extent that science has limited its research methods to observing the tangible world alone, it has failed to deal credibly with the awkward evidence that the world it studies is part of a larger, integrated reality—much of which is not amenable to precise objective measurement. This is where the humanities hold sway. Science needs to be saved from itself and an over-reductionist approach. And the converse is also true for the humanities.

I am willing to predict that visionary leaps ahead will bridge some of those limitations, presaging a major expansion of the role and scope of scientific discoveries. Friedman also said:

> Not only is our present scientific paradigm too narrow, but it is time for a broadening—and deepening—of the general worldview. We would expect that a change in the fundamental framework employed in scientific investigation would make itself felt throughout human culture, in precisely those areas where we now sense that our old philosophies no longer serve.[377]

The current polarization between intellect and feelings, between the Two Cultures, between inner and outer, between science and religion, denote the way of thinking from the past. I foresee that building bridges to reconcile the philosophical divide between head and heart will characterize the next phase for leading-edge thinkers, whatever their discipline.

Chapter 3 discussed mastery—both outer, subject-matter mastery *and* inner, self-mastery. All efforts in that direction are laudable, reflecting considerable dedication and effort. But those who are most likely to heal this rift are the very ones working to accomplish Integrated Mastery.

---

[377] *Op. cit.*, Friedman, Norman, 282.

They have been acquiring remarkable clarity in both the inner and outer realms — with a foot solidly and confidently planted in both. The paradigm that emerges will be rooted in an integration that rests on those bridges. Stuart A. Kauffman, a biologist, brings in the role of the sacred in healing those differences in *Reinventing the Sacred*.

> Part of reinventing the sacred will be to heal these injuries — injuries that we hardly know we suffer. If we are members of a universe in which emergence and ceaseless creativity abound, if we take that creativity as a sense of God we can share the resulting sense of the sacredness of all of life and the planet can help orient our lives beyond the consumerism and commodification the industrialized world now lives, heal the split between reason and faith, heal the split between science and the humanities, heal the want of spirituality, heal the wound derived from the false reductionist belief that we live in a world of fact without values, and help us jointly build a global ethic. These are what is at stake in finding a new scientific worldview that enables us to reinvent the sacred.[378]

I can also see that a parallel shift is required on the humanities and inner-awareness side of the equation. They too must be able to bring a degree of analytical rigor to the awareness of feelings and inner states. This is a core necessity for grounding.

Efforts toward accepting integration need to be made on an individual level by those able to see past the apparent differences imposed by each sphere of knowledge or professional fiefdom. The need is clear, but is the necessary Will to deal with it present?

I predict that these changes to how we all view fields of expertise will be the stuff of leading-edge science for the coming generation. To my way of thinking, the signs are pointing in that direction. And in the mood of the investigative spirit, some far-seeing scientists can be expected to lead that change. And they will probably be called visionaries — after the dust has settled.

---

[378] Kauffman, Stuart A., *Reinventing the Sacred: A new view of science, reason, and religion* (New York: Basic Books, 2009), 9.

Chapter 18 - Following the Spiritual Route of the Heart

Spirituality seeks a direct personal relationship with the divine, which is accessed by going within; whereas, religion is a system of beliefs about God and the important questions in life. Each religion started as an inspired vision.

The Fundamental Difference Is Love

The visionaries most at home in the realm of the heart are the mystics. They seek divine truth, against which all else is considered less important. Mystics are the "rocket scientists" of the inner realm, the most specialized and single-minded in their pursuit. But these pioneers sharpen and fine-tune the heart's perception, rather than the mind.

While mystics are few in number, the religious and spiritual matters they grapple with touch each of us is where we are most solitary and vulnerable. So, the references to "mystics" here do not apply only to mystics, but to those who pursue the inner journey.

Following the route of the heart presents special challenges since customary measures of proof do not apply. Mario Beauregard said in *The Spiritual Brain*, "Mystics are akin to pioneer scientists, deep-sea divers, or astronauts, offering themselves as volunteers in the search and accepting the outcome."[379]

"Mysticism" is derived from a Greek word (muo) that means "to conceal." Mystics seek access to levels of consciousness concealed from everyday life — rather as if they are obscured by a mist or a mystery. This quest is also hidden from view simply because it exists within the individual, so what it entails is not readily observable by others. It touches our deepest core concerns.

Mystics explore the inner realm — out of the reach of conventional thinking, disengaged from objective validation. Such esoteric knowledge cannot be acquired through the physical senses or reason. On this journey, the heart leads and the mind and body follow. The individual learns to read the subtle signals that arise in their inner recesses.

Although the mystics engage the most determined devotion to the wisdom of the heart, everyone is challenged to give greater credence to those deeply felt influences in our lives. Gaining inner maturity requires developing a proper balance of head and heart in the quest to understand the inner world.

Mystics move toward wholeness by polishing and improving the inner lens, dealing with the outer world only to the extent that it insists. Visionaries in all other subject areas seek to establish a vision that will *make things in the world better*; whereas, mystics have relatively little interest in the normal world, except as it furthers their connection to God.

---

[379] Beauregard, Mario and O'Leary, Denyse, *The Spiritual Brain: A neuroscientist's case for the existence of the soul* (New York: HarperOne, 2007), 103.

Evelyn Underhill's *Mysticism* is the classic work that put the spotlight on those mystical states:

> The business and method of mysticism is love.... It is the eager, outgoing activity whose driving power is generous love, not the absorbent, indrawing activity which strives only for new knowledge that is fruitful in the spiritual as well as in the physical world.... Mystic love is total dedication of the will; the deep-seated desire and tendency of the soul towards its Source. It is a condition of humble access, a life-movement of the self: more direct in its methods, more valid in its results—even in the hands of the least lettered of its adepts—than the most piercing intellectual vision of the greatest philosophic mind.... [God can be found only] by love of thine heart. He may not be known by reason, He may not be gotten by thought, nor concluded by understanding; but He may be loved and chosen with the true lovely will of thine heart.[380]

This chapter describes the challenges of those who search for truth as apprehended by the heart—on the spiritual wing of the visionary path. It includes spiritual and religious matters, along with the quest for ultimate reality. About half of this chapter describes religious trends in modern America.

It does not attempt to distinguish between Religious, Spiritual, or Mystical Experiences (RSMEs), treating them as similar, though not equivalent. Any of those terms will be used without elaborating on the very real distinctions between them (unless specifically germane).

Mystics can be found in any of the major religions or spiritual traditions. "All mystics," said Saint-Martin, "speak the same language and come from the same country. As against that fact, the place which they happen to occupy in the kingdom of this world matters little."[381] Their primary loyalty is to knowing God.

Every religion or philosophical system has its own particular take on these topics, their dogma. Bumping into some sacred cows is probably unavoidable, but that is not my intention. Substitute whatever terms that comport with your beliefs.

Information in this chapter reflects my own thinking, derived from a lifetime on the spiritual path. I understand what it demands and what its rewards are. As a person named Faith, these topics are more than a passing interest to me. Understanding the nature of faith has been my prime mandate.

This chapter speaks of "God" since most who go this route desire a more intimate relationship with the divine. However, there are many names for God: Source, Spirit, Yahweh, the Universe, Allah, The One, Ultimate Reality, Truth or Justice (virtues with a capital letter), All that Is, the Tao, Ultimate Reality, Great Spirit.

---

[380] Underhill, Evelyn, *Mysticism: A study in the nature and development of man's spiritual consciousness* (New York: E.P. Dutton & Co. Inc., 1961), 85.
[381] *Ibid.*, xiii.

Whatever your personal beliefs about God happen to be, please accept that sincere people can and will differ on any of these matters. I have attempted to be even-handed, without stepping on anyone's spiritual toes.

Love is not just about being warm and fuzzy. As Christian essayist, Chesterton pointed out "To love means to love the unlovable. To forgive means pardoning the unpardonable. Faith means believing the unbelievable. Hope means hoping when everything seems hopeless." Perplexities abound and some of this is paradoxical indeed.

Mysticism Is the Science of Love

Let me state out front that spiritual searchers and mystics are not perfect. They take their pants on and off every day like everybody else. Those on the spiritual path have the same psychological needs and frustrations to contend with as others. They are not saints, and would be the first to disown any claim to specialness. Such individuals don't deny they must struggle with their baser impulses, but they strive mightily to rise above them. Underhill said:

> [They seek] the expression of the innate tendency of the human spirit towards complete harmony with the transcendental order.... This tendency, in great mystics, gradually captures the whole field of consciousness; it dominates their life and, in the experience called 'mystic union,' attains its end.[382]

> Mysticism, in its pure form, is the science of ultimates, the science of union with the Absolute, and nothing else, and that the mystic is the person who attains to this union, not the person who talks about it. Not to know about, but to Be, is the mark of the real initiate.[383]

Mystics desire access to a consciousness beyond man's limits. In this, they are motivated by love rather than curiosity or personal gain. Many of them have no desire to improve anything in the visible universe, since their sight is focused on God. However, their spiritual practice may include a commitment to serve others or to relieve suffering, so they don't fully disengage from life's obligations.

Mystics attempt to live in a way that avoids anything that could interfere with their inner life. In that sense, even the pursuit of visions is viewed as a distraction. Between moments of contact with divinity, they try to live with as few external or unnecessary influences as possible.

Mysticism is not about the self or making the individual more important. Quite the contrary—it seeks to shrink the role of a separate identity, so the inherent unity with all that exists can blaze forth. Again, to quote Underhill:

> In mysticism the will is united with the emotions in an impassioned desire to transcend the sense-world, in order that the self may be joined by love to the

---

[382] *Ibid.*, xiv.
[383] *Ibid.*, 72.

one eternal and ultimate object of love; whose existence is intuitively perceived by that which we used to call the soul.... In magic, the will unites with the intellect in an impassioned desire for supersensible knowledge.... Obviously the antithesis of mysticism, though often adopting its title and style.[384]

Mystical experience is considered an advanced state of self-transcendence, whereby the sense of a separate self is abandoned. It is the removal of the separateness of "I, Me, Mine," which, being finite, separate us from that which is infinite.

Even a mystic doesn't have mystical spiritual experiences often. But those committed to this quest don't lose sight of their overriding desire for any evidence of being connected with God. And they are keenly aware of all the distractions that must be circumvented in order to stay available.

My Path and the Spiritual Path

I encountered Underhill's *Mysticism* when I was sixteen. No single book has had a greater impact on my personal development. That same dog-eared copy was used for the quotes included here. But my strong interest in spiritual matters predates that.

I was born in Alaska to a Jewish father and a German Lutheran mother (not a likely match, but I like to think there was divine orchestration involved). By the time I was born, they were both Bahá'ís. (It is call the Bahá'í Faith—hence Faith being one of my given names.) That is relevant here because Bahá'ís draw on the central truths of all the world's major religions, and I grew up exposed to ideas from many religious traditions.

That not only contributed to my being eclectic, but it also helped me see their common threads without my judgment being obscured by a preference for a single religion. Later, I attended a Methodist liberal arts university and acquired a major in philosophy-religion (along with concentrations in psychology and business). For eighteen years as an adult, I lived in a spiritual community devoted to rigorous inner work that was also quite eclectic in scope.

I knew I was on the spiritual path for as long as I can remember. Being spoken to by God at twelve, when I was told my life purpose, left me no doubt in that regard. That auditory vision has been the mainspring of my wide-ranging life activities.

Each time I found myself at a crossroads, I revisited my twelve-year-old mandate and would consider the words I heard then in light of the decision at hand. While that vision never steered me wrong, it is equally true that the meaning of the original message has continued to expand and change, as I've grown and refined my perspective.

---

[384] *Ibid.*, xiv.

This path reflects my personal life mission. But because of that mystical experience at such a young age, I had an extra responsibility: pay attention, notice, prepare yourself to be a witness and a voice for what you find. I have paid my dues, and can speak of this topic because I've been preparing for over half a century.

About forty years ago I made a pledge to make my life a living example that spiritual devotion and family life can work together, so they make each other stronger. I was attempting to challenge the widespread assumption that a person must choose one at the expense of the other.

I like to think my life choices demonstrated that it is possible—and worth it! It is not easy, nor merely a slogan. Maintaining the will to serve both my higher purpose and my everyday life honorably is an intricate balancing act that must be reaffirmed on a minute-by-minute basis.

Flavors of Love

The ancient Greeks identified four different kinds of love:
- Storge—affection, as within a family
- Philos—friendship
- Eros—romantic or sexual love, usually between a man and a woman
- Agape—the love of God or unconditional love

> Those devoted to spiritual growth are most attentive to agape. I am adding another with a slightly different emphasis—Divine Creative Intelligence. I believe that what we experience as Divine Love is the unfolding of an Intelligence that evolves through the experience of creation.

We humans are part of the created universe; we can sense its reality through who we are or choose to become. We participate in divinity by our efforts to create as well. Those with a spiritual calling are often found within a religious setting, which provides a measure of training, community, and protection from the pressures of the everyday world. Most devotees live as relative hermits or in spiritual communities, looking to inhabit a defined space that is neither "*in* the world" nor "*of* the world."

In my opinion, these desires for greater spiritual connectedness are stirring with greater vigor in many more people these days. As our tug-of-war between head and heart resolves into greater cooperation between them, this yearning toward living from one's authentic self will be stronger still.

To the extent that pursuing those inner summonses becomes more acceptable and widespread, some people will not feel as obliged to abandon everyday living in order to explore the mysteries of life.

W.T. Stace wrote extensively about mysticism. He distinguished between two types of mystical experiences:

- Extrovertive: Nature, art, music, or mundane objects facilitate mystical consciousness. Suddenly, they are transfigured by awareness of the One.
- Introvertive: The One is found 'at the bottom of the self, at the bottom of human personality.'

Generally, Stace regarded introvertive mysticism as much more important historically, because it escapes the limitations of the senses.[385]

Some spiritual searchers make the introvertive route primary. However, none of these experiences are the exclusive province of those on a visionary or spiritual path. They reflect a human predisposition to find meaning that resides in every heart. One need not turn to any particular philosophical stance or religion to make it flame bright.

Stace's distinction shows why people can be deeply immersed in mystical and spiritual experiences without any need for formalized religion. For them, the transcendent experiences of nature or art permit a direct connection to sublime awareness. Those will not be the main focus of this chapter, although some aspects do overlap.

Being and Becoming

Another way of addressing the progression of spiritual growth is through the Being versus Becoming Paradox. All efforts to find God or the ultimates are about "becoming closer and ever closer" —*almost there*. "Becoming" is incremental and relative. "Being," on the other hand, is absolute and non-relative. It is the unshakable certainty of being *always, already there*. Nothing more is needed or desired.

All systems of religion are dealing with Becoming issues. But transcendent experiences arise as Being, and we sense them through our very Being. That is why they are so transitory. What is known and obvious via Being is perplexing in any other state. Most spiritual practice attempts to maintain a ceaseless contact with that state.

References to a spiritual path are clearly about an incremental and gradual development. When one is immersed in Being, words and explanation add nothing. But they are the lifeline for the rest of the time, as we function in Becoming. Trying to put words to this paradoxical disjuncture ties the mind in knots, but it accounts for many of the hard-to-discuss efforts that attend creativity or "out-of-this-world awareness."

Experiences of Now are from Being, as are flashes of certitude and Being in a sea of Becoming. Being encompasses Becoming, but knowing that is not much help when one is not sensing the full truth from one's Being. Those two states coexist—each an accurate reflection of big "R" Reality and small "r" reality.

---

[385] *Op. cit.*, Beauregard, 187.

Love is a quality of Being, so all the talk of love in this chapter speaks to that level.

In *The Spiritual Brain,* Mario Beauregard and Denyse O'Leary speak of the unavoidable paradox.

> Mystics often describe their quest in apparently paradoxical ways.... Often the intention is to point to a state of mind in which striving is absent, and labeling of mental activities ceases. The mind of 'no effort' strives neither for thought nor for no-thought. Paradoxes apprise the hearer that mystical consciousness is different from the normal human thought streams.[386]

What Mystics Want

The Deepest Discovery of the Interior Life

Mysticism is about a soul's profound, intimate, and heartrending relationship with God. It includes the unassailable discovery that God is living within oneself. That realization usually comes only after a long journey of opening and deepening. But finding that truth fundamentally alters how a person looks at everything in their prior life, as well as how they live afterward.

Mother Clare Watts describes being touched by a direct experience of God.

> To experience the presence and reality of God, and to experience that this immense and all-knowing Being has an individual knowing and love for you, will break your heart open and submerge it in the most wonderful new life that in comparison makes all previous knowing and living seem meaningless and dull.
>
> Once you are touched and opened by that warmest and greatest of loves, nothing in the worlds of matter or spirit looks the same. Now everything has the tincture of the divinity and the love, affecting how you understand, relate to and feel about it. Nature looks more magnificent, material pursuits more spurious, and human beings can no longer be thought of as anything less than sons and daughters of God in the making. You will see all people in terms of how close or far they are from God and God's love rather than by any other ways you would have understood them before. And all human love will pale in the face of experiencing the love God has for you.[387]

Mystics Crave and Long for:
- A lost home, a better place, which makes them a pilgrim or a reformer
- A heart for a heart, for the perfect mate or companion (the divine), which makes them a lover (mystical marriage)

---

[386] *Ibid.,* 191.
[387] Mother Clare Watts, "Christian Mysticism," *Wisdom Magazine,* December, 2009, http://wisdom-magazine.com

- Purity and perfection, which makes them an ascetic, who denies their earthly desires or base impulses

Stages of the Path

There is an orderly progression toward spiritual maturity that reflects a person's inner growth. That is the Becoming track. However, individual striving aside, Divine Love can manifest at any point or stage. It is not just the carrot dangling ahead or only dished out in heaven.

Underhill divided the path into five sections (in contrast to the usual three: Purgation, Illumination, and Union).

Stages of the Spiritual Path:
1. The Awakening of Self — vision, inspiration, metanoia; turning toward the light
2. The Purgation of Self — removing oneself from the distraction or temptations of the world (or of the ego)
3. Illumination — total merging of the individual self with God
4. The Dark Night of the Soul — the test of surrender, giving up the limited relationship with God for a higher level of comprehension and Being
5. The Unitive Life — even a search for God (or identification with the process) is purged, leaving only that which is unbroken and whole — Being

It bears noting that "Illumination" falls in the middle, not at the end. If one considers that to be enlightened, that stage is not the grand climax, followed by a state of unending bliss.

Popular expectations to the contrary, one can (and does) touch that state in transcendent moments — a quick round-trip to Being. It is also not true that being enlightened makes all one's problems go away. Problems do arise, but they are handled very differently — without ego identification or judging. In spiritual mastery, one is sufficiently developed to access those states "at will."

One key distinction in any discussion about God is whether God is *out there* (God Transcendent) or *in here*, within me (God Immanent). Those who go very far along this path are striving for an intimate relationship with the infinite. The link that allows that to happen is Love.

> In certain types of psychological and spiritual training, you can be introduced to a full spectrum of stages of consciousness and bodily experiences right from the start — as a peak experience, meditative state, shamanic vision, altered state, and so on. The reason these peak experiences are possible is that many of the major states of consciousness ... are ever-present possibilities. So you can very quickly be introduced to many higher states of consciousness.
>
> You cannot, however, be introduced to all the *qualities* of higher stages without actual growth and practice. You can have a peak experience of higher states ...

because many states are ever-present, and so they can be "peek" experienced right now. But you cannot have a peak experience of a higher stage (like being a concert-level pianist) because stages unfold sequentially and take considerable time to develop. Stages build upon their predecessors in very concrete ways, so they cannot be skipped.... This is one of the many important differences between states and stages.

However, with repeated practice of contacting higher states, your own stages of development will tend to unfold in a much faster and easier way."[388]

Transformation of the Individual

Losing One's Limited Self in the Absolute

There are three significant transformations along the spiritual path. Each seems finished and totally sufficient at the point it is completed. In one sense, that is true since they each connect one to Being. However, until all transformations are realized, what is learned cannot stay grounded or embodied. The awareness of Unity eliminates the apparently random flip-flopping between Being and Becoming.

Saying: Mental transformation is relatively easy, it only takes a few years. Emotional transformation is hard and takes a very long time. Physical transformation almost never happens, but it never goes away.

Order of Personal Transformations:
- **Mental Transformation**—fastest and easiest to acquire; this involves learning physical, mental, and emotional discipline. It involves devotion, often to a specific religious tradition. People who reach this stage sometimes wrongly assume they are enlightened or "saved" (they have seen the light), but it is a temporary honeymoon. They still face the grueling next stages where unity with the divine can take root.

- **Emotional Transformation**—this one is the toughest because the person might think they've already arrived because of mental transformation (so this feels like a wrong turn, rather than the next stage). Everything within the individual that is not governed by love and compassion is being honed and refined.

- **Physical Transformation**—the body, which had been left behind or controlled in the quest for God or meaning, is found to hold divinity, and it is recognized as a reservoir of esoteric knowledge. The flesh never

---

[388] Wilber, Ken, *Integral Spirituality: A startling new role for religion and the modern and postmodern world* (Boston: Integral Books, 2007), 10-11.

doubted or lost its way, but existed, as does all matter, as a perfect creation.

In the Unitive Life (the final stage, *a la* Underhill), the person knows himself or herself to partake in the unity of all things. One knows with every fiber of one's body, mind, and heart that all is God (or one of the absolutes).

This awareness of being one with God is referred to as "God Immanent" (God *in me* and *as me*), compared to "God Transcendent" (God out there and far away), which is the province of religions and philosophies.

Enlightenment Is Great, But...

Anyone with a body has to live in the material world. However, another meaning of enlightenment is that the body itself can hold more light within the cells. It's imbued with the most refined energy. That is one reason there is so much concern about purification and avoiding negative (sinful) influences. It is no small matter that many religious traditions refer to the body as the "Temple of the Holy Spirit."

An enlightened person sees with the most inclusive lens and with the focus of true compassion—that is mastered passion. Along the way they have given up most personal preferences and see through the light of Perfection, infused with divine energy—and that is glorious!

Contrary to popular belief, reaching enlightenment (or nirvana) is not the end of the spiritual journey. Neither is heaven, which must await our physical death. (Not that I am denying anybody's beliefs about the afterlife. I am only referring to what can be realized here, while still alive.)

Enlightenment is greatly to be desired and worked toward. It is one of the major markers for spiritual seekers. However, mystics know that anything less than realization of union is just a way station.

When flirting with enlightenment, attempts to understand through words are doomed to fail. One can only *know through identity* what is known, through Being. Enlightenment (meaning infused with light and delight) is beyond dogma—although all the teachings are vigorously trying to explain it and build a path to reach it. And that is any religion's proper role—but it cannot be more than a path—one of many. Again, quoting Underhill:

> [Mysticism] is non-individualistic. It implies, indeed, the abolition of individuality; of that hard separateness of 'I, Me, Mine' that makes of man a finite isolated thing. It is essentially a movement of the heart, seeking to transcend the limitations of the individual standpoint and to surrender itself to ultimate Reality; for no personal gain, to satisfy no transcendental curiosity, to obtain no other-worldly joys, but purely from an instinct of love. By the word 'heart,' of course we here mean not merely the seat of the affections, 'the organ of tender emotion,' and the like: but rather the inmost sanctuary of personal being; the deep root of its love and will, the very source of its energy and life.

> The mystic is 'in love with the Absolute' not in any idle or sentimental manner, but in the vital sense which presses at all costs and through all dangers toward union with the object beloved.[389]

The notion of enlightenment has become tarnished by its extensive use in popular literature. It is often treated as the Black Belt of spiritual achievement or the Ph.D. of godliness. I hate to puncture any treasured beliefs or desires, but the nature of one's core identity has little concern for that. It simply Is. Enough said.

> The word enlightenment conjures up the idea of some superhuman accomplishment, and the ego likes to keep it that way, but it is simply your natural state of felt oneness with Being. It is a state of connectedness with something immeasurable and indestructible, something that, almost paradoxically, is essentially you and yet is much greater than you. It is finding your true nature beyond name and form.[390]

One of the blinding discoveries, signaling the end of searching, is this: the need to search was only an illusion because God's Love is recognized as the nature of the universe, and "who you are" as well. That realization has been interspersed along the path, and keeps being re-discovered over and over. To Being, it is obvious; to Becoming, it is something to discover once again.

The final stage consists not in discovering that, but in no longer forgetting it. The illusion is known to be just that—even feeling lost helped to reveal the illusion of distance.

No religion or spiritual path has a lock on God, Divine Love or any of the virtues. Those surpass the religious form or man's highest level of devotion. That which is infinite cannot help but exceed man's capacity to comprehend it—hence the need for humility and a sincere trust in Grace—both of which remove the entire path from the context of accomplishment.

> [Tolle said] The present moment has always been available to spiritual seekers, but as long as you are seeking you are not available to the present moment. 'Seeking' implies that you are looking to the future for some answer, or for some achievement, spiritual or otherwise. Everybody is in the seeking mode, seeking to add something to who they are, whether it be money, relationships, possessions, knowledge, status ... or spiritual attainment.[391]

The blinding truth that comes in Being experiences is the realization that *you both have and are what you have been seeking*. The Unity of absolutely everything is unassailable. And you are neither greater than, nor lesser than, everything else because you know that to be true.

---

[389] *Op. cit.*, Underhill, 71-72.
[390] Tolle, Eckhart, *The Power of Now: A guide to spiritual enlightenment* (Novato, CA: New World Library, 1999), 10.
[391] *Ibid*.

Developing Spiritual Discipline

Listening to Silence

According to existential philosopher Paul Tillich, "The first duty of love is to listen." Those on a spiritual journey do not just listen to the wisdom of the heart within, but also strive to hear and see signs of God and love in life—in others and within the world of matter.

They don't avoid engaging with the messiness of life because it is too coarse and hostile. But, attuned to the signs of divinity, they see (and listen for) its presence everywhere.

In order to develop the practice of listening as a sacred art, three qualities work together in a way that enhance awareness about oneself, higher reality, and the value of other people. **Silence** creates the space for listening to God. It provides time to explore our relationship to Source. The practice of being in this silence nurtures our capacity to listen to others.

> **Reflection** gives us access to listening for our inner voice. The practice of taking a few breaths before responding to a situation, question, or comment gives time for your true wisdom to reveal itself. It's a slowing down, waiting, practicing patience.
>
> **Presence** is the awareness of listening to another, of connecting at the heart level. The practice of taking a mundane, ordinary activity and giving it your full attention.[392]
>
> It is important to slow down our thinking process, take time to reflect, listen to the still, small voice at the essence of our being, and open up the possibility of understanding. It not only takes time to listen like this, it takes practice to remember to do so. The blessing comes in feeling profoundly related to others, especially those whose beliefs are different from our own.[393]

Of course, these same practices are also conducive to making the creative juices flow. One "listens" in order to flow with insights as they arise—tapping the abundance of "knowing" that comes forth. You don't have to be an artist or highly creative to benefit from enlarging these abilities. They can add to each person's quality of life in countless ways.

Finding an Empty Space Within for Intuition and Grace

We find our divine purpose through the way we manifest it in our lives. In this regard, the mystics are no different than everyone else who is caught up in everyday concerns. According to William McNamara, "The mystic is not a special kind of person; every person is a special kind of mystic."

---

[392] Lindahl, Kay, *The Sacred Art of Listening: Forty reflections for cultivating a spiritual practice* (Woodstock, VT: Skylight Paths Publishing, 2002), 16.
[393] *Ibid.*, 70.

In *The Corporate Mystic,* Gay Hendricks and Kate Ludeman explain the unnatural space in which mystics operate.

> Intuition dwells in the gap between ordinary thoughts. Much of the time our thoughts seem jumbled together so tightly that there doesn't seem to be any space between them but if you look carefully, you will see that there is open space between and behind all your thoughts. Intuition occurs in this gap.
>
> The gap is the province of the mystic. Mystics are comfortable in the gap, while non-mystics experience fear when they're there. Non-mystics are comfortable only in the predictable territory of their known thoughts. Mystics cannot live in the zone of the known for very long without feeling stultified. To find intuition and make it your friend, you must enter the gap.[394]

In the context of spiritual matters, grace is one of the paradoxes. What comes into our lives through Grace are not rewards for good behavior. Grace signifies that knowledge about the divine cannot be earned or gained by rational notions. It is a gift only.

~ Make a Space for Grace ~
A BonBon ~ Faith Lynella

God comes in the little spaces between—between activities, between thoughts, between people. That's the brief moment where there's a "space for grace." It's not felt as grand and glorious, but close and intimate—because God becomes alive to us that way. That's really how we connect—not through large gestures but in the wee, small, personal and intimate ones.

But for that to occur, we must leave space that's unfilled with other matters. Make space between all those jostling concerns sucking up your attention and energy. Make space for the presence of God, and it will be filled.

Space between events brings peace and freedom (though brief).
Space between people brings respect, and often love.
Space within yourself brings joy.

P.S. Make a space for Binkles!
Every space IS a Binkle!

From *BonBons to Sweeten Your Daily Life*; Or from *More BonBons*.

---

[394] Hendricks, Gay and Ludeman, Kate, *The Corporate Mystic: A guidebook for visionaries with their feet on the ground* (New York: Bantam Books, 1996), 110.

Faith Is a Safety Net

"Faith is believing when it is beyond the power of reason to believe," according to Voltaire. Faith is for the mind or emotions, something to hang onto when one cannot be sure of what to trust. Faith is mostly about holding fast to our hoard of beliefs when the full force of certainty is not present. But faith has no purpose in the light of illumination—one simply knows.

Faith is often contrasted with doubt concerning the reality of God (or some other religious belief). People assume they must not yield to doubt because that is a failure of their devotion. However, as Paul Tillich points out, "Doubt is not the opposite of faith; it is one element of faith."

Doubts can lead us out of rigid or outgrown beliefs, and to a higher perception of truth. We should respect our doubts, yet be clear-sighted about what can be learned from them. Disabilities advocate Joni Erickson Tada said, "Faith isn't the ability to believe long and far into the misty future. It's simply taking God at His Word and taking the next step."

Faith needs open eyes. Inspired certainty is beyond faith. Faith is like a ladder, but once you arrive at the topmost point of clear sight it serves no further purpose. Clinging to faith instead of trusting what you see would represent a step back, or down.

Identification with Divinity

For those on the spiritual path, the fork in the road takes him or her away from total identification with everyday reality (Caesar's world in the biblical sense). Some profound experience could lead them to metanoia—a *turning from* their normal reality and toward God, nature, beauty or any of the ultimates.

For long stretches of the spiritual path, a person is torn between the otherworldly reality that is encountered on occasion, and the normal world of the senses: between the divine and the mundane, between desires of the spirit and of the flesh. For some, that inner turmoil leads to them to cease being totally identified with the everyday world and shifting their primary allegiance to the profound.

Chief among identifications is each person's identification with their own ego, which is casually treated as "who I am." But the ego has a narrow view of a particular person's authentic self. Every person is much greater than the scope of their ego and a spiritual life seeks to find out how. Reining in the ego, or its self-aggrandizing ways, must occur before one's core, and larger, identity can be seen clearly.

Also, the psychological notion of being "identified" with something is a step removed from being authentic. That elevates a concept or object (what the person is identified with) above their authentic identity, or even God. It is one of the most seductive of mental habits since it is seldom challenged or unmasked. Tolle also said:

Identification with your mind creates an opaque screen of concepts, labels, images, words, judgments, and definitions that block all true relationship. It comes between you and yourself, between you and your fellow man and woman, between you and nature, between you and God. It is this screen of thought that creates the illusion of separateness, the illusion that there is you and a totally separate 'other.' You then forget the essential fact that, underneath the level of physical appearances and separate forms, you are one with all that is.[395]

Identification relates to the first of the Ten Commandments given to Moses in the Old Testament: "You shall have no other gods before Me."[396] Accordingly, the only acceptable identification is with God (or your own authentic self). Anything else is not one's true identity, hence it is false.

Whatever (or whomever) a person is most identified with is in danger of being placed first — whether it is money, status, emotional attachments to a particular person(s), or stuff. Authentic and transcendent experiences cannot become dominant for someone as long as one's identifications hog all the air in the room. Their increasing nakedness ferrets out such unrecognized identifications, so they can be demoted to their rightful place.

A Person's Sequence Works this Way:
1. Identified with normal life — our natural and default condition; starting point
2. On the spiritual path — become identified with the vision, God, or one's primary mission
3. Brings vision and creative efforts into sync — grounding inspiration and otherworldly influences
4. Growing in skills of both realms; finding the appropriate degree of harmonious balance and accommodation. It is no longer an identification but rests on one's integrated identity — the authentic one

Reduction of the Ego

A spiritually directed path works hard to reduce the desires of the world or egotistical tendencies. Taking vows like chastity, poverty, and obedience, that some spiritual traditions mandate, are efforts to minimize normal life concerns. In *Breakfast at the Victory*, James P. Carse clarifies the relationship between ego and soul.

> Mystics often distinguish between the ego and the soul, or the ego and the self. The terms are not so important, but the distinction is. The ego is the dualist in us. It is the habit we have of seeing ourselves over and against someone else. As

---

[395] *Op. cit.*, Tolle.
[396] *Bible*, Exodus, 20:3.

ego, my inwardness remains inward because it is completely closed off to you by my outwardness. As ego, my wealth, intelligence, moral goodness, social class are what they are only in contrast to the person next to me. Whether or not we are believers, we oppose the natural and the supernatural; we are here and worldly; God is there and otherworldly. In fact, belief and unbelief are strictly issues for the ego; you can't be an unbeliever unless there are some believers against whom you are an unbeliever. All such oppositions are creations of the ego.

From the perspective of soul, however, we are each opposing either/or as a conjoined both/and. We can be here only because we are not there; in this way the 'here' and 'there' belong together. 'That comes from this, and this comes from that—which means that that and this give birth to one another. Life rises from death and death from life'....

The still center, the soul does not oppose anything. Not opposing anything, it does nothing. As soul, we do not act; we are. Ego, we cope with the world, change it, arrange it, try to improve it. We cope with ourselves, too, becoming our own projects, struggling to be who and where we are not.[397]

The True Nature of the Heart and Love Are a Mystery

Although I have tried to be careful in my use of the words "heart" or "love" throughout this book, it is time for candor about them. **Nobody knows precisely how they work**. Despite all human efforts to figure them out, despite whole libraries and philosophies devoted to explanations, it must be admitted that we do not know.

That is not to say they cannot be known, however. Each of us can know the truth of it and have times when we do—without a doubt. We know love through being one with it. We sense our unity and identity with the larger reality, the big R one. Whether that comes as a Now moment, a binkle, a vision, or full Mystical Union, we know it with every fiber of our being—or Being.

That knowledge cannot be conveyed except through direct experience. However, anything less than that full and immediate awareness does not, and cannot, be mistaken for it. That reality will always remain The Mystery.

What we read or hear about it are either from memory, hubris, or a state of "lesser" fullness (from "becoming"). For more, revisit Chapter 6.

What the heart knows is that it is the link between the self which is limited and the self which is not. It is also the link between oneself and others, as well as with the divine and the larger reality. The heart is a hub that connects our numerous realities and energetic states. The work for all humans is to purify

---

[397] Carse, James P., *Breakfast at the Victory: The mysticism of ordinary experience* (New York: HarperCollins, 1994), 11-12.

one's heart. If it is energetically congested with old emotions, hurt, grief, or distrust, then the richer and fuller connection with divinity is distorted.

Each of us has a juvenile picture of intellect being in the wrinkled-up brain and feelings being in the valentine-like heart. The images are useful metaphors, but the relationship between heart and mind is far more complex. And we treat our choices or preferences as being between one or the other, as though it were that simple. It isn't.

They are intermeshed, and constantly influence each other. It is human nature to want to figure this out, but it defies anything that logic can throw at it.

The current set of principles and schools of thought regarding heart versus head or intellectual versus emotional intelligence are sadly lacking. They are all missing something we (humans) do not yet know or have not yet realized. Perhaps that is because they are *not* separate functions but blended capacities that operate in some sort of invisibly ordered chaos.

Emotions play a valuable and important role in the development of our everyday perspective. Emotions are the language of 3-D reality. They motivate or halt any activity, warn us of danger, and connect us to those we love. It is now common knowledge that feelings and emotional impulses course through the entire body and brain, triggering chemical reactions. They, in turn, affect our muscle tone, heart rate, organ function, and blood pressure, while also stirring up mental pictures, thoughts, beliefs, and stored programs.

Emotions are frequencies. They are vibrations which are translated and interpreted by our learned beliefs about what is happening in our reality. But we are not automatons, at the mercy of each stimulus that "pulls our chains." Greater self-awareness can call forward a higher vibrating and alternate emotional response, literally from within oneself.

We can learn how to intervene on primal and habitual responses arising from our animal/instinct nature with responses that are more aligned and harmonious with our authentic identity the divine—our true self.

Becoming attuned to the heart's energy opens us to a larger scope of possibilities. It starts with energetically and emotionally cleaning out one's heart space—shine it up, air it out and begin to live there.

The heart operates as our power source. One's heartbeat and internal rhythms are connected to the oscillating frequency of the planet. It is each person's heart-based purpose to consciously use that power source in their own inimitable way to radiate love and appreciation for self and all, every moment of every day.

Whittling Down the Ego

The dilemma, of course, is how one can successfully disengage from so-called love that operates from self-interest and embrace in its stead the model of divine love, familiarly known in public discourse as "unconditional love." That requires the involvement of the higher "energy-intelligent centers," which are not rooted in this plane of reality (a conditional reality).

Unconditional love is not an emotion at all, but is first and always, a choice—a conscious choice. Sometimes, the heart gets to feel the fullness and satisfaction of that choice, but other times the heart is feeling things that seem contrary to that choice. The point is, the choice never changes, it is the constant, and it must occur first always.

It is also a choice that often must be made repeatedly until the ego fully gets the message and gives up all its foot-stomping. The emotions don't drive that choice, they respond to it.

Compassion is not ego-oriented. It permits a person to look at the world, and other people, through the lens of unity and heart-based caring. It has no ulterior motives beyond experiencing the love itself. It arises with the recognition that at our core identity we are all the same.

The Expanding Emotional Focus:
- Self-centered—"I feel *my* pain," and that is what matters the most
- Empathy—"I feel *your* pain," reflects awareness of personal similarities with someone else; often leads to sharing, aid, or reciprocity
- Compassion—"I feel *our* pain," reflects an awareness of unity with everyone, does not feel separate from anyone

Your heart is a gateway that connects you to your higher self, to one another, to the life on this planet, and to all dimensions that connect with ours. It is the intelligence of your heart that holds truth and wisdom. And it is within the heart that the process of transformation takes place.

Having acknowledged the trickiness of any discussion in this area, I still feel the need to point out a distinction related to the heart, where many people get stuck.

The Desiring Heart and the Caring Heart

Each of us has multiple ways that we engage the heart in making practical life choices. "The heart wants what the heart wants." But the nature of those desires indicates the extent to which the ego is exerting its influence. Progress along the spiritual journey could be tracked by someone's movement along a continuum: between the Desiring Heart (the default) at one end and the Caring Heart, which is more compassionate, at the other. That progression tracks with the development of greater spiritual and psychological maturity.

The two approaches co-exist within each person's heart, but the worldviews that each signifies compete for expression. They differ as to what is treated as primary or in what they mean by "love." Movement indicates a growing level of self-mastery regarding what's considered ideal.

They coexist to varying degrees within each of us. The Caring Heart is largely dormant unless it is carefully developed and nourished. Lacking that, it is not unusual for someone who has been subjected to the crucible of great personal suffering to awaken through an epiphany to the existence of this inexpressible divine state. Once experienced, there's no going back.

The two approaches, each authentic and sincere, have very different desires and capacities that reflect a difference of maturity. The two expressions of heartfelt desires are not at odds exactly, but as long as the Desiring Heart is in the forefront, it drowns out any ability to perceive the other in most situations.

The Desiring Heart is totally involved in the material world and one's exterior life, while the Caring Heart is more attuned to the higher principles of unity and love. It also concerns itself about the likely impact on others, if its desires are met. But it is not an either-or choice since it is made from the awareness that both approaches are valid and have a role to play. It is usually a matter of answering to both in appropriate proportion.

The Desiring Heart sometimes displays out-of-control mood swings, depending on whether or not it gets what it wants. At its most undisciplined, the Desiring Heart displays the willful demands of a petulant child. While it can get smarter about expressing those desires, the driving force is still ego-based and acquisitive: "I want that," *or* "I deserve that." (It is always about "me.")

The Desiring Heart is the prevalent dictator in modern life—in both adults and children (neither of whom seem to know any better). However, it is ominously unwise to let it run the show. It is need-driven and want-driven.

The Desiring Heart wants to acquire in things or thrills whatever can compensate for what's not being satisfied on the inside—the lack of genuine love or authenticity. Of course, anything that's not genuine cannot satisfy the deep hunger.

Rigor is required in the training of the heart—a putting aside of the willfulness of "what I want" that is self-centered in favor of greater concern for others or the larger picture. While the Caring Heart is more values-driven, it is the combination of them together that brings wisdom and caring into the lives of those who let it flower. We could all benefit from more of that.

Religion and Spirituality—A Changing Relationship

Going Directly to God

Religions provide systems of beliefs about God and morality. Each is a vessel that maintains its founders' teachings and the rituals for relating to the divine. Many of them combine meditation, contemplation, worship, and the quest for personal salvation.

Spirituality and religion are not the same thing. Although there can be considerable overlap, the two operate with different priorities and methods. In *Spiritual But Not Religious,* Robert C. *Fuller explains the historic trend.*

> Before the 20th century the terms religious and spiritual were used more or less interchangeably. But a number of modern intellectual and cultural forces have accentuated differences between the 'private' and 'public' spheres of life. The increasing prestige of the sciences, the insights of modern biblical scholarship, and greater awareness of cultural relativism all made it more difficult for educated Americans to sustain unqualified loyalty to religious institutions. Many began to associate genuine faith with the 'private' realm of personal experience rather than with the 'public' realm of institutions, creeds, and rituals.... Those who see themselves as 'spiritual but not religious' reject traditional organized religions as the sole — or even the most valuable — means of furthering their spiritual growth.[398]

Spirituality seeks a direct personal relationship with the divine, which is accessed by going within. But religion is a system of beliefs about God and the important questions in life. Each religion started as an inspired vision, by a solitary person who found a way to plant the seeds of belief in others.

Every religion functions with more or less: structure, symbolism, formal rituals, and a cast of various intermediaries — all designed to connect to God. As such, most of them have more in common with large organizations (Chapter 14) than with a rapturous ascetic striving to unite with God.

Avenues to God:
- Through the heart — love and good works; service to others, animals, and the earth
- Through the mind — scholarship of sacred texts, theology, philosophy
- Through mastery of the flesh, spiritual practices that control and redirect natural impulses or emotions; either control or escape from the body

Each avenue appeals to certain individuals more than the others, but all three approaches can be accommodated within the major religions. Spiritual practices usually involve meditation and acts of devotion like: good works, training devotees, preaching, symbolic rituals, and missionary activities.

Churches are fraught with Flame and Vessel issues, as described in Chapter 8. All existing religions are examples of vessels and have the challenges to support light and inspiration, without attempting to supplant it.

Surveys in the U.S.A. show that most religious groups have lost ground. Even while the number of Christians has declined, many more people are exploring their own spiritual frontiers, and have fallen off the faith map entirely. There is a growing trend for people to look outside their church for a sense of inner peace and a direct experience of connection to "something more" or the holy.

So many people claim "no religion at all" that that category outranks all Christian religious groups, except the Baptists and Catholics. Those who

---

[398] Fuller, Robert C., "Spiritual, But Not Religious," excerpt from the book, *Spiritual But Not Religious* (New York: Oxford University Press), 2001.

identify their religion as "None" now make up 15% of the population. In addition, nearly three million people identify themselves with dozens of spiritual movements.

In *How God Changes Your Brain,* Andrew Newberg *et al.* speak to the evolving relationship between religion and spirituality.

> All of the research that we and others have accumulated allows us to make a prediction about the future of God. Clearly, God is not going go away, but it won't necessarily be the God depicted in our sacred texts. According to a recent Barna survey, the biblical views of an all-powerful, all-knowing creator is waning. What will take its place?
>
> If our survey sheds any light on the question, it will be a God that maintains its mystery, a very intimate experience that cannot be captured by words. And if the trend toward personal spirituality continues, we should see a world where many notions of God coexist. Hopefully, this will inspire greater tolerance between people of different religious faiths as they realize the underlying unity and diversity of these experiences....
>
> Religion and spirituality are constantly changing and evolving, and this is a good thing, for both society and the human brain. New ideas challenge us to think more deeply about personal values and survival, and the more you think about the mysteries of human nature, the more likely it is that you'll have an epiphany that can improve the inner quality of your life. For most Americans, that is what spirituality is about.[399]

Writers have noted that many people treat God as a form of personal hobby, rather than as a deep personal commitment, as was the case when churches played a more central role in community life. Numerous surveys have found that confidence in organized religion has fallen significantly. But that is not to say that most people do not care about the ultimate questions, like the meaning of life or man's place in the scheme of things. They have simply moved away from treating any single religion as a "one-stop shop."

"Spiritual but Not Religious"

Spirituality is being redefined in our culture to be something separate from, and very much broader than religious faith. "Spirituality is something everyone can have—even atheists. In its most expansive sense, it could simply be taken to refer to any individual's particular quest to discover that which is held sacred."[400]

---

[399] Newberg, Andrew and Waldman, Mark Robert, *How God Changes Your Brain: Breakthrough findings from a leading neurologist* (New York: Ballantine Books, 2009), 82.
[400] Mooney, Chris, "Spirituality Can Bridge Science-religion Divide," *USA Today*, September 12, 2010.

A *USA Today* article by Chris Mooney found that most people did not consider God as separate from them.

> When we asked our survey participants to describe their spiritual experiences, many talked about God as an emotional presence, using words like peace, energy, tranquility, or bliss. God was not a separate entity, but rather a force that permeated everything. God didn't create the universe, God was the universe, a radiance that extended throughout time and space. God was light, God was freedom, and for many people God was consciousness itself.[401]

Conventional religions are very hierarchical, with God at the top; the church is in the middle; and individuals (believers) are at the bottom. As with other institutions, people are less satisfied to be at the bottom of the pecking order. The church used to be the individual's primary link to God.

Now institutional religion is largely optional since people find their inspiration in a variety of other settings and practices as well. They are able to find the holy outside of the religious framework. Andrew Newberg also found:

> [Social scientists are] good at explaining how people make judgments about harm and fairness, but they still struggle to explain the feelings of awe, transcendence, patriotism, joy and self-sacrifice. Which are not ancillary to most people's moral experiences, but central. The evolutionary approach also leads many scientists to neglect the concept of individual responsibility and makes it hard for them to appreciate that most people struggle toward goodness, not as a means, but as an end in itself.[402]

Atheists Care about God, Too

Those who claim that God does not exist are not indifferent to spiritual concerns. They have a belief system about God, but it is oriented 180° away from that of those who consider themselves religious. In many respects, atheism acts as a religion—a rather defiant one. As such, it concerns itself with many of the same issues as the faithful.

Atheism has all the marks of a belief system. Most atheists put their trust in the mind and dismiss any "evidence" about divinity that does not satisfy objective reason. But how could it? The mind does not operate on that channel.

Let's be honest here. That is a rigged game. The burden of proof as to whether God is real *cannot* be met—period. The heart's arguments cannot prove it and the mind's arguments cannot disprove it. Framing it as the burden of proof uses the wrong tool, the wrong, standard—guaranteed to result in a standoff, which is what we have now.

The flaw with the burden of proof approach is not in the correctness of the competing arguments themselves—it is in thinking that arguing can resolve it.

---

[401] *Op. cit.*, Newberg, 112.
[402] Brooks, David, "The End of Philosophy," *New York Times*, April 7, 2009.

Believers and atheists alike can be moved by awe and wonder—of something beyond our puny comprehension. If one chooses to call that "God," and the other calls it "not God," it is still the same experience (and I am not just talking about labels).

Einstein was addressing such a sensation when he said: "The most beautiful emotion we can experience is the mystical. It is the power of all true art and science. He to whom this emotion is a stranger, who can no longer wonder and stand rapt in awe, is as good as dead!"

It's not such a great accomplishment to point out the flaws in religious beliefs, or all the ways religion leads man astray, or its inconsistencies between the espoused principles and execution. All religions have a poor track record in such matters. But that's largely a reflection of human frailties and arrogance. That does not negate that there could be something more to religion than that.

Being "anti" is a phase, like adolescence. The guy in heaven in a white beard is a caricature of anything holy, and does not deserve blind devotion. But neither is it such a coup to point that out. Atheists play a form of "the emperor has no clothes," which points out the big lie.

But then what? That is hardly a comprehensive philosophy or a way to live. Having toppled the "false gods," what does a person hang their hat on instead? What do they put in its place, or mature into? Thinking along these lines can get stuck in defiance, and seems to lack a second act.

It's possible to remove "God in the sky" from the discussion of spiritual concerns and still connect with the ultimates: values, ethical behavior, or the grandeur of the natural world. Doubt is not a special achievement of the naysayers. It is integral to any religion or philosophy. Doubt is the sibling of faith, and it is the dance between them that makes any belief system strong and vibrant.

Being an agnostic says "I do not know" (from the Greek, A- + GNŌSTOS, unknown or unknowable). If that means the person is holding an open mind and heart, that's the road to knowing in a new way. "The purpose of education is to replace any empty mind with an open one," said business commentator, Malcolm Forbes. That puts a premium on receptivity.

This book praises the *value of not knowing* as a very exalted state (Chapter 7). It is fully engaged in the question. The risk in wearing the agnostic or atheist labels is when it calcifies into "I don't know and I don't intend to." That is just being stuck and proud of it.

Finding Divinity in the Ordinary

Extraordinary moments of feeling one with God and all creation are not the province of an elite few (mystics and religious adepts), but are available to anyone. As the heart opens, the presence of a higher order of truth can be seen and experienced everywhere. James P. Carse speaks to learning the true significance of what is being seen in *Breakfast at the Victory*.

> Mystical vision is seeing how extraordinary the ordinary is. I saw but I didn't see that I saw. My seeing was strictly in the mode of ego.... The mystical is thoroughly worldly.... But its inherent indifference to the world seems to leave the world exactly as it is.[403]

Margaret Cropper addresses the need for the fully-developed interior life to engage with material reality in *The Life of Evelyn Underhill*

> Where [Underhill] perhaps struck new ground was in her insistence that this state of union produced a glorious and fruitful creativeness so that the mystic who attains this final perfectness is the most active doer for the Kingdom of Heaven, and not the hidden and secluded dreaming lover of God.[404]

An intimate relationship with God does not require a cloister or forsaking normal life. One can engage higher awareness and direct experience of the most profound type through the most common of experiences. That is also the nature of the Way of the Return—bringing the profound into life because of the recognition they are the same.

Anybody can find the sacred in their everyday experiences. In learning to see all things with the eyes of love, humility, and compassion, one is connecting their inner and outer realities in a harmonious way. That is how each of us who wish to grow in spiritual ways can do so without leaving the life we are living. But rather, one can be living it more fully, more lovingly.

In this way, a person can see through the mist, helping to ground it in the here and now.

Christian philosopher Teilhard de Chardin said, "Someday after mastering winds, waves, tides and gravity, we shall harness the energies of love. And then, for the second time in the history of the world, man will discover fire."

An Evolving Relationship with Divinity

I once heard it said that God represents our next level of understanding—as we grow, so does our understanding of the divine. It is our own limitations that get in the way of seeing the fuller possibilities latent in each moment—and God's presence in each moment. In moments of awe or inspiration we see and know beyond doubt, from Being—not someday but right now.

As a person grows and changes, they are capable of having a maturing relationship with that which is highest and most profound for them. Religious

---

[403] *Op. cit.*, Carse, 15-6.
[404] Cropper, Margaret, *The Life of Evelyn Underhill: An intimate portrait of the groundbreaking author of Mysticism* (Woodstock, VT: Skylight Paths Publishing, 2002), 47.

doctrines attempt to have a set of answers and beliefs that are true for everybody—the official version.

Beliefs that are appropriate for a child too young for complex thinking, will not suffice for an adult taking stock of their belief system. Living a life of faith does not mean blind acceptance, or a life without discernment or inner growth. Commitment to one's spiritual and religious life should never require putting on blinders, let alone closing down either the heart or mind.

A person's relationship to divinity matures along with their level of understanding generally. A child can relate to God as a father figure, just as an adolescent (as stage, not age) is rather critical and questioning about what notions they will accept. Various apparently contradictory ways to view God reflect the developmental level of the believer.

That grows and changes as the individual can learn to relate to greater complexity. The nature of the divine is not changing, but an individual's level of comprehension is.

> The great Masters, who appear in different ages and civilizations to point the way, are born on this earth with an awareness of being which transcends the ordinary human condition. Their truth and example reinforce the truth within ourselves and strengthen and direct us in our quest. But the quest must be our own. A great teacher can only quicken in us a Light which waits the moment when we will allow it to shine in all its purity.[405]

Back to Two-Winged Birds...

In fairness to the mind's approach (end of Chapter 17), the heart-centered approaches have their share of one-winged birds, too. Too often, the emotions are excessive and sentimental, the reasoning lacks precision, and it is likely to be ungrounded. But finger-pointing gets us nowhere, and it certainly does not end the War of the Two Cultures.

On one level, there is the standoff between the humanities and spirituality. Ken Wilber (in *One Taste*) points out the uneasy relationship that religion and spiritual matters have with the broader fields of the humanities. These rivalries must be addressed and reconciled as part of the shift to a more collaborative and integrated approach.

> Science did not kill spirituality; the humanities themselves did. The problem is that the humanities rejected introspection, interiority, and subjectivity, and rejected them with an aggression and thoroughness that didn't even give scientific materialism a chance to get its hands on them. (Oh, it would reject them, too, it just never had a chance.)[406]

---

[405] Fausset, Hugh I'Anson, *The Flame and the Light, Meanings in Vedanta and Buddhism* (New York: Greenwood Press, 1958), 34-5.

[406] Wilber, Ken, *One Taste: The journals of Ken Wilber* (Boston: Shambhala, 1999), 276.

Visionary thinking, with a dollop of originality, yields better solutions than either mental or emotional approaches can produce alone. To be able to participate fully in what life has to offer, we must find ways to step off the unconsciously-defended turf and onto the common ground of our making. Good will demands it — our beckoning possibilities are being held hostage until we do.

"While consciousness lies in the no-man's land between religion and science, claimed by both yet understood by neither, it may still hold a key to the apparent conflict of these two great human institutions," according to B. Alan Wallace, a Buddhism scholar.

There could be a great pay-off in getting science and humanities to hold hands and work with a shared purpose. We might even discover that more birds can fly. Frederick and Mary Ann Brussat speak of the reconciliation in *Spiritual Literacy:*

> Our spiritual life needs the soul-stuff of ritual, story, image, sensation, memory, and quotidian happenstance. Our secular lives need the vision, reverence, piety, values, reflection, service, and commitments offered by a spiritual sensibility. When each side of this split is affected and reconfigured by the other, then we might see a reconciliation of the two, and both our spirituality and our secularity might enjoy qualities of the soul, which, according to many ancient teachings, is the factor that makes us human.[407]

---

[407] Brussat, Frederick and Mary Ann, *Spiritual Literacy: Reading the sacred in everyday life* (New York: Scribner, 1996), 10.

Chapter 19 - Shifting the Paradigm

Something new is calling forth our clear-sighted capabilities. Doors previously closed and barring "outsiders" now stand wide open because so many "insiders" have dropped the ball. A new kind of visionary thinking is starting to make itself felt.

We Interrupt the Regularly Scheduled Program for an Urgent Message!

The paradigm is shifting! Repeat, the paradigm is shifting! The area affected is Planet Earth.

Right now! It has begun! Prepare for massive winds of change blowing across the globe. No person is safe from it. No institution will remain unscathed. Remain on high alert!

Early damage reports are coming in. This is "the big one!" Every person is warned to take adaptive measures because all of us are in for years of massive primary and secondary tremors. Normal life has been suspended — actually cancelled. It is up to us to build a different model to replace "life as we know it."

Do not panic. Repeat, do not panic. Large segments of the population are fighting pitched battles to resist these unrelenting forces and keep the *status quo* intact. That is futile. Efforts would be better applied to charting the storm's course and taking corrective action. The smart money is betting on going with these forces of nature, rather than going against them.

This is not a natural disaster, but the ripening of seeds and choices already planted. It is both revolutionary and evolutionary. You, yes you, have a vital part to play. Close ranks so you can assist your friends, family, and community through these challenging times. We need to support each other in order to get through this (and will grow stronger because we do). Kindness is advised.

Getting Attention and Getting Aboard

This is a big deal, but massively underreported. Most people are still under the mistaken impression that: (1) it is temporary or only affecting a few groups or places; (2) it is somebody's fault and they can or should fix it: and (3) we can ride this out until it passes. None are true.

This is far more extensive and destructive than an earthquake, hurricane, flood, or wildfire, but has elements of them all. Its effect is to clear the field in preparation for renewal on a global scale. This is not a calamity, but the early phase of a rebirth. And it is not going away any time soon, nor before it has run its course.

The intelligent strategy is to pull one's head out of the sand, foreswear fear or finger-pointing, and deal with the opportunities this offers in a positive, capable, and collaborative frame of mind. We must also open our hearts, for this paradigm shift is toward a more heart-directed way of life. For those who want to return to business as usual, it is too late. That locomotive has sailed.

A paradigm shift is not like flipping a switch: Before – FLIP – After. One view – CLICK – Another view. It is a process where the established view begins to fade while the emerging one comes into greater and greater focus. Right now, we are in the midst of such a process, so the decisions each of us make contribute to a tipping-point moment. We will still be making related decisions down the road, but they will not have such disproportionate impact as those made in the near term.

There are two things of which we can be sure: (1) The changes will be enormous, and they will affect every one of us and every aspect of modern life; and (2) every person has an active role to play—actually multiple roles. And the way we perform them will collectively set the course for where the changes take us.

There are many forces at work these days tearing down all types of social and organizational structures. We cannot yet know what is emerging to replace what is fading because so many of the elements are still in our hands. What prevails is being hammered out by decisions many of us are still in the process of making. Each person is both an instigator of the new course of action, while being swept along by its accumulating force.

Why are things different now? Why do I think this is the time for the visionary spirit to move to the forefront? Four main factors are converging to create a zeitgeist more receptive to insightful solutions.

1. The impetus of grassroots, bottom-up movements—people saying "Enough already!"
2. Collapse of unresponsive institutions, along with discredited values and assumptions
3. The Uranus Factor—the force of abrupt and unpredictable change
4. The Internet and methods that redefine the nature of commerce, collaboration, and community

The Ever-Changing Focus

Connecting Enough Dots

Gathering more and more dots of information reflects a picture that is getting clearer, more encompassing, more detailed. At some point, a connection is made in the brain, a "click" of realization about what they mean. One sees! One knows!

Connecting dots tracks with more brain neuron connections as well. The effect is to link something new, which includes the particular idea (dots) with a significance that was not already apparent. What is seen is no longer just information, but *meaningful* information.

References to connecting dots appear throughout this book. It also points out many of the dots about the visionary experience that I have connected.

However, just as many of the insights described here relate to being a living, breathing, thinking human being. We are designed to spot connections and to make sense of them. There will always be more dots to be found and more connections to be made by anyone alert to their significance. I find that exciting!

Twenty-five hundred years ago, Aristotle said: "The whole is more than the sum of its parts." That can be rephrased: A picture is more than the sum of its dots. As we view experiences from a variety of perspectives and scales, we gain an added wholeness, a sense of evocativeness to the impression.

Humanity is in the midst of a perceptual shift that is much more significant than making sense of accumulated facts (dots). Increasing clarity is strengthening our individual and collective *capacity to use them* more fully. It is not the quantity of dots that adds the meaning. *How we see them* in that moment of insight briefly expands our perceptual frame—and with it a larger scope of possibilities.

Later, the rational meaning of what was seen is added to our body of knowledge, even though the energy of the insight fades. Humans require meaning because experiences that do not make sense to us lead to fear and anxiety. High levels of turmoil shake our comprehension and confidence. We require meaning and a sense of predictability and all this turmoil has undermined it.

Gregg Easterbrook said, "A transition from material want to meaning want is in progress on an historically unprecedented scale—involving hundreds of millions of people—and may eventually be recognized as the principal cultural development of our age."[408]

Even beyond the click of meaning or insight, it is possible for us to take a *step further* with experiences (although doing so is entirely optional). We have the capacity to *perceive a larger pattern involved* as well, from an increasingly solid vantage point. On what will we rely? In my opinion, the dominant rational basis of finding what to trust must give way to a heart-mind-body alliance.

These days that capacity to spot the over-arching, but hitherto largely invisible, patterns is being engaged by more people, more often. That is at the root of how the next paradigm differs from the existing one. Those who can perceive the *added meaning* gain an advantage over those who don't. They are among the first to see and adopt what is coming into focus.

Amassing more dots does not argue for any specific image or conclusion so much as to demonstrate how one can move among various points of view (and their attendant lenses of meaning), as appropriate. In the process, we both see and understand *from a different angle* than before.

---

[408] Pink, Daniel H., *A Whole New Mind: Why right-brainers will rule the future* (New York: Riverhead Books, 2005), 219.

Frances Moore Lappé, cofounder of the Small Planet Institute, said, "My intent is to enable us to see what is happening all around us but is still invisible to most of us."

The Nature of Paradigm Shifts

Shifting a paradigm reflects a change in how we assign meaning. The specific dots don't change, but *what they signify to us* does. We view them, and the interrelationship among them, in a different way than we used to.

There is not a single paradigm that everyone accepts, even within a certain historic period or field of interest. Already the emerging paradigm shift is redefining humanity's zeitgeist (as well as smaller frameworks). Signs of where we're headed are not hard to find. Science fiction author William Gibson said "The future is already here — it's just unevenly distributed."

As the new shift gains steam, some people begin to notice what occurs in a different light. That allows them to make new associations, to attend to areas of perplexity previously avoided, and to drop assumptions that no longer apply. One moves into questioning their prior givens.

Elements of the Incoming Paradigm:
- Grassroots, widespread, and driven by local initiative
- Greater transparency — that which has been hidden will be revealed
- Less "either-or thinking" or one-size-fits-all answers (that really don't fit)
- More visionary thinking; greater acceptance of unconventional individuals and opinions
- Dissipation of apathy; more engaged personal passion (Chapter 13)
- More inclusive and integrated, while also being more diverse and widespread
- More values oriented; not just focused on practical goals
- More intuitive and accessible; makes added sense both mentally and emotionally
- More flexible and responsive to both large-scale and tiny-scale changes
- More spontaneous and expansive in scope
- Greater personal responsibility for self and toward others; a recognition that it is no longer about me but *us*

Before we fully arrive, a diverse variety of far-sighted pioneers will formulate philosophies that will turn out to characterize the next paradigm. At some future point, it will be… oh so evident. But for now, each of us can put our mark on the parts that matter to us most — by fleshing out our desired changes through our current behavior.

We are, both individually and collectively, already in the process of defining the form our shared reality will take.

A fundamental shift that the new paradigm is already hinting at is the demise of the totally self-centered, me-only frame of reference. Humanity is outgrowing it. No, of course it won't be gone any time soon. But it also will not be given a "pass," or be treated as a "given" or a birthright. The strengthening alliance between head and heart, mentioned so often in these pages, assures the brain-only, me-first, my-way-or-the-highway approaches are going the way of the dodo bird.

In an interview with Tami Simon of Sounds True, poet and author David Whyte said:

> Our 'frontier identity' is the leading edge of our being, the part of us that ventures beyond territory we have already covered, the part of us that actively seeks the unknown. This frontier is where I want to live. Not in the realm of thinking thinking thinking, but in the realm of being—or, one could say, right at the edge of the wave.[409]

One of the new elements that will define the in-coming paradigm is our growing ability to reside "right at the edge of the wave," without losing our bearings. There is no such thing as being "settled" there, for it is a state of full engagement with life that constantly changes. If our attention flags, we default to our everyday (static) point of view.

Being on the sidelines from the flow of things until one re-engages is not so bad, really. Sometimes, we simply need to rest and restore our energy. That ebb and flow of engaged and disengaged is a proper rhythm, not necessarily just flip-flopping between succeeding and failing.

There are many elements still to be seen that are gradually unfolding, just as there are infinite ways each of us can help to tip the balance toward these developing trends we most want to happen. Human beings are writing a different kind of social contract, not as petitioners, but as envisioners, who have the ability to make our grandest desires come to pass.

The uncertainty of these times is unleashing massive fear and backlashes in a host of forms. Those clinging to what is on its way out will suffer more than those who are resonant with the fresh possibilities. The advantages go to those who are most flexible and open to what is developing. But bear in mind that a person is likely to be more supportive of some changes than others.

Bottom-up and Top-down Views

Starting from particular dots is largely about looking through the telescope from the "broken bits" end. That is the bottom-up view, the normal perspective, the human default state wherein we see the details, but not always how they

---

[409] "To Think or Not to Think?" Tami Simon Blog, June, 2010, http://www.soundstrue.com/tami-simon/

connect in the larger scheme. If all one has are the dots—the details—there is a need to put them together in order to see how they add up.

However, from the other end of the telescope, one sees the connectedness of dots from a unity perspective. It is a more inclusive awareness, rooted in the quantum perspective of everything *already being connected* up as a whole.

That is the top-down view. That is not yet humanity's normal frame, but that can be experienced nonetheless as brief glimpses of vision and inspiration. That broadest of outlooks is outside of the forest *or* the trees, and it is aware of how all is connected (Chapter 2).

Sometimes (rarely) the top-down view and bottom-up view merge and become one and the same. When that occurs, one is in touch with his or her full capacity, for that transcends the one *or* the other view. It is an integration wherein every component fits.

Connecting enough dots can deliver a perspective that is bigger and more enduring than one's prior commonplace view. But occasionally, the meta-patterns of unity and harmony can be glimpsed as well. These experiences of unity within oneself transcend time and space, the here-and-now, or one's personal limitations.

Some of those take the form of broad-scoped visions that invite the envisioner to bring them into reality. As with Fingertip Smarts, the overview and particular dots can coexist and add more depth of field.

Getting unstuck from old ways of thinking pulls us out of mental ruts, so other views become more available. That fresh input is worthwhile in itself, but often opens doors to fresh areas of exploration.

Along with the greater clarity that comes with seeing more of the big picture, our gaps in understanding, inaccuracies, and illusions dissipate—as they recede in importance. Therefore, any shifts in the direction of the larger view can be considered growth—a step toward using one's maturing judgment with greater ease.

All our lives, each of us collects dots through our specific observations and experiences. If we can also gain a broader perspective and same emotional distance, they can connect up in additional and different ways.

Steve Jobs, former founder/CEO of Apple, Inc., points to the time factor in the way we see meaning in to varied events in our own lives (from the Stanford Graduation Address, 2005).

> Of course it was impossible to connect the dots looking forward when I was in college. But it was very, very clear looking backwards ten years later. Again, you can't connect the dots looking forward; you can only connect them looking backwards. So you have to trust that the dots will somehow connect in your future. You have to trust in something—your gut, destiny, life, karma, whatever. Because believing that the dots will connect down the road will give

you the confidence to follow your heart even when it leads you off the well-worn path; and that will make all the difference.[410]

He also notes the need to trust that there is (or will be) meaning to the dots, and that more of their significance becomes clearer over time. That trust in a larger-frame meaning keeps the attention sensitized to something larger than the details or "random" elements.

What Does Progress Look Like?

Any successes that a visionary achieves in the near term are certainly gratifying, but probably won't reflect the true impact of their discovery. A visionary's activities build on each other and could add up to a significant body of work and influence over the long haul. Viewing the full scope of their contribution could also reveal a maturing of their capabilities.

Denise Shekerjian found that in her interviews with MacArthur Fellows for *Uncommon Genius*.

> It is hard to know when the time has come to judge the merits and possibilities of one's work. Still, there is one small way of easing this difficulty.... It is to think about one's effort as a 'work-in-progress,' that is, a temporary resting place in a continuous creative process.... [One has] the feeling of settling for something less than they had perhaps imagined, of making do with this particular work, and hoping that in the next try they will be able to narrow the gap between what was dimly envisioned at the start of the project and what was produced in the end. The same holds just as true in the sciences, where 'fact' is regarded merely as a temporary resting ground until the next discovery, the next clarification. Whether in science or in art, then, the ability to judge that a work is finished is more an act of commitment to the continuousness of the creative process than it is a sign of having expressed the last word.[411]

Even that approach uses a much-too-narrow perceptual lens since it looks at an individual's effort alone—from the scale of personal accomplishment or impact. Individuals seldom act alone or without influencing others (and being influenced by them). Effective collaboration can speed discoveries along much faster than any single person's efforts can. And collaborative discoveries, and ways of operating, will be even more in evidence in the new paradigm.

A visionary cannot determine the extent to which he or she succeeded by only looking at *how the vision fared*, or whether what they worked to achieve ever caught on. Nor can the visionary process be judged simply on the basis of looking within, and leaving the material world out of it. It is the interweaving of those inner and outer elements that cements the gains.

---

[410] Jobs, Steve, Commencement Address at Stanford University, 2005.
[411] Shekerjian, Denise, *Uncommon Genius: How great ideas are born* (New York: Viking, 1990), 172-3.

Of course, the customary measures of success apply. But so too do the width of one's Straddle-span and the openness of one's heart to the subtle influences at work. Who can say which factor has the greater impact? How securely has a person anchored their innate sensibilities and cultivated skills to each other?

The seeker of truth must forge some degree of linkage between their inner and outer states. That is a maturing quality that only becomes evident as we gain life experience and emotional wisdom.

Award extra marks for including happiness, joy, and binkles because they reward both our inner and outer natures. These are all potential benefits of the journey, too. Judging from those measures, the visionaries are no different than everyone else, since it is through enjoying life that we resolve the human riddle.

Those ahead of the curve are seldom able to recognize their degree of progress in the short term because there are so few markers. When engaged in specific projects, the context of an entire life's work seems too remote. Besides, a person's attention is caught up in the immediate obstacles and small victories as they arise, so they can't be sure if they are gaining or losing ground.

When seeking early signs of change and progress, we usually need to look beyond specific individuals for pockets that harbor new approaches and fresh thinking. The give-and-take among peers, competitors, and colleagues often improves and fine-tunes the labors of everyone involved.

Their broader, shared knowledge base and the hands-on results they communicate about can urge each other on. (See Chapter 15 on supportive environments.)

Out of the Rubble of Dinosaur Thinking

Daniel H. Pink has been tracking changes in attitudes in modern America, to what he calls the Conceptual Age. In *A Whole New Mind* he argues that effectiveness requires balancing our left brain [L-Directed] reasoning with six essential right brain [R-Directed] aptitudes. Together, these six aptitudes can help us to develop the new "whole mind" that the next phase will demand.

Aptitudes for the Conceptual Age:
1. Not just function but also DESIGN
2. Not just argument but also STORY
3. Not just focus but also SYMPHONY
4. Not just logic but also EMPATHY
5. Not just seriousness but also PLAY
6. Not just accumulation but also MEANING[412]

---

[412] *Op. cit.*, Pink, 65-6.

> Design. Story, Symphony. Empathy. Play. Meaning. These six senses increasingly will guide our lives and shape our world.... The high-concept, high-touch abilities that matter most are fundamentally human attributes. After all, back on the savannah, our cave-person ancestors weren't taking SATs or plugging numbers into spreadsheets. But they were telling stories, demonstrating empathy, and designing innovations. These abilities have always comprised part of what it means to be human. But after a few generations in the Information Age, these muscles have atrophied. The challenge is to work them back into shape. Anyone can master the six Conceptual Age senses. But those who master them first will have a huge advantage.[413]

What the right brain contributes by itself has serious limitations because much of that emphasis is concerned with correcting imbalances that have favored the rational left-brain dominance. In my opinion, right-brain engagement is yet another stage along the way to full-functioning integration. Framing our challenge as right brain or left brain ignores the larger scope, of which we are capable. Also, the new paradigm represents the next step, wherein they are not treated as separate functions but rather a seamless and inseparable unit.

The only part of us that can shepherd a run-away brain, even a higher functioning integrated whole-brain, is the fully-functioning heart. Becoming an integrated human requires all parts of the self to participate at the decision-making table — the feeler, the analyzer/organizer, the imaginer, the contemplator, the actor, the critic, with all sharing leadership based on the strength of each. Additionally, they only take action with consensus from all.

Everyone Has a Role to Play

A Call for Visionary Thinking

I began this book writing about the qualities of visionaries and the visionary process itself. Along the way, my focus has evolved from the visionary *think<u>ers</u>* to include visionary *think<u>ing</u>*. That broadens the scope of players from the die-hard forerunners to almost everyone who exercises their urges to find novel and effective solutions — on any scale. That is a single example of changing one's perceptual lens as related to the incoming paradigm.

I foresee, off in the distance, that the widespread adoption of visionary thinking itself will evolve in the way that visions do, until it is so widely accepted as to represent the normal view for many people. The new approach ceases to be a matter of controversy or comment because it makes so much sense. Most people will come to treat it as settled truth.

I urge nothing less than a new norm, where everyone is engaged to some degree in visionary thinking and seeing, wherever they are, toward whatever they care

---

[413] *Ibid.*, 67.

about passionately. That is where each person applies his or her skills in the laboratory of their own experience.

And like objective scientists, each of them assesses results and confirms their beliefs through the measure of what is working for them.

The combined impact of greater individual clarity leads to all of us living in a fundamentally different paradigm. We have moved from linear and hierarchical structures *to* grassroots synchronicity in ways that are more broad-based and diverse. The new paradigm is also less mind-focused and money-focused — more responsive to the influences of heart, synergy, and the larger community.

Everyone is being forced to experiment with fresh approaches because much of what we were accustomed to no longer works like it did. In the long run, that is a good thing. It opens us and opens doors — while making it more likely we will go through them. It helps when we train ourselves to look for a larger picture and engage a more inclusive approach.

> The capacity to see the big picture is perhaps most important as an antidote to the variety of psychic woes brought forth by the remarkable prosperity and plentitude of our times. Many of us are crunched for time, deluged by information, and paralyzed by the weight of too many choices. The best prescription for these modern maladies may be to approach one's own life in a contextual, big-picture fashion — to distinguish between what really matters and what merely annoys.[414]

Visionary think<u>ing</u> is a more extensive grassroots phenomenon that is showing up all over the place, often as "no big deal." It is how we take the next step forward with our growing capacities engaged. It's moving toward being broader, more inclusive, and refined.

The ability to tap into untold possibilities is available for anyone who lets curiosity or a more expansive drive lead them on. Our sparks of insight burn brighter to the extent they are valued, given credence, and put into practice. That is to the good because engaging in visionary thinking need not be as zealous or jealous (of other interests) as was demanded previously by the visionary path.

Improving the quality of one's thinking in a step-by-step fashion can be accomplished without the draconian commitment required on the visionary path. Anyone with an ounce of motivation to do so is capable of finding ample answers that are much fresher and have a slightly different slant than they used to.

While the ability to push the envelope is one of our species' inborn capacities, it is a "muscle" that needs exercise. Each person decides on their own: what would be sufficiently intriguing for me to extend the extra effort?

---

[414] *Op. cit.*, Pink, 143.

Visionary thinking bridges the limits of rationality and the sensory world to reach a greatly expanded view. Increasingly, the ability to employ such a broad perspective will not be the province of only a few. Leaping ahead will provide the evidence of greater beyond-the-brain activity and it will arise from many more people, and from more directions than ever.

There will always be a few intrepid forerunners who follow the demanding visionary path, but some of the irritants that provoked them to leave the conventional mainstream in the first place will not be as offensive — so that choice of route is no longer the only course open for less conventional thinkers/creators.

The phase that caused one to feel like a misfit or an outcast will largely be optional or briefer (or won't hurt so much) because its role in the creative process will be better understood.

The visionary path is a faster track or a more challenging track because it streamlines the growth process and minimizes certain kinds of distractions. But the destination can be reached in a variety of less intense ways. The urge to live a full and meaningful life is built into every single person. How we respond to that desire is part of what makes each of us unique.

The visionary path accelerates the traveler's refinement process and raises the stakes. While the growing involvement is about grounding the vision, it also engages the drive to ground the individual's core humanity in tangible ways. Part of what I see on the horizon is that as we become more at ease with our inner development, it won't be considered such a risky undertaking.

Making Our Deepest Desires Felt

Economic disruption, ecological instability, social alienation, and governance incompetence are converging to produce a widespread uncertainty, with no clear sense of direction. Where do you find yourself with regard to this unnatural lull, this pregnant moment when the forces of change are gathering? Some elements of modern life are in collapse or in free fall, while various long-stuck places are now freer to move in more ways.

Our responses fall on a continuum between fundamentally pessimistic (and braced for the worst) at one end, and eager to make change work at the other. Do you find yourself focusing on the positive or negative possibilities? Both will turn out to be true, but which most influences your choices?

Individuals who have been nursing their grand visions feel that *this is their moment*. They are poised and ready to move. But for most people, who would rather have life be a bit more predictable and "sane," this doesn't feel like what they want. The scale and scope of uncertainty is too great, and they feel torn (even if mildly hopeful).

Consider this phase as seeding your ground that will grow to be a rather lovely garden in time. What flowers/plants would you want to have in it? You do not have to be a master gardener, just someone who has a few seeds to plant—specific results you'd like to see included. Not only are your contributions entirely subjective, but the chosen seeds planted by each person are distinctly different.

Christian philosopher Thomas Moore said, "There is no way to re-enchant our lives in a disenchanted culture except by becoming renegades from that culture and planting the seeds for a new one." This in-coming paradigm will be a new garden, with many different plants than before, and many familiar ones missing that can no longer be sustained in these new and rarified conditions. There is ample room for diversity and whimsical "because I like it," along with some things never before seen.

The social side of our lives is also being reformed to include different types of relationships that are rooted in energetic affinity and deep emotional resonance. Desmond Tutu, an African human rights advocate, speaks of the heart's desire for beautiful and transcendent experiences. The Brussats said in *Spiritual Literacy*:

> We are made to enjoy music, to enjoy beautiful sunsets, to enjoy looking at the billows of the sea and to be thrilled with a rose that is bedecked with dew.... Human beings are actually created for the transcendent, for the sublime, for the beautiful, for the truthful.... And all of us are given the task of trying to make this world a little more hospitable to these beautiful things.[415]

Finding ways to make these desirable ends hang together requires engaged involvement and many hands. As more and more of us can maintain a high degree of desire for the future (garden) we would prefer to live in, we weave the best notions into solid form. We discover how to sustain a rhythm of creativity: the in-breath (inside, the sparks of inspiration) and the outbreath (doing, grounding in the tangible world) makes something delightful and new happen. It is marked by grace and beauty, coupled with functionality.

Everyone is feeling immense pressure to make changes on many fronts. The issue each of us must answer is whether it is toward greater use of humanity's full palate of possibilities, or settling for less. Each person is being asked to demonstrate: How big is your vision for the future?

We Are Driving the Change Together

The visionary journey has a quest built into it, but so, too, does life. In that sense, living compels each person to deal with unknowns and lack of control that compel us to try something new. It might only come up in a last-ditch effort, but sooner or later, one runs out of ideas.

---

[415] Brussat, Frederick and Mary Ann, *Spiritual Literacy: Reading the sacred in everyday life* (New York: Scribner, 1996), 275.

That's where something fundamentally different might get a hearing. Luckily, the full scope of unplucked fresh ideas is available to anybody.

As Marcel Proust said, "We do not receive wisdom, we must discover it for ourselves after a journey through the wilderness which no one else can make for us, which no one can spare us, for our wisdom is the point of view from which we come at last to regard the world."

Just by being alive, we keep redefining our scope of understanding — along with our individual skills and motivations to make things work. At some point in time, without our conscious awareness of it, we are being changed in more ways than any of us realize. This is not so much about the scale of our impact as the ripening consequence of having lived. That, when coupled with social disruptions, add up to a new future of our making.

A Role for Everyone

I am a true believer in what daring individuals can do — and how important their collective contributions are to building a positive future that works for everybody. However, I also recognize that such intense and single-minded dedication is not a suitable or feasible pursuit and lifestyle for most people.

Those on the leading edge of change will always be few in number compared to the larger majority who can and do benefit from their efforts.

Socrates said, "The unexamined life is not worth living." Life offers everybody the opportunity to examine who they are beneath the surface — to broaden their focus of perception and develop a unique flavor of creative expression at every step. How readily a particular person embraces those possibilities cannot be predicted. How they go about doing so is equally unpredictable. But one standard against which anyone can be measured is did they make the attempt?

The Purpose of Vision and Creative Energy

There are an infinite number of paths leading us toward achieving our individual or collective sense of purpose. Each of us discovers and defines our own — humans are wired to do so. A chosen path could be a craft that we work with our hands, or a refinement of a personal quality (like cultivating serenity), as well as acting within any of the recognized fields of knowledge.

Subject matter mastery integrates all the tasks and skills learned in executing the specific craft or discipline. It makes someone an insider in their field. Likewise, an array of people skills must be mastered in building a platform for the vision — and leading from there.

The various routes taken to self-fulfillment are equally valid, and each individual's lifetime provides countless opportunities for him or her to bring originality into what they do. In that way, the visionaries are no different than everyone else.

The urge and opportunities are there for anyone who is inclined to spread their wings and see where it takes them. The visionary path is simply a way of turning up the heat—adding energetic intensity, sharpened clarity, and a more precise focus into the business of living.

"The only way to let your dreams come true is to wake up," said French poet Paul Valéry. Grounding one's highest hopes and vision is about the outer journey. It combines ideas with the foot-on-the-ground and taking the next step.

The "waking up" part is about the inner journey, while building the capacity to see the larger view and have them coexist in a larger frame of reference. The new paradigm is the path of waking up—not by the few, not merely in flashes, but as a shared reality.

Encouraging More Transparency and Diversity of Opinion

What Was Hidden Will Be Revealed

All of us are encountering new choices, options, and values. Self-centered and ego-based priorities are losing ground—compelled to yield to other considerations and the needs of others. That is one of the meta-patterns that will characterize the new paradigm.

Many groups and individuals are expressing abhorrence and growing intolerance of political, corporate, and cultural manipulation and lies. They are standing up and speaking out. "Enough already!" The old game is over. And that agitation is global.

These times are showing a heightened demand for transparency. Standards for behavior are changing too. More accurately, the gap between public pronouncements and private behavior is becoming glaringly apparent. That is especially true for those in positions of power. Sexual peccadillos, back-room deals, blatant greed, and unfair strategies are being unmasked.

For those accustomed to getting away with outrageous behavior, displays of hypocrisy and hubris act like wearing a "Kick Me" sign. It smells; almost nobody is fooled. Watch the news; people are not behaving worse than ever, but what is unseemly is not being hidden or tolerated any more.

> Transparency is not just a new buzzword. It matters. It makes anonymity—one thing sure to lead to no good—impossible. And new communications tools suddenly transform 'transparency' into useable information.[416]

The Uranus Factor Describes the Dynamics

Uranus is the symbol for the mindset of the "winds of change" that are now blowing through. Its destructive intensity is allied with fresh modes of thought

---

[416] Lappé, Frances Moore, *Getting a Grip2: Clarity, creativity, and courage for the world we really want* (Cambridge, MA, Small Planet Media, 2007 and 2010), 109.

and ideals. The Uranus Factor means abrupt and unexpected change to advance a new paradigm.

Uranus is merely the *symbol for the type of change going on* — not the cause of it. This reference to Uranus does not refer to any astrological concepts.

The Uranus Factor coincides with the demise of business as usual while opening the door to large-scale change. Uranus represents big-picture revolution over a long duration (across generations). Prevailing norms are replaced by entirely new ways of seeing or resolving the world's challenges. Whatever has been concealed will be brought to light (particularly if those secrets protected established power structures).

The Uranus Factor Accelerates Shifting Priorities on a Grand Scale:
- Promotes large-scale forces of freedom and creativity
- Brings massive destabilization, upheaval, rebellion, and total change
- Shatters conventions in order to pave the way for more diverse and inclusive arrangements
- Breaks with tradition to create a new mold, a new world order
- Destroys restraint by breaking down customary standards; encourages erratic or bizarre behavior
- Ushers in sudden, sometimes violent, usually unforeseen, changes of direction
- Supports society's upward climb toward the light of freedom
- Exposes what has been kept secret
- Shifts individuals from a self-orientation to large-scale social way of thinking

In the hope of discovering truth (either big T or small t), the more perspectives and disparate input, the better. However, no matter how much we claim to want to know the truth, we have to want it even more than our desire to be right. We have to be open to what we don't already know. As Josh Billings said, "As scarce as truth is, the supply has always been in excess of the demand."

Welcoming Diverse Perspectives

Being able to draw upon the widest scope of backgrounds and skills is our greatest hope of finding a way out of this mess. Diversity is about tolerance and acceptance of our individual and group differences. It rejects any view that some individuals or groups are inherently superior or inferior to others. The same human rights apply for all.

Diversity is also a belief that the world is a big enough place for almost any form of unique expression or belief system to find a place. But that is not to say all beliefs are equal or equally beneficial. Demeaning and destructive beliefs or philosophies that do harm to others do not deserve our praise. Discernment is important, but it rests on a consideration of basic integrity and the quality of the person's activities.

People are feeling emboldened to speak up and speak out. But also, more people are starting to listen. Long-ignored voices are being heard. American anthropologist Margaret Mead said, "If we are to achieve a richer culture, rich in contrasting values, we must recognize the whole gamut of human potentialities, and so weave a less arbitrary social fabric, one in which each diverse human gift will find a fitting place."

Many more opinions from diverse perspectives are making themselves felt. As Bill Bishop said in *The Big Sort*:

> National institutions have splintered. The idea of community has been 'miniaturized,' observed Francis Fukuyama. 'Rather than seeking authoritative values in the national church that once shaped society's culture, people are picking and choosing their values on an individual basis, in ways that link them with smaller communities of like-minded folk.' That ability is both liberating and exciting. In this new world, there will be greater differences nationally among communities but fewer differences within the smaller groups.... There will be both more diversity and more conformity. But missing will be any sense of the whole.[417]

The very nature of democracy itself is up for grabs in every country that claims to be democratic because "by the people" is taking on a new urgency. However, the form of government does not seem to be a serious barrier to individuals everywhere demanding dignity and the right to have their opinions heard.

But this is not about politics. Political parties, as now constituted, are complicit in the me-first thinking that is no longer trusted. Grassroots efforts are claiming their power and giving voice to the full range of human values. That represents a quite different attitude than competing interest groups fighting over the spoils.

Each of us benefits by thoughtfully considering new and unfamiliar ideas that show promise. This comports with the "informed citizen," who is the bedrock of a democratic society. Being open to new ideas is less about us making political choices or staying up on technological discoveries, than about us choosing carefully from among the best ideas modern life has to offer.

Terence, a playwright in ancient Rome, said, "I am a human being; nothing human can be alien to me." That is the bedrock on which our sameness rests. We may appear different on the outside, but by virtue of being human, we are alike.

Everyone really is the same under the skin. Starting from there, the mental and emotional gymnastics to make it seem true (like political correctness) are unnecessary. Our current social structures based on group identity that perpetuate distinctions and barriers are crumbling these days. As we go

---

[417] Bishop, Bill, *The Big Sort: Why the clustering of like-minded America is tearing us apart* (New York: Houghton Mifflin, 2008), 302.

forward, what is needed is *not* an emphasis on what divides us but rather on *what unites us.*

What more can each of us do to notice and appreciate bright ideas as they come along, without prejudging them or the messenger? Alexander Elliot said, "Intolerance is the father of illusion and evil deeds. Tolerance is not its opposite; tolerance is neutral. The opposite of intolerance is creative imagination, sympathetically exercised in the service of ever illusive truth."

It is already possible to spot early signs of success by those attempting to reframe our collective vision of where we are headed. They are weaving novel elements into actual behavior. On small and large-scale matters, millions are changing their minds and their lives, not down the road, but now.

~ "Do Not Judge" Is a Place, Not a Verb ~
A BonBon ~ Faith Lynella

The admonition "do not judge" has been taken to ridiculous lengths in modern life. Even the most absurd, inappropriate, or self-serving behavior rates a PASS by those determined not to criticize. Discernment is jettisoned willy-nilly to avoid the appearance of being judgmental or reluctant to understand.

We're all the poorer for it, since relevant nuances of thought and behavior go determinedly unnoticed.

It sounds noble and open-minded to declare, "I won't judge." The statement implies: I don't think I'm better than you. My behavior isn't any different than yours. It further implies external standards don't apply. All words and deeds are equal.

Refusing to judge has become the unchallenged and worthy (see, that's a "judgment" word) objective. A statement of fact (even if totally true) that sounds the least bit judgmental brings instant rebuke from all directions, "Don't judge!"

That phrase defines our culture — with everyone busily not judging… or noticing… or standing up for any notion that could be construed as "better," or "higher," or "good for the world."

The reasoning goes like this: To judge someone else is bad (oops, one of those darned judgment words, though it's usually permitted in this case). So I refuse to do it. Instead, I must do the opposite — which is to avoid judging.

So when I do that I'm good and fair (more of those darned words). The problem is, that's a simplistic example of either-or thinking — judge versus not judge — choosing between opposites. Either one is a verb — *something one does*. To attempt to do both (avoiding either one) sounds less judgmental, but leaves one paralyzed.

The phrase "do not judge" has been totally misunderstood and misapplied. It's not about doing something (or not). It refers to resisting the urge to judge (or not), **so you can be free to try something entirely different**. It refers to a place within yourself where judging isn't possible.

Go there. Disengage momentarily from trying to change or fix things. Suspend your preferences. Appreciate what's unfolding, without the need to understand it. Ahaaaaaaa… There's nothing needs doing. Peace reigns.

See, it's a place within—an awareness, a place of clarity. And its name is DO NOT JUDGE. Whatever makes you want to criticize or "fix" yourself or anyone else is a reminder to go there.

From *BonBons to Sweeten Your Daily Life*; Or from *More BonBons*

Diversity Yields More Ideas and More Kinds of Ideas

What is needed is a breaking down of the institutional and systemic barriers that impede fresh ideas from being launched or accepted. That includes banishing pigeon holes and categories, the cornerstone of bureaucratic and linear thinking. That also diminishes the top-down model in favor of broader participation and interaction throughout the organization. We should be vigilant about imposing undue constraints that stifle fresh thinking.

A new model for change and solving the world's problems is in the offing. I am confident that the groundbreakers of the present and near future will find ways to resolve the many seemingly intractable difficulties besetting humanity and our besieged planet. And they won't stop there.

The spirit of curiosity and innovation can take us beyond solving problems to also serve our innate desires to live fully. We will find ways whereby our species can flower—by drawing on the full array of our individual potentials.

I propose a slogan that serves the interest of both transparency and diversity: **More Vision—Less Division**. In fact, I cannot think of any arena where that slogan won't improve the quality of cooperation and communication.

More Vision – Less Division

Diversity Close to Home

I am the oldest child. When my sister was born prematurely, her survival was in doubt and she spent her first month in an incubator. Hers was next to an incubator with an Eskimo boy, who was also fighting for his life. His mother had left him at the hospital on the assumption that he wouldn't live, and certainly would die if she took him back to her home village.

At some point, the head of the hospital had a talk with my mother. He suggested she take both babies home, with the hope that at least one would survive. They both did — without ill effects from their rough start.

My brother and sister grew up being called "the twins:" Madelon, delicate and blond-haired and Ray, black-haired and a solid oriental build. They never tired of the shock value of telling strangers "We're twins" and watching their puzzled reactions.

As a young child, my mother taught us, "We are all the leaves of one tree and the flowers of one garden." I believed her when she said people are all the same on the inside — where it counts. My point is, our family was diverse. It was not something we struggled to achieve.

We were indifferent to racial stereotypes — although it was painfully evident to us that many people are not. I recall the hurt our whole family felt from rejections and racial slurs directed at Ray and our mixed-race family.

The type of racial blindness I grew up with sees each person directly, without making labels or stereotypes more important than their particular qualities. And our openness to individual differences wasn't only about race or religion. Our mother's open-minded approach made our home feel like a clubhouse for non-conformists and "interesting characters." For me, outsiders feel like home.

My siblings: Madelon, Ray and Geneva as children

That way of seeing everyone as fundamentally the same as me *inside* turned out to be a signal advantage when I lived in Arizona. I helped to start an organization for tribal economic development, called the Native American Economic Coalition. As a result of the group's success, the Governor of Arizona appointed me to a four-year term on the Arizona Commission of Indian Affairs (making me the token Caucasian). That board stayed on top of significant concerns that affected all twenty-one Arizona tribes.

I think the reason I was able to fit into the Native American community so gracefully was because, apparently to them, I did not "think or act like a white person." Their acceptance came only after the initial puzzlement that I didn't focus on the "gee-whiz—you're Indians" that is woven into so many of their interactions with the wider culture.

I really was indifferent to such typecasts and easily related to each Native American on a person-by-person basis. For that perspective, I certainly give thanks and credit to growing up with Ray.

I share my personal story because for too long we have given lip service to acceptance, while treating race, gender, sex, religion, economic status, and various physical characteristics as grounds for magnifying our differences. That is "old paradigm" thinking. A different take on diversity is one of the signal ways that the incoming and fading paradigms will differ.

Tolerating differences is not at all like embracing the full palate of human qualities and possibilities. As a friend once said to me, "If we were just the same or agreed on everything, one of us would be redundant." In the spirit of accepting greater diversity, our differences add to the fullness of humanity. In truth, there are no redundant people.

Making a Difference through Grassroots Efforts
New Grassroots *By* All of Us—*For* All of Us

We are at a tipping point in history when the most imaginative possibilities could gain traction in short order. Many of today's most widely respected notions started as controversial grassroots movements. That approach can be an entry point for hands-on experimentation, as well as radical ideas. But most fundamentally, grassroots activities are about people solving the problems that affect them.

One of the biggest shifts of the paradigm is the "let someone else do it" attitude fading away in some arenas. Hello—*you* are that someone else. And so am I. You and I are the special forces who are landing. You and I are Mighty Mouse—here to "save the day." Of course, Gandhi said it most forthrightly: "Be the change you want to see in the world."

We water the fresh, grassroots notions that could replace old-growth behemoths that have ceased to be relevant or responsive. A strategy that's good for us all: Dismantle limitations and one's habitual reactions. Be open to what is vital and wholesome. But the most important thing we all can do is take greater responsibility for letting the best thinking shine.

As author and transformational thinker Werner Erhard said:

The problems we have now in communities and societies are going to be resolved only when we are brought together by a common sense that each of us is a visionary. Each of us must come to the realization that we can function and live at the level of vision rather than following some great leader's vision. Instead of looking for a great leader, we are in an era where each of us needs to find the great leader in ourselves.

A good way to start is by reacting to difficulties with vision and determination, rather than with complaints, indignation, and finger-pointing. We cannot afford to act with the stridency of petulant adolescents who protest that life is unfair. Rather we need the determination of an adult who has the will to find a way to make things work out better. That's fair.

~ Democracy through Action ~
A BonBon ~ Faith Lynella

We don't just vote at the ballot box. We vote in our daily lives as citizens—for those causes and concerns we believe in and against those things of which we disapprove.

We vote with our time—whether we invest it in cultural or civic activities, or in the movies and TV programs we watch.

We vote with our money—with regard to which products and charities get to receive our patronage.

We vote with our kind and supporting words—to a young person making an effort to learn, to an old person making an effort to stay involved.

We vote with our behavior—whether we drive with safety and with courtesy, or whether we are wasteful.

What happens at the polls or through government affects us a lot less than the frequent votes each one of us casts every day. Make your votes count. Choose the activities which give you pleasure. Cast your ballot for beneficence in your world.

See yourself as a citizen of the universe and vote for its survival and betterment with every choice and every activity. In this way democracy becomes a living force, with you choosing the world you want to live in. You have the power to improve whatever you touch, so why not vote for it?

From *BonBons to Sweeten Your Daily Life*; Or from *More BonBons*

Building Bridges—Taking Down Walls

Transformation of today's existing institutions will mostly be by the back door. The front door approaches have meant getting around the array of gatekeepers and power players. We must find different answers than the ones we've been settling for. Back door and grassroots methods have been treated as so unlikely to prevail that the guard is not up to block them.

But low-key under-the-radar, non-aggressive, very determined methods provide the very advantage most natural and suitable for such motivated individuals. Philosopher Eckhart Tolle said in an interview with *What is Enlightenment? Magazine* (Fall-Winter, 2000):

> Transcending the world does not mean to withdraw from the world, to no longer take action, or to stop interacting with people. Transcendence of the world is to act and to interact without any self-seeking. In other words, it
>
> means to act without seeking to enhance one's sense of self through one's actions or one's interactions with people. Ultimately, it means not needing the future anymore for one's fulfilment or for one's sense of self or being. There is no seeking through doing, seeking an enhanced, more fulfilled, or greater sense of self in the world. When that seeking isn't there anymore, then you can be in the world but not be of the world. You are no longer seeking for anything to identify with out there.[418]

People are quietly going about making the changes they need in order to make their lives work. They are desperately looking for ways to deal with certain urgent needs and desires that have been left out of the profit-based, power-manipulated priorities of the greed economy. We must engage people on the periphery to support the changes, rather than going head to head with those in the chain of command.

Such visible doers are quietly going about making changes without calling attention to themselves, or without fanfare for what they accomplish. But they provide a powerful model of how authentic change actually happens and are themselves living examples of "critical mass theory" in practice.

Something new is calling forth the clear-sighted capabilities that are not yet engaged. Doors previously closed and barred to "outsiders" now stand wide open because so many "insiders" have dropped the ball. A new kind of visionary thinking is starting to make itself felt. We are starting to see energetic pioneers activated and stripped down to essentials (naked) right out of the starting gate.

The combination takes the dream from the unseen realm into the world as we know it. But it is a child of both. Do not forget that the dream is the mother; the doing is the father. What they make has a life of its own—a new beginning, with all the promise that implies. Now, *that is* creativity in action.

> Such enlightenment, in which death is moment by moment transformed into life, and blindness into seeing, is not just a personal achievement. Were it so,

---

[418] Tolle, Eckhart, Interview—"Ripples on the Surface of Being," *What Is Enlightenment? Magazine*, Fall-Winter, 2000, http://www.wie.org/j18/tolle.as-*Eckhart Tolle*

the pursuit of it would be valueless and foredoomed to failure. It is like all true acts of creation and recreation, a cosmic event, which changes the balance of forces in the world, as it changes them in the individual, and to the less extent, in all with whom he enters into relationship.[419]

The new future that is emerging is not like our version of normal life but an enhanced perception of it that harmoniously connects both the abstract and concrete realms. And the visionary spirit (in whatever form it appears) has been learning to swim in those otherworldly waters all along. The divine-but-human creature is amphibious—equipped to function with potency in either environment as needed.

Making a Significant Difference

David C. Korten is an advocate for grassroots development, who founded the Living Economies Forum and *Yes! Magazine*. He points out some of the factors gaining currency for the shift underway.

> In my career in international development, I saw, time and again, that the most successful projects were not the largest or the most carefully, centrally planned; they were the ones that arose from the bottom up. Likewise, successful social movements are emergent, evolving, radically self-organizing, and involve the dedicated efforts of many people, each finding the role that best uses his or her gifts and passions. Their scope and their success may not, at first, be readily apparent.
>
> Social movements grow and evolve around framing ideas and mutually supportive relationships instead of through top-down direction. New ideas gain traction, or not, depending on what works for those involved in the movement. Some alliances are fleeting; others endure.
>
> The organism, not the machine, provides the appropriate metaphor. The relevant knowledge resides not in the heads of outside experts but in the people who populate the system. The challenge is to help them recognize, organize, and use that knowledge in ever more effective ways.
>
> This is the model I think of when I think about what it will take to build the new economy—one based on fulfilling the basic needs of people and planet—that we need. It's also the way that that economy is already being built: step by step, in creative and surprising ways, by people looking for alternatives to a system that isn't working for them.
>
> To bring down the institutions of Empire, we must begin to build the rules, relationships, and institutions of a New Economy. These must be lived into being from the bottom up.

---

[419] Fausset, Hugh I'Anson, *The Flame and the Light: Meanings in Vedanta and Buddhism* (New York: Greenwood Press, 1958), 66.

So how do you know whether your work is contributing to a big-picture outcome? If you can answer yes to any one of the following five questions, then be assured that it is.

1. Does it help discredit a false cultural story fabricated to legitimize relationships of domination and exploitation and to replace it with a true story describing unrealized possibilities for growing the real wealth of healthy communities?

2. Is it connecting others of the movement's millions of leaders who didn't previously know one another, helping them find common cause and build relationships of mutual trust that allow them to speak honestly from their hearts and to know that they can call on one another for support when needed?

3. Is it creating and expanding liberated social spaces in which people experience the freedom and support to experiment with living the creative, cooperative, self-organizing relationships of the new story they seek to bring into the larger culture?

4. Is it providing a public demonstration of the possibilities of real-wealth economy?

5. Is it mobilizing support for a rule change that will shift the balance of power from the people and institutions of the Wall Street phantom-wealth economy to the people and institutions of living-wealth Main Street economies?

These are useful guidelines for setting both individual and group priorities. Bear in mind that in a systems-change undertaking of this magnitude, there is no magic bullet and no one is going to make it happen on their own, so don't be discouraged if the world looks much the same today despite your special and heroic effort yesterday.[420]

Transforming Our Future

The Visionaries of Tomorrow

I see forces at work that are fundamentally altering what it means to be a visionary in our culture. Historically, walking the visionary path was usually an emotionally costly and tortured lifestyle choice. Few people were so driven, but there was no place for them in the larger society. These days, that is not the only choice for those who hear a distant drummer.

---

[420] Korten, David, "The Big Picture: 5 Ways to Know if You're Making a Difference," adapted from Agenda for a New Economy: From phantom wealth to real wealth, *Yes! Magazine*, June 21, 2010, http://www.yesmagazine.org

This book describes what makes the very real challenges of the visionary path worth the effort. But in many ways, that path is not so far removed from what we all desire—to live a full and satisfied life, to feel we've made a difference. Everyone is walking on the path to self-fulfillment, albeit at different rates and with different degrees of impact or enjoyment.

While it makes no sense to urge anyone to be a visionary if they are not called to it, every single one of us can gain by allowing *more insightful thinking* to take root in our individual lives. Ideas that come through inspiration are imbued with added energy that makes thinking more crisp and perceptive.

It can be found by listening closely to one's own unique notions, as well as by paying greater attention to the ideas espoused by others that have a bit of originality.

Long stretches of the visionary path are solitary, until the developing notion can be shared and accepted by others. But the solitary, dispossessed, outsider visionary is not the only model available. However, individuals should be free to leave the beaten path without being treated as outcasts or weirdoes.

I also recognize that such an arduous approach is not for everyone. It is certainly not the only way to introduce novelty into daily life. Anyone can benefit by weaving their insights and micro-visions into his or her ordinary activities.

While visionaries push the margins when they can, others fill in the intervening steps and help to ground what's new. The combination of visionary leaps by a few and insightful steps taken by many means visionary thinking is rather widespread on a wide variety of scales. We can expect to see more of this.

What Is Around the Corner?

The shift underway is not pointing to something *totally* new. We've been longing for some elements of it for a very long time. Deep down, we are awakening to a desire to express more of the qualities of consciousness that are already resident within us. The increasing balance of heart, mind, body, and spirit permits each of us to tell what is primary and what is peripheral as we make decisions.

The old is dying because something newer and more fundamentally humane is arising in its place. That more integrated approach has been biding its time until now. But it allows us to make the wisest and fairest choices. This capacity leads to a broadly shared sense that we are drawing on our best—the best of all of us.

> The shift is subtle and at the same time profound. It is a shift in our being, in the quality of our consciousness.… This represents a true quantum leap of consciousness. When people first hear this term they often think it means some huge leap in consciousness. But in modern physics, a quantum leap is the smallest possible leap. At the atomic level, a shift from one energy state to the next does not occur as a smooth transition, but as a discrete change—an

instantaneous transition from one state to another. Similarly the shift from a tense mind to a relaxed mind is a discrete shift.[421]

Human evolution moves through unfolding stages from survival to higher states of consciousness. That sequence progressively shifts a person's self-centered point of view first from me, then to us (a group), then to all of us (global). Its focus is less and less personal. At the same time, people and their cultures progress through myriad forms of growth, so a point of view is always in flux.

When growing, each stage "transcends and includes" the prior one. The developing view goes beyond what existed before, yet it still includes and maintains many of its values.

Purposes of the Shift toward Integration:
- Acquire greater awareness and inner maturity — ability to ground the normal ideas along with the abstract ideals
- Movement from polarization to reconciliation — from focus on differences to focus on similarities
- Freedom from one's total ego control; ego in its right and necessary place
- Stripped of illusions and personal baggage (distortions)
- Character and values drive our behavior
- Emotional neutrality (not the same as the emotions turned off)
- Mental and physical discipline about responsibility for each other
- Trust in the source of one's own vision and greater awareness
- Evading deceptions inherent in a low-energy reality

Our children's generation will have a very different world. For them, the new paradigm will feel normal. Some of them are already attuned to very different forms of energy and relationships than their elders of the past. For instance, hierarchies are largely anathema to them. They refuse to put their opinions about what really matters aside in order to satisfy rules in which they find no value.

Most adults are not attuned to the more egalitarian view that the young ones experience. Like an immigrant family in a country with an unfamiliar language, the children pick up the new dialect and translate for the parents. As long as those who are older or in power are tone deaf to the newer messages, they will not be able to make good judgment calls. We need to all get on the same page.

Finding Peace with Oneself
Whatever economic or cultural changes the future brings, each of us will be challenged as individuals as well. We must draw upon as large an array of our

---

[421] Russell, Peter, *Resurgence*, "Natural Mind," September/October, 2009.

own personal abilities as possible. Being able to call up one's internal "teamwork" is no small achievement.

That points to a life skill, a lifelong activity that is not totally dependent on external circumstances. But it builds resilience and judgment for what life brings.

Among the inner places needing to be built by each of us is a structure that permits one to move fluidly within ourselves that is responsive to changing circumstances. Jean Houston, author and scholar in the human potential movement, developed a term and concept that addressed the healthy functioning of the full range of all our personal roles: "polyphrenia."

Her approach permits a person to orchestrate and accept the depth of the many aspects of "who I am."

> [Individuals exhausted from too many demands can] move into another kind of awareness: seeing themselves as a theater of selves, a troupe of actors playing different roles according to the scene and script for the day. I have often suggested that if schizophrenia, the self that is split against itself, is the disease of the human condition, then polyphrenia, the orchestration of our many selves, may be our expanded health.... The brittle raft of a solitary ego is an uncertain vessel in the sea of so much change. The polyphrenic person is able to keep a large cast of characters active, calling them to stage front as needed for the many roles we have to play. Each character brings new energies and a new set of skills. If one feels blocked or inadequate in some area, move one persona over in the psyche, and one stands a good chance of finding an aspect of the self which is not blocked and is quite willing to tackle some dreaded activity.[422]

As more of our habitual distortions fall away, we are freed from the minute deflections that prevent us from sensing a connection with the larger frame of reference. That connects every person to their unique, inherent, and wholehearted identity. Increased self-awareness reveals the extent of our power and purpose. And the awareness of that brings a sense of joy and awe.

Heading Toward Nakedness and Authenticity

Consciousness is naked—unadorned and uncomplicated. For someone to most fully engage life, he or she must become more simple and authentic in their outlook, too. Our inspired moments of vision or otherworldly clarity are so liberating, the physical limits of flesh or the normal world are left behind. One knows oneself to be whole. That is the big T Truth—the Naked Truth.

Sometimes, life resembles a game of strip poker. The challenge is not just to take it off, but to *leave it off*, so we stay open to life. But that works best if others around us are willing to strip to the essentials as well. Otherwise, people are playing by different standards and at cross-purposes.

---

[422] Houston, Jean, "Jean Houston Writes about Her Working Muse, *Soul Food Café*, 2000, http://www.dailywriting.net/Houston.htm

Each of us can know the full rush of greater clarity occasionally—discovered without warning in inspired and special moments. We briefly know what is true and abiding within every fiber of our being, so we chaff at lesser truths as the imposters they are.

Each moment of living offers each person a variation of the same choice: embrace or hold back; trust or fear; expand or contract; create something new for yourself or stand pat. Fear and insecurity urge wearing protective garb. By contrast, novelty relies on what comes to hand in the moment—spontaneity.

There's an ideal balance to be found, of course. Creative expression puts a premium on nakedness because it avoids distortion and old ideas that no longer apply. That flux opens us to a wider, more genuine, range of experience.

Greater nakedness prevents being identified solely *with one's own* perspective or goals, without a sensitivity to the larger context, as well as our impact on where we live and work. What to wear? Not bare-assed naked, but clothed appropriately—discarding the clothing/ideas that are out of date or don't ring true any longer. Each person can get in touch with the naked consciousness of "who I am"—their essence. Starting there, whatever they do or wear fits perfectly.

In remaking the world, we should be mindful of it being a world with valuable qualities of its own (unrelated to our human interests). People don't just make their mark on it, but *vice versa*. So irrespective of the desirability or usefulness of our vision, what we set out to do with it must also *make things better*.

That includes an emotional resonance infused with worthwhile values. Improving the world is about being able to ground all the components in an integrated way.

The urge to create and bridge from the familiar to something better is as much an innate right as the pursuit of happiness, and sometimes the very same thing. It's in our mental and emotional DNA. The forces for creative change are innate and universal, worth every effort to experience them. Let's stand up for a world where everyone is responding to the urge to "do what they're here to do."

Chapter 20 - Creating an Incubator for Visionary Thinkers

*Somehow, those who are most involved with their visions and
creativity have carved out areas of freedom for them in their lives.
Each has figured out a way to get the special fuel needed to keep going.
That includes finding protections from toxic influences around them.*

A Vision of My Own

Walking the visionary path represents an enormous challenge. The attrition rate is ridiculous for those who set out. Most of their ideas die on the vine. There is typically a high personal cost to those pursuing their vision. But there is an even greater loss to the world if they don't, since what these individuals offer is so badly needed.

Challenges on the visionary path are daunting by any measure, made even more by so few hazard signs or landmarks for guidance. Heading off the beaten track is likely to be rough going and lonely.

Each intrepid pioneer who goes *anyway* is responding to his or her own reasons for separating from the herd. Why couldn't there be more signposts to guide them? There must be some way to improve the odds of getting through the maze of hazards, on the way to bringing their visions to life.

For years I've pondered what might assist more budding visionaries to brave the strenuous early phases, or help them hang on until their visions bear fruit. The visionary path represents a complicated growth cycle, with much more involved than reaching some far-off finish line. A person growing into their vision must work through innumerable challenges and learning curves—testing them in every possible way.

I want to encourage more unbridled creative expression of what drives them. I want those off the beaten path to move more unerringly through the high-risk spots—where they often bog down or lose their drive. Granted, every single stage entails its own risks, but how much of this journey is spent repeatedly "reinventing the wheel?"

Challenges are necessary for the visionary's inner and outer development. Some relate to the individual's personal growth and competence, others with building a conceptual package for the vision and gaining traction for it. And some come from being perceived as an "outsider."

But that doesn't mean every visionary must repeat each challenge in order to be successful. They might be able to benefit from the experience of others who preceded them. It is not a given that each traveler must do every step of it on their own.

One of my goals is to stimulate greater understanding about the crucial role visionaries, their unique outlook and contributions, play in the change process. Having lived my life ahead of the curve, it's comforting to think the time might be ripe for such a possibility. I anticipate an emerging new outlook about what it means to be a visionary and that it will be diffused into the wider culture. That should lead to a relaxation of the 'we-they' thinking that sanctions rejection of non-conforming and highly creative individuals.

This chapter describes some of my evolving notions about how to encourage those committed to their visionary aspirations. I have already gone through several revisions in my thinking. Most of what I foresee is still in the ungrounded-vision phase that will remain in theoretical form until more components come together, or until more people take it on.

Getting Organized

I recently formed a non-profit corporation in Massachusetts called Center for Visionary Brilliance to accomplish a number of the activities described in this chapter. No effort is made here to distinguish what I intend to do from what that organization, or the online community will do. Also, many of the choices about its priorities or the direction this goes will depend on what participants want.

I envision a Center and/or organization devoted to sorting out fact from fiction about the visionary process. This book is an integral part of bringing forth my own multi-faceted vision. This overview could help individuals prepare for their journey, find the courage to leap, and reinforce their resolve along the way. Such a resource might buttress the skills needed to launch and sustain their efforts.

Visualizing an Incubator

An incubator maintains a nurturing environment to stabilize growth at the infancy stage. It compensates for under-development until all systems become viable on their own. Such a place/space is transitional, but it often spells the difference between survival and not.

Once a person discovers a spark of vision, what is the best way for them to "blow on the spark" so it grows and catches fire? What form of protective nest can best keep such precious sparks alive? Finding answers along those lines is a key aspect of designing an Incubator for visionary thinking.

What I describe as an Incubator is not a fixed place, like a "Camp Visionary," but a place of disengagement for the individual. It is an "Ollie-ollie in free," a safe time-out, where one can catch one's breath before returning to the fray.

Designing an Incubator:
- What would it do?
- Who would it be for?
- What would be required for it to work?
- Who would do the "heavy lifting"?

- What would be the upside for visionaries? For their respective fields? For the larger community? For the long term? Also, what would be the likely risk or downside for each?
- What can be done to encourage those engaged in the visionary process without distorting it, distracting them, or frightening them by acknowledging the scale of that to which they aspire?
- How much of the struggle and need for isolation is inevitable and necessary? To what extent? In what ways is the struggle crucial to the vision's realization itself?
- What are my own assumptions or perceptual biases about this?
- What is needed to speed up the present pace of gaining acceptance? Better yet, to speed up recognition that it's precisely what we need at this point in our evolution? What is optional? What have we entirely failed to notice?

Some parts of the Incubator are for the benefit of visionaries themselves. But it is also to gather expertise about visionary matters that can be used by allied groups and interested professionals. The Center will also collect and organize relevant information about the visionary process in a systematic way.

Aspects of the Incubator/Center:
- Define or develop support services customized for common visionary challenges
- Encourage a community of visionaries that promotes their individual and shared goals; Maintain a virtual clubhouse for camaraderie
- Expand awareness about the visionary process (and its necessity to our progress) in the larger culture
- Post real-life examples of visionaries and their visions in action who are gathering notice and momentum
- Conduct studies; locate, collect, and organize relevant research being done elsewhere
- Build a knowledge base, compendia, archive dealing with visionary topics

Many of these functions can be accomplished online within a virtual environment. The online space/place will serve as a commons, a gathering place for members of this self-selecting community—some active contributors, some more occasional participants, some deeply interested who actively use the resource, while preferring to remain socially invisible. This is a fully inclusive community, respecting every drop in our vast ocean of creative human capital.

Those who are involved will play a direct and active role in the form and direction of this project. This whole Incubator concept is itself a visionary undertaking. To a large extent, its very existence is my way of testing out central principles of the visionary process.

Some of the initial "data" will emerge as a consequence of getting activities launched so data can be collected. But its true value will depend on the visionaries in the trenches and their ability to decide what is desirable, and what is not. This will evolve.

The research side of the Center will examine the mechanics of how individuals ground their original notions in satisfying and sustainable ways. The approach I have in mind will shed a different light on the creative-change process itself by being attuned to the omnipresent and underlying energetic and emotional influences.

That emphasis will bring attention to factors totally ignored in other research methods. The place I envision is fundamentally different than a typical think tank, training facility, or non-profit organization, although it will perform some similar functions.

A Fish Tank—Not a Think Tank

The saying goes: A fish cannot see the water in which it swims. Meaning, we tend to ignore or unconsciously take for granted the milieu that influences our experience—the water. Our Center will also gather meta-research that is specifically about *studying the water itself*—the emotional and energetic backdrop of creativity.

Think tanks value thinking. They're designed for analysis and strategic planning. They produce reports, forecasts, and policy recommendations. Their work is usually funded by organizations and special-interest groups to further organizational priorities. Such an institution is comprised of well-trained minds that work together to solve problems within the restraints of their moral principles.

But there's usually a philosophical or political basis for the topics explored— whether it is quite outspoken or covert about those guiding principles. So findings are often biased in favor of the organization's overall mission.

The way think tanks function discounts the non-rational, emotional, and energetic influences, which are neither valued nor trusted in rational inquiries. Such factors are treated as unwelcome distractions to the singularly valued thought process. On the other hand, clarifying these influences that defy logical analysis is exactly what our Center will attempt to do.

Finding solutions to any particular problems will be secondary because what is being studied is the *process of inventiveness*—with an eye on the inner and energetic surrounds. Thinking indicates being mental, rational and logical, all of which are rooted in narrowing the perceptual focus.

Instead, our Center is interested in what might be discovered by turning 180° away from that intellectually narrow approach. Such a radical change of emphasis could very well alter what is observed, measured, or discovered. I'm sure it will.

Nurturing Sparks of Brilliance

Supporting Creative Energy and Freedom

Somehow, those who are most involved with their visions and creativity have carved out areas of freedom for them in their lives. Each has figured out a way to get the special fuel needed to keep going. That includes finding protections from toxic influences around them. (Maybe they wanted more than they got, but they didn't settle for "none.")

Such individuals realize that meeting their own inner needs is essential to their survival within a society that considers them "strange." But it's worth noting that they tend to be "strange" in similar ways, in ways that they can appreciate in each other. Those on the visionary path tend to recognize in each other a comparable drive to find what's missing in normal life.

For them, taking the visionary path, and all it entails, is not a passing phase. Nor is it dependent on whether their ideas "click" or they become a media darling. That urge is a "need that cannot be denied," a desire to stand tall and breathe free in a world where what they "know to be possible" is allowed to thrive.

Nothing short of attempting that suffices. And these forerunners do not want that freedom only for their own good, but for anyone else who wants their version of that as well. The nature of the Incubator is to beat the drum for such a space. Even if it is largely virtual and internal, it encourages conditions conducive to visionary thinking predominate. That place/space has an energy-level component as well as a mutual-affinity component.

Visionaries at Various Stages

The Center is not intended to be a clubhouse *only* for those who are on the visionary path. Its purpose involves mapmakers (preferably from various fields), who have documented the lay of the land and how various conceptual maps connect to other.

By determining where the quicksand is, or whether bridges are out, or which remedy works for certain maladies, some of the confusion or frustration can be reduced. Each of the stages has its own flavor of snags and identity issues, so those will be addressed as well.

The Incubator was initially conceived by me for individuals who *already knew* they were visionaries, who had found their voice and leaped. Those individuals knew they were somewhere along the visionary path.

But it soon became clear that a far wider range of individuals than the already initiated would find these ideas useful. Many incipient visionaries are dealing with the early challenges of the visionary process well *before they find their voice* or are becoming cognizant of the pervasive need for more creative expression in their lives. I call them Emerging Visionaries. Age appears irrelevant.

On the other hand, age is a factor in a way—not so much in years of life as the stage to which the person's inner maturity has progressed. How self-directed are they? How much actual life experience have they acquired, and in the process, how many of the essential seeds of wisdom?

The front-burner needs of those who are driven, but not yet focused, are very different than the needs of those who have already found their voice and vision (who know their *what*, even if not the *how*).

In many cases, the person has a vision and/or voice, but has not yet developed a following. Others have emerged as an acknowledged voice for their cause, but are already struggling with mastery-level issues (with mixed results).

Specific Subsets of Visionaries:

- Emerging or Unfocused Visionaries—those who are still finding their unique voice and self-confidence

- Fledgling Visionaries— those who made the leap and are still getting their act together: message, packaging, stamina, and growth issues

- Flying Visionaries—those who are in the thick of building their vision and are "on the wing"

- Mature Visionaries—those who are at later stages of the visionary path, dealing with mastery-level issues

- Late Bloomers as Visionaries—those older individuals who get on the visionary path late in life, as a second act; they have many of the issues of fledgling visionaries, but have lived long enough to develop some wisdom, necessary skills, and a broader perspective

- Innocent Visionaries—those who are children who have extraordinary capacities engaged from the beginning. But they will not remain children. How are their needs and abilities different than other visionaries? What happens to them once they mature? Is this category a new kind of hybrid that doesn't have the same needs for support? Are there ways we can support the adult parents of such clear-sighted children?

This list is neither exhaustive nor definitive. It is bound to grow larger as our feet hit the ground in the school of experience. The Center must figure out technological solutions that honor contributor's input, ideas, feedback, desires, and sharing of best practices.

Along the way, we will without a doubt discover a great deal more about the true scope of visionaries, their visions—great and small. We need to know what they want and need to fulfill their callings, their missions, and their grandest dreams.

Forming Natural Clusters

It is probably wise to avoid setting up categories to the extent possible. The Center won't try to fit a theory or to define taxonomies — that represents the old-school model. That is much too linear and boundary-prone for our purposes. Visionaries are not inclined to be joiners or their own demographic group. But even those who are outliers or rare share some traits in common.

I'd like to see communities of related visionary interest groups. Or They might form spontaneously around pockets of leadership or philosophical interest. This speaks to natural affinities and being dynamic, rather than fixed relationships. This way of connecting up is sometimes referred to as "tribes."

This becomes particularly important if the relationships or support structure happens mostly online. It could also be shared via appropriate social media. I would hope it is not just driven by professional field or causes because that could interfere with cross0pollination and a sense of shared community.

Extending the Support Range

An aircraft carrier acts as a man-made island, an outpost in the middle of the ocean. It allows planes and jets to stop long enough to get the necessary fuel, maintenance, and supplies needed before resuming their journey. The same applies for the pilot, who needs food, rest, updated information, and a brain break. That floating pit stop recharges their mental, psychological, and creative energies.

An aircraft carrier operates as a temporary home base for those far from their mainland supply lines. Planes don't stay any longer than necessary, going off to their next mission as soon as they're replenished. In some respects, the Incubator resembles that aircraft carrier that individuals can draw on as they need some R&R from their leading-edge vision pursuits.

On a related note, over time an oasis space/place like that also discovers precisely what to have on hand so travelers (visionaries) can get to their destination successfully and safely. To that end, the Visionary Incubator will constantly experiment with how the visionary process can be tweaked to proceed more smoothly.

Although our Center will be predominantly a virtual space, its primary purpose is to be a welcoming, gratifying, and resourceful gathering place for all things visionary. Nearly all of its functions will occur online or through digital publications and resources that people worldwide can tap.

The only requirement is desire. Although there is a social and communal component of this virtual clubhouse, there's no barrier to creating an actual meet-up with others in the same local area who might have similar or aligned interests.

Cultivating Visionary Aspirations

A Sense of Finding "My People"

Being immersed in the visionary experience sets a person apart from most of their contemporaries in significant ways. Many are mavericks or outsiders, to some degree, since so many social conventions do not suit their single-minded priorities.

But that is not to say these individuals do not have a fundamental need to be social to some degree, or to be valued, or to be "understood." Often those desires have been thwarted so repeatedly that they have few expectations about being accepted on a personal basis—and for the "right reason." That is why it seems important that there be a social and interactive component for the community I envision.

Many visionaries are outsiders—perhaps not in every area of their lives, but in areas vis-à-vis their visions where they have jumped out of the orbit of "normal." Many have a hard time getting validated for their personal aspirations and choices. That is why finding a few others out on the fringes who might "get" what is meaningful to them is doubly important.

Finding those who can say "that makes sense to me" is like a bystander offering a drink of water during a marathon. Everyone appreciates validation that "you're not crazy" at certain points, especially when the mounting evidence suggests that you are. Only another person who has faced (or is facing) those same difficulties can comprehend what is involved—let alone respond with compassion.

The Individual Must Get Around Two Common Confusions:

- "Ugly Duckling" issue—when the community of ducks leads the person to feel they are "wrong" or inadequate ducks; visionary types don't flourish as ducks, but without different role models they feel trapped and unsure of themselves

- The perception of visionaries as too different from the rest of us—their status seems too remote for a person who hears their own distant drummer to feel a kinship with them

Finding one's most closely aligned peers in the ranks of visionaries helps a person gain a more accurate perception of their true nature, true self. Those who have mostly been told you're wrong or foolish by the world-at-large for their eccentric or extravagant ideas, will more likely encounter "me too!" reactions from fellow visionaries with the same concerns.

This community is more about exchanging energetic like-mindedness than particular information or data. In some visceral way, members can "see" each other, and there is no substitute for that level of recognition.

Encouragement in the Early Stages

Most of the initial signs of visionary tendencies are likely to be missed (or rejected) by anyone who is not themselves dabbling in leading-edge matters. It's the psychological support that is the most heartening.

The sooner those with visionary tendencies identify their proclivities and strengths, the greater the likelihood that they won't burn out or give up. The community can find ways to encourage members to accept their unique abilities early on. That is not easily done because it can take a long time for someone to realize he or she is "onto something" new and significant.

The quality or completeness of the person's vision is less important than their singular devotion to it. That determination to hang on reflects the combination of the uniqueness and persistence of the individual's emerging perspective. Our acknowledgement for those efforts doesn't depend on results nor does it have to wait for them. That is entirely contrary to the way most visionaries have been treated in the past.

If we want the fabulous advancements they deliver to continue streaming into our lives and improving the quality of life for everyone on the planet, then we better start changing the way we treat them right now. I intend to walk my talk on that one and invite you to join me.

Support with "Inventing Their Wheels"

If incipient visionaries can better understand the nature of the journey they're on, they won't be so easily caught unaware. Even for them to realize that it is a process, with certain helpful rules, is a huge step forward. Being able to read the signals better reduces considerable mystery and grounds for self-doubt from the outset.

Those who have traveled that route have already figured out many survival skills that can be passed along to those who follow. However, the uniqueness of each individual argues against any single formula or cookie-cutter approach. But everyone can benefit by using existing wheels or by adapting what's already available. Given how visionaries function, expect somebody to design newer and more functional wheels, too.

Mentoring New Voices

A community is comprised of individuals who often represent the full spectrum of abilities. The give and take among all kinds of like-minded travelers grows into a shared group dynamic.

Visionaries are discerning and able to spot the signs of genuine novelty quite early, before it has gelled. That ability can make them valuable mentors to still-unfocused developing visionaries. A group that encourages new voices invites each to bring a song of their own to the chorus.

But this community is not about those who know something telling those who don't. All participants are in a position to share their hard-earned insights. It operates as a two-way street, meaning everyone will be a giver at times, a receiver at others.

That sort of receptivity and reciprocity comports with the new emerging paradigm. What we're all feeling compelled to do is to break out of 'either-or' thinking and narrowly-defined roles to a greater extent.

Mentoring of all kinds exists within many fields of interest. The arts thrive because the more accomplished are willing to tutor the up-and-coming talent. The various forms of mentoring cannot be praised too highly, whatever the field. We need much more of it and for many more areas of interest. I hope there will be active cross-pollination between this community and others, as opportunities permit.

What makes this different from what any of them do is to look for the *common threads* most visionaries encounter *without regard to their expertise or chosen area of interest*. Involvement is not field-specific.

The Center/Incubator pays attention to the overall visionary perspective and the dynamics it stirs up within a person. It seeks to find the most basic and intimate qualities of creativity that can be found operating when creative talents are engaged. Maintaining contact with others who are "holding more creative energy" can ratchet upward as individuals are able to integrate more of their gains.

Studying Vision-driven Change

Things That Matter, Things That Don't

I think it is possible to study the dynamics of visionary thinking *as it is occurring* by those most accustomed to practicing it. However, finding answers to specific problems will not be the sole or primary goal of this research. It also seeks a clearer understanding about ways to support the growth and effectiveness of those engaged in visionary pursuits. What magnifies and reinforces their efforts? Or what factors have a dampening effect?

Although it feels like a lifetime ago and remote to me now, I was trained as a social scientist with a specialty in research design and statistics. So I am sensitive to the need for accuracy and precision in framing such research. Some analysis of the visionary process will include surveys and empirical studies backed by statistical analysis.

But it will also include anecdotal data and group dynamics components that don't fit into tidy conceptual or measurable boxes.

In most research, uncontrolled or uncontrollable elements, like emotions, are treated as distractions or confounding factors. So their influence is minimized (controlled for) to the extent possible. But I'm persuaded that many of those below-the-surface influences also deserve to be acknowledged, better understood, and factored into conclusions.

Imagine what can be discovered about the subtle, unstructured, spontaneous, and uncontrolled factors that need to be free to *arise as they will* as a person moves through the visionary process.

Just as important are the energetic factors, for they fuel creative efforts. The amount of lift-off energy available is a limiting factor as to an individual's ability to sustain clarity in a world of complex challenges.

All of us are learning how to function in a higher-level energetic reality. Figuring out how having more energy alters each of our beliefs and behavior is part of the task at hand. The real advantage in being attentive to our energy levels is so causes of energetic leakage or decline can be recognized and minimized. As a consequence, our creative bursts can get more mileage.

Studying the Visionary Process
The Center is itself a laboratory for study and defining the dynamics of creative energy at work and at play. What I foresee supports an approach where participants are both the subjects and beneficiaries of what is discovered. One need only compare their own before-after experiences to gauge what works. The structure and methods employed at the Center could develop a steady output of high-octane answers and tools.

I sometimes refer to this as "visionary science" but that is not exactly accurate. It is about studying the visionary phenomena and collecting data, but that collection is not constrained by the rigid methodology of the "scientific method." Investigations may use them, but with the caveat that the Center's goal is to supplement and build upon additional ways of gathering knowledge. If it incorporates the visionary mindset, all the better.

What is being studied is much broader and deeper than any single field of inquiry. It is not only rational or scientific data being gathered, or even the experiences of visionaries themselves. Picking the lock on that treasure chest calls for an interdisciplinary approach that draws upon many different frames of reference and skills.

All manner of experiences, irrespective of the contributor's age, gender, expertise, formal education level, or motivation, need to be part of the emerging picture of the visionary process. That interplay of factors makes our alliance with each other organic and able to grow in an expansive, fluid way.

Goals of Visionary Research:
- Develop language precise enough to be able to express meaningful distinctions within the internal landscape
- Collect and consolidate relevant research about visionaries and the visionary process

- Eliminate our own distorting preconceptions about this topic to avoid getting stuck in old thinking
- Study the visionary phenomena *as they happen,* rather than in retrospect or impersonally
- Determine what assists, and what interferes, with the creative-manifestation process
- Monitor how efforts to define and study the visionary process make it more transparent and available to broader discussion and investigation
- Advocate for visionaries and inspired answers

One element of this undertaking is to develop a clearer understanding of the potential value of such unconventional approaches to research, and how their results might be best applied. Having broken free of conventional goals or analyses, what new vistas are opened?

I do not think the dynamics inherent in the visionary process will yield their secrets easily, but who better to pick that lock than visionaries themselves?

Assessment of results will include (in part) the Hawkins Scale of Consciousness (below). The Hawkins scale is included to assure that the consciousness vibration level of any of the Center's recommendations or conclusions are held to a high standard.

Consciousness Energy Data Base and Archives

In August, 2001 I first encountered David Hawkins and his germinal book, *Power vs Force: The hidden determinants of human behavior.*[423] He developed a measure of the consciousness energy level of any object, person, concept, place, etc. The higher its calibrated score on the Scale of Consciousness, the more consciousness it embodies.

Reading Hawkins crystalized a number of notions I was ruminating over at the time, so I saw its revolutionary implications immediately. I contacted Dr. Hawkins soon thereafter and spelled out a way I wanted to apply his Scale of Consciousness. He graciously approved my request. Some of the structure of the database or archives at the Center derive from what I foresaw at that time.

Any person (living or dead) or object can be quickly calibrated to find precisely where it falls on his Scale of Consciousness. His scale (between zero and 1000) allows someone to ascertain the consciousness energy level of what is being assessed. With something as nebulous as consciousness, accurate measurement or comparisons will always be thorny. But Hawkins' approach gets around much of that subjectively. Since it's a logarithmic scale, even a small numerical increase represents a significant increase in consciousness energy level.

---

[423] Hawkins, David R., *Power vs Force: The hidden determinants of human behavior* (Sedona, AZ: Veritas Publishing, 2000)

By using Hawkins' method of calibration to determine the level of consciousness, I've become accustomed to measuring and tracking where a person or object falls on the scale. This technique has also been very useful to verify that efforts at inner growth are working.

Everyone's consciousness level is influenced by the energetic levels of the company they keep, or the quality of activities pursued. Moments of vision and inspired clarity are very high on the scale, so they temporarily elevate a person's level far beyond his or her customary point on the scale.

Above 500 on the Hawkins Scale, love energy begins to predominate. Any person whose score exceeds 500 is becoming more heart-based, and is learning to balance their head and heart influences more effectively. Further up the scale, a person's head and heart become allies and start to work in unison. That collaboration is especially germane to the creative process.

The average consciousness energy level for mankind continues its gradual upward climb, as more people take steps to move away from fear and low-energy pursuits. Widespread high-octane energy nudges many who weren't previously attuned to their inner growth and toward greater insight — including the inner maturity that corresponds with it.

The scale provides a different way of interpreting what we think we already know about anyone's behavior — relative to its energetic level. This approach permits getting a handle on the energetic affinity of both tangible and intangible influences.

The masters or giants reside on higher points on the scale than their contemporaries. Anyone operating above 700 (very few in number, but mighty powerful in their influence in the world) sees events through a vastly different perceptual lens than almost everyone else. These individuals are beacons of moral authority, who impart true wisdom.

Establish a High-consciousness Energy Archives

The archives developed by the Center would be a treasure trove of tools, resources, and how-to with particular relevance to the creative processes. The archive will protect, organize, and share information about the collected wisdom related to these topics. Its long-term goal is to broaden the discourse and lead to greater scholarship and analysis about vision and creativity.

Part of the Incubator/Center is setting up a database and an archives of books (and other kinds of creative works). All the books in it are chosen because they calibrate at 500 or higher high on the Hawkins Scale.

Books are selected for the collection on the basis of their high consciousness energy level, a whole new basis for inclusion than libraries use now. Books have never been selected and organized on the basis of their energy/truth level. It would be like deciding to have a library only of books with blue covers.

Books and Materials in the Archives Are Chosen by:
- Consciousness calibration level
- Topics related to the visionary process or individuals
- Books/works *for*, *about*, or *by* visionaries
- Authors of high consciousness level; recognized visionaries
- Reference books and general information (which won't be calibrated)

For my own reading, I seek out authors who score as high as possible. In my home library, I make a practice of calibrating favorite authors (alive or dead) as well as to determine the score of the specific book they wrote.

An author always has a higher score than their writings—but not by much. And his or her score can change as their body of work matures. Calibrating their work helps me decide which writers or concepts are more trustworthy.

These archives will have a physical location and a constantly expanding collection. But the information about the chosen books, the database itself, can be accessed by anyone over the Internet. These resources are integral to the research and findings of the Center.

Imagine the energy of such a physical space; actually *feel the highly charged intensity* of such a space. Such a resource would be used for research and to protect creative works that would otherwise be lost. The archives will track down out-of-print or hard-to-find titles, along with some never-published works. Researchers from a variety of fields may conduct research there and delve into the collection.

The collection may have to make electronic versions of some works where the books themselves are not available. Or it may bring some out-of-print editions back into print (or into electronic formats).

However, I feel the printed books themselves matter and they hold an energetic signature aside from the words/message inside the covers. So to the extent possible the archives will prefer hard copies to electronic versions alone.

Making It Happen through Collaboration

As far as I'm concerned, this project is a labor of the heart and mind, of art and science, of idea and practice dancing together. To make all needed leaps and landings requires more hands (legs) than a single person can provide.

But even if my contribution of effort could be infinite, it would still be mine—constrained by my limits and point of view. The undertaking would gain immeasurably by involving the widest possible array of viewpoints and participants.

That's especially true since many participants in this group are anything but typical. They've been on an extraordinary journey and have acquired great depth of knowledge. We can all learn from fellow travelers if there is a way to spur the dialog.

The Incubator/Center I described provides a multi-pronged approach for us to better understand the visionary experience. If it is to happen, it must involve many people over a long time window. At this point I simply continue throwing rock after rock into the pond, knowing their ripples continue on.

I've been on the leading-edge phase of numerous start-ups and visionary undertakings. I love it! I love the roll-up-the-sleeves challenges and sense of achievement as it grows. It's been a large portion of my life. As I've lived with the vision of this Center and its purpose, I see something else as well (and it was slow to dawn on me).

I'm retiring, but will stay engaged with the visionary community primarily as a mentor and advocate. Nothing has made it clearer to me than the evolving nature of this chapter what my role should be going forward. I look at this Center and Incubator through the eyes of the visionary. I've shared some of what it could accomplish and have no doubt it is possible.

I have a different role to play from here on. Having shared this vision, I see myself in a new place in this process, and in my life. Much of what I'm describing is going to be the work of others. These ideas will go into the world. Some will take root. Some may be buzzworthy enough or viral enough to influence the discourse about what matters.

While I will continue with projects close to my heart and those well-underway, I have a new function. When I first "saw" the Incubator, I visualized myself in the thick of it—involved in the day-to-day and missionary functions. I've been surprised by the number of tasks that have shifted to the "That's not for you to do" column.

At first I thought it was a recognition of my own limits or a bow to practicalities—since it is not from a lapse of interest by me. But I've come to understand the rightness of my new role. I think we are on the cusp of a more creative and participatory way of life. Some of us have worked long and hard to get here. We've prepared the ground and moved public perceptions to reach this watershed time.

So just being where we are as a species is the completion of a very long, uphill preparation phase. What's on the verge of happening (Chapter 19) is going to reflect the next wave of insights and visions to lead our species on. Every visionary trick will be required—and then some. I see myself as contributing perspective and experience to those at the forefront.

Between my input, the Center, and those who commit to share some part of my vision, there could be a community ready and able to encourage those embarked on this arduous process.

Making the Center a Reality

It has started to happen. People reading this and visiting the websites are opening the door to greater interest in this topic. Discussing the visionary process at all is altering the scope of what such a place/space can accomplish. It sounds rather like a visionary quest, does it not?

    http:// visionaryfountain.com
    http:// nakedvisionary.com

When some trait is considered rare or unexpected its appearance is treated like a fluke, a random happenstance. But when it is seen as a process, each dot is treated as a detail in a bigger picture, a step in a longer progression. It will take many more dots than those I found and noted to bring clarity to the visionary process.

I am counting on readers reacting to what I've written with: I know something she missed. I have some pieces to fill in the blanks. This book and the projects briefly described here are themselves an open invitation for those who are deeply engaged in the visionary process in any capacity to share their information and provide feedback about what you have discovered.

Let's see what dots can be connected by collaboration, by those who know the most about the visionary process and the related worldview(s). I invite emails at:

    editor [at]visionaryfountain.com (replace [at] with @)

Chapter 21 - Taking the Next Step

*I don't care if it is called "the human race," it is not a race
and there is no finish line, except maybe death. It is a parade, with
everyone stepping forward. No one is on the sidelines of this parade.*

One Small Step for Man...

At some time before I was a year old, I reached out for the bright sparkle of my father's pocket watch. With my eye focused on the prize, my short arms reaching forward, I followed the steadily receding watch across the room. I took one step, then another—without being held up except by the eagerness of my pursuit.

In the end, and unbeknownst to me, I walked. I stepped forward with my wobbly little feet without any intention to walk on my own. Those first steps were taken while my attention was focused on something just out of reach. At that moment, stepping forward on my own was not hard—simply the natural thing to do.

Similarly, the early steps someone takes toward what they envision are taken without an awareness of their significance. The excitement of grasping what sparkles and beckons is enough—for the moment. We grasp for that bright and shining thing, thinking it is within reach.

It is, but more elusive than we bargained for. We look until it is found, then stretch a little further and grasp once more. Then it slips away again. Step by little step, we reach out and follow.

The attractive power of the bright and shining thing that is *almost* within reach lingers—even without much reward beyond the tantalizing anticipation. The degree of desire for what is out of reach influences our overall level of drive: from casual interest to single-minded pursuit.

That tentative reaching out describes how each of us moves toward our own larger purpose as well. One stumbly step; then another, not so tentative... As we embrace what we have seen in the mind's eye, it becomes ever more real for us.

Then Another Step...

When Neil Armstrong first stepped on the moon in 1969, he said the famous words: "That's one small step for man, one giant leap for mankind." His point was clear: one step from the earth to the moon was a large step, but he took it for all human beings.

We cannot follow his footsteps, but we can all share in the achievement. What Armstrong did allowed us to enjoy reaching the bright and shining thing that people long assumed to be out of reach.

His feat showed us the moon was no longer an insurmountable distance away. That statement was about taking a single step—from here to there. What does it matter that "over the horizon" (there) is off the planet? Monumental obstacles cannot define what humanity is capable of doing, when there is enough determination.

In another sense, what Armstrong did is a classic example of what every pioneer attempts to do. He or she goes somewhere far away and unexplored—then returns home to tell us of their discovery.

Going to the moon was a visionary act, not all that different from those by others who left the safe and familiar behind to pursue what beckons. Stepping on the moon involved a supporting cast of thousands, who worked as one to attain another Everest "because it is there" achievement. But their combined effort still added up to just one step. That single step was indeed a singular achievement, a great leap forward. But it was not the *only* step, nor will it be the last.

Such Victories Remind Us that:

- Difficult does not mean impossible
- Individuals, and humanity collectively, rise to challenges; we keep trying until we get it done
- Each of us takes the same step in pursuit of a bright idea when we resolutely plunge into the unknown, or we go where fear or logic insists "don't go"
- It is the *mental* step—not the footstep that makes the great leap forward—then the "feet on the ground" move us forward
- It is not the first step alone that matters, but continuing to step out, even when uncertain about what comes next

Taking that "next step" represents *vision over reluctance*—trusting "what I can see" over "I can't" or "I don't know how." Each person who finds a way to take that next step *anyway* is elevating a desire, a hope, a dream above the limits of the mundane and earthbound. He or she is not deterred because the task at hand might appear hard, or "foolish," or unlikely to succeed.

In reaching for that unclaimed possibility that seems to have one's name on it, the larger-frame question should be: Where is it taking me? Is it a vision that is grand enough to inspire my best efforts? Once that is clear to your satisfaction, don't spare the horses.

Not all steps are equal or equally fateful. A step over the edge could be inspired and courageous—or sheer madness. The move might appear to be the same in either case, yet the motivations behind them could not be more different. The person's journey is defined as much by their motivation as by what they discover.

A worthy aspiration stirs us to act in remarkable ways. It is up to each of us to "fill in our own blank" about what kind of vision deserves our unreserved devotion. Pursuing a personal vision despite high costs and risks can be seen as an evolutionary step. That capacity remains latent in us *until we take that step*. Then we attempt to ground what is not yet real except in the mind's eye.

Another thing about steps—they are discrete. Each is a completion and invites a new "leap" forward—a commitment to the course of action all over again. Without the rededication to taking another *next* step, the effort sinks into autopilot.

An infusion of more energy is required or signs of entropy will start to appear. A challenge inherent in going forward is to remain engaged, alert, and "awake at the switch." That is where our inner strengths come into play, since acting on our core beliefs buttresses both determination and staying power.

From Taking a Step to Making a Road

In the sweep of history the visionaries are most likely to be out front—the intrepid pioneers. They are recognized as the forerunners, the advance scouts who are the first to venture down remote paths. Contingents of those who later follow convert some trails into roads. The roadway is being constantly groomed and altered by the collective efforts of all feet which use it.

It is human nature to find ways to weave our desires and daydreams into concrete form. The visionaries might make the largest and most dramatic intuitive leaps, but that same process defines how each of us makes a life—our individual life.

The web of progress is driven less by the work of rare giants and forerunners than by the countless unidentified individuals who span their own gaps between idea and performance—who make something new. All those little steps add up in countless ways in the march of progress.

That "next step" happens person by person, moment by moment, decision by decision, challenge by challenge—over and over, day in day out. That is what taking the next step is really all about. Those collective steps of insight move us all.

It is also human nature to work toward accomplishing something beyond mere survival. We care about principles and values; we want them to matter in how we live. When practical concerns consume all our time and attention, we suffer individually, but so does the larger culture.

Giving credence to a grand vision raises our sights above the humdrum. By contrast, leaving out deep and enduring values is like marching in place.

Cultivating a Culture of Creativity

Curiosity and the urge to be creative are inborn. Living with curiosity and an enthusiasm for figuring things out makes our creative efforts as natural as walking. Each person brings their one-of-a-kind flavor into what they make. In the process of *creating through doing,* each of us builds an identity as unique as our fingerprint.

In *Women Who Run with the Wolves,* Clarissa Pinkola Estes speaks to the changeable nature of creativity:

> Creativity is a shapechanger. One moment it takes this form, the next that. It is like a dazzling spirit who appears to us all, yet is hard to describe for no one agrees on what they saw in that brilliant flash. Is the wielding of pigments and canvas, or paint chips and wallpaper, evidence of its existence? How about pen and paper, flower borders on the garden path, building a university? Yes, yes. Ironing a collar well, cooking up a revolution? Yes. Touching with love the leaves of a plant, pulling down 'the big deal,' tying off the loom, finding one's voice, loving someone well? Yes. Catching the hot body of the newborn, raising a child to adulthood, helping raise a nation from its knees? Tending to a marriage like the orchard it is, digging for psychic gold, finding the shapely word, sewing a blue curtain? All are of the creative life.[424]

Life invites us to bring our inimitable style of creative novelty into whatever we do. But the consequences of rising to that challenge are not merely personal. We are changing our future, *the* future. We are doing it together.

Creative living is not just about taking a leap, making something work, or the eventual success of any particular notion (or series of them). Through the collective influence of many people, history is being redirected. Each of us should trust our individual, and shared, vision and ingenuity enough to let their clarity lead the way.

Can we build upon each other's contributions for the good of us all? *That* would be a worthy goal. Let us resolve to fan the flames of our sparks of brilliance. The combination of all of our individual creativity and uniqueness assures unlimited variability and a full spectrum of options.

Twyla Tharp, renowned dancer and choreographer, remarked:

> Creativity is more about taking the facts, fictions, and feelings we store away and finding new ways to connect them. What we're talking about here is metaphor. Metaphor is the lifeblood of all art, if it is not art itself. Metaphor is our vocabulary for connecting what we are experiencing now with what we have experienced before. It's not only how we express what we remember, it's how we interpret it—for ourselves and others.

The capacity to find innovative answers is innate, and every person is given an opportunity to let them shine through their manner of living and thinking. Personal vision is about each of us clarifying our particular global desires within the reality of what life presents to us.

---

[424] Estes, Clarissa Pinkola, *Women Who Run with the Wolves* (New York: Ballantine Books, 1992), 298.

Since our earliest stirring of longing, each individual's sense of personal purpose has been drawing him or her forward. Despite personal successes or failures in reaching our particular distant goals, we are being carried toward a larger purpose through the combined efforts of all of us.

We are in pursuit of a still elusive future, that each of us is helping to create. Singularly and together, everyone is moving toward greater awareness of our collective unity. We are part of something larger than our individual and separate selves. Realizing that makes *every step* consequential. Author and mystic Thomas Merton said "There is in all visible things … a hidden wholeness."

The Human Race Is Really a Parade

I don't care if it is called "the human race," it is not a race and there is no finish line, except maybe death. It is a parade, with everyone stepping forward from wherever they happen to be. No one stands on the sidelines of this parade, and everyone has an important role to play. Every person alive is part of a parade that is marching toward the future.

Each of us is proceeding at our own pace somewhere along the cavalcade. This is a parade not only of those living in the present, but follows on the heels of our ancestors, and in due course, will be joined by generations to come. Every gradation of personality, style, eagerness, or speed is represented in this parade.

Speed is irrelevant in this procession, and concepts like winners and losers don't apply. Nor is it competitive since each individual proceeds according to their own individual goals, timetable, and measures of success. Each participant is moving toward greater comprehension, purpose and simplicity — irrespective of how long it takes them.

Within that company, each person must take his or her own steps, and chart their own course, and stick their own neck out. In the process, they are forging a unique life, largely of their own making. It is the human race, the collective "we." All of us arrive somewhere when any one of us does.

Each individual shares in the accomplishments, and likewise also contributes to them. One comes to know that there are no lone actors or anyone left out in the larger scheme of things.

Over time, it is the spirit of curiosity and a desire for something more, rather than any particular ideas, that alter the route we are all traveling. Together, we weave the collective visions of all which have been brought to flower into the fabric of a shifting direction.

A Rallying Cry for More Vision

I foresee a time, in our near future, when the visionary thinkers are no longer considered flukes or outsiders because their capabilities are widely accepted and practiced as a new kind of norm. Think of having sparks of genius on tap.

I will always beat the drum for the bold visionaries eager to make "the next big thing" happen. But I am even more excited to beat the drum for those who act on their micro-visions—the motivated, insightful "next steps" that are possible in any circumstances.

The pervasiveness of vision will become even more evident in the way people feel inspired to carry on in the paradigm shift that is in the process of settling into place. An article by Kurt Anderson in *Time* said:

> We are in a state of shock. In a matter of months, half the value of the stock market, and more than half of Wall Street's corporate pillars have disappeared, along with several million jobs. Venerable corporate enterprises are teetering. But as we gasp in terror at our half glass of water, we really can—must—come to see it as half full as well as half empty. Now that we're accustomed to the unthinkable suddenly becoming not just thinkable but actual, we ought to be able to think the unthinkable on the upside, as America plots its reconstruction and reinvention.[425]

The messes in the world, almost everywhere we look, serve as calls to action for any person or group with a better idea. Each of us can find unprecedented ways to bring the power of vision into practical solutions right where we live and work. Start with my Problem D'Solver slogan: Every problem is an invitation to open your mind and heart.

Plenty of invitations are going out, and we'll see who takes them to heart. The scale of the challenge means less than the appropriateness of the *action taken*. There are enough needs to go around to suit anybody's talents. Find yours and do something about it.

The fading and collapse of what has long been established acts like a vacuum. It *will* be filled. What replaces it is, to some extent, within our individual power to influence. But the serious need to mobilize vision on a larger scale is also coming to the fore.

You cannot assume the "other guy" will have an answer you would like as well as what you could come up with. We, as consumers of products and ideas, will be able to select those that matter the most to us.

Each of us has an active part to play in this transition from the present situation now in stark decline to a future that is better, fuller, more enriching, in ways that serve us all, no one left out. A series of fortuitous circumstances has disconnected us from the old circular thinking and self-serving decisions that characterized our past.

And there is enough urgency to accept that *this is the time* to declare our creative participation in the redesign of our world.

---

[425] Andersen, Kurt, "The End of Excess—Why this crisis is good for America," *Time Magazine*, April 6, 2009.

Much like the lull after a tornado has left our material life in rubble, we realize that we must build back from scratch. But we now have the opportunity to build a home, or neighborhood, or town, or community, with *vision*!! We can design for energy efficiency, build "smart" homes and businesses, consider efficient mass transit systems and pedestrian friendly commons instead of the concrete and parking lots there before. The possibilities are infinite. What are we to do?

SEIZE THE SPARK

Seize the Spark—your bright sparks, as well as the sparks of others that inspire you. Blow on them. Encourage them to burn bright. That is the way for us to achieve a bright future. If you want a wink with that, try:

CARPÉ SPARKEM

Failing to seize the moment and reach for the highest and best vision could waste this special moment in history. Let us proceed intelligently, drawing upon the strengths each of us embodies, so we can all accomplish the particular dreams every one of us cherishes for ourselves. That is possible if we abide by Gandhi's counsel, "We must be the change we wish to see in the world."

Looking even more deeply, we should also use such opportunities to embrace our nakedness to a greater extent. After all, our inner self is where the spark resides—the flame that lights our entire being, both inner and outer.

As poet/philosopher Mark Nepo said, "I have come to believe that we are destined to be opened by the living of our days, and whether we like it or not, whether we choose to participate or not, we will, in time, every one of us, wear the deeper part of who we are as a new skin."

Creativity Gives the Wee Small Voice a Megaphone

Your wee small voice is being echoed by the wee small voices of many other people, so they are becoming a groundswell with power. It is no longer so wee or easy to ignore, but *WE standing tall*. Those who trust the might of vision at work in the world are a grassroots force to be reckoned with. And it is on the march. The *status quo* and its defenders are quaking.

Those responding to their visions are less inclined to question the wisdom of acting on them. They are more inclined to speak up and speak out—with passion and determination. Those individuals have gotten on the pulse of change, and they have a megaphone that demands to be heard. Wee small voices are getting louder in everyone and it takes more to tune them out.

They speak for fairness, honesty, and good judgment. They point a bright light on the duplicitous and unseemly. They claim the high moral ground and insist, "We can do better, and we *must do better.*"

We not only hear and heed our own inspired notions but recognize that we want others to be able to do the same. The distant drummer is not so distant, since we are in the process of discovering that we, our very selves, are the drummers who are inspiring others to march with us. We are not just responding, but defining the messages, rhythms, and goals of the parade.

An over-riding sense of larger purpose and unity is woven into these visions, whether they are personal or collective. I commend all who give credence to what inspires them enough to let it flower. This renewal is much more than overt acts, however, since this also nourishes the spirit and the whole person. We must pay attention to our aspirations, for that adds legitimacy to our efforts.

"We need a renaissance of wonder. We need to renew in our hearts and in our souls the deathless dream, the eternal poetry, the perennial sense that life is miracle and magic," said American educator and poet E. Merrill Root. Who can't get excited about that?

We can *take the next step*, our equivalent of Armstrong stepping on the moon. It is done by each of us individually, but also as Everyman. We cannot know ahead of time which steps might be foolhardy. But making the evolutionary leap "feels like it must be." We are ignoring the limits imposed by prior under-expectations. No one is insufficient if their heart is open and functioning and the wee small voice is given a microphone.

To Spot a Fish

Not long ago, my son Ross and I were strolling across a long bridge on a lazy Sunday afternoon. It was a pleasant way to enjoy the warm sun and balmy spring breeze, while spending time together. He is a fly-fisherman—the catch-and-release kind. We stopped and leaned over the railing, where he and I looked down at the river for a while.

Ross would point to a place on the slow-moving water. "See that? There's a fish. See it?" It took a while for me to get a fix on where he was pointing. I was as likely to respond, "Where?" as "Oh! I see it."

We watched the water some more until he would point, "See? There's another." After a bit, I got better at seeing where he pointed, and I was not so slow to find the fish for myself. When I tried to point one out unassisted, he'd calmly explain that what I saw was leaves or a dip in the flow caused by rocks.

The leisurely pace of our exchange was pleasant enough at the time. But when I later reflected back on the experience, I realized Ross had been trying to show me something more. He was teaching me *how to read the water*, or more accurately, how to see what was *under* the water. "The fisherman even has a phrase to describe what he does when he studies the patterns of a river. He says he is 'reading the water.'"[426]

Ross patiently fine-tuned my eye and attention. He was helping me learn to see something more beneath the surface. On one level of my awareness, it was just

---

[426] Maclean, Norman, *A River Runs Through It* (Chicago: The University of Chicago Press, 1976), 65.

water flowing by, but on another level there were fish going about their business.

With the right focus and patience, I got to see a bit more. Except for Ross's prompting, I would have missed the whole thing. On a rational level I knew there were fish in the river, but they had nothing to do with me. Now I cannot wait to try it again—and find out what more I can see on my own.

Some years ago, I heard a speech about the gracefulness of fly-fishing. The speaker quoted from *A River Runs Through It*, which is a reverential homage to becoming one with the river. I have since seen the movie (with Brad Pitt) and read the book. I was struck by the profound peace and elegance Maclean described in the absolutely tranquil settings where nature is putting on its most beautiful face. Here is an example of Maclean pointing out some subtle signals.

> All there is to thinking is seeing something noticeable which makes you see something you weren't noticing which makes you see something that isn't even visible.[427]

> It was a beautiful stretch of water, either to a fisherman or a photographer, although each would have focused his equipment on a different point. It was a barely submerged waterfall. The reef of rock was about two feet under the water, so the whole river rose into one wave, shook itself into spray, then fell back on itself and turned blue. After it recovered from the shock, it came back to see how it had fallen.

> No fish could live out there where the river exploded into the colors and curves that would attract photographers. The fish were in that slow backwash, right in the dirty foam, with the dirt being one of the chief attractions. Part of the speckles would be pollen from pine trees, but most of the dirt was edible insect life that had not survived the waterfall.[428]

Fly-fishing requires careful attention to the most miniscule of signals, so that what is below the water can be spotted. To do so, a person must stop the busy mind and let the world shrink to only what is present right then with all senses fully engaged, attuned to the barest of signs.

There is abundant information to be "read" in those ripples—and not just about fish. But to engage them, it is necessary to leave the rest of the world long enough to slip into that frame—not as an intruder, but as just another object in the landscape.

I have no desire to take up fly-fishing. The fish themselves interest me less than the realization that I am no longer blind to that world. But my heart leaps at the possibility of being able to see what was previously opaque to me.

---

[427] *Ibid.*, 92.
[428] *Ibid.*, 16-17.

I have always loved to be able to look beneath what is apparent, to see what I was blind to until some collection of elements became a more encompassing whole for me. Reading the river, even a little bit, tells me there are meaningful signals in murky waters, and I could get better at reading them, if I keep at it.

There is a moment when the dots of information became a detailed picture, when the apparent noise turns into an intelligible signal. You spot the pattern whenever a meaningful signal emerges from apparent noise or randomness. That ability is well worth cultivating.

Looking Below the Surface

But for the moment, I'd like you to visualize me as Ross, with you and me standing on the bank of a river. Throughout the book I have been pointing out various fish and describing how to read some signals beneath the surface. Can't you imagine yourself being able to read those signals too?

To distort the metaphor a bit, a vision is like a fish that swims through your river. You won't notice it unless you're paying close enough attention to read the clues—as well as valuing what they have to tell you. Your life is your very own pond or stretch of river.

Look with fresh eyes, whether you see minnows or whoppers. It is *your ability* to read the signals or spot a few fish that makes your insights remarkable. All of that can add a dimension to your life beyond what is apparent to you now.

What more can you see beneath the surface that you did not notice before? Has your eye been trained to discern even more, the more diligently you look? Are you motivated to appreciate what you find when you look anew?

To my way of thinking, such abilities as discernment and taking decisive action should be developed as part of each person's bag of tricks. The determination to act on what is discovered characterizes the visionary approach. But it works for anyone. The scale of possibilities that opens for each of us is immense! It is that same skill, with varying levels of mastery, which makes us whole.

This is what visionary seeing or thinking can provide. Amateur or giant, the challenge is the same: Can you see beneath the surface? And having seen, what more do you know? What will you do with what you discovered? Taking such discoveries seriously is the nature of the visionary path.

Crank up your ability yet another notch to see more. *That's* where the adventure is. And it is precisely where you will benefit most from seeing beneath the surface of *your own* thinking. No doubt, you will discover some visions very close to home—something remarkable. Are you hooked yet?

~End~

Back - Appendix
50 Ways to Get Naked

Too Many or Not Enough?

All these flavors of "nakedness" are metaphors for stripping away or disrobing. That is required in service to the person's vision. Meanings of being naked focus on the nuances of inner and outer wisdom.

These qualities or roles are not unique to the visionary path since many people encounter some of these, in one form or another. Bear in mind, no single visionary encounters all of them, even over a long lifetime—and certainly not all at the same time.

The ideal is for these various flavors to combine into a well-seasoned stew. Delicious and unique to the individual visionary. How complete is someone's experience with each? How intense and multi-faceted? Over time the visionary is becoming a master of such distinctions.

Each aspect of nakedness represents a spectrum—from a small degree to fully developed.

How many of these do you sense nudging to the fore within your own experience? Or is this treated like a list of banned books—examined to make sure that none of them crossed your path (or were missed)?

Personal Qualities of the Visionary

1. Naked as Newborn
Everyone comes into the world naked, having nothing but humanity's original, natural form. And at death nobody gets to take anything material with them. *Tabla rosa* as the blank slate that life "writes" upon through our experiences. Training and maturity apply the lacquer-like layers that reflect a person's culture, social standards, and values. To become naked, once clothed, means to return to the fundamental basics.

2. Naked as Innocent
Original and pure, not yet touched by tragedy. Devoid of the scars from bearing life's burdens. The natural state of every human. Unclothed and without shame. Implies going back to the Garden of Eden (pre-knowledge).

3. Naked as Open, Receptive, and Trusting
Superficial awareness that doesn't doubt or question. Not being in control—or feeling a need to be. Easily manipulated. Accepting things to be exactly what they appear to be. Having no clue of the odds stacked against them, as in "fools rush in where angels fear to tread."

4. Naked as Untested and Naïve
Gullible and earnest. Too simple to be suspicious or defensive, even when it is called for. Blissfully unaware, Bambi. Unsophisticated as to what lies ahead — or how to read the warning signals. Not calculating or able to foresee the consequences of the choices being made. An initial phase of the process.

5. Naked as Totally Self-exposed
A solitary voice speaking out with an unpopular viewpoint. Speaking "truth to power" to people and institutions that have no desire to hear it. Unmasked — without embarrassment, humiliation or shame. Self-exposure usually requires a high degree of trust, so to disrobe without there being any trust may raise suspicions or invite attack.

6. Naked as Unarmed
Revealing one's self to be harmless — not a danger. Showing one's cards. Abandoning one's defenses definitely raises the ante regarding the level of commitment — a point of no return.

7. Naked as Candid
No convoluted communication — intense direct interactions and honest expression. Plain-spoken. Can say "the emperor has no clothes." To remove customary smoke screens.

8. Naked as Fanatical and Obsessive
Single-minded to the point of ignoring everything unrelated, except with reference to the primary interest. Tireless and total devotion. Unbalanced, fixated, maybe to the point of being unhinged. All-consuming passion.

9. Naked as Without Barriers and Boundaries
Totally accessible, with one's guard down. Inviting another type of interaction with few social conventions. Also, abandons the limitations of restrictive relationships. being so. To invite intimacy (non-sexual) of a sort that usually only arises after mutual trust is established.

Along the journey, one discovers the extent that personal boundaries are increasingly permeable. The visionary process is expansive, prone to break down limitations in any form in which they appear.

10. Naked as Vulnerable
To unilaterally drop one's customary safeguards, to let oneself be seen as defenseless. To dismantle one's personal protective walls. Foolhardy to the point of tempting fate. Letting others into one's private space without preconditions — even when it is unwise to trust them. Risky behavior since may incite others to assert control.

11. Naked as Not Fearful or Defensive
Not putting trust in anything external as an adequate shield or protection. Refusing to live in fear. Trusting that one's strength lies elsewhere within or in

the realm of the vision. Relying on one's inner awareness or guidance for protection when needed.

12. Naked as Lacking Pretense
Has few delusions—neither an inflated nor deflated sense of self, or of others. Without embroidery to put oneself in the most favorable light. Blunt and unadorned. No attempt to "sell," justify, or influence the impression—especially to oneself.

13. Naked as Congruent
Has dismantled inconsistencies and compartments in one's own thought processes. All aspects of the personality and message work harmoniously. Results in consistency between intention and performance.

14. Naked as Unadorned
Not gussied up. Not using trappings or superficial traits to make a statement regarding one's status or taste. Clashes of style and fashion are about external appearances, but the visionary sows confusions by refusing to play that game. Avoids sending a message defined by cultural standards, rather than matters of greater worth. Permitting oneself to be underestimated by those who only see the obvious.

15. Naked as Alone or a Loner
Solitary, perhaps lonely. An early phase of the process, before gaining followers. Could be the seed of a movement, but that's not yet apparent. Still seems too small and unpretentious to provide a clue about what may come. Acts like a seed crystal, the core around which structure forms. Easily undervalued or dismissed.

16. Naked as Without Possessions
Having other priorities, so doesn't care very much about having material things and all the attention they demand. Prefers to be engaged in the pressing matters of the stuff of the vision. Unfettered. Reduced interest in ownership also indicates a step away from the community and what most people in it consider important.

17. Naked as Having Nothing to Lose
That's not absolutely accurate since a visionary could lose life itself, which occasionally happens to those who challenge authority. (The word for that is martyrdom.) But there's not much of anything in the way of image or possessions that can be lost. Those have been whittled down along the way and are of minor concern, compared to the animating power of the inspired vision.

The bigger risk is not the loss of social status or possessions but the loss of clarity. For example, Joan of Arc illustrates the horror of finding her resolve or vision fade. When one feels there's nothing left to lose is precisely the point when one discovers how much is left. The hidden, unsuspected reserves or supports come into play.

18. Naked as Emptied Out
Having let go of so much personal baggage, the visionary is maximally receptive to personal growth. A worthy spokesperson and model for their cause. Not carrying many unresolved personal issues.

19. Naked as Humble
Modest and unassuming. Not puffed up with a sense of importance or entitlement. The road is long and difficult so courage, determination, stamina, and brutal honesty are repeatedly put to the test. If these qualities are not will develop in the visionary's character at the outset, the process assures they develop. Once the external frills fall away, the person loses the aspects of personality that are out of alignment.

20. Naked as Clothed in Grace
The radiance that sometimes develops around spiritual masters. Having been stripped down to the essence functions from Being, the transcendent self. Their vibrational signature is the "halo." An inspirational and translucent presence. A palpable energy field; some would describe it as a loving and warm energy.

21. Naked as Disconnected in Time and Space
In moving from the conventions of the larger community, the person and their message are less and less defined by time and location. It moves toward greater generality—more philosophical and universal. Since visions are often rooted in timeless verities, they rise above the local or the particular. Why so many visionaries are ahead of their time.

22. Naked as Bare Flesh
The body animated by life as it reveals itself through the textures and rhythms of living cells. The body is engaged in the dance of life, expressed in the cycles to which it corresponds. Physical flesh is alive, both uniquely individual and the embodiment of all forbearers. It carries the genealogy and emotional legacy of those who came before. That will, in turn, be passed along to that person's lineage.

23. Naked as Out of Step
Non-conformist. One who hears their own drummer. Free spirit; individualist. Refuses to do what everybody else does.

24. Naked as Master of One's Impulses
Has developed a level of self-discipline that includes inner and outer states. Responsible and discerning about what is most important for them to do. Doesn't bow to the whims of the crowd or own baser instincts.

25. Naked as Being Without Limits
One's identity doesn't stop with the skin of the physical body. The energetic body. One partakes of the Divine nature of infinite and unchanging being. Infinitely expansive with minimal boundaries.

26. Naked as at Peace with Oneself
Able to remain calm and exude goodwill toward others despite external stresses. Lack of drama or venting. Equanimity.

27. Naked as Playful
Able to laugh at life's ups and downs. Good humored; light hearted. Fun loving; lots of laughter. High spirited; joyful.

Ways the Visionary Is Perceived

28. Naked as Being Without Clothes
Totally bare, shocking in its starkness. Revealing oneself to the world. Erasing the distinction between one's private and public appearance. Presenting the same face in all circumstances, without holding back.

29. Naked as Gadfly
Provokes a reaction by throwing a stink bomb into genteel discourse without regard for propriety. Those who upset the *status quo* by posing upsetting or novel questions. Disrupts as a way to get noticed or compel a response. Seen as an annoyance rather than a serious threat.

30. Naked as Authentic
Displays a high degree of self-confidence and self-acceptance. Comfortable in one's own skin. Unafraid to appear in an unflattering light or to uncover distortions that imperil communications. Literally, what you see is what you get. Letting everything show — warts and all.

31. Naked as Without Deception
Blatantly obvious, without any slight-of-hand or efforts to control the perception of others. Receptive to shared cooperation or creativity on an equal footing. Not holding anything back; nothing hidden. Not manipulating anyone else or trying to gain an advantage over them.

32. Naked as Undisguised and Transparent
Removing the false face and uniforms of conventional roles. Not operate with a primarily ego-based point of view. No overt justification or effort to spin the image presented. To the extent possible, the same face is shown consistently to everybody.

33. Naked as an Outsider
The maverick on the margins of society. Isolated from one's reference group, without the protective "herd mentality" and closeness. Defies the norms of society — or fails to notice them. Tone deaf. Behavior is unfathomable to those who abide by social conventions. May be perceived as a threat to the group, so is rejected or driven off.

To the extent the group considers the new notion unacceptable, they can appreciate no use for it. They close ranks against the person or the notion. If the visionary isn't "careful," the response could turn from ignoring to rejecting, or even to attacking.

34. Naked as Eccentric
To display weird and puzzling behavior that is at odds with normal standards. Anywhere from mildly quirky to crazy enough for the loony bin. Unusual way of dealing with the practicalities of life.

35. Naked as Unfashionable
Being naked is a refusal to "wear the uniform." Intentionally inappropriate. Not dressed for success or according to established standards. However one presents himself or herself in order to go out into the world. Totality of their impression one makes — includes not merely garments, but also manners and social graces.

36. Naked as Exemplar
The accurate representative of a particular philosophical point of view — evident in thought and deed. To fully embody and demonstrate one's message. Walking the talk.

37. Naked as Inappropriate and "Wrong"
Not doing what is expected or meeting the standards of the community. Being different is often perceived as bad or wrong. When others are critical it calls forth the person's own doubts and fears. Having one's "buttons pushed." Who does not forever hear their mother's nagging voice in their heads?

38. Naked as Cutting Edge
Operating at the point where change occurs. Where new growth happens. Visionaries inhabit the interface between society's current location and what they foresee emerging. The way that visionaries distinguish these two points is the placement of the cutting edge.

39. Naked as Heroic and Archetypal
To stand up for something without flinching; courageous. Putting everything on the line. Holding nothing back or running for protective cover. Willingly accepting the consequences of such a brazen stance. Mythic; ventures into archetypes like hero, guru on the mountain top, spiritual warrior, muse, messenger.

40. Naked as Daring
Putting oneself to the test — totally committed. To have the courage to act on an unpopular impulse — coupled with the tenacity to hold on. Not content to be a dreamer or sit on the sidelines.

41. Naked as Clear Seeing
Discerning. Not distracted by glamour, flattery, wishful thinking, or temptations of popularity. No longer see "through a glass darkly" since distorting mindsets are falling away. Clarity of perception.

42. Naked as Intimate
To invite others into one's most concealed space, motivated by self-revelation. Letting someone into one's "poetic space" the inner recesses which one seldom shares. Exposing that which is most private, serene and hidden. To erase privacy boundaries.

The Visionary's Impact

43. Naked as Revolutionary
One who brings about a drastic and far-reaching change in ways of thinking and behaving. The person who has radical ideas or opinions. Stands up for something — to death if necessary. Advocates radical change. Rabble-rouser; extremist with own agenda.

44. Naked as Competitor
Presents an alternative to what's already widely available. Promotes the new concept or invention for its improvements and benefits.

45. Naked as Homeless
A wanderer who has left the home (and security) of youth behind in search of a larger world. Not provincial; disengaged from hometown priorities. Unencumbered. A Citizen of the World. A member of faceless humanity.

46. Naked as Activist
Engaged citizen supporting a worthy cause; engaged in community governance. Supports grass roots causes. Could be a zealot.

47. Naked as Pilgrim
One who leaves the normal world to go in search of a lost home or better country; Seeking Eldorado. On a quest or pilgrimage.

48. Naked as Leaper
Willing to make a leap of faith; does not hang back in fear and doubt. Trusting one's impulse to act decisively and without hesitation. A precursor to taking flight.

49. Naked as Removing the Veil
Giving up one's prior illusions and fuzzy thinking. Insisting on precision of thought and emotion. Looks at things with mature acceptance and willingness to accept what is evident. Avoids denial as a way of coping. No longer plays a role in a play written by others or society.

50. Naked as a Model or Reflection
To be naked acts as a mirror, reflecting back to the one who looks at it. What does the viewer perceive about the visionary and why? Reveals the inherent group dynamics. Who is trusted enough for the visionary to be naked in their presence? Does it show a group practice that applies to the inner circle of followers?

Glossary

A

Adjacent Possible – Some events or choices can only arise after others occur because opening one door gives access to related ones. Theory developed by Stuart Kauffman.

Art of Seeing – Seeing without preconception; scanning the span of knowledge to spot connections that are not apparent through casual observation or habitual assumptions.

Atemporal – Independent of or unaffected by time; timeless.

B

Being and Becoming – Two states of existence. **Being** is absolute and unconditional; a different level of reality. **Becoming** is the default condition of manifest, 3-D reality.

Binkle – A measure of etheric energy. The uplifting *energy* that is felt; the zizz, a moment of sensed perfection. Related to Krindle and Laphe. **Krindle** – the *meter* or battery that detects and holds the special binkle energy, located within the physical body. **Laphe** – (pronounced, "laugh") the sense of being full of binkles; acts as a *balanced feeling* that is centered within.

Black Swan – The appearance of a rare or improbable event; also described in book by Taleb of that name.

Breakthrough – A sudden, dramatic, and important discovery or development; overcoming a major obstacle that allows a process to complete. Usually occurs within a level and can be lost or forgotten, as compared with a change of state, which cannot be lost since it results in an identity change.

C

Canny Outlaws – Organizational insiders who subvert unbending rules in order to broaden the creative choices. Described by Barry Schwartz in *Practical Wisdom*.

Coincidence – An event that might have been arranged although it was really accidental. It can be persuasively argued that there is no such thing as a coincidence *or* that *everything is a coincidence*. Your choice.

Cultural Lag – When the "disruptive" part of culture gets out ahead of the "adaptive" part of culture. Defined by William Ogburn.

D
Default State – A mental and physical condition we naturally slip into when external pressures are removed; the natural condition; one's personal *status quo*.

E
Either-or Thinking – Also called black-or-white thinking because it assumes that one choice or answer excludes its opposite. Very linear and ignores numerous other possibilities.

Emerging Visionaries – Those who are dealing with the early challenges of the visionary process well *before they find their voice.*

Essence – The intrinsic or indispensable properties that serve to characterize or identify something.

F
Fingertip Smarts – Another kind of knowledge that's not quite the same as rational thinking or gut level intuition, but incorporates them both (and more). From the German, *Fingerspitzengefühl* meaning "keeping one's finger on the pulse."

Fledgling Visionaries – Those who made the leap and are still getting their act together.

Flying Visionaries – Those who are in the thick of building their vision and are "on the wing."

I
Incipient Visionaries – Those who are feeling the pull of their inner calling, but have not yet defined their vision or committed to it.

Innocence of Perception – To see without reliance on prior knowledge or expectations; frame of reference that is open to what can be encountered when events are engaged in new ways.

Innocent Visionaries – Those who are children who have extraordinary capacities and commitment engaged from the beginning. Issue: how does their path and purpose differ from prior visionaries?

Intrinsic Motivation – That which is done for the pure enjoyment of doing it; not motivated by other benefits that may also arise.

L
Level Shift – Same as a **change of state**; see Breakthrough.

Lift-off Energy – High-octane energy that fuels insights and creative efforts.

Linear Thinking – Linear thinking is a step-by-step approach to solving a problem or completing a task. Events and ideas follow in a simple progression, where each step triggers the following one; logical thought.

M

Map of Consciousness – Method developed by Dr. David Hawkins using applied kinesiology to determine the frequency or vibrational rate of the energy of consciousness, verifiable by human muscle response which stays strong in the presence of love and truth. Described in *Power vs Force*.

Mature Visionaries – Those who are at later stages of the visionary path, dealing with mastery-level issues.

Metanoia – To make an abrupt change of direction, a conversion from a prior state; repentance.

Mission Leap – Resembles mission creep, where a project keeps expanding beyond the initial goal, or in the case of visionaries, leaps further than they intended.

N

Naked – A state of being innocent, open, simple, trusting, unpretentious, non-defensive.

Naked Vision – What someone can see by means of "innocence of perception" coupled with their own congruency; grounded in the here and now.

Non-linear Thinking – Contrasted with Linear Thinking. See Breakthrough.

O

Open Questions – Areas of inquiry that are able to yield many levels of meaning; cannot be reduced to a single or simple answer.

Out of the Box – To move out of one's familiar frame of assumptions or habits; may yield breakthroughs. Sometimes treated as a synonym for creative thinking.

P

Paradigm – A set of assumptions, concepts, values, and practices that constitutes a way of viewing reality for the community that shares them. One that serves as a pattern or model.

Paradigm Sift – A fundamental shift in the way information is viewed and interpreted within a discipline; as described by Thomas Kuhn in *The Structure of Scientific Revolutions*.

Persistence of Thought – To view the world and events from one's customary mindset.

R
RSME – Stands for Religious, Spiritual or Mystical Experiences; they are not equivalent.

Resistance – Inertia; the physical or psychological inclination for things to stay the same, to oppose change; the default condition.

S
Scale Shift – A person's change of identity; a movement to a different level of awareness, a permanent move out of their prior comfort zone. See also Breakthrough.

See with Fresh Eyes – To be able to see/look at something without one's customary frame of reference or assumptions. Gain a first impression with something familiar.

Serendipity – Accidentally discovering something fortunate, especially while looking for something else entirely.

Status Quo – The way things already are; how they stand; the universal default state; what is considered "normal." Latin phrase.

Straddle-span – The distance between your feet-on-the-ground reality and your top-of-the-mountain states. Develops as one learns to anchor a connection to both inner and outer perceptual frames *simultaneously*.

Synchronicity – An experience when two or more events that are not causally related occur together in a supposedly meaningful manner.

T
Time Horizon – The farthest time frame that a person can formulate goals and carry them to completion. Based on a theory regarding work and time by Elliott Jaques.

Z
Zeitgeist – The spirit of the age and its society; a German language term.

References

A

Andersen, Kurt, "The End of Excess—Why this crisis is good for America," *Time Magazine*, April 6, 2009

Arrien, Angeles, *The Four-fold Way: Walking the paths of the warrior, teacher, healer and visionary* (San Francisco: HarperSanFrancisco, 1993)

B

Beauregard, Mario and O'Leary, Denyse, *The Spiritual Brain: A neuroscientist's case for the existence of the soul* (New York: HarperOne, 2007)

Belsky, Scott, *Making Ideas Happen: Overcoming the obstacles between vision and reality* (New York: Portfolio, 2010)

Bishop, Bill, *The Big Sort: Why the clustering of like-minded America is tearing us apart* (New York: Houghton Mifflin, 2008)

Brooks, David, "Drilling for Certainty," *New York Times*, May 27, 2010
____ "The End of Philosophy," *New York Times*, April 7, 2009
____ "Fragile at the Core," *New York Times*, June 19, 2009
____ "The Humble Hound," *New York Times*, April 9, 2010
____ "The Sandra Bullock Trade," *New York Times*, March 30, 2010
____ *The Social Animal: The hidden sources of love, character, and achievement* (New York: Random House, 2011)

Brussat, Frederick and Mary Ann, *Spiritual Literacy: Reading the sacred in everyday life* (New York: Scribner, 1996)

C

Calonius, Erik, *10 Steps Ahead: What separates successful business visionaries from the rest of us* (New York: Portfolio/Penguin, 2011)

Cameron, Julia, *The Artist's Way: A course in discovering and recovering your creative self* (London: Pan Books, 1994)

Carr, Nicholas, *The Big Switch: Rewiring the world, from Edison to Google* (New York: W.W. Norton & Company, 2008)

Carse, James P., *Breakfast at the Victory: The mysticism of ordinary experience* (New York: HarperCollins, 1994)

Chatzky, Jean, "Emotion-Free Investing," *Newsweek*, October 3, 2011

Chesterton, G.K., "The Queer Feet," *The Father Brown Omnibus* (New York: Dodd, Mead & Company, 1951)

Clark, Taylor, *Nerve: Poise under pressure, serenity under stress, and the brave new science of fear and cool* (New York: Little, Brown and Company, 2011)

Collins, James C.V. and Porras, Jerry I., *Built to Last: Successful habits of visionary companies* (New York: Harper Collins, 1997)
____ *Good to Great: Why some companies make the leap…and others don't* (New York: Harper Business, 2001)
____ *How the Mighty Fall: And why some companies never give in* (New York: Harper Collins, 2009)

Colvin, Geoff, *Talent is Overrated: What really separates world-class performance from everybody else* (New York: Penguin Group, 2008)

Covey, Stephen M. R., *The Speed of Trust: The one thing that changes everything* (New York: Free Press, 2006)

Covey, Stephen R., Merrill, A. Roger, Merrill, Rebecca R., *First Things First: To live, to love, to learn, to leave a legacy* (New York: Simon & Shuster, 1994)

Cropper, Margaret, *The Life of Evelyn Underhill: An intimate portrait of the groundbreaking author of Mysticism* (Woodstock, VT: Skylight Paths Publishing, 2002)

Csikszentmihalyi, Mihaly, *Creativity: Flow and the psychology of discovery and invention* (New York: HarperCollins, 1996)
____ and Gardner, Howard, *Good Work: When excellence and ethics meet* (New York: Basic Books, 2002)

D
Daumal, René, *Mount Analogue* (Baltimore: Penguin Books, 1952)

Darnton, Robert, *The Case for Books: Past, present and future* (New York: PublicAffairs, 2009)

E
Eagleton, Terry, *The Guardian*, December 19, 2010

Epstein, Joseph, "Past Their Prime (Rate)," *Newsweek*, March 16, 2009

Estes, Clarissa Pinkola, *Women Who Run with the Wolves* (New York: Ballantine Books, 1992)

F
Farson, Richard, *Whoever Makes the Most Mistakes Wins* (New York: Free Press, 2003)

Fausset, Hugh I'Anson, *The Flame and the Light: Meanings in Vedanta and Buddhism* (New York: Greenwood Press, 1958)

Fields, Jonathan, "Ride the Butterflies," http://www.jonathanfields.com/blog

Florida, Richard, *The Great Reset: How new ways of living and working drive post-crash prosperity* (New York: Harper, 2010)
____ *The Rise of the Creative Class: And how it's transforming work, leisure, community and everyday life* (New York: Basic Books, 2002)

Freidman, Thomas L., "Are We Home Alone?," *New York Times*, March 22, 2009
____ "The New Untouchables," *New York Times*, October 20, 2009

Friedman, Norman, *Bridging Science and Spirit* (St. Louis: Living Lake Books, 1994)

Fuller, Robert C., "Spiritual, But Not Religious," excerpt from the book, *Spiritual But Not Religious* (New York: Oxford University Press, 2001)

Fuller, Steve, *Kuhn vs Popper: The struggle for the soul of science* (Cambridge, England: Icon Books, 2003)

G

Gardner, Howard, *Changing Minds: The art and science of changing our own and other people's minds* (Boston: Harvard Business School Press, 2004)
____ *Extraordinary Minds: Portraits of 4 Exceptional Individuals and an Examination of our own extraordinariness* (New York: Basic Books, 1998)
____ and Csikszentmihalyi, Mihaly, *Good Work: When excellence and ethics meet* (New York: Basic Books, 2002)

Gawande, Atul, *The Checklist Manifesto: How to get things right* (New York: Henry Holt and Company, 2011)

Garreau, Joel, *Radical Evolution: The promise and peril of enhancing our minds, our bodies – and what it means to be human* (New York: Broadway Books, 2005)

Gilkey, Charlie, "How to Think About Possibility – And why it matters," http://www.productiveflourishing.com

Girard, Bernard, *The Google Way: How one company is revolutionizing management as we know it* (San Francisco: No Starch Press, 2009)

Gladwell, Malcolm, *Outliers: The story of success* (New York: Little Brown and Company, 2008)

Godin, Seth, *Tribes: We need you to lead us* (New York: Penguin Group, 2008)

Goleman, Daniel, *Working with Emotional Intelligence* (New York: Bantam Books, 1998)
____ *Primal Leadership: Realizing the power of emotional intelligence* (Boston: Harvard Business School Press, 2002)

Gotswami, Amit, *Creative Evolution: A physicists resolution between Darwinism and Intelligent Design* (Wheaton, IL: Quest Books, 2008)

Gottlieb, Robert, *George Balanchine: The ballet maker* (New York: HarperCollins, 2004)

Granger, Russell H., *7 Triggers to Yes: The new science behind influencing people's decisions*, (New York: McGraw Hill, 2008)

Grayling, A.C., *Ideas that Matter: The concepts that shape the 21st century* (New York: Basic Books, 2010)

H
Haidt, Jonathan, *The Happiness Hypothesis: Finding modern truth in ancient wisdom* (New York: Basic Books, 2006)

Hall, Edward T., *Beyond Culture* (New York: Doubleday, 1976)

Harford, Tim, *Adapt: Why success always starts with failure* (New York: Farrar, Straus and Giroux, 2011)

Hawkins, David R., *Power vs Force; The hidden determinants of human behavior* (Sedona AZ: Veritas Publishing, 2000)

Healy, Jane M., *Different Learners: Identifying, preventing and treating your child's learning problems* (New York: Simon & Shuster, 2010)

Heath, Chip and Dan, *Made to Stick, Why some ideas survive and others die* (New York: Random House, 2007)

_____ *Switch: How to change things when change is hard* (New York: Broadway Books, 2010)

Heath, Joseph and Potter, Andrew, *Nation of Rebels: Why counterculture became consumer culture* (New York: HarperBusiness, 2004)

Hendricks, Gay and Ludeman, Kate, *The Corporate Mystic: A guidebook for visionaries with their feet on the ground* (New York: Bantam Books, 1996)

Hertzinger, Kim, Ed., *Not-Knowing: The essays and interviews of Donald Barthelme* (New York: Random House, 1997)

Hoffer, Eric, *The Ordeal of Change* (New York: Harper and Row, 1963)
_____ *The True Believer: Thoughts on the nature of mass movements* (New York: Harper & Row, 1951)

Hoffman, Reid and Casnocha, Ben, *The Start-up of You: Adapt to the future, invest in yourself, and transform your career* (New York: Crown Business, 2012)

Houston, Jean, "Jean Houston Writes about Her Working Muse", Soul Food Café, 2000, http://www.dailywriting.net/Houston.htm

Howe, Jeff, *Crowdsourcing: Why the power of the crowd is driving the future of business* (New York: Crown Business, 2008)

I
Ibarra, Herminina, *Working Identity: Unconventional strategies for reinventing your career* (Boston: Harvard Business School Press, 2003)

J
Joel, Mitch, *Six Pixels of Separation: Everyone is connected. Connect your business to everyone* (New York: Hatchette Book Group, 2009)

Johnson, Christopher, *Microstyle: The art of writing little* (New York: W.W. Norton & Company, 2011)

Johnson, Steven, *Where Good Ideas Come From: The natural history of innovation* (New York: Riverhead Books, 2010)

Jokoupil, Tony, "Old People Are More Innovative," Newsweek, August 24, 2009

K

Kauffman, Stuart A., *Investigations* (New York: Oxford University Press, 2000)
____ *Reinventing the Sacred: A new view of science, reason, and religion* (New York: Basic Books, 2009)

Kawasaki, Guy, *The Art of the Start: The time-tested, battle-hardened guide for anyone starting anything* (New York: Penguin Group, 2004)

King, Stephen, *On Writing: A memoir of the craft* (New York: Pocket Books, 2000)

Knafo, Saki, "Bringing 'Where the Wild Things Are' to the Screen," *New York Times*, September 6, 2009

Koestler, Arthur, The Act of Creation (New York: The Macmillan Company, 1964)

Korten, David, "The Big Picture: 5 Ways to Know if You're Making a Difference," adapted from *Agenda for a New Economy: From phantom wealth to real wealth*, Yes! Magazine, June 21, 2010, http://www.yesmagazine.org

Kotter, John P., *Leading Change* (Boston, Harvard Business School Press, 1996)

Kuhn, Thomas S., *The Structure of Scientific Revolutions* (Chicago: The University of Chicago Press, 1997

L

Lagace, Martha, "Oprah: A Case Study Comes Alive," *Working Knowledge, Harvard Business School*, February 20, 2006

Lappé, Frances Moore, *Getting a Grip: Clarity, creativity, and courage in a world gone mad* (Cambridge, MA: Small Planet Media, 2007)
____ *Getting a Grip2: Clarity, creativity, and courage for the world we really want* (Cambridge, MA: Small Planet Media, 2007 and 2010)

Lehrer, Jonah, *How We Decide* (New York: Houghton Mifflin Harcourt, 2009)

Levitin, Daniel J., *This Is Your Brain on Music: The science of a human obsession* (New York: Plume Books, 2006)

Lewis, Thomas, Amini, Fari, and Lannon, Richard, *A General Theory of Love* (New York: Vintage Books, 2000)

Lindahl, Kay, *The Art of Listening* (Woodstock, VT: Skylight Paths Publishing, 2008)

Lynch, Dudley and Kordis, Paul L., *Strategy of the Dolphin: Scoring a win in a chaotic world* (New York: Balantine, 1990)

Lyubombirsky, Sonja, *The How of Happiness: A scientific approach to getting the life you want* (New York: Penguin Group, 2007)

M
Maclean, Norman, *A River Runs Through It* (Chicago: The University of Chicago Press, 1976)

MacLeod, Hugh, *Ignore Everybody* (New York: Portfolio, 2009)

McKinney, Michael, "The Persistence of Vision," LeadershipNow.com

McLaren, Karla, *Language of Emotions: What your feelings are trying to tell you* (Boulder, CO: Sounds True, 2010)

McTaggart, Lynne, *The Intention Experiment: Using your thoughts to change your life and the world* (New York: Free Press, 2007)

Margolis, Howard, *Paradigms and Barriers: How habits of mind govern scientific beliefs* (Chicago: University of Chicago Press, 1993)

Merrill, Douglas C., *Getting Organized in the Google Era* (New York: Broadway Books, 2010)

Metcalfe, Bob, "The Visionary Thing," *Wired Magazine*, Issue 7.11, Nov., 1999

Michalko, Michael, *Cracking Creativity: The secrets of creative genius* (Berkeley, CA: Ten Speed Press, 1998)

Monsaingeon, Bruno, "The Cardinal Virtues, Conversations with Nadia Boulanger," *Knowledge of Reality Magazine*, Issue 17

Mooney, Chris, "Spirituality Can Bridge Science-religion Divide," *USA Today*, September 12, 2010

Moore, Geoffrey A., *Crossing the Chasm: Marketing and selling disruptive products to mainstream customers* (New York: Collins Business Essentials, 1999)

N
Nanus, Burt, *Visionary Leadership: Creating a compelling sense of direction for your organization* (San Francisco: Jossey-Bass, 1992)

Newberg, Andrew and Waldman, Mark Robert, *How God Changes Your Brain: Breakthrough findings from a leading neurologist* (New York: Ballantine Books, 2009)

O
Orsi, Jannelle, "Cooperative Law for a Sharing Economy," *YES! Magazine*, Sept. 10, 2010

P
Patterson, Kerry, Grenny, Joseph et al., *Change Anything: The new science of personal success* (New York: Business Plus, 2011)

Peters, Tom, *Thriving on Chaos* (New York: Alfred A. Knopf, 1988)

Pink, Daniel H., *Drive: The surprising truth about what motivates us* (New York: Riverhead Books, 2009)

___ "Ever Felt Like Your Job Isn't What You Were Born to Do? You're Not Alone," *The Telegraph*, February 26, 2011, http://www.telegraph.co.uk

___ *A Whole New Mind: Why right-brainers will rule the future* (New York: Riverhead Books, 2005)

Pinker, Steven, *The Stuff of Thought: Language as a window into human nature* (New York: Viking, 2007)

R

Rich, Adrienne, *Poetry and Commitment* (New York: W.W. Norton & Company, 2007)

Rich, Frank, "What We Don't Know will Hurt Us," *New York Times*, February 21, 2009

Roam, Dan, *The Back of the Napkin: Solving problems and selling ideas with pictures* (New York: Penguin Books, 2008)

Root-Bernstein, Robert and Michele, *Sparks of Genius: The thirteen thinking tools of the world's most creative people* (New York: Houghton Mifflin, 1999)

Ross, Alexander, "The Long View Of Leadership," *Canadian Business*, May 1992

Russell, Peter, "Natural Mind," *Resurgence*, September/October, 2009

S

Schwartz, Barry and Sharpe, Kenneth, *Practical Wisdom: The right way to do the right thing* (New York: Riverhead Books, 2010)

Seligman, Martin E.P., *Authentic Happiness: Using the new positive psychology to realize your potential for lasting fulfillment* (New York: The Free Press, 2002)

Senge, Peter, *The Fifth Discipline: The art and practice of the learning organization* (New York: Broadway Books, 1990)

___ Senge et al., *The Fifth Discipline Fieldbook: Strategies and tools for building a learning organization* (New York: Doubleday, 1994)

Shekerjian, Denise, *Uncommon Genius: How great ideas are born* (New York: Viking, 1990)

Shell, G. Richard and Moussa, Mario, *The Art of Woo: Using strategic persuasion to sell your ideas* (New York: Portfolio, 2007)

Shirky, Clay, *Here Comes Everybody: The power of organizing without organizations* (New York: Penguin Press, 2008)

Sigismund, Charles G., *Champions of Silicon Valley: Visionary thinking from today's technology pioneers* (New York: John Wiley & Sons, 2000)

Simon, Tami, Tami Simon Blog, "To Think or Not to Think?," June, 2010 http://www.soundstrue.com/tami-simon

Sims, Peter, *Little Bets: How breakthrough ideas emerge from small discoveries* (New York: Free Press, 2011)

Smilor, Ray, *Daring Visionaries: How entrepreneurs build companies, inspire allegiance, and create wealth* (Holbrook, MA: Adams Media Corp., 2001)

Snow, C.P., "The Two Cultures", Rede Lecture, delivered 1959, Cambridge, and subsequently published as *The Two Cultures and the Scientific Revolution*

Steffen, Alex, "How to Change the World," May 16, 2004, (New York: Riverhead Books, 2010) http://www.worldchanging.com

Sulloway, Frank J., *Born to Rebel: Birth order, family dynamics and creative lives* (New York: Vintage Books, 1997)

T
Taleb, Nassim Nicholas, *The Black Swan: The impact of the highly improbable* (New York: Random House, 2007)

Tapscott, Don and Williams, Anthony D., *Wikinomics: How mass collaboration changes everything* (New York: Portfolio, 2006)

Thaler, Richard and Sunstein, Cass R., *Nudge: Improving decisions about health, wealth, and happiness* (New Haven, CT: Yale University Press, 2008)

Tharp, Twyla, *The Creative Habit: Learn it and use it for life* (New York: Simon & Shuster, 2003)

Thompson, Gabriel, *Calling All Radicals: How grassroots organizers can save our democracy* (New York: Nation Books, 2007)

Tolle, Eckhart, *The Power of Now: A guide to spiritual enlightenment* (Novato, CA: New World Library, 1999)

U
Underhill, Evelyn, *Mysticism: A study in the nature and development of man's spiritual consciousness* (New York: E.P. Dutton & Co., Inc., 1961)

W
Watts, Mother Clare, "Christian Mysticism," *Wisdom Magazine*, December, 2009, http://wisdom-magazine.com

Wheatley, Margaret J., *Leadership and the New Science: Discovering order in a chaotic world* (San Francisco: Berrett-Koehler Publishers, 1999)

Whitehead, Alfred North, *Adventures of Ideas* (New York: The Free Press, 1933)

Wilber, Ken, *Integral Spirituality, A startling new role for religion and the modern and postmodern world* (Boston: Integral Books, 2007)
____ *One Taste: The journals of Ken Wilber* (Boston: Shambhala, 1999)
____ *The Simple Feeling of Being: Embracing your true nature* (Boston: Shambhala, 2004)

Williams, Roy H., "When Divergence Becomes Convergence — And It All Comes Together," November 8, 2010
http://www.mondaymorningmemo.com/newsletters/read/1898

Wright, Robert, *Nonzero: The logic of human destiny* (New York: Vintage Books, 2000)

Y

Young, Dean, *The Art of Recklessness: Poetry as assertive force and contradiction* (Minneapolis, MN, Graywolf Press, 2010)

Z

Zachary, G. Pascal, "Genius and Misfit Aren't Synonyms, or Are They?" *New York Times*, June 5, 2007

Zander, Rosamund Stone and Zander, Benjamin, *The Art of Possibility: Transforming professional and personal life* (New York: Penguin Books, 2000)

Index

1% Inspiration 25, 133
3-story Human Factory 335-6
99% Perspiration 25, 132, 343, 453, 404

A
Adams, Scott 318
Adjacent Possible 242-3, 537
Agents of Change 57-9, Chapter 9
Aiken, Howard 70
Alaska 8, 18, 67, 452
Anderson, Kurt 588
Anthony, Susan B. 176
Armstrong, Neil 519
Arrien, Angeles 24, 77, 541
Artistic Expression Chapter 16
Art of Seeing 311-3, 321-2, 537

B
Balanchine, George 13-14
Barker, Joel 24
Baudelaire 313
Beauregard, Mario 449, 455, 541
Belsky, Scott 35, 74, 134, 138-9, 184, 211, 231, 273, 383, 541
Bible 11, 151, 209, 463
Billings, Josh 489
Binkle 341, 353-6, 406-7, 461, 519, 537
Bishop, Bill 490, 541
Black Swans 91, 122-4, 246, 375
Boulanger, Nadia 113, 546
Boundary Crossers 393-4
Bradbury, Ray 108
Brande, Dorthea 409
Breakthrough 307, 405, 537
  Breakthrough, Compared to Level Shift 224, 307
Brooks, David 53, 63, 98, 196, 242, 372, 374, 470, 541
Brussat, Frederick 474, 486, 541
Buchholz, Esther 174
Burnout 191-2

C
Calonius, Erik 99, 541
Cameron, Julia 130, 182, 425, 541
Campbell, Joseph 38, 265
Canny Outlaws 395-7, 537
Card, Orson Scott 96
Carr, Nicholas 377, 400, 427, 541
Carse, James P. 441, 464, 472, 541
Casals, Pablo 294
Catalyst, Vision as 35, 101, 432
Center for Visionary Brilliance 9, 504
Change Chapter 9
Chardin, Teilhard de 304, 472
Chatzky, Jean 226, 541
Chesterton, G.K. 194, 225, 419, 451, 541
Clark, Taylor 129, 215, 541
Coincidence 158, 163, 537
Collaborative Visionary 133
Collins, James C.V. 248, 359, 361, 365, 369, 371, 376, 542
Colvin, Geoff 91, 357, 363, 378, 387, 418, 542
Commitment 180-3
Coolidge, Calvin 109
Covey, Stephen M.R. 76, 362, 392, 542
Covey, Stephen R. 186, 298, 542
Cropper, Margaret 472, 542
Csikszentmihalyi, Mihaly 23, 85, 97, 118, 130, 136, 158, 178, 188, 210, 292, 316, 413-4, 542
Cultural Lag 54, 237, 245, 537

D
Darnton, Robert 252, 542
Daumal, Rene 441-2, 542
DaVinci, Leonardo 7, 286, 419
Delacroix, Eugene 91
De Mille, Agnes 108
Descartes 105
Devans, William Stanley 125-6
Dickinson, Emily 327, 324
Diderot, Denise 68
Diffusion of Innovations 251
Doerr, John 404
Drucker, Peter 95, 201, 233, 268, 359, 361, 371, 390

E

Eagleton, Terry 421, 542
Easterbrook, Gregg 477
Edison, Thomas A. 25, 317
Ego 225-6
Einstein 54, 74, 208, 273, 277, 281, 296, 420, 431, 437, 471
Elliot, Alexander 490
Elliot, Walter 89
Eliot, T.S. 40, 187, 413
Emerging Visionaries 507-8
Emerson, Ralph Waldo 5, 19, 59, 60, 87, 304
Energetic Intelligence 189, Chapter 13
Energy Management 187-90, 226, 337
Entropy 218, 337, 521
Entrepreneur 375, 379-82
Epstein, Joseph 42, 542
Erhard, Warner 494
Estes, Clarissa Pinkola 522, 542
Exemplar 433, 534

F

Farson, Richard 325, 384, 542
Fausset, Hugh l'Anson 143-4, 199, 473, 542
Fields, Jonathan 197-8
Fingerspitzengefühl 195-7, 386, 538
Fingertip Smarts 195-7, 386, 538
Firestone, Robert 167
Flame and Vessel Paradox 220-1, 468
Fledgling Visionaries 508
Florida, Richard 246, 248, 254, 257, 358, 377, 389, 401, 542
Flying Visionaries 508
Forbes, Malcolm 471
Franklin, Benjamin 312
Freedom 298-302, 507
Freidman, Thomas 229, 543
Friedman, Norman 434, 447, 543
Frost, Robert 38-9
Fuller, Buckminster 137
Fuller, Steve 438-9, 543

G

Galileo 128, 200, 203
Gandhi 97, 302, 494, 525
Gardner, Howard 41, 90, 104, 122, 163, 269, 279-80, 412, 543
Garreau, Joel 237, 340, 374, 444, 543
Gauguin, Paul 312
Gawande, Atul 208
Genius, Meaning of 148, 342
Gerber, Michael 426
Gibson, William 478
Gilkey, Charlie 243, 543
Girard, Bernard 60, 381, 399, 543
Gladwell, Malcolm 285, 287-8, 543
Godin, Seth 89, 128, 219, 234, 381, 543
Goldberg, Elkhonon 303
Goldman, Emma 24
Goleman, Daniel 294, 366, 368, 414, 543
Gotswami, Amit 443, 543
Gottlieb, Robert 14, 543
Granger, Russell H. 217, 543
Grayling, A.C. 433, 435, 543
Grudin, Robert 119
Gurdjieff 336

H

Haidt, Jonathan 142, 284, 544
Hall, Edward T. 72-3, 161-2
Harford, Tim 246, 318, 370, 413
Harmon, William 214
Harris, Robert 421
Hawkins, David R. 149, 166-7, 342, 514-5, 544
Hawthorne, Nathaniel 66
Hayes, Helen 170
Healy, Jane M. 280-1, 544
Heath, Chip and Dan 45-6, 263, 265, 269, 290-1, 544
Heath, Joseph 300, 305-6, 544
Hendricks, Gay 182, 395-6, 461, 544
Hertzinger, Kim 416, 544
Hock, Dee 313, 385
Hoffer, Eric 205, 207, 227, 229, 236, 264, 268, 273, 275, 319, 544
Hoffman, Reid 141, 379, 544
Houston, Jean 500, 544
Houston, Sam 31-3
Howe, Jeff 270-1, 379, 428, 544
Humility 166, 459
Hugo, Victor 56
Huxley, Thomas 109

I
Ibarra, Herminina 142, 258, 544
In Praise of Trees 47-50
Incipient Visionaries 44, 507, 511, 538
Incubator for Visionaries Chapter 20
Ineffable 161
Innocence of Perception 24, 133, 197, 216, 311-3, 325, 339, 538
Innocent Visionaries 508, 538
Innovation Chapter 9, 23, 377-8, 401, 414-5
 Innovation, Stages of 250
 Innovation, Diffusion of 251
Innovative Collaboration 252-3
Integrated Mastery 65, 73, 448
Intrinsic Motivation 277, 287, 292-3, 369, 538

J
James, William 70, 403, 407
Jaques, Elliott 373-4, 540
Jobs, Steve 113-5, 266, 480-1
Joel, Mitch 191, 249, 544
Johnson, Christopher 419, 545
Johnson, Steven 125-6, 152-3, 238, 242, 360
Jonze, Spike 360, 545
Jung, Carl 80, 87, 181

K
Kaiser, Henry J. 178
Kauffman, Stuart A. 200, 448, 537, 545
Kawasaki, Guy 263, 372, 383, 545
Keats, John 193
Keller, Helen 137
Kierkegaard, Søren 315
King, Stephen 110, 545
Koestler, Arthur 97, 231-2, 322, 412, 415, 545
Korten, David 497, 545
Kotter, John P. 359-60, 363-4, 385, 545
Krindle 355-6, 407, 537
Kuhn, Thomas S. 432-4, 545

L
Lagace, Martha 298, 545
Lappé, Frances Moore 71, 294, 404, 477, 488, 545
Leadership Chapters 14 and 15

Laphe 355-6, 407, 537
Lehrer, Jonah 193-4, 320, 406-7, 417, 545
Level Shift 307, 538
Levitin, Daniel J. 258, 418, 545
Lewis, Thomas 416, 545
Lift-off Energy 333-5, 338, 340-1, 347, 354, 513, 539
Lincoln, Abraham 16
Lindahl, Kay 247, 460, 545
Lorde, Audre 105
Love Chapter 18
Lynch, Dudley 247, 545
Lyubombirsky, Sonja 351, 352, 388, 546

M
Maclean, Norman 526-7, 546
MacLeod, Hugh 24, 167, 168, 174, 188, 203, 282, 351, 546
McKinney, Michael 313, 546
McLaren, Karla 79-80, 546
McLuhan, Marshal 55, 105
McTaggart, Lynne 55, 546
Maddi, Salvatore 215, 247
Margolis, Howard 433, 434-5, 546
Maslow, Abraham 25, 289
 Maslow's B-Values 294-5
 Maslow's Hierarchy of Needs 338-9, 406
Mature Visionaries 508
May, Rollo 319
Mental and Emotional Challenges 221-4
Merrill, Douglas C. 287, 346, 546
Metanoia 181, 293, 439, 456, 462, 539
Metcalfe, Bob 364, 546
Michalko, Michael 316, 318, 546
Michelangelo 41, 133
Mission Leap 93, 555
Miller, Henry 61
Monsaingeon, Bruno 113, 546
Mooney, Chris 470, 546
Moore, Geoffrey A. 177, 250, 381-2, 546
Moore, Thomas 485
Motivation/Drive Chapter 10
Mousetrap Maker 59-60, 67, 183, 380, 432
Mysticism Chapter 18

N
Naked/Nakedness Chapter 3, Appendix A
Naked Messenger 72-7
Naked Message 84-6
Naked Vision 27, 312-3, 323-4, 328-9, 539
Nanus, Burt 175-6, 365, 546
Negative Capability 193
Needleman, Jacob 332
Nepo, Mark 525
Newberg, Andrew 469-70, 546
Nin, Anaïs 312
Not Knowing 192, 194, 197-8, 471

O
Ogburn, William 54, 537
Open Questions 192-3, 539
Oprah 298
Organizational Structure Chapters 14 and Chapter 15
Orsi, Jannelle 406, 546
Out of the Box Chapter 12

P
Paradam 441-3
Paradigm Chapter 17
  Paradigm, Definition of 433
  Paradigm Shift 432-9
Passion 109-115
Pasteur, Louis 158
Patterson, Kerry 226, 278, 546
Pauling, Linus 431
Perot, Ross 378
Persistence of Thought 313, 318, 540
Peters, Tom 361, 362, 365, 366-7, 547
Pierson, Louise 117
Pinchbeck, Daniel 415
Pink, Daniel 114, 287, 319, 378, 393, 394, 482-3
Pinker, Steven 164, 315, 547
Problem D'Solver Laws 322
Prometheus 19

R
RSMEs 159, 450
Resistance 180, 217-8, 343, 540
Rich, Adrienne 420, 547
Rich, Frank 328
Richmond, Nigel 137

Road Not Taken, The (poem) 39
Roam, Dan 314, 547
Rogers, Everett 283
Roosevelt, Theodore 286
Root, E. Merrill 526
Root-Bernstein, Robert and Michele 25, 127, 132, 145, 315, 547
Ross, Alexander 373, 547
Russell, Bertrand 132, 444
Russell, Peter 499, 547

S
Saint-Martin 450
Scale Shift 92, 307, 540
Schlemmer, Oskar 315
Scientific Consensus 434-5
Schwartz, Barry 303, 392-3, 396, 537
Seligman, Martin E.P. 280, 284, 547
Senge, Peter 148, 159, 166, 183, 197, 331, 435, 613
Serendipity 163, 341, 540
Shekerjian, Denise 106, 127, 148, 189, 272, 296, 418, 481, 547
Shell, G. Richard 257, 271, 547
Shirky, Clay 53, 126, 133, 399, 401, 547
Sigismund, Charles G. 26, 367, 391, 547
Sills, Beverly 20
Simon, Tami 479, 548
Sims, Peter 279, 406, 548
Smilor, Ray 347, 380, 548
Smith, Kenneth 424
Snow, C.P. 445-6, 548
Spiritual Path, Stages of 456
Stace, W.T. 454
Status Quo 30, 540
  Status Quo, Definition of 217
Steffen, Alex 254-5, 548
Stein, Gertrude 77, 313
Straddle-span 307, 348-50, 481, 540
Stravinsky, Igor 157
Sulloway, Frank J. 220, 228, 548
Suzuki, Shunryu 82
Swift, Jonathan 24, 214
Synchronicity 163, 341, 540

T

Taleb, Nassim Nicholas 23-4, 123, 375, 537, 548
Tapscott, Don 134, 253, 270, 379, 134, 253, 270, 378, 548
Terence 490
Tesla 150, 311
Thaler, Richard 120, 548
Tharp, Twyla 125, 158-9, 173, 299-300, 303, 522, 548
Thompson, Gabriel 191, 548
Thoreau 25
Thurmond, Howard 112
Time Horizon 22, 373, 540
Tolle, Eckhart 225, 327, 328, 459, 463, 496
Twain, Mark 124, 212
Tutu, Desmond 486

U

Ueland, Brenda 102
Unconditional Love 453, 466
Underhill, Evelyn 157, 159-60, 165, 450, 451-2, 456, 458-9, 472, 548
Uranus Factor 476, 488-9

V

Valéry, Paul 487
Van Gogh 203-4
  VanGogh Fallacy 213
Vision Chapter 6
  Vision, Grounding Chapter 4
  Vision, Meanings of 27, Chapter 6
  Vision, Your Personal 140-2
  Visions, Known as 147
Visionary 36, Chapter 4
Visionary, Challenges for Chapter 8
  Visionary Distortions 179-80
  Visionary Process, Elements of 17
  Visionary Process, Stages of 204
  Visionary, Subsets of 508
  Visionary Thinking 483-4
Visual Seeing 27, 314

W

Watts, Mother Clare 455, 548
Wharton, Edith 24
Wheatley, Margaret J. 69, 548
White Queen (C.S. Lewis) 99
Whitehead, Alfred North 181, 230, 315, 435-6, 437, 441, 445, 548
Whyte, David 125-6
Wilber, Ken 155, 186, 206, 207, 261, 424, 446-7, 457, 473, 549
Wilde, Oscar 24
Williams, Roy H. 194-5, 549
Wilson, Colin 213
Wilson, Woodrow 24
Wordsworth, William 416
Wright, Robert 54, 271, 549

Y

Young, Dean 197, 416, 549

Z

Zachary, G. Pascal 253, 436, 549
Zander, Rosamund and Benjamin 93, 104, 332, 549
Zeitgeist 36, 540
Zero Tolerance Policies 240-1
Zukov, Gary 24

www.ingramcontent.com/pod-product-compliance
Lightning Source LLC
Chambersburg PA
CBHW062136160426
43191CB00014B/2298